The Ninth Vermont Infantry

ALSO BY PAUL G. ZELLER

The Second Vermont Volunteer Infantry Regiment, 1861–1865 (McFarland, 2002)

The Ninth Vermont Infantry

A History and Roster

Paul G. Zeller

McFarland & Company, Inc., Publishers
Jefferson, North Carolina, and London

LIBRARY OF CONGRESS CATALOGUING-IN-PUBLICATION DATA

Zeller, Paul G., 1946–
The Ninth Vermont Infantry : a history and roster / Paul G. Zeller.
p.   cm.
Includes bibliographical references and index.

ISBN 978-0-7864-3279-0
illustrated case binding : 50# alkaline paper ∞

1. United States. Army. Vermont Infantry Regiment, 9th (1862–1865)
2. Vermont — History — Civil War, 1861–1865 — Regimental histories.
3. United States — History — Civil War, 1861–1865 — Regimental histories.
4. Vermont — History — Civil War, 1861–1865 — Registers.
5. United States — History — Civil War, 1861–1865 — Registers.
6. Soldiers — Vermont — Registers.   7. Soldiers — Vermont — Pictorial works.
8. Virginia — History — Civil War, 1861–1865 — Campaigns.
9. United States — History — Civil War, 1861–1865 — Campaigns.
I. Title.
E533.59th.Z45   2008   973.7'443 — dc22   2008003376

British Library cataloguing data are available

On the cover: Colonel George J. Stannard, first commander of the
9th Vermont (USAMHI); Block House on Bogue Sound, NC;
detail map of Vermont ©2007 Pictures Now

Manufactured in the United States of America

*McFarland & Company, Inc., Publishers
Box 611, Jefferson, North Carolina 28640
www.mcfarlandpub.com*

ACKNOWLEDGMENTS

My wife, Sally, was pivotal in my being able to start and finish this book. After taking eight years to write my first book I told her I would take a break, and I did, kind of, for a year. Then I just had to start on this book, and, being the trooper she is, she continued to be my research assistant, travel agent, editor and best friend. Without her love and support I could not have finished this project. I only hope she will be as tolerant with the next one.

I again have to give special thanks to my Vermont friends, Euclid and Priscilla Farnham and Brad Limoge. Euclid and Priscilla have put us up during our research trips to Vermont and Euclid supplied me with photographs of his ancestors in the 9th Vermont and one of their 1865 diaries. Brad Limoge spent many hours going through Civil War era copies of his newspaper, gathering letters written by members of the 9th Vermont. His newspaper during the Civil War was the *Lamoille Newsdealer*. Today it is the *News and Citizen*. The help and encouragement of these friends is much appreciated.

There are several other individuals who were important in making this book possible. They are Tom Ledoux, Webmaster of "Vermont in the Civil War," Greg Dely, Jim Wilson, William L. McKone, Marie Kittel, Joe Kittel, and Krista W. Ainsworth.

The following historical societies, libraries and institutions provided me with research assistance, copies of letters, diaries and photographs and other materials: William M. Aldrich, Norwich Historical Society, Norwich, Vt.; Bill Branthoover, Montgomery Historical Society, Montgomery, Vt.; Paul Carnahan and Marjorie Strong, Vermont Historical Society, Barre, Vt.; Daniel T. Cole, Charlotte Historical Society, Charlotte, Vt.; Dwayne Cox, Special Collections and Archives, Auburn University, Auburn, Ala.; Chris Curran, Chester Historical Society, Chester, Vt.; Elaine C. Fairbanks, Halifax Historical Society, West Halifax, Vt.; Kathie Gilman, Vermont Veteran's Home, Bennington, Vt.; Angela Hallock and Sherrel Adams, Vermont Public Records Division of the Department of Buildings and General Services, Middlesex, Vt.; Audrey C. Johnson, Senior Rare Book Librarian, the Library of Virginia, Richmond, Va.; Phyllis L. Lavelle, Bradford Historical Society, Bradford, Vt.; Nina P. Long, Wistar Archives, The Wistar Institute, Philadelphia, Penn.; Carol Mowry, Hartland Historical Society, Hartland, Vt.; Barbara Mallory, Memphremagog Historical Society of Newport, Newport, Vt.; Lorna Quimby, Peacham Historical Association, Peacham, Vt.; Lew Shattuck, Hardwick Area History Advocates, Hardwick, Vt.; Jenny Stoner, Greensboro Historical Society, Greensboro, Vt.; Gary Wade, Wallingford Historical Society, Wallingford, Vt.; Doris E. Wickman, Orwell Historical Society, Orwell, Vt.; John D. Wright, Weathersfield Historical Society, Weathersfield, Vt.; Kent Young, Windham County Historical Society, Newfane, Vt.; Brooks Memorial Library, Brattleboro, Vt.; Martha Canfield Library, Arlington, Vt.; Susanne Greenhagen, SUNY Morrisville College Library, Morrisville, N. Y.; Jeffrey D. Marshall, Bailey/Howe Library, University of Vermont, Burlington, Vt.; Charlene Peacock, the Library Company of Philadelphia, Philadelphia, Penn.; Pat Ritter and staff, York County Public Library, Yorktown, Va.; Sarah C. Smith, Martha Canfield

Memorial Free Library, Arlington, Vt.; Swem Library, College of William and Mary, Williamsburg, Va.; Vermont Department of Libraries, Montpelier, Vt.; Mary West, Morristown Centennial Library, Morrisville, Vt.; the staff at the National Archives, Washington, D.C.

The following historians took time during their busy schedules to review parts of the manuscript to insure its historical accuracy: Robert E. L. Krick, Richmond National Battlefield Park; Jeff Bower, Harpers Ferry National Historical Park; Diane K. Depew, Colonial National Historical Park, Yorktown; Steven A. Cormier.

I would especially like to thank the following descendents of the men of the 9th Vermont whom I contacted in various ways looking for letters, diaries and photographs. Although not all of them had such articles, they all took time to reply and wished me the best in my endeavor. Their enthusiasm kept me going. Jan Arnold, Lynn Atkinson, Diane Ball, Alan Barker, Galer Barnes, Brian Bashaw, Daniel A. Bellware, Alson D. Braley, Jim Britton, Margaret Burwell, Peter A. Chamberlin, Patricia A. Clark, Eva C. Clough, Mary Comiskey, Ellen Cook, Allen Freeman Davis, Elaine C. Fairbanks, Charlotte Fox, Susan Fox, Shane Gower, Pat and Jim Geary, Doug Green, Jan Harmon, Peter Jefferds, Kirsti Kenny, Robert E. Kilbourne, Thelma S. Kiley, Doris M. King, Alan Lathrop, Anne Levine, Joanne Liberty, Rick and Betsy Lloyd, James Madsen, Kimberly Marchshyn, Cathleen S. Marshall, Mary Mitchell, Edward Mobbs, Noreen Mobbs, Jim Monical, Joe Morits, Mary Murphy, Barbara Pahlow, Michael Pierce, Thomas E. Rice, David Prentiss, Julia W. Ritterbush, Chris Sawtelle, Richard Shea, Joanne and Bruce Shedrick, Raymond E. Simonds, Jr., D. William Sleeper, Clyde Smith, Wayne Thompson, James J. Ticehurst, Allison and Gary Wade, Charles Wheeler, Joel E. Wheeler, Robert S. Whitmore, Jr., Anna Marie Wilson, Donna B. Winauski, Duane Wolfe, Jerry Young, Charles Yow, Arlie Avery, Cheryl MacKinnon.

I also owe a debt of gratitude to George Skoch, who drew the maps for this book. As with my first book, George's beautifully detailed maps greatly enhance my narrative. Thanks, George, and I look forward to working with you again.

I sincerely hope I have not left anyone out of this acknowledgement. If I have, I apologize.

TABLE OF CONTENTS

Acknowledgments   v

List of Maps   viii

Preface   1

1 — "Every man should be willing to do what he can for his country."   3

2 — "As helpless as rats in a cage."   36

3 — "We are penned up here like *sheep*."   55

4 — "A fools errand."   78

5 — Another Battle Lost   116

6 — The Battle of Fort Harrison   158

7 — "Richmond is ours. The whole thing."   199

Epilogue   221

Appendix A — Acronyms and Abbreviations   225

Appendix B — Ninth Vermont Infantry Regiment Roster   226

Chapter Notes   305

Bibliography   321

Index   327

LIST OF MAPS

Map No. 1 — The State of Vermont   4

Map No. 2 — Northern Virginia and Maryland   27

Map No. 3 — Map of Fort Sigel drawn by Valentine G. Barney (Vermont Historical
    Society)   27

Map No. 4 — The Battle of Harpers Ferry, September 15, 1862   45

Map No. 5 — Southeastern Virginia   80

Map No. 6 — The Siege of Suffolk, Virginia, April 11–May 4, 1864.   82

Map No. 7 — Sketch of the 9th Vermont's camp at West Point, Virginia, drawn by
    the regiment's chaplain, Lucius C. Dickinson, on the back of one of his letters
    to his wife (courtesy Steve Wakefield)   98

Map No. 8 — Eastern North Carolina   118

Map No. 9 — Newport Barracks and Vicinity   119

Map No. 10 — Map of the Battle of Newport Barracks, February 2, 1864, drawn by
    Josiah O. Livingston (National Archives)   136

Map No. 11 — Richmond and Petersburg, September, 1864   161

Map No. 12 — The Battle of Fort Harrison, September 29, 1864   168

Map No. 13 — The Second Battle of Fair Oaks, October 27, 1864   187

Map No. 14 — Richmond, April 1865   210

PREFACE

In response to a request of the governor of Vermont, Edward H. Ripley, former commander of the 9th Vermont Infantry Regiment, wrote the following letter on July 9, 1866:

Dear Sir:

Below I have the honor to hand you list of engagements requested in yours of the 2nd Inst. Viz:

Harpers Ferry	Sept 13 & 15 of 1862
Newport Barracks	Feb 2 of 1864
Chapin's Farm	Sep 29 of 1864
Fair Oaks	Oct 27 of 1864

The regrets that I often used to feel struggling with the pride I felt in looking in the numerical and physical strength of the regt. are felt now oftener and deeper than ever, that the 9th's name is not more intricately woven into the historic pages of the past 4 years by association with the names of some of our great successes.

The Regt. have passed away, & with it most probably will pass away with its ephemeral brilliancy & perfection, but not so those whose colors are placed such memorializing names as cover the flags of the old Brigade.

The contrast now is without relief a sad one, as though between mortality and immorality. And yet there is a satisfaction, a deep one that I feel, that in the records of your office the testimony is borne & *you* cannot forget that the 9th strove to do its whole duty & though with great elate is deserved it — a consciousness of its modest integrity & reliability is its right.

Ripley's letter, which is almost an apology for his unit's record, is one of the reasons I decided to write the history of the 9th Vermont. Most Americans root for the underdog and I am no exception. The 9th Vermont worked hard and tried its best, but was in only one battle that was a Union victory. At Harpers Ferry, September 15, 1862, it was captured, along with the rest of the garrison, when surrounded by Stonewall Jackson's Corps. It spent the winter of 1862–1863 guarding prisoners of war in Chicago while waiting to be paroled. In the spring of 1863 it participated in the Suffolk Campaign and saw very little action. It fled in retreat February 2, 1864, at Newport Barracks, North Carolina, when it was overwhelmed by a superior Confederate force. On October 27, 1864, as part of the XVIII Corps, it was defeated at the second battle of Fair Oaks. The only battle in which it was ever successful was the battle of Fort Harrison on September 29, 1864, where it distinguished itself in capturing Battery No. 11.

The other Vermont units in the Civil War, especially those that were in the "Old Vermont Brigade" with the Army of the Potomac, were badly bloodied and won many accolades. The 9th Vermont, though it fought its heart out, seemed always to be at the wrong place at the wrong time. This endeared them to me as much as the trials and tribulations of the 2nd Vermont Infantry Regiment, which was the first regimental history I wrote.

As with my first book, I have let the men of the regiment tell their own stories through their letters and diaries. I have left the spelling and punctuation in the passages as they appeared, except for where they had run-on sentences, in which cases I added periods for ease of reading.

Vermont towns are not followed by Vermont since they are mentioned so often, except where it would be confusing for the reader with towns such as Peru and Holland, Vermont. Many of the primary sources came from descendents of members of the regiment. Others were from libraries, universities and historical societies. I also poured through the men's military service records and pensions records at the National Archives in Washington, D.C.

The vast majority of the men in the 9th Vermont were farmers and factory workers, and had never been very far from the village in which they had grown up, much less out of the state. Most of then had joined the army to save the Union, not to free the slaves. Although there was an abolition movement in Vermont at the time, most of the men had never seen a Negro, much less cared about their plight in the South. This attitude would change, however, as the Vermonters spent more and more time in the South and saw the way slaves were treated. I have in no way tried to gloss over the men's offensive and sometimes insulting remarks about Negroes as written in their letters and diaries; nor do I condone it. For the purpose of understanding from where we have come, and to be historically accurate, the passages from the men's letters and diaries remain as written and are in no way meant to insult African Americans.

I have made every effort to ensure this book's historical accuracy, and I accept full responsibility for any inaccuracies that may be found. Even though this book is the history of what one could call a "bad luck unit," I hope it will make not only the soldiers' descendents proud, but all the citizens of Vermont.

Paul G. Zeller
Williamstown, Vermont
Spring 2008

1

"EVERY MAN SHOULD BE WILLING TO DO WHAT HE CAN FOR HIS COUNTRY."*

The clouds of war had hung over the nation for a little over a year when Vermont's governor, Frederick Holbrook, on May 21, 1862, received the order to raise another infantry regiment. The country had sent over a half million men off to war, nine thousand of whom were from Vermont. In fact, in April it was thought that enough men were under arms to end the rebellion, thus recruiting had ceased across the nation. Hardly anything had gone right for the Lincoln administration the previous year, with the loss of Fort Sumter in April followed by the humiliating defeat at Bull Run in July. The year 1862 started out bright with Major General Ulysses S. Grant's capture of Fort Henry and Fort Donelson in Tennessee in February, only to be followed by his near defeat at Shiloh two months later. At the time of Lincoln's call for more troops Maj. Gen. George B. McClellan's campaign on the Virginia Peninsula was moving at a snail's pace.[1]

This call for troops produced Vermont's ninth infantry regiment. The 1st Vermont Volunteer Infantry Regiment was mustered into service in May 1861 to serve three months. As soon as it left for war President Lincoln called for 42,034 more volunteers to serve for three years, and the 2nd, 3rd, 4th, 5th, and 6th Vermont Infantry regiments were raised and formed the famous Vermont Brigade. The 7th and 8th Infantry regiments were raised in the winter of 1861–1862 and were stationed in and around New Orleans. Vermont had also supplied one cavalry regiment and two light artillery batteries.[2]

The current call for troops found Vermont with an empty bag, but state officials quickly established recruiting offices in the towns of Bennington, Bradford, Brattleboro, Burlington, Hyde Park, Irasburg, Middlebury, Perkinsville, Plainfield, Rutland, St. Johnsbury, and Swanton. Thankfully, the men of Vermont readily answered the call to arms. About a third of these men were veterans of the 1st Vermont Volunteer Infantry Regiment.[3]

The company from Hyde Park was typical of how the 9th Vermont's companies were raised. The local newspaper was the first place the recruiting official started. The recruiting ad pictured on this page appeared in Hyde Park's newspaper, the *Lamoille Newsdealer*, on May 30. In the same edition were an editorial appealing to the men's patriotic duty to enlist and an article about Charles Dutton, Lamoille County's recruiting officer, and his effort to enlist recruits. The following is an excerpt from the editorial:

Our readers have, ere this, learned that Vermont has been called on for another regiment of volunteers to assist in putting down the rebellion. We hope they will respond to the call with promptness. Let none who can consistently go, hesitate a moment. If any man, young or old, has any misgivings on account of the necessity of leaving behind a wife, a sister, or a sweet-heart, let him lay the case

*Quoted from *Hyde Park Lamoille Newsdealer*, May 30, 1861.

3

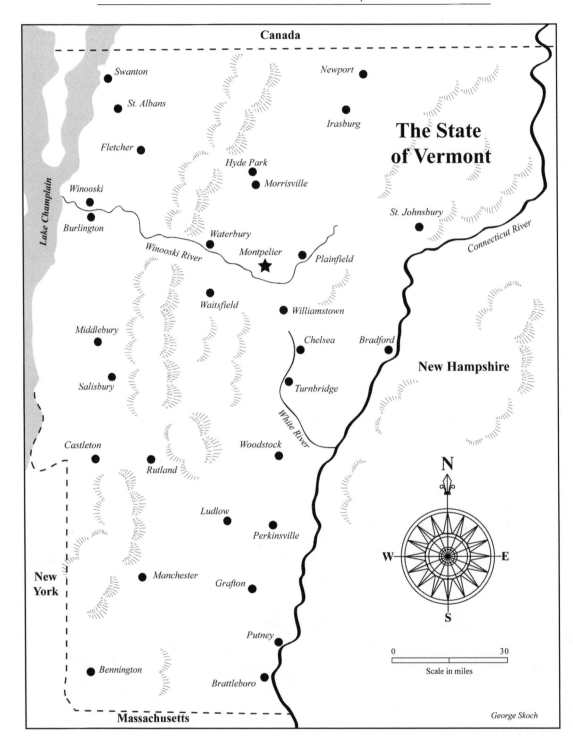

State of Vermont.

before them, and in nine cases out of ten, their decision will be in favor of going; and in many instances they will express regret that they are not men, too, that they might go.[4]

The article about Mr. Dutton's recruiting efforts was as strongly worded as the editorial:

Charles Dutton, recruiting officer for this county, is actively at work. He has appointed for his assistants Zerah W. Strait in Cambridge, U.A. Woodbury in Elmore, C.F. Douglas in Stowe, and Willard Fuller in Johnson. They are all actively at work and up to Wednesday night had obtained the names of about 25 who propose to enlist. It is expected that in less than three weeks, enough to form a company will have enrolled their names.

We are glad there are so many who are willing to go, and hope that none who can consistently leave will hesitate because they are not sure of an office. Every man should be willing to do what he can for his country, and to take the position in which he can best serve her interests. In this enterprise there should be no bargaining — no figuring for office in order to *sell out*, but every man should enlist to serve his country. Vermont pays her sons well. The way to promotion is open to all, and merit will not long remain unrewarded.

In a day or two more we expect to hear the familiar notes of the fife and drum as an accompaniment to the military evolutions of men taking their first lessons in the art of war.

We hope next week to be able to give the names of a goodly number of patriotic hearts, who will have signified their readiness to fight for the "Stars and Stripes." Other States are sending their men by thousands, and Vermont will not be behind.[5]

MORE VOLUNTEERS !
WANTED.

A recruiting office has been opened at the
AMERICAN HOUSE,

in Hyde Park, where volunteers for the Ninth Vermont Regiment will be received. The men now called for are to be employed as reserves to hold places now or hereafter taken. The pay and bounty will be the same as heretofore.

The call of our Country is urgent ! treason is still unsubdued, and all who love their Country should come forward manfully to fill up the ranks of the army now fighting to maintain the Institutions established by the blood of our revolutionary fathers. If the rebels are traitors, let us show that we are patriots, and freely offer ourselves to save our country from ruin.

Rally to the Standard !!

and show that "Spunky Lamoille" has still those who are ready to do and die for the Constitution.
CHARLES DUTTON, Recruiting Officer.
Hydepark, May 28, 1862.

Advertisement for volunteers to join the 9th Vermont from the June 6, 1862, edition of the *Lamoille Newsdealer* (Morristown Library).

The assistants chosen by Mr. Dutton were men with reputations that would help in the recruiting drive. Zerah W. Strait was a longtime member of the Vermont militia and was selected as the captain of company H of the 2nd Vermont the year before only to be rejected during the medical examinations just before the regiment mustered. Urban A. Woodbury went to war with the 2nd Vermont in June of 1861 and had his right arm torn off by an artillery shell fragment at the battle of Bull Run, which earned him the grim distinction of being Vermont's first "empty sleeve" of the war. He would later serve a term as the governor of Vermont. One can only assume that the other two men were of equal stature.[6]

Mr. Dutton's recruiting strategies worked. By the middle of June, 43 men enlisted. On June 24, the recruits drilled in Hyde Park. At about 8:00 P.M. that evening, sporting their new uniforms, they marched four miles to Morristown Corners where they were treated to lemonade and beer. Following these activities they were saluted by the firing of guns and the raising of the American flag in the town square. They then marched another mile to Morrisville, where again they were treated to lemonade and beer and then were invited to dinner by various villagers. This type of publicity worked and within the next day or two 93 men enlisted, filling up the company.[7]

The Hyde Park company was officially organized on Friday, June 27, and its officers elected.

Abial H. Slayton of Stowe was elected as the captain. Guy H. Guyer of Morristown was elected first lieutenant and Calvin R. Loveland of Hyde Park was elected as the company's second lieutenant. Voting for captains and lieutenants was a common practice in volunteer units during the Civil War, with the governors issuing commissions to those so selected. Eden native Stillman Stone was chosen as the company's first sergeant and David P. Barnes of Elmore was chosen as the second sergeant. It was decided the rest of the noncommissioned officers would be chosen after the company went to its camp of instruction. After the company organized it marched to the local grocery store where one of the men of the town treated all the troops to a glass of beer.[8]

Since the company had orders to move to its camp of instruction on Monday, June 30, the men were released to go home to say their good-byes, with instructions to report back to Hyde Park at 10:00 P.M. Sunday night. By 1:00 A.M. Monday morning all of the men had returned and at 2 A.M. the company loaded into five wagons and a coach for transport to Waterbury to catch the train for Brattleboro. As the horses plodded out of town pulling the wagons loaded with soldiers, a tearful crowd waved and yelled good-bye. By 4:30 that afternoon the wagons rolled into Stowe, where the men had an hour's rest and were treated to beefsteak, coffee and other good eats. Then, in a drizzling rain, they were off again. The company reached Waterbury, boarded the train, and before long was on its way to Brattleboro. Upon reaching its camp of instruction, the Hyde Park company was officially designated as Company H of the 9th Vermont Infantry Regiment.[9]

Governor Holbrook chose 41-year-old George Jerrison Stannard of St. Albans, Vermont, to lead the regiment. At that time Stannard was serving as the lieutenant colonel of the 2nd Vermont Infantry Regiment on the Virginia Peninsula. Stannard was born in Georgia, Vermont, on October 20, 1820. After completing public school at age 15 he worked on the family farm and taught school for five years. In 1845 Stannard went to work as a clerk at the St. Albans Foundry Company and by 1860 was a joint owner of the company, where he remained until the outbreak of the war. Stannard joined the Vermont militia as a private at the age of 16 and rose through the ranks. He was commissioned as colonel of the 4th Regiment in 1858. When President Lincoln

Colonel George J. Stannard, first commander of the 9th Vermont. Purported to be the first Vermont volunteer of the war, he would be a major general by the end of the war (U.S. Army Military History Institute).

called for troops after the fall of Fort Sumter, Stannard wired the governor offering his services. Thus, it is believed, he was the first man in Vermont to volunteer for the war.[10]

The 9th Vermont was organized like most Civil War infantry regiments, with a regimental staff and ten infantry companies. The regimental staff consisted of commissioned and noncommissioned officers. The commissioned officers consisted of the colonel, lieutenant colonel, major, adjutant (first lieutenant), quartermaster (first lieutenant), surgeon, assistant surgeon, and chaplain. The noncommissioned staff members were the sergeant major, quartermaster sergeant, commissary sergeant, hospital steward, and principal musician.[11]

The man chosen to fill the position of lieutenant colonel was Dudley Kimball Andross, a five feet ten and one-half inch miller from Bradford. He was born into an old Vermont family in Bradford on September 12, 1832. In his early life Andross worked as a lumberman, then as a railroad builder, and as a gold-miner in California. Initially Andross was chosen as the captain of the 9th Vermont's company G, but was soon replaced by William J. Henderson when he was selected as the regiment's second in command. Andross previously served as a captain in the 1st Vermont Infantry and at the battle of Big Bethel, June 10, 1861, was the first Vermonter atop the rebel earthworks.[12]

Lieutenant Colonel Dudley K. Andross. Resigned from the regiment due to chronic bronchitis, May 22, 1863 (U.S. Army Military History Institute).

Edwin S. Stowell, a 33-year-old, five-foot ten-inch farmer from Cornwall, was chosen as the regiment's major. At the time he was chosen, he was serving as the captain of Company F of the 5th Vermont Infantry on the Virginia Peninsula. Stowell was born in Cornwall on January 27, 1829, and he entered Norwich University in 1848. He dropped out of Norwich in 1850 to take up farming, raising blooded horses and sheep. He joined the 5th Vermont when it was raised in September of 1861, and he was reputed to be one of the best line officers in that regiment. Stowell remained with the 5th Vermont through the current campaign on the Virginia Peninsula and would not join the 9th Vermont until September.[13]

The adjutant was John C. Stearns of Bradford. He was the son of John and Elizabeth Chandler Stearns and was born in Chelsea on February 11, 1831. He started his career as a clerk in a general store in Bradford. For six years he was a member of the firm of Brooks & Stearns, which was engaged in trade in Worcester, Massachusetts, where he became a member of the Massachusetts militia and on his return to Vermont enlisted in the Bradford Guards, where he worked his way up through the ranks to lieutenant. He enlisted in Co. D, 1st Vermont Infantry May 2, 1861, as a private. Soon after enlisting he was promoted to sergeant major of the regiment, a rank which he held until the regiment mustered out of service August 15, 1861.[14]

Major Edwin S. Stowell. Resigned from the regiment May 11, 1863, due to illness (Dennis Charles).

Francis O. Sawyer, an agent for an express company from Burlington, was selected as the regiment's quartermaster. His expertise in logistics earned him a promotion to captain and a position on higher level staffs in the summer of 1864.[15]

Dr. Charles L. Allen of Middlebury was initially chosen as the regiment's surgeon, but Colonel Stannard wanted Benjamin Walter "Walt" Carpenter as his chief surgeon. Carpenter was serving at the time with Stannard in the 2nd Vermont Infantry as that regiment's assistant surgeon. He not only had proven himself a competent doctor, but he exhibited great coolness under fire. Carpenter, like Major Stowell, would remain on the Virginia Peninsula until the campaign was over and would not join up with the 9th Vermont until September.[16]

The assistant surgeon was Dr. Horace P. Hall of St. Albans.[17]

Adjutant John C. Stearns. Resigned from the regiment May 1, 1863, due to illness (Dennis Charles).

Postwar photograph of Quartermaster Francis O. Sawyer. His organizational skills would carry him to higher level staff positions before the war's end (Vermont Historical Society).

Surgeon Benjamin W. Carpenter. He had served in the 2nd Vermont as assistant surgeon until selected as surgeon for the 9th Vermont, June 1862 (U.S. Army Military History Institute).

Chaplain Lucius C. Dickinson (U.S. Army Military History Institute).

Assistant Surgeon Horace P. Hall. He was believed to be incompetent by most members of the 9th Vermont. He resigned March 13, 1863, because of ill health (Vermont Historical Society).

Sergeant Major James T. Gorham. By the end of the war he was the captain of Co. H (U.S. Army Military History Institute).

The Rev. Lucius C. Dickinson, a 39-year-old Methodist Episcopal preacher from Cavendish, was appointed chaplain and remained with the regiment through its entire time of service.[18]

The regiment's noncommissioned officer staff was:

Sergeant major, James T. Gorham from Ludlow.[19]

Theodore S. Peck of Burlington, quartermaster sergeant.[20]

Commissary sergeant, Davis J. Pattee of Georgia, Vermont.[21]

The position of hospital steward remained vacant until August 10, when 21-year-old medical student Henry D. Belden from Burlington was selected to fill it. Belden previously had served as a private in the 1st Vermont Infantry and enlisted as the first sergeant of Company H on June 2, 1862.[22]

Drum major (later referred to as principal musician), Robert G. Hardie from Brattleboro.[23]

Quartermaster Theodore S. Peck. He had previously served in the 1st Vermont Cavalry Regiment as a private. He would attain the grade of captain by the war's end (U.S. Army Military History Institute).

Captain Valentine G. Barney, Co. A. Promoted to lieutenant colonel June 19, 1863 (U.S. Army Military History Institute).

First Lieutenant Linus E. Sherman, Co. A (Vermont Historical Society).

Mirroring other Civil War regiments, the 9th Vermont's ten companies were lettered A through K, minus J. The letter J was not used because in hand written orders and reports it was easily confused with the letter I. A captain commanded each company, which was subdivided for command and control purposes into two platoons. One platoon was commanded by a first lieutenant and the other by a second lieutenant. Each platoon was divided into two squads, each of which was under the supervision of a sergeant. The company was also authorized one first sergeant (often referred to as the orderly sergeant), eight corporals (two per squad), two musicians, one wagoner, and between 64 and 82 privates.[24]

The following are the 9th Vermont's companies, the towns in which they were recruited, and the officers elected to lead them:

Company A, Swanton: Capt. Valentine "Val" G. Barney, First Lt. Linus E. Sherman, Second Lt. Erastus W. Jewett.

Company B, Rutland: Capt. Edward H. Ripley; First Lt. Samuel H. Kelley; Second Lt. Alfred C. Ballard.

Company C, Middlebury: Capt. Albert R. Sabin, First Lt. Herman Seligson; Second Lt. Elijah B. Sherman.

Company D, Perkinsville: Capt. Charles Jarvis, First Lt. Asaph Clark; Second Lt. Justus Dartt.

Captain Edward H. Ripley, Co. B. He became the fourth commander of the 9th Vermont and by the end of the war was a brevet brigadier general (U.S. Army Military History Institute).

Second Lieutenant Erastus W. Jewett, Co. A (Dennis Charles).

Company E, Irasburgh: Capt. Amasa Bartlett; First Lt. Elisha M. Quimby, Second Lt. Curtis A. Hibbard.

Company F, Burlington: Capt. George A. Beebe; First Lt. Eugene Viele; Second Lt. John T. Bascom.

Company G, Bradford: Capt. William J. Henderson; First Lt. Edwin A. Kilbourne; Second Lt. William C. Holman.

Company H, Hyde Park: Capt. Abial H. Slayton; First Lt. Guy H. Guyer; Second Lt. Calvin R. Loveland.

Company I, Plainfield: Capt. Albion J. Mower, First Lt. Josiah O. Livingston, Second Lt. Oliver C. Campbell.

Company K, Brattleboro: Capt. David W.

First Lieutenant Samuel H. Kelley, Co. B (U.S. Army Military History Institute).

Second Lieutenant Alfred C. Ballard, Co. B. He wrote numerous letters to the *Rutland Herald* chronicling the events of the regiment (Dennis Charles).

Captain Albert R. Sabin, Co. C. Resigned his commission December 24, 1862, due to ill health (Dennis Charles).

Lewis, First Lt. Joseph C. Brooks, Second Lt. Henry H. Rice.[25]

There were many reasons why the men readily enlisted. Some enlisted because they wanted to experience the excitement of war, while others wanted to see something besides their farms. A few probably joined to free the slaves. While Vermont had its share of abolitionists and was part of the underground railroad system, which shuttled escaped slaves north, the majority of the men joined to preserve the Union. The following editorial from the *Vermont Phoenix* of July 17, 1862, illustrates the point:

First Lieutenant Herman Seligson, Co. C. Promoted to lieutenant colonel July 20, 1865 (U.S. Army Military History Institute).

The few secession sympathizers in this state and in the North are unceasing in their attempts to stigmatize Vermont as given over to "abolitionism" and her people as "abolitionists," devoid of patriotism and its associated virtues. The sources from whence such stale and senseless charges come do not entitle them to any consideration; but when they are repeated it is only necessary to point to the honorable position which Vermont has taken to sustaining the national government in the hour of

Second Lieutenant Elijah B. Sherman, Co. C. He was passed over for promotion and resigned January 7, 1863 (U.S. Army Military History Institute).

Captain Charles Jarvis, Co. D. Shot in the stomach by a Confederate soldier December 1, 1863, and died the same day (Dennis Charles).

First Lieutenant Asaph Clark, Co. D (U.S. Army Military History Institute).

trial. Under the call for seventy-five thousand men for three months she sent her regiment at an early day. Under the call for five hundred thousand men she put in the field nearly nine thousand good soldiers. Under the recent call she is the first to respond with a regiment of her best men. Let these facts be the sufficient and only answer to the little miserable brood of cavilers who seek to aid and abet traitors and rebels to the full extent of their ability. When they shall be remembered no more the record of Vermont patriotism will shine with untarnished lustre.[26]

Unlike the majority of the preceding Vermont regiments, most of the companies of the 9th Vermont were uniformed where they were recruited. The exception seemed to be Co. A, which was outfitted after it arrived

Captain Amasa Bartlett, Co. E. Died of disease March 16, 1864 (Dennis Charles).

First Lieutenant Elisha M. Quimby, Co. E (Vermont Historical Society).

Postwar photograph of Second Lieutenant Curtis A. Hibbard, Co. E (Vermont Historical Society).

Captain George A. Beebe, Co. F. Died of disease August 10, 1862 (Vermont Historical Society).

First Lieutenant Eugene Viele, Co. F (Dennis Charles).

Second Lieutenant John T. Bascom, Co. F (Dennis Charles).

Captain William J. Henderson, Co. G (Vermont Historical Society).

First Lieutenant Edwin A. Kilbourne, Co. G (Vermont Historical Society).

Second Lieutenant William C. Holman, Co. G. Captured February 2, 1864, during the battle of Newport Barracks, North Carolina, and exchanged May 6, 1863 (Dennis Charles).

Captain Abial H. Slayton, Co. H. Resigned December 8, 1862 (Vermont Historical Society).

Above: First Lieutenant Guy H. Guyer, Co. H. Resigned February 13, 1863 (U.S. Army Military History Institute). *Right:* Second Lieutenant Calvin R. Loveland, Co. H (Vermont Historical Society).

First Lieutenant Josiah O. Livingston, Co. I. Pictured here as a captain (U.S. Army Military History Institute).

Captain Albion J. Mower, Co. I (Vermont Historical Society).

Left: Postwar photograph of Second Lieutenant Oliver C. Campbell, Co. I. He resigned December 20, 1862, due to ill health. He enlisted in the Veteran Reserve Corps until July 6, 1863, and served until mustered out November 15, 1865 (Vermont Historical Society). *Right:* Captain David W. Lewis, Co. K (Dennis Charles).

Left: First Lieutenant Joseph C. Brooks, Co. K. He was promoted to major April 21, 1864 (Dennis Charles). *Right:* Second Lieutenant Henry H. Rice, Co. K (Dennis Charles).

at the camp of instruction in Brattleboro. Captain Valentine "Val" G. Barney, a 37-year-old five-foot nine-inch clerk from Swanton and commander of Co. A, complained to his wife on June 22, "We have been very busy for a few days past in distributing clothing to the men and you cannot imagine what a pile of stuff it takes to fit out a company ready for service." The men's uniforms consisted of a dark blue wool frock coat with a skirt that extended to the mid-thigh and had nine brass buttons on the breast. When in the field the men usually wore a dark blue wool sack coat with four brass buttons. Under the coat the men wore flannel shirts. The trousers were also made of wool and were sky blue. Several different styles of caps and hats were authorized for wear, but the men in the 9th Vermont wore the more popular dark blue forage cap, also called a kepi. A stamped brass hunting horn, the insignia for infantry, was affixed to the top of the cap. Above the hunting horn was a brass number for the number of the regiment. Inside the loop of the horn was a brass letter signifying the man's company and, below, brass letters for the abbreviation of the state from which the regiment originated.[27]

Worn over the blouse was what was referred to as one's "equipments" or "traps," which consisted of a belt over the left shoulder. From this belt hung the leather cartridge box, which rested on the right hip. The cartridge box held 40 rounds of ammunition. Over the shoulder belt and positioned just above the cartridge box was the waist belt. The waist belt was fastened by a lead-filled brass oval belt plate with the letters "US" on the front. Attached to the waist belt was a bayonet in a leather scabbard suspended over the left hip and a cap box containing the percussion caps on the right front between the buckle and a brass keeper on the belt over the right hip. The waist belt was worn over the shoulder belt to keep the cartridge box against the right hip when the soldier was running. Slung over the right shoulder, and hung just above his left hip, was the haversack, which contained the soldier's rations. Resting atop the haversack was the soldier's canteen.[28]

Haversacks usually were made of black waterproofed cloth, similar to oil cloth. They had an inner cloth lining that could be removed and washed. The linings usually did not last long, leaving the inside of the haversack greasy, grimy and smelly from carrying cooked meats, butter, and other foods, which often spoiled.[29]

The men in the 9th Vermont wore shoes, or "bootees," as they were called, square toed and ankle high with leather soles and heels and rawhide laces.[30] To finish off the soldier's ensemble was a knapsack that carried all his belongings. The knapsack usually weighed between 50 and 70 pounds.

The 9th Vermont's companies reported in piecemeal fashion to Camp Davis, their camp of instruction in Brattleboro, during the last half of June. Camp Davis, named for Vermont's quartermaster general, George F. Davis, was located about a mile from town on a high treeless plain that was soon covered with freshly planted evergreens to provide shade. The Brattleboro Union High School's athletic fields cover the site today.[31]

The men were quartered in wall and Sibley tents (which they took with them several weeks later to Washington) and were kept busy with daily squad and company drills.[32] Although the men kept busy learning the rudiments of military duty, they were fed well. Captain Barney wrote on June 22, "I have just returned from church and finished my dinner which was composed of baked beans, bread & butter, raw egg & cold boiled ham."[33]

The men started receiving their weapons on June 27. With the number of men that had been called to arms since the beginning of the war, the best weapons the state's quartermaster general could obtain were old smoothbore Belgian muskets. Second Lieutenant Alfred C. Ballard, of Co. B, native of Tinmouth, wrote several days later, "On Friday we went down again and got our muskets, and strange to say, no one was hurt. (Guns are very dangerous things in the hands of raw recruits, even if they have neither stock, lock, or barrel!)" The next several months would prove Ballard's words to be quite prophetic.[34]

Although a Tinmouth, Vermont, native, 27-year-old Second Lt. Alfred Ballard had taught school in Clarence, New York, east of Buffalo, for two years before the war. He came home to enlist while the 9th Vermont was being recruited. Even before the regiment rendezvoused at Brattleboro, Ballard wrote letters to the *Rutland Herald* chronicling the events of his unit and continued to do so through the entire war.[35]

On the way back to camp with their muskets the men were treated to refreshments by some young Brattleboro ladies as noted by Second Lieutenant Ballard:

On our way back with our guns—and some had two—and, by the way, I had two more than belonged to me—we halted to rest in a pleasant shade by the road side, and while there we were assailed by a detachment of fair women and fairer girls, armed with pails of clear, cold water, and sparkling glasses, and each soldier drank his own health, and I doubt not, asked a blessing on the head of the giver of the refreshing draught—and as I watched them ministering to the wants of those strange soldier boys, I could not but think, that among them all, they might have fathers and sons, and husbands, and brothers, and lovers far away in some sunny and more unhealthy clime—and if so, may they in their greater need than ours, find as fair hands and kind hearts to minister to them, as we on that afternoon, when we first begot our guns.[36]

The next day Ballard commented:

The Rutland Company (Co. B) has been four days under canvas, though for a time it was a question with us whether we should not be first under water, as it rained when we got here Tuesday, and after it got tired of raining, it began to pour, and kept it up until Thursday noon.[37]

In a drizzling rain the 9th Vermont was mustered into United States service on July 9 by Major William Austine, the regular army mustering officer for the State of Vermont. With the men of the regiment standing in formation, Governor Holbrook presented the regiment its regimental colors and its American flag. The governor made a short speech and the regiment's commander, Col. George J. Stannard, replied with a speech complimenting the regiment on its fine appearance, stating he had the fullest confidence in the men, and that the men would shed the last drop of their blood before they would prove traitors to the trust that the governor and the people of the state had placed in them. After the flag presentation, the governor reviewed the regiment, which at that time numbered 920 officers and men. One of the soldiers in the ranks remembered, "the day passed off pleasantly for us all."[38]

The men of the 9th Vermont had a pleasant surprise on Saturday, July 11, with the appearance of the paymaster, who doled out a month's advance pay. One of the men in Co. H recorded:

After the boys got their pay to day, the Captain was besieged on all sides by the boys for passes to go to the village. He being officer of the day had all he could attend to, but the boys teased so hard he had to let them go, and for some reason they are rather more noisy to-night than usual, some of them feel quite salubrious, others are trying to borrow money, some are sporting new watches and chains, while others still remember the dear ones at home, and are writing letters which doubtless will enclose some of the Green Backs.[39]

As far as pay was concerned, the Vermont troops were more fortunate than the troops from many states. When war broke out in 1861 the Vermont legislature passed a bill appropriating money to supplement its soldiers' federal pay with seven additional dollars. For a private that meant $20 a month versus $13.[40]

On Tuesday, July 15, with orders in hand to move his regiment to Washington, Colonel Stannard had his men up at 3:30 A.M. After roll call and breakfast, the regiment formed at 6:00 A.M. and in a driving rain departed for the depot in Brattleboro, where it arrived at half past seven. Amid cheers from families, friends, and citizens of Brattleboro, the train pulled out at 9:15 A.M. The train rolled to a stop at Springfield, Massachusetts, at 1:30 P.M. and was received by an artillery salute from the guns at the U.S. arsenal located there. At the depot the regiment was treated to music by the town band. To the men's surprise a group of Springfield citizens boarded the train and handed out cakes, crackers, cheese, sandwiches, and other goodies. The train then chugged on to New Haven, Connecticut, where it pulled into the depot at 6:00 P.M. Here the regiment transferred to the steamer *Bay State* and started for New York City.[41]

The *Bay State* arrived at the pier in the East River at the foot of 23rd Street at 7:00 A.M. Wednesday, July 16. The regiment debarked and marched amid cheering crowds to Madison Square, where tables loaded with food awaited their arrival. The men stacked arms, loaded their plates and sat down on the grass to eat their breakfast. The regiment's officers were treated to breakfast and lunch at the Fifth Avenue Hotel by New York City's "Sons of Vermont." During the trip and while in the city a number of the men tried to get their fill of John Barley Corn, as Captain Barney described to his wife:

We have got along so far very well and the men have kept very straight though I have emptied [the men's] 4 containers of whiskey for different ones since we started and I will have more today I presume as some of my men are bound to be drunk all the time if possible and it keeps me on the lookout to keep them sober.[42]

At 2:00 P.M. the men were treated to a lunch of roast beef, bread and vegetables. An hour later they marched down Fifth Avenue, Nineteenth Street, and Broadway to the North River to take the ferry to New Jersey for the next leg of their journey. As they marched along, the regiment was cheered with "huzzas" by the people thronging the streets. During the march the regiment stopped in front of the hotel where President Lincoln's wife was staying and the drum corps gave her a parting salute. At the ferry, Horace Greeley, editor of the New York *Tribune*, made a patriotic speech from the wheelhouse of the boat. At Jersey City the men boarded a train on the Camden & Amboy Railroad and arrived in Philadelphia at 2:00 A.M. Thursday, July 17. From Philadelphia the Vermonters traveled to Baltimore.[43]

The trip from Philadelphia was uneventful, but the situation upon reaching Baltimore was another matter. Due to an ordinance forbidding locomotives from running through the city, troops had to detrain so horses could pull the cars, forcing the units to march down Pratt Street from President Street Station to the Baltimore and Ohio Railroad's Camden Street Station. Being within a border state a large part of the population of Baltimore sided with the Confederacy. In fact, on April 19, 1861, the 6th Massachusetts Infantry Regiment had been attacked by armed citizens while marching between the two stations and lost 4 men killed and 31 wounded.[44]

Having come through Baltimore with the 2nd Vermont in June 1861, and having experienced the angry mood of the citizens, Colonel Stannard was not taking any chances, so he had his men load their muskets for the march. Thankfully, only a few angry scowls were experienced and the Green Mountain Boys, with some trepidation, boarded a train of cattle cars at Camden Street Station for the final leg of their journey.[45]

The 9th Vermont finally arrived in Washington at 10:00 P.M. where it was quartered in some dirty barracks north of the Capitol and, according to Sgt. Joel C. Baker of Co. B, "Three days were spent there accustoming the well fed sons of Vermont to the worst fare which they were required to live upon during their entire service." During their three day stay in the nation's capital, Stannard's boys traded in their old Belgian muskets for Springfield rifles that Capt. Edward H. Ripley, the 22-year-old commander of Co. B from Rutland, thought were the most beautiful Springfields you can imagine."[46]

The rifle Captain Ripley raved about was the Model 1861 Springfield rifle musket. It was a muzzle loader that was 58.5 inches long and weighed 9.75 pounds, with the bayonet attached. It could fire a bullet with man-killing accuracy over 800 yards, although most soldiers were not very accurate past 300 yards. The rifle was fired by the hammer striking a brass percussion cap that was placed on the rifle's nipple. A soldier was expected to get off two to three rounds per minute from his Springfield. The bullet used with the Springfield was the .58 caliber lead minie ball.[47]

The minie ball was invented in 1848 by French Army captain Claude-Etienne Minie. The U.S. Army adopted a similar bullet in 1855 that retained Minie's name. The American minie ball was not a ball at all, but a soft lead conical bullet with a cone-shaped cavity in its base with three external rings cut into its lower body. When the rifle was fired, gasses forced the sides of the bullet into the barrel's rifling grooves, causing the bullet to spin, giving it considerable accuracy. When a minie ball hit a man, the result was not a small hole like a modern jacketed bullet. The minie ball struck at a low velocity and expanded like a dum-dum bullet, splintering bone and tearing tissue, leaving a large exit wound.[48]

Although the rifle musket was introduced into the U.S. Army in 1855, the doctrine for tactical formations did not change. During the Civil War, and even up to and through World War I, tactical offensive formations remained shoulder to shoulder close order formations, in two ranks. The two ranks allowed the attacking force to throw its firepower along a broad front, have the sustaining power of the second rank, and allowed commanders greater command and control. Unfortunately, once the rifled musket was introduced, the two-rank offense could not overcome the fire power of the defender. The defenders could engage the attacking force at a greater distance, pour in a more accurate fire, and keep the attackers under fire for a longer time. The wholesale bloodletting caused by this mismatch between technology and doctrine would be repeated in battle after battle during the four years of the Civil War.[49]

The Vermonters were assigned to the Army of Virginia, which was created on June 26, 1862. Although named the Army of Virginia, it was more a collection of units than a real army. Its mission was to protect Washington and the Shenandoah Valley and to move east of the Blue Ridge Mountains to draw Confederate troops away from Richmond, where Maj. Gen. George B. McClellan's attempt to take the Confederate capital was floundering. It consisted of three corps with a strength of about 47,000 men and was commanded by Maj. Gen. John Pope.[50]

After experiencing New York and Philadelphia, the 9th Vermont boys must have found the sight around their camp in Washington a disappointment. In 1862, the nation's capital was a ramshackle, dirty town with hogs running loose through its unpaved streets. First Lt. Linus E. Sherman of Company A complained: "Washington's a dirty uncleanly city. No decent street in the city except Pennsylvania Avenue." The smell was worse than the sight, for the city's sanitary conditions were appalling. A defective sewage system that drained directly onto tidal river flats, and the city's numerous privies, had always been odorous in warm weather. The newly arrived regiments, whose camps lacked adequate latrine facilities, only added to the filth. Captain Barney added, "I tell you I don't think much of the Southern country and if Washington and Baltimore are examples of Southern cities I don't think the whole South is worth fighting for very hard, for they are the dirtyest of all places that ever I saw."[51]

Although the Vermont boys were not very impressed with the nation's capital, they were ready to fight, as Pvt. Charles A. Flanders, a 22-year-old farmer from Corinth in Co. G, wrote his mother on July 18:

> I've good courage yet. don't worry about me. There were seven pickets shot last nite about ten miles from this city and brought in dead. We are among Rebels. That's so every time. It is the rite place for us. It is what suits us. We want to fite and that aint all. We have got to fite.[52]

On July 19, Colonel Stannard was ordered to take his regiment across the Potomac and report to Brig. Gen. Samuel D. Sturgis, whose brigade was encamped in the vicinity of Cloud's Mill, west of Alexandria.[53]

Colonel Stannard had his men up and on the road at 8:00 A.M. on Sunday, July 20. The regiment marched from its barracks to the Potomac River, where it crossed the Long Bridge to Alexandria. Corp. Charles F. Branch of Co. C wrote later of the march:

> Marching out of Washington this terrible hot Sabbath, we crossed the Long Bridge and into the streets of Alexandria. As we marched we began singing "John Brown" keeping step with the song, but our Lieut. Col., probably thinking it was not a Sunday song, rode back down the line and commanded "every mother's son of us to stop that d----d singing."[54]

Then the regiment marched four more miles to Cloud's Mill. Even though the day was reasonably cool, the men who were not used to marching with loaded knapsacks soon started dropping out of the column even before they reached the Potomac River. Hundreds of their knapsacks littered the roadside. These knapsacks were gathered and brought to camp in wagons and were returned to the men with an admonition from Stannard that if they threw them away again they would go without. The 9th Vermont reached its camp at Cloud's Mill near 3:00 P.M. with only about 450 men. The stragglers marched in later, and there were so many of them that Pvt. Charles H. Hodge in Co. H wrote that the men in camp "began to cheer for the 10th Vermont; in fact they looked almost like a regiment."[55]

The 9th Vermont's camp at Cloud's Mill was located in a hilly area a little over four miles west of Alexandria and about a half mile north of the Orange & Alexandria Railroad. The area had been the site of a skirmish the year before, and the remains were a sobering reminder to the men that they were about to engage in serious business, as Captain Ripley mentioned in one of his letters: "We are encamped upon a ground where the skirmish of Cloud's Mill took place, soldier's graves, demolished houses, and shattered trees are the silent, but forcible reminders to the boys." First Lieutenant Linus Sherman noted, "One may pick up spent bullets in any quantity on the side hill above us. The mill is well battered with bullets." Capt. Val Barney commented on what the ravages of war had done to the surrounding area, "The country is in a horrid state and not a fence is to be seen."[56]

There was another reality of field service the men would face at Cloud's Mill—field rations. Lieutenant Sherman noted on July 21, "Tomorrow the men have got to begin to eat hard bread [hardtack]. They have not had any yet. I suppose they will complain some but they have got to eat that or none."[57]

Army field rations during the Civil War consisted of hardtack, salt pork or salt beef, coffee, sugar, and salt. Hardtack was a cracker made of flour and water about three inches square and nearly half an inch thick. It was solid and very hard, but nourishing. Ten slabs usually constituted a day's ration. When on the march or when time was short, hardtack often was crumbled in a cup of coffee and eaten with a spoon. When the men had time they would toast the cracker over a fire or soak it in water and fry it in pork fat or beat it into a powder and mix it with boiled rice and serve as a griddlecake.[58]

Salt pork and salt beef usually were fried in a skillet which the soldiers made from half of a canteen with a wire handle attached. On the march, the meat often was eaten raw or broiled on a stick over a fire and eaten with hardtack. Occasionally, the meat was issued rancid and, sometimes, crawling with worms. This brought loud complaints from the ranks.[59]

The army seemed to live on coffee. Veteran soldiers learned to carry a small canvas bag in which they mixed ground coffee and sugar. The ration was ample for three or four pints of coffee a day. When on the march, a halt of more than five minutes found men making little fires for boiling coffee. If rest halts were too far apart, men often fell out, built a fire, boiled coffee, drank it, and then plodded along to catch up to their regiment.[60]

The Green Mountain Boys also encountered poisonous snakes at Cloud's Mill. As Second Lieutenant Ballard related, "Before we had been in camp an hour, we killed a 'copper head,' and rattlesnakes were visible to the ear frequently." As though snakes were not enough, he went on to say, "Before I had been in bed five minutes last night [July 21], I discovered a *huge* spider preparing to make a descent upon me, but I routed him — and not long after a bug was discovered lurking in my whiskers; but I very soon *shelled* him out."[61]

On Wednesday, July 23, just as the Vermonters were getting settled in their new camp, Colonel Stannard got orders to report to Brig. Gen. Abraham S. Piatt at Winchester, Virginia. This order was quite a disappointment to the men, as they had expected to be assigned to the Vermont Brigade in the Army of the Potomac. That night the entire regiment was up scurrying around getting ready for the next morning's departure. Captain Ripley reported home: "Our marching orders came Wednesday night. We cooked rations and distributed ammunition. I was up all night getting the men ready to strike tents and march at 3 o'clock."[62]

Stannard had his men on the road to Alexandria at 4:00 A.M. the next morning. Little did anyone realize the human toll this trip would take. At Alexandria the regiment boarded the mail boat *Columbia* to cross the Potomac. Here the first injury occurred while the men were unloading the regiment's baggage from wagons and loading it onboard the boat. Thirty-seven-year-old Wyman Wetherell and his younger brother Ephraim, both privates in Co. H from Waterville, were among the men detailed to transfer the baggage. As he was lifting a box, Wyman lost his balance and the box fell on him. His brother quickly grabbed the box to take the weight off Wyman, but not before he had sustained a painful hernia in his groin. That was the last duty pulled by Wyman Wetherell. He was discharged with a disability two months later on October 20.[63]

After crossing the Potomac the Vermonters waited all day under Washington's hot sun for the train that would take them to Winchester. Finally the train arrived and the regiment departed at 6:00 P.M. The train was a far cry from the one the men had been on for the trip down from Vermont. They left on what Captain Ripley described as "a rickety train of old cattle cars, and crept at a snail's pace all that night." The cars were so full that some of the men had to ride on the platforms at the ends of the cars and others on the roofs of the cars. Private Hodge of Co. H remembered the miserable conditions on the inside of the cars:

They did not use us as well as they would cattle, for they put us in box cars and not ventilated at that. Our company was put in three cars. They were so full that we could not all lie down spoon fashion. After we had rode a while we were almost suffocated. Then we thought it about time to have a little fresh air, and we just made a few loop holes through the side of the cars large enough for a six pound columbaid [cannon]. The car we were in was so low that we could not stand up straight in it, so we made up our minds to take things as they came, and rode on very well contented, but rather uncomfortable. Some of the cars were made of iron, so the boys could not ventilate them and they suffered severely.[64]

While the Vermonters waited for their train in Washington, General Pope fired off a telegram at 11:48 that same morning to the Union commander at Winchester stating, "I send you to-day the Ninth Vermont regiment, 950 strong, as an addition to your force. Push forward your works a rapidly as you can." He finished the note with a rather ominous warning: "You may have to use them soon."[65]

The trip from Washington to Harpers Ferry took all night and most of the next day. Private Charles Hodge described the scenery along the way:

It is an awful rough country till we got to Frederick Junction. Then it is a most beautiful country to the Point of Rocks. From Point of rocks to the ferry the mountains come close to the river banks, and it is very rough, but beautiful mountain scenery. The houses, many of them, are destroyed; mills burned up, and it looks very much like rebeldom. We arrived at the ferry at 4 o'clock P.M.[66]

When the train was a few miles south of Baltimore it had to change to the Baltimore and Ohio Railroad tracks running west. The junction was called Relay House. Here the train stopped for a while and two tragic accidents occurred. As the train rolled into the station Pvt. Joseph Lawrence of Co. E, a 26-year-old farmer from Newport, one of the men riding on the platforms at the end of one of the cars, somehow fell between the cars. The rear car ran over him, severing both of his legs near his thighs. He died within minutes. Lawrence was survived by his parents, Jonathan and Angeline Lawrence, who were disabled and had depended on him for their support. One resident testified that the younger Lawrence, through clothing, food, and money, had contributed nearly $100 a year to his parents' support for the three years prior to his enlistment. In 1868, his mother received a pension of $8.00 a month from the government. Private Hodge of Co. H wrote, "One other fell on the track and had his fingers cut off." The soldier Hodge referred to was Private Charles M. Batchelder, an 18-year-old farmer from Bradford in Co. E. Apparently, Batchelder's injury was not too bad, as he remained in the regiment until discharged for chronic diarrhea September 10, 1865. He died in Bradford September 23, 1930, and was buried in the village cemetery there.[67]

Before the entire regiment moved out of Harpers Ferry an advance party led by Captain Ripley was sent out first. Ripley wrote of his experience:

Here [Harper's Ferry] we were detained till in the late evening, but after innumerable and vexatious delays, I was finally sent off in charge of the advance, consisting of a ridiculous old engine and six cars. This railroad has been habitually torn up, by either "Stonewall" Jackson, or the Union leaders, about every other week. The railroad is composed of logs for ties and the "strap rail." Of course we ran off, and as it happened to be just at the time the engineer thought he could hurry up a little, we got a pretty severe jam-up. Quite a number of the boys were thrown out the door, but miraculously escaped crushing. I went on to Winchester to get a stronger engine, and more tools. We got there at 3 in the morning.[68]

The rest of the Green Mountain Boys remained at Harpers Ferry. First Lieutenant Edwin Kilbourne complained on July 26: "We were & are still cooped up in cattlecars— as in a cage — and no place to sit down or lie down. The boys are about worn out being packed into the cars so closely — nothing to eat but 'hardtack' and no meat, coffee, or anything of the kind." They finally left at 1:00 A.M., on July 27, and took nearly five hours to cover the 35 miles to Winchester. According to Private Hodge:

It was the most beautiful country, but the roughest railroad that I ever rode over; nothing more than timbers laid down with bars of iron spiked on them. The country through the valley shows the effects of war to a considerable extent — houses burned and pillaged, bridges torn out, fences gone, corn and grain choked out by weeds, and things generally look as though they have had a "severe letting alone" for the past season.[69]

While the train was lumbering along between Harpers Ferry and Charles Town, Virginia, it jumped the track. The sudden lurch and abrupt halt slammed men and material around inside the cars. Captain Barney reported that Co. A fared pretty well in the mishap:

Between here and H. Ferry the train of cars which I with my Co. were on run off the track but as we were not moving very fast and there being ledges and rocks on each side of the track but little harm was done though two cars were really smashed up no harm was done to any of my Co. except that 3 or 4 of them lost their caps.

Private Ephraim B. Wetherell, a five-foot nine-inch 32-year-old carpenter in Co. H, who had helped his brother out of a jam only hours before, was not so lucky. He was smashed under the weight of four or five men that fell on top of him, along with a barrel of hardtack. Luckily, he survived the ordeal but received a spinal injury that had him on crutches for years and plagued him the rest of his life. After his injury he spent most of his time in the service in army hospitals until he was discharged with a disability on December 30, 1862. Despite his injury he lived until August 9, 1923. Ephraim's injury left only two of the four Wetherells in Co. H healthy.[70]

At that time, the garrison at Winchester was under the command of Brig. Gen. Abram S. Piatt. With the addition of the 9th Vermont, Piatt's brigade numbered roughly 3,000 men. Several days after the Vermonters arrived Piatt was replaced by Brig. Gen. Julius White. White was a 56-year-old lawyer and legislator from Illinois and a friend of President Lincoln. Like Stannard and his Green Mountain Boys, White was a volunteer and had entered the service in September 1861 as the colonel of the 37th Illinois Infantry Regiment. In the spring of 1862, he was promoted to brigadier general for gallant conduct in the battle of Elkhorn Tavern (Pea Ridge), Arkansas. The Vermonters took a quick liking to White, as Captain Ripley wrote several days after White had taken command: "Gen. Piatt has been superseded by Gen. Julius White, a Volunteer, and a pretty able man we begin to think. He is prompt, precise and energetic, and knows what he is about." Private Hodge was also impressed with General White, as he indicated in a letter to the *Lamoille Newsdealer*: "Brig. Gen. White, one of the heroes of Pea Ridge, is commander of the post; and a more polite and energetic man cannot be found. Evidences of improvement are everywhere manifest since he took command."[71]

Since the beginning of the war, the Shenandoah Valley had been troublesome for the Federals. The Valley was of great military importance because it was a corridor through which the Confederate armies could move rapidly over its well-maintained roads. Even when the roads were blocked with wagons, the land was cleared so neatly and cultivated that soldiers could march unimpeded through the fields. As important as its strategic transportation network was, the Shenandoah Valley also was known as the granary of Virginia. Thomas Lewis correctly stated in his book, *The Guns of Cedar Creek*, "the valley was a linchpin of the Southern Cause and a primary target of the Northern war machine."[72]

The town of Winchester was a prosperous commercial center of 4,400 people that lay at the junction of several roads, including the macadamized Valley Pike. The town's location determined its fate in the war. The town lay on a natural transportation corridor. It was also only about 70 miles from the U.S. capital in Washington, D.C., and 20 miles from the Baltimore & Ohio Railroad at Harpers Ferry.[73]

The 9th Vermont's camp, named Camp Sigel after Maj. Gen. Franz Sigel, who had been run out of the Valley by Stonewall Jackson two months before, was located on a hill about one-half mile northeast of Winchester. "The hill we are on is not high," recalled Captain Ripley, "yet we can see the entire valley spreading around us, encircled by the Blue Ridge, on all sides looking as though our position was a center from which a circumference of mountains was described, with a radius of about thirty miles." The camp was on the grounds of a plantation owned by the Confederate minister to England, James M. Mason. By now the house was ravaged by war, as Co. H's Private Hodge described: "The house occupied by him is a perfect ruin. It was a beautiful stone mansion, but the wood work has been entirely torn out, so that the owner will find very uncomfortable quarters, if he should ever return again." Captain Barney was not impressed with the area at all and informed his wife on July 27, "The country is a sorry looking place and if this war should last 3 years more I would not give much for Va."[74]

The reception the Green Mountain Boys received from the citizens of Winchester was anything but congenial. One of the townsmen hailed Corp. Charles Branch with "Hello, you belong to the new troops just arrived." "Yes," Branch replied, "this is the 9th Vermont." The Southerner said, "Well! by G-- if it isn't another lot of G-- D----- Yankee S--- of b------." Upon the last remark Branch knocked the man to the ground and warned him about how he addressed Vermonters.[75]

One of the women of Winchester wrote, "My contempt of the Yankees is so great that I cannot feel afraid of them. I know I can cow them and make them afraid of me whenever we come into collision." Another remembered how she would watch a Federal officer approach her on the street, intending to speak, and then turn her back just as he opened his mouth. Captain Ripley noted:

> The women here are worse than in New Orleans. Col. Stannard told me yesterday that it would be justifiable if we shot these rascals who insult our Flag and our men — and shot the women too who shoot our men — believing that petticoats should no longer be used as shelter.[76]

Private Zenas H. Bliss, a 20-year-old, five-foot-seven-inch farmer from Calais in Co. I, also complained about the hostile townspeople:

> Well we are in the worst hole in Va. I mean as far as the rebels are concerned. They are all rebels here and all mightily saucy. It makes me mad when passing through the city to the picket post to have them stand along the sidewalks and make faces and say that we should never come back alive. I would like to put a minie through some of them.[77]

The Vermonters' two main duties at Camp Sigel were picket duty and assisting in the construction of a large fort known as Fort Sigel [also called Star Fort because of its shape]. The men dubbed the fort "Fort Rip Raps" after the Union military prison located on a small island in Virginia's Hampton Roads where the prisoners busted stones with sledge hammers. Captain Ripley gave a glimpse of the effect the hard fatigue duty had on his men when he wrote:

> Our poor men are having a pretty hard time of it, for green ones, and my Co. B, which has kept up longer than any other, is now giving way. They work hard in the trenches ten hours per day in this intense heat and intolerable dust, or do quite hard guard duty and then sleep in the Fort or in the rifle pits or outside the stockade almost every night.[78]

On Sunday night, July 27, Confederate guerrillas attacked the picket line at Winchester. Within 20 minutes the regiments were assembled to reinforce the pickets. Captain Ripley described the scene:

> There was a tremendous flying around and some trembling — a great many boys thought their time had come. We formed and marched out and occupied the line of rifle pits facing the town, and after waiting there an hour and a half, we marched back again. We searched some houses and found arms and ammunition. The most important *capture* made was that of the celebrated "Belle Boyd," the female spy. She used to enter Fremont's and Seigel's line with perfect ease and impunity, whenever she wished, in spite of their efforts to the contrary. They say she is a wonderfully keen intriguer. She was sent to Washington this morning [July 30], under strong guard.[79]

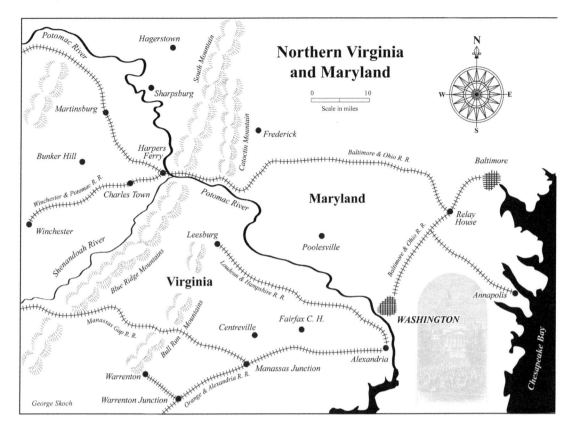

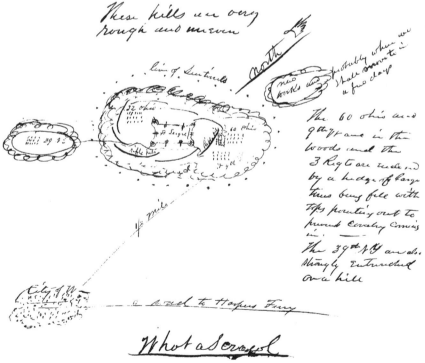

Top: Northern Virginia and Maryland. *Bottom:* A map of Fort Sigel drawn by Valentine G. Barney (Vermont Historical Society).

Charles Hodge also remembered the exciting night:

Last night about 10 o'clock the picket alarmed the camp, the "long roll" beat, and such a falling out and falling in I never saw before. The Col. ordered "Lights out," and then such a confusion. Some could not find their guns, others could not find their equipments, and although perfect silence was required, one would think the camp was infested by a horde of rebels. Many of the boys were pretty excited and although strict orders were given not to load a gun, many of them had to load before they could take their place in the ranks. One poor fellow came to me with his gun under one arm, and cartridge box and belt over the other, and begged of me to load his gun, for he did not know how, and he expected the rebels then every minute. I told him not to load until he had orders, and he had better take his place in the ranks. Capt. Slayton and Lieut. Guyer were as calm as men could be. Lieut. Loveland was not very well, but he was on hand. Some of the sick boys turned out that were not really able. After we had formed in line near the rifle pits, and stood about an hour, an orderly came and said all was right and that we might go to our quarters.[80]

Some of the men in Co. A, also involved in the skirmish, nabbed several prisoners as noted by Captain Barney: "[M]y guards have brought in 6 rebel scouts. They are rough looking customers and one of them makes believe crazy but they will bring him around to his senses I think for I have just detailed six sergeants to go and dig a grave for him."[81]

The spy Captain Ripley referred to was Isabelle "Belle" Boyd, an 18-year-old young lady who had supplied detailed information to Confederate forces for more than a year. She had grown up in the area and using her feminine wiles was able to freely move in and out of the Federal camps, thus supplying the Confederacy invaluable information about Union troop strengths and positions. Being a "wonderfully keen intriguer," as Captain Ripley called her, was her downfall. She was betrayed by her boyfriend, who she thought was a dashing Confederate cavalry officer, but was in fact a Union spy. She was captured on July 29 at her home in Front Royal with enough evidence that she was arrested. That same day she was taken to Brigadier General White's headquarters in Winchester. The next day she was taken to Washington and incarcerated.[82]

Private Charles Hodge saw Belle after she entered the Union lines and commented, "She is not as good looking as some have represented her to be, although she would pass for a fair damsel. The age of Belle has been reported at nineteen, but if we have the genuine Belle here, she is at least six years older, unless much care-worn."[83]

On July 29, another senseless accident occurred in Co. A. As Augustus T. Bushnell, a 26-year-old musician from Georgia, Vermont, in Co. A, unloaded his pistol he accidentally shot and mangled the index and middle fingers of his right hand. What was left of his fingers was amputated a short time later by Dr. Hall. Captain Barney reported home, "He will probably get his discharge soon. I am sorry to lose him as he is one of the best boys in the regt. and a good musician." Bushnell in fact was discharged for disability on May 28, 1863.[84]

Several days later there was another accidental shooting in the regiment. Corporal Abner B. White, a 26-year-old farmer from South Hero in Co. A, was sitting in the barracks with First Lt. Linus Sherman and Second Lt. Erastus Jewett cleaning their revolvers. Someone near by shoved another soldier who in turn fell against White. Somehow Corporal White discharged his revolver and the bullet lodged in his left knee joint. He was evacuated to E Street General Hospital in Washington, D.C. The bullet could not be removed. White was discharged for disability October 18 and had a bad limp the rest of his life for which he received a meager pension. Abner White married Charlotte Rodgers on February 28, 1875, in Kankakee County, Illinois. He died January 14, 1902, and his wife received a widow's pension until her death December 10, 1910. Their daughter Nasa A. White, born October 30, 1899, had Mary White of Story, Iowa, appointed as her guardian and received a pension of $12.00 a month commencing September 11, 1911, until she turned 16 years old in 1914.[85]

Even though most of the Vermonters itched to have a shot at the rebel troops, picket duty in the middle of the night could be scary business, as 30-year-old Stratton native Corp. James Grout of Co. K related:

> I went out on picket a few nights ago. There was some firing some ways from me but have not learnt what it was for. But one of my men that was posted about 25 rods from whare I was [was] some what skeerd and come to whare I was and said he thought that he would be ready to run if there was any danger. But there was not, so he went back to his post and staid until morning. Our camp has been alarmed twice. The first time we were drawn out in line of battle. The next time we were taken out but were not drawn up in line of battle. Thair was a union soldier taken prisoner about 2 miles from here two or three days ago.[86]

On the night of July 29, the rebels returned again as Captain Barney recalled:

> Last night we were called into line again and from the amount of firing among the pickets one would have thought they were having quite a battle. We were kept in line about one hour and dismissed. When the old guard were relieved and our men came in I learned the reason for once of the firing as some of my men were stationed at that point. Some rebel cavalry were scouting about the country and came upon and fired into our pickets with no harm being done. Our men returned fire and one of my men (John Sabberville of Alburgh) shot one of them from his horse but did not get the body as it was taken off by the rest of them immediately.[87]

Corporal James Grout, Co. K (Kent Young).

The arduous labors of the Vermonters started to take its toll as the days passed. Nor did the weather help the situation, as Corporal Grout complained: "We have very hot days and cool nights. The sun burns like holding a shovel full of coles to your face. I think some of the nights are cooler than I ever see in Vermont at this time of the year." The work on the fort was also producing its share of injuries. In late July Pvt. Joseph Douglass, a 38-year-old farmer from Stowe in Co. H was partially paralyzed on his left side by an injury and was discharged April 10, 1863, with a total disability. On August 20 Pvt. William V. Wetherell, one of the four Wetherells in Co. H, was injured while helping to construct the fort's magazine. While working with several other men to move a log with levers the log got away from them and rolled over Wetherell, hurting his back and causing a hernia in his scrotum. He was in the hospital when Winchester was taken by the rebels and was sent to Libby prison in Richmond where he contracted jaundice. He was paroled September 21 and discharged for disability December 30, 1862. He was drafted in 1863, but was rejected because of his hernia. He was married twice and had a total of six children. He died September 30, 1908, and was buried in Waterville. Corporal Horace W. Brown of Co. E got a hernia while pushing a wheel barrow loaded with dirt and had to be discharged October 17, 1862.[88]

The hot days and cold nights seemed to exacerbate the all too common camp diseases, and the number of men in the regimental hospital started to climb. On August 9 the regiment lost its first enlisted men to death from disease. Rufus B. Tucker, a 40-year-old, five-foot seven-and-one-half inch private in Co. D from Bridgewater, died of dysentery. When Tucker married his wife, Betsy Bates, August 21, 1853, his occupation was listed in the marriage book in the village of Tunbridge as a farmer, but in the 1860 census he was listed as a pauper and he and his family were living in the poorhouse. When he enlisted he gave his occupation as laborer. Private Tucker's platoon leader, First Lt. Asaph Clark, wrote to Tucker's wife on August 7:

by the request of Mr. Tucker I write you to let you know that Mr. Tucker is quite sick. we have hopes of him and hope he will be up in a few days. he has just as good care as any man can have in camp. he has been sick ever since we left Clouds mills which was two weaks to day it is the Disentary that ales him he is the only one in the Co that is very sick. He is very [illegible] and appers to be resince [resigned] to his fait. Let it be as it will and that makes it better for him. If he does not get able to write himself I will write again soon or if there is any chang I will write and let you know often how he is.

But on August 9 Clark had bad news to tell Mrs. Tucker:

It is with Sadness that I etempt to address you through the paper this morning for the tidings I have to communicate are ... Mr. Tucker has parted this life. He died this morning about sun rise he died very easy and was sensible to his fate. we shall miss him much but no so much as you must but Gods gibeth and taketh away and he [illegible] all things right. He will be burried to day I expet and I shall most likely write again and send you what he has left here behind that we can send if there is any and now I will close by Saying God be with you all.

The following is an inventory of all Rufus Tucker had left in this world: Cash $8.50, Wallet $.05, 2 Pocket knives $.50, 1 Bible $.33, 1 Needle Case $.50, 1 Pocket Hand Knife $.25, 1 Over Coat $6.20, 1 Blouse $1.50, 1 Shirt $.44, 1 pr Shoes $1.00, 1 Cap $.50, 1 Wool Blanket $2.75, 1 Rubber Blanket $1.50, for a total of $24.08.[89]

By November of 1862, Tucker's wife had remarried and his six children were wards of the state and placed in various homes. Each child received a small monthly pension from the government.[90]

The other enlisted man to die on August 9 was Pvt. Stephen Parker, a 33-year-old farmer from Hinesburgh in Co. F; like Tucker he died of dysentery.[91]

That same day 23-year-old Capt. George A. Beebe of Burlington had the misfortune of being the 9th Vermont's first commissioned officer to die of disease. Like Parker and Tucker, he died of dysentery. Beebe's death was quite a blow to the regiment as he was well respected and liked. His death was taken hard by his friend Capt. Edward Ripley, who wrote:

I went with Beebe more than with any other officer. He was a fine hearted, gentlemanly fellow, and universally beloved. His death afflicts everyone. He was the officer I spoke of, as, next to me, the youngest in the line, and besides me, the only beardless one. We sent his body home at our expense, in a metallic coffin.[92]

Before the war Captain Beebe had been a clerk in Burlington and had previously served in the 1st Vermont Infantry. When the 9th Vermont was being formed he had been elected as the captain of company F. Beebe's body was shipped by rail to Burlington, where it arrived August 14. The coffin, draped with the American flag on top of which was a wreath of evergreens and flowers, was taken to the town hall for a memorial. The hymn "Hark from the Tomb" was sung and a prayer was offered by a local minister. Beebe's body was then taken to his family's hometown in Highgate and buried.[93]

Second Lieutenant Alfred C. Ballard noted, "Last Sabbath Capt. Beebe was as well and strong as any of us," but by the 10th he was dead. Justified or not, Captain Ripley blamed the regiment's assistant surgeon, Horace P. Hall, for Beebe's and the other two men's deaths:

If we had a decently managed medical and hospital department, we would not have lost them. Dr. Carpenter has but just come on. Until now the sick have been under the care (lessness) of Dr. Hall, Asst. Surgeon. I have not let any of my men go into the hospital at all, but in three or four cases have taken them into my own tent, put them on beds, and nursed them myself, and they all have got well. Beebe would have been cured himself, and when Dr. Carpenter came, it was too late.[94]

Second Lieutenant Linus Sherman referred to Dr. Hall as a "Blockhead."[95]

The Vermonter's camp was moved on August 15 closer to the Valley Pike, but this was not as nice a spot as the first one, as Captain Ripley lamented:

Our old camp ground was delightful, but this is within 5 or 6 rods of the dustiest roads I ever saw, along these roads there is a continual flood of Gov't stores pouring into the Fort all day and all night.... The great trouble with the men is the perfect impossibility of keeping clean. Their tents are whirling full of dust night and day. They have hardly time to bring water to drink, the spring is so far, and their conveniences for bathing are about as good as in the desert of Sahara.[96]

As bad as the camp's location might have been, Edward Ripley indicated, in his snobbish way, that he and his fellow officers were bonding:

You have no idea how much I enjoy Major Stowell's being here. We are together very much while off duty, and his warm-harted friendship is all I enjoy down here. The line officers I do not like. Ballard, my 2nd Lieut., for a literary man does tolerably; but still he is one of those that licks his knife assiduously, before he takes his butter, and blows his nose with his fingers and wipes them on his breeches! There are pleasanter men at mess, you know—but still do not think I complain. Even they have their humorous side.[97]

Although the strenuous labor was taking a toll on the Green Mountain Boys they were at least eating well, as Lieutenant Sherman noted in one of his letters home:

We live just as well as we could ask. Have fresh vegetables & blackberries, good butter and eggs etc. etc. The men have a good variety for the army. They have to eat hard bread now but we are building a bakery and then they will have soft bread. Our bread we get outside the lines for eighty cents a loaf and just as good as you ever tasted. We got honey too. There is any quantity in the country. The valley in which we are in is rich fertile & produces large crops of hay & grain. We are appropriating some of it for our own use. A detachment of cavalry brought in 50 head of cattle Friday night and also some sheep.[98]

Captain Barney also mentioned how well they were eating:

Today we have been moving our tents and leveling the ground under them and in my tent (by the way Sartwell & I have a tent by ourselves) Sartwell has dug a cellar to keep our butter & milk in. You would think it a funny cellar it is about 2 feet square and about as deep. We get milk most every day and today I went out and bought 6 lbs. of very nice honey and some eggs. He also gets nice fresh bread every day of a Union family about one mile from here. Yesterday I went out with him and traveled around the country till we got tired and returned. We picked 3 qt. of B. berries and ate as many more. I did not know but they would make me sick but I find myself all right yet and but five minutes ago ate a lot more in milk for my dinner.[99]

Their labors apparently did not diminish their Yankee entrepreneurial spirit either. Corp. James Grout wrote his niece:

I sent to Plimpton to have him send me a box of stuff to sell here in camp. I expect he will send me 50 lbs. of maple shugar, 8 or 10 lbs. of tea and a lot of chewing tobacco. If he does I can more than double on it besides paying the expressage on it.[100]

By the middle of August Confederate activity around Winchester started to increase, causing General White to hurry up the completion of the fort. By Monday, August 18, Fort Sigel was armed with heavy siege guns. The orchards and timber around the fort were cleared away, rifle pits and abatises [obstacles made of trees felled toward the enemy] were constructed, and the magazine was filled with ammunition. That morning General White held a ceremony to officially dedicate the fort. The American flag was raised with full military honors, speeches were made and the troops passed in review.[101]

Several evenings earlier the cannons had been fired to determine their ranges. One of them had been positioned to fire over the city of Winchester, but it did not have enough elevation and when fired sent a solid cannon ball through a brick building. The round went through the brick wall into a bedroom, taking out the headboard of a bed, continued through an interior wall and exited through the other side of the building. Fortunately for the residents of the house the cannonball came through the first floor and they just happened to be on the second floor at the time. Captain Kilburn opined, "The boys were much elated about it. Would like to see the whole city served in a like manner. I wouldn't care much myself. Rather think I could look on with a great degree of complacency."[102]

At 8:30 P.M. the same evening as the ceremony in the fort, a contingent consisting of the 9th Vermont, parts of the 32nd and 60th Ohio, the 39th New York, a detachment of the 1st Massachusetts Cavalry, and an artillery battery — in all about 200 men — were sent out after Confederate cavalry raiders. Corporal Edwin R. Smith of Co. K was not able to go along because of a boil on his ankle as he complained to his mother:

> I was very sorry last night that I was lame. I could have given almost any thing if I had been well. The reason was Co. K was sent out at 8 o'clock last night with some cavalry and one battery. (The battery was 9 pieces. They are carried on the backs of mules. Two men can carry one easy enough. They are brass and throw grape. Are made for only close action are very distinctive.) Our Co. took one days rations. They may be back to night. Perhaps they will not be back until tomorrow morning. I wanted to go badly. They expect fighting. The officers were very particular that each man should have 40 rounds of cartridges. They are going among the rebels. Where they have some force. The boys were all glad to go somewhere. It is the first time they have been sent out on any such expedition. We have got about through digging trenches and will have fun enough out scouting or foraging.[103]

The mission was not as exciting as Corporal Smith had anticipated. Fourteen civilians were arrested that night but were released the next morning. Although several of the raiders were occasionally seen, none was captured. The Federal troops made about 40 miles before returning to Winchester at 8 o'clock the next evening. Although it was a hard march the Vermonters still had time to forage for food, as Corporal Grout reported home:

> At one place some of us got all the honey we could eat. At another place Jason Goss [Pvt. Jason E. Goss from Stratton in Co. K] and I went into a house and they gave us a good dish of bred and milk which was a fine treat as we have had to live on hard bread all of the time since we have come here.[104]

Even though the expedition was a bust, Corporal Grout indicated his willingness to go after the rebels again: "Our boys most of them are pretty lame and sore today but for my part I should like to start out again and I think I shall before long. I would like to get a crack at one of them bloody rebels."[105]

The 9th Vermont suffered another tragedy on Thursday, August 21. Private William H.H. Greenslit, a 26-year-old farmer from Waitsfield in Co. I, shot himself with his own rifle. He was found dead with a hole through his chest with his rifle and ramrod by his side. He apparently had used the ramrod to push the trigger. Second Lieutenant Ballard recalled that "Greenslit ... shot himself intentionally without doubt. He had been sick and somewhat out of his head." Private Hodge also noted Greenslit's strange behavior: "He had appeared melancholy through the day, and partially deranged at times."[106]

The rebel raids around Winchester reached a high point on Saturday, August 23, when a detachment of about 30 men from the 12th Virginia Cavalry Regiment, under the command of First Lt. Milton Rouss, placed an obstruction on the railroad tracks midway between Summit Point and Wade's Depot and stopped the train coming to Winchester from Harpers Ferry. The rebels robbed the train of $4,000 of Army paymaster money, the U.S. mail it was carrying, and a number of express boxes. The only casualty was the express agent, who was shot in the leg while trying to escape. For a while the rebels had a high old time eating the goodies and drinking champagne from the express boxes. When they had eaten their fill they set fire to the train and sent it on its way to Winchester without the engineer aboard. The train finally came to a stop three miles short of its destination. The Green Mountain Boys were more upset about the loss of their mail than they were about the loss of the Army payroll.[107]

As the Vermonters went about their business in camp on August 24 they heard the muffled sound of cannons far off to the southeast. Although they did not realize it at the time, they were listening to the prelude of the second battle of Bull Run.[108]

Toward the end of June General McClellan, mistakenly believing he was facing overwhelming odds, ended his attempt to take Richmond and retreated to the James River. By July 3 his Army of the Potomac was encamped at Harrison's Landing. General Robert E. Lee realized that McClellan's position was too strong to attack and for the next six weeks rested and reorganized his Army of Northern Virginia.[109]

Lee was now in a very tenuous position. The Army of the Potomac lay on the outskirts of Richmond. Maj. Gen. Ambrose E. Burnside, with an army of 7,500 men, was at Newport News. Burnside was something of a wild card, with the ability to march up the Peninsula to reinforce McClellan or move up the south side of the James and attack Petersburg. Lastly, Pope could drive south from northern Virginia to link up with McClellan.[110]

Lee watched and waited. Then, on July 12, Pope moved south from Washington. Knowing he could not wait and withstand an attack from the combined forces of McClellan and Pope, Lee sent Maj. Gen. Thomas J. "Stonewall" Jackson with two divisions to intercept Pope. The two forces clashed at Cedar Mountain on August 9, with the Federals being forced to fall back.[111]

By now, Lee knew that McClellan's army was being withdrawn from the Peninsula to reinforce Pope. Seeing an opportunity of striking Pope before this junction could take place, Lee ordered Maj. Gen. James Longstreet's corps to join Jackson. On August 24 Lee's and Pope's artillery dueled across the Rappahannock River, but due to a series of Confederate blunders, Lee's anticipated attack never materialized and Pope was allowed to escape. This was the cannonading the Vermonters heard at Winchester.[112]

Refusing to be denied a victory, Lee adopted a bold plan to send half his force on a wide strategic envelopment to get astride the Federal line of communication and then to follow a day later with the rest of his army. On the morning of August 25 Jackson, along with Maj. Gen. James E.B. "Jeb" Stuart's cavalry, set out on his raid.[113]

On the evening of August 27 Jackson's men destroyed the Federal depot at Manassas Junction. Pope moved to Manassas on August 28, but the Confederates were gone. Getting reports of the enemy in Centreville, and assuming this was the entire Confederate force, Pope ordered all his units to converge there. On August 29–30 the second battle of Bull Run was fought. On the first day of the battle Pope conducted a series of piecemeal frontal attacks, all of which failed to drive Jackson's men from an unfinished railroad cut. On the second day the Federals again attacked, but were repulsed with heavy losses and, as in the first battle of Bull Run, the blue-clad troops retreated back to Washington.[114] By his own recommendation, General Pope was relieved from command on September 2, and McClellan was given overall command of both armies. For the next week the whole Federal army was busy reorganizing.[115]

After the second battle of Bull Run, Lee's army disappeared from the Federals' view for a short while, but was soon found to be heading to Maryland. Lacking sufficient resources in northern Virginia to feed his army, both men and horses, Lee decided to take his army north. In addition to the full larder in Maryland, he hoped the invasion might cause an uprising by the already sympathetic Marylanders. With Washington surrounded by a large Confederate force, Lee reasoned the Federals would stay north of the Potomac, taking the pressure off Virginia. Lastly, a significant victory in the north might earn diplomatic recognition from Great Britain and France and thereby garner military aid.[116]

Lee's first destination in Maryland was the city of Frederick. The most direct route to logistically support this campaign was the Valley Pike running down the Shenandoah Valley. This would take his wagons through Winchester and Martinsburg and then straight to Hagerstown, his next destination. Unfortunately, the Federal garrisons at Winchester, Harpers Ferry and Martinsburg precluded the use of this route. Lee hoped that by putting his army between Washington and the Shenandoah Valley the Union troops stationed in the valley would retreat, giving him his needed supply route without a fight. Until then he would have to use a time consuming circuitous route through Gordonsville, Virginia.[117]

Once Lee had captured Hagerstown and opened his supply line through the Shenandoah Valley he would have unlimited possibilities to use his army. The Baltimore & Ohio Railroad could be held or destroyed, and the army could move from Hagerstown to Harrisburg, Pennsylvania. West of Harrisburg the Pennsylvania Railroad could be interdicted. Then the eastern part of the United States would be cut off from the western part, except for the slow and circuitous route by the Great Lakes. Lee would then be free to defeat McClellan, who could not be reinforced by Federal forces from the west. After defeating McClellan, Lee could march on Philadelphia, Baltimore, or even Washington.[118]

As Lee's army moved north, enemy activity increased around Winchester. During the night of August 26, Union cavalry from Winchester captured 10 Confederate cavalrymen near Newtown and brought them to Fort Sigel the next morning. Captain Barney remembered:

> Our men surprised them in the morning before they were up and took them with out resistance. I went down to the guard tent and looked them over. They are real tough, fat, healthy looking fellows. They were very well dressed with gray jackets & pants. I told them that they did not look as though provisions were very severe at the south and one of them said that they did not go hungry much as long as there was Union men in the country who they could steal from.[119]

Earlier in the day the Confederates had also taken some prisoners. As Pvt. David Steele, a 34-year-old iron worker from Weymouth in Co. C, was coming off picket duty he fired his rifle to clear it. The cap exploded and a piece hit him in the right eye. Before he could get back to camp for medical aid Steele and about 43 other soldiers were scooped up by rebel cavalry. They were taken to Richmond and incarcerated in the prison on Belle Isle in the James River. Steele was paroled after about two months and sent to Camp Parole in Annapolis, Maryland, and then sent to Chicago to rejoin the regiment. A short time later he got a furlough to go home. He was suffering from scurvy and was so sick he could not return to Chicago for two months. After returning he enlisted in the 17th Infantry on January 17, 1863, and deserted on February 8. He was arrested at home and sent to Forrest Hall Prison in Georgetown, D.C. He was discharged from the prison for disability December 18, 1863, because of the loss of sight in his right eye.

Steele applied for a pension after the war and his platoon leader, Charles F. Branch, wrote on December 12, 1881:

> Private David Steele of Co. C 9th Vt. Vols. is an applicant for a pension. He is a deserter and borne upon the rolls as such. His story of a prison life is to be winked at as his capture was always considered as a premeditated affair. The government has already more that paid him for the service he has rendered. He was always a shirk and a coward. I have this day disapproved of his testimony favoring a pension.

David Steele died January 29, 1892, without ever receiving a pension.[120]

As Confederate troops got closer and closer to Winchester, Maj. Gen. Henry W. Halleck, commander and chief of the Federal armies, ordered General White to withdraw his command to Harpers Ferry. On Tuesday afternoon, September 2, White issued orders to his commanders to prepare immediately to abandon Winchester and be ready to move. The men working on Fort Sigel were told to stop work and pile up all tools, wheelbarrows, sand bags and any other combustible material and set it ablaze. At the same time the cannons that had just been installed in the fort were dismounted from their carriages and then spiked (metal objects such as nails or files driven into the vent hole so the cannon could not be fired without a lot of repair). At 8:00 P.M. the Green Mountain Boys were ordered to fill their canteens, pack their knapsacks and prepare two days' rations. With all preparations made, White's command left Winchester at 11:00 P.M.[121]

Captain Edward Ripley wrote later, "Just before we started, my baggage wagon came, loaded with 28,000 cartridges, upon top of which, I was told, I might put my Co. Baggage. I got in one company mess chest, the Sibley tent, our mess chest, one wall tent and two of our beds, our trunks, and that was all." Then, he added, they marched into the "deepest darkness and silence."[122]

Left behind in the darkness was Captain Powell of the U.S. Engineers and a handful of men whose job it was to explode the fort's ammunition magazine and burn the army storehouses in Winchester. The man Powell selected to blow up the magazine was Pvt. Charles H. Sweeney of Wolcott in Co. H of the 9th Vermont. Under Powell's direction, Sweeney quickly scattered a thick layer of gunpowder on the floor of the magazine, lit the fuse and ran for his life. The rest of the 9th Vermont was about four miles away when the magazine went off. Everyone turned toward the sound of the explosion, which shook every house in the town, and witnessed the column of flame shooting skyward from the magazine, as well as the fires from the storehouses which lit up the night sky. Charles Hodge wrote, "[S]uch a conflagration was never seen by many of the boys before."[123]

Also left behind were about 40 members of the 9th Vermont too sick to make the journey. Surgeon Walt Carpenter also stayed behind to tend to his men. The next day the Confederates took Winchester, and Dr. Carpenter and his wards became prisoners of war. Among those too sick to leave were four officers, Captain David W. Lewis and lieutenants Linus E. Sherman, Erastus W. Jewett and Justus Dartt. Also left were the four Wetherells in Co. H. The only one of them not injured was 45-year-old William, probably a cousin to the other three, who was suffering from hepatitis. All four Wetherells would be paroled on September 21 by the rebels. William would be discharged for his disease on December 30. All four men returned to Vermont as disabled veterans without ever seeing combat. Leaving the sick men behind did not suit Captain Ripley, who reported home: "The saddest thing connected with the whole affair was we were ordered to leave behind all our sick. *I cannot say we had to do so, for I think they ought to have been brought away, and could have been.*"[124]

Winchester was entered unopposed the next day, September 3, at 11:00 A.M., by Confederate forces under the command of Lt. Col. John H. S. Funk, 5th Virginia Infantry. The retreating Union troops had attempted to destroy everything useful to the rebels, but Funk's men still managed to capture 90 Union prisoners, a large quantity of stores, a large amount of ammunition, guns, medical stores, tents, cooking utensils, etc. After the town was secured General Lee designated it as a Confederate depot. So far Lee's plan was on track.[125]

2

"As helpless as rats in a cage."*

Brigadier General White's retreating column from Winchester moved quickly through the early morning hours of Wednesday, September 3. Captain Edward H. Ripley wrote of the march:

> Our poor men suffered much, many were sick, many just recovering from sickness, and so long a march, carrying 40 rounds of cartridges and their knapsacks broke them down completely. We could get no ambulances, but could help a man broken down by a ride on a baggage wagon, once in a while.[1]

The fear of being scooped up by the Confederates kept down straggling even though the men were exhausted. Even with the fear of being captured several men still fell behind. One was Pvt. Emery S. Wilder, a 19-year-old, five-foot nine-inch farmer from Jamaica, Vermont, of Co. K, who was snatched up by the rebels. He was paroled September 15 and rejoined the regiment a few days later.[2]

At daybreak the column forded Opequon Creek, which was running about breast high, and at 7:00 A.M. they stopped at a place called Pleasant Point to rest and have breakfast. Two hours later the men formed up and were on the road again.[3]

As the regiment left Winchester, First Lt. Edwin A. Kilbourne, a Bradford native in Co. G, spied a bridle laying along the roadside and picked it up in hopes of finding a horse along the route. Soon after the breakfast halt his wish came true, as he explained:

> I was very fortunate in the last part of the march in securing me a horse, thus enabling me to ride about half the distance, which rested me "a heap." I came across a horse by the wayside. I just caught him, bridled him, & "jumped aboard," and pretty soon was fortunate enough to get a saddle off one of the teams belonging to an Ohio Regt., and then I was *full rigged* for a march. As I was Acty. Adjt. I rode along beside the Col. and the Surgeon in the rear of the Regt. & had a very comfortable time of it the rest of the way in.[4]

As the temperature rose and the march got longer the men started to jettison their belongings and the road from Winchester became littered with knapsacks, overcoats and blankets. During the morning Captain William J. Henderson of Co. G, who had been sick with a fever for a week, dropped by the roadside. Colonel Stannard had him put on one of his mounts and he continued on with the column.[5]

At 4:00 P.M., after a 34-mile forced march, the depressed and weary troops slogged into the safety of Harpers Ferry. When the Vermonters finally reached Harpers Ferry, entire companies sank to the ground, according to Captain Barney: "We came on again and did not stop more than 10 minutes at a time till we got here, which made us a very hard march and my company was very tired so that they, as well as myself, just lay right down and did not move for some time after we stopped."[6]

As the men lay panting on the ground they had time to reflect on the events of the last 24

*Quote from Captain Edward H. Riploy, U.S. Army

hours. Why they had "skedaddled" from Winchester was a mystery to the officers and men in the ranks. Captain Barney complained to his wife: "The fact is we are all mad to think how we were obliged to work to fortify ourselves and then to come away as we did and leave so many behind but such is the fate of soldiers." Private Hodge lamented:

> What all this skedaddle has been for we do not at present know. One thing is sure — we should have preferred to stop till we had seen something to run for. It is a very good time to run when one is obliged to. Everyone in the regiment is indignant at this operation but we have to obey orders.[7]

The town of Harpers Ferry lies on a small flat area at the confluence of the Shenandoah and Potomac rivers. About a mile to the rear of the town rises a 600-foot vertical bluff known as Bolivar Heights, which stretches from one and one-quarter miles from the Potomac on the north flank to the Shenandoah on the south flank. To the southeast, across the Shenandoah River, stands Loudoun Heights, which reaches an altitude of 1,200 feet. To the northeast on the Maryland side of the Potomac is Maryland Heights, which reaches a height of 1,450 feet. Harpers Ferry was an important piece of real estate because of its location, its industry and the Baltimore & Ohio Railroad that ran through it. The town was built around the ferry and the U.S. armory that was established there. It also was well known because John Brown chose the location for his failed attempt to arm slaves and start an insurrection. Brown and his comrades were captured at the armory on October 18, 1859. In the spring of 1861, Stonewall Jackson trained troops there. By September 1862, the town had changed hands several times.[8]

The garrison was under the command of Colonel Dixon S. Miles, a 58-year-old regular army officer. Originally from Sweet Air in northwestern Baltimore County, Maryland, he had been in the army since he entered West Point in 1819 at the age of 15. Miles graduated in 1824 and fought in the Mexican War. After the Mexican War he spent most of his 42 years of service fighting Indians at various outposts from Florida to New Mexico. At the outbreak of the Civil War he was commander of the 2nd U.S. Infantry Regiment at Fort Leavenworth, Kansas. In the first battle of Bull Run on July 21, 1861, Miles commanded a division of 6,000 troops, which was held in reserve. At some point in his career, he developed a fondness for the bottle, and during the battle of Bull Run he was inebriated and spent most of the day riding around criticizing his subordinate's troop dispositions. As the Federal army started to collapse, Miles was ordered to shore up the Union right flank, to which he replied, "I have something else to attend to." He was soon relieved from command and a short time later was brought up on charges. During the course of the court of inquiry Miles got off clean when it was learned that, because of an ailment, a surgeon had prescribed brandy for him.[9]

After being cleared of his scrape at Bull Run, Colonel Miles, with a force of about 1,000, was stationed at Harpers Ferry to guard the Baltimore & Ohio Railroad in March 1862. By the next month his "Railroad Brigade" had grown to about 3,600 men. Shortly after Miles' assignment, Maj. Gen. Stonewall Jackson became quite active in the Shenandoah Valley in an attempt to keep Union forces there from reinforcing McClellan's campaign on the Virginia Peninsula. As Jackson's activity increased, Brigadier General Rufus B. Saxon was assigned to command at Harpers Ferry and Miles became his chief of staff.[10]

Saxon took immediate steps to improve the defense of Harpers Ferry. Hundreds of troops were used to haul two 10-inch navy Dahlgren cannons, one 50-pounder Parrott, and three 12-pounder guns up the steep slopes of Maryland Heights. They were emplaced about halfway up the mountain and were trained on the terrain beyond Bolivar Heights, which Saxon thought was the most likely route of a Confederate advance. Saxon's thought was proven correct when Jackson's troops arrived in front of Bolivar Heights on May 28. Jackson assaulted the Union troops on the heights to no avail. On May 30 the Confederates assaulted again and almost broke through when one of Saxon's regiments broke and fled. To strengthen his lines, Saxon pulled all his units back to Camp Hill halfway between Bolivar Heights and Harpers Ferry. Jackson even put sharpshooters on Loudoun Heights to harass the Federals, but the distance from the mountaintop to Camp Hill made rifle fire useless. Then, on May 31, due to a threat 50 miles to his rear, Jackson gave up the effort. The Federals mistakenly thought their defense at Bolivar Heights and Camp Hill had caused Jackson to give up his attempt to capture Harpers Ferry.[11]

In June, several changes occurred that affected the garrison at Harpers Ferry. Saxon departed, leaving Miles in command again, and Maj. Gen. John E. Wool took command of the Union Army's Middle Department headquartered in Baltimore, of which Miles' command was a part. Wool had little use for the volunteer officers that were flooding the army and put his trust in regular army officers like Miles. Even as Wool funneled troops to Miles he wrote to Secretary of War Stanton on June 14: "I have examined Harper's Ferry, and find it in a very indefensible position." Then he asked for even more troops for Miles' command. With the arrival of Brigadier General White's command the number of men at Harpers Ferry swelled to nearly 12,000.[12]

On September 4, the day after arriving at Harpers Ferry, in an apparent attempt to retain the outranked Miles in command, General Wool ordered White to leave his command with Miles and take command of the troops at Martinsburg. White left the next day to assume command of the 4,000 men stationed at Martinsburg, 10 miles northwest of Harpers Ferry.[13]

On the same day that White received his order to take command of Martinsburg, Lee's lead units crossed the Potomac at White's Ford, Cheek's Ford, and Noland's Ferry, the nearest of which was only a little over a dozen miles from Harpers Ferry. Although reports brought in by his scouts indicated Lee's forces were getting close, Miles refused to accept the information, even though Wool had wired him that day to "Be energetic and active, and defend all places to the last extremity."[14]

The 9th Vermont experienced its first death in its new camp on September 5, as Captain Barney explained: "There has been but one death in the Regt. since we came here and that by a young man who had been detached in the battery [at Winchester] and acted as Corporal. He declared that he would never go back to the Co. as a private so he cut his own throat with his jack knife and bled to death before he was found. He was a member of Co. D." The man Barney referred to was John W. Spafford, a 23-year-old farmer from Sherburne (present day Killington).[15]

Also on September 5, with the number of units under his command increasing, Miles organized them into four brigades for better command and control. The brigades were organized as follows:

1st Brigade — Col. Frederick G. D'Utassy
    39th New York Infantry Regiment — Col. Frederick G. D'Utassy
    111th New York Infantry Regiment — Col. Jesse Segoine
    115th New York Infantry Regiment — Col. Simon Sammon
    15th Battery, Indiana Light Artillery — Capt. John C. Von Schlen

2nd Brigade — Col. William H. Trimble
    60th Ohio Infantry Regiment — Col. William H. Trimble
    126th New York Infantry Regiment — Col. Eliakim Sherrill
    9th Vermont Infantry Regiment — Col. George J. Stannard
    Wilder's Indiana Battery — Capt. Silas F. Rigby

3rd Brigade — Col. Thomas H. Ford
    32nd Ohio Infantry Regiment — Col. Thomas H. Ford
    1st Maryland Potomac Home Brigade (one battalion) — Maj. John A Steiner
    5th New York Heavy Artillery, Co. F — Capt. Eugene McGrath
    1st Maryland Potomac Home Brigade Cavalry (one detachment) — Capt. Charles H. Russell
    7th Squadron Rhode Island Cavalry — Capt. Augustus W. Corliss

4th Brigade — Col. William G. Ward
   12th New York Infantry Regiment — Col. William G. Ward
   87th Ohio Infantry Regiment — Col. Henry B. Banning
   5th New York Heavy Artillery, Co. A — Capt. John H. Graham
   32nd Ohio, Co. F Artillery — Capt. Benjamin F. Potts

Miles retained the following under his direct command:
   1st Maryland Potomac Home Brigade (one battalion) — Col. Maulsby
   1st Maryland Potomac Home Brigade Cavalry (several companies) — Capt. Henry A. Cole
   8th New York Cavalry Regiment — Lt. Col. Benjamin F. "Grimes" Davis[16]

Colonel D'Utassy's First Brigade was assigned to the right portion of Bolivar Heights running from the Potomac River along the heights to a point about halfway to the Charles Town Pike. The Second Brigade's line connected with D'Utassy's left and continued on to the Charles Town Pike.[17]

After being given their assignments, Trimble and Stannard rode out to examine the part of the defensive line where their units would be placed. Both agreed that it was a weak point in the defense of the garrison. Stannard recommended that a swath of timber and cornfields be downed for clear fields of fire and to deny the enemy a place to hide in preparation for an attack. Trimble carried the recommendation to Miles. According to Stannard, Miles examined the area and denied Trimble's request, saying the troops were too tired for the job and that he did not want the farmers to lose their crops and timber. Stannard and Trimble then devised another way to defend the area and asked Miles to allow them to entrench and lay a line of abatises above the unguarded ravines that ran from the Charles Town Pike to the Shenandoah River. Miles nixed this idea, allowing that artillery posted on Bolivar Heights could enfilade an infantry attack, plus the ravines running up from the river were impassable.[18]

The Third Brigade, under the command of Colonel Ford, was assigned to Maryland Heights on the Maryland side of the Potomac, which was the key to the defense of Harpers Ferry. Like Trimble and Stannard, Ford reconnoitered his position and found it weak. The only artillery was the battery of heavy guns positioned on the mountainside which could fire only toward Bolivar Heights. There were none to protect the heights from an attack from the back side. According to Ford, "It was covered with timber, and in all other respects in its natural condition." The key to protecting Maryland Heights was to hold Solomon's Gap six miles to the north. It was the first saddle in the ridge where the enemy could gain access to the heights. Ford advised Miles of this, and Miles promised to give him the artillery and men to do so, but as with so many other of Miles' promises, nothing ever materialized. In the meantime, Ford posted a picket line at the gap so he would not be surprised by the rebels. Colonel Ward's Fourth Brigade was posted on Camp Hill where Saxon had made his stand in May.[19]

Although Miles' force had grown to nearly 12,000 men, most of the units were as green as the 9th Vermont. In fact, the four New York infantry regiments had been in active service only three weeks. How they would react in combat was anyone's guess.[20]

It is interesting that Miles did not allow Trimble, Stannard and Ford to improve their positions, since General Wool had visited Harpers Ferry in mid–August and had ordered Miles to do that very thing. In fact, he went a step farther and told Miles to entrench Bolivar Heights and place abatises on Camp Hill, but for some reason Miles chose to ignore the order.[21]

While Miles rearranged his units on September 5, Col. Grimes Davis's 8th New York Cavalry was out on patrol where one of his detachments captured Confederate First Lieutenant Milton Rouss. It was Rouss and his men who had captured the train bound for Winchester on August 23. When captured, Rouss claimed he was wounded in the thigh, but no one took the time to see if he was wounded, which he was not. After reaching Harpers Ferry Davis took Rouss to headquarters to be interrogated by Colonel Miles, but Miles was out. While waiting for Miles to return Rouss complained about his wound so much that Davis sent him to the hospital accompanied by a surgeon. As the doctor proceeded to the hospital, Rouss kept limping and lagging behind. Finally, he was so far behind the surgeon that he had ample time to escape.[22]

The next day Lieutenant Rouss was recaptured and returned to Harpers Ferry. This time Miles was in and interrogated the rebel lieutenant for over an hour behind closed doors. What transpired between Miles and Rouss is unknown, but what is known is that Rouss was paroled and promised not to take up arms again until officially exchanged. Miles accepted Rouss's word and allowed him to leave Harpers Ferry through the lines on Bolivar Heights. This was the second time in as many days that Rouss was allowed to observe the troop positions inside Miles' lines. Why Miles thought that Rouss would not pass such valuable intelligence on to his army one can only wonder. The men in the 9th Vermont thought it was strange also and many started to question Miles's loyalty.[23]

There were other reasons besides Rouss's release that caused the Vermonters to question Miles's loyalty. Day after day virtually no work was done to improve their defenses. Everything around them was going on in a listless, lackadaisical way. On September 7, Miles wired his last message to Wool a little before midnight and just before the rebels cut the telegraph wire. It read, "The enemy is steadily pressing on my pickets, and is establishing batteries on the plateau opposite Point of Rocks, but I am ready for them." Nothing could have been further from the truth and most of those at Harpers Ferry knew it. As inexperienced in military matters as Capt. Edward Ripley was, he wrote, "Now was the time when we would have been glad to dig by day and night...."[24]

Also, during General Wool's August visit to Harpers Ferry, he had ordered Miles to build a blockhouse on Maryland Heights. He even went so far as to send Miles an engineer officer to supervise the job. Again, Miles chose to ignore the order and let the engineer cool his heels for several days before sending him as a courier to Washington. By the time the engineer completed his courier mission Harpers Ferry was surrounded, so he returned to Wool's headquarters in Baltimore.[25]

In addition to Miles not improving the fortifications on Maryland Heights, a number of his subordinate officers pleaded with him to occupy Loudoun Heights. Colonel Stannard, who had reconnoitered the heights, offered to take the 9th Vermont to the summit and, with the addition of a battery, assured Miles that he could hold it against any attack. Miles, however, made light of Stannard's offer and insisted that it was impossible for Stannard or the rebels to get cannons up the steep mountainsides. One has to wonder why Miles would have made this statement, since the Confederates had done that very thing when they attacked Harpers Ferry in May.[26]

In the first four days after arriving at Harpers Ferry the Vermonters relocated their camp six times. The moving finally ended on September 8, with a campsite behind the town on Bolivar Heights. The regiment's right flank rested on a little redoubt where the Charles Town Pike crossed the heights and then ran just north of and parallel to the pike. First Lieutenant Kilbourne wrote, probably with a little bravado, of the position:

> Our Regt. (the left of it) rests across the Charlestown Turnpike, & in case of an attack we undoubtedly should be somewhat cut up. The left of the Brigade was assigned to the 9th Vt. I suppose on account of Col. Stannard's having seen considerable service. It is a *post of honor* & yet of danger. But I reckon we are good for it.[27]

Colonel Stannard soon had his men back into the military routine of squad, company and regimental drills, picket duty and the evening dress parade. This was the first time he was afforded the opportunity to drill his men since leaving Vermont in July, and their poor performance bore witness to that fact.[28]

One downside to being stationed at Harpers Ferry was the men's inability to supplement their army rations as they had at Winchester. Captain Ripley complained to his mother:

> This is the poorest country to forage in we have seen yet, it is stripped bare; no butter, no milk, no potatoes, nothing but an occasional ear of green corn to be bought, or ginger snaps in town.[29]

Some of the Vermonters were determined to supplement their diets regardless of orders to the contrary. While on a foraging expedition on September 8, Second Lt. E.B. Sherman let the men of his platoon leave the march to pick fruit in a farmer's orchard. When confronted by his commanding officer, Capt. Albert R. Sabin, Sherman tried to defend his men's actions. The next day Sherman was charged with neglect of duty and disrespectful language to a superior officer. Somehow he beat the charges.[30]

A foraging party, of which Company G of the 9th Vermont was a part, was sent out on September 9 by Colonel Miles. The mission was to confiscate food and animal forage from the farm of John A. Washington, a secessionist serving in the Confederate army. First Lieutenant Kilbourne wrote later of the experience:

> It was a most beautiful tract of land. Beautifully situated & covered with most splendid growth of fruit trees I ever saw. But war makes *horrid work with it*, as with *every* farm within reach of the army. Alas, for the seductive influence of "state rights." The "Old Dominion" is *gone forever*! But I'll not stop now soliloquies on the evils of Succession [*sic*]. Suffice to say we see it in its boldest forms.[31]

While the Federal units were getting into their defensive positions, Lee's Army of Northern Virginia was bivouacked in and around Frederick, Maryland, trying to resupply itself and recruiting, but by September 9 the supply of food, shoes, forage and recruits Lee expected had not materialized in a quantity to do his army much good. Nor could Lee continue to maintain his supply route through Culpeper Courthouse. To move on west to Hagerstown he must have the Valley Pike. Although Winchester had fallen to his forces on September 3, the Federal troops stationed at Martinsburg and Harpers Ferry had not retreated as he expected. To remedy this situation Lee boldly decided to split his army, ordering Jackson, with six divisions, to secure Harpers Ferry while the rest of the army moved on to Hagerstown.[32]

Lee's Special Order No. 191, issued on September 9, explained his intentions. His plan was to capture Harpers Ferry by hitting it from three different directions simultaneously. Stonewall Jackson, with three divisions, was to take the route toward Williamsport, Maryland, cross the Potomac and by Friday morning, September 12, take possession of the Baltimore & Ohio Railroad, capture any Union units remaining in Martinsburg, and by securing Bolivar Heights intercept Union troops attempting to escape from Harpers Ferry. Major General Lafayette McLaws, with his division, and that of Maj. Gen. Robert H. Anderson, was to follow Maj. Gen. James Longstreet. On reaching Middletown, Maryland, Anderson was to take the route to Harpers Ferry and by Friday morning seize the commanding position of Maryland Heights. Brig. Gen. John G. Walker, with his small division, was to cross the Potomac and take Loudoun Heights by Friday morning. Then, after capturing Harpers Ferry, Jackson, along with McLaws' and Walker's commands, was to rejoin the army at either Boonsboro or Hagerstown, Maryland.[33]

Meanwhile, Longstreet's command, with the reserve, supply and baggage trains of the army, was to proceed on to Boonsboro and halt. Maj. Gen. Daniel H. Hill's division was to form the rear guard of the army and follow Longstreet. Lastly, Maj. Gen. Jeb Stuart's cavalry was to screen the route of Longstreet's and Hill's commands. The next day Longstreet's destination was changed to Hagerstown.[34]

Jackson's divisions left Frederick at 5:00 A.M. Wednesday morning, September 10, and 12 hours later bivouacked at Boonsboro, Maryland. Miles was notified by scouts twice that Jackson's units were in the area, but Miles dismissed them as foraging parties.[35]

By Thursday, September 11, 1862, Jackson's divisions were crossing the Potomac below Williamsport, Maryland. Running behind schedule, his infantry scattered Union cavalry blocking their way and pushed on. Meanwhile, Brigadier General White's scouts kept him informed of Jackson's strength and progress.[36]

While Jackson marched toward Martinsburg, McLaws' infantrymen poured over South Mountain into Pleasant Valley to the rear of Maryland Heights. Union officers on the top of the heights watched all afternoon as more and more Confederates moved into the valley below. By suppertime McLaws had some artillery brought forward and shelled Ford's pickets out of Solomon's Gap, but due to the rain and the onset of darkness he halted for the night. Later that night Miles sent eight additional infantry companies to reinforce Ford.[37]

Near midnight Miles sent his last message to Halleck in Washington before the rebels cut the remaining telegraph wires leading from Harpers Ferry. The telegram read somewhat melodramatically:

> My eastern front is threatened. My pickets at Solomon's Gap shelled out. The ball will open to-morrow morning. Force opposing me is estimated at ten regiments of infantry with proportionate artillery, before dusk; others have come into camp since. General White will abandon Martinsburg some time to-night, and I expect this will be the last you will hear of me until this affair is over. All are cheerful and hopeful. Good-bye.[38]

McLaws' attack started at first light on September 12 and was spearheaded by the brigades of Brig. Gen. James L. Kershaw and Brig. Gen. William Barksdale. Kershaw made his way south on the spine of the ridge running from Solomon's Gap to the top of Maryland Heights, while Barksdale's troops went along the east slope of the ridge. Both Kershaw's and Barksdale's men traded shots with the Union pickets as they moved through the woods and underbrush. Two of McLaws' other brigades remained in Pleasant Valley to protect against attack from the rear. Another brigade set up its two guns to cover the turnpike and railroad. Meanwhile, McLaws and the rest of his units moved south down the center of the valley. About 4:00 P.M. the 600-man 126th New York arrived on Maryland Heights to reinforce Ford. By 6:00 P.M. McLaws' men were partway up the heights when they ran into an abatis, and a sharp skirmish broke out with Ford's men. Darkness ended the firefight with both sides resting on their arms where they had stopped.[39]

With Jackson closing in on Martinsburg, the outnumbered White and his 3,000 troops left Martinsburg in a driving rain at 2:00 A.M. September 12, and arrived at Harpers Ferry about noon. They were ordered to bivouac on Camp Hill. White's units consisted of the 12th Illinois Cavalry Regiment, 65th Illinois Infantry Regiment, 125th New York Infantry Regiment and John C. Phillips' Battery M of the 2nd Illinois Artillery, which brought Miles' troop strength up to nearly 15,000 men.[40]

Earlier in the morning, not long after General White's arrival, and to everyone's disbelief, Colonel Miles paroled 16 Confederate prisoners that had been captured by cavalry patrols and held for several days in the town. As with Lieutenant Rouss, Miles let them leave through the lines on Bolivar Heights. Colonel Stannard happened to be the field officer of the day and was in charge of the picket line there. The prisoners approached and announced that they had been paroled and were to pass through the line. Stannard was aware the prisoners had been allowed to wander around Harpers Ferry and that they knew the number and locations of the Union troops, and, with the enemy approaching his front, he refused to let them pass and held them until almost dark. Then a staff officer rode up with a pass signed by Miles to let the rebels out and Stannard reluctantly let them go. Unbelievably, Miles did the same thing the next day. This was more reason for the Vermonters to question Miles' loyalties.[41]

Early Saturday morning, September 13, Brigadier General White published an order relinquishing command to Colonel Miles, even though he outranked Miles. White's rationale was

Miles' greater knowledge of the terrain at Harpers Ferry and the troop dispositions; he also was aware of Wool's preference for Miles. Almost immediately Miles published an order acknowledging White's magnanimous gesture and stated that the command must obey any orders from White as though they were from Miles himself.[42]

As Miles and White were writing their orders, McLaws resumed his assault on Maryland Heights at 7:00 A.M. Like the day before, the spearhead of the Confederate attack was the 2,000 veteran troops of Kershaw and Barksdale. The 126th New York and the 32nd Ohio formed the Union defense. The Union troops held their line until about 10:30 A.M. At that time the 126th New York's commander, Col. Eliakim Sherrill, was wounded in the jaw. As he was carried to the rear, blood poured from his mouth and his tongue was cut so badly he could not talk. The sight spooked his green troops and not long afterward someone passed the word to fall back and they broke. A little after the New Yorkers broke in confusion, Colonel Downey, with the 600 men in his 3rd Maryland Potomac Home Brigade, arrived in time to help stem the Confederate advance. The Union boys were pushed south about 400 yards, but there they held for six hours.[43]

A number of attempts were made to get the New Yorkers back up the hill, but it was like trying to push a string. Miles rode up the mountain to take control of the situation, but even he and his aides could not get the New Yorkers back into position. When Ford expressed fear that he might not be able to hold the position Miles replied, "You can and you must." Then, instead of insisting Ford hold to the last man, Miles added that Ford could withdraw if his force gave way again. Miles then left for his headquarters in town.[44]

Miles ordered Col. Simon Sammon's 900-man 115th New York Infantry up Maryland Heights, but then he and Ford decided to use them to support the heavy guns near Ford's headquarters rather than sending them to the summit to reinforce the troops that were being pressured by McLaws' men. Several officers asked that Miles and Ford make a counterattack with the reserves on the mountain, but Miles refused.[45]

While the battle raged on Maryland Heights, Jackson's division arrived on School House Ridge about 1,000 yards in front of Bolivar Heights at about 11:00 A.M. Before long, two batteries were unlimbered on the Charles Town Pike and opened up on Capt. Silas F. Rigby's and Capt. John C. Von Schlen's batteries, to which the Union artillery answered in kind.[46]

The new sounds of combat to the west got Miles' attention. He left his headquarters and rode to Bolivar Heights and by 1:00 P.M. or so he and his aides were on-site directing the defense. Around 3:30 P.M. one of Miles' aides directed his attention to Maryland Heights. Miles could hardly believe his eyes. Ford's 4,000 men were streaming down the mountainside. According to the chaplain of the 115th New York, Colonel Miles exclaimed, "God Almighty, what does this mean? They are coming down! Hell and damnation!" But, it was too late to do anything about it.[47]

As if matters were not bad enough, about the time Ford left Maryland Heights, Brigadier General Walker's battle flags were seen atop Loudoun Heights. He had reached his objective: Harpers Ferry was now surrounded. At the time, the Federals gave little importance to Walker's appearance since they were led to believe that it was impossible to get artillery to the summit and it was too far away for small arms fire to be of any threat. As Captain Ripley remembered later, "[W]e laughed at their mispent exertions." The Vermonters would not be laughing for very long. At dusk the artillery duel petered out and an eerie silence settled in over Harpers Ferry.[48]

One of the Vermonters on picket definitely was not laughing at the rebels. Private Louis Murray, a 19-year-old farmer from Addison, was hit in the left wrist with a Confederate minie ball. While the wound was not very bad, it was serious enough to cause him to lose strength in his thumb and middle finger and he was discharged for disability on November 23, 1862.[49]

As Miles' men were being shelled on Saturday afternoon, McClellan moved his Army of the Potomac into the camps around Frederick, which the rebels had abandoned four days earlier. Here, one of the most fantastic opportunities of the Civil War occurred. Unbeknownst to Lee, one of the copies of his Special Order No. 191 was lost in one of the abandoned campsites and found by a Federal soldier who forwarded it up the chain of command to McClellan. McClellan now had an opportunity to totally destroy Lee's splintered force. He also knew of Lee's plan to capture Harpers Ferry and had enough time to save it.[50]

At about 9:00 o'clock Saturday evening, Miles sent for Capt. Charles H. Russell of the 1st Maryland Cavalry and asked him if he, along with some of his men, could pass through the enemy's lines and get word to the Army of the Potomac of their predicament. Russell said that he thought he could. Miles then told him to get to any general of the United States Army, or to any telegraph station, or, if possible, to General McClellan himself. He was to report that Miles thought he could hold out forty-eight hours, but if he was not relieved by that time he would have to surrender. Russell successfully delivered his message to McClellan at 9:00 the next morning.[51]

As Captain Russell was riding through the darkness in search of McClellan, McClellan wired General Halleck around midnight:

> This army marches forward early to-morrow morning, and will make forced marches to endeavor to relieve Colonel Miles; but I fear, unless he makes a stout resistance, we may be too late.
> A report came in this moment that Miles was attacked to-day, and repulsed the enemy; but I do not know what credit to attach to the statement. I shall do everything in my power to save Miles if he still holds out.[52]

After verifying the authenticity of Lee's lost order, McClellan issued orders to his corps commanders. He gave Maj. Gen. William B. Franklin, commanding the VI Corps, the picture in detail, telling him about the finding of Lee's lost order and explaining the positions of Lee's troops. Franklin was ordered to move at daybreak, September 14, for Crampton's Gap. Once through the gap, his first duty was to cut off, destroy or capture McLaws' command and relieve the Union troops at Harpers Ferry. After that, depending on events, he would either rejoin the main army at Boonsboro or move west to Sharpsburg to cut off Lee's retreat. To make it perfectly clear, McClellan added, "My general idea is to cut the enemy in two and beat him in detail." Unfortunately, McClellan did not emphasize the sense of urgency.[53]

While the VI Corps was to be taking Crampton's Gap, McClellan's First and IX Corps were to force passage through Turner's Gap, seven miles to the north. Clearing Turner's Gap would open the way for the rest of the Army of the Potomac to attack the other half of Lee's divided army.[54]

Not a man to exceed his orders, Franklin did not move until the next morning, September 14, at 6:00 A.M.; then, at a leisurely pace, he crossed Catoctin Mountain. The division that was spearheading the VI Corps bumped into Confederate pickets in the village of Burkittsville, Maryland, around mid-morning and quickly cleared them out, but instead of trying to secure Crampton's Gap, Franklin halted his men for lunch while he assessed the situation.[55]

At Harpers Ferry the breaking dawn found the Confederates in possession of the summit of Loudoun Heights. During the night they had, with much exertion, brought 10 long-range cannons up to the top of the mountain and had them in firing position by 8:00 A.M. but did not open fire. Jackson had sent Brig. Gen. John G. Walker an order the previous afternoon that read, "Harper's Ferry is now completely invested. I shall summon its commander to surrender. Should he refuse I shall give him twenty-four hours to remove the non-combatants, and then carry the place by assault. Do not fire unless forced."[56]

By mid-morning Walker was aware that the battle for Crampton's Gap was underway and he was getting nervous with the rear of his troops exposed. Walker signaled Jackson around

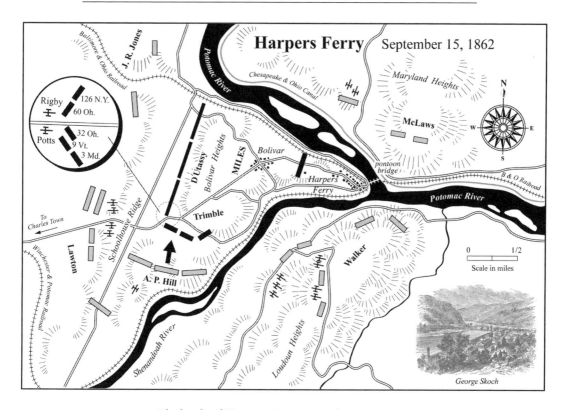

The battle of Harpers Ferry, September 15, 1862.

noon and informed him of the action at the gap and that Yankees were in the valley behind him. Jackson replied that it was nothing more that a cavalry engagement. Walker knew better and against orders he decided he was going to be "forced" to open fire. A little before 1:00 P.M. he sent two of his infantry regiments out into the open and, as he expected, the Union artillery on Camp Hill opened fire on them, but with no effect because the guns could not be elevated enough to hit the top of the hill. Walker now had an excuse to return fire. At 2:00 P.M. Gen. A. P. Hill's artillery west of Bolivar Heights opened up and at 3:00 P.M. McLaws joined the fray from atop Maryland Heights. If Jackson seriously had considered asking Miles to surrender before opening fire, Walker's action had ended any hope of it. Paul R. Teetor, in his book *A Matter of Time: Treason at Harper's Ferry*, presents an argument that Jackson already had an agreement with Miles to surrender, with Lieutenant Rouss being the go-between. However, we may never know with certainty if that was the case.[57]

About 1:00 P.M. the 9th Vermont's Maj. Edwin S. Stowell and Capt. Edward Ripley were lying on their backs in the grass behind their tents watching the shells from the Union artillery fly up toward the top of Loudoun Heights. They noticed the Union shells were falling short, but then suddenly they saw half a dozen puffs of smoke where the rebel artillery was positioned. Both men jumped to their feet, clapped their hands and yelled with joy that their artillery finally had gotten the range. Suddenly, in the center of White's brigade came a half dozen explosions, and columns of smoke and dirt shot skyward. Stowell figured out what was happening before Ripley and exclaimed, "It's their guns!"[58]

Captain Ripley described what happened next:

In an instant the bivouac turned into the appearance of a disturbed ant hill. Artillery, infantry, and cavalry were mixed in an absurd and laughable melee, as the panic increased. The rebel batteries were now in most rapid play, and as the fugitives came streaming towards us, the shells followed them with unerring practice. All at once one dropped into our camp, and Stowell sprang up with the exclamation that it was getting to be no laughing matter and we had better be taking care of ourselves. Then in a cool and quiet way our four companies in camp fell into line, in their company streets; and, as the shelling increased, at the word of command from Stowell, marched by the flank up the slope of Bolivar Heights, and lay down over the crest, where the shells skipped over our heads into the valley beyond. Again we laughed, but only for a moment, and for the last time in Harpers Ferry. We lay peering over at Loudoun Heights, and with occasional scannings of the front at our left, where we could see the rebel lines moving in and out of the fringe of woods, and batteries going into action. Suddenly, immediately behind us, we heard new concussions shake the earth, and to our dismay, right across the open ground where the Shepherdstown Road entered a fringe of woods, was an appallingly long bank of cannon smoke not over 1,000 yards away. We could plainly see the brass guns as they were run out of the woods. In an instant the air seemed alive with the exploding shells. We were between two fires, and there was no shelter that would protect a rabbit.[59]

Colonel Miles' aide wrote in his journal during the bombardment: "The cannonade is now terrific. The enemy's shot and shell fall in every direction; houses are demolished and detonation among the hills is terrible."[60] Even though the Union artillery could not reach the top of Loudoun Heights they kept firing. Captain Ripley wrote later that "The wicked waste of ammunition went on for hours unchecked."[61]

The surprise barrage caused the 125th New York to become panic-stricken and the men ran for the ravines or hid behind boulders, trees or anything else they thought would provide them shelter. The 9th Vermont, to avoid being blown to bits by the incoming artillery, moved as a unit over one slope after another as the Confederate artillery got their range, thereby allowing the Vermonters to come through the shelling without any men killed or wounded.[62]

Jackson's strategy to take Harpers Ferry relied on his experience from the previous May. To fool Miles into thinking he was going attack Bolivar Heights again he ordered one brigade and an artillery battery to secure a lightly defended prominent hill on the Federal right, which quickly was accomplished around 3:00 P.M. This action kept D'Utassy's brigade occupied.[63]

About the same time as the attack on the Union right, Jackson ordered A.P. Hill to move along the left bank of the Shenandoah River, turn the enemy's left flank and be prepared to enter Harpers Ferry the next morning. Hill first shelled the woods over which his route lay and then moved obliquely to his right until he struck the Shenandoah. After reaching the river, he noticed a hill on the extreme left of the Yankees' line bare of earthworks and protected only by abatises made of fallen timber. Hill ordered the brigades of Brig. Gen. William D. Pender, Brig. Gen. James J. Archer, and Brig. Gen. John N. Brockenbrough to gain the crest of the exposed hill. Those of Brig. Gen. Lawrence O. Branch and Brig. Gen. Maxcy Gregg were ordered to march along the river during the night and secret themselves in the ravines that ran from the river and be prepared for a daylight assault on the Yankees' rear. By 5:00 P.M. the artillery duel ceased and A. P. Hill's brigades increased the pressure against the Union left.[64]

Colonel Downey's 3rd Maryland Potomac Home Brigade was hit by Pender's and Brockenbrough's brigades. Downey called for reinforcements and Colonel Trimble ordered Colonel Willard to take his 125th New York to Downey's aid, but Willard said that his unit was too demoralized and would not move. Trimble then ordered Colonel Stannard to take four companies of the 9th Vermont to support Downey, which was accomplished in a matter of minutes. A little later a portion of Colonel Ford's 32nd Ohio also was sent to reinforce Downey and, with the aid of Rigby's battery, near the Charles Town Pike, they held the Confederates at bay.[65]

Corporal James Grout, a 30-year-old farmer from Stratton in Co. K, told of his experience in the fight:

We had something of a fight at the ferry. The shot and shell come among us like fury. We had one man in our company wounded by a musket ball in the hip. One of the Maryland boys stood by me was wounded in the cheek and one by me on my right hand was shot dead. You may calculate the bullets flew rite smart. They whisked round my ears like bumblebees and rather close I tell you.[66]

The man wounded in the hip was Pvt. Seneca W. Taylor of Co. K, a 25-year-old, five-foot five-inch, farmer from Plymouth, Vermont. He was hit in the left hip by a rebel minie ball that, fortunately, missed the thigh bone and passed on through his hip. Later he was sent to the Naval School Hospital in Annapolis, Maryland. He rejoined the regiment in Chicago and for the rest of the war, because of his wound, worked in the regiment's hospital. After the war he returned to Plymouth, where he worked as a grocer and then a tin peddler. In 1878, Taylor moved to Iuka, Kansas, where he became the postmaster and a successful department store owner. He married there and had one son. He died June 30, 1926.[67]

Sergeant Nelson L. Wandell, a 24-year-old five-foot three-inch carpenter from Brattleboro in Co. K, recorded the action against the 9th Vermont's skirmish line:

Just as the sun was going down they advanced. Gen. A.P. Hill's brigade to flank us on the left, they filed down the hill opposite through a cornfield. We retreated at [up] the hill and were fired on by their advances. Retreated behind a rail fence and collected the pickets to make a Stand.

Here we fired several rounds and the rebels advanced in good order. We were not strong enough to withstand them, again we retreated, but kept up a steady fire. We formed again behind a rail fence and some stumps and bushes. Here we were reinforced by the 32d Ohio.

It was getting to be quite dark and the men were hollering out your shooting our own men. Here we made a stand for half an hour and then retreated towards the fort to a better position. The rebels did not advance on us. At nine O'clock P.M., we went down to the cross roads on the Charleston [Charles Town] pike and staid all night.[68]

Near the Charles Town Pike the 9th Vermont laid down in a peach orchard for the night in front of Rigby's battery as his support. As Co. K and the other two companies of the 9th Vermont had fallen back in the darkness, Captain Ripley's Co. B, which was on the extreme left flank of the Federal line and deployed down the side of the bluff overlooking the river, was left behind. Ripley wrote later of his experience:

As I was in a measure isolated in the darkness, the companies connecting on my right had orders to keep up a careful contact with us. After a while the firing on the right seemed to drop back as though our line had given way, and I heard a confusion to the right of our front. Creeping carefully up in the darkness I discovered our line gone and the rebels pushing in between me and it. Without an instant to spare, I whispered my orders to the men, and we slid silently down the slope and made our way within our new line by the bank of the river, after we were supposed to have been cut off and captured.[69]

Around 8:00 P.M. Pender assaulted Rigby's battery that had been such a bother all evening, but his men were no match for the double shots of canister that Rigby poured into them and the rebels retreated. (A canister is a round similar to a small paint can filled with cast-iron balls, making the cannon somewhat like a large shotgun. In this case each cannon was loaded with two rounds at a time.)[70]

General White saw a chance to launch a counterattack on Pender's retreating command and ordered Colonel Ward's 12th New York to support the attack, which would have isolated Branch's and Gregg's brigades, but Miles got word of the counterattack and countermanded it. He claimed that Camp Hill, where Ward's regiment was positioned, had to be held.[71]

By 9:00 that night A.P. Hill's troops were in position for the next morning's attack and the firing gradually died down. In some places Hill's troops were within 150 yards of the Federal line. Captain Ripley remembered later:

That night we could hear the rebels very busy across the Shenandoah exactly in rear of our left flank. We were withdrawn from Colonel Downey's line during the night, and lay in a young peach orchard underneath and perhaps fifty yards from the guns of Rigby's battery, to support it from an attack along the Charles Town Pike. As far as the eye could reach in the circle, from the Shenandoah to the

Potomac, was the lurid glare of Jackson's campfires, close up around us. The darkness of the night, with the protection it brought us, was so grateful that we wished we might always be enwrapped in it, so inevitable was the hopeless contest to be forced on us with the first streak of dawn.[72]

At 8:15 Sunday night Jackson sent Lee a message that read, "Through God's blessing, the advance, which commenced this evening, has been successful thus far, and I look to Him for complete success tomorrow. The advance has been directed to be resumed at dawn tomorrow. I am thankful that our loss has been small." At least in Jackson's mind the fate of the Union troops trapped in Harpers Ferry was sealed.[73]

During the late afternoon, while Stannard's Vermonters helped to fend off A.P. Hill's men, Franklin's troops, including the "Old" Vermont Brigade, battled McLaws' men in Crampton's Gap. By nightfall the gap, as well as the other side of the mountain in Pleasant Valley, was secured. The Confederate troops that had been pushed out of the gap were put in a defensive line about a mile and a half south of where the Yankees had stopped for the night. It appeared that the next day Franklin would relieve Miles' force bottled up in Harpers Ferry.[74]

On September 13, Lt. Col. Benjamin F. "Grimes" Davis, commander of the 8th New York Cavalry Regiment, tried to convince Colonel Miles that the cavalry was of no use at Harpers Ferry and they should try to cut their way through the surrounding Confederate lines and escape. His plan was to ford the Shenandoah River half a mile above the ferry and make his way around the base of Loudoun Heights. Then, the blue column would push down the south bank of the Potomac River to Washington. At first Miles agreed, but then he changed his mind and denied Davis's request.[75]

Because the cavalry was extremely vulnerable to the Confederate bombardment and because the horses would be a delectable prize if Harpers Ferry was taken, Davis approached Miles again on Sunday about permission to escape. At first Miles refused to let Davis go, but when Davis told him he would go with or without Miles' consent, Miles agreed to the plan with the provision the cavalry would cross below Harpers Ferry and proceed toward Sharpsburg, to which Davis consented. Miles also ordered everyone involved with the breakout not to let any of the infantry units know, as he was afraid if they knew the cavalry was leaving they might stampede. At 8:30 that night 1,500 cavalry quietly departed Harpers Ferry. For two hours, in columns of two, the cavalrymen snaked across the river on a pontoon bridge and trotted off into the darkness.[76]

Although the cavalrymen encountered a number of Confederate pickets along the way, they easily evaded them and continued on through the night. Near Sharpsburg, Maryland, the column met with a sheet of flame from rebel rifles. Davis quickly changed direction and headed his men toward Falling Waters on the Potomac to find an easier point to penetrate the Confederate line. At Boonsboro they again bumped into the rebels, who lobbed several artillery shells at them, but on they plodded. Just before dawn, near Hagerstown, the blue-clad cavalrymen came upon a 60-wagon rebel supply train belonging to Major General Longstreet, which they promptly captured. With the rebel wagons in tow, the Union cavalrymen continued on until they crossed the Mason-Dixon Line and came to a halt at 9:00 A.M. in the safety of Greencastle, Pennsylvania, completing one the most daring escapes of the war.[77]

Colonel Miles was right that the infantry would want to break out also if they learned the cavalry was going to leave. When Colonel Stannard found out about the plan he was livid. He asked Miles for permission to take his regiment out with the cavalry, but Miles refused and stated that his pickets would not permit the infantry to pass out. Stannard countered that he would take possession of the picket line with his own men and leave. According to Stannard, "Miles then became excited, used 'very strong language,' swung his saber in the air, and ended all further discussion by saying that he had been forty years in the army and did not care to be lectured by one who bad been a soldier but a few months."[78]

When dawn broke on Sunday, September 15, Harpers Ferry was shrouded in a thick fog, which shortly lifted, and Jackson's artillery opened up as soon as the gunners could see their targets. The 9th Vermont could not have been in a worse spot, as Rigby's and Capt. Benjamin F. Potts' batteries were the rebel's main targets. The Vermonters lay almost in a direct line between Potts' battery and a Confederate battery that had been set up during the night in a cornfield across the Shenandoah in the Federals' left rear. Captain Ripley felt that they were as "helpless as rats in a cage."[79]

Ripley continues the story:

There was not a tree trunk in the orchard an inch in diameter, or with foliage enough to make a screen, and we lay on our faces plainly exposed to at least three batteries. All we could do was to lie still and wait until these batteries got the range on us and then Stannard would coolly jump us up and throw us forward at a double-quick as far as he could move to the front and then drop us flat again. When they got this range, we would jump up and double-quick back under Rigby's guns. In this way the regiment was most skillfully preserved from a heavy loss.[80]

Major Edwin S. Stowell had a very close call during the bombardment, as he later explained:

One shot struck in the midst of Co. B, Capt. Ripley's. The men jumped and I thought they were ago-ing to break and getting up from my blanket where I was sitting watching matters and things when a 12 pound shrapnel [cannonball filled with lead bullets] struck my blanket, exploding, scattering bul-lets by the hundreds in all directions. None for me, as usual.[81]

Soon after the artillery bombardment started, Corporal Grout of Co. K was sent out to find where A.P. Hill's skirmishers were. He wrote to his mother later of his experience:

I went out from my company by order of our Lieutenant to see how they were advancing and I went a little to far. I git by their skirmishers and when I come back they hailed me to take me, but I had no notion of being taken, so I kept on. And they fired a voley of 25 or 30 shot at me and the way they rattled my ears was a sin.[82]

When Grout returned, his lieutenant, Able E. Leavenworth, asked him why he had not sur-rendered. His reply was, "I might have perished, but surrender, I would not in sight of my com-rades."[83]

The only casualty in the 9th Vermont during that morning's bombardment was First Lt. Josiah O. Livingston of Marshfield and Co. G. Instead of staying down on the ground, Liv-ingston stood on the rail of a rail fence to see what Hill's infantry was up to and was hit in the left ankle by a shell fragment. The wound was slight, and he was able to remain with his com-pany.[84]

First Lieutenant Edwin Kilbourne barely escaped with his life during the shelling, as he later remembered: "The last day of the fight a 6 pound cannon ball went so near me as to draw blood on the bridge of my nose. My head was turned sideways to the battery & the ball passed me & struck just beyond at my feet. [I] was lying down on my belly at the time with all the oth-ers."[85]

Although the men of the 9th Vermont generally withstood the shelling without breaking, there were a few exceptions, as Major Stowell admitted later:

Well we lost but few men. We supposed matters were about the same other wheres, for then our noble men stood exposed more (but every other Regiment had skedaddled and hid in woods and ravines) than any other Regiment there and apparently more than any I ever saw before not a man hardly offering to leave the ranks. I say "hardly." There were two— one I knocked down with my pis-tol and the other I snapped a cap at him. Fortunately for him being a poor one and not discharging the pistol. No more skadaddling after that I assure you.[86]

About 7:00 A.M. the Federal guns started running out of long-range ammunition. Colonel Miles talked with General White about the possibility of surrender. White suggested that the brigade commanders be consulted, which Miles did. They all agreed that the only way to avoid a slaughter was to surrender. With his officers in agreement, Miles ordered the white flag raised. Slowly, one rebel battery after another ceased firing. As the artillery fire subsided, Maj. Gen. A.P. Hill, who had been selected by Jackson to oversee the surrender of the garrison, sent an aide to the Union lines to ask if they in fact were going to surrender. Miles assured him they were and asked General White to ride out to see Hill about the terms of a surrender.[87]

The Green Mountain Boys were shocked by the sudden surrender. Captain Barney confessed, "I never had such feelings come over me as at that time and could hardly suppress the tears." The Confederate troops, of course, had the opposite feeling and, according to Captain Barney, as soon as the white flag went up cheer after cheer went up from the rebels."[88]

After confirming Miles' intent to surrender, Jackson sent the following message to General Lee at about 8:00 A.M.:

> Through God's blessing, Harper's Ferry and its garrison are to be surrendered. As Hill's troops have borne the heaviest part in the engagement, he will be left in command until the prisoners and public property shall be disposed of, unless you direct otherwise. The other forces can move off this evening so soon as they get their rations.[89]

After a 15 minute lull in the artillery fire the Confederates opened up again. One of the rounds landed near Colonel Miles and a fragment of the shell tore away most of his left calf and then sliced his right one. One of his aides, Lieutenant Henry M. Binney, ran to his boss and tied his handkerchief around Miles' left leg just above the knee for a tourniquet. Binney then called for a group of nearby men to help move Miles to an ambulance. Two of the men were from the 9th Vermont, Corp. Joseph B. Graham and Pvt. Daniel Sullivan, both of Co. B and Rutland. The others were Capt. Benjamin Lee and four enlisted men from the 126th New York. The men put Miles on a blanket and started carrying him toward the ambulance. According to Graham and Sullivan, as they passed Rigby's battery, which refused to lower its flag after the surrender, Miles said to Lieutenant Binney, "Why don't they haul down that God damned flag? It has been the death of me." Miles' remark could be taken two ways. One way is that Miles was a traitor and was cursing the flag. The other way is that he was angry that Captain Rigby had not taken down his American flag and was the cause of the renewed bombardment. Which version is true, or even if he really made the comment, will probably never be known for sure.[90]

On the way to the ambulance another shell struck close to the men carrying Miles, causing the men to drop him. One of the shell fragments wounded Captain Lee and blew Miles' hat off. But the men got back up and finally got the colonel to the ambulance. Soon after Miles left the field, the Confederate fire ceased.[91]

Miles lingered in terrible pain until 4:30 P.M. the next day, when he died. His body was escorted by his staff to Baltimore and then through Baltimore County to the graveyard at St. James Episcopal church, near his home in Sweet Air, where he was buried Friday, September 20.[92]

When the word reached the 9th Vermont that Miles had surrendered, Stannard swore that he would never surrender and got the regiment on its feet and double-quicked them down a ravine to a road that ran along the river. His intention was to pass through the town and cross over a pontoon bridge spanning the Potomac River and try to cut his way through to McClellan in Maryland. But before Stannard got to the town, Hill had started rounding up the Federal units. When the 9th Vermont was found missing, several staff officers were sent to locate the missing Vermonters. They were intercepted just as they breathlessly reached the pontoon bridge. At first Stannard refused to obey the order to return, but after being informed of the penalties that would be imposed on the other troops if he violated the terms of the surrender, he reluctantly agreed to return.[93]

The terms negotiated by General A.P. Hill and General White stipulated that all the troops under Colonel Miles' command, with all munitions of war and public property belonging to the United States, would surrender to Hill. The officers and men would be paroled and would not bear arms against the Confederate States until properly exchanged. Lastly, the officers would be allowed to keep their sidearms and personal property. Hill allowed the Federal officers to retain enough wagons to transport their personal possessions, but the wagons were to be returned. They were returned as requested, but for some reason not until two months later after Hill had "made repeated calls for them."[94]

The surrender netted the rebels 11,000 prisoners, about 12,000 stand of small arms, 70 pieces of artillery, harness and horses, about 200 wagons, and a large number of commissary, quartermaster and ordnance stores. Jackson gained this victory with the loss of only 39 men killed and 247 wounded. The Union loss also was light, considering the pounding they had received, with only 44 killed and 173 wounded.[95]

As strange as it may seem today, paroling prisoners during the first three years of the Civil War was a necessity for both sides. Neither side was prepared to transport, house, or feed the number of prisoners that they captured. Brig. Gen. Ulysses S. Grant summed up the problem of capturing 12,000 prisoners at Fort Donelson when he wrote his superior on February 17, 1862: "I am now forwarding prisoners of war to your care and I shall be truly glad to get clear of them. It is a much less job to take them than to keep them."[96]

The word parole came from the French term *parole d'honneur* and was a pledge under which a prisoner was released with the understanding that he would not bear arms until exchanged. At the start of the war in 1861 there was a body of widely recognized customs, usages and principles regulating the taking, paroling and exchanging of prisoners. It was not until February 1862 that the first discussions between Confederate and Federal officials took place to work out a system to exchange prisoners. One reason for the delay was that the Union did not recognize the Confederacy as a nation and felt that to enter into negotiations would give the South tacit recognition. On July 22, 1862, the Federals and Confederates developed a cartel for exchange that was based on rank. For example, one general equaled sixty enlisted men, one colonel equaled fifteen enlisted men, one lieutenant equaled four enlisted men, and one sergeant equaled two enlisted men. The parole system worked well during the war because on both sides it was effectively self-enforced.[97] To make the Confederate's job more difficult in issuing paroles, Stannard would not have his regiment paroled as a unit and insisted that each man be issued his own parole. This caused the rebel officers many more hours of work.[98]

Earlier, while Stannard and the staff officers were in deep discussion at the head of the pontoon bridge, the company officers quickly tried to devise a way to save their regimental colors. Captain Ripley remembered huddling around Color Sergeant Felix Quinn, a six-foot two-inch farmer from Roxbury in Co. I, with a number of other officers debating what to do. Ripley suggested having Quinn take off his coat and cut the flag loose, wind it around Quinn's body, and then put his jacket back on. Ripley whipped out his pocket knife to cut the flag loose, but several of the others stopped him, stating that would be the first place the Confederates would look. Someone suggested cutting the flag up and distributing the pieces to various individuals. Ripley said later that he carried a piece of the flag in his pocket through the entire war. Others of the regiment remembered it differently. Colonel Stannard thought it was cut from the staff by Quinn, who carried it off under his blouse as Ripley had suggested. Lieutenant Theodore S. Peck and others thought that it was torn into strips and distributed among the officers. First Lieutenant Edwin A. Kilbourne, acting adjutant at the time, believed that it was wrapped around some sidearms belonging to him and several of the other officers and thrown into the river.[99]

Because of these stories Vermont's adjutant and inspector general Peter T. Washburn often said that none of Vermont's units ever lost their colors during the war. However, after the war, the Confederate government buildings in Richmond were cleared out by Federal troops and taken to Washington. Years later, George G. Benedict, while researching and writing *Vermont in the Civil War, 1861–1865*, found the 9th Vermont's regimental standard in the collection of Union flags captured by rebels in a government office in Washington, D.C.[100]

While Captain Ripley and others tried to save the regiment's flag, others tried to keep the rebels from getting their weapons, as Captain Barney described: "Many [officers] threw away their swords and revolvers and many of the boys broke their guns over stumps."[101]

After agreeing to honor the surrender, Stannard marched his men back to Bolivar Heights. As they crested the heights they saw the long rows of stacked arms, to which the Vermonter's reluctantly added theirs. The troops then were released to their camps, which they found full of rebels who were freely pillaging their possessions in spite of the terms of surrender.[102]

Incensed by what was happening, Lieutenant Quimby went up to a group of mounted Confederate officers who were watching the goings on and asked one of the bearded men, "Are you Stonewall Jackson?" Jackson replied, "Yes." With his Vermont dander up, Quimby said, "Did you not agree to protect us under the terms of the surrender?" Jackson replied, "Yes." Now having worked himself into a lather Quimby blurted out, "Then, by God, sir, I want you to drive these lousy thieves of yours out of my camp and stop them robbing my men." The other Vermonters who were watching recoiled in terror at Quimby's last remark and waited for Jackson's fiery response, but Jackson calmly said, "This is all wrong and I will see it stopped." He turned to one of his staff and ordered him to chase the rebel troops out of the Vermonters' camp, but it was too late to save a lot of the men's belongings. Sergeant Nelson Wandell wrote in his diary that night, "The rebels stole my knapsack with all my things."[103]

One rebel officer rode up to the 9th Vermont's second in command, Lt. Col. Dudley K. Andross, and said, "Colonel, I will exchange horses with you." Andross' horse was a fine looking bay named Frank that had been given to him by the citizens of his hometown of Bradford when he went off to war. According to Corp. Charles F. Branch of Co. C:

> Andross with tears in his eyes dismounted, exchanged his good horse for a poor old bob-tailed black mare, and as the regiment stood in line (having stacked arms) rode up and down, driving his Mexican spurs into the flanks of his beast, and ordering her with a twitch on the bridle to "Get up here, you ____ Southern Confederacy!" One of the regiment's officers finally was able to protest to General Jackson about Andross' treatment and his horse was returned.[104]

The Vermonters were less than impressed with the rebel soldiers who had captured them. Major Stowell described them as "the dirtiest, lousiest, greasiest set of half-starved rag muffins ever seen on the face of the earth." Captain Barney called them "the rustyest looking set I ever saw."[105]

Another Vermonter affected by the looting was Lieutenant Samuel H. Kelley, a Clarendon native in Co. B. He was forced to give up his saber to one of A.P. Hill's staff officers, in direct violation of the terms of the surrender. The rebel strapped his own saber to his saddle and rode off wearing Kelley's. A little while later the Confederate officer dismounted and left his horse with an orderly. While the orderly was not watching one of Kelley's men stole the Confederate officer's sword and gave it to Kelley. It was better than the one the rebel stole and Kelley wore it through the rest of the war.[106]

Once the looting stopped the soldiers of both sides started mixing and talking. Captain Barney wrote, "Before an hour rebel and Union soldiers were all mixed up together and in conservation and telling jokes, swapping canteens &etc." Major Stowell remembered:

> We really had a very fine time with them considering the circumstances etc. Their officers being very gentlemanly & sociable. They wished us all sorts of good luck but success in subjugating the South as they state it, hoping they might meet us again under different circumstances & etc.[107]

The next morning the Union troops were issued a day's rations by the Confederates and ordered to start for the parole camp at Annapolis, Maryland. As the 9th Vermont neared the pontoon bridge strung across the Potomac River, the men noticed a large group of Virginia planters standing on the bank looking for Negroes who might be trying to escape by mixing in with the column. In fact, one was with the Vermonters, as Captain Val Barney remembered: "I tried to bring a negro who had been cooking for the Co. but did not succeed." One of the planters thought he saw another Negro in the ranks and grabbed the man by the arm. To the Virginian's surprise the man let out a string of oaths in French and knocked the man to the ground. Instead of grabbing a Negro, the planter had grabbed Pvt. Jesse Gerard of Co. B, a 38-year-old, five-foot eight-inch laborer from Pittsford. Because Gerard was a French Canadian with a dark complexion, black eyes, and black curly hair, the planter had mistaken him for a Negro.[108]

The regiment's chaplain, Lucius C. Dickinson, wrote of Gerard:

> He is of Co. B good sized and quite dark. He is a Canadian Frenchman. I think is part Indian. He is a first rate hand to tend and break a horse. He is a smart man by nature, but cannot read nor write. He has as good a head as Gen. Geo. B. McClellan. Is well posted on almost any subject. I have learned a good many things from him.[109]

By mid-morning the Federals were on the road. The first day's march brought them within two miles of Frederick, Maryland, where they spent the night in the rain without tents. The only solace to the miserable night was that they were still free and not on their way to prisoner of war camps further south.[110]

On Wednesday, September 17, the Harpers Ferry garrison marched to Frederick and then three miles to the right of the town to await orders. While lounging in this camp the men could hear the battle on Antietam Creek raging in the distance. Although they did not know it at the time, they listened to the bloodiest one-day battle in American history. The Union loss was 2,108 killed, 9,549 wounded and 753 missing. The Confederates lost 2,700 killed, 9,024 wounded and 2,000 missing.[111]

The next day, Thursday, September 18, the column started again. First the men marched to Frederick and then they took the Baltimore Turnpike toward Baltimore. They made about 20 miles and camped on a steep hillside where it started to rain about 9:00 P.M.; according to Sgt. Nelson Wandell, they "got quite wet."[112]

Friday's march brought the Green Mountain Boys within 11 miles of Baltimore. Captain Ripley reported home:

> We reached here last night about 8 o'clock, after a weary march of 23 miles. That is for the poor boys whose feet are badly blistered, footsore and leg weary. I never felt livelier in my life.... It is pretty unpleasant taking care of the boys, and we have to be pretty severe now. They have formed the idea [because they were paroled] they are not under discipline now as they are prisoners of war, and are inclined to be impudent and do as they please. Still, by hard work on the part of the officers, we have kept up a splendid column and have not, after these sixty miles, more than twenty stragglers, while every other regiment is sprawled from Frederick to Baltimore.... Every Captain has to march in the rear of his Company, and report every man who enters a house or garden without permission, $5.00 being deducted from such private's pay, and if the officer neglects to report such men, he is cashiered. Our Colonel is rigorously severe; we have 2 Captains now under arrest for leaving their companies one half hour to get a cooked dinner. I haven't dared to leave my company 5 rods since I left Harper's Ferry. I lay right down where my place in line is when we break ranks, and sleep there. I don't intend to be disgraced by having to march in the rear of the regiment, swordless.[113]

At 10:00 A.M. on Saturday the Vermonters were on the road again. They backtracked two miles and halted until 2:00 P.M., when they again were ordered to move out. They reached the Washington Turnpike at sundown and camped for the night. Earlier in the day near Ellicott Mills Captain William J. Henderson collapsed again as he had on the retreat from Winchester. Colonel Stannard had him sent by train to Annapolis.[114]

On the last day of the march, Sunday, September 21, the column was on the road at daybreak. The men marched four miles and then stopped to fix breakfast. After a 24 mile march they reached their camp two miles from Annapolis, having covered nearly 100 miles in the previous six days.[115]

Corporal Edward N. Phelps, a 22-year-old farmer from Waterbury in Co. I, wrote his mother of his experiences over that week:

> We have been through the pleasantest country that I ever saw. It was a rolling plain well watered & there are a great abundance of fruit & the buildings here are much nicer that they are any where that I have been here in the south. The Baltimore Pike is macadamized road built wide enough for two teams to pass at once & the ruins of toll gates every 10 miles but there seems to be nothing like taking toll at present. Where we stopped at Frederick I saw the affects [sic] of the barbarity of our southern neighbors. It was the remains of the railroad bridge across the river which they burnt. It is larger than the long bridge below the village. It is a shame they destroy all they cannot take with them. But I hope they will get their pay now. The last 2 days of our march I went with the teams & got my load carried & messed them so that I got along some easier than I did on the rest of the journey. We made a long march on Sunday & arrived here just about sundown & are camped in the open field. All the house we have is made of bushes set up in the ground. There are a great many paroled prisoners here.[116]

Corporal James Grout also wrote about the march: "We marched all of the way and carried our knapsacks. It is about 100 miles. You may think that we are tired boys, but we all got here safe and sound with the exception of blistered feet. I stood it first rate. My feet are not sore any."[117]

The officers fared no better than the enlisted men on the grueling march, as noted by Captain Ripley: "I have eaten so much rancid pork that my lips are very sore, and my left heel has felt as if it were rapidly disappearing, but a bath in salt water, a shave, my hair cut and a shampoo which the Major and I took, were wonderful restoratives."[118]

The Lincoln administration lost no time in determining what had gone wrong at Harpers Ferry. On September 23, a military commission was assembled to look into the matter. After weeks of testimony by the majority of the unit commanders captured at Harpers Ferry, the commission published its findings and concluded that Col. Thomas H. Ford should never have been put in command of Maryland Heights, as he did not have the ability to command such an important position, and that he abandoned it without sufficient cause. He eventually was dismissed from the service.[119]

Colonel Dixon S. Miles was tried in absentia. The commission did not find him guilty of treason, as the Vermonter's thought he was, but instead found that "Colonel Miles' incapacity, amounting to almost imbecility, led to the shameful surrender of this important post."[120]

3

"We are penned up here like *sheep*."*

As soon as the Vermonters reached the parole camp at Annapolis, Maryland, on September 21, they heard rumors that they would not be staying long. Their final destination, though, was uncertain. Corporal James Grout wrote not long after arriving, "I suppose we shall go from here within a day or two. It is said for Shecaggo, but I don't know whare we shall go. Some think we shall go home but I think not." Corporal Edward Phelps of Co. I also noted the camp rumors: "There is some talk of sending us to Chicago to winter & some that we are going to Minnesota to fight the Indians. But I cannot tell where we go till we get there." Looking on the bright side of the prospect of leaving he continued, "If we go west I shall have a chance to see something of the world."[1]

The officers, of course, were privy to more accurate intelligence than the enlisted men, as seen in one of Capt. Edward Ripley's letters: "I reached here at 5 P.M., where we got the delightful information that transports were already in the Bay to take us to Baltimore, on our way to Camp Douglas, Chicago, in which place we are to rot, instead of here." Ripley's information was correct. The Green Mountain Boys were in fact going to Chicago, and soon.[2]

The 9th Vermont broke camp in the early morning hours of Thursday, September 25, and boarded the Steamer *John Tucker* in Annapolis for the trip to Baltimore. The regiment arrived in Baltimore at 12:30 P.M., but did not board the train for the journey west until after dark. Sergeant Nelson Wandell remembered that they "rode all night in poor miserable cars."[3]

The regiment arrived in Altoona, Pennsylvania, at 4 o'clock Friday afternoon and by 3:30 A.M. Saturday it was in Pittsburgh, where the troops were treated to a good breakfast. By 5:00 that evening the regiment had crossed into Ohio. Early in the next morning the train rolled into the depot at Louisville, Ohio. As the train lurched into the station Pvt. Charles A. Luce, a 20-year-old farm hand from Royalton in Co. D, was thrown from the top of one of the box cars on which he was riding and killed.[4]

The train crossed the Indiana state line Sunday morning at 10:30, September 28, and made a stop at Fort Wayne, Indiana, a little after noon. At the station the Vermonters were met by a flood of town folk who brought them all sorts of good food. After lunch the train departed and arrived in Chicago at 10:00 P.M. Lieutenant Ballard summed up the trip in a letter to the *Rutland Herald*:

> We came through as usual for soldiers, in freight cars with one passenger car attached for the "field and staff" officers, and the sick; those who have been for eighty-five hours in a car with the soft side of a board to sleep and sit upon, can realize how the soldiers of the 9th felt when we arrived.[5]

The regiment marched two miles out of the city and camped in a grove of trees near the grave of Stephen A. Douglas. The men bedded down in the open without tents and without supper, but by this time they were so tired they didn't care. To add to their misery it started to

---

*Quote from Second Lieutenant Elijah B. Sherman

rain about midnight. Captain Barney remembered, "There was no more rest for us that night as we were obliged to keep walking about to keep warm and from that time to this it has kept up a steady rain and the mud is almost knee deep and as half of our men are nearly barefoot and naked it makes it rather unpleasant. According to Lieutenant Ballard, "In the morning the regiment presented a decidedly 'drowned rat' appearance."[6]

On the first morning in Chicago, September 29, a senseless accident occurred in Co. B. Private Nathan Spaulding, an 18-year-old farmer from Tinmouth, was squatting down by a fire cooking his breakfast. One of his comrades walked by and kicked a gun barrel lying on the ground into the fire that Spaulding was using. Within seconds the loaded barrel discharged and Spaulding was hit in the right hand. The bullet entered the palm of his hand and exited between his middle and ring fingers taking tendons and muscle with it. After the wound healed his index and ring finger were permanently contracted. He was discharged April 24, 1863, for disability, with a monthly pension of $8.00.[7]

Camp Douglas was named for (Illinois) U.S. senator Stephen A. Douglas and was located very near the Douglas property. Ironically, Douglas was born in Brandon, Vermont, April 23, 1813, where he lived until age 16, when his family moved to New York. Later he moved to Illinois, where by age 32 he served as Illinois secretary of state, a state supreme court justice and a congressman. In 1846 he was elected to the U.S. Senate. In 1856 Abraham Lincoln challenged Douglas's senatorial seat, but Douglas retained it by a narrow margin. In 1860 Lincoln and Douglas challenged each other for the U.S. presidency, with Lincoln, of course, the victor. Douglas died in Chicago on June 3, 1861.[8]

The reason for building Camp Douglas at that location was that the prairie extended for miles around, yet it was only four miles from downtown Chicago. Although the camp was located in a sparsely inhabited area it had public transportation in the form of horse-drawn street cars. The downside was its foul drinking water and the sewage situation. The soil could not absorb all the waste generated by the thousands of humans and animals stationed there.[9]

Camp Douglas was built in September 1861 as a series of camps where Illinois volunteer regiments received their initial military training. By the next year it had grown considerably and had been used, just before the arrival of the 9th Vermont, to confine Confederate prisoners of war from the western campaigns.[10]

The camp's stockade fronted an area known as Cottage Grove, and extended west four blocks to Kankakee Avenue (present-day Martin Luther King Drive). It was bounded on the north by East 31st Street (present-day Ridgley Place), and on the south by East 33rd Street (present-day College Place). The enclosed area contained about 80 acres and was made up of three distinct sections. The eastern section, known as "Garrison Square," contained officer's quarters, post office, post headquarters and a parade ground. Adjoining Garrison Square to the south was White Oak Square, where the enlisted men's barracks were located and where prisoners were housed until a separate section was built later known as Prisoner Square. On the west side was Hospital Square, which held the post hospital, warehouses and surgeons' quarters. Surrounding the camp, and separating the different compounds, was a six-foot high board fence.[11]

The barracks inside the camp were built of wood and were 105 feet long and 24 feet wide, each housing 180 men. Each barracks was divided into three rooms, each containing two stoves. The walls were made of a single thickness of pine boards with narrow wooden strips covering the seams and were roofed with tar paper.[12]

By the time the 9th Vermont arrived the interior of Camp Douglas was filled with 8,000 newly raised Illinois troops in training. Outside the camp's wooden fence, quartered in tents, were several units paroled at Harpers Ferry. Because of this lack of space, the Vermonters were marched the next day to the fairgrounds, which extended two blocks from Camp Douglas, where the men were assigned horse stables for barracks. This camp was named Camp Tyler for its commander, Brig. Gen. Daniel Tyler.[13]

Daniel Tyler was born in Brooklyn, Connecticut, in 1799 and graduated from West Point in 1819. He served in the Army from graduation to 1834, when he resigned his commission. When the Civil War broke out Tyler was commissioned as colonel of the 1st Connecticut Infantry on April 23, 1861, and was promoted to brigadier general on May 10, 1861. He commanded the 1st Division at the battle of Bull Run, but was caught up in the blame for the loss of that battle and was mustered out of the army August 11, 1861. He came back on active duty on March 13, 1862, and successfully commanded a brigade at the battle of Corinth, Mississippi. He had the reputation of being a no-nonsense man and a strict disciplinarian.[14]

Even though the Vermonters had to bunk in the stables, Captain Ripley thought it was not as bad a deal as it seemed:

> We are at present quartered in the horse stables ranging around the fairgrounds; the barracks were, thank heaven, full, before our Brigade reached here. They are filled with vermin and dirty, even if you keep them as clean as you can.
> These stables have had horses stand in them only during a few days of the Fair, and are clean; an abundance of hay makes them luxurious in comparison to our sleeping quarters during the last two weeks. The idea of their being horse stables was immediately seized upon by the discontented ones, to make capital out of.[15]

Writing several days later Captain Barney thought that the stables were the least of their problems:

> We have not been furnished yet with cooking utensils and the boys have to eat the pork raw or cook it on the end of a stick over the fire. The boys find a great deal of fault and about ½ of the Regt. are away all the time staying down town and at private houses about and many refuse to even stand guard around our camp. This is rather a bad state of affairs but I don't know as I should blame the men much if they all left though I do my best to help them all right and try and have them think that all is for the best.[16]

Private Hodge in Co. H also complained about the rations:

> As to rations we have suffered very much, not having drawn anything fit to eat since we came here. Our bread has been bad, coffee poor, and meat worse, being smoked a little and alive with maggots. We would prefer killing and dressing our own meat, rather than have it in such a condition.[17]

The discontent among the enlisted men of the regiment had actually started before they arrived in Chicago. Captain Ripley indicated there had been trouble even before they had left Baltimore:

> We got away from Baltimore at dark after a very unpleasant time, trying to keep the boys straight. An impression prevails to a great extent in some companies, and but among 8 or 10 lawless characters in my own, that paroled prisoners are not under the authority of the U.A. [Union Army], but are prisoners of Jackson's, and amenable to his authority. A few are disposed to be impudent, and resist discipline, but as soon as we can get once settled, these fellows will get an Iron Hand laid on them, of which they have hitherto had no idea.
> Our men have ever been very mildly treated, no case of severe punishment has occurred; and they are disposed to think 24 hours in the guardhouse the extreme extent of punishment; if we stay here any time, they will find out differently.[18]

Lieutenant Ballard wrote on October 3:

> Those paroled prisoners have some strange notions in their heads; as for instance, that they ought no longer be subject to military relations, but should be allowed to roam around the city at will, where there are beer shops at every corner, and two between, and liquors of all kinds at every beer shop. Some are apparently so scrupulous as to regard it a violation of their parole to take up arms to do guard duty around camp; and one of the three regiments on the Fair Grounds, the Garibaldi Guards

[39th New York Infantry Regiment], refused this morning to do guard duty at all. A few individuals in the 9th also refused this morning.[19]

The men's insubordination stemmed from the parole system. While still at Harpers Ferry one of Maj. Gen. A.P. Hill's brigade commanders, Brig. Gen. Lawrence O. Branch, harangued the Union troops and told them the parole excluded them from the performance of any kind of military duty until exchanged. So the enlisted men felt they had no obligation to obey their officers or perform military duties. As bad as the situation seemed to the 9th Vermont's officers, the two other paroled units at Camp Tyler were in a situation that was far worse. In a letter written to the War Department on October 3 complaining about the insubordination of the 39th and 125th New York Infantry Regiments, Brig. Gen. Daniel Tyler included the sentence, "Colonel Stannard's Ninth Vermont, unarmed, is the only reliable regiment here."[20]

The *Chicago Tribune* ran an article on Oct 1 that was picked up by the *Burlington Daily Free Press* on Oct 4. It read:

> Yesterday, the 9th Vermont Regiment were drawn up by Col. Tucker [commander of Camp Douglas], and ordered to take arms and go on guard duty. They utterly refused, and further manifested their contempt for the authorities by groaning Col. Tucker. The latter then ordered up the 93rd Illinois and gave the order to charge, when the Vermonters sullenly consented to go on guard.[21]

The article, which was incorrect, incensed the Green Mountain Boys. Captain Val Barney explained what really happened:

> Those paper reports were to a great degree false. Only 10 men from each company were sent under Capt. Jarvis over to Camp D to get guns to do guard duty. On their arrival the Ohio boys gathered around them and as they had refused to do guard duty they put the same spirit into our men. Though 4 from my company took them. Capt. J sent for Col. Stannard and on his arriving there they all took the guns willingly and we have done our guard duty ever since. The Ill. Regt. were not called out to charge on our men at all.[22]

Within a few days after arriving at Camp Tyler the number of paroled units increased. In addition to the 9th Vermont there were the 32nd and 60th Ohio infantry regiments, 65th Illinois infantry regiment, 39th, 111th, 115th, 125th, and 126th New York infantry regiments, 1st Independent artillery, 15th Indiana artillery, 5th New York artillery and 2nd Illinois artillery. On October 5 Brigadier General Tyler wrote:

> Our camp has at least for the present become quiet and orderly. Yesterday the Thirty-ninth (Garibaldi Guard) and the One hundred and twenty-fifth New York, Colonel Willard, both of which had refused to do any duty, being ordered on duty at a particular hour each regiment fell in obedience to orders.
> What I exact of these paroled men is (1) regular police in their camps; (2) inspections, &c., as ordered from time to time; (3) keeping guard over their own camp; (4) company and battalion drill without arms. These exactions the men now acquiesce in and can or could be carried out, but today's Tribune, published at Chicago, contains the enclosed slip publishing the cartel between Generals Dix and Hill, 22d July last, and by referring to the fifth paragraph of that instrument it would seem that if these men are considered a "surplus," they are forbidden to perform "field, garrison, police, guard or constabulary duty." Indeed, under the last clause of article 6 the parole forbids performance of field, garrison, police, guard or constabulary duties.[23]

The men had also read the newspaper article and it only stiffened their resolve not to perform any kind of military duty, and this mutinous attitude worsened daily.[24]

The problem was exacerbated by the fact that most of the officers did not live in camp. They boarded and ate their meals at the Arcade, a small hotel near the camp. Captain Barney would have liked to have stayed at the Arcade, but as he explained to his wife, "Nearly all the officers board at a hotel near by and I don't know but I would if I had any money but I am destitute and so have to depend on the Co. for my rations and lodging." Ever the snob, Captain Ripley called the Arcade "a one horse hotel — and a sort of cheap suburban Sunday resort."[25]

Although by October 5 the rains had stopped and the mud started drying up in camp, which made the place more tolerable, Brigadier General Tyler had locked down the camp. Second Lieutenant Elijah B. "E.B." Sherman of Co. C complained, "We are penned up here like *sheep*. We cant go to the city without a written pass, not even a commissioned officer. Nor stay after 8 o'clock. We cant get leaves of absence *any way* unless backed up by a surgeon's certificate of disability."[26]

The citizens of Chicago did not help the matter any, as Private Hodge explained:

The citizens talk as though our room would be preferable to our company, and are continually taunting us of being Harper's Ferry cowards, etc. We surly feel our insignificance, but we have some human feelings left. We do not consider that we were to blame for the Harper's Ferry affair, or that we ought to be treated like brutes for it.[27]

As a result of being cooped up in camp with nothing to do, the men soon became edgy. On the morning of October 10 one of the men in Co. G was arrested by the guards for some infraction of the rules. Private Thomas O'Brien, another Co. G soldier, took exception to the arrest and tried to prevent the guards from arresting the man. Captain Val Barney of Co. A approached the group to quell the mutiny and O'Brien threatened him. For this act O'Brien was arrested. He was charged with starting a mutiny and threatening a superior officer. He was brought before a regimental court-martial the next day. To set an example Colonel Stannard sentenced O'Brien to be confined for the rest of his enlistment and to lose all pay and allowances during his time of confinement.[28] Four days later, Co. K's wagoner, George A. Chase from Whitingham, refused to do the duty he was assigned. He was court-martialed and sentenced to 15 days confinement and a $5.00 fine.[29]

The 9th Vermont's chief surgeon, Walt Carpenter, who had been treating Union prisoners of war at Winchester, Virginia, rejoined the regiment not long after its arrival in Chicago. Carpenter had a small hospital built, which was completed on October 11, raising the morale of the men in camp who were sick. Captain Ripley reported home:

We moved our sick into a new establishment our carpenters have just finished, and we are now very pleasantly arranged compared to what we have been hitherto. Our ward has accommodations for 25 men, who have nice, clean straw ticks, clean white sheets, feather pillows, white cases, but there is a scarcity of shirts and drawers suitable to be sick in. Jellies, preserves and such things are almost entirely wanting.[30]

By the middle of October the Vermonters were issued new uniforms and two hours of drill were added to their daily schedule. A return to some type of military regimen helped reduce the men's insubordination, but did not totally stop it. A number of the men tired of the situation started deserting. A number of others were discharged for various disabilities.[31]

Private Edward H. Lane, a five-foot eight-inch farmer from Newport in Co. E., was discharged for deafness from what the doctor diagnosed as scartilina maligna (scarlet fever). His platoon leader, First Lt. E.M. Quimby, annotated on Lane's discharge paper, "Said Lane is so deaf that he is in my opinion unfit to perform the dutys required of a soldier." Assistant surgeon Hall stated, "This man has narrowly escaped being shot while on picket duty because of not hearing the challenge. In my opinion said Lane is an unsafe soldier because of said deafness. I hope he may be discharged from service. Said difficulty existed at time of enlistment in my opinion. Degree of disability is one-fourth." Lane was discharged October 17 for disability.[32]

Lane apparently regained his hearing, as he reenlisted in the 9th Vermont on December 21, 1863. He served the rest of the war without incident and was mustered out with the regiment on December 1, 1865. After the war he moved to Castle Grove, Iowa, where he met Jane Eliza Lane. They were married July 4, 1867, and had a son on June 18, 1868. Jane, with their son, left Lane in 1870 and moved in with a Mr. Joseph R. Valentine in Golden, Colorado. Edward divorced Jane in 1879, charging her with adultery. On April 29, 1889, he married Margaret M. Dalton of Northampton, Massachusetts. Edward Lane died January 13, 1895, of typhoid fever.[33]

Private Ara M. Carlisle of Co. D was also discharged on October 17, but his character was nothing like Lane's. His company commander, Capt. Charles Jarvis, wrote of the 43-year-old farmer from Chester, "Carlisle was found to be too lame for drill or duty at Cloud's Mills, Alexandria, Va., where we were stationed 25th July last. It seemed a chronic disorder and had made him a burden to his officers & the same ever since wherever we have been." Assistant surgeon Horace P. Hall stated the reason that Carlisle should be discharged was because of "Rheumatism chronius." About Lane's character the doctor wrote, "Said Carlisle has been the most worthless soldier in the 9th Vt. never having done one days full duty since his enlistment. In my opinion, he will never be of any service to the Government. I hope he may be discharged. Said difficulties existed at the time of enlistment. Degree of disability one-fourth." Carlisle got his disability discharge, but unlike Lane he did not rejoin the regiment.[34]

Some of the ailments from which the men suffered were self-induced, according to the regiment's chaplain, Lucius C. Dickinson. After leaving Camp Douglas Dickinson wrote of Pvt. William T. Wright, a Newbury native in Co. G, "Bill 'Wright' (wrong) the Lt. Col.s hostler we left in Chicago. All used up with the rheumatism, bad whisky and other *bad* things such as Chicago affords an ample supply of. He is trying to get his discharge and I presume *may* succeed sometime." Wright was transferred to the Veteran Reserve Corps November 1, 1863. The Veteran Reserve Corps was an army organization where men with slight disabilities would continue to serve doing light duty away from the front such as guard duty at military hospitals, and as nurses, clerks, warehousemen, etc. He finally got his disability discharge on July 1, 1865.[35]

Not long after arriving at Camp Tyler camp sickness began again. The first man to succumb to disease in Co. B was Pvt. Benjamin Mann, Jr., a 37-year-old farmer from Ira, who died of typhoid fever on October 13. Apparently, Mann's family was well off and his body was sent home rather than being buried in Chicago. Captain Ripley wrote, "He was laid out in his shirt, drawers, pants, necktie, stockings and blanket & his body sent to his home for burial. The remainder of his effects were packed in the outside box containing the coffin & sent with it."[36]

In addition to camp diseases, other ailments were taking their toll on the regiment. On October 7 Pvt. George H. McGrath of Co. A was discharged for disability. The 45-year-old, five-foot-five-and-one-half-inch farmer from Georgia, Vermont, had never been of much use to the regiment. The surgeon noted, "Said McGrath has never been able to do but half duty, was always behind on marches and in my opinion he can never do *full* duty as a soldier." He was discharged for old age and intemperance.[37]

All the other units paroled at Harpers Ferry, except the 9th Vermont, were moved into Camp Douglas on October 17. Private Charles Hodge complained that "by the noise they make occasionally I should think they were in Bedlam."[38]

During the week of October 8 the insurrection among the paroled troops started literally to heat up. One night that week the 60th Ohio burned a row of barracks that would have housed about 1,000 men. During the night of Thursday, October 16, another row of barracks was burned and about 1,000 feet of the wooden fence around Camp Douglas was torn down. The next day 500 feet of the fence was rebuilt, but that night it was torn down again. On the night of October 18 the 9th Vermont was visited by the fire bug. It was reported in the Chicago paper the next day that the Vermonters started the fire, but the letters of a number of the Green Mountain Boys say differently. According to them, three men of the 115th New York started the fire in the camp's guardhouse. The guardhouse was situated about 15 feet from Co. B's barracks and it did not take long for the fire to jump from the guardhouse to the barracks. Before it was contained, both companies B and C were burned out and lost all their new clothing.[39]

Although it appears that the boys in the 9th Vermont were innocent of the crime, Captain Ripley indicated their attitudes were getting worse:

> From all these overt acts, the 9th Vermont is yet free, but there is a bubbling at the bottom and considerable excitement. The men are getting jealous of their officers, manifest a little spite, as if they thought them responsible for their confinement here. We are fast losing ground among them.[40]

Part of the problem with the men Captain Ripley blamed on Lieutenant Colonel Andross. Soon after arriving at Camp Tyler, Colonel Stannard was chosen by Brigadier General Tyler to serve as acting brigade commander, leaving the day-to-day running of the 9th Vermont to Andross. Ripley complained in a letter home:

> Stannard has his hands full with the brigade, and Lt. Col. Andross is not the man for the hour. He tries to govern discontented men by flattering, pandering and finally yielding. Two or three difficulties I have had, he has "gone back on me," and failed to sustain me, when I was trying to enforce discipline and order among men who were anxious to prove that officers and privates, as paroled prisoners, are on a level, and that we have no authority over them; Andross *proved it* by the course he adopted.[41]

Alcohol, as usual, was part of the problem. A typical example happened on the night of October 20. Private Peter Brady of Co. C, a 22-year-old Irish immigrant from Middlebury, was drunk and disorderly after tattoo. In the attempt to subdue him, Brady was disrespectful to his commanding officer and "disclaimed publicly the president of the U.S. and other authorities." To make matters worse, the next morning he tried to set his company's barracks on fire. Fortunately, he was stopped by his comrades before he could do any damage. Brady was brought before a regimental court-martial on October 25 and sentenced to serve six months at hard labor and to forfeit all pay and allowances during his incarceration. Brady, however, did not stick around for his punishment and deserted on November 28 and did not return until April 1, 1863. Whether or not he served his sentence does not appear in his records.[42]

A detail of 125 men from the 9th Vermont was sent to Camp Douglas in the late afternoon of October 21. Upon arriving, a large group of the paroled men threatened that if the Vermonters remained there after nightfall they would be in trouble. Sure enough, after dark a large contingent of the paroled prisoners attacked the Vermonters. Since the rifles the Green Mountain Boys were carrying had had their barrels filled with sand and pebbles, so they could not fire, they could barely defend themselves. The paroled men began pelting them with rocks. Major Stowell was hit three times, a man in Co. K had a leg broken and several other men were slightly injured. They were lucky to have escaped without a fatality.[43]

As November wore on, more men deserted, got sick or died. By the middle of the month 15 men in the 9th Vermont had died of disease since their arrival in Chicago. By the end of the month all the New York regiments had been exchanged and left for the front, but the 9th Vermont, 65th Illinois and 2nd Illinois artillery still remained at Camp Douglas wondering what would become of them. Second Lt. E.B. Sherman of Co. C gave an idea of how things were when he wrote:

> All the N.Y. Regts. have been exchanged and put into the field and we an older Regt. left behind. Well we do not feel grateful for the compliment, but we can live through it never the less. But if we stay here this winter our Regt. will be nearly worthless in the spring, some deserting, some dying and the rest demoralized by idleness and *rum*.[44]

On October 10, 1862, Pvt. John Mickman of Co. E refused to perform the duty that had been assigned him by his platoon leader, Lt. Elisha L. Quimby. Quimby ordered several other men to take Mickman to the guardhouse. In the process of getting Mickman to the guardhouse he called Quimby a "God dammed son of a bitch." Mickman was brought before a regimental court-martial on October 25 and sentenced to be confined to the guardhouse for 60 days and to forfeit his pay during that time.[45]

Another regimental court-martial was held on October 30. Private John Bolton, a 31-year-old farmer from Danville in Co. E, seemed to have had a habit of coming and going as he liked. On the march from Harpers Ferry to Annapolis he had refused to march with his company and would shadow it from a distance only to show up after dark. In the morning before the time to march he would take off again. Bolton was even bold enough to try to get other men to join him, but apparently no one took him up on his offer. At Camp Tyler Bolton was AWOL from October 15 to 19 and again from October 20 to 25. He was found guilty of desertion, but for some unknown reason the court was lenient in its sentence and his only punishment was a $10 fine.[46]

Privates Edward Balaw, Frank Sylvester and Joseph Wells, all of Co. I, refused to take muskets for guard duty on October 21. Although justice was slow in this case, all three were brought before a regimental court-martial on November 5 and sentenced to 15 days hard duty and fined $5.00 apiece.[47]

Captain Ripley wrote on November 20 that the governor of Vermont had sent an emissary to Washington in a attempt to get the regiment exchanged: "I received a letter from Gen. Baxter yesterday, stating as a result of his trip to Washington, a promise from Secretary Stanton to get the 9th exchanged at once, which he said meant that we were to be included in the exchange then being negotiated." But Baxter's visit to the secretary of war was not as fruitful as Ripley had hoped and the 9th Vermont was nowhere near being exchanged.[48]

Private Otis B. Smith, one of the youngest men in Co. I at age 17, was discharged for disability on November 5. The five-foot four-inch teenager from Montpelier suffered from ague and was generally run down. He had been unfit for 52 days out of the previous 60 as of October 19, 1862. Dr. Carpenter wrote on his disability certificate, "In my opinion he was too young when enlisted and should be discharged from service."[49]

A fight broke out in Co. D's barracks on November 10 between Pvt. Leonard M. Stevens, of Claremont, New Hampshire, and Pvt. John Finchon, of Tunbridge. First Lieutenant Asaph Clark entered the building and ordered the two men to break it up. Stevens turned on Clark and punched him. Three days later Stevens was tried by a regimental court-martial and sentenced to 15 days hard labor and had to forfeit $15.00 of his pay.[50]

Brigadier General Tyler was relieved of command of Camp Douglas on November 20. His hardnosed attitude of drilling and training paroled troops could no longer be overlooked by the War Department. Colonel Daniel Cameron, the Scottish-born commander of the 65th Illinois, was put in temporary command of the camp. Cameron's time in command would be short, however, as the secretary of war did not think it was proper for a paroled officer to be in command of the camp.[51]

With the departure of so many of the other paroled units that had been exchanged, the 9th Vermont was able to move into Camp Douglas on November 23. The Green Mountain Boys were finally out of the horse stables and in real army barracks.[52]

As if to rub salt into the wound, another insult was laid on the units wasting away at Camp Douglas in December. The War Department had issued General Orders 154 and 162 on October 9 allowing regular army units to recruit from volunteer units. In December, recruiting officers from the 14th U.S. Infantry arrived at Camp Douglas and started recruiting. Many of the men in the 9th Vermont, tired of cooling their heels while other Vermont units were at the front engaging the enemy, decided to join the regular army. Recruiting from any unit was in direct violation to the 22nd and 23rd Articles of War. The 22nd Article of War, which was superseded by General Order 154, stated that no soldier could enlist in any other unit without a discharge from his parent unit, and if he did, he would be charged with desertion. The 23rd Article of War, which was superseded by General Order 162, stated that any officer or soldier convicted of trying to persuade any soldier to desert his unit would be punished severely, to include the possibility of a death sentence.[53]

Toward the end of December Captain Ripley complained:

> The Gov't gave us a kick by sending here recruiting officers from the Regulars, to take 100 or 150 of our best men from us. We had already lost 60 men by disease, discharge and broken down, and 100 good men taken away from us would utterly ruin us. The Major fired up at the insult. No better officers, if as good, to come here now and try to domineer it over us, rob us of our commands because we are just poor, damned, miserable volunteers, and they are *Regulars*.[54]

Under the provisions of General Order 154, Pvt. William A. Otis, a 24-year-old shoemaker from Ausable Forks, New York, in Co. F, enlisted in the 14th U.S. Infantry on December 8 and apparently tried to induce other members of his company to do the same. He was arrested later in the day and charged with desertion and being in violation of articles of war 22 and 23. He was brought before a court-martial on December 26, where he pleaded innocent to the charges, using the War Department's General Order 154 as his defense. Unfortunately, Otis became the pawn that the officers at Camp Douglas were going to use to fight the War Department.[55]

The trial lasted two days, with the prosecutor bringing in officer after officer who testified that since the articles of war were vetted by Congress they superseded any general order issued by the War Department. In addition, all the officers felt that since Otis was a paroled prisoner of war, with or without General Order 154, he was duty bound not to bear arms until exchanged. At the end of the trial Otis was found guilty and sentenced to hard labor for 90 days and to forfeit his pay and allowances during his time of incarceration. Otis, however, was not in the courtroom to hear his sentence read. The night before, with the help of a Lieutenant Miller of the 14th U.S. Infantry, he escaped from the guardhouse and fled Chicago. On March 23, 1863, when the case reached the headquarters overseeing Camp Douglas the commanding general wrote on the cover of the proceedings:

> Proceedings, finding and sentence on this case are disapproved. Private Otis having been regularly enlisted in the 14th U.S. Inf. in accordance with orders from the War Dept. cannot be considered a deserter from the 9th Vermont Vols., and no such charges should have been entertained by the court. Private Otis will be released from confinement and returned to duty in the 14th Regt. U.S. Inf. and reported discharged on the rolls of his former Regt.[56]

Otis's case did not seem to have scared men of the 9th Vermont from being recruited by the regulars. By the time the recruiting effort was over 57 men had enlisted. At least this was not as bad as the 100 to 150 men that Captain Ripley feared would be lost.[57]

General Order 154 galled nearly all the officers at Camp Douglas, as Captain Barney expressed to his wife:

> As I said before our reg. is very small and according to a Gen. order issued by the Sect. of War the Regulars have a right to enlist from the Vol. service 10 men from each Co. and they have already enlisted 15 from mine and Lieut. Jewett is going down to the city to arrest the whole lot tomorrow as we have had no official notice of the enlistment. The Gen. order has caused a very hard feeling among volunteer officers and we got together yesterday and signed a document to be sent to congress setting forth the evils arriving from the order. It was signed by nearly every officer in camp and what will come out of it I can't say. We are in hopes *good*, but possibly we will all be dismissed from the service, but should it be so I should consider it an honor for no one knows how much trouble it has made us here and in fact we can have no discipline as long as that contemptible order is in effect for if a man commits a crime he will hold out the threat that he will enlist in the Regulars if we punish him so in order to keep our men together we have to suffer almost any thing and I am just mad and Col. Andross has tendered his resignation on account of it but I presume it will not be accepted.[58]

The following is a copy of the document that was sent to the Senate and House of Representatives protesting General Order 154 by the officers at Camp Douglas that Captain Barney referred to:

Camp Douglas, near Chicago, Illinois,
January 19th, 1863.

To the Honorable United States Senate and
    House of Representatives in Congress Assembled:

The Undersigned, volunteer officers, and loyal citizens of the United States, would respectfully memorialize you in reference to "General Order, 154" from the War Department. They consider it calculated to greatly impair the efficiency of the Volunteer Service. And thereby to do serious injury to the cause in which they are enlisted. They would state, generally, the following as their objections to the order named, which they trust you will consider and act upon, as the importance of the interests affected demands.

The order is in palpable conflict with the spirit, and, in the opinion of the undersigned, with the letter of Articles of War, Nos. 22 and 23, said Articles being, with others, an Act of Congress, and the sworn rule for the Government of the Armies of the United States, and the order named setting them aside being merely as emanation from the War Department.

It is an undeserved indignity upon the Volunteer Service, impliedly saying — since it invites and rewards enlistments from the Volunteers into the Regular Service, without requiring any extension of the term of original enlistment — that the former arm of the service is largely lacking in efficiency, as compared with the latter. It is further an indignity upon commissioned officers of the Volunteer commands, inasmuch as it makes them, in effect, mere recruiting sergeants for the Regular Service.

It is unfair to the officers of the Volunteer Service, since it takes from them commands, which, in recruiting, they were led to believe they should retain, unless forfeited by misconduct of their part, of which trial and conviction should first be had.

It is in violation of good faith with Volunteer officers, since it takes from them, without remuneration or apology, men whom they have at large expense recruited, and for whose safekeeping, discipline and instruction they have been held responsible.

It is again unjust, since it allows Volunteer regiments to be largely depleted by enlistments into the Regular Service — rendering such regiments liable, under Senator Wilson's bill (which will probably become a law), to be consolidated, and half of their officers thrown out in consequence of such depletion for which such officers are in no way chargeable, and for which they cannot in justice be made to suffer.

It promotes misconduct and insubordination generally among the enlisted men of Volunteer commands, since it encourages them to hold over their officers in *terrorism* the threat, that, *if opposed, they will join the regulars*, and since such enlistment furnishes to misconduct a too ready relief from punishment.

Its operation tends, in many ways, too patent to need enumeration here, to demoralize and break up Volunteer commands.

It tends, to the extent to which enlistments take place under its provisions, to diminish that pride and enthusiasm which each State feels for her own Volunteers; and thereby to dissipate the interest with which the several States should regard the common cause.

Should a draft be rendered necessary to fill up Volunteer commands, through their depletion, under the operation of the order, such draft would be in effect for the regular service.

The advanced bounty of Forty Dollars to each recruit, under the order, contemplates the expenditure of millions of money — an outlay, which, considering the financial embarrassment of the country, in the opinion of the undersigned, finds no compensation in the proposed transfer.

It promotes an unprofitable jealousy between the two arms of the service, through its discrimination in favor of the one against the other.

Its operation — as the experience of the undersigned, and probably that of every other officer who has witnessed it, shows— is and must be attended by meanness, trickery and misrepresentation on the part of recruiting agents; while, on the part of officers who have been in charge the business of recruiting under its provision, "conduct unbecoming an officer and a gentleman" is and must be the rule, and courtesy and honorable dealing the exception.

The restrictions imposed by a subsequent order (162) avail only to invite fraud to assist in the work of disorganization which misrepresentation has begun.

In every way the Order seems objectionable — as conflicting with the Articles of War, as doing indignity and injustice to Volunteer officers, and as calculated seriously to injure the cause of the Union, by impairing the efficiency and ruining the integrity of Volunteer commands, and thus destroying in them that *esprit de corps* so essential to success.

What are the two arms of the service, and what have they done, that the more important of the two should be ruined in order to strengthen the other?

We pray you consider this earnest petition and remonstrate, and if possible, and as soon as possible, redress the wrong of which we complain.

And your petitioners will ever pray, etc.

Signed by

Field, Staff and Line Officers of the 65th Illinois and 9th Vermont Infantry Volunteers[59]

In the end none of the officers who had threatened to resign over the General Orders went through with their threat and the crisis gradually faded away.[60]

Christmas finally arrived, which lifted the men's spirits. Apparently Pvt. Thomas B. Ripley, a 19-year-old farmer from Shrewsbury in Co. B, had a little too much Christmas spirit. In a drunken rage Ripley broke out one of the windows in the mess quarters and then went into his barracks and ripped up a bed tick and started tearing the bunks apart, board by board. His company commander, Capt. Edward H. Ripley, no relation to Thomas, ordered the drunken young man to be taken to the guardhouse. As the men who the captain had ordered to subdue him tried to grab him, Ripley broke away and ran outside the barracks. As the men tried to retake him Ripley started throwing bricks at them. Finally, a contingent of the guard force had to be called out to capture him. What punishment Thomas Ripley received is lost to time.[61]

Captain Ripley apparently had his hands full. That same day, 18-year-old Pvt. William Williams, Jr., an Irish immigrant also in Co. B, got drunk and without provocation started throwing cups and plates at the cooks in the cookhouse and then tried to beat them up. Sergeant James L. Slason of Co. A had Corporal David Buffam and Privates Oliver Jones and James C. Freeman subdue Williams and take him to the guardhouse. Williams violently broke away from the men and ran away. He was caught a short time later and brought before Captain Ripley. Williams asked Ripley what the charges were against him. When Ripley told him Williams said, "Put them through then if you want to. I don't care." For this Williams spent several weeks in the guardhouse. For almost two years afterward Williams was a good soldier. He was promoted to corporal on October 19, 1864, but was, for some reason, reduced to the ranks on April 4, 1865.[62]

As the year 1863 arrived the 9th Vermont was still not exchanged. On January 1 the regiment's morning report showed an aggregate of 704 officers and men, of whom 147 were sick and 21 absent without leave. Since its arrival in Chicago the 9th Vermont had lost 170 men by death, discharge or desertion. The weather was miserably cold and the men, tired of the months of inactivity, were deserting at will. Many voluntarily returned after an absence of several days to several months, but there seemed to be no consistency to the punishment meted out. Some men were court-martialed while others were forgiven for their crime.[63]

The new year also brought in a new commander to Camp Douglas, Brigadier General Jacob Ammen, who had formerly commanded Camp Dennison in Ohio. Like Brigadier General Tyler, Ammen was an old school regular army officer and a strict disciplinarian. He was born in Virginia in 1806, but grew up in Ohio. After graduating from West Point in 1831, he remained at the academy and taught mathematics, infantry tactics and philosophy. Later he was transferred to South Carolina, where he served as a military civil engineer until he resigned his commission in 1837. After leaving the service he taught mathematics in colleges in Kentucky, Mississippi and Indiana. He entered the war in April 1861 as a captain in the 12th Ohio Infantry Regiment six days after the bombardment of Fort Sumter. He was soon promoted to colonel of the 24th Ohio Infantry. He was promoted to brigadier general July 16, 1862.[64]

General Ammen was well respected by the Vermonters, as evidenced in one of Captain Ripley's letters: "General Ammen is in command here now. He has put us under good, healthy, invigorating strict discipline that is doing us all good. We are fast regaining a healthy Winchester time again." Lieutenant Ballard wrote in one of his articles in the *Rutland Herald*:

> Our camp is now under command of Gen. Ammen, and very strict discipline is maintained. But few citizens are allowed inside, owing, no doubt, to the fact there are a great many "copperheads" [Northern Democrats opposing Lincoln's war policy] about here, and it would disgrace even "butternuts" to associate with them.[65]

The new year also saw many changes in the ranks of the regiment's officers that had started with its arrival in Chicago in September. Second Lieutenant Justus Dartt of Co. D, who had been left sick with pneumonia in the hospital at Winchester, resigned due to his health. He was replaced by Sgt. Charles W. Haskell, a 23-year-old farmer from Weathersfield. Captain Albert R. Sabin, the commander of Co. C, resigned because of his invalid wife and aged mother. He was succeeded by First Lt. Herman A. Seligson. Sergeant James F. Bolton, a 32-year-old farmer from Danville, replaced Seligson. Captain Abiel H. Slayton of Co. H resigned and was succeeded by First Lt. Guy H. Guyer. Guyer resigned in February due to lawsuits (from before the war when he was a sheriff) and was replaced by First Lt. Lewis H. Bisbee, a 23-year-old lawyer from Derby. Second Lieutenant James T. Gorham of Coventry was promoted to first lieutenant on the advance of Bisbee. Second Lieutenant Calvin R. Loveland of Co. H resigned because of ill health and was succeeded by Sgt. Stillman Stone. Second Lieutenant Oliver C. Campbell of Co. I was forced to resign due to failing health and was succeeded by Co. I's First Sgt. Alvan P. Vaughn, a 24-year-old carpenter from Woodbury. On February 17, Capt. William J. Henderson of Co. G

Second Lieutenant Charles W. Haskell, Co. D (Dennis Charles).

First Lieutenant James F. Bolton, Co. C (U.S. Army Military History Institute).

resigned due to liver disease and partial deafness and was succeeded by First Lt. Edwin. A. Kilbourne. Kilbourne's vacant position was filled by Second Lt. William C. Holman and Co. G's First Sgt. John Whitcher was promoted into Holman's billet.[66]

Captain Lewis H. Bisbee, Co. H (Dennis Charles).

Second Lieutenant Stillman Stone, Co. H (Vermont Historical Society).

Second Lieutenant John Whitcher, Co. G (Vermont Historical Society).

Second Lieutenant Alvan P. Vaughn, Co. I (U.S. Army Military History Institute).

With all the turmoil in the officer ranks, unit politics and hard feelings surfaced. A month prior to the changes in Co. C, Second Lt. E.B. Sherman, a 31-year-old native of Fairfield, got wind that Captain Sabin was going to resign. Sherman figured that Co. C's first lieutenant, Herman A. Seligson, would be promoted into the captain position. He complained to his brother Alva that Co. C's first sergeant, James F. Bolton, would most likely be promoted to the vacant first lieutenant position rather than himself:

> If we cannot go into the service again sometime I think I shall resign and go into study. I cannot afford to be still & do nothing for country & self. Besides to tell you the truth Sabin has never used me very well, giving me as far as possible without seeming to the cold shoulder & influencing Lieut. Seligson to do the same. They have intended to compel me to resign but I wont for them. Sabin, I am told, though not by *him* for he avoids treating me to any confidences, intends to resign soon which I hope he will do and he and Lieut. S. are working to get the Col. to place *Bolton* as 1st Lieut. over me saying to someone "if he doesn't resign then he will be a fool." Well I wont make a devilish fool of myself by swilling brandy & guzzling beer and for this I suppose they hate me. Let them go on I shall come out all right some way. I have many friends among the officers and men of the Regt. and can manage to live without the approbation of selfish unprincipled men. Sabin is a *knave* having been a drunk and for some time in college.... I am not very popular with the Col. I don't drink and smoke & swear like some devils as he and Lt. Col. do. Such men as can go that treat [illegible] one favorite. That is a *fact*. I am conscious of being better fitted for civil than military life and shall rejoice when I can make the change.[67]

First Sergeant Bolton was in fact promoted to the first lieutenant position and, true to his word, Sherman submitted his resignation. It read:

> My Father is a confined invalid, bed-ridden and utterly helpless, demanding constant and unwearied care night and day. While my Mother is now seventy two years of age.
> For some years before enlisting the service my brother Lieut. Co. A, 9th Vt., and myself have attended alternately upon our parents.
> When the call for 300,000 volunteers came out, we were in different parts of the State and simultaneously engaged as recruiting officers, each thinking that the other would still be left for a helpless Father and aged Mother.
> We have both served till the present time, but my Mother becoming more feeble, it now seems but right and just that while one serves in the field the other be permitted to discharge filial obligations, no less sacred than those to our country.
> For these reasons I most respectfully resign my commission a Second Lieutenant Co. C 9th Vt. Vols., trusting they will be deemed sufficient for its acceptance.

Sherman got his wish and was discharged January 7, 1863; however, instead of going home to look after his parents he almost immediately enrolled in the University of Chicago, graduating with a degree in law in 1864. He remained in Chicago and became a successful lawyer. In 1876 he was elected to the Illinois house of representatives where he served two years. In 1879 Sherman was appointed a judge in the U.S. circuit court for the northern district of Illinois. He married Hattie G. Lovering of Iowa Falls, Iowa, in 1866. E.B. Sherman died May 1, 1910, of pneumonia at the age of 77 and was buried May 3 in Rosehill Cemetery in Chicago.[68]

Captain Val Barney did not feel that E.B. Sherman, nor Sherman's younger brother Linus in Barney's Co. B, were worthy of promotion, as he explained in a letter to his wife:

> [Linus] Sherman's brother has resigned. He was a Lieut. in Co. C. The reason was because he was soon to be jumped and so to avoid it he resigned, and was there a Capt. to be made in this Co. our Sherman would be second in the same manner as they both stand about the same.[69]

On the evening of January 2, Corp. Charles W. Howe, a Sharon native in Co. D, came into the company barracks and asked where Pvt. David Squires was. Someone yelled out that he was in his bunk. Howe went over to Squires' bunk, rolled him over and tried to pull him out. Squires, a 22-year-old farmer from Cornish, New Hampshire, said, "What do you want, Charley?" Howe replied, "I want you to come down to my bunk." Squires tried to ignore him, but Howe grabbed him by his collar and pulled him out of his bunk. Howe then pulled Squires over to his bunk. The other men in the barracks, almost all of whom were under the influence of alcohol, or totally drunk, ignored the row since Howe was always fooling around. At Howe's bunk Squires told Howe to stop, that he did not want to hit him. This made Howe even madder and he started choking Squires and told him he could not hit him even if he wanted to since he was Squires' superior. Then Squires called Howe a fool and Howe started choking him even harder saying, "Do you call me a fool?"[70]

By this time it was apparent that the two men were not just fooling around and Pvt. Leonard M. Stevens yelled out to Howe to let Squires go or he would come over and "black his face." Howe did not stop, so Stevens went over to Howe's bunk and pulled the two men apart and punched Howe in the nose. Howe immediately retreated to the space between the upper and lower bunks of his bed. Stevens told Howe to come out from between the bunks and as Howe started out Stevens punched him in the eye. Of course, Howe jumped back between the bunks. Stevens said, "What do you want to crawl in there for?" Howe replied, "To get out of the way." Stevens reached in and grabbed Howe and pulled him out and punched him in the eye again. Stevens was ready to hit Howe again, but Pvt. William Piper stepped in and broke it up.[71]

Stevens was arrested and charged with striking a superior officer. He was tried by a general court-martial the next day, and found guilty and sentenced to 14 days of solitary confinement. Howe and Squires apparently got off scot-free.[72]

"The bloody Ninth is exchanged at last and soon will be marching along towards Dixie's land," declared Pvt. Zenas H. Bliss of Co. I. It was true. On January 10, the 9th Vermont was finally exchanged and the men were issued brand new Enfield rifles. "We have armed again, not this time with the splendid Springfield sixty-ones," wrote Captain Ripley, "but with a very respectable new Enfield, better than any I ever saw before, and I feel very satisfied." Company and battalion drills were resumed and the men settled down into regular military routine, and the spirit of the whole regiment revived. All were confident that it would not be long before they would soon be facing the rebels again. That wish came true, but not as they had expected, as Sergeant J. Webster Stebbins of Co. K noted:

> Well since I wrote last there has been quite a change in our expectations. Then we expected to have been in the field before this time. But here we are yet and expect to stay here for the present and may be for some time. The Capt. said last night that we are to be jailors. It is reported that some rebel prisoners are coming here to stay and we are to guard them. If it is true, and the Capt. Says it is, we will not go from here this winter and there is no knowing when we shall go.[73]

Company K experienced a bit of a disturbance at drill on January 24, 1863. First Lt. Abel E. Leavenworth, the acting commander, reprimanded Corp. Asa Cutting for some minor offense and Cutting replied with some disrespectful words. Cutting was tried before a regimental court-martial the next day and was reduced to the ranks for "too frequent & unguarded use of his tongue."[74]

Toward the end of January the men's disappointment in Chaplain Dickinson started to appear in their letters home. On Sunday, January 26, Sergeant J. Webster Stebbins of Co, I complained:

> It is almost time for us to go to Sabbath School and I will write but little more before we go. After the Sabbath School we have a sermon. Brother Dickinson is to preach. He is not liked very well as a chaplain, for he does not manifest much interest for the spiritual welfare of the men. His sermons are not about the soul but about the duties of soldiers as such. We have meeting every Sunday, Tuesday and Friday evenings but Dickenson [sic] does not come near them. He scarce ever visits the hospital and when he does, he merely goes in and if he says any thing to the sick, it is about their sickness but not about their relations to their God.[75]

Stebbins was not the only one in the regiment who did not think much of Chaplain Dickinson. Captain Edwin Kilbourne wrote some time earlier, "Our chaplain is not a very energetic man, rather dead metaled & sluggish in his movements & not smart at all in his preaching.[76] The unhappiness with their chaplain would reappear in the men's letters many more times before the war was over.

The Confederate prisoners of war started arriving at Camp Douglas on January 27. Their appearance was apparently quite a shock for the Green Mountain Boys. Captain Barney wrote several days after their arrival:

> You will see by the paper I send you that 1500 of the rebel prisoners have arrived here. They are the Rustyist looking lot of human beings I ever saw together. Some have old bags for blankets, some old pieces of carpeting, old bed quilts and any thing that will keep them warm. When they arrived here they had been 27 days on the boat and cars and had not seen any fire or had any thing but raw bacon and hard bread to eat in that time and I tell you they were sorrowful looking fellows. They are very ragged and dirty and their hats are of all shapes and some have none at all, but have an old piece of carpet to cover their head. Quite a number of them were sick when they got here and had to be brought up in wagons and 5 or 6 have died since their arrival. They are all sick of the war and are anxious to have it closed. They claim to have been pressed into service. They are from the Murfresboro [sic] fight and we expect a lot from Arkansas Post this afternoon.[77]

Captain Kilbourne was as shocked as Barney. He informed his wife, "They represent almost every state in the So. Confederacy and such a filthy, dirty, lousy, hatless, shoeless, coatless, blanketless, 'God forsaken' set of mortals I never beheld, or ever care to again."[78]

Nearly everyone in the regiment was disappointed that they would be guarding prisoners of war rather than going to fight the rebels in Virginia. Captain Edward Ripley was especially disappointed. His brother, Lieutenant Colonel William Y. Ripley, had joined the famous Berdan's Sharpshooters in 1861 and won accolades for bravery. William was currently at home recuperating from a severe gunshot wound in his left ankle which he had received at the battle of Malvern Hill, just below Richmond on July 1, 1862. Edward Ripley was not only arrogant and snooty, but dreamed of military laurels like his older brother. He wrote to his brother William on January 30:

> I was utterly thunderstruck when met by the morning paper to hear of the unexpected arrival of 1300 Murfreesboro, Tenn., prisoners and nearly 4000 from Arkansas Post, and my courage sank within me, as I foresaw months of this disgraceful service in store for me.[79]

Lieutenant Ballard was not as upset with guarding the rebels as Ripley:

> We have to do guard duty once in three days, and on such an occasion as night before last, it is "right smart" cold business; but when off duty we have comfortable barracks, as the cracks on one side let the wind out as fast as it comes in on the other. We have good stoves, a comfortable supply of fuel and bedding, and enough to eat and to spare. Certainly, this style of warfare is not very romantic, and does not afford many opportunities for gathering "laurels," but we can afford "to labor and to wait," trusting that the good time will surely come. I hope our friends at home will not think this guarding poor, miserable, ragged, half frozen rebels to be a disgraceful business, but remember that prisoners must be kept as well as taken. We are unfortunate victims of Harper's Ferry notoriety, and though we were not to blame, yet we feel it quite unpleasantly.[80]

By the time the prisoners stopped arriving in early February, they totaled about 4,000. As Captain Barney mentioned in his letter, the rebel prisoners started dying as soon as they reached Camp Douglas. Although they contracted the normal diseases associated with Civil War camps, the most serious was the outbreak of small pox. Both the Confederate and Union soldiers suffered from this scourge. Corporal Stebbins noted, "There are some 30 or 40 in the pest house with small pox. Most of them are rebels. Some die, but most of our men get along well. I have been vaxinated and it worked well." Captain Ripley reported:

> Sent a man out of my company yesterday with it. Every afternoon the undertaker who has the contract for burying us all — Secesh and Union alike — comes up and gets his load, and puts them into very respectable pine stained coffins, and buries them in the United States Army Cemetery [Rosehill

Confederate prisoners at Camp Douglas.

Cemetery] about 8 miles out from here. Each coffin and grave are numbered, and he keeps a big book, containing the descriptive list on each one, copied, so it is kept very straight and proper.[81]

As the rebel prisoners continued to die on a daily basis, the War Department had two respected doctors evaluate the conditions at Camp Douglas. The following is an excerpt of their report published April 5:

We desire most earnestly to call the attention of the Sanitary Commission and the Government to the condition of these hospitals. In our experience we have never witnessed so painful a spectacle as that presented by their wretched inmates; without change of clothing, covered with vermin, they lie in cots without mattresses or with mattresses furnished by private charity, without sheets or bedding of any kind except blankets often in rags, in wards reeking with filth and foul air. The stench is most offensive. From January 27, 1863, when the prisoners (in number about 3,800) arrived at Camp Douglas, to February 18, the day of our visit, 385 patients have been admitted to the hospitals, of whom 130 had died. This mortality of 33 per cent does not express the whole truth, for of the 148 patients then remaining in hospital a large number must have since died. Besides this about 130 prisoners had died in barracks, not having been able to gain admission even to the miserable accommodations of the hospital, and at the time of our visit 150 persons were sick in barracks waiting for room in hospital. Thus it will be seen that 260 out of the 3,800 prisoners had died in twenty-one days, a rate of mortality which if continued would secure their total extermination in about 320 days. Under the circumstances the rate of mortality would increase rather than diminish.[82]

By the time the report was released the prisoners had already been exchanged and were back with their own forces.

With the number of men going AWOL and returning without punishment, Pvt. John Sabbeville (sometimes found as Sabberville), an 18-year-old laborer from Alburg in Co. A, must have irritated one of his officers to have been court-martialed for what seemed to be a minor infraction. He was arrested for trying to persuade another soldier to run away with him. How the incident was discovered or when Sabbeville was arrested is unknown, but on Wednesday, January 7, he was arrested for violation of Articles of War 38 and 23. Article of War 38 specifies that any soldier that sells, loses or ruins through neglect any of his equipment will be court-martialed. In Sabbeville's case he had either sold or lost his government issue blanket. Violation Article of War 23 carries the penalty of death or lesser punishment for any member of the army that tries to entice another member to desert. Sometime in January Sabbeville asked Pvt. Birchard E. Webster, a Hartford boy in Co. A, to run away with him. To both charges he pleaded innocent. During questioning by the prosecutor Private Webster swore that Sabbeville had asked him to desert with him after they had been paid off. Private Sabbeville was found guilty of both charges, but received a very light sentence. He was fined $5.00 and confined to seven days hard labor in Camp Douglas.[83]

Private Sabbeville, whose real name was John B. Sabre, succeeded in deserting from Camp Douglas on March 4. Sometime later he joined the 2nd New York Infantry as John Barney and received a large bounty. With his newfound riches Sabre must have had a good time, as he was treated for gonorrhea in February 1863 and again in March 1865. Sabre survived the war and became a grain dealer in Cowell, Massachusetts. He died on April 24, 1909, and was buried in Chazy, New York.[84]

In the early part of the evening of February 8, James C. Town, Co. H's wagoner, a 34-year-old teamster from Stowe, barged into First Lt. Lewis H. Bisbee's quarters to complain about the lieutenant refusing to give him a pass to go to town. Captain Guy H. Guyer was sick in bed and Lieutenant Bisbee was temporarily in command of the company. Bisbee told Town that when a soldier came to see him he expected the soldier to follow the rules posted at the door: to knock, be told to come in, remove his cap, quickly conduct his business and leave. Bisbee told Town that he had not had a good upbringing, that he was rough and had no manners. Town told the Lieutenant he knew "how to be a gentleman" but he still did not remove his cap. The two quarreled for almost an hour over these and other issues that caused each not to like the other. As the conversation heated up, Town let fly with a few words that he should not have, such as "Go to Hell" and "I will do as I please in spite of you" and "I don't care a damn for you." One of the topics which helped heat up the quarrel was leadership. Town told Bisbee that he preferred the leadership style of Colonel Stannard, whom the men loved. Bisbee said he preferred that of Major Stowell, to which Town replied that Stowell's style was like that of Bisbee's, whom the men hated. Bisbee said that was not true and that he had a big heart. Town said he did not know that because Bisbee had never shown one. Town then brought up the way Bisbee had spoken harshly to him on several other occasions. The conversation finally got back to the rules posted at the door, which seemed to incense Town. The lieutenant said he had power over him and he would make Town follow the rules. Town replied, "Do not feel so damned big of your shoulder straps," followed by "Kiss my ass!" Bisbee told Town that he would suffer for that remark. At that, Town turned and left, saying, "I will never darken your door again!"[85]

Town was arrested and put in the guardhouse. He was charged with being in violation of the 6th article of war, disrespect toward a superior officer, and was court-martialed on February 27. He was found guilty and reduced to the ranks, required to perform 30 days of police duty and fined three months' pay.[86]

Although Bisbee was soon promoted to captain he was apparently something of a martinet and not liked by many of the men in his company. Company G's Second Lt. Charles H. Hodge of Stowe wrote of Bisbee:

> The fact is although he made a very good Capt. the boys never came to like him as they did Capt. Slayton [company G's original captain] who showed himself to be a man on all occasions. His word was inviolate and was probably the most respected by the field officers of any Capt. on the line and would now have been, if he had staid, a field officer himself.[87]

On February 9, Pvt. Clark J. Beede of Co. G obtained a pass to go to Chicago. By afternoon he was in a bar on Canal Street drowning his sorrows. Several days before, the 39-year-old, five-foot-nine-inch, farmer from Orange received a letter from home telling him his wife was very sick and might not live. He asked about a furlough to go home, but was turned down. As the afternoon wore on and the flow of alcohol continued, the thought of his five children being left with no mother became too much to bear and he decided he had to go home. He borrowed some civilian clothes from the owner of the bar and left for Vermont. It would be several months before his company commander would hear from him and even longer before he would return.[88]

The same night that Beede deserted, a group of men from the 65th Illinois got mad at their officers and tore down the sutler's store, robbing him of everything he had. Next they started to tear up the 9th Vermont's sutler's store. They had hardly gotten the windows broken out when Lieutenants John T. Bascom, Co. F, and Sylvester C. Burlingame, Co. K, fired their revolvers at them and the men retreated. The Illinois boys regrouped and were getting ready to make another rush on the store when the guards were ordered out and charged them with fixed bayonets. It seems their grievance was they had been forbidden to trade with an old lady who lived nearby. She had a cut hole through the fence around the camp and would sell stuff to the men, but the officers of the 65th had the hole covered up. The men declared they would destroy every sutler's store in camp if they were not allowed to trade with the woman. Fortunately the Illinois ruffians did not carry out their threat. Captain Val Barney felt that "If the officers of that Regt. would stay with their men I think there would be no trouble, but they are all away almost every night and the men do as they please."[89]

While the deaths from disease at Camp Douglas were tragic, the death of Corporal James Grout of Co. K appears to be the most tragic of all. Grout, who was cited for bravery at the battle of Harpers Ferry, died of tuberculosis on March 2, leaving behind three orphaned children:

Ella, age 9, Hellena, age 5, and Leon, age 2. Grout had married Caroline A. Pike in 1852. Caroline was badly burned October 10, 1861, when an oil lamp she was trying to light exploded. James's sister, Pamelia, was with her when the accident happened and had smothered her burning dress, but not before Caroline was badly burned from the waist up. She suffered for 13 agonizing days with James at her side until she died on October 23. He remained with his children until June 1862, when he felt it was his duty to join the army. He left his children in the care of his brother-in-law, James W. Kelly. After Grout's death Mr. Kelley received an $8.00 a month government pension, plus $2.00 for each child until they turned 16. James Grout's body was sent home to his father-in-law, Moses Pike, and he was buried next to Caroline in Pike Hollow Cemetery in Stratton, Vermont.[90]

James' brother, Joel Grout, also in Co. K, wrote on March 18:

> James and I were both in the camp hospital when he died. he had been sick for some time as I had too but neither of us had been in the hospital but a few days. he had had a bad cold and cough for some time. He was detailed to work on the barracks and could [not] get excused by the boss carpenter without going to the surgeon or he would have gone to the hospital before he did. his cough was very bad but I did not think he was dangerous until a few moments before he died.
> The surgeon opened him and found that the phleym had filled his lungs so hard that one lung had burst. This was the cause of his death.[91]

James Grout's platoon leader, First Lieutenant Abel E. Leavenworth, wrote Grout's mother after his death: "As a soldier, he was brave almost to rashness. As a companion and friend, he was honest and trustworthy."[92]

In addition to tuberculosis, smallpox and other camp sicknesses, the camp was plagued with lice, as Corporal Stebbins complained:

> If you were penned up in here as we are where you could see nothing but the same thing every day and the persons and the largest part of them these dirty ragged, and lousy rebel prisoners, the sight of whom is enough to make one sick to the stomach, if not actually to throw up "Jonah." One of them said that after another died he saw him and there was not a place on his body so large that you could put the end of your finger down without hitting a louse. What do you think of that. I can feel them crawl all over me every time I think of it, or hear any thing about the "line backs" as they are called. They are lice what are lice now! A full grown one is as large as a big louse you find on cattle. I have never found any on me but once, and then I got rid of them in short order, I will assure you, by boiling all my clothes in salt and water.[93]

Another tragedy occurred on February 15. While getting the camp ready to receive the rebel prisoners of war, Pvt. John E. Robbins, a 25-year-old, five-foot nine-inch farm boy from Brownington in Co. E, was gravely injured. He was helping erect a barracks when a timber fell from the roof and hit him in the small of his back. The timber apparently injured his spine and he was paralyzed from the hips down. He also started having convulsions. He was discharged May 8, 1863, with a full disability. Robbins recovered from his injury and enlisted in the 3rd Massachusetts Cavalry and survived the war. He married Rebecca Pirl September 1, 1860. In 1873 she committed adultery with a Mr. Charles McKneel. Robbins divorced his wife in Yorkville, Illinois, January 27, 1874. Who got custody of their son, born March 6, 1861, is not clear. He married Mary H. Hubbell September 10, 1874, in Batavia, Illinois. From that marriage were born Grace Amanda Robbins, June 27, 1875, and Ralph Roy Robbins, September 28, 1884.[94]

On the last day of February or the first day of March (the record is not clear) there was a serious incident at one of the 9th Vermont's guard posts. One of the guards was relieved for some reason and Corp. Bradford T. Scott of Wardsboro in Co. K temporarily replaced him. As Corporal Scott was walking his beat a man from the 65th Illinois, who had a pass to go to town, returned and for some unexplained reason climbed over the fence to enter Camp Douglas rather than coming in the main gate. He came over the fence near Scott's beat. Scott ordered him to halt, but the man ignored him. Scott fired, intending to wound the man, but the Illinois trooper dodged at the last second and took the full brunt of the minie ball and was killed instantly. Several days later Scott was brought before a court of inquiry and not only found free of any wrong doing but was complimented for doing his duty. This was just another example of the senseless loss of life in garrison. Now, hardened by incidents such as this, Lieutenant Ballard said of the killing, "So goes life."[95]

The Green Mountain Boys got some bittersweet news in early March when they learned that Colonel Stannard was to be promoted to brigadier general and assigned to replace the commander of the Second Vermont Brigade, who had been captured by Confederate partisans. The Second Vermont Brigade was formed in August 1862 by President Lincoln's call for 300,000 militia to serve for nine months. The brigade was composed of the 12th, 13th, 14th, 15th and 16th Vermont Infantry regiments. The brigade's first posting was in the defense of Washington. On December 12, 1862, the Second Vermont Brigade's commander, Brig. Gen. Edwin H. Stoughton, was ordered to move his brigade near Manassas, where they set a five mile picket line along Bull Run and Cub Run. Stoughton established his headquarters at Fairfax Court House. At the time, at age 24, Stoughton was the youngest brigadier general in the army. On March 9, 1863, Capt. John S. Mosby and 30 of his partisan rangers infiltrated the Vermonter's picket line and entered Fairfax Court House undetected. Mosby and several of his men knocked on the door of Stoughton's headquarters, saying they had a dispatch for the general. They were admitted and went to the general's room, where it is said that Mosby removed the sleeping general's covers with the tip of his sword and then slapped him on his rump with the flat of the blade to awaken him and inform him that he was a prisoner of war. In addition to the general, Mosby made off with 2 officers, a telegraph operator, the post postmaster, a photographer, 15 enlisted men, and 55 horses. President Lincoln said of the incident that he did not so much mind the loss of the brigadier general, for he could make another one in five minutes, "but those horses cost $125 apiece!"[96]

Although Stannard was a strict disciplinarian the men held him in the highest respect. It is certain Lieutenant Ballard's feelings were not unique in the 9th Vermont when he wrote:

> The fact that most concerns the regiment is the appointment of Col. Stannard as Brigadier General, of which we were apprised last night. We are all glad of it, on his account, for those who know him best and respect him most, think the men are few who are more deserving; but it is a hard thing for the regiment.[97]

The effective date of Stannard's promotion was March 11, but he did not leave Camp Douglas for two weeks. Within a few days of his promotion, in a show of their love and respect, the officers presented him with a beautiful horse. The noncommissioned officers and enlisted men purchased him a complete set of equipment for his new mount. General Stannard rode the horse through the rest war and took him home to Vermont where the horse died of old age many years later.[98]

Lieutenant Colonel Dudley K. Andross was selected to replace Stannard as the regiment's colonel, with a promotion date of March 23. The elevation of Andross to colonel created a cascade of promotions in the regiment. Major Edwin S. Stowell filled the position of lieutenant colonel vacated by Andross and Captain Edward H. Ripley replaced Stowell. Ripley's position as commander of Co. B was filled by Samuel H. Kelley.[99]

Upon Captain Ripley's departure, in appreciation of his leadership at the head of Co. B, the noncommissioned officers and men presented him with new sword at the cost of $75.00, which was no small sum at the time.[100]

By the middle of March the weather started warming up and drying out the camps. Captain Val Barney happily told his wife, "We are having the finest kind of weather and it seems like Summer and now many of the boys are out playing ball and enjoying themselves."[101]

A new flag pole was raised in the Vermonter's camp on March 16. Captain Kilbourne remembered:

> One of the boys in Co. E climbed the liberty pole last night [March 16] over a hundred feet high and put a rope through the pulley and come down again. Paid him $15.00 for it. We then raised the stars and stripes with 3 hearty cheers and a tiger. The rebels I noticed didn't cheer. Couldn't look at it in the light they ought. Poor deluded creatures.[102]

"A sad accident occurred in camp yesterday afternoon," wrote Lieutenant Ballard on March 24: "Newton of our company was seriously wounded in the thigh by the accidental discharge of a musket. One of his legs was broken, and the result will be, at best, long days and nights of pain, and weariness, and maybe permanent disability, if he should live through it. He is, I think, the youngest and smallest of our company and is numbered among our most faithful men."[103]

Private Charles W. Newton, a five-foot three-inch farmer from Mt. Holly, was the youngest man in Co. B. Although his enlistment papers had his age as 19, Newton had lied about his age and was actually only 15 when he had enlisted. The wound was much worse that Lieutenant Ballard could have known. While on guard duty March 23, one of the pickets stumbled and accidentally discharged his musket. The ball entered the outside of Newton's left thigh, passed through his thigh, broke his pubic bone and continued on, shattering the right thigh bone, and stopped just before exiting the right thigh. Several of the men nearby picked him up and rushed him to the regimental hospital, where he remained until March 30. His wound was so severe that he was finally taken to the Marine Hospital in Chicago on March 30. Because of all the internal injuries the wound was beyond anything medical science could repair at that time and he was given opiates and stimulants to ease the pain until he died on April 1 at age 16.[104]

"Let us rejoice!" read Lieutenant Ballard's newspaper article written on March 29: "The regiment has received marching orders. We go to City Point on the James River, Va. and are to take these rebel prisoners with us. Two companies go tomorrow, and so on till Friday, when Co. B is expected to start." The 9th Vermont had the daunting task of moving 2,500 Confederate prisoners of war halfway across the country. City Point [present day Hopewell] was located some 10 miles southeast of Petersburg, Virginia.[105]

The first two companies to leave were companies A and F under the command of Lieutenant Colonel Stowell. The units went by train from Chicago to Baltimore, passing through Fort Wayne, Indiana, Harrisburg and Pittsburgh, Pennsylvania. From Baltimore they boarded ships for the voyage down the Chesapeake Bay and up the James River to City Point. Each group had stories of their trials and tribulations to tell.[106]

Between them, companies A and F had 451 prisoners. After reaching Baltimore on Thursday, April 2, the Vermonters and their wards were put on the steamer *Long Island* for the last leg of their journey. The trip to City Point was uneventful and they successfully delivered their prisoners to the Confederate authorities on Saturday, April 4. The conditions at City Point surprised the Vermonters, as Lieutenant Sherman described it, "City Point is 16 miles from Richmond and 40 or 50 miles inside the rebel lines. It was totally destroyed by our forces. Hardly a house remains & there is not an inhabitant anywhere now. Only rebel soldiers."[107]

Their trip back down to Fort Monroe was not as smooth as the one up the river. Just after leaving City Point the vessel ran into a severe storm and had to drop anchor until the next morning. After arriving at Fort Monroe the *Long Island* was ordered to Norfolk for some minor repairs on Monday, April 13. Since the quartermaster could not find tents for the Green Mountain Boys they stayed aboard ship and accompanied it to Norfolk, where they stayed for one day and two nights. The next day, at least some of the Vermonters were allowed shore leave to look around Norfolk. First Lieutenant Linus Sherman recalled:

Saw where the rebel *Merrimac* was destroyed. Saw also the wreck of the *Cumberland* which she sunk. Norfolk is a good clean city of some 30,000 inhabitants before the war. Contrabands help keep the streets clean & hogs are not permitted to roam at large by an order of the Provost Marshall. On the whole it is a good looking place.[108]

On Wednesday companies A and F were back at Fort Monroe. After debarking from the ship the two companies marched to Camp Hamilton, just outside the fort in the vicinity of present day Phoebus, where they set up camp.[109]

Company K deposited their prisoners from the steamer *Matamora* at City Point on April 7 and picked up a load of exchanged Union prisoners. Sergeant Nelson Wandell remembered:

> Tuesday morning at 10 O'clock 129 paroled Union troops from Richmond arrived. 78 of them belonged to the 1st Vermont Cavalry. The Secesh left and they came aboard. Our men were stripped of everything, some even of their pants and caps, and had to wear the rebels old clothes. Left City Point at 1 O'clock noon, at 4 O'clock P.M. met the Steamer *Columbia* going up with a load of the devils.[110]

Company D experienced a serious accident before it reached Baltimore. While passing through western Ohio at about two o'clock in the morning the train of five or six cars ran off the track. The train was not moving very fast and no one was seriously hurt, which was a miracle, as one of the Vermonters stated: "If the train, at the time, had been running as fast as it had only a short time previous, another great Railroad slaughter would have been chronicled, as the cars were filled to overflowing with the prisoners and their guard."[111]

Even loading the rebel prisoners aboard the train could be hazardous. While Pvt. Joseph Douglass, Jr., a 19-year-old farmer from Stowe in Co. H, was herding a group of prisoners to the train he jumped over a ditch and felt a tear in his groin. The jump caused a hernia in his groin that one doctor reported "was as large as a goose egg." Douglass was transferred to the V.R.C. and was discharged with a disability on November 28, 1865. Because of the disability due to his injury he had to sell his farm in 1869.[112]

Companies B and E left Chicago on April 3. The trip was going as planned until they left aboard ship from Baltimore. Lieutenant Ballard related one of his unit's experiences in one of his letters to the *Rutland Herald*:

> ... about daylight we embarked for Fortress Monroe, on a nameless, nondescript craft, called a "transport." It was formerly the *West Point*, and was sunk on the Potomac while running the rebel blockade about a year or so ago. It has been raised and rebuilt, but the name was washed off in the Potomac, and has not yet been replaced. This is her first trip and we hope it may not prove a perfect failure. As we got near the mouth of the Potomac, last night, it was discovered that our boat was leaking badly, and we turned into Point Lookout, on the Maryland side of the river, and reached the dock just as the water was putting our fires out. We turned the boat up side-wise, and stopped a leak, and thought it all right, but very wisely concluded to stay there till morning, and at 4 o'clock this morning we started again, but soon found the water gaining on us, and we put back for repairs. About 10 o'clock A.M. we started again, and now about 1 P.M., we are making good headway over a quiet sea. We are enjoying the trip very much, though the prospect of a salt water bath in a cold day was not pleasant.[113]

Of the 502 men on the 9th Vermont's morning report on April 1, only 400 were actually present for duty. The others were either AWOL, absent on furloughs or on details. Sixty were left behind in the hospital and 50 were left buried in graves on the shore of Lake Michigan.[114]

By April 15 all the 9th Vermont's companies had delivered their prisoners to City Point and were quartered at Camp Hamilton, where the men fixed up their tents with board floors and got back into a military routine. Early that morning Colonel Andross received orders to move the regiment to Suffolk, Virginia, on the other side of Hampton Roads.[115]

4

"A FOOLS ERRAND."*

The events that caused the 9th Vermont to move to Suffolk were started in motion several months before. After the battle of Fredericksburg, December 13, 1862, General Robert E. Lee and his victorious Army of Northern Virginia went into winter camp along the south bank of the Rappahannock River. This part of Virginia had been occupied, almost continuously, from the start of the war and consequently had been stripped of anything to sustain an army. The food shortage plagued not only Lee's army but the entire Confederacy. Because of a drought, the 1862 harvest had been extremely poor. The situation had gotten so desperate that by November 1862 the commissary general of the Confederate army could not guarantee that meat stocks would last past January. The supply of forage for the army's animals was so severe Lee was forced to disperse his artillery and cavalry to other areas where forage could be found.[1]

After its loss at Fredericksburg, the Army of the Potomac was encamped on the north side of the Rappahannock River facing Lee's butternut-clad troops. In January 1863, the Federal commander, Maj. Gen. Ambrose E Burnside, attempted one more attack on the Army of Northern Virginia, but foul winter rains bogged the army down in what would become known as Burnside's Mud March. Burnside was soon after relieved of command and Maj. Gen. Joseph Hooker was placed as the commander of the Army of the Potomac. Instead of being dismissed from the army after he was relieved, Burnside was given command of IX Corps, which he had commanded prior to ascending to command of the Army of the Potomac. On February 14 Burnside and his 15,000-man IX Corps were reassigned to Newport News.[2]

The movement of the IX Corps only added to Lee's problems. While his army could prevent Hooker from marching south to Richmond, there were hardly any Confederate troops between Newport News and the Confederate capital. There were only about 5,000 rebel troops around Richmond and about 6,000 in the Petersburg area. The Federals, however, had nearly 15,000 troops at Suffolk, 60 miles below Petersburg, as well as another 10,000 stationed at Yorktown, Norfolk and Ft. Monroe, not counting the IX Corps. Burnside's new position gave him the ability to move on Richmond as McClellan had done in 1862 or open another front in North Carolina.[3]

To counter this threat, Lee sent Maj. Gen. George E. Pickett's and Maj. Gen. John B. Hood's divisions of Lt. Gen. James Longstreet's corps to Richmond. Pickett's division left on February 15, followed by Hood's division on the 17th. These two divisions beefed up the troop strength in Richmond by nearly 16,000 men. To coordinate the defense of the capital and North Carolina, Lee ordered Longstreet several days later to join his two divisions. Longstreet was assigned as the commander of the Department of Virginia and North Carolina and established his headquarters in Petersburg. In addition to Pickett's and Hood's divisions, Longstreet commanded Maj. Gen. Daniel H. Hill's division, then stationed in North Carolina, and Maj. Gen. Samuel G. French's division, which had been operating unsuccessfully against Suffolk for months.[4]

*Quote from Colonel Edward H. Ripley, U.S. Army

One of Longstreet's first decisions in his new capacity was to order Pickett's division to Petersburg and Hood's to Falling Creek, about eight miles north of Petersburg, along the Richmond & Petersburg Railroad. This also accomplished Longstreet's second objective, which was to be able to quickly send his two divisions back to Lee in case Hooker decided to cross the Rappahannock. In early March, shortly after relocating his two divisions, Longstreet was given a third mission, which was to collect subsistence for the Confederate army in the enemy-held northeastern portion of North Carolina, which was rich in salt fish, bacon and corn.[5]

To accomplish this new mission, Longstreet ordered D.H. Hill to attack the enemy garrison at New Bern, North Carolina. To beef-up Hill's force, Longstreet sent Brig. Gen. Richard B. Garnett's Brigade of Pickett's division, but Hill was unsuccessful in taking the town. Next, Longstreet ordered Hill to attack the Federals at Washington, North Carolina, and sent another of Pickett's brigades, Brig. Gen James L. Kemper's, to ensure a successful operation. While this attack also failed, Hill's men were successful in foraging in the eastern portion of the state.[6]

In early March Longstreet sent Brig. Gen. Micah Jenkins's brigade of Pickett's division to the Blackwater River, where he took command of French's division while French was in Petersburg. On March 19, the majority of Burnside' IX Corps left Newport News for Ohio. With Burnside no longer a threat, Lee gave Longstreet permission to attack Suffolk.[7]

By March 26, Pickett and his two remaining brigades were encamped at Ivor Station, 25 miles northwest of Suffolk on the Norfolk & Petersburg Railroad. Longstreet relocated his headquarters there on March 30. Hood moved his division from Falling Creek to Petersburg on April 2, and awaited orders from Longstreet to move south. During this time Longstreet recalled Pickett's two other brigades from North Carolina.[8]

On April 10, Pickett's, Hood's and French's divisions were camped in and around the town of Franklin along the banks of the Blackwater River 20 miles west of Suffolk — all told, about 18,000 men. Longstreet had his units on the move early on April 11. French's division crossed the Blackwater at South Quay south of Franklin, followed by Pickett. Hood crossed a little farther upstream at Franklin. Pickett advanced up the Somerton Road, and then spread out toward the Dismal Swamp on the south side of Suffolk. French's division would approach Suffolk from the west and Hood from the north side of the Nansemond River.[9]

Suffolk was one of the oldest communities in the Old Dominion. The first settlement was attempted in 1617, but the Indian massacre of 1622 frightened the English away. The Nansemond Indians of the region had always been unfriendly and settlement was not tried again until they were wiped out in the war of revenge in the years following the massacre. By 1637 enough Englishmen were living on the Nansemond River to qualify as a county, which was named after the river. Although the courthouse was located at the end of deep water, there were so few homes near it that the town of Suffolk was not recognized until 1742. The little village was pillaged and burned to the ground in 1779 by the British but was rebuilt after the Revolutionary War. For many years it slumbered peacefully as the county seat of Nansemond County until the outbreak of the Civil War.[10]

The Confederate as well as Federal commanders had realized the strategic importance of Suffolk as soon as hostilities broke out in 1861. Suffolk was located at the head of navigation of the Nansemond River 18 miles upstream from Hampton Roads. Suffolk was the key to the entire Norfolk area. It was located at the intersection of two major railroad lines; the Seaboard & Roanoke Railroad from North Carolina and the Norfolk & Petersburg Railroad from Petersburg.[11]

Fearing attack by overwhelming odds from either North Carolina or McClellan's army on the Virginia Peninsula, Confederate forces retreated from Norfolk, Portsmouth, and Suffolk on May 9, 1862. On May 10, Federal troops under the command of Maj. Gen. John E. Wool captured the city of Norfolk unopposed. Union cavalry entered Suffolk on May 12, and the town

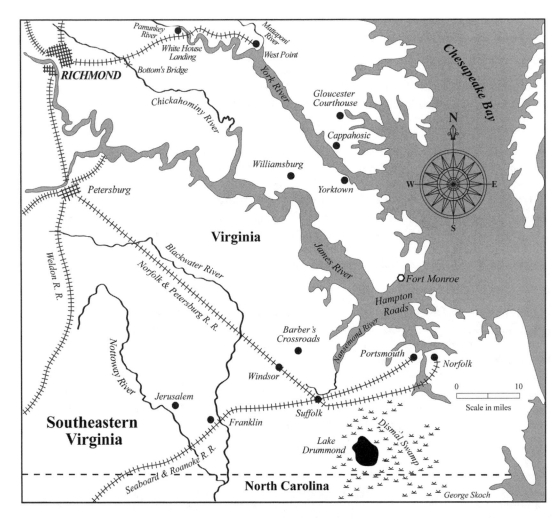

Southeastern Virginia.

would remain in Union hands for the rest of the war. Prior to the war, Suffolk's population was about 1,400; however, by 1862 the town was minus several hundred young men who had enlisted in the Confederate army.[12]

Suffolk was under the command of Maj. Gen. John A. Dix, commander of the Department of Virginia and the VII Corps, headquartered at Fort Monroe. The commander on the ground in Suffolk was Maj. Gen. John J. Peck, commander of the 1st Division of the VII Corps. Peck was born in Manlius, New York, on January 4, 1821, and graduated from West Point in 1843 with a commission in the artillery. He had served in the Mexican War and on the western frontier. He resigned from the army in 1853 and became a banker and railroader. He was commissioned a brigadier general of U.S. Volunteers on August 9, 1861. In the fall and winter of 1861-1862 he commanded the Third Brigade of Buell's Div. in the defense of Washington. In the spring and summer of 1862 his brigade was part of the 1st Division of the IV Corps of the Army of the Potomac and participated in the Peninsula Campaign. In the Seven Days' Battles he commanded the 2nd Division of the IV Corps. He was promoted to major general in July 1862. The following September he was assigned as commander of 1st Division of the VII Corps in Suffolk.[13]

Although Suffolk had been garrisoned by Federal forces since May 1862, few defensive fortifications had been constructed. Peck made this his first priority, and by the spring of 1863 Suffolk was surrounded by a series of forts and earthworks that made the place virtually impenetrable by taking advantage of the Nansemond River and the Great Dismal Swamp. The southernmost fort was Fort Union. To the right, or northeast, of Fort Union stood Fort Dix, which guarded the approach of the White Marsh Road. To the north of Fort Dix was Fort Halleck, which secured the Portsmouth Road and the site where the Norfolk & Petersburg Railroad crossed the Jericho Canal.[14]

A half-mile northwest of Fort Union, Fort McClellan guarded the approach along the Somerton Road. Three quarters of a mile west of Fort McClellan, Fort Nansemond also guarded the Somerton Road as well as the Norfolk & Petersburg Railroad. Battery South Quay and Fort Rosecrans, north of Fort Nansemond, guarded the approaches along the Carrsville and South Quay Roads running east from the Blackwater River to Suffolk. Forts Corcoran and Peck, as well as Batteries Mansfield, Drawbridge, and Onondaga stood on the bluff overlooking the Nansemond River on the north

Maj. Gen. John J. Peck. Edwin R. Root (United States Army Military History Institute).

side of town. A continuous ring of earthworks around the town connected all of the forts and batteries. The eight-mile stretch of the Nansemond River north of Suffolk to Cahoon's Point was unfortified but patrolled by one navy and two army gunboats.[15]

When Longstreet had moved his two divisions to Petersburg in early March, Peck got nervous and requested reinforcements. On March 13, Brig. Gen. George W. Getty's 5,000-man 3rd Division of the IX Corps was sent to Suffolk. Unlike most of Peck's other regiments, Getty's men were seasoned combat veterans. This brought Peck's strength up to 17,407. By the time Longstreet's troops crossed the Blackwater River, Peck was ready for them.[16]

Hood's column scattered Union pickets as it pushed toward Suffolk. By nightfall his troops were digging in on the north side of the Nansemond River opposite the town, and the men in French's division were entrenching on the South Quay Road. Pickett's division would not arrive until the next day.[17]

On April 12, Pickett's two lead brigades marched up the Somerton Road, driving in the Federal pickets. When they hit the southern perimeter of the town, they were pummeled by Peck's artillery in Forts Nansemond, McClellan and Union. The intensity of the fire caused the rebels to stop and start throwing up breastworks. Although Longstreet's and Peck's troops sparred with each other over the next several days, Longstreet knew he could not successfully penetrate the Union defenses without severe loss of life that neither he nor the Army of Northern Virginia could afford. He contented himself with laying siege to the town while his men scoured the area for food to feed Lee's army.[18]

On April 15 Major General French placed two artillery batteries at Hill's Point to ward off the Yankee gunboats. Hill's Point was of great strategic value on the Nansemond River. It provided high ground for artillery just above the confluence with the Western Branch at a place where the Nansemond suddenly narrowed, or suddenly widened, if one was heading downstream. French had returned from Petersburg and taken over his division, which Longstreet had given to Jenkins. Longstreet offered French command of the artillery, but French chose to retain command of his division and be an advisor to the artillery. At Hill's Point, French stationed

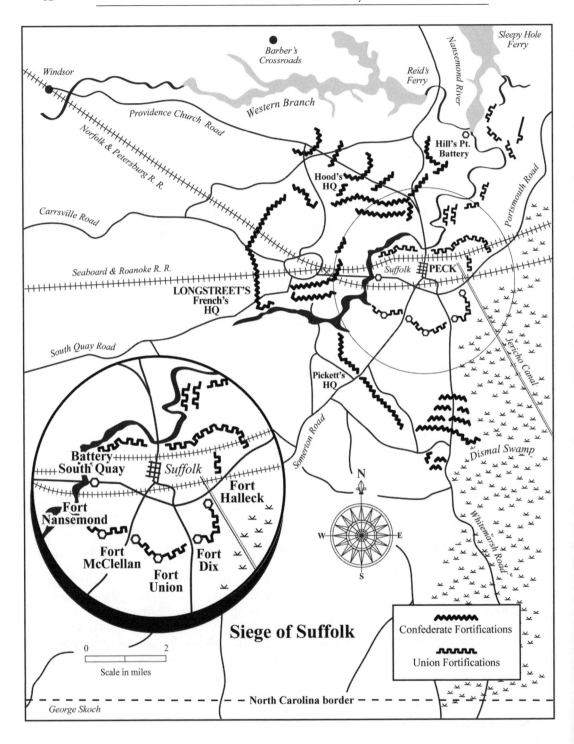

The Siege of Suffolk, Virginia, April 11–May 4, 1863.

Capt. David L. Smoots' Alexandria (Virginia) Battery, which was positioned in sunken positions to protect them from the gunboats, and Capt. Robert M. Stribling's Fauquier (Virginia) Battery occupied Fort Huger, which had been deserted by Confederate forces when they pulled out the previous spring. The artillery was supported by two companies of the 44th Alabama Infantry. A mile to the rear of the fort, the 55th North Carolina was stationed as a general reserve.[19]

Peck, in the meantime, was scrounging the Hampton Roads area and Washington for all the units he could find. By April 23, another 10,000 reinforcements had arrived in Suffolk.[20]

The 9th Vermont was one of the regiments caught up in Peck's request for reinforcements. In a driving rain, on April 15, the Vermonters broke camp at Camp Hamilton about noon and by dusk had loaded aboard the steamer *Champion* and were heading for Norfolk. The regiment arrived in Norfolk during the night, but remained aboard the boat until morning. After unloading their equipment, the Green Mountain Boys boarded open rail cars for the last leg of their journey to Suffolk. The regiment arrived in Suffolk at 10:00 A.M. and went into a temporary camp near the railroad tracks.[21]

The Vermonters were assigned to the Third Brigade of the 3rd Division of the IX Corps.

Twenty-four-year-old Colonel Arthur H. Dutton commanded the brigade. In addition to the 9th Vermont, the Third Brigade consisted of the 21st Connecticut, 13th New Hampshire, 25th New Jersey, and 4th Rhode Island. The 3rd Division, commanded by Brig. Gen. George W. Getty, was holding the right of the lines along the east bank of the Nansemond River.[22]

As the number of Hood's troops increased on the far riverbank, Peck feared the gunboats were not enough to keep Longstreet from throwing a pontoon bridge across the river. As reinforcement units arrived, Peck raced them downriver as soon as they came in. The 9th Vermont moved 3 miles downriver to Fort Connecticut on April 17, near Sleepy Hole Ferry, where it established a camp which the men dubbed "Camp Wood Tick." For the first time the men were sleeping in shelter tents. Shelter tents, very much like the ones used by our army today, were made of two cotton halves approx-

Post-war photograph of Brigadier General Gen. George Washington Getty, commander of the 3rd Division of the IX Corps (Civil War Library and Museum MOLLUS, Philadelphia, Pennsylvania).

imately five feet by five feet with buttons along two sides and corresponding button holes along the others. Each man was issued one panel, and two or more men had to join forces to have a complete tent.[23]

Sgt. John W. Bennett remembered having to be ready for an enemy attack every morning at daybreak: "We have to get out by four o'clock in the morning, and stand on our arms till sunrise; so you see it will be very difficult for the enemy to catch us napping." "No fighting yet," wrote Lieutenant Ballard several days after arriving in Suffolk, "though a considerable picket firing last night, and the enemy made a dash for one of our field batteries early this morning, as they did for one of our earthworks yesterday morning, but were repulsed on both occasions." Even though they could see and hear combat all around them, the men's sprits were high as Ballard continued: "Our boys are very cheerful; our fifer is playing merrily, and today one of our boys got out his fiddle, and Nero like, fiddled away to the sound of the enemy's cannon. It is well that men can get accustomed to anything — even to the horrors of war."[24]

Even though the Green Mountain Boys had been at Suffolk for less than a week, Maj. Edward Ripley was fed up with the constant stress of an imminent attack. "I wish they would decide whether Longstreet or Peck belongs here by one day's good fighting, and then wind up; not that I am 'spilin for a fight,'" he wrote, "I candidly confess I am not, but this constant suspense is wearing."[25]

In front of the Vermonter's camp was a battery of Federal 20-pounder Parrott guns on the bank of the river. The rifle fire between the pickets on the opposite banks of the river was almost incessant, and artillery duels were frequent. Captain Valentine Barney wrote about his experience on picket on April 18 along the Nansemond River:

> My Co. was detailed to go on picket out on the bank of the river and as our position was a very important one we got little or no rest that night. Our orders were to watch the opposite shore and see if any attempt was made to cross the river or lay a pontoon bridge.... About noon yesterday the enemy sharpshooter on the opposite shore commenced firing at us and at some others who were throwing up earthworks to protect some artillery near by and though none of us were hit some of the bullets came so near as to make it rather uncomfortable. As I was looking through a field glass at the opposite bank an orderly stood at my side and about a foot from me and one whistled right between us and struck in the ground about two rods to my rear. I had not thought of getting behind any thing before but then I was not long in getting behind a tree but while watching again another struck about 3 or 4 ft. from me which I picked up and now have. For some time every one of us who showed our head got fired at but no harm done, but we returned the fire and our artillery fired a few rounds at them and we silenced them for an hour or two when they again opened but accomplished nothing more than to prevent our men from work for a while. We were relieved at dusk last eve and we came here and found our camp in this nice little pine thicket and our cooks had got our tents up so all we had to do was to drink our coffee and eat our crackers and pork (which by the way is all we can get here) and crawl into our nests which is a rubber blanket laid on the ground and a wool blanket over us with our coat as a pillow. To keep warm we snuggle up close together and get along fine.[26]

Although rifle fire and artillery duels were a daily occurrence back and forth across the river, the heaviest action around Suffolk was between the Federal gunboats and the Confederate artillery. The artillery at Hill's Point was especially troublesome for the gunboats. The worst attack was on April 14, when the 500-ton steamer U.S.S. *Mount Washington* was all but sunk. Navy Lieutenant Roswell H. Lamson, commander of the Upper Nansemond Flotilla, tired of the pounding his boats took each time they passed around the point, devised a plan to capture it.[27]

On his trips by Hill's Point Lamson had noticed that although the front of Fort Huger, because of nature and man's efforts, was impossible to assault the rear was virtually unguarded. When the Confederates built the fort in 1861, they occupied Suffolk and did not need rear security. Now the rear was an open, unguarded cornfield. Lamson figured he could land troops on the upriver side of the point and take the batteries before the rebels could react. He sold his plan to Getty, and at 1:00 A.M. Thursday, April 16, Lamson, Getty and 200 Union troops executed the plan. Unfortunately, the operation fell apart almost as soon as it got started. The troops were successfully landed, but after moving inland about 50 yards they encountered several rebel pickets and scurried back to the boat.[28]

Lamson talked Getty into trying the plan again in the early morning hours of April 19, but this time with 500 troops. Again the attack failed before it even got started when the troops showed up two hours late for embarkation, leaving too little time before sunrise for the attack. The naval officers were furious and threatened to pull out the upper river flotilla.[29]

Still determined to capture the menacing guns on Hill's Point, Lamson, along with Capt. Hazard Stevens from Getty's staff, reconnoitered the rebel batteries a few hours after the second failed attempt. Stevens suggested they try a daylight attack since the enemy knew the ground better in the darkness. Lamson agreed, and they returned upstream to sound out Getty. Getty liked the idea and set the time of the attack at 6:00 P.M. that evening.[30] Finally, the plan came together. At 5:30 P.M. 130 men from the 8th Connecticut and 140 from the 89th New York boarded the U.S.S. *Stepping Stones*. With the decks shrouded with canvas to conceal the infantrymen, the *Stepping Stones* was soon heading downstream to Hill's Point.[31]

At approximately 6:00 P.M., under the cover of fire from gunboats below the point and Getty's artillery across the river, the *Stepping Stones* chugged up to the landing point. About 30 yards from shore, she hit a piling and went aground. Fortuitously the Confederate pickets were not on duty or the operation would have ended in disaster. Sizing up the situation, Captain Stevens jumped overboard to check the water depth and was able to wade ashore. Infantrymen, with rifles and cartridge boxes held over their heads, were soon in the water behind Stevens, slogging to the riverbank, still undetected by the rebels.[32]

Lamson soon had the vessel back under control and nosed it into the riverbank. The rest of the infantrymen who had not jumped overboard to get to shore jumped ashore as soon as the vessel made contact with dry land. Also, four 12-pounder howitzers were brought ashore.[33]

As soon as the Federal cannonade started, orders were sent to the 55th North Carolina to come forward, but for some reason the orders arrived too late. Also, again for some unexplained reason, the Alabama infantry at the fort was not in position, and within 10 minutes the surprised rebels were captured. The Federals captured 130 prisoners—nine of whom were officers—five field guns, and a large amount of ammunition. Not stopping to fire their rifles or needing to use their bayonets, Getty's men caused no casualties among the rebel cannoneers. The Federal casualties on land were three killed and 10 wounded. The navy lost three sailors killed and one wounded onboard the gunboats.[34]

As soon as the fort was taken, the *Stepping Stones* started ferrying reinforcements across the river. The reinforcements consisted of the remainder of the 8th Connecticut, five companies of the 10th New Hampshire, four companies of the 117th New York, companies D and F of the 9th Vermont under the command of Captain Jarvis, and a detachment of Battery A, 5th U.S. Artillery—in all, about 1,000 men.[35]

Soon after daylight on Monday, April 20, a Confederate force charged the captured works at the point, but artillery from the fort and the gunboats forced the butternut-clad troops to fall back to the cover of the woods. That would be the only attempt by the rebels to retake their captured works. As the day progressed, the troops continued to strengthen their position, but not long after the rebel attack Getty decided that Hill's Point was not worth holding. He reasoned that the 1,000 men he had there could stop an enemy crossing only at that one point, leaving weak places in the rest of his lines along the river. He relayed his concern to Peck, who concurred. The artillery was removed in the late afternoon and the infantry soon after dark.[36] The loss of the fort was quite an embarrassment to Longstreet, for which he blamed French. The feud between the two generals lasted for more than 30 years.[37]

The capture of Fort Huger was the last major action in the siege of Suffolk and the Union soldiers quickly got back into a normal camp routine. One of their favorite things to do was complain, as Maj. Edward Ripley did in one of his letters home: "The stores are all sold out in Suffolk and the people will go hungry in a week more, unless Gen. Peck allows merchants to run one or two trains to Norfolk for provisions. Our living is truly luxurious, the hardest, stalest crackers, and black water, and we lie in open fields in the wet four nights out of five." Several days later he wrote, "The country is worse stripped than upper Virginia, and the Sutlers are a set of villains. Mighty poor butter is 50 cents per pound, milk unknown, except in rare cases one runs across the 'Expressed Essence of Cow,' as the boys facetiously call solidified milk. It is a great institution. We got one can and lived high."[38]

The troops also resumed shooting at one another back and forth across the river, as Captain Barney recounted:

While we were at work yesterday on the fort a rebel sharp shooter got behind a large tree on the other side (being about 500 yds. off) and fired a number of times at us but we did not think him a very good marksman as he was not able to hit any of us while about 150 men were exposed all the while. Our men fired their muskets at him a number of times but he cared little. But when a twelve pound solid shot was put through the side of the tree he took himself away as fast as his legs could carry him.[39]

On Thursday, April 23, the 9th Vermont was transferred to a newly organized reserve brigade commanded by Colonel David W. Wardrop of the 99th New York. The brigade consisted of the 19th Wisconsin, 99th New York, 188th New York, and the 152nd New York.[40]

After the capture of Fort Huger, there were only five more minor confrontations between Longstreet's and Peck's forces, one in which the 9th Vermont participated. On April 24, General Peck decided he had to determine the rebel strength on the south side of Suffolk and sent out two reconnaissance forces. The largest, totaling 5,500 men under Col. Robert S. Foster, was to march down the White Marsh Road, while another of 1,200 men commanded by Col. Charles H. Buehler proceeded down the Somerton Road.[41]

The 9th Vermont received orders to move four miles to the left early in the morning of April 24 and in a drizzling rain moved out at 11:00 A.M. The Green Mountain Boys were to be a part of a large reserve, which would remain behind the protection of forts between the White Marsh and Somerton roads. The advancing columns moved out a little after 1:00 P.M., and serious contact was made with Pickett's men about an hour and a half later. Major Ripley noted, "Our forces drove the enemy about five miles; *they retiring pretty obstinately.*"[42]

The rebel artillery soon caused the Union troops to halt and then to fall back. "It was quite a little affair for the Union troops.... The Rebs handled their Artillery Capitally," Ripley recalled later. Not wanting to bring on a full-scale battle, Peck ordered his units to return to their own lines. The 9th Vermont was soon ordered to return to their original position downriver. Ripley continued:

> As we were about half through dinner, an order came from Gen. Peck, to have the 9th Vt. hurry back to their post in the defense of the Nansemond. Reached camp about 11:30 at night, found a big scare, for we could plainly hear the Rebs hard at work right across the river, chopping, shoveling, talking, trace chains rattling, etc., etc. Our batteries opened and stopped their labors. We then *slept on our arms*, the boys terribly tired for its muddy beyond anything you know in Rutland, having rained for four days.[43]

During the evening of April 25, two new assistant surgeons reported in from Vermont: Dr. Story N. Goss and Dr. Walter S. Vincent. Dr. Goss was a 32-year-old physician from Georgia, Vermont. He had been appointed to the regiment the previous September, but had been ordered to remain in Vermont on duty at the general hospital at Brattleboro. Twenty-five-year-old Walter Scott Vincent was a physician from Plainfield and had graduated from the Vermont Medical College in 1861. "We have now two assistant surgeons in our regiment, and can well afford to be sick occasionally," wrote Second Lieutenant Ballard upon their arrival: "They appear to be very fine fellows, and that is more than half of a good army surgeon."[44]

On April 27, the Green Mountain Boys were mustered for four months' back pay. Sergeant J. Webster Stebbins acknowledged a couple of days later in a letter to his brother:

> I think I shall have money enough without sending home for any as I now get $34.00 a month more than I did. I hope I can let you keep the $17.00 that you get. That will give me $7.00 a month to spend here and it will take that, I think. I must have some tea, butter, etc. any way. Don't know as I can get any tea here, guess I can at the city. I bought ½ peck potatoes for 25 cts. which makes them 2 dol. Per bbl. Butter is 40 cts. Sugar 16 cts. After which D. and I went down to the brook and washed up and feel much better.[45]

The 9th Vermont moved its camp back toward Suffolk to Fort Union, replacing the 4th Rhode Island, on Friday, May 1. The Vermonters now got a closer look at the town. Sgt. Charles H. Hodges of Co. H described Suffolk in a letter home:

Left: Assistant Surgeon Story N. Goss (Vermont Historical Society). *Right:* Assistant Surgeon Walter S. Vincent (Vermont Historical Society).

We are now camped in a direction east of Suffolk and only separated from it by a ravine. Suffolk was once a very pretty place about the size of Montpelier I think. Now a sad looking place indeed. Most of the white inhabitants have left and their once beautiful residences are now inhabited by *cullud persons* and Uncle Samuel's employees. We have traveled about this place considerable in our line of duties and I must say if there was a beautiful place in Virginia *this* was one. The farms about here were old but have the appearance of having been well cultivated. The buildings were very fine also.[46]

Once in their new camp, the men got back to picket and fatigue duty. Captain Barney mentioned a problem he had with one of the men while on fatigue duty at one of the forts:

I was in command of one hundred men yesterday at work on a fort near by and I got along first rate. Only one thing happened to make it unpleasant. One of Co. D men was some saucy. I was obliged to tie [him] up to a stick of timber and keep there. I suppose he thought because he could say what he pleased to his own officers he could do the same to others, but he got snubbed that time.[47]

Sergeant Stebbins explained the trials and tribulation of being on picket:

We cant always finish a letter here when we commence it as you see by this. When I commenced this we were on picket and I write until it began to rain and as we had no shelter I was obliged to stop. We had a little shower after which I layed down and fell a sleep and woke up some 3 hours later finding the sun shining very bright and warm and myself sweting from the heat. It was then 4 ¾ o'c. I got up and made the necessary arrangements for the night and soon the lightning flashed and the thunder rolled telling us of a shower. There were 5 of us on the post (i.e.) 2 men, myself, and the Lieut. We sent a man to camp for some coffee. He had just got back and we had nearly got through supper when it began to sprinkle. We set some crotches and put on some poles, then threw our rubber blankets over which made a shelter. Soon the rain come a perfect torrent and the wind blew the blankets off which let the rain and 2 or 3 pails full of water that stood in the blankets where they saged between the poles, square onto us which wet us no little. Well then each man took care of himself the best he could. I sat on my wool blanket, overcoat & haversack to keep them dry and put my rubber over me and kept from getting any more wet. Well as it happened the shower last all night [illegible] some at 2 or 3 times it stopped ½ or ¾ of an hour. You may reckon none of us got any sleep that night. I could have slept but for having something to do every little while. In the morning at 7½ we were relieved and went to camp wet cold and hungry. Our guns all covered with rust. We were soon informed that we were to have inspection of arms and be mustered. We went to cleaning guns. I worked on mine ¾ of an hour and then did not get it clean. After muster we got something to eat and made a fire and went to drying blankets etc. which took till night when we layed down to sleep.[48]

Events occurred on April 29, that would hasten the end of the siege of Suffolk. On that day Hooker's units started crossing the Rappahannock River to begin the spring campaign against Lee's Army of Northern Virginia. Lee sent word for Longstreet to return, but it would take several days to recall all his foraging parties and disengage from the ring around Suffolk. The battle of Chancellorsville was fought on May 3–4 before Longstreet could return. Without Longstreet, Lee went in with one hand tied behind his back, but Stonewall Jackson's famous devastating flank attack on Hooker's XI Corps turned the tide of battle. By May 6, all the Federal troops were back on the side of the river from where they had started.[49]

Longstreet did not get his troops out of Suffolk until the night of May 3. His divisions returned along the same routes they had used to move to Suffolk. On May 6 his units started loading aboard trains at Ivor for the trip north to join Lee. Longstreet's mission had been a success. He had forced the Union to bleed off troops for Suffolk that could have been used to bolster Hooker, and he had collected tens of thousands of bushels of corn and possibly as much as one million pounds of bacon. The experience at Suffolk had not been any more enjoyable for the rebels than it had been for the men from Vermont. The men of the 8th Georgia Infantry regiment remembered Suffolk as "the best place to move from" and "a wretched place," as well as "a detestable hole."[50]

The Confederate human loss had been rather steep during the siege, with 400 to 500 killed and wounded, 400 captured, and 500 deserted, compared to the Federals' 44 killed, 202 wounded and 14 missing. The 9th Vermont was lucky and did not sustain any combat losses during its time in Suffolk. Many years after the war, Pvt. Albert A. Niles, a Morristown native in Co. H, related one unusual casualty the 9th Vermont suffered:

In June 1863 I was detailed as one of the color bearers of the Regt. which position I held until November when I returned to my co. for promotion. While with the color guard, at the battle of Suffolk, a minie ball struck the staff of the state colors, which I was carrying between my hands, which can be seen today at the state capital at Montpelier.[51]

When the rebels left, Peck sent Brig. Gen Michael Corcoran's division in pursuit. Corcoran did not accomplish much, but left destruction in his wake. According to the 9th Vermont's Sgt. Charles H. Hodge:

When the Rebels left this place on the 3rd of May Gen. Corcoran went out to give them chase and on one days march of probably 35 miles burned over twenty of those most beautiful mansions to ashes. Reason. He found rebel soldiers who from sickness and inability to keep up with the retreating army convalesced in them and destroyed the houses and took the inmates prisoners.[52]

The 9th Vermont was sent four to five miles south of Suffolk near the Dismal Swamp to level Confederate fortifications on Tuesday, May 5. Major Ripley wrote home:

I am here with 300 men, with 150 spades and shovels destroying some very formidable Rebel earthworks; the first line of which only our forces felt the strength of when they made a reconnaissance eleven days ago. The embankments are made very solid, earth well rammed, and cypress boughs through and through, so it is quite as much work to destroy as to build originally.[53]

After three days of extremely hard work, the Vermonters returned to camp, but not without a little more extra work, as Pvt. Nelson L. Wandell of Co. K related: "Finished throwing down the breastworks at 12 O'clock M. Started for camp so we thought but we went over on another road where they had a breastwork some few rods of rifle pits. It took us but a few minutes to demolish them, returned to camp."[54]

Lieutenant Colonel Stowell resigned his commission on May 11. He had been sick off and on since the fall of 1861 when he was in the 5th Vermont. His loss would be deeply felt, as he was one of the most popular officers in the regiment. Upon hearing the sad news, Captain Barney wrote, "We were all taken by surprise this morning on hearing of Col. Stowell's resignation. So we have lost our best officer and the regt. will feel it much. I presume the vacancy will not be filled at present nor till the regiment is recruited up and no one knows who will be the lucky man." Major Edward Ripley felt bad about Stowell's resignation as well: "Stowell's resignation is finally put through and accepted and he will be in Vermont before long. I feel terribly at this; he is the reliance of the whole Regt., *a rare officer, and has more military ability than all the rest of us simmered down together.* I dread the future now. Andross feels his lack of experience, and used to depend on Stowell, and I certainly distrust myself."[55]

In addition to his health, Stowell had other problems, as Major Ripley wrote: "Stowell's farm was going to the devil, his wife's health broken down. There was two of us here to command a small Regt. and he thought he was not needed, so he went home." With Colonel Andross sick in the hospital, Ripley was now temporarily in charge of the regiment, and the thought of being promoted to lieutenant colonel did not exactly please him, as he confided to his mother: "This unfortunate decision of Stowell to resign puts me in a mighty unpleasant situation. I don't want to be *Lt. Col.* It is nothing but perfect "Bullhead luck" that keeps carrying me up. I am at best a boyish looking Major, how much more boyish *LT. Col.*"[56]

Although Ripley himself had some feelings of self-doubt about the enormous responsibility of leading the regiment, most of its officers and men did not. Lieutenant Alfred Ballard wrote, "Our Major is making a good officer. Wherever there is any scouting to be done or a new line of pickets to be posted, there you may look for the Major." Ripley was promoted to lieutenant colonel May 16.[57]

Upon his departure from the army, Edwin S. Stowell returned to his farm in Cornwall, Vermont. He continued to be plagued by ailments from his days in the service, one of which was severe constipation. On May 27, 1877, he had a colostomy, but the operation did not solve the problem, and he died September 11, 1880, at the age of 49 of a bowel disease.[58]

Ripley moved the regiment to a field about one-quarter mile south of Suffolk on May 14, where it was brigaded with the 99th New York, 118th New York and 19th Wisconsin. The brigade was commanded by Brig. Gen. Isaac J. Wistar and became an independent brigade of the VII Corps.[59]

Wistar was born November 14, 1827, in Philadelphia, Pennsylvania. He graduated from Haverford College with a degree in law and commenced practice in his native city. He entered the army in June 1861 as a captain in the 71st Pennsylvania Infantry and by that

Brigadier General Isaac J. Wistar. (Katherine Vanderensuce Collection, U.S. Army Military History Institute).

November was the regiment's colonel. He was wounded in the right arm in the battle of Ball's Bluff, October 21, 1861, causing his arm to be permanently bent in a crooked position. He was wounded in the left shoulder at the battle of Antietam September 17, 1862, which paralyzed his left arm. He regained enough use of his right hand that he could, with much effort, write with a modified pen and could barely ride a horse. He was promoted to brigadier general on March 16, 1863, but the promotion was backdated to November 29, 1862.[60]

The regiment had to supply 80 men a day to work on the fortifications and drill, which the boys of the 9th Vermont had not done since arriving at Suffolk. "We drill three hours a day," wrote First Lt. Linus E. Sherman of Co. A, "but it all comes before 10 o'clock A.M. & after 6 P.M. so we are not troubled by the heat." Even with daily fatigue duty and drill, the men still had time to relax. Private James Martin, a young man from Calais in Co. I, wrote his friend Harry in Vermont: "I went a fishing the other day. I caut five eels." Private George W. Bisbee, a carpenter from New Haven, Vermont, in Co. C, noted in his diary May 19, "Had a great game of ball with the 118th N.Y." Bisbee did not record which unit won the game.[61]

Colonel Andross submitted his resignation on May 19. In a written statement Dr. Carpenter noted, "He is suffering from chronic bronchitis, which has troubled him in a greater or less degree for the past six months; affecting his voice at times so that he is unable to utter the necessary commands to his regiment with sufficient force of voice to be heard. He is also often afflicted with acute tonsillitis induced by the exposure which is unavoidable to a soldier in the field." Andross was discharged on May 22. He returned to Bradford, Vermont, and after recuperating from his illness, resumed his life as a farmer. He died November 28, 1906, of heart disease.[62]

To his surprise, Lieutenant Colonel Ripley received orders late Wednesday morning, May 20, to prepare the regiment to move out. Its mission was to protect working parties engaged in tearing up the railroad tracks between Suffolk and the Blackwater River. The men were ordered to quickly cook three days' rations, pack up and fall in with blankets and tents. Shortly after receiving the movement order, Ripley got another surprise when he learned that Colonel Andross, who was in the hospital in Suffolk, had submitted his resignation. Twenty-three-year-old Edward H. Ripley was now officially in command of the regiment.[63]

By noon the Green Mountain Boys was moving out of camp. The day was hot and sultry and the road was very dusty. The Vermonters reached the village of Windsor at about 7:00 P.M. after marching 16 miles. The men were too tired to put up their tents and laid out in the open for the night. "The worst of it was the dust blew so that we could hardly breathe sometimes, and you could guess we were dirty looking fellows," complained Sgt. Stebbins. "Some of the men one could hardly know at all. When we got to Windsor I was quite tired and the bottom of my feet were soar and all most blistered."[64]

The next morning the men were ordered to pitch their tents and had just settled down to rest when they were ordered to fall in. By 11:00 A.M. they were on the road again heading in a northeasterly direction. Because the regiment was so deep in enemy territory and the road ran through a thick pine woods, Lieutenant Colonel Ripley had skirmishers out in front of the column, which made for a slow and torturous march. Corporal Edward N. Phelps of Co. I complained that they had marched "through dust so thick we could hardly see and the sun pouring down his rays like a heated furnace."[65]

To defend against ambush, Civil War era doctrine prescribed an advancing column divide into three parts: first the skirmishers, then the main body and finally the reserve. The skirmishers were placed several hundred yards ahead of the column and on the flanks, about five paces apart from each other. The line could extend a quarter mile or so from the road. To keep ahead of the column, the skirmishers had to keep up a fast pace over fields, fences, creeks, swamps, and through woods. To make matters worse, they were in full uniform, carrying knapsacks, haversacks, canteens and muskets with fixed bayonets. The skirmishers cleared the way for the main body and reserve. If the skirmishers were checked by the enemy, they would fall back on the main body, which then deployed in line of battle and opened fire or charged with fixed bayonets.[66]

Five miles out of Windsor the regiment reached Barber's Crossroads, where it filed into the front yard of the Ely plantation. Lieutenant Colonel Ripley had the regiment drawn up in line of battle under the shade of the trees in the Elys' yard. Pickets were selected and posted around the farm. Guards were posted around the Elys' house and outbuildings to make sure that none of the Vermonters destroyed or stole anything. The rest of the men were allowed to stack arms and lie down in the shade for a rest. Instead of resting, some of the men who were running low on rations bought bacon, corn meal, cider, and hoecakes from the Elys. Sgt. Stebbins admitted later that while Mr. Ely was busy selling rations other men of the regiment "stole as much again as they bought."[67]

Hoecakes were a novelty to the Vermonters. Lieutenant Ballard was so taken with them he wrote about how they were made in one of his articles in the *Rutland Herald*:

> The inevitable "hoe cake" appears on every table, and is about all the bread in use. I have found out how to make it, and for the benefit of friends at home I will describe the process: Take cold water and stir in meal, making a thick batter. Don't put in any salt — they don't have any here. Bake it the best way you can and eat it without any fixings. Such is hoe cake here.[68]

Early Saturday, May 23, the regiment's quartermaster, Francis O. Sawyer, and quartermaster sergeant, Edward D. Barber, rolled into the Elys' yard with a wagonload of rations. It was now apparent that the Green Mountain Boys were going be out of Suffolk for a while.[69]

Later that morning some of the members of the company of the 11th Pennsylvania Cavalry that had accompanied the 9th Vermont set one of the Elys' outbuildings on fire. The cries from Mrs. Ely brought a group of Vermonters to the scene and the fire was quickly put out before the building was very badly damaged. The Vermonters, however, were not without their scoundrels who also bedeviled the Ely family, as Capt. Valentine Barney admitted later to his wife: "The men don't feel very kindly toward the family. I see they have painted their wagon with tar which will not make it very nice to ride in."[70]

Saturday night provided a little excitement for the Vermonters. Several Confederate cavalrymen approached the pickets, and shots were exchanged. The only casualties were one of the Pennsylvanian troopers, who was slightly wounded in the hand, and one man in the 9th Vermont's Co. C who had the toe of his boot shot off. Other than three rebel stragglers rounded up by the Pennsylvania boys, Saturday night's exchange of gunfire was the only contact made with the enemy during the entire mission.[71]

Near 4:00 P.M. on Sunday, May 24, Lieutenant Colonel Ripley pulled the regiment back from the Elys' house to a gristmill and set up camp. Then, on May 26, the regiment marched back toward Suffolk and bivouacked three miles from where they had started the week before. Corporal Edward N. Phelps wrote, "...before we left the mill where we were camped I think it was unfit to grind any more grain for the Sesech."[72]

Phelps continued:

> We were marched the most crooked round about way that I ever saw turning a corner at every new farm. We marched ahead about 3 miles of the town when we turned into a field of shrub oaks and made a pail of coffee and had just laid down and got fairly to sleep when we heard the major sing out Fall in. A sound that at this time I assure you was not so welcome. But it was cheerfully obeyed and in less than ten minutes the Regt. was in line again with their blankets on their backs when we were forwarded quick time into camp. This was 10 and we had just got ready to lay down again in camp as the watch noted the hour of 12.[73]

Several weeks later Lieutenant Colonel Ripley summed up his view of the Barber's Crossroads expedition:

I see you have been reading the imaginative columns of the New York papers, for the especial benefit of some politician in straps. Something like my gallant affair at Barber's Crossroads—vide the N.Y. Herald, where the "enemy was gallantly repulsed," great loss. I don't think there were over 3 Rebels hurt, if that.

This is disgusting to me, and I pray to get into a respectable department under an energetic leader, where we can do something besides die in camp.[74]

While in camp, Captain Barney had time to write his wife. In the letter he told her of having to discipline his orderly sergeant:

I have reduced my orderly [John S. Halbert from Fairfax] to 5th Sergt. on account of absenting himself without leave while we were out on picket. He is smart and capable of filling any position but there are some things about him that I could not reconcile to such as putting himself forward and out of his place. At first I thought of reducing him to the ranks but thought perhaps the punishment would be to severe and I think what I have now done will be of great benefit to him and I hope he will so conduct himself as to be worthy of promotion. I have made Sergt. Cleveland [Edmund F. Cleveland of Richford] my orderly. He was formerly a Corp. and is deserving of the place and I am not at all concerned but that he will perform his duty faithfully.[75]

The men had barely gotten their camp set up when orders were received on Friday, May 29, to be ready at a moment's notice to move out with five day's rations. Lieutenant Sherman noted the next day:

Second Lieutenant John S. Halbert, Co. A. Reduced from first sergeant to fifth sergeant in May 1863. Promoted to second lieutenant November 28, 1864 (U.S. Army Military History Institute).

Our orders to be prepared to move at a moments notice is withdrawn & we again breathe freely. There is a prospect of our having good wall tents for officers & Sibley tents for the men, which looks as if we were to remain here sometime for if we go into the field we cannot transport them. *One team* is allowed to transport the baggage, cooking arrangement, tents & etc. for all the line officers, besides the company mess things. So you may judge we cannot have a very large amount each. We drill 3 hours per day and do a very small amount of guard duty and that is all.[76]

Val Barney wrote several days later:

When I last wrote you we were under marching orders and expected to leave every day, but the order was countermanded yesterday [June 1] and my mind is not so much in a moving mood and we are allowed to unpack our knapsacks and let our blankets remain unrolled. We expect to exchange our little tents in a few days for the wall tents. I don't know how I shall feel to again live in a tent where I don't knock my hat off every time I go into it or get well soaked every time it rains, but I reckon the change will not be very disagreeable.[77]

The same day the marching orders were rescinded, Captain Kilbourne complained:

This is a very dusty camp—being situated upon plowed ground—and I can scarcely make a move but dust will follow thus keep me completely enveloped in a cloud of dirt and sand from morn to night. The weather is *very hot* and sultry. And I sweat like rain every day enough in six months to make a common sized river.[78]

While waiting for movement orders, the regiment continued the daily drill periods. Some of the men had apparently forgotten how to march, as Captain Barney mentioned:

We are having a good opportunity to drill and the men are improving very fast. There are a few men in ea. Co. who are careless and willfully helpless and they have been put into a squad by themselves called the "awkward squad" and are drilled two hours per day. We had a brigade drill last Friday and our regiment got compliments for its good appearance and knowledge of the drill.[79]

With time on their hands, the officers began to speculate who was going to get promoted into the regiment's vacant positions. Captain Valentine Barney wrote his wife on June 11:

The fact is it is awful dull here and I am getting tired of the monotony. We expect here every day to hear of some promotions in our Regt., but no one knows who are to be the lucky ones. As I wrote before I don't have any idea of getting a promotion. I know the line officers and (almost without an exception) in favor of my having a place but *their* say don't go very far. I would not wonder if one of our junior Capts got promoted to Major as Capt. Brooks is a constant companion of Col. Ripley and of the same stamp. My Co. are doing finely in drill and quite a number of officers have told me I have got the best drilled Co. in the Regt.[80]

Three days later he told his wife:

I have heard nothing as yet from the new promotions but we expect every day to get some news of them and see the newly promoted gents come out with new straps on. I expect my orderly will be 2d Lieut., but of some other Co. Every old 1st Lieut. will be Capt. except Sherman and there would be no hope for him if he should be in the Regt. till dooms day. In fact no more than there is for me to get promoted and I don't think as much for he is looked upon as "small potatoes" by all the officers and there is no doubt that if I had had a different 1st Lt. I would have been better off myself, but what cant be cured must be endured (don't mention the above).[81]

Lieutenant Colonel Ripley was promoted to colonel on June 12, with his commission back-dated to May 22. He wrote his mother on June 16:

The change from Leaves to Eagles I should scarcely notice, were it not for the serenades, congratulations etc., etc., for my care is no greater and my work no greater. The hardest work now before me is to fill the many vacancies in the Regt.[82]

At age 23, Edward Hastings Ripley was a full colonel. The lanky six-foot-tall young man had no military training and before enlisting had been a student at Union College in Schenectady, New York. He apparently exhibited a natural leadership ability as well as having the luck of being at the right place at the right time. He came from a wealthy family in Rutland. His father was William Y. Ripley and had made his fortune in the marble business. His mother was Jane Betsy Warren. He had three brothers and four sisters. Edward left school early in his third year, in 1861, to replace his brother William in the family business. William had joined the 1st Vermont Infantry, a three-month regiment, and had deployed in May to Hampton, Virginia. Edward returned to school in the fall of 1861 but left early again in the spring of 1862 to join the 9th Vermont.[83]

Ripley's promotion, along with several resignations, caused quite a ripple effect in the regiment. Ripley's new position required him to learn how to deal with state politics. He wrote his mother:

Colonel Edward H. Ripley (U.S. Army Military History Institute).

I have made recommendations to Governor Holbrook, but he lugs in politics, and begs leave to differ, and asks if I don't think such and such a person should have them, naming men who have great political influence at home, and who would help him next fall to a re-election, or perhaps by and by, to the Senate, but who have not a particle of military taste or ability, and who are, in fact, rather nuisances than otherwise.[84]

The regiment's adjutant, John C. Stearns, resigned May 1 due to chronic diarrhea and was replaced by Josiah O. Livingston. Although he thought he had no chance for promotion, Valentine G. Barney was selected as the regiment's lieutenant colonel. Captain Charles Jarvis of Co. D was picked to be the regiment's major. First Lieutenant Linus E. Sherman, who Barney thought did not stand a chance of promotion, became captain of Co. A. Second Lieutenant Erastus W. Jewett filled the position left vacant by Sherman, and Sergeant Edmund F. Cleveland replaced Jewett. First Lieutenant Samuel H. Kelley was promoted to captain in Co. B. Second Lieutenant A.C. Ballard filled Kelley's old position, and Sgt. William A. Dodge replaced Ballard as Co. B's second lieutenant. First Lieutenant Asaph Clark rose to captain of Co. D, followed by Charles W. Haskell as first Lieutenant and Sgt. Asa H. Snow as second lieutenant. Captain Lewis H. Bisbee resigned June 3 and was replaced by First Lt. James T. Gorham. Second Lieutenant Stillman Stone replaced Gorham as first lieutenant, and Sgt. Charles H. Dodge was elevated to Co. H's second lieutenant position. Sergeant Patrick Hobon of Co. C was appointed as second lieutenant of Co. I.[85]

Charles Jarvis was born in Weathersfield on August 21, 1821. He entered the University of Vermont at age 14 and was the school's youngest graduate when he graduated in 1839. After graduating from college, he studied law, but after the death of his brother he returned to the family farm to assist his father, who died a few years later. In March 1862, he raised company B of the 9th Vermont. When questioned by his friends about his decision to join the army, he is reported to have said, "There are things dearer than life. I would rather die for my country than live in ease at home." Because of his age and his giving personality, he was called the "father of the regiment."[86]

One of the most unusual promotions occurred earlier on June 8, which Lieutenant Ballard

Left: Second Lieutenant Edmund F. Cleveland, Co. A (Vermont Historical Society). *Right:* Second Lieutenant William A. Dodge, Co. B (Vermont Historical Society).

mentioned in one of his articles to the *Rutland Herald*: "Fifer [Edward M.] Edgerton, by the way of Co. B, is promoted to 4th sergeant because of his faithful services in training our drum corps. We have now the best music in the neighborhood, and it improves every day."[87]

While cooling their heels in Suffolk, General Wistar assigned the 9th Vermont the task of inflicting punishment on some New York troops, as Captain Barney mentioned on Sunday, June 14:

> The 99th N.Y. Reg. (one of our Brig.) had some trouble after they left here and got into quite a mutiny. Twenty of the ring leaders were arrested and sent back and our men have been guarding them. They are kept marching constantly night and day and now are on their third day. They have only bread and water to eat and carry their knapsacks. When they refuse to march they are gagged and bucked for four hours which is worse than marching. The Gen. says he wants to almost kill them before he lets them off.[88]

After reconstituting and reorganizing his Army of Northern Virginia, Robert E. Lee started it on another invasion of the north on June 3. It took several days for the Federal high command to determine Lee's intentions, but when they did, the Army of the Potomac was sent in hot pursuit. In an attempt to draw off Confederate troops, Maj. Gen. Halleck, on June 14, ordered Maj. Gen. Dix, with his 32,000 troops stationed around Hampton Roads, to demonstrate against Richmond. Halleck was quite specific in his instructions to Dix:

> Lee's army is in motion toward the Shenandoah Valley. All your available force should be concentrated to threaten Richmond by seizing and destroying their railroad bridges over the South and North Anna Rivers, and do them all the damage possible. If you cannot accomplish this, you can at least occupy a large force of the enemy.[89]

Because all available troop transports in his department had been ordered to Aquia Creek to evacuate the Army of the Potomac's wounded from Fredericksburg in the aftermath of the Chancellorsville Campaign, Dix could not start moving any of his units from Suffolk until June 17. In the meantime, he developed his plan of attack. He would land his force at White House on the Pamunkey River and send one column northeast to destroy the railroad bridges of the North and South Anna rivers. As a diversion, he would send another column to Bottoms Bridge to make it appear he was trying to reach Richmond from that approach.[90]

Colonel Ripley received orders on Wednesday, June 17, to be ready to move with the rest of the reserve brigade by 3:00 P.M. The destination was Yorktown. At 5:00 P.M. tents were struck and the Vermonters marched to the rail station in Suffolk. As usual the train was not on time and the men had to wait until 8:00 P.M. before it arrived and they could board. The regiment reached Norfolk and was loaded aboard the steamer *Paconi* about 9:00 P.M.; they sailed to Fort Monroe, where they anchored for the night. While at Fort Monroe, Captain Barney was taken to the Chesapeake General Hospital with malaria, where he would remain until July 7. During his hospitalization he would be promoted to lieutenant colonel. The Green Mountain Boys reached Yorktown at noon Thursday, June 18, just ahead of the rest of Wistar's brigade. After seeing the conditions inside the fortifications General Wistar had Ripley form up his regiment and march them several miles from Yorktown before going into camp.[91]

Wistar wrote years later in his autobiography about the appalling conditions he found at Yorktown:

> I transported my brigade of four regiments and a battery, on four steamers, and calling to report arrival to the Brigadier-General [Rufus King] in command, lately a western newspaper editor, I found him lying incapacitated in his quarters under the pious care of a pretty hard-looking staff, who called the affliction "malaria" [liquor], a disease which seems to have much to answer for in morals, politics and war. The general condition of affairs was the most disgusting I have ever seen in a military post. The fortifications enclosed perhaps a couple of hundred acres, inside of which, besides the dirty, idle, and neglected troops, were gathered over 12,000 refugee negroes supported in idleness on

Government rations, and lying about without order under any ragged shelter they could get, in every stage of filth, poverty, disease and death. The roadways, parade ground, gun platforms, and even the ditches and epaulements were encumbered by these poor wretches; the soldiery was ragged, filthy and idle, and unless all military signs were at fault, a raid by a handful of resolute and well-led men could have captured the place, with all its stores and its 3000 so-called troops, in a few minutes.

Though nominally and legally placed under command of the creature who was responsible for all this, I sternly insisted on keeping my hard-worked Brigade clear of the mess; and taking post some miles in front of the place, allowed no interference, and permitted no person within its camp without my own pass, keeping my troops hard at work, picketing, patrolling and drilling.[92]

The commander at Yorktown was Maj. Gen. Erasmus D. Keyes, a lackluster general whom McClellan had jettisoned after Keyes' failed attempt to take Richmond the year before. Since the end of the Peninsula Campaign, August 1862, Keyes, commanding the IV Corps, had been cooling his heels at Yorktown. Under Keyes' command was the recently formed division of Brig. Gen. Rufus King. Like Keyes, King was also in exile. In the Second Bull Run Campaign of August 1862, he had prematurely withdrawn his division from Gainesville, forcing Brig. Gen. James R. Rickett's division to abandon Thoroughfare Gap, thus allowing Longstreet's Corps to join Stonewall Jackson's on the main battlefield. At the opening of the battle proper, part of King's division was assailed by Jackson's men at Groveton and performed heroically, but there were reports that King himself was drunk. Although no charges were preferred against him, he was shunted off to southeastern Virginia within weeks. (In addition to his other problems, he was an epileptic.)[93]

Yorktown was established in 1691 on bluffs 50 feet above the York River. Its claim to fame was being the town where American independence was won October 19, 1781, when Lord Cornwallis's army surrendered to General George Washington. In 1861 Confederate Maj. Gen. John B. Magruder had improved and modified the British fortifications around Yorktown and dug new works that ran from Yorktown across the Peninsula to Mulberry Island on the James River.[94]

The historical significance of Yorktown was not lost on the Green Mountain Boys. Captain Edwin Kilbourne wrote his wife the day after arriving:

This Jennie is truly historic ground. Here it is right on the ground even that Lord Cornwallis surrendered up his sword to Washington. I last night went to the very spot marked by a monument where the deed was consummated. I cut off from a part enclosing the spot a small piece of wood and enclose it in this for you to keep. It can be marked (Father can do it) and laid up with the curiosities in the parlor. Also a few leaves from a tree beside the same spot. All around the place where the monument stood are the fallen dead of the battles of just a year ago. Mostly marked the 11, 12 and 15th of June 1862. Little wooden slabs with an inscription (their name, time of death with the Co. and Regt. they belonged to) is all that marks the spot of the fallen brave. All honor to these defenders of their country and their country's rights. As I walked in among the little mounds I could but weep inwardly at the loss of many a fond Mother now mourning for her only child, never to comfort and to bless her save perhaps in the satisfaction attending his death and the glorious sacrifice he made upon the alter of his country. God bless our Mothers. I noticed one head board of a fellow from N.Y. on which was written in lead pencil beneath his name "The last of three brothers fallen in the service of their country and a widowed Mother still to mourn." It affected me, but I dried my tears and went on and soon came across 2 Vermonters named Oakes [Pvt. Joseph Oakes, Co. A, 6th Vt., from Bristol, died April 25 of wounds received April 16, 1862] and Flint [Pvt. Royal Flint from Roxbury, who died of disease June 15, 1862] Co. H 6th Vermont Vols. Also some from the 2nd N.H. They most all died or were killed about the middle of June/62. A large field of them.[95]

Apparently a lot of soldiers during the siege of Yorktown the year before had visited the site of the surrender and had taken pieces of the monument that marked the spot, as Capt. Linus Sherman noted:

The place where Cornwallis surrendered his sword *was* marked by a monument of granite, but it has been carried off piece by piece till there is not a grain as large as a *bean* to be found. The place called to mind scenes in history very vividly. The old fort is here but the new one built by the Rebs is ten times as large. McClellan's trenches are all around & across the fields.[96]

As soon as the Vermonters made camp, they were put on alert for the upcoming operation. Instead of going to White House, Wistar's brigade was again designated as the reserve and would be stationed at West Point. The officers and men were ordered to pack away everything they could not carry. Captain Kilbourne wrote:

> Our men have stored their knapsacks and all we have for a tent is just the "shelter tent," carry it on our backs. All of us. Officers and all. We are going to move in light marching order when we do move and not be encumbered with baggage of no utility to the soldier. We expect marching orders every minute. All transportation they allow us is simply 2 teams to a Regt. and I'm cut down to a small valise. When we go on the march can't take but a shirt, 2 pair stockings and a pocket handkerchief and a little writing material.[97]

Kilbourne went on to explain how he had hired a local ex-slave to be his servant: "I have a smart negro with me now. He brings all the water for my cook and my own use. Blacks my shoes, brightens my equipments and does everything I wish him to do. Makes up my bed and on the march he is to carry my shelter tent and blankets so as to relieve me from much weight. Niggers are not a bad thing after all, eh!"[98]

While in camp awaiting movement orders, there was a bit of a row in Co. K caused by Sgt. Sylvester C. Burlingame. Burlingame had served in the 4th Vermont Infantry, but was discharged for disability March 5, 1862. After regaining his health he enlisted in the 9th Vermont. For some reason, over the last month or so he had become surly. He frequently found fault with the officers in his company and was quite verbal about it. He also sided with the enlisted men in his company in minor squabbles. On March 22 he finally went too far. During morning inspection, he was caught with a dirty rifle and was reprimanded by his company commander, Daniel W. Lewis, to which Burlingame uttered some disrespectful comments. The next day, June 23, Sergeant Burlingame was reduced to the ranks in a regimental court-martial.[99]

Orders to load aboard transports finally came on June 25. The Vermonters were on the beach in Yorktown by mid-morning, but did not get loaded aboard the steamer *Kennebec* until 4:00 P.M. The regiment reached West Point about 7:00 P.M., but it was near midnight before it was completely unloaded. The Confederates had some time earlier burned the wharf, and the men had to be taken ashore in small boats.[100]

The village of West Point was located on a triangular parcel of land formed where the Pamunkey and Mattapony rivers join to form the York River. The area was originally called Pamunkey Neck, but in 1650 Captain John West established a farm a mile up the Pamunkey River and the name soon evolved into West's Plantation, then West's Point, and finally West Point. The town was not incorporated until 1870 and then had a population of only 75.[101]

Captain Edwin Kilbourne's Co. G was the first to land and was sent out on picket. Kilbourne described the operation:

> The night we landed here the Genl. called on me and my Co. to go out some 2 or 3 miles and post a chain of picket guard from one river to the other. I was the first one that landed. Went ashore in a small boat and my Co. the same. Was then growing dark and it *rained like suds*. I immediately landed and through out my Co. as skirmishers and pressed forward gradually into the woods feeling my way along gradually. Not knowing but what I might stumble upon the enemy at any moment. Thus in the darkness of the night and amidst a severe rain storm I felt my way out in advance some 2 miles and coming across a little earthwork of rifle pits running parallel to my front I halted and took up a position for the night. After halting my men I made a tour of observation from the left of my command resting on the Pamunkey to the right resting as I afterwards made it on the edge of an impassable swamp which swamp ran to the Matapony river as I found out by waking up a negro who lived in a little log hut in the woods beside this swamp. He gave me the information of the lay of the land around which I wanted and which I found to be invaluable. I then posted my men anew but *very quietly* and kept a sharp lookout for the enemy or bushwhackers which might be hovering in the woods

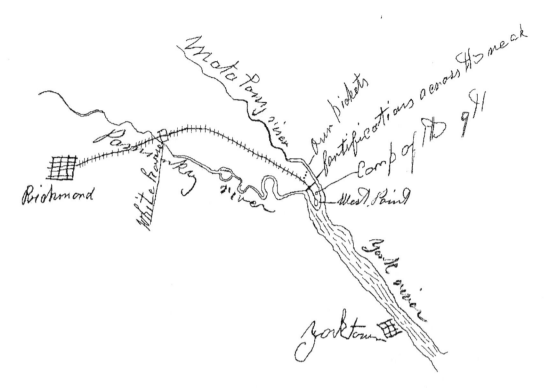

Sketch of the 9th Vermont's camp at West Point, Virginia, drawn by the regiment's chaplain, Lucius C. Dickinson (Steve Wakefield).

around. Twas near 12 P.M. before I felt sure I had a tenable position. I got wet through to my skin. *Saturated completely through.* I was relieved the next day about noon.[102]

After landing, the rest of the 9th Vermont and the 19th Wisconsin camped on the river bank. The next morning the troops tore down two small buildings and constructed a wharf so they could unload the 16th New York Artillery still aboard the transport. Then Brigadier General Wistar moved his men a mile or so up from the tip of West Point. For the next ten days Wistar's men lay at West Point as the reserve doing picket duty and picking blackberries.[103]

Charles Hodge griped on June 27, "We shall probably stay here to guard this miserable swamp, until some move is made that will relieve us."[104]

Not wanting to be part of the reserve, Colonel Ripley wrote his mother the day after landing: to say so "I regret we are to be detached on any side show, for if this is not to be a fools errand, and we are really to try and do something, I had rather be with the main Column."[105]

Several days later Ripley complained to his brother:

I am paid so many dollars per annum for taking care of the 9th Vt. Vols., I agree to fight as well as I can, when we are the victims of poor strategy and poor generalship, I agree to loaf around West Point (Va.), to the terror of a few women and the niggers, drill the Regt. regularly as well as I can, do picket duty in front as well as I can, and try and imagine there is something here for us to do, if the Gov't. wishes me to. All the while, Lee is upon our soil, the Gov't in terror is calling the Penn. Dutch to hurry up and take the place of those old veterans Regt. who are alone able to confront Lee's veteran Army with any chance of success, but whom the Gov't, with ineffable stupidity, has set as far out of the way as they had means to do in the short space of time given them.[106]

The only excitement while at West Point was the news about the fall of Vicksburg, Mississippi, and Meade's victory at Gettysburg, Pennsylvania. Colonel Ripley wrote his mother,

"Tonight we are all excitement over rumors yelled ashore from a boat passing, that Vicksburg has at last fallen, and that Meade has taken 40,000 prisoners in Pennsylvania. But we have no idea of the truth of it, except the low rumbling of heavy guns in the direction of Fortress Monroe, which we fondly hope may be in honor of a great victory."[107]

What the Green Mountain Boys did not know was that Brigadier General Stannard had become one of the heroes of the battle at Gettysburg. On the second day of the battle, July 2, his brigade held the left slope of Cemetery Ridge until he was ordered farther to the left in the afternoon to oppose Lieutenant General Longstreet's assault after the route of the Union III Corps. His brigade closed the gap, saving two artillery batteries, retaking another and capturing two Confederate guns. The next day Stannard, with three of his regiments, was instrumental in stopping Pickett's charge. Stannard hit the right of the advancing rebel column, causing a portion of it to stop. In this action Stannard was wounded in the right leg by canister ball, but did not leave the field until after the battle. After recuperating from his wound, on September 8, 1863 he commanded troops in New York City until he was given command of the First Brigade, 2nd Division, XVIII Corps in May 1864.[108]

General Dix had been shuttling troops from Suffolk to White House Landing as quickly as he could. On June 24 he sent a cavalry force north to destroy the Virginia Central Railroad bridge across the South Anna River. The mission was accomplished, and the cavalry returned on 27 June. In addition to destroying the railroad bridge, the cavalry destroyed the Confederate quartermaster's depot at Hanover Courthouse. It also brought back 700 animals, 35 army wagons, $15,000 in Confederate bonds and other property. In addition, it captured Robert E. Lee's second eldest son, Brig. Gen. William H.F. "Rooney" Lee, who had been wounded June 9 at the battle of Brandy Station and was recuperating at Hickory Hill, his father-in-law's plantation, in Hanover County.[109]

By June 28, Dix had 18,730 troops at White House. To complete the destruction of the railroad bridges across the South Anna River, Brigadier General Getty was sent up the left bank of the Pamunkey on July 1. He arrived at the Richmond and Fredericksburg Railroad bridge on July 4, but retreated when he discovered it was too heavily guarded for him to attack with his force. He did, however, manage to destroy three miles of railroad track before returning to White House.[110]

The same day Getty left on his mission, Dix ordered Major General Keyes with three brigades to Bottom's Bridge as a diversion for Getty. He got as far as Bottom's Bridge, but retreated after his first encounter with Confederate resistance, allowing the Confederate force to be moved to the South Anna to oppose Getty. Seeing no further advantage to his operation, Dix started pulling his troops back downriver on July 5. The total loss for the Union force was only two killed and seven wounded.[111]

With the expedition over, the 9th Vermont, along with the 16th New York Artillery, loaded aboard the steamer *Hero* just before midnight on Tuesday, July 7, for the trip back down the York River. When the Vermonters sailed away from West Point, they left two of their comrades behind. Privates Orlando Whitney and William H. Metcalf, both of whom had died of disease, were buried in field graves. Private Orlando Whitney, a 20-year-old farmer from Tunbridge, died July 3. His body was reinterred a year after the war in the Yorktown National Cemetery. His family placed a memorial stone in the family plot in the Whitney Hill Cemetery in Tunbridge. His mother and father received Orlando's $175.00 bounty after his death. After his father's death on July 11, 1865, his mother, Arathisa, tried to work the family farm herself, but after several years she was too old to do so. She finally applied for and received a widowed mother's pension from the government. William H. Metcalf, one of Co. B's musicians, died on July 5. If his body was reinterred in the Yorktown National Cemetery, it is one of the many unknown soldiers buried there.[112]

The Green Mountain Boys arrived back in Yorktown at 10:00 A.M. Wednesday, July 8, and returned to their old camp. Once settled in, Colonel Ripley complained to his mother:

We are all now West Point graduates, finishing I hope in this one term of about two weeks, all the labors we shall ever do at that deserted watering place. So again, has the Mirage in the sky of Richmond taken allured an Army to its gates, and then gently faded away, leaving it dispirited with all this wearying pursuit of a phantom. Can one fathom the impenetrable mystery of all this seemingly idle and resultless marching to and fro?[113]

On Thursday morning, July 9, Ripley was ordered to move his regiment to the interior of the fort surrounding Yorktown. The men were able to move into log barracks that measured 60 × 20 feet, very spacious accommodations compared to their shelter tents. However, the entire area occupied by the Vermonters had to be cleaned up. Several hundred cartloads of rubbish had to be hauled away before they could move in. Wistar's brigade was now permanently stationed at Yorktown.[114]

Above: **Private Orlando Whitney, Co. D, died of disease in West Point, Virginia, July 3, 1863 (Euclid D. Farnham).** *Below:* **Present-day photograph of the Yorktown National Military Cemetery (Sarah Zeller).**

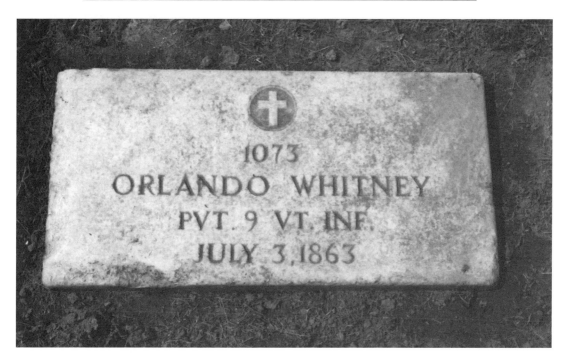

Present-day photograph of Private Orland Whitney's grave stone in the Yorktown National Military Cemetery (Sarah Zeller).

Ripley was not at all happy at being stuck in Yorktown and blamed it on General Wistar's injuries, as he told his mother: "Wistar's Brigade is permanently located here, garrisoning Yorktown and Gloucester. I have moved the Regt. inside the fortifications, am in barracks and it looks like my spending the summer here.... This comes of being a Brig. Gen'l who is hewed and hacked with wounds, and crippled. Wistar has a fine reputation that would put him in a more responsible position, would his health permit."[115]

The Vermonters were formed up in a hollow square on Sunday, July 12, to hear Chaplain Dickinson preach. "The chaplain preached to us for a few minutes, but not very interesting, for he isn't a *live* man enough for the army," complained Capt. Edwin Kilbourne.[116]

Because of his poor performance in the operation against Richmond, Major General Keyes was relieved of command at Yorktown on July 12 and assigned administrative duties until he resigned from the service May 6, 1864. After his resignation, he moved to California, where he engaged in gold mining, banking and wine making. Brigadier General King left three days later, leaving Brigadier

Present-day photograph of Private Orlando Whitney's memorial stone in the Whitney Hill Cemetery, Tunbridge, Vermont (Euclid D. Farnham).

General Wistar the commander of the Eastern District of Virginia. King resigned from the army the next year due to ill health.[117]

Within a few days after assuming command at Yorktown, Wistar found out just how bad the "pretty hard-looking" staff of General King's really was. The garrison provost marshal was selling oystering permits in the York River to the Negroes in Yorktown and pocketing the money himself. The garrison quartermaster had a crew of 400 contraband (runaway slaves called "contraband" so the U.S. Army did not have to return them to their masters), which were being paid $8.00 a month, to handle supplies and do manual labor, and he was skimming off some of the money himself. As was his military prerogative, Wistar fired the entire staff and selected trustworthy officers from the regiments in his brigade to replace them. From the 9th Vermont, Doctor Carpenter was selected as chief surgeon of the garrison and put in charge of the fort's hospital, the Nelson General Hospital, located in the Nelson House. First Lieutenant Able E. Leavenworth, Co. K, was made the acting assistant inspector general, and First Lt. Erastus W. Jewett, Co. A, was selected as the garrison engineer. The regiment's quartermaster, Francis O. Sawyer, was selected as the garrison's acting assistant quartermaster. Captain Joseph C. Brooks of Co. F was chosen as provost marshal. Wistar noted Brooks as being "a competent officer of zeal, force and integrity." In addition, Wistar chased off the sutlers, or "rouges," as he called them, that had been overcharging the troops and trading with the enemy.[118]

While it was flattering that Brigadier General Wistar thought so highly of the Vermont officers, several other officers were selected for court-martial duty and a few were sent back to

Brigadier General Isaac J. Wistar's staff November 1863. First Lieutenant Able E. Leavenworth remained on Wistar's staff until June 1864 (courtesy of The Wistar Institute, Wistar Archive Collection, Philadelphia, Pennsylvania).

Vermont on recruiting duty, which depleted the regiment of most of its leadership. At one time during the summer 15 officers of the 9th Vermont were on some type of special duty.[119]

Another action Wistar took soon after taking command was to get all the Negroes out of the fort. Several thousand yards outside the fort he had a piece of land surveyed and laid out in two and four acre plots with streets and building lines. Then he had all the able-bodied Negroes set to work building log cabins of prescribed form and dimensions. The soldiers called the place "Slabtown," which stuck until the community was purchased by the Federal government and destroyed in the early 1970s to add more acreage to the Yorktown National Battlefield. The Vermonters called the settlement by another name, as Lieutenant Colonel Barney mentioned in a letter home: "We have a negro village just outside the fort named Jewettville after First Lieutenant Jewett on account of his overseeing the building of it and I presume it will be called by that name for years to come." Slabtown was located on land to the rear of the present day Yorktown National Military Cemetery.[120]

Captain Kilbourne related one of his visits to the contraband camp:

I went outside the fortifications to a negro settlement about a mile out and attend the regular afternoon meeting which they have on the Sabbath. I was much interested in hearing them speak and pray. One old negro, who seemed to be the best informed among the number, rose and read a passage of scripture concerning the Kingdom of heaven and the wise virgins and etc. Then he went on to expatiate upon it using his peculiar dialect common to the negroes, but in the main using very good language and withal a vast deal of good common sense. But the point where the gazelle came in was where he got up to the highest pitch of his voice laying it down in strong terms what they must do if they wanted to die in peace. Then the women began to *moan* and *grown* [*sic*] and sway their bodies one side and the other and forward and back and look up and holler and yell and O my! I cant begin to tell what they did. It was ludicrous. There was one old woman directly in front of me (as I was sitting on my horse in the open air). She was black enough to be seen distinctly in the darkest night you ever saw! Well, she just opened her mouth, tiped back her head and my goodness, if she didn't "sing aloud" much to my amusement, this I would say so. It was all I could do to "hold in," but I did manage to, out of respect for the poor creatures, and the subject they was considering, but when they came to sing from "Watts Hymns" I could not contain myself any longer I had to laugh a little. There [*sic*] singing I am not able to imitate, much less, portray. I only wished you could have been present and heard them. There was upwards of 200 at the meeting, and I felt *well paid* for going. Think I shall go out again some Sunday and hear them. They certainly are sincere and earnest in all that they do. For this I respect them.[121]

Just after midnight on July 18, Pvt. Timothy Steady, an 18-year-old farmer from Hinesburg in Co. F, was at his guard post walking his beat at the commissary building near the quartermaster's wharf on the York River when he was taken with severe cramps in his stomach. He called for the corporal of the guard but apparently was not heard. Because the cramps were so severe, he had to sit down. After the cramps gradually subsided, Steady fell asleep. At 3:30 A.M. the corporal of the guard made his rounds and found Steady sound asleep. Steady was put under arrest, thrown into the guardhouse and charged with sleeping on his post. He was court-martialed on August 3 and pleaded guilty. In his defense, he called his first sergeant, Elias L. Brownell, as a character witness. Brownell testified that prior to this offense Steady had been a good soldier, and when asked by the judge advocate, "Have you had any reason to complain of him in regard to his duty?" Brownell replied, "Nothing more than in some slight case." Then he stated, "I understood he was a self made boy at home, he has always been a willing boy. I have heard that he only had a father and a brother." What Brownell did not mention was Steady had deserted earlier in the year at Camp Douglas, but had returned and was not charged.[122]

Steady then explained to the court why he had fallen asleep, followed with, "I was fifteen years old on the 2nd day of Sept. last." The court found Steady guilty of sleeping at his post, which could have been punishable by execution, but he was sentenced to only forfeit two months' pay. A note in his court-martial records reads, "The court are lenient on account of the extreme youth of the prisoner & also on account of his apparent ill health." Steady continued to serve as a good soldier until honorably discharged June 13, 1865.[123]

While Colonel Ripley was in a meeting with General Wistar on the evening of July 22, he had quite a scare, as he related to his mother:

> Gen. Wistar astonished me last night by telling me that Gen. Foster had ordered a Military Commission to be assembled to examine and recommend for discharge all incompetent officers. He then stopped talking a moment and went to thinking, and I in agony, felt my heart sink within me, for I have feared lest I might be brought before one, for my own short-comings and mistakes, and now confidently expected he would recommend me. But instead, I was almost as badly frightened when he resumed the conservation by saying, "And I have sent your name to Gen. Foster at the Fortress, as Colonel of the Committee." Well, I bid the Gen. a kind of stupefied adieu, hurried home, pulled out Tactics, Regulations, Orders from Adjutant General '60, '61, '62, and '63; "Current Series," "Jominie," "Military Dictionary," etc., and read everything from funeral through table of pay, ordinance blanks and index; and finally went to bed toward morning in despair.[124]

Colonel Ripley received orders on July 24 for an expedition to Gloucester Court House the next day. The purpose of the trip was to capture some rebel cavalry reported to be in the area and to confiscate all firearms, horses and mules fit for cavalry or the quartermaster's use. The order also stated there would be no pillaging or unnecessary injury to civilians or private homes. The men were ordered to have one day's rations in their haversacks, full canteens, and 40 rounds of ammunition in their cartridges boxes.[125]

The Vermonters were to land at Cappahosic, where Ripley would lead six companies to the courthouse, while Lieutenant Colonel Barney would wait two hours, giving Ripley time to reach the courthouse, and then march to Gloucester Point, searching farms for animals and firearms as he went. At 4:00 P.M. two squadrons of the 2nd Massachusetts Cavalry, with two ambulances, and the 118th New York Infantry, with two sections of the 8th New York Artillery, were to leave Gloucester Point and rendezvous with Ripley at the courthouse.[126]

Cappahosic was a small settlement on the east bank of the York River that had been settled in 1712. It was named for the local Indian tribe and in 1863 consisted of two storehouses, a boathouse, a couple of farmhouses, and a barn or two, together with a large cornfield.[127]

As ordered, the 9th Vermont departed from the quartermaster's wharf at Yorktown at 2:00 P.M. on Saturday, July 25, on the gunboat *Commodore Jones*. It sailed up the York River to Cappahosic, but because there was damage to the pier there the regiment had to be landed in small boats, leaving onboard the officer's horses. Companies A, B, C and D remained with Lieutenant Colonel Barney, while the other six companies left with Colonel Ripley for Gloucester Court House. Being in enemy territory, both columns marched with flankers and a rear guard. The weather was extremely hot, and several men fell out, but Barney confiscated a wagon to use as an ambulance and left no one behind.[128]

Confiscating the horses and mules necessary for farming was difficult for the Green Mountain Boys, most of whom were farmers themselves. Lieutenant Colonel Barney confessed, "It was pretty hard to see the women cry and take on while we took their horses but I told them I would rather see them shed a few tears than to be obliged to walk."[129]

At the courthouse, Ripley met the 2nd Massachusetts Cavalry, which had captured a Confederate mail carrier with a bag of mail from Richmond. With information from the local citizens that the Confederate cavalrymen had left the day before for King and Queen County, Ripley started his troops down the peninsula to Gloucester Point. The rebel mail carrier was not happy about having to walk, as one Vermonter remembered: "The fellow seemed to detest the style of making him walk, and using his team to advance the interests of the advance guard." About 10 miles from the courthouse, Ripley's and Barney's columns reunited at Hickory Fork, where they took an hour break and were cooled down by a heavy downpour. After the break,

Present-day photograph of Gloucester Court House, built circa 1766 (Sarah Zeller).

the column proceeded on to the point, which it reached just before sunset, and crossed the York River on the ferryboat *Winnimsimet*.[130]

The entire operation had gone as planned, except for the escape of the rebel cavalrymen. The two columns did, however, collect 40 horses, three mules, two wagons and a number of shotguns and pistols. The most important prize was the rebel mailman and his satchel of mail. Best of all, there were no casualties.[131]

On the evening of Tuesday, July 28, 18-year-old Pvt. John Finchon, a five-foot-three-inch Tunbridge native in Co. D, was assigned a guard post in Fort Yorktown. He told the officer of the guard before being posted that he was sick and wished to be relieved from guard duty, but the officer ignored him. At 11:00 P.M., while making his rounds, the officer of the guard found Finchon a short distance from his post asleep. He was awakened and sent to the guardhouse, where he stayed a short time before being admitted to the hospital. He was brought before a general court-martial on August 20. He was charged with leaving his post before being regularly relieved, to which he pleaded guilty. He explained to the court what had happened and that he had been in the hospital ever since, but he was still found guilty and sentenced to three months hard labor at the fort.[132]

Wednesday, July 29, was one of the best days in the Vermont camp for a long time. This was the day the paymaster arrived and everyone got two months' back pay. They were now paid up through the month of June.[133]

During the month of July, camp sickness started to plague the Vermonters again as it had at Camp Douglas. Lieutenant Colonel Barney noted:

The health of our regiment is not first rate at present. We have about 50 sick but deaths are not few compared with the amount of sickness. We are favored however when we consider the health of the other regiments here. The 19th Wis. have 250 sick and more coming down every day. We are doing every thing we can to keep the men healthy and to keep clean is one great object.[134]

Captain Sherman noted the sickness in camp was getting worse: "I am well but many of the men are sick with intermittent fever.... Today nearly 100 men excused from duty."[135]

In mid–July, Captains Linus Sherman and David Lewis were assigned court-martial board duty that would last into September. Sherman shared his experience on the board with one of his friends back in Vermont:

I am now & have been for twenty days detailed as member of General Court Martial & am likely to continue thus for twenty days to come. Have nothing to do with my company, except what I *chose* [*sic*] to do. Can go where I please except when court is in session without asking permission of anybody which is quite a relief after being under control for so long. Before I could not go a half mile hardly without asking Col. Frequently adjourn for a day & sometimes two days & then I have a nice time. My dear friend & classmate Partridge is signal officer at Gloucester Point just on the other side of the river and I enjoy his society very much.

Sherman's attitude toward his responsibility as a company commander was probably the type of thing Lieutenant Colonel Barney did not like about him.[136]

The following article appeared in *The Cavalier*, a newspaper printed in Yorktown by the Union troops, on August 3, concerning the use of alcohol in Yorktown:

On Saturday last, the order prohibiting the sale of spirituous and malt liquors to enlisted men went into effect in Yorktown. The bad quality of the water in the Fort caused porter and ale to be used here pretty extensively as a substitute, and as the supply from Baltimore was scarcely equal to the demand, it was seldom permitted to attain to a sufficient age to be a wholesome beverage. The more cooling drinks now supplied to soldiers, such as lemonade, mineral water, sarsaparilla, etc., will, it is thought, be more conducive to the health of the men, or if they are not relished, a sufficient quantity of ice may be purchased for the same amount of money that a couple of glasses of the exploded beverage have cost to make the water palatable. The ration of whiskey now furnished by the commissary department will be found to supply all the stimulant necessary to health, and will prove a consolation to those who love their beer. Regular authorized regimental sutlers, we believe are still permitted to sell malt liquors in small quantities to commissioned officers, and we recommend those who wish a good glass go to the 9th Vermont, who can supply an article of stock ale that cannot be beaten anywhere.[137]

As the summer progressed Sherman and Lewis spent the majority of their days in the sweltering courtroom listening to boring testimony. On August 4, Captain Sherman wrote his brother a letter during one of the trials:

While we are waiting for a witness and seeing there is pen & paper handy I will write a line. You may be sure we have a *gay* old time on court martial. Every little while we have to have a story or something to pass the time. This is the 9th day of our court & we are on our second case. Have three others on hand one of which will take at least a week and more likely ten days. We are taking testimony now but it is so *dull* that I have to do something to keep awake. One member is fast asleep at this moment. There, this witness has done and there being a little stir member asleep wakes up to find a paper ball elevated just ready to be thrown at his head. Remarks by Capt. C. just before he wakes "see how near you can come to his nose." The testimony thus far has amounted to nothing and we have become almost disgusted with proceedings.[138]

By August 4, the diseases in camp were getting out of control. Lieutenant Colonel Barney wrote to his wife of the dilemma:

We had out for review only about 150 men, but we report about 300 for duty. The 19th Wisconsin reg. have nearly 400 men on the sick list and had out for review only about 70 men. The medical director came up here from Ft. Monroe yesterday and examined the different camps to find out if possible the cause of the sickness. He complimented our regiment very highly for their cleanliness and neatfulness of our camp. But I understood he reported quite unfavorably as to the other regiments and especially the 19th Wis.[139]

On the same day Captain Kilbourne also mentioned the problem:

Sickness in this command is alarmingly on the increase. Some 20 per day are coming down in our Regt. with intermittent fever. The 19th Wisconsin and 99th N.Y. are more sickly than we. They are dying off very fast. We are going to take rations of whiskey and quinine every day as a remedy for these chills and fever so prevalent among the men. I think it will be a good thing.[140]

Along with the sickness was the incredibly hot humid Virginia weather which Second Lieutenant Stilllman Stone of Co. H complained about: "The weather is very hot, (if hot is any name for it) the mercury getting as high as 110 in the shade, nearly every day for the past days." Captain Kilbourne also described the miserable heat:

O this wretched *hot weather*! This oppressive sultry dead morning. The thermometer runs up to 105 degrees and in the shade and holds for a number of days, perhaps a week at a time. Last night I laid almost in the open air with nothing over me and then could not get to sleep for some hours the heat was so prostrating and the air so heavy.[141]

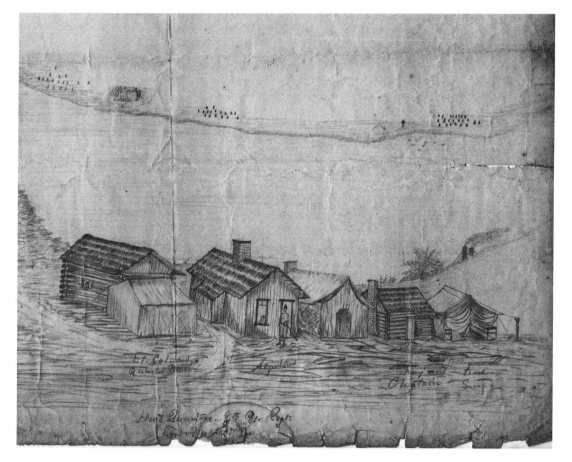

Sketch of the 9th Vermont's staff quarters in Yorktown, Virginia. From the left in the foreground: Lt. Col. Valentine G. Barney's and Quartermaster Francis O. Sawyer's quarters, Adjutant John C. Stearns quarters, unidentified, Major Charles Jarvis's and Chaplain Lucius C. Dickinson's quarters and Assistant Surgeon Story N. Goss's quarters. Across the York River are Union camps on Gloucester Point (Vermont Historical Society).

Present day photograph of the Nelson house, built circa 1730. Used by the Union forces as a hospital (Sarah Zeller).

Two days later he wrote, "I'm growing poor and if we don't have a cessation of hostilities on the part of fleas and the like and also an abatement of the *hot hot wretched hot weather* there will not be enough left of me by next winter to get a furlough." Lieutenant Colonel Barney was also vexed by the insects: "I would have rested finely had it not been for the fleas. They are very thick here and we are completely covered with their bites and I don't know but I would prefer living in a tent to a log house."[142]

Toward the end of August, General Wistar selected companies E, G, B and K of the 9th Vermont to man the large cannons that bristled from the top of the walls of the fortifications that surrounded Yorktown. "I like the drill quite well but there is a slight difference between handling pieces weighting 11 lbs. and 9,000 lbs!" wrote Captain Edwin Kilbourne. "We are to drill every morning and evening (5:30 A.M. and 4 P.M.). We are out learning the uses and ranges of different projectiles, the time of flight, length of fuses and elevation and etc. and all this to kill men. To destroy life and limb and make mothers and sisters and wifes mourn their loss."[143]

On August 29th Corp. Samuel Hartley of Co. C forged an order from his company commander, Capt. Herman Seligson, to enable him to buy alcohol from the 9th Vermont's sutler, John Moore. Hartley, a 25-year-old Irishman who had deserted the British Army in Canada to enlist in the 9th Vermont, had an excellent record in the regiment up to this point and had been promoted to corporal December 1, 1862, at Camp Douglas. Captain Seligson had issued an order earlier: "That no man should procure ale or beer unless by an order signed by said Captain Seligson." Apparently, the boredom at Yorktown and his desire for alcohol had gotten the best of him. Corporal Hartley was brought before a regimental court-martial on August 31 and charged with forgery. He was found guilty, and on September 13 he was reduced to the ranks, confined to one month at hard labor, and had to forfeit one months' pay. The stiff punishment seemed to improve Hartley's behavior, at least for a while.[144]

As September approached, the health of the men in the regiment got even worse. The main illness was malaria. There were so many cases that Vermonters started calling the fort surrounding Yorktown "Fort Malaria." On September 5 Lieutenant Colonel Barney wrote, "The truth is this is a very unhealthy country and a person who can stand it through the summer and not get sick is as tough as iron. About 130 of our Regt. are on the sick list and although our sickness is extensive the deaths are very few we having lost but one man for a month past." By the end of the month it was a different story. "Since I last wrote we have lost by death six of our men," Barney recalled. "Four died in two days." Unfortunately, it would only get worse.[145]

Private Jesse Gerard of Co. B, the man who had been mistaken for a Negro at Harpers Ferry, was discharged with a disability from chronic rheumatism on September 2. Because he had not been able to perform military duties, he had been assigned as the regimental mail carrier on June 11, but now he could not even handle that duty. He would suffer with rheumatism on his left side for the rest of his life.[146]

Four members of the 9th Vermont who deserted while the regiment was in Chicago were returned and court-martialed in early September. Privates Alva W. Elmer of Co. E and Hiram Wood of Co. B were tried on September 7. Elmer had deserted October 23, 1862, and had been returned to the regiment August 30. Wood had deserted on January 26, 1863, and had also been returned August 30. Each was found guilty. Elmer was sentenced to one year of hard labor and forfeiture of all pay and allowances during his time of incarceration. Wood was sentenced to hard labor on fortifications at Portsmouth, Virginia, for the rest of his term of service. On February 14, 1864, Wood wrote the following letter to Colonel Ripley:

Dear Sir:

I take this opportunity to drop you a few lines letting you know that i am still a prisoner and doing heavy duty every day and hoping that the time is not far distant when i shall return to my regt. and be a soldier and do a soldier's duty. When you saw me last fall you said you would have me released if it lay in your power to release me. i wish you would and i will try and do my duty as a soldier and a man.

Apparently Ripley could not, or would not, get Wood released early, and he was dishonorably discharged from the service June 13, 1865.[147]

Seventeen-year-old Pvt. Herbert Barden of Co. B from Wells was tried for desertion on September 11. Barden left the regiment on December 10, 1862, to join an Illinois cavalry regiment. For some reason he was brought under arrest to Camp Douglas July 23, 1863, as a deserter and was returned to the regiment August 29. He was found guilty and sentenced to one year of confinement at hard labor plus loss of pay. Barden's father wrote the following letter to President Lincoln in an attempt to get young Herbert's sentence reduced:

Wells Vermont Dec 7th 1863

To Abraham Lincoln Esq.

Dear Sir

I hardly no how to wright a few lines to you in the present occasion.

I had a boy of about seventeen years old inlisted in the 9th Regiment Company B of Vermont Vol. he inlisted with out my consent as I considered him to young for the service, but he was anxious to go and went. he has been unfortunate. They were taken prisoners at Harpers Ferry and paroled and sent to Chicago and then the Boy complained that they fared rather hard. he tried to get a furlough to come home but could not obtain one. he said the officers would give one another furlows to go home but he could have no furloughs. we wrote him to be as content as he could and their circumstances might be in a short time as good as any other regiment. he stayed there I believe about five months and then inlisted in to the Illinois Cavalry. he wrote home stating what he had done, and I answered his letter immediately saying to him that I thought he had made a poor move as he had parted with all his Vermont friends and stated his age in my letter and told him that he had better not go there and told him to show my letter to his officers and they might let him off. he left there under circumstances I no not, but did not return to the 9th Vermont as I supposed he would. Since then he has been taken as a deserter and sentenced to one year hard labour and close confinement with out pay.

Now Mister President I acknowledge the boy to be to blame but in the first place a boy was patriotic to inlist as young as he was and with the hard fare that this Regiment had it wasn't verry strange that he should git sick of it but he did not dezert as I understand it to get out of service but to go to actual service, and my letter not meaning any harm was undoubtably the cause of his leaving there.

The boy I believe has never been paid but once and that was verry small I believe not but a month and a half or two months which I think is more favorable to him than if he had got all of his pay before he left, and none. Sir it seems hard to the Boy's Father and mother, say no further to think of a boy in that situation. he has had to under go the hardships of a broken arm besides other sicknesses with out any pay since the first payment which did not last long to buy necessaries that a soldier needs.

Now Mr. President excuse me for wrighting this imperfect letter to you. I should not have done it had not duty caled me to it. Will you be so kind as to have some proper officer at least give the case a small investigation.

        Yours Respectfully

           John Barden

P.S. The Boys name is Herbert Barden. he sometimes put in a middle (H). I do not no whether he did when he inlisted or not. (He is in a camp near Portsmouth, Va. 4th Rhode Island Vol. Company A).[148]

Mr. Barden was mistaken; Herbert was not confined in Portsmouth, Virginia, but his exact whereabouts are not recorded in his court-martial record. Young Barden was incarcerated October 15, 1863. Whether President Lincoln actually saw Mr. Barden's letter or one of his staff handled the matter is unclear, but Barden's sentence was remitted. Of course, the wheels of government turn slow, and he was not released until May 4, 1864, only four months short of his sentence. Herbert Barden had no more trouble with the military and was honorably discharged June 13, 1864, when the 9th Vermont was mustered out of service.[149]

Private John Frisbie of Co. B, who had deserted October 26, 1862, was court-martialed September 12. Like the others, he was sentenced to a year at hard labor.[150]

About the middle of September the weather turned cold. What few men were able started building winter quarters, since it looked like the regiment was going to spend the winter there.[151]

Chaplain Dickinson held a service for the regiment on Sunday, September 20. Again Captain Kilbourne felt the chaplain was not doing his job properly:

We had a chapter read and a prayer offered at dress parade tonight but our chaplain is not very interesting and I could wish we might exchange him for a more live and active man, one who would preach to us and take more interest in the men. A chaplain can be a very useful man if chooses to be, as it is the one we have is no better than none.[152]

The stillness of the night in Yorktown was interrupted at 11:00 P.M. on Wednesday, September 23, by the crack of gunfire, and Pvt. Henry E. Morse, a five-foot-six-inch, 34-year-old farmer from Wells River in Co. G, was dead. Morse had recently been detailed a cook for the officers in Co. G and, in addition to his cooking, he was building the officers a new set of quarters. He was able to scrounge enough material to build the quarters, but was short on window sashes. Several of the officers indicated he could get some sashes from the old deserted rebel barracks about half a mile from the fort. In the dark of night, Henry Morse and another man eluded the camp guards and sneaked out to the old barracks. What the two Vermonters did not know was that a captain and several men from the 6th North Carolina Colored Infantry Regiment were recruiting in the area and had taken up residence in one of the barracks that day. The noise of the two men prying out the sash awakened the new residents, who then tried to capture Morse and his accomplice. The two men made a break for it, and the captain of the Negro unit fired two pistol shots at them without effect. He then ordered his men to fire, and a Pvt. Nathaniel Simmons put a minie ball through Morse's head, killing him instantly. Morse's companion escaped uninjured. Morse's company commander, Capt. Edwin Kilbourne, was quite upset over the incident:

> He had no right outside the fort after six P.M. If he had obeyed he would have saved his life, but he did not and death was the penalty. The man was my cook, Henry Morse, one of the recruits from Wells River. A good man and we all mourn his loss very much. I don't know when I have been so pained as I was on hearing of his death and in this manner. He leaves a wife and 4 pretty children. Too bad. I pity her very much for her loss is truly great.[153]

Captain Kilbourne was wrong about the number of children Morse had. He had five instead of four, ranging in age from one to thirteen. Morse's wife, Marion, received a widow's pension after the war of $18.00 a month plus $2.00 for each child. In statements supporting Marion Morse's pension claim, Henry's comrades in Co. G, James T.H. McLure, Seldon F. Learned, Stephen Hix, and Carlos E. Bolton, stated that Captain Kilbourne and the other officers in the company instigated the stealing of the window sashes. Seldon Learned went so far as to state that Lieutenant John Whitcher was the other man with Morse.[154]

The stay at Yorktown was wreaking havoc on the regiment's morale. About 4:00 P.M. Saturday, October 10, Pvt. John Mickman of Co. E refused to do his assigned duty. His platoon leader, First Lt. Elijah L. Quimby, ordered him to the guardhouse. Prior to this, Mickman had been a good soldier, but by now his nerves were frayed. In the process of going to the guardhouse Mickman called Lieutenant Quimby a "God dammed son of a bitch." He was brought before a regimental court-martial on October 25 and sentenced to be confined to the guardhouse for 60 days and to forfeit his pay during that time. After his confinement, Mickman continued to be a good soldier until he was killed in action September 29, 1864.[155]

At 3:00 A.M., October 4, the sergeant of the guard was making his rounds, checking on the guards posted in and around Fort Yorktown, and found Pvt. George W. Davis of Co. E asleep at his post. The 21-year-old carpenter from Derby was brought before a general court-martial on November 24 and charged with sleeping on post. In his defense, he submitted a statement written by his company commander, Capt. Amasa Bartlett. Captain Bartlett stated that he had known Davis since Davis was a child, that he was one of the best soldiers in Co. E, and that Davis was the sole supporter of his family, his father being totally blind. He also indicated that Davis had returned from detached duty in Vermont on September 29 and was put on guard the next day and not relieved until Thursday, October 1. That same day, Davis

Private George W. Davis, Co. E, court-martialed November 24, 1863, and confined to hard labor for 30 days. He was promoted to corporal February 2, 1864, and was killed in action September 29, 1864 (Dennis Charles).

volunteered to help out on company fatigue duty. The next day, October 2, he was back on guard duty again without sufficient rest. The court considered Bartlett's statement but found Davis guilty and sentenced him to be confined at hard labor for 30 days.[156]

Although Colonel Ripley was on temporary duty at Fort Monroe, he was in frequent contact with the Governor of Vermont, trying to get his regiment relocated to a place that was more conducive to good health. He first tried to get his regiment reassigned to Norfolk, but the general commanding would not exchange a strong full-up one for one that had its ranks thinned by disease. With the influence of Vermont's Governor John G. Smith and Vermont's Senator Solomon Foot, the 9th Vermont was finally scheduled to go to North Carolina. Lieutenant Colonel Barney noted on October 11:

> I presume by two or three days we will be down in North Carolina at Beaufort or Newbern. The reason of our going is on account of the great amount of sickness in the regiment and it is thought we will be better by a change of climate. For the last few days we have had one or two deaths per day, but with all our sickness we have not suffered from it as much as any other Regt. in this vicinity. The 16th N. York Battery numbering only 80 men have lost 17 within six weeks.[157]

Getting the 9th Vermont away from Yorktown was not as easy as it sounded, as Captain Kilbourne wrote several days later: "The order came for us to move on Tuesday afternoon [October 13] and we expected to embark that night or Wednesday morning. But Wednesday morn came and with it came an order countermanding the order of the previous day." Lieutenant Ballard wrote in the *Rutland Herald*:

> All the rest of the Brigade have gone, infantry and artillery; we alone remain, a ghastly skeleton of the Ninth Vermont. But better days are before us, I trust, and though it may not be said of us that we have passed through the ordeal of fire, it cannot be denied that we have been compelled to grapple with disease in its strongholds, and the loss, of necessity, is ours.[158]

Also on October 13, Assistant Surgeon Story N. Goss submitted his resignation. In his letter of resignation he stated, "My wife is in a feble state of health and has no other protector but myself. She has the care of a young child which makes it very difficult for her to get along alone. I feel it my duty to resign knowing that the gain to my family will be greater than my loss to the government." His resignation was accepted up the chain of command, and he was discharged on October 15. Dr. Goss returned to the service in 1864 and was assigned to the Smith General Hospital in Brattleboro for a short time until the battle of the Wilderness, when he was reassigned to the Fairfax Seminary Hospital in Alexandria, Virginia. He again returned to the service a short time later and served in the Baxter General Hospital in Burlington and again in the Smith General Hospital in Brattleboro. After the war he returned to his practice in Georgia, Vermont, and in 1870 settled in Chelsea.[159]

Every day, the Vermonters hoped to leave Yorktown. Lieutenant Colonel Barney complained to his wife:

> We were ordered away day before yesterday and got everything packed up and the steamer was at the wharf ready to receive us when the order was countermanded so we were the second time disappointed in getting away from this place of sickness and death, but still we expect to leave any day for Newbern.[160]

Captain Kilbourne felt he knew why the regiment remained on the bluffs overlooking the York River:

> We still remain in a state of suspense not knowing whether we shall ultimately go or not. The order was for us to go to Newbern, N.C. and we all felt much elated about it. The reason for our not going was this: Gen. Wistar commanding this post received information that a large body of the enemy was coming down on the opposite side of the river and in considerable force, had driven in our pickets and it was thought probable our service might be required in repelling an attack.[161]

In October the sickness in the 9th Vermont surged to epidemic proportions. Corporal Stebbins wrote on October 15:

If this Reg. don't go from here soon, they will have it all in the hospital at Ft. Monroe. Some 16 of our Co. are there now, and some more will go soon I guess at least they aught to have gone yesterday with the others. Five in number. Denny [Mason] was one that went yesterday. He is better than he was when I came.[162]

Lieutenant Ballard described the condition in company B:

Within the last eighteen days every eighth man of Co. B has fallen, and we expect every hour to hear of the death of another, J.C. Freeman, of Pittsford. God grant that a widowed mother may not have to mourn the untimely death of an only son; but I fear it must be. Of those who have died since I wrote you last, the first was C.W. Cooley, of Granville, Addison County. He had a furlough and started for home, and got to Fortress Monroe, where he died the next day. The next was D.N. Hill of Mt. Holly; he died the 6th, very suddenly. He sat up in a chair and took his breakfast, and in an hour after he was dead, having died without a struggle. The last was E.A. Woodward of Mt. Holly, I think, who died this morning after a comparatively short illness, thus making six men in eighteen days out of forty-seven present in this place. Our company seems to be the fated one this time, although the other companies are losing many men. I think the health of the regiment is improving slowly now, yet one of our largest companies reports but one man for duty to-day.[163]

On October 17, 19-year-old Pvt. Porter S. Niles of Co. H died in the Chesapeake General Hospital in Hampton of malaria. He had taken sick on September 26. "He did double duty for a long time at Yorktown in taking the place of comrades who were sick, by doing so he contracted malaria & typhoid," wrote his older brother, Albert A. Niles. He went on to record that his brother's death "was a hard blow to me and made me sad and lonely. He was a good soldier, faithful & true, loved and respected by all." Young Porter Niles was buried in what is now the Hampton National Cemetery in Hampton, Virginia.[164]

Private Charles H. Isham of Co. H died at the Chesapeake General Hospital on October 26. Isham's mother received the following letter from the hospital's chaplain a week later in an attempt to console her:

He had every care and comfort possible. His surgeon was Dr. Bayles of N.Y., and his nurses were careful and attentive. His disease was diarrhea, chills and fevers, and the effects of that malarial poison of the country where he was encamped. He was no doubt kept too long at Yorktown before he was sent away.

Our wards were warm and comfortable, and nurses night and day to administer to his wants. I talked with him upon his spiritual interests in Christ—pointed him to the Lamb of God that taketh away the sins of the world, and every Tuesday night and Sunday we had religious service in the ward where he was, and he was furnished with religious reading, when able to read—but his disease took a fatal turn and he suddenly died. But I trust the means of grace brought to bear upon his heart and mind in prayer and singing, and talking and reading, were blessed of God to lead him before he died to put trust and confidence in the merits of our blessed Redeemer. I was not present when he died, and therefore I did not get his last thoughts and wishes. I inquired of the nurse, but he said he died easy without speaking at all. He loved his mother. How they talk of a mother's love and kindness, and a mother's prayers in their behalf. Never despair of praying for a child from home. God hears those prayers.

He was buried Oct. 12th, 1863, in the Hospital Cemetery (Chesapeake), with military honors and religious services. A military escort preceded the corpse borne by eight soldiers. I walked between the escort and the body. Everything was conducted in the most proper and solemn manner. I read from the 15th chapter of 1 Cor., and talked and prayed, after which his body was lowered in the grave and over it the soldiers discharged "their farewell shots." His coffin has his name on the top so that if the head-board should be removed ever, when the grave is opened their [sic] will be no difficulty in identifying the body. The cemetery is fenced around, and every grave is marked. The remains can be removed at any time in cold weather.

I deeply sympathize with you in the death of your son. He died in a noble cause; you should be proud of the sacrifice for your country. He honored the name and honored you in helping to sustain the great empire of civil liberty. He fell by the way-side of life — his mission completed. God called him away. I trust to a higher sphere of usefulness. Our Heavenly Father doeth all things well. May this death — so common to so many homes — be sanctified to spiritual good. Life's hardest lesson is submission to God's will. When you can pray, "Not my will O God, but thine be done," then you too will be ready to go home.

You now have one less attraction upon the earth — I trust one more in heaven. May God bless and sustain you and give you grace to be led by his divine hand in the way of eternal life.[165]

On Friday, October 23, the 9th Vermont finally got orders to move. Colonel Ripley, who had returned from Fort Monroe a few days before, wrote his father, " I write in haste as we expect to sail this P.M. Report says to Newbern, which may be true.... We have sent some more of the sick to the Fort, who are expected to be sent on to Vermont. 125 in all."[166]

One of the men left at the hospital at Fort Monroe was Orin J. Fisk, a 23-year-old, five-foot six and one-half-inch laborer from Randolph who was suffering from malaria. Sometime later he was transferred to Baxter General Hospital in Burlington. He was discharged on March 7, 1864, with a disability and returned home. In 1997, Larry Towne of Randolph was renovating his back porch and found a gravestone under the ground at the base of his steps. When Towne turned the gravestone over he found a flag engraved at the top under which was inscribed:

Orin J.

only son of

David E. and Huldah Fisk

DIED

May 27, 1864

AD. 24 yrs. 5 ms. and 24 ds.

Member of Co. G 9th Regt. Vt. Vols.[167]

Towne mentioned the gravestone to his neighbor, Joe Kittel, who in turn told the story to his daughter Marie, a local social studies teacher. Kittel and his daughter were fascinated by the discovery of Fisk's gravestone under Towne's porch and soon started doing research to solve the mystery. Their journey through history was not an easy one.

From a copy of the *Revised Roster of Vermont Volunteers* in their local library, the Kittels learned that Orin J. Fisk of Randolph had enlisted in the 9th Vermont August 11, 1862, was mustered into the service September 22, 1862, and had been discharged from the service March 7, 1864. From the *Historical Vermont Gazetteer* they found that an Orin J. Fiske (spelled with an "e") in the 9th Vermont had been transferred from Co. G to Co. I on June 1, 1864. While Orin Fisk had been transferred from Co. G to Co. I, the date in the *Gazetteer* would have put the transfer after Fisk's death. Could there have been both a Fisk and Fiske in the 9th Vermont? They ordered the compiled service record and pension record for both Orin J. Fisk and Orin J. Fiske from the National Archives. The National Archives had records only for Orin J. Fisk, so Fiske had been a misspelling of his name.

While they were waiting for Fisk's records from the National Archives, the Kittels went to the office of Randolph's town clerk and looked up the death certificates of Fisk's parents, David and Huldah. They learned that they both had died in East Somerville, Massachusetts, in 1893. The Kittels then looked up David Fisk's obituary in the August 3, 1893, edition of their local paper. In the obituary they learned that Orin J. Fisk had died in Randolph on July 27, 1864, not May 27, 1864, as the inscription on the gravestone indicated. After receiving Fisk's records from the National Archives, they learned that the army had mistakenly used May 27, 1864, as Fisk's date of death.

Since Orin Fisk had been supporting his parents prior to his death, his mother applied for a government pension in 1879 and used May 27, 1864, as Fisk's date of death. After Fisk's mother died his father applied for a pension and also used May 27, 1864, as Orin's date of death. The Kittels speculate David and Huldah Fisk were advised that it would be easier to use the May 27, 1864, date of death than try to convince the government of their mistake. Both Orin's mother and father were successful in obtaining their pensions.

Fisk is buried in Randolph's South View Cemetery and listed on the family gravestone. Apparently the government had purchased Fisk's gravestone and used the wrong date of death, so the stone was not used. But why was the gravestone under Larry Towne's back porch steps?

With more research through town records the Kittels found that Orin Fisk's sister Ruth and her husband, Will Curtis, had owned, and probably built, the house owned by Larry Towne. Being frugal Vermonters the Curtises put Fisk's misdated gravestone to good use. The mystery of Orin J. Fisk's gravestone was finally solved.[168]

Near midnight, October 23, the 9th Vermont left camp for the last time and marched down to the wharf on the York River and, along with the 99th New York, loaded aboard the Streamer *John Rice*. Its destination was Newport Barracks, North Carolina.[169]

5

ANOTHER BATTLE LOST

The *John Rice* did not leave Yorktown until 6:00 A.M. on Saturday, October 24, 1864. Instead of heading straight for New Bern it had to lay over at Fort Monroe to take on coal. With two regiments aboard, plus horses and baggage, Colonel Ripley felt the vessel was too cramped and he ordered up another vessel. Companies H and K stayed on the *John Rice* while eight companies, numbering about 320 men, under the command of Lieutenant Colonel Barney disembarked and were loaded aboard the steamer *United States*.[1]

Both the *John Rice* and the *United States* left Fort Monroe on Sunday morning. Unfortunately, during the night a severe storm set in causing the going to be quite rough. Being a larger ship, the *John Rice* continued on to North Carolina, but the *United States* turned around just past Cape Charles and headed back to the sheltered waters off Fort Monroe. Lieutenant Colonel Barney related what happened next:

> The Capt. concluded that he could not go through so turned about and got back to the Ft. about 4 O'c P.M. I tell you we were pleased to get back for nearly every man was seasick and where the men were stowed away so thickly the vomit was of a good thickness on the floor and all presented a sorry sight. I immediately went ashore and requested that the men be shifted on to some other boat or made more comfortable in some way. As they concluded to send us a lot of straw and this was good as far as it went but still the men were wet and cold. We remained aboard till yesterday noon and then it was thought best to put ashore so we landed and came out here. Got some tents, camp kettles, etc., and got very comfortably fixed by night and the next morning the men were feeling quite fine. Some of them are sick yet with the ague. We sent 11 to the hospital and before this morning one of the number (Austin Kennedy) died. He was one of my old boys and yesterday while on the boat he came to me with tears in his eyes and asked to be sent to the hospital with the others. I called the surgeon's attention to him and he did not consider him very sick but thought best to send him and this morning the poor little fellow is dead. I have not had any thing make me feel as bad for a long time for he was a young, nice little boy about 17 or 18 years old. I don't know who his parents are or where they live.[2]

Another sad incident occurred during the night of October 25, while the regiment was still aboard the ship. While the *United States* lay tossing at anchor Lieutenant Colonel Barney was startled out of a sound sleep around midnight by someone shouting "Man overboard!" He raced to the main deck and looked over the side and saw the form of one of his soldiers splashing around in the water. The vessel's crew threw the man a rope, but he did not seem to notice it and sank beneath the surface. A small boat was put over the side, but it was too late. Barney decided to let his men sleep and did not have a roll call until the next morning when it was discovered the missing man was Pvt. Vilas Smith of Co. I, an 18-year-old, five-foot four-inch farmer from Marshfield. His body was recovered on the beach at the fort on November 12, and was buried the same day in the cemetery at Chesapeake General Hospital. It was later removed to the Hampton National Cemetery in Hampton, Virginia. Barney remembered Smith as "One of our best men."[3]

Finally, on Wednesday, October 28, Lieutenant Colonel Barney and his men loaded aboard the steamer *Maple Leaf* and sailed for Beaufort, North Carolina. While Lieutenant Colonel Barney and his men waited to get away from Fort Monroe, Colonel Ripley and his two companies were at sea in a terrible storm. One unnamed soldier in Co. H wrote to the *Lamoille Newsdealer*:

> Some enjoyed the rough sea finely, but as for me, I will say "A life on the ocean wave" reads well and sounds pretty when sung by a sturdy band of marines, but I could not realize exactly where this fun came in. I don't know but when a vessel rises up mountains high on a towering wave, and begins to tip so that every man has to hold on for dear life, with twenty or thirty horses down below all in a heap kicking and smashing about, myself looking over the side of the vessel down into the deep, seething, surging boiling cauldron, feeling that surely we shall go over, is a pleasure to some, but for me, give me dry land or a very small pond or narrow river, where I could swim ashore or touch bottom if an accident should happen. Some expressed a willingness to re-enlist for nine years with the privilege of going home by land rather than go home in a vessel around Cape Hatteras. The gale was so furious off Hatteras that the vessel had to put out to sea fifty miles or more.[4]

The *John Rice* arrived safe and sound at Beaufort on Monday, October 26. The storm they sailed through was so violent a New York newspaper had reported the *John Rice* lost at sea. After unloading their equipment from the steamer Ripley's two companies were loaded aboard a train and taken to Newport Barracks, 26 miles inland. Barney and his eight companies caught up with the rest of the regiment on Saturday, October 31.[5]

Upon arriving in North Carolina, Colonel Ripley and Dr. Carpenter reported to Brigadier General Peck, commander of the district of North Carolina, whose headquarters were at New Bern. Peck had been assigned to New Bern after the siege of Suffolk. Peck put Ripley in command of the garrison at Newport Barracks. "Gen Peck assures me 'tis the key to Beaufort and the surrounding country, and seems a little scared, but then everybody who was with Peck at Suffolk knows him to be a timid old Granny," Ripley wrote later.[6]

The country around Newport Barracks was level, sandy terrain cut up by numerous swamps and streams and covered with low growing bushes and tall pine trees. The chief cash crops in the area were tar and turpentine from the pine trees. The locals referred to their tracts of pine trees as "pitch orchards." Also, the Vermonter boys were about to see things that most of them had never seen before — Spanish moss, alligators, and poisonous snakes.[7]

In the first week the Vermonters sized up the local citizens and were less than impressed with them. Captain Edwin Kilbourne wrote:

> I haven't seen but 2 natives since landing here and they are fine specimens of the genus homo. Fine types of the poorer class of people which live and inhabit this southern clime. They are much below the African in intelligence and native wit and powers. In fact they are not to be put on the level with a *good intelligent horse*.[8]

Captain Sherman also showed his disdain for North Carolinians: "Did I tell you all the women around here *chew* snuff? Well they do and suck a rag on the end of a stick too. They are lax in their style of dress, lax in housekeeping & loose in morals and everything else. This applies to all classes from fine lady to filthy nigger." Sherman would later, however, learn to overlook the bad habits he wrote of in exchange for the women's attention.[9]

Ripley's command at Newport Barracks consisted of about a thousand men comprised of Co. F 19th Wisconsin, Co. D 2nd Massachusetts Heavy Artillery, Co. A 5th Rhode Island Heavy Artillery, and troops A and B of the 23rd (Mix's) New York Cavalry Battalion, in addition to the 9th Vermont. Ripley was responsible for a picket line that ran from Bogue Sound, about three miles from the barracks, to a point on Gale's Creek, seven miles west of the barracks— in all, a line about 15 miles long. At the Bogue Sound end of the line was a log blockhouse that mounted a small cannon and was surrounded by earthworks. The blockhouse was built by the 9th New Jersey Infantry in August 1862.[10]

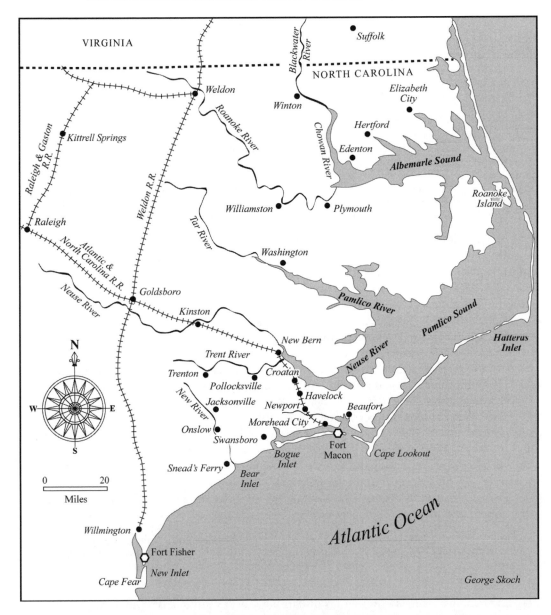

Eastern North Carolina.

Newport Barracks lay one mile north of the village of Newport, a small village consisting of about 15 houses, four stores and a church. The barracks had been built by the 7th North Carolina Infantry in 1861. The two log barracks were located at the junction of Mason Town Road (also known as the County Road) and the Atlantic & North Carolina Railroad. The officers lived in tents until quarters could be built. The land on which the camp was located was sandy soil, so the regiment would not be troubled by mud as it had been in Chicago the winter before. Colonel Ripley, however, was less than happy with what he found:

> The barracks were in tumble-down condition, no quarters for the Field Staff, Post Commissary and Post Quartermaster. The camp was intolerably dirty, the Forts, wretchedly constructed in a shifting soil, were rapidly going to destruction. The Cavalry I found lawless and undisciplined.[11]

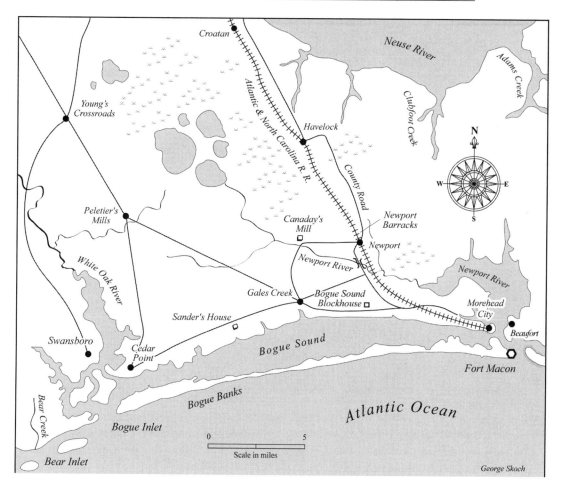

Newport Barracks and vicinity.

The barracks were protected by earthworks, with walls about 12 feet high with abatises in front. They had been built by the 9th New Jersey Infantry during Maj. Gen. Ambrose P. Burnside's occupation of the area in the spring of 1862 to guard the railroad trestle and the county highway bridge located nearby. The earthworks were now armed with one 32-pounder gun and three 12-pounders.[12]

Colonel Ripley's first priority was to improve the camp and strengthen the fortifications. But lacking the necessary number of men to perform guard and picket duty and rebuild the fortifications, he issued the following special order:

> The Provost Marshal of the Town and surrounding District of Newport is hereby empowered and ordered to collect all able-bodied male Negroes in his district. None will become exempt but those who have a tar-kiln burning, those already in the employ of the Government or Government employees, those excused by Dr. Carpenter, Post Surgeon. The Provost Marshal will assess a tax upon them of three days' work per man each week.[13]

The officers in the regiment knew it was against General Peck's wishes to employ Negroes and they were also concerned what Maj. Gen. Benjamin F. Butler, the commander of the Department of Virginia and North Carolina, would think. Captain Linus Sherman wondered, "We are all anxious to know what policy our new commander will pursue in the field where he [Butler] first called niggers 'contraband of war.'" On November 20, Colonel Ripley found out how

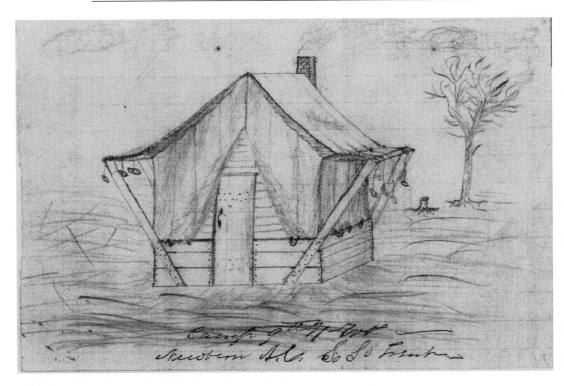

Drawing of Lieutenant Colonel Barney's tent at Newport Barracks, North Carolina (Vermont Historical Society).

Butler felt about using Negroes: "General Butler dropped in upon me yesterday rather unexpectedly, waddled around the fort and drove away my fears by endorsing my Conscription act. So now I can issue rations and pay them."[14]

The 9th Vermont's first mission in North Carolina came on October 29 when Lieutenant Colonel Barney was ordered to take two companies out on reconnaissance. The column traveled down the railroad toward Newbern. One company was posted at a station called Havelock and the other at Croatan. Neither unit observed any enemy activity. Colonel Ripley sent out a scouting party of cavalry and infantry on Friday, November 6, near Swansboro to capture a rebel schooner but neither the schooner nor any rebels were found. But according to Ripley the scouting party did accomplish something:

> An expedition to Swansboro of the Infantry, and Cavalry furnished me an opportunity to draw up the strings, which resulted in some twelve men being court martialed, for straggling, depredating, etc. These got from ten to fifteen days each fatigue work; adding some strength to my dusky — or, as they call themselves — "de Cunnel's culld guard."[15]

Toward the end of November Captain Kilbourne, who had been detailed as the provost marshal of Newbern, attended a local wedding that he recorded in a letter home expressing how he felt about the North Carolinians:

> I will tell you about a wedding I went to the other night. I can but laugh every time I think of it. Upon invitation of Mr. Durant Bell, the justice who married the parties, I went out with him and another man about four miles towards Canaday's Mills to a Mr. [illegible]'s. His daughter was married to a Mr. Mann, both simple ignorant little idiots! They were married just at candle light as they call it. The bride and groom came switching along into line before the justice, just as a little boy and girl would do on going to a fair or other great day. Just as soon as the ceremony was over the couple went into another room out of the way entirely and staid there until the call for supper, for such they

call it in this beautiful country. Everybody is expected to sit down and everybody considers himself invited. Mr. Bell kindly invited me to take a seat by him at the head of the table, next to the bride. Of course I accepted. While at the table I attempted to converse with the bride, but she was not inclined, so I gave up the undertaking as a lost cause and thought during the evening I would try one more lady. If she was or proved to be of the same pattern I would retire in disgust. Well I did so and found both alike. I was not long in coming to the conclusion that there was more society in my Meerschaum than in the whole crowd of women under cover of that roof. I forthwith proceeded to the piazza, filled up my good sociable pipe and took a smoke with the crowd outside. After the supper was over the table was cleared and removed from the room and the old and young went in for a general break down. Had a little dance and a few games and then went home. But the primitive character of all the people and in which everything was conducted was certainly a rarity to me and I enjoyed it very much.[16]

It appears Colonel Ripley did not have enough to keep him busy at Newport Barracks. He complained in a letter home:

This irregularity of the mails is the greatest drawback to our thorough enjoyment of this Post. One has nothing then to do but to resolutely shut out thoughts of home and friends, and I drive deepley and earnestly into work here.... I want to be with "La Grande Armee." What have I to show for my year and a half of service, what to boast of? Not a thing! Harper's Ferry — Suffolk — "Dix Blackberry Raid," what a record for a would-be soldier.[17]

Since the regiment had not been paid in quite a while and everyone was low on money, Colonel Ripley issued a circular inviting all the officers and men to join in a hunting expedition to kill wild game for Thanksgiving dinner. The expedition did not go quite as well as Ripley had planned, as one member of the regiment remembered:

The directions for the proceedings not being understood by all, or not heeded, the result was perfect confusion, and each man hunted for himself, and thought himself very lucky that he came out of the woods with a whole skin, for the balls and shot whistled through the woods in every direction, and the game fled to secure retreat. The tired hunters returned to camp hungry if not wiser men. Thanksgiving day our Quartermaster, who is always contributing from his private purse to the comfort of the men, purchased a sufficient quantity of such articles as the market offered, to give to the men in this regiment a good substantial dinner, of which all partook with a relish.[18]

November 30 was a joyous day for the 9th Vermont, with the much anticipated arrival of the paymaster with two months' back pay. The next day, however, proved to be the worst in the regiment's short history.[19]

Major Charles Jarvis and a squad of about 10 cavalrymen left Newport Barracks on Tuesday, December 1. Although there are several different versions of the nature of their mission, the one most often recorded is that one of the Union cavalrymen assigned to the command at Newport Barracks had committed some sort of depredation on a nearby residence. The aggrieved citizen gave a general description of the cavalryman in question and also a description of the trooper's gray horse. Major Jarvis rounded up the men who came closest to the description and took them out to the man's house to be identified. As they rode along the White Oak Road toward Swansboro, they learned from one of the local residents there were three Confederate soldiers in the area. Jarvis quickly determined that capturing the rebels was a higher priority than his original mission and took his men in pursuit. Near Cedar Point they came upon the three Confederate soldiers. As soon as the rebels saw the approaching Yankees they quickly ran for the cover of the woods. Earlier, Jarvis had sent three of the horsemen about four hundred yards ahead of the main body and they got into a running gunfight with the fleeing rebels. Two of the gray-backs reached the woods, but the third saw he was not going to make it and turned and made a determined stand. Major Jarvis rode up behind the lead cavalryman who was the rebel's immediate target and said, "Go in and I will support you." About that time one of the conical balls from the rebel's navy Colt revolver hit Jarvis in the stomach, knocking him off his horse. The bullet entered about three inches to the right and a little below his bellybutton, severing a small artery. The bullet continued upward and severed another artery near his spinal column. Then it glanced off his spine and lodged in the muscles of his back.[20]

The first two rebels escaped, but the one who shot Jarvis was captured. As one of the troopers was getting Jarvis back on his horse, the cavalryman holding the rebel asked if he should kill the man. Demonstrating the type of man Jarvis was, he replied, "No, he is a soldier. Take him prisoner." It was later learned that the three men were members of a North Carolina infantry unit returning home on furlough.[21]

Jarvis remained on his horse for a mile of so, but the wound soon became so painful, and he so weak from the loss of blood, he had to dismount. One of the cavalrymen confiscated a cart from a nearby farm and the wounded major was loaded aboard and continued slowly toward Newport Barracks. Soon after the gunfight one of the troopers was ordered back to the barracks to get the doctor. Assistant Surgeon Vincent, Colonel Ripley and Chaplain Dickinson, escorted by two companies of Vermonters, hurried out to meet the party bringing Jarvis back. After reaching Jarvis's side, Dr. Vincent determined the wound was mortal and the major was taken to the Sander's house, a nearby farm, to be made as comfortable as possible. He lived until about 10:30 P.M. that night, speaking calmly with those around him, sending messages to his friends, and expressing his resignation to the will of God before succumbing to his wound. Major Jarvis was the first man in the 9th Vermont to be killed by a rebel bullet.[22]

The 42-year-old bachelor major was the most popular officer in the regiment and his loss was deeply felt. Colonel Ripley stated later, "He passed away as he had lived, a brave soldier and simple-hearted, devoted Christian; and left an example whose impression will never fade from our hearts." Captain Linus Sherman wrote, "He was a noble man and a Christian, beloved by all who knew him & called by some the father of the regiment." Lieutenant Colonel Barney related, "His loss will be much felt in the Regt. for he was a father to every one and the most strictly honest man and conscientious Christian I ever saw."[23]

An escort under the command of Capt. Amasa Bartlett accompanied Charles Jarvis's body home, where he was buried in Weathersfield's Bow Cemetery. His tombstone reads:

> Jarvis, Major Charles, b. Aug 21, 1821, d. Dec 1, 1863. Mortally wounded near Newbern, NC, Civil War. A noble disinterested Christian patriot, exemplary in every duty, he took up his sword as a cross in the cause of his country and his God. "I had rather be a martyr for my country that to remain at home in ease. For me to live is Christ and to die is gain."[24]

The officers of the regiment wore the badge of mourning (a band of black crepe worn around the left arm above the elbow) for thirty days and published the following resolutions of respect on December 3 in the memory of their gallant major:

> *Whereas,* It having pleased an all wise Providence to remove from us our esteemed friend and brother in arms, Major Charles Jarvis, who fell mortally wounded in an encounter with the enemy near Cedar Point, N.C., Dec. 1st, 1863, therefore:
> *Resolved,* That in the loss of Major Jarvis the Regiment has lost a valued officer, the State one of her most honored and worthy sons, the Country a man of eminent zeal and patriotism, and the World a consistent Christen.
> *Resolved,* That the deceased was distinguished alike for his gallantry as a soldier, his efficiency as a companion, and his kindness as a friend! That he was faithful in the discharge of every duty, and ever watchful of the interests and happiness of both officers and men.
> *Resolved,* That we tender our sympathies and condolence to the friends and relatives of the deceased, commending and pointing them to the God of Battles for consolation and support; while with them we mourn his loss, we recognize the hand of Devine [sic] Providence in this dispensation, and bow in humiliation to his will.
> *Resolved,* That the officers of this Regiment, as a token of respect to his memory, wear the usual badge of mourning for thirty days.
> *Resolved,* That copies of these resolutions be sent to the family of the deceased, and to the Vermont Journal for publication, with request that the State papers copy.[25]

The 9th Vermont's most fervent abolitionist, First Lt. Erastus W. Jewett, commanding Co. A, enlisted the regiment's first Negro, Benjamin Franklin, on December 4, 1864. This was a very rare occurrence, as most Negroes were enlisted in Negro regiments or were hired as civilian cooks and servants. This appears to be the only one of three Negroes enlisted in the 9th Vermont. The other two were never mustered. One deserted and the other was asked to leave by Colonel Ripley. The 9th Vermont is the only Vermont unit to enlist Negroes. Franklin was an escaped slave from Onslow County, North Carolina, and was enlisted as an under cook. At the time of his enlistment, December 4, he was a 20-year-old, stood five feet six inches tall and indicated his occupation was a farmer. Having been a slave and not allowed an education, Franklin signed his enlistment paper with an X, which was witnessed by Co. A's Second Lt. Theodore S. Peck. Franklin served with the regiment until August 21, 1865. His compiled service record at the National Archives indicated he had deserted the regiment on that date, but on July 18, 1890, his record was corrected to show he was honorably discharged under the provisions of an act of Congress approved March 2, 1889.[26]

In addition to enlisting a Negro in the regiment, the 9th Vermont's Co. C picked up a young male slave named Ben Robinson. According to *The History of Braintree, Vermont*, 10-year-old Robinson was cultivating a cornfield as Co. C marched by. Several of the Vermonters called for the boy to join them, but he replied he would have to check with "Massa." The boys of Co. G convinced him that they would deal with his master and Robinson joined them. Robinson's surname, as was the custom during the time of slavery, was taken from his current master, named Furby, but later he changed his last name to Robinson after his first owner. For his first several months in the regiment, young Robinson worked for Pvt. John Manny. Manny got sick in April 1864, and on April 20 was transferred to the Veteran Reserve Corps until he was discharged on July 9, 1865. When Manny left, Robinson worked for other soldiers. He eventually went to work for First Lt. William Holman of Co. G, who had been captured on February 2, 1864, and returned to his company in May 1865. Holman was so impressed with the boy that when he was discharged from the army on June 13, 1865, he took Ben Robinson home with him to East Braintree, Vermont.[27]

Holman assumed guardianship of Ben and sent him to school. When Robinson reached the age of 21 Holman gave him $200 to start his life. Unfortunately, the naive Ben Robinson loaned the money to a man who never repaid him. However, Robinson was an industrious young man and was soon supporting himself. For years he worked on farms in the Braintree area and as he got older he got a job as a night watchman in a mill in Randolph. Robinson was contented in his new home and was often heard to say that he did not believe

Gravestone of Ben Robinson. He was freed from slavery in North Carolina as a boy by men of Co. G. He went to Vermont with William Holman, who raised him like a son. Robinson's gravestone reads: "Under God and the strong army of our American Republic the Negro slave is free" (Euclid D. Farnham).

there was another place in the world where, in spite of his dark skin, he would be treated so "white."[28]

Ben Robinson died of heart disease on May 31, 1910. In accordance with his request he was buried with full military honors by the U.S. Grant Post No. 96 of the Grand Army of the Republic in South View Cemetery in Randolph. On his tombstone is chiseled, "Under God and the strong army of our American Republic the negro slave is free." Every Memorial Day an American flag is put on his grave by the Randolph Post of the American Legion.[29]

After the excitement of Major Jarvis's death and everything settled down again, Colonel Ripley went into the horse trading business to help occupy his time. He wrote his older brother William on December 17 about exploring another moneymaking idea:

> The other scheme is a turpentine one. There is a machine at work in Burlington distilling turpentine from pine wood roots, knots and refuse stuff. It pays well even in Vermont. What would it not do here in this country. It would not interfere at all with the present production of turpentine, for it would take the hundreds of thousands of cords of refuse timber that are now unused, and which will cost but a song. Labor is not very high, Government will encourage it as much as possible, as it will add greatly to its resources. Col. Heaton, the Special Supervising Agent of the Treasury, who has charge of this State, is delighted with the project, and perhaps will not impose the 5% tax of Government. What do you say to pitching in, securing the right for the entire state, and going in on a big scale? It must pay like the devil. I'll be able to invest a couple thousand, and give you my *enormous* interest for two more. But seriously, I think it a chance for great enterprise if well and discreetly managed.[30]

The inactivity at Newport Barracks was apparently affecting a number of the officers in a negative way. Sergeant John W. Bennett, a 57-year-old farmer from Weathersfield in Co. D, wrote:

> A private in the army who has independence of character needs considerable patriotism to sustain him when we consider how liable he is to be imposed upon by little simple minded drunken tyrants for officers which mere favoritism has placed in power as a reward not for meritorious service, but for their drunken brutish habits as it would seem. Of course there are some noble exceptions, but truth I am sorry to affirm compels me to say that the above description to [sic] faithfully describes the majority.[31]

Boredom was also getting to the enlisted men. On December 18, the regiment's quartermaster sergeant, Edward D. Barber, a 25-year-old bookkeeper from Middlebury, showed up drunk in front of the regimental formation, and Lieutenant Colonel Barney had him arrested. Barber was court-martialed on December 24 and reduced to the ranks. Private George C. Chamberlain of Bradford in Co. G was selected to replace him as the regiment's quartermaster sergeant on February 27, 1864.[32]

Not long after arriving at Newport Barracks, several officers and enlisted men were sent to Vermont to recruit men to fill the regiment's badly thinned ranks. Recruiting for the entire Union army had been difficult nationwide since the beginning of 1863 — so bad, in fact, Congress passed the Enrollment Act in March 1864, allowing the Federal government to draft men into service. Even though volunteer enlistments had been steadily declining since the previous fall, the draft was very unpopular with the American public and by mid-summer led to wide-scale rioting. To draft men from their congressional districts was quite embarrassing to local politicians. To preclude running a draft, local authorities added additional money to the already existing $300.00 bounty the Federal government was offering for three-year volunteer enlistments.[33]

The men who volunteered in 1862 to serve in the 9th Vermont were resentful that men now had to be threatened with being drafted or offered a large bounty to enlist. Shivering from the cold while on picket duty on December 18 at Canaday's Mills, one of the members of the 9th Vermont's Co. E, who remains anonymous, penned the following complaint about the draft and bounties:

It seems that the good people of Vermont are now agonizing the bare thought of the impending draft and are willing to give any thing in the shape of enormous bounties that the bitter cup may be passed from their lips. An old soldier is greatly at loss to comprehend how the services of eleventh hour men are so much more valuable than the services of those who went to the war long ago, and that cheerly too, without the stimulant of such glittering bounties or the fear of an impending draft, which simply requires of the citizen that he shall defend his country against the foe. The reason of the big bounties is obvious: it is to avoid the draft which shall come to the mansion as well as to the hovel. It would be well for the reputation of the State hereafter that it served all the soldiers alike.[34]

Toward the end of December the regiment's officers' quarters were finally completed. Lieutenant Colonel Barney described his to his wife: "This is quite a stylish building 18 by 36 feet and my room is 18 by 12 feet. I have got a man putting up a chimney this morning." He also mentioned getting a new servant: "I have got a new darky now. My old one had a wife in Yorktown so could not stay. The one I have now is darky all over and very full of his tricks. His name is John Franklin."[35]

On December 22, a number of the 9th Vermont's officers were promoted to fill vacant positions. Capt. Amasa Bartlett of Co. E was selected to replace Major Jarvis. First Lieutenant Elisha M. Quimby replaced Bartlett as commander of Co. E and Second Lt. Edward L. Kelley of Co. B was promoted to first lieutenant to replace Quimby. First Lieutenant Eugene Viele of Co. F, a 28-year-old clerk from Hinesburgh, was promoted to captain of Co. I in place of Albion J. Mower, who had resigned in July. Sergeant Elias L. Brownell was promoted to second lieutenant of Co. F and Sgt. Joel C. Baker to second lieutenant of Co. K, replacing Lieutenant Henry H. Rice, who had resigned in June.[36]

Second Lieutenant Edward L. Kelley (Vermont Historical Society).

Second Lieutenant Elias L. Brownell, Co. F (Vermont Historical Society).

In addition to the promotions, Capt. Edwin Kilbourne had been selected to be the provost marshal of New Bern and Capt. Linus Sherman the provost marshal of Newport. Sherman explained his new duties to a friend of his back in Vermont:

Second Lieutenant Joel C. Baker, Co. I (U.S. Army Military History Institute).

My duties are varied and numerous, but mostly in the office, which is worth something this cold rainy weather. I have a horse and I can ride out when it is pleasant. I draw forage for a horse and the pay of a Captain of Cavalry which is ($10.00) ten dollars per month more than a Capt. of Infantry. On the whole it is a good place. I shall retain the place so long as pleases the General Commanding District. I have to see justice is done to all citizens and give them passes and permits to trade etc. All the disputes and lawsuits which usually come before a civil court come before me. I am the justice of the peace, judge and jury, besides counsel for both sides. I have had to grant two Letters of Administration to settle the estates of persons deceased etc. etc. The past week I have had to enroll the names of all able bodied men, white & colored, between the ages of 18 & 45 and it has made me an extra amount of labor. I have a very good clerk, and of course I make him do most of the work.[37]

Colonel Ripley and 75 men of his men were ordered out on a raid to destroy some Confederate saltworks on Bear Creek south of Newport on Wednesday, December 23. The Vermonters were a part of a larger force commanded by Col. James Jourdan, commander of the 158th New York Infantry and commander of the Sub-district of Beaufort, N.C. The Green Mountain Boys, along with 125 men of the 158th New York Infantry and eight men and one gun of the 2nd Massachusetts Artillery, loaded aboard the gunboats *Howquash* and *Daylight* for the trip and departed Morehead City on the morning of December 24.[38]

The artillerymen and about half of the infantry disembarked in small boats at Bear Creek Inlet. The boats were rowed up the creek about three miles where the saltworks were found and destroyed. Here the men remained for the night. It was an uncomfortable night, as Colonel Jourdan noted in his report of the operation:

> During the night of the 24th instant, the men suffered intensely from the cold, having been obliged, owing to the shallowness of the water, to wade from the boats to the land, but I am happy to say that both officers and men, soldiers and sailors, did their duty promptly, without grumbling or complaint.[39]

The next day, Christmas Day, the men who were still on the gunboats went in small boats two miles toward Swansboro and destroyed another saltworks. Then, the entire command again boarded the gunboats and steamed up Bear Creek six or eight miles where they destroyed a large quantity of salt stored in some buildings. After completing this task the command set sail and reached Morehead City at sundown. Although it had been a grueling mission, Lieutenant Colonel Barney reported, "The boys felt well over their trip and are anxious for another." It would be another month before the Green Mountain Boys would get their wish.[40]

By the light of a flickering candle Corporal Charles Noirel, a 19-year-old five-foot five-inch laborer from Albany, New York, in Co. C, sat in his quarters on December 30 and penned the following letter to Secretary of War Edwin M. Stanton:

Secretary Stanton

Sir:

It is only under the express necessity that I make the following application to you.

I have been in the service now nineteen months. I am not Seventeen years of age; my mother resides in Albany, N.Y. and has had very poor health for the last few months. For me I cannot stand the hot weather and after marching my legs will swell and confine me to my quarters for several days.

These are the reasons I make application to you for a discharge.

I await your answer very anxiously.

I remain yours respectfully and Obedt. Sevrt.

Charles Noirel[41]

Noirel actually got a reply back from a staff officer in the secretary of war office, but not to his liking. Probably with a smile on his face, Brig. Gen. Edward R.S. Canby wrote on February 2, 1864:

Your application of the 30th of December last to be discharged in consequence of your being under seventeen years of age and your inability to "stand hot weather" has not been favorably considered by the Secretary of War.[42]

Brigadier General Canby's reply came back to the regiment through the chain of command. When Lieutenant Colonel Barney saw the letter he was less than amused by Noriel's going straight to the top. Barney wrote the following endorsement on the back of the letter:

Corp. C. Noirel I think rather over goes his bounds when he makes application for a discharge in the improper way. Our surgeons do not consider him a fit case for a discharge. He has suffered some from fever and ague, but is at present looking well and is able for any duty we have to do.[43]

What Barney said to Noirel is not found in the records, but one can only imagine it was not very pleasant.

The year 1864 found the 9th Vermont with only 499 officers and men. Two hundred and ninety-seven were present for duty, 183 were sick in various hospitals, 16 absent with leave, 2 absent without leave and 1 in confinement. Seven companies remained at Newport Barracks, while Co. B was stationed at the Bogue Sound Blockhouse, Co. H at Gales Creek, and Co. E at Canaday's Mills.[44]

On January 17, Pvt. Charles A. Flanders, a 23-year-old farmer from Corinth in Co. G, was sent to Dr. Carpenter, the regiment's surgeon, on sick call. Flanders' behavior was growing more and more bizarre and Company G's commander and first sergeant wanted to know what was wrong with him. Flanders began acting strange while the regiment was in Yorktown, but he seemed to return to normal when the regiment first moved to North Carolina. But before long Flanders' behavior was worse than ever. Dr. Carpenter stated, "I will add that at first the disease resembled the type usually induced by religious excitement, although I know of no exciting causes." Dr. Carpenter felt that Private Flanders' behavior was now so severe that he ought to be institutionalized and he recommended he be sent to the Government Hospital for the Insane in Washington, D.C.[45]

The case worked its way up the chain of command to Major General Peck. On March 10, Peck issued Special Order 70 sending Private Flanders, accompanied by an escort, to Washington, D.C.[46] Private Flanders was released from the government hospital in Washington on May 12, 1864, and returned to his parents' home in Corinth. His parents were very poor and Flanders was their main source of support since he was a young man. Now, without his army pay, and being unable to work, his parents could not support him and he was assigned a guardian September 10, 1864. A short time later Flanders wandered away and was found lying in a cornfield in Maine completely out of his mind; he was sent to the Maine Insane Hospital in Augusta. He eventually escaped from the asylum and drowned while trying to cross a river on September 3, 1869.[47]

Without Charles' financial support, his mother worked as a spinner to support herself and her disabled husband, but after several years the infirmities of old age forced her to quit and she and her husband became wards of the town of Corinth. Mrs. Flanders applied for a dependant mother's pension based on Charles' army service and was awarded a pension of $12.00 a month in 1883 until her death on March 7, 1889.[48]

As far as military operations were concerned, the month of January was a quiet month for the Green Mountain Boys until Wednesday the 27th. At 4:00 P.M. 100 men from the 9th Vermont, under Colonel Ripley, 125 men of the 158th New York, 125 men and one howitzer of the 12th New York Cavalry and 80 men of the 23rd New York Cavalry left Newport Barracks and marched to Young's Crossroads. Again, Colonel Jourdan was in command. The objective of this foray was to clear out the enemy in the area of Swansboro and Jacksonville and capture a Confederate schooner reported to be loaded with turpentine.[49]

With the cavalry preceding them, the infantry trudged all night through the pine forests and over the swamp roads, some of which were knee-deep with mud. At 12:30 P.M. on Thursday, January 28, the infantry column reached the White Oak River near Young's Crossroads and stopped. The men had marched nearly 30 miles since the previous afternoon.[50]

The cavalry had reached the White Oak River near midnight on the 28th and a detachment of 50 troopers was sent across the river to sweep the country toward Swansboro and Jacksonville. Before returning, the detachment surrounded and captured a Confederate outpost consisting of a lieutenant and 27 cavalrymen with 30 horses and equipment. A large number of arms and ammunition that could not be carried away was destroyed on the spot. The cavalrymen returned about 5:00 A.M. Learning the schooner had sailed three days before, Jourdan marched the command back to Newport Barracks.[51]

Before reaching the barracks the 9th Vermont halted at Young's Crossroad for a break. The men stacked arms and took off their equipments to get comfortable. While stacking his musket, Pvt. Charles Morgan of Co. A, a 19-year-old laborer from Milton, was wounded when his weapon somehow discharged one of the other muskets that had been left loaded and capped. The minie ball ripped off part of the thumb and index finger of Morgan's right hand. He was treated by the regiment's assistant surgeon and when the regiment reached camp, Morgan was sent on to the hospital at Morehead City. While in the hospital, gangrene invaded the wound and the remaining part of his thumb and most of his index finger were amputated. Afterward the wound healed properly, but without his thumb and index finger he could not cock or shoot his musket and was transferred to the Veteran Reserve Corps on October 18, 1864. He was discharged from the service with a $4.00 monthly disability June 29, 1864. After the war Morgan moved to Stuben County, Indiana, where he married Rebecca Ann Berger, who died on January 20, 1873. The next year he married Isadora Halstead on May 16 and settled down in Hamilton, Indiana, where they raised seven children. Morgan worked as a farmer until he died of apoplexy on May 30, 1922.[52]

The Vermonters reached Newport Barracks at 8:00 P.M. and, according to Corp. Nelson Wandell of Co. K, "The regt. returned this evening footsore and weary." Private Warren E. Stearns of Co. G also noted how the expedition had taken its toll:

> The night that I got into camp I took my shoes off and the bottoms of my feet were blood shot whare they blistered but I stood it and that was all. We had some 400 cavalry with us and their horses were used up about as bad as we Infantry fellows. One of their horses dropt down dead in the road. Where ever we would get a rest and get up to start again you would think we were all cripples, horses and all untill we got limbered up.[53]

Lieutenant Colonel Barney related later, "Our men did not effect the capture but the cavalry who did were supported by our men so we claim some of the honor ourselves."[54]

On the morning the Vermonters left on the raid, 345 recruits arrived from Vermont to fill the regiment's depleted ranks, bringing its strength up to 844 officers and men. One of the new men, Edward H. Lane, had served in the 9th Vermont before. He had been discharged October 17, 1862, due to deafness. Apparently he had recovered from the ailment that had affected his hearing. He made it through the rest of the war without anymore serious illnesses or injuries.[55]

Colonel Ripley and Major Bartlett, along with several enlisted men, left Newport Barracks on Saturday, January 30, to escort rebel prisoners to department headquarters at Fort Monroe. Both Ripley and Bartlett had other missions besides escorting prisoners. Ripley had a personal audience with Major General Butler to try to retain his quartermaster officer, Francis O. Sawyer. It appears that Major General Wistar had been impressed with Sawyer while the 9th Vermont was stationed in Yorktown and wanted him on his staff. Colonel Ripley felt that Sawyer was irreplaceable and wanted to plead his case to Butler. After meeting with Butler he was successful in retaining his quartermaster, at least for the present. Bartlett was headed to Vermont to bring back more recruits. Lieutenant Colonel Barney was left in command of Newport Barracks and Capt. Edward L. Kelley, commander of Co. E and being the senior captain present, was put in temporary command of the regiment.[56]

The raids in which the 9th Vermont had participated were minor ones compared to other Union operations in eastern North Carolina in 1863 and the first month of 1864. Major General George E. Pickett, commander of the Confederate Department of North Carolina and South Virginia, had been asking the Confederate War Department for additional troops since taking command of the department in September, but to no avail. On December 20, 1863, he wrote the war department concerning a raid in the vicinity of Elizabeth City, North Carolina. According to Pickett, the Yankees' Negro troops had hung one Confederate soldier, manacled ladies and taken them off in irons, and burned bridges. Showing his frustration he complained, "With my force it is impossible to protect such distant points. Still it makes my blood boil to think of these enormities being practiced, and we have no way of arresting them."[57]

On December 20, General Robert E. Lee wrote President Davis recommending the capture of New Bern, North Carolina. He indicated that until spring he had the troops to spare to do the job and felt the garrison at New Bern had become complacent with no Confederates to challenge them. Lee went on to say that the U.S. Navy ships helping to secure New Bern could be captured to cooperate with a land force. Davis bought the concept and Lee went to work on the plan. Lee picked Brig. Gen. Robert F. Hoke, a North Carolina native who helped him develop the plan, to lead the operation. The Confederate War Department, however, felt an officer with more rank and experience was needed and Pickett was the natural choice.[58]

Lee gave Pickett command of the brigades of Brigadier Generals Hoke, Thomas L. Clingman, Matthew W. Ransom and Seth M. Barton. In addition, Pickett would have four unbrigaded infantry regiments, five cavalry regiments and an assortment of artillery units under his command. To conduct the waterborne portion of the operation Colonel John Taylor Wood was chosen to lead eight midshipmen from the Confederate Naval Academy and a detachment of Confederate sailors and marines to capture the U.S. Navy ships in the Neuse River. By the last week of January, Pickett had his command of 13, 300 troops marshaled at Kinston, North Carolina, ready to strike.[59]

General Barton, with his own brigade and that of Kemper, along with three regiments of Ransom's brigade, 14 artillery pieces and 600 cavalry, were to leave on the on the morning of the 30th. With his cavalry Barton was to cut the railroad and cross Brice's Creek, take the forts on the bank of the Neuse, cross the railroad bridge, and cut off any Federal reinforcements from New Bern.[60]

Later the same day, the 15th and 17th Virginia Infantry Regiments were to report to Colonel James Dearing on the north side of the Neuse River. With these two regiments, the 67th North Carolina Infantry, three artillery pieces, and 300 cavalrymen Dearing was to attack and, if it was possible, capture Fort Anderson at Barrington's Ferry. By taking Fort Anderson, Dearing would be able to have direct fire on the town and enfilading fire on the works in front of it.[61]

Pickett would accompany Hoke's brigade, which was reinforced with three additional regiments, 10 artillery pieces, and 30 cavalrymen. Hoke was to depart on the evening of the 30th. Colonel Wood and his detachment of 33 officers and 220 men were to leave on January 31. Wood, after capturing the gunboats, would cooperate with Pickett's force by pounding the Federals from the captured vessels. All of Pickett's forces were to attack simultaneously on Monday, February 1.[62]

To provide a diversion for Pickett's operation, Maj. Gen. William H.C. Whiting, commanding the District of the Cape Fear River and the Defenses of Wilmington, headquartered at Wilmington, North Carolina, was to send a force to threaten the Swansboro area. Whiting selected Brig. Gen. James G. Martin to lead the mission. Martin would have the 17th and 42nd North Carolina infantry regiments of his brigade plus several companies of cavalry and a battery of six guns, in total about 2,000 men. His objective was Newport Barracks. To get there in time, Martin would have to leave Wilmington on January 28.[63]

Martin would prove to be a tough adversary. James Green Martin was born in Elizabeth City, North Carolina, on February 14, 1819, and graduated from West Point in 1840. He served in the Mexican War and lost an arm at the battle of Churubusco, but won a brevet promotion for bravery. At the outbreak of the Civil War he resigned his commission in the U.S. Army, joined the Confederacy and was appointed brigadier general on May 15, 1862. He was known for his bravery and loved by his men, who once carried him around on their shoulders giving cheers for "Old One Wing."[64]

All three columns of Pickett's command departed as planned with high expectations. By the evening of Sunday, January 31, Hoke's column was approximately 10 miles from New Bern and two miles from the Union outposts. After a few hours' rest, a little after 12 o'clock Monday morning, February 1, Hoke had his men up and on the march and crossed Batchelder's Creek at daybreak. Unfortunately, the firing by the pickets alerted the Federals, who had already been reinforced by troops from New Bern. Hoke's troops, however, pushed the Yankees aside and got to within a mile of New Bern before halting to wait for the sound of Barton's guns.[65]

Picket and Hoke, however, would never hear Barton's guns because he ran into some serious Federal fortifications at Brice's Creek. Instead of using his element of surprise, Barton brought up his artillery and then went forward to reconnoiter. Feeling the fortifications were too strong to attack Barton halted where he was. He sent several messengers to notify Pickett, but none reached him until the next day. Dearing had a similar experience when he encountered Fort Anderson. He also felt he could not successfully carry the works and halted in place to await orders.[66]

While Confederate ground forces were trying to get to New Bern, Colonel Wood and his men, in 14 launches, rowed 60 miles down the Neuse River, reaching New Bern at 4:00 A.M. on February 1. Unfortunately, the fog was so thick Wood could not find any gunboats. To keep from being discovered when the sun came up he went back up the river to Batchelder's Creek, where he secreted his men and boats until nightfall. While his men were resting, Wood and a subordinate reconnoitered New Bern in daylight and found only one Federal gunboat, the *Underwriter*. The *Underwriter* was a side-wheel steamer mounting four guns and a crew of about 84 officers and men. Wood went back upstream and developed a plan to attack the *Underwriter* at 10:00 P.M. that night. After a short but violent and bloody action, the *Underwriter* was in

Confederate hands. During the Confederates' boarding, some of the *Underwriter*'s crew jumped overboard and swam ashore. As soon as the Union sailors reported what had happened, the shore batteries were ordered to fire on the captured vessel. Finding the steam pressure too low to maneuver the vessel, Wood and his crew set her on fire and made good their escape.[67]

While Pickett was being thwarted in his attack on New Bern, Brigadier General Martin was steadily closing in on Newport Barracks. He reached Jacksonville on Saturday, January 30. The next day he pushed on to the White Oak River. There he sent pickets across the river to arrest anyone that might warn the Yankees of his approach. The river had to be bridged so the rest of the command could cross, which took until the next morning. During the day he caught a Yankee deserter from whom he obtained lot of valuable intelligence as to the position, strength, and condition of the Federals at Newport Barracks. He got so much information that he felt the man "should be treated differently from the other prisoners."[68]

Martin's command crossed the White Oak River on Monday, February 1, and before nightfall he and his men were within 10 miles of Newport Barracks, where he stopped for the night. It rained all night, and, fearing the condition of the roads, Martin sent most of his wagons back over the White Oak. With the rain still coming down on Tuesday morning he pressed on to Newport Barracks.[69]

The first Federals encountered by Martin was a cavalry picket near Gale's Creek at about 8:00 A.M. The 25 cavalrymen had been sent out in advance about two miles and after mixing it up with Martin's cavalry, the lieutenant in charge of the Federal cavalrymen, with blood streaming from a saber cut to his shoulder, hurried his men rearward as the rebels pressed forward. An hour later Martin's men hit the 9th Vermont's Co. H picket line, which fell back post haste to the rest of the company posted at Gale's Creek.[70]

As soon as the pickets came in Captain Gorham formed his men to meet the rebels. The new recruits, who were unarmed, were sent to the blockhouse near Bogue Sound where Co. B was stationed about three miles away. The Green Mountain Boys did not have long to wait before the enemy's infantry and artillery came in on another road leading directly toward them. The pickets that Gorham had placed just outside the camp fired a volley into the advancing rebels and fell back to the main line formed around an old meetinghouse the company had been using as a barracks. The volley from the Vermonters only angered the gray-backs, who soon brought up a battery and commenced shelling the barracks. The enemy charged with their infantry and Gorham, seeing he was greatly outnumbered, ordered his men to fire one more volley and fall back to the woods.[71]

After finding some cover Co. H attempted to delay the rebel advance. As Gorham shouted orders and rebel bullets zipped through the leaves, Private Stephen Burrows, a 24-year-old farmer from Wardsboro in Co. H, felt a searing pain in his left hand as a minie ball tore across it. He was able to bandage it up and retreat with the rest of his company. At the hospital his index, middle and part of his ring finger on his left hand were amputated. He was transferred to a hospital in Newark, New Jersey, on May 4 and then to Sloan General Hospital in Montpelier, where he was discharged for disability December 16, 1864.[72]

Realizing he was going to be overrun, Gorham ordered his men to retreat through the woods and swamps to Newport Barracks. While retreating, twelve of Gorman's men fell behind or got lost and were captured, six of whom would die in Confederate prisoner of war camps before they could be paroled.[73]

After chasing off Co. H the Confederates hit the 9th Vermont's Co. B at the Bogue Sound Blockhouse at about 11:00 A.M. The company was under the command of First Lt. Alfred C. Ballard, with about 62 men. Half of these men were recruits who had just received their rifles and a pocket full of cartridges that morning, but with the old howitzer mounted inside the blockhouse and the firepower of his men's rifles, Ballard was determined to make a stand.[74]

"BLOCK HOUSE" ON BOGUE SOUND, N. C.
(Built by Company K, 9th New Jersey Volunteers.)

Bogue Sound Blockhouse from *The History of the Ninth New Jersey Veteran Vols.* (The Library of Virginia).

As soon as they got their guns in position, the Confederates unleashed a barrage on the blockhouse. The first round passed clear through the log structure, but Ballard and his men held on for about half an hour. Then Martin sent in Co. A of the 17th North Carolina as skirmishers with another company behind it to storm the building and force the Vermonters out. When they were within about 200 yards of the blockhouse the Tar Heels charged. Corporal William J. Sisco pulled the lanyard on the old howitzer for one last shot, then Ballard and his men came pouring out. "The Company then put for the woods at a very quick step, for the swarms of rebels were after us screaming and yelling as victorious soldiers know how to do," Ballard wrote later. Ballard and his men fell back firing at the rebels until they could make their escape to Morehead City. As the Confederates left they set fire to the blockhouse.[75]

As soon as Co. B left the safety of the blockhouse men started getting hit. Private William P. Smith, a 21-year-old farmer from Poultney, had a minie ball ricochet off the occipital lobe on the back of his head, fracturing his skull. He was carried along with his comrades as they pulled back and was left at Mansfield Hospital in Morehead City. On March 26, a doctor removed a piece of his skull as big as "a Spanish dollar." By May 3 the wound had healed. Smith was evacuated to Baxter General Hospital in Burlington to recuperate and did not rejoin his company until August 1. He was admitted to the Bermuda Hundred Hospital, in Virginia, with a serious illness in September and was transferred to the V.R.C. on December 20, 1864. He was discharged from the service March 9, 1865, with a disability and a $4.00 a month pension. He would suffer from partial deafness in both ears, dizziness, headaches and sometimes nervous excitement for the rest of his life.[76]

Soon after Smith was wounded, Pvt. Nathan DeForge, a 38-year-old, five-foot five-inch farmer from Shrewsbury, went down with a moan when a bullet hit him in the left leg. The minie ball hit him in the back of the left calf and traveled down his leg, coming out the front just below the ankle joint. This wound kept him from returning to his company and he was transferred to V.R.C. on October 11, 1864. Years after the war, unable to work because of his wound and infirmities of old age, he entered the Vermont Soldier's Home in Bennington on April 16, 1894, at the age of 66. At the time, he was receiving a $12.00 a month military pension. He died at the home on September 13, 1894, and was buried in the cemetery there. On his application for admission to the Vermont Soldier's Home DeForge indicated he was not married, which was not true. He had married Jennie Livernoise in Shrewsbury on February 29, 1854. Apparently he could not support her on his pension and placed himself at the mercy of the soldier's home. How she survived while he was in the home is unknown. After his death Jennie applied for and received a veteran's widow's pension until she died December 10, 1910.[77]

Because Company B was moving so fast, both Smith and DeForge were left behind and captured, but they were so severely wounded the rebels paroled them and left them at a neighboring farmhouse. Privates Franklin Caswell, Henry W. Fletcher, John Grant, Franklin Ives, William B. Jenks, Thomas B. Ripley, Thomas Rudd, and David Weller were also captured. Caswell, Ripley and Weller were incarcerated in the infamous Confederate prisoner of war camp, Camp Sumter (generally referred to simply as Andersonville), at Andersonville, Georgia, where they died of disease. Ives was sent to the Confederate prisoner of war camp in Salisbury, North Carolina, where he died four months later of disease on May 30. Jenks was paroled in November and Fletcher in December; both returned to the regiment.[78]

Private Thomas Rudd, a 25-year-old Canadian laborer, survived the horrors of being a prisoner of war and was paroled at Charleston, South Carolina, December 16, 1864. He was evacuated to Baxter General Hospital in Burlington where he died of pneumonia on January 10, 1865. In the military files of the 9th Vermont's Quartermaster the author found the following note:

Baxter General Hospital, Burlington, Vt.

January 10, 1865

To R.W. Blake: Pvt. Thomas Rudd, Co. B, 9th Vt. died in the hospital of typhoid pneumonia this day — will you please furnish a coffin for his remains.

A.D. Tagert
Ward Surg.

As an afterthought Dr. Tagert scratched, "Length of coffin 6 feet." With that, Pvt. Thomas Rudd was gone.[79]

Earlier in the morning, Lieutenant Colonel Barney got word that Capt. Russell H. Conwell, commander of Company D of the 2nd Massachusetts Heavy Artillery, had been out to Canaday's Mills the night before to check on some of his men and had been shot while about halfway between Newport Barracks and the mill. Conwell claimed he would have been killed had the watch in his breast pocket not stopped a bullet. Barney sent Second Lt. John Whitcher of Co. G and 25 enlisted men, along with Captain Conwell, out toward Canaday's Mills to see if they could round up the men who shot Conwell. Barney ordered Whitcher to return in three hours, but to leave half of the men in ambush near where Conwell had been shot. The detachment left at 9:00 A.M. Lieutenant Whitcher and half of his men returned at 1:00 P.M. without Conwell. Conwell proceeded on to Croatan, about 14 miles away. There, the telegraph operator reported that Newport Barracks was under attack. Conwell procured a horse and for some unexplained reason rode to New Bern.[80]

As soon as Colonel Jourdan learned of the attack he took a train from Morehead City to Newport Barracks, arriving about noon. Upon his arrival he told Lieutenant Colonel Barney to withdraw the pickets from Canaday's Mills. Then Jourdan ordered Barney to hold on as long as possible and if he had to retreat to do so slowly, falling back on Morehead City. If he was cut off from that direction, he was to fall back on Newport village and there make a stand on the opposite bank of the river, destroying the bridges in his front, and if driven from there to retreat to Beaufort. Jourdan then instructed Barney to use the artillery at the barracks as long as possible, and if they were overrun the guns should be brought with them or thrown in the Newport River. If that could not be accomplished he was to spike the guns and break the gun carriages and wheels. With his orders issued, Jourdan had all the sick men and part of the quartermaster's supplies at the barracks loaded aboard the train, and he headed back to Morehead City.[81]

After Colonel Jourdan's departure, the long roll sounded in the Vermonter's camp and the regiment fell into line. After a short stirring speech from Captain Kelley the men were marched toward Bogue Sound, in the direction of the latest firing, at about 2:00 P.M. Most of the men were new recruits that had only been issued their muskets at 4:00 that morning. Lieutenant Colonel Barney stated, "New recruits composed nearly all our force having about 60 or 70 of the old men present." Kelley halted the regiment about two miles from camp. Here the regiment was deployed in the edge of the woods in a thin single line since there were not enough men to form a proper double line of battle, and a skirmish line was quickly thrown forward. The left of the skirmish line, under the command of First Lt. William C. Holman, rested on the railroad. First Lt. Theodore S. Peck commanded the right of the skirmish line. Peck was ordered forward with his portion of the skirmishers to see if they could make contact with Co. B. Peck, of course, could not find the missing company as it had already retreated down the coast road to Morehead City pursued by a swarm of angry North Carolinians.[82]

After advancing about two miles from the Bogue Sound Blockhouse, Martin's column emerged from a thick woods into a clear area and ran into Peck's skirmish line. Martin formed the 17th North Carolina in line of battle on the right side of the road and the 42nd on the left. He then ordered his artillery forward, which quickly unlimbered and started throwing shells at the Vermonters.[83]

Firing as they moved forward, the rebel infantry hit Lieutenant Peck's skirmish line. Realizing he was outnumbered Peck ordered his men to fall back to Newport Barracks and "for every man to take care of himself." Just before the Vermont skirmish line fell back, 20-year-old Pvt. James H. Grace, a farmer from Starksboro in Co. C, fired his last shot and while bending over to pick up his ramrod was struck in the head by a minie ball. Although the bullet was nearly spent, it still had enough momentum to penetrate his scalp about four inches above his right ear where it lay embedded between the scalp and the skull. Grace was knocked down but, amazingly, was not stunned and was up on his feet before his two comrades, Privates George Atkins and Joseph Carl, could come to his aid. Grace wrapped a towel he had with him around his head and continued to fall back with the skirmish line along with Atkins, Carl, Benjamin Stokes and Simon "Simmy" Day. Before they reached camp Grace attempted to jump a small stream, but caught one of his boots on a vine and fell flat on his face on the other side. When he hit the ground a small stick stuck him in the inside corner of his right eye. He quickly got up and put his hand to his eye and found that blood was running down his face, but the rebels were so close he kept on running.[84]

As the Green Mountain Boys and the gray-backs were blazing away at each other James F. Bolton of Co. C was hit by a minie ball that tore across his back. The ball entered near the left shoulder joint and exited under the right arm, but fortunately for Bolton it did not hit his lungs. Bolton survived his wound, but was discharged from the army the following fall on November 22. After returning to Vermont he had to give up farming because of the effects of his wound. He eventually went to Washington and got a job as a clerk in the War Department. In 1880 a doctor said of Bolton, "As he has grown older his disability increases, and that there is a marked and general weakening of the whole system as a result of his wound."[85]

In the midst of the smoke from the black powder both of the Osier brothers from Monkton in Co. C were hit. Joseph was killed on the spot. Lieutenant Peck was standing near him when he was hit and related later that Joseph Osier was "a fine looking little fellow only 18-years-old, and a new recruit. He died fighting bravely." When the regiment returned to Newport Barracks several days after the battle they found Joseph's nearly naked body. He had been stripped of all his clothing except for his shirt and drawers. Joseph's older brother, 19-year-old Peter, was only wounded, but was left behind and captured by the rebels. Peter survived his captivity and was paroled December 6, 1864, at Charleston, South Carolina, and taken to Division No. 1 Hospital in Annapolis, Maryland, where he died December 15. He was buried in Ash Grove Cemetery, now the Annapolis National Cemetery.[86]

As soon as the rebels reached the Vermonter's main line, Capt. Eugene Viele of Co. I. prepared to answer the rebel artillery fire with an artillery piece that he and several men from Company D of the 2nd Massachusetts Heavy Artillery had dragged by hand from the barracks. Stationing the field piece in the middle of the road Viele opened fire. One of his rounds hit a rebel caisson and blew it up. Then he switched to canister rounds to help slow the Confederate advance. As the artillery fire continued, Pvt. Charles W. Stoddard, a 36-year-old farmer from Dover in Co. K, was hit with a shell fragment in the left thigh about three inches below the hip joint. The piece of steel cut through his flesh to the bone. One of Stoddard's comrades, Pvt. Aurelius Pettee, from Dummerston, saw him go down and, with the help of Pvt. Edgar F. Copeland, got him into an army wagon. The next morning Stoddard was admitted to the hospital in Beaufort. The wound healed, leaving a formation of hard calloused tissue surrounding the affected area. Surprisingly, Stoddard rejoined the regiment four months later on June 20.[87]

Private Matthew Riley in Co. G was also hit in the left thigh by a shell fragment, but he was not as lucky as Stoddard. Riley, a 28-year-old farmer from Randolph, was taken on the retreat by his comrades but died in Hammond General Hospital in Morehead City on February 6. He was buried the next day. After the war his body was reinterred in the New Bern National Cemetery.[88]

As the firing continued, a minie ball bored into the right arm of Pvt. Thomas P. Garry, a 21-year-old Irish immigrant in Co. D. The bullet hit in the front of the upper arm four inches below the shoulder joint. It traveled through the arm in a downward path, destroying the brachial nerves and causing paralysis in the arm which left his right hand in a permanently constricted fist. Garry was discharged from the service with a disability on February 27, 1865, with a pension of $4.00 a month. The next year his pension was raised to $16.00.[89]

Private George F. Durkee, a 28-year-old, five-foot-seven-inch farmer from Chittenden in Co. B, was shot in the left leg just below the knee joint. The bullet traveled down his tibia, breaking it, then went through the ankle joint and finally exited through the arch of his foot. Durkee spent four months in the hospital at Morehead City and was transferred to the U.S. Gen-

Private George F. Durkee, Co. B, displaying the wound on his left leg for the U.S. Pension Bureau (National Archives).

eral Hospital in Newark, New Jersey. From New Jersey he was transferred to the Baxter General Hospital in Burlington and eventually to Governor Smith General Hospital in Brattleboro. After he recovered from his wound Durkee was transferred to the 2nd Battalion V.R.C. on December 4, 1864, and was discharged from the service on September 14, 1865, with a disability. By the 1880s the leg was numb, atrophied and one inch shorter that the right one and he was unable to do any manual labor. He died February 29, 1892, in Jewell, Kansas.[90]

As the gunfire intensified, a Confederate minie ball tore into the right leg of 19-year-old Pvt. Nelson Roberts of Co. A from Sharon. The ball entered about three inches below the knee joint, fracturing the tibia, and exited out the back of the leg. Corporal David Paine helped Roberts to the rear. Roberts was eventually transferred to Sloan General Hospital in Montpelier, but the wound, still not healed, was inflamed. After arriving at Sloan Hospital Roberts was given a furlough but did not return on time. An officer was sent to arrest him and found him at his father's house in Sharon suffering from the wound in his leg and recovering from an illness. He said he was unable to travel at the time his furlough expired and his attending physician had forwarded his affidavit to military authorities and he thought his time had been extended. Roberts returned to the hospital when he was able to travel and was deemed fit for the Veteran Reserve Corps, but he had had enough of the army and wanted his discharge. He was discharged from Sloan General Hospital in Montpelier June 24, 1865. Roberts died April 4, 1880, of consumption.[91]

One of the new recruits, Pvt. Nathan C. Smith, a 27-year-old farmer from Brookfield in

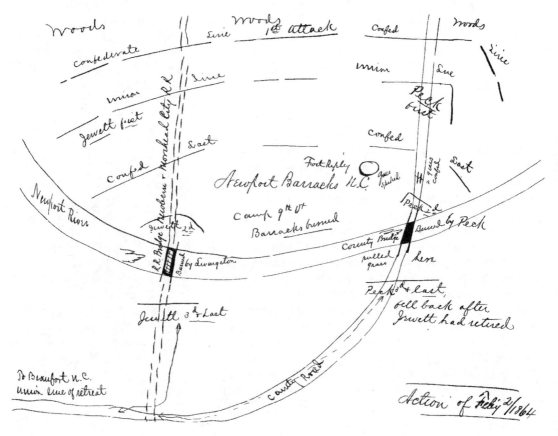

Map of the Battle of Newport Barracks, February 2, 1864, drawn by Josiah O. Livingston (National Archives).

Co. D, was hit with a minie ball and killed instantly. When his personal effects were inventoried after the battle, all he had to his name was a watch and $13.00.[92]

Because the regiment was without any field officers, Surgeon Carpenter was at the front and assisted Captain Kelly by observing and reporting Martin's troop movements and carrying orders to the various portions of the command. Between 3:00 P.M. and 4:00 P.M., the other half of the detachment that had been out on the Gale's Creek Road in ambush, as well as the pickets from the Gale's Creek post, returned and added to the regiment's strength. The Green Mountain Boys fought as well as they could, along with the newly armed recruits who "were armed at 4 A.M., and at 10 o'clock they were fighting like demons," but being outnumbered, they were gradually pushed back towards Newport Barracks. The men were halted wherever a strip of woods or bushes afforded cover and by repeated stands held the enemy in check for several hours. By 5:00 P.M. the regiment had been pushed back to Newport Barracks where Lieutenant Colonel Barney and Captain Kelley planned to make a final stand under the cover of the artillery in the fortifications there.[93]

As the regiment slowly retreated a new recruit, 45-year-old Burke native Pvt. William Melcher, fell behind and was captured. He died August 30 at Andersonville. Melcher's wife, Rhoda, collected in return for her husband's sacrifice a $16.00 a month pension for herself, her 15-year-old daughter and her four-year-old son.[94]

Also while falling back, 37-year-old First Lt. William C. Holman of Co. G from Braintree was somehow snatched by the rebels. He was imprisoned in prisoner of war camps in Savannah and Macon, Georgia, and Charleston and Columbia, South Carolina. While in Camp Sorghum in Columbia, Holman escaped on November 4 with a number of other Federal officers, but because of his weakened condition caused by chronic diarrhea he could not keep up with the other men and was recaptured. He was exchanged May 6, 1865, but remained in the hospital until the end of May before he rejoined the regiment in early June. He was mustered out on June 13, and as mentioned earlier he returned to Vermont with Ben Robinson in tow.[95]

After Holman's capture, First Lt. Erastus W. Jewett's Co. A replaced Holman's Co. G on the left of the skirmish line.

After reaching Newport Barracks, the Green Mountain Boys found the artillerymen had spiked their guns and fled. With Captain Conwell AWOL the men had panicked at the sound of the approaching rebels and retreated to New Bern, spreading the report that the 9th Vermont had been cut off and captured. Captain Conwell was later court-martialed for "shamefully abandoning his command in the face of the enemy" and was dismissed from the service.[96]

Seeing that he could not hold his position at Newport Barracks, Lieutenant Colonel Barney did as ordered and fell back to the village of Newport, where another artillery battery was stationed. He had the regiment fall back slowly to a crest near the County Bridge that crossed the Newport River. Before leaving, at about 5:30 P.M., Barney had several of his men set the barracks and storehouses on fire.[97]

Another Vermonter captured was Pvt. Alfred Tatro, an 18-year-old farmer from Charlotte in Co. F. He died in Andersonville from chronic diarrhea August 16, 1864. His mother, Angeline Tatro, applied for and received an $8.00 a month pension starting August 17, 1864, which was raised to $12.00 a month March 19, 1886. She died July 24, 1903. A farmer named Rufus Enos that Alfred and his father worked for stated that he had known the Tatros for 30-some years and that from 1854 to 1860 they lived in his house. He said of Alfred:

> Alfred Tatro and his father Jarvis Tatro worked for me during the time they lived in my house and that all his [Alfred's] earnings were payed to his father for the help to support the family, they being very poor and I can say that he was one of the best boys that I ever had to work for me. That said Alfred being a young boy at that time about 15 years of age and that said Alfred was full of ambition and always trying to help his parents.[98]

Left: Private Franklin Averill, Co. I, captured February 2, 1864, at Newport Barracks, N.C. He died in the Confederate prisoner of war camp at Andersonville, Ga., July 25, 1864 (Mary Comiskey). *Right:* Corporal Charles Averill, Co I, brother of Franklin Averill. Charles survived the war but lost his corporal stripes for some minor infraction of military discipline July 12, 1864 (Mary Comiskey).

Here on the crest, with the Newport River to his back, Lieutenant Colonel Barney was determined to hold Martin's troops off until he could get his men across the river. As the Green Mountain Boys formed their defensive position, Martin extended his line around the right of the 9th Vermont. At the same time, the force that attacked Co. B at the blockhouse moved in on the Vermonters' left and occupied the railroad track, cutting off any chance of retreat in the direction of Morehead City. Barney had to cross the Newport River and head toward Beaufort. Accordingly, he sent Adjutant Josiah O. Livingston with orders for Lieutenant Peck to cover the County Bridge and Lieutenant Jewett to hold the railroad bridge. Each were to burn the bridges after the regiment had gotten across. Barney told Livingston to impress upon both officers "the bridges must be burned at all hazards."[99]

Barney retracted his line slowly as he got more and more of his men across the County Bridge, until only Lieutenant Peck and his company, forming the rear guard on the right, were left. The place where the 40-foot long County Bridge crossed the Newport River was very narrow but very deep. On the other side the area was full of marshes, with the road running through it. Lieutenant Peck was told by Livingston there would be cavalry on the far side with plenty of turpentine and tar to ignite the wooden structure and that the bridge must be burned at all costs to keep the rebels at bay. While his rear guard was holding off the rebels, Peck sent one of his sergeants to see if everything was ready to set fire to the bridge as soon as they arrived. The sergeant returned and told Peck there was no sign of the cavalry or turpentine. Leaving one-half of his men to hold off the rebels, Peck rushed with the other half to the bridge. At the bridge he found that some of the planks were not nailed down, he had some of his men stack up the planks while several other men went off to gather dried marsh grass for kindling. When all was ready to fire the bridge Peck called in his other men and got them safely across the bridge.[100]

After crossing the bridge, Peck got his men in position and resumed firing at the North Carolinians, while several other of his troops set the bridge on fire. Martin's troops were as determined to take the bridge as Peck was to destroy it. The rebels brought up artillery and started showering the other side of the river with canister balls.[101]

Just as the bridge was starting to catch fire, Peck was told that Sgt. Charles F. Branch of Co. A had been wounded and was on the other side of the river, unable to pull himself across the bridge. Peck immediately rushed across the burning bridge, scooped up Sergeant Branch and carried him back across the bridge in the midst of a shower of Confederate minie balls and canister fire. Just after Peck got across, the bridge became a flaming inferno and soon collapsed into the river in a mass of glowing embers.[102]

While Peck was destroying the County Bridge, Lieutenant Erastus W. Jewett, with a detail of about 70 men, had the mission of burning the railroad bridge about three-quarters of a mile downriver from Peck. Jewett stated later:

> We held the bridge and twice drove the enemy back to the cover of the woods. They then shelled us with a battery at about 600 yards, for fifteen minutes, but as soon as they stopped, we were at them again with our muskets, and succeeded in keeping them back from the bridge till it was burned, so that they could not cross the river.[103]

While Jewett and his men held off the rebels, Livingston set fire to the bridge, receiving a wound in his hand in the process. On September 8, 1891, Jewett, Livingston and Peck were awarded the Medal of Honor for their heroic efforts in destroying the bridges, which ensured the successful escape of their regiment.[104]

A number of stragglers, mainly the new recruits who did not know the territory, lost their way and were captured. Others reached the river too late to cross the bridges, so they plunged into the river and swam across.[105]

While the rear guard was holding the Confederates at bay at the bridges, the rest of the 9th Vermont reached Newport village where Lieutenant Colonel Barney expected to find artillery support. Instead, the Vermonters found that the artillerymen had spiked their guns without firing a single shot and were standing in formation outside of the fort about to retreat. Finding it impossible to hold this position, Barney had his men retire under the cover of darkness in the direction of Beaufort. One of the guns in the fort at the barracks was brought away, another stuck in the mud and abandoned and the balance rendered unserviceable. Just before the Vermonters left the village, Capt. Linus Sherman and his provost guard fired the government storehouses there that were filled with a large quantity of barrels full of turpentine.[106]

After the bridges were destroyed, the rear guards followed the rest of the regiment, which was making its way in the dark in a long 23-mile detour around swamps and inlets to Beaufort where the lead elements arrived at sunrise the next morning.[107]

During the retreat to Beaufort, Capt. Linus Sherman and his men were following the regiment as part of the rear guard. Later, Sherman told of his experience during the night: "I started on horseback & rode 5 or 6 miles & found a man shot through the foot. I let him ride and the scamp rode on and I have not seen him since. During the march the wagon master kindly offered to let me ride & I rode a few miles more."[108]

Stumbling through the darkness, one of the new recruits, Pvt. Benjamin E. Stokes of Co. C, a 34-year-old farmer from Starksboro, tripped on a fallen tree and severely hurt his right leg and caused a double hernia, yet he limped on with his retreating comrades. He was admitted to the hospital in Morehead City February 4 and returned to his company nine days later. The injury Stokes received that night troubled him so much after the war he received a disability pension.[109]

With the bridges destroyed and darkness rapidly closing in the rebels put a halt to their pursuit of the Vermonters. Martin and his men stayed in the area for several days before being ordered back to Wilmington. Although he had not been able to capture the Federal troops at Newport Barracks, his portion of the Confederate attack had been a success. He had captured four dirt forts, three blockhouses, one regimental flag, 10 pieces of artillery, 20 barrels of powder, several hundred small arms, one cannon, 200 boxes of fixed ammunition for artillery, a considerable quantity of forage and other stores and 1,000 barrels of turpentine belonging to the United States Government. He also destroyed two county bridges, three railroad bridges, some trestle work and some of the track at Croatan. Additionally, he captured one lieutenant and 73 men, mostly Vermonters.[110]

The 9th Vermont's losses in the attack were three killed, 13 wounded and 48 captured. Two of the wounded died later of their wounds. Of the 48 men captured 29 died in Confederate prisoner of war camps, most of them in the infamous camp at Andersonville, Georgia.[111]

On Wednesday, February 3, the 9th Vermont was taken by boat to Morehead City where it was reunited with the men of Co B. who had retreated there from the Bogue Sound Blockhouse. Then the 9th Vermont was loaded aboard a train and taken a short distance from the city to the outer fortifications to await another Confederate attack during a long and chilly night. Thankfully for the exhausted Vermonters the expected attack never came. The next day the men were put to work strengthening fortifications. They were relieved at dark and finally got a good night's rest. Most of the men in the regiment had lost everything they owned at Newport Barracks and had to endure the cold weather with no overcoats or any extra clothing. Although they were miserable, Lieutenant Ballard commented, "Since the day of the fight, Feb. 2d, we have had quite cool weather, and men and officers alike have endured many hardships, but they have borne it without a murmur."[112]

Having lost the battle and being captured at Harpers Ferry and now losing the battle at Newport Barracks, the sprits of the officers and men in the 9th Vermont were at an all-time low. Lieutenant Colonel Barney, trying to convince himself and his wife that the 9th Vermont had done its best, wrote from Morehead City, "I have been told by Col. Jourdan commanding this district that I done the very best that possibly could be, so I feel that I have not been disgraced even if I was obliged to destroy every thing and retreat."[113]

While the rebels held Newport Barracks they tried to play a psychological game with the telegraph operators in Morehead City. On February 3 they sent a telegram to Colonel Jourdan stating that everything was all right at the barracks and signing Colonel Ripley's name to the dispatch. The telegraph operators in Morehead City knew Colonel Ripley was at Fort Monroe and the rebels were trying to play a trick. A dispatch was sent back, directing Colonel Ripley to hold the place at all hazards. Several dispatches went back and forth when at last the Morehead City operator sent word that the steamer *S.R. Spaulding* had arrived with 4,000 troops. After that the rebels cut the lines.[114]

Colonel Ripley returned from Fort Monroe on February 5 and took command of the regiment. That afternoon Colonel Jourdan ordered the 9th Vermont back to Newport Barracks. Under Jourdan's command, the 9th Vermont, along with the 21st Connecticut Infantry Regiment and an artillery piece, were loaded aboard a train at 2:00 P.M. and arrived at the barracks at 6 o'clock that evening. The New Englanders found that Martin's men had vacated the area just two and one-half hours before they arrived. Colonel Jourdan sent a cavalry patrol out to find the enemy, which they did about 11 miles away.[115]

Virtually nothing remained intact in the old camp. The barracks were nothing but mounds of smoldering ashes and the railroad track was torn up in a few spots. The three Vermonters killed during the fight were found stripped of their shoes and uniforms. Two severely wounded Confederate soldiers had been left behind, and their comrades, believing they would soon die, had stripped them of their belongings. The wounded rebels were cared for by the 9th Vermont's doctors and both survived.[116]

The regiment was pulled back past the town of Newport on the night of February 6 in anticipation of a rebel attack that never came. The next morning the Green Mountain Boys returned to Newport Barracks. The outposts at Gale's Creek, Canaday's Mills and Bogue Sound were reestablished and life at Newport Barracks got back to normal.[117]

Just as the weather was taking a turn for the worse on February 13, the Vermonters were issued tents and over the next two days they were issued new uniforms and overcoats. The tents and clothing had arrived just in time. On Thursday, February 18, Newport Barracks got three inches of snow.[118] Seventy more recruits from Vermont arrived at Newport Barracks on February 11, bringing the regiment's strength up to 876.[119]

As busy as things were at Newport Barracks, Colonel Ripley still had time to think about his turpentine venture. He wrote his brother William on February 12:

The late raid puts a new future on the turpentine question. What a cleaning out there would have been, had we put up a Machine. I should have lost my little all had I found a chance to invest it. Still, the thing ought to be put through vigorously. Did I know you were actually coming I would buy a plantation of a thousand or so acres, mighty cheap, and kill the old trees on it. A large trade has been spoiled by the ravages of a destructive fire. It cannot be used for turpentine, but must be cut down for tar, as they have no way of extracting the turpentine. Could I buy this cheap I would make money on it like the devil, provided the machine came on. Can you not come down here? We'd have a splendid time, and you could look up the turpentine business thoroughly, you have just time before Spring opens.[120]

Colonel Ripley was so excited about getting into the turpentine business that sometime between February 12 and 17 he issued a general order taking away a number of the U.S. Treasury trade permits from local businessmen, thereby shutting them down. On February 17, he invited the local U.S. Treasury agent to his quarters on the pretext of "some important business connected with my command, and in course of which I hoped to get some useful information from him casually and by direct inquiry." He also made up an explanation for his arbitrary general order so as not to have a "misunderstanding" with the Treasury agent. By March 1, William used both his and Edward Ripley's savings to purchase the patent for the machine that extracted turpentine from scrap pine. However, William admonished his younger brother: "I do not like to see you engaging in speculation with residents of North Carolina. I am afraid they will compromise your official position. It would kill Father and Mother."[121]

As the scheme to corner the turpentine market matured, William went so far as to travel to North Carolina to procure wood, but it took so long to get the wood north the business struggled. To add to the problem of the wood supply, the price of turpentine fell off sharply the following October and William was barely able to get out of the business with what the two brothers had invested. That was Edward Ripley's last business venture while in uniform.[122]

On February 21, Privates James H. Grace, Joseph Carl and Benjamin Stokes, all Starksboro natives and members of Co. C, walked out of Newport Barracks about three-quarters of a mile to look for Stokes' rifle. During the retreat Stokes had tossed his rifle away and after returning to Newport Barracks Stokes' platoon leader told him he would have to pay for the rifle if he could not find it. While wandering around trying to find the missing rifle, the trio was surprised by five armed Confederate soldiers and taken prisoner. The rebels, led by a Lieutenant Martin of the 10th North Carolina Infantry, had been on leave at Martin's father's house in Beaufort and were returning to their regiment. The three Vermonters were taken to Richmond by way of Goldsboro, North Carolina, and Petersburg, Virginia. They were incarcerated in Richmond's infamous Castle Thunder. Because of his head and eye wound, Grace was eventually sent to the Crew and Pemberton Hospital at the intersection of Richmond's 21st and Cary Streets. Privates Grace, Stokes and Carl, along with a little over 1,000 other Union prisoners of war, were exchanged on March 20 and sent to Camp Parole in Annapolis, Maryland. After being told at Camp Parole that they would not get the 30-day furlough they expected, the three men deserted and headed for Vermont.[123]

Joseph Carl was arrested at his home in Vermont on April 12 and sent to Brattleboro, but escaped enroute on April 18. James Grace and Benjamin Stokes were never apprehended. All three men surrendered to military authorities in May 1865 under a presidential proclamation of amnesty for deserters and were given honorable discharges. Initially, all three men were charged with deserting to the enemy, but their records were corrected after the war.[124]

General Peck and his entourage arrived at Newport Barracks on February 22 to look over the camp's security. Ripley wrote later:

> Yesterday was quite a big day for Newport Barracks. Major General Peck, and his brilliant staff, and Colonel Jourdan and his, visited the place, to take consideration of the changes of Camp and fortifications, and outpost defenses I have so urged upon them since the skirmish here. The general finally gave his approval to all the plans, and [gave] me instructions to work day and night in completing them. As I write at 11 o'clock tonight, the work goes bravely on. I can do what I have tried to impress upon them should have been done months ago, and if they had been done, would have insured a totally different result to the late disastrous affair here. I think now I have arranged things with my commanding Gen'l at last, so that I will be less tied by fear of laws and regulations than heretofore, and free to go ahead with the best of my ability to the task set before me here.[125]

Colonel Ripley moved the regiment's camp to the east side of the railroad and work began in earnest. The work went on day and night for almost a month. Bonfires were used so the men could see to work at night. "Even the Sutler sweats in a pit with a shovel," noted Colonel Ripley. The fear of the rebels' return was so great that even white and black residents of the area voluntarily pitched in as one Vermont soldier mentioned in a letter home:

> The rebels were said to be again advancing upon our lines and every effort was made that could be, to be prepared for them, even to the arming of the citizens and negroes, who did good service in the rifle pits. The citizens expressed their willingness to work a month if necessary but did not relish the idea of taking up arms as most of them are deserters from the rebel army and runaways from the conscription and are therefore afraid of the consequences should they be captured by the enemy.[126]

The existing fortifications were strengthened and new rifle pits were dug. Corporal Nelson Wandell of Co. K chronicled the progress of the work in his diary. On February 29 he wrote, "Worked on the rifle pits and slashing the woods in front, worked part of the night." On March 1, he recorded, "We were mustered this forenoon at 11 A.M., went to work slashing the woods, worked till dark." The next day he was slashing again and on Thursday, March 3, he noted, "Took charge of forty two darkies slashing the woods on the east side of the railroad in front of the rifle pits. Worked till 2 P.M."[127]

One Green Mountain Boy wrote on March 10, "We have had very busy times for the past two weeks, felling timber, blocking roads, building breastworks, etc., so that it now looks like a very different place from what it did on the 2 Ult., when the rebels called to pay us their respects."[128]

To protect the left flank, a gunboat with a howitzer was stationed at the mouth of Gale's Creek on the sound.[129] As the men toiled there were constant reports of rebels in the area. Colonel Ripley complained on February 28:

> I am receiving telegrams half hourly from Maj. Gen. Peck in reference to an immediate attack expected. He tells me *I am to die in the last ditch ere Newport is given up; etcetera, etcetera*; and to oblige him I have the entire command out *preparing* in the utmost haste a *ditch suitable for the purpose.*
>
> The rattling of axes, *the songs of the boys, and their laughter as they toil away*, all present a Sunday night scene that would have a singular effect on the popular mind in Rutland could they see it, and especially were all able bodied citizens in Rutland ordered out to work, as they are here tonight.
>
> I am much disposed to poke fun at the whole scare, and bet my commission no attack will take

place, but am not going to be careless, *or do any less to provide for all emergencies than as though I knew it was to come.*

Then he got more philosophical about his regiment's image which had been maligned in several Vermont newspapers:

If there is to be another fight here, it has got to be fought by the 9th Vt., and for the benefit of the 9th, and if there is any fight in them, several unpleasant chapters in the history of the Regt. will pass away, or the Regt. will die in the attempt.

I hope to be able to prove to the croaking, carping, fault-finding "stay at homes" in Vermont, that these men are brave, as noble a body of men as has been sent out of the State, as worthy to carry her state flags; and I hope to prove to them that the boys were urged on to their death by the remembrance of their wrongs at the hands of the people of Vermont; and may this remembrance never cease to haunt the minds of certain ones I [write] of in Vt.[130]

Just as the work on the fortifications was nearly complete sickness broke out among the new recruits. Measles, typhoid and dysentery were the main culprits. In March the 9th Vermont had 192 men on the sick list, the largest number since leaving Yorktown. Eighteen of the cases of disease proved fatal. In addition to the deaths from disease, Pvt. Herman Belding, of Co. E from Bridgewater, was accidentally shot in the stomach and died on March 11. Belding's body rests today in the National Military Cemetery in New Bern.[131]

Fear of another rebel attack caused the U.S. Government to recruit five regiments of North Carolinians, as noted in one of the Vermonters' letters dated March 10 and published in the *Vermont Journal* on March 26, 1864:

There are five North Carolina Union regiments completed and in process of completion, three of which are colored. There is now one company of the North Carolina 24 (white) regiment doing duty here. With what feelings they must have heard of the recent hanging at Kingston of twenty of their number who were so unfortunate as to be captured by the enemy on his late raid. The time is not far distant when the lives of those men shall be *avenged.* If the press of this state reflect the sentiments of the people there are strong evidences that North Carolina, long restless under the yoke of Jeff Davis, will soon arise in its might and throw off the most merciless despotism that ever enslaved a free people.[132]

The hangings referred to were ordered by Major General Pickett. When the Confederates made their failed attempt to take New Bern they captured between 300 and 500 Yankees. Thirteen of the prisoners were identified by their former Confederate comrades as deserters. Being a deserter was bad enough, but when Pickett learned they had joined the Union army he supposedly said, "God damn you, I reckon you will hardly ever go back there again, you damned rascals. I'll have you shot and all other damned rascals who desert." Instead of shooting them Pickett had them hanged on February 15. Because of this incident, Pickett was one of the few Confederates charged with war crimes after the war. As soon as he heard of the charges against him, Pickett, with his wife and daughter in tow, fled to Montreal, Canada. He eventually wrote to Lt. Gen. Ulysses S. Grant, an old friend of his from before the war, and asked him to intervene. Grant was able to secure a special pass for Pickett to re-enter the country without being arrested. On Christmas Day, 1868, Pickett was issued an amnesty by President Andrew Johnson.[133]

Major Amasa Bartlett died suddenly of spinal meningitis on Wednesday, February 16. He had been sick only a day or two and died in the tent that he and Lieutenant Colonel Barney shared. His death hit the regiment hard, but no harder than it hit Barney. "Maj. Bartlett was one of the finest men I ever knew, and has always been a firm friend of mine. Since his promotion he has tented with me and I assure you it is quite lonely for me now. He died here in my tent and on my bed," Barney wrote home on March 19. Bartlett's coffin was escorted to the train at Newport Barracks on February 19 for its journey back to Vermont. Captain Sherman said of Bartlett, "He was a *patriot* & a Christian, beloved by all his men and fellow officers."[134]

Captain Joseph C. Brooks, commander of Co. F, was promoted to major in Bartlett's place on March 20. First Lieutenant John T. Bascom filled Brooks' vacant position in Co. F.[135]

By the end of March, Captain Sherman was back at his duties as the provost marshall in the town of Newport and back to chasing the ladies. "I have made the acquaintance of a few young ladies but none very well cultured or refined. Most of them 'dip' which means 'chewing snuff.' A most abominable *filthy* habit," he wrote to a friend of his in Vermont. Although he had complained several times about the women in North Carolina dipping snuff this habit never seemed to keep him from seeking their attention.[136]

One lady who Captain Sherman was especially fond of was a Miss Millie Bell, who lived in Newport. On May 1 Sherman noted in his diary, "Visited Millie a few minutes this evening." Several days later they had a small spat: "Had a long talk with Millie and she thought I threatened to put her in guardhouse. Am sorry she is feeling so badly about it for there was no intention on my part." Then the next day he recorded, "Millie asks me to forgive her and feels badly about thinking so hard of me." In his last entry about Miss Bell on June 9, Sherman wrote, "Had quite a long visit with Millie and staid quite late with her." That was Sherman's last diary entry concerning Millie Bell. Whether or not they had a falling out is not known.[137]

Colonel Ripley was taken from his command again on April 6. While Colonel Jourdan was home on leave Ripley was temporarily put in command of the sub district of Beaufort, headquartered in Morehead City. This, of course, left Lt. Col. Val Barney in command of Newport Barracks again. Barney did not welcome the assignment. He complained to his wife: " I will take command of the post but I am not anxious to have so large a command but if the responsibility is placed on me I will assume it."[138]

Assistant Surgeon Erastus P. Fairman (Vermont Historical Society).

The day after Colonel Ripley departed to replace Colonel Jourdan, Private Rufus Nicholson was brought before a court-martial. The 19-year-old Tinmouth farmer in Co. B had deserted from Camp Tyler on October 7, 1862. He tried to make his way back to Vermont to see his parents, but in Ohio he ran out of money. He went to work for a man in Ohio for almost a year until someone found out he was a deserter and turned him in. Nicholson was arrested by the local sheriff and sent to Camp Parole in Annapolis, Maryland. From Camp Parole he was sent to Fort Monroe and then to Yorktown, where he reported to the regiment October 16, 1863. Since the regiment was expecting to move any day he was put back on duty rather than in the guardhouse. At his court-martial he was found guilty of desertion and sentenced to be confined to hard labor for one year and forfeit all pay during that time. Nicholson spent his time at hard labor at Fort Macon, South Carolina, and returned to the regiment May 1, 1865.[139]

Erastus P. Fairman, a 36-year-old physician from Wolcott, arrived in the 9th Vermont's camp on April 9. He had enlisted in the 17th Vermont Infantry Regiment as a private on February 29, 1864. While in camp of instruction a few days after he enlisted, he met Dr. Samuel W. Thayer, surgeon general of the State of Vermont, with whom he was acquainted. Dr. Thayer inquired if Fairman had enlisted as a private and Fairman acknowledged that he had. Dr. Thayer said, "I have a place for you. You go home and stay there until I send you a commission." Not one to disobey an order, Fairman complied. On April 1, he received a commission as the assistant surgeon of the 9th Vermont. Fairman started the next day for Newport Barracks to join his regiment, but was held up in New York City three weeks waiting for a steamer. He finally reported to Colonel Ripley on April 27, and was mustered into the regiment.[140]

Sergeant J. Webster Stebbins of Co. K was grousing about Chaplain Dickinson again on April 11. In a letter home he complained:

> I wish I might call in and hear a good sermon from some good preacher. Since Maj. Jarvis was killed we have had no religious meeting at all. Sunday night at dress parade the Chaplain sazes a fiew words about our duties as soldiers; reads a chapter in the bible and makes a prayer, but never preaches about Jesus and heaven and a judgement. Such a preacher is more than useless. The men do not respect him at all. They say "all he cares for is his pay." But I am not his judge.[141]

By the middle of April the weather had warmed up enough that snakes were emerging from their hibernation. Sergeant Stebbins noted in a letter home, "Snakes are beginning to show themselves. Captain Lewis has three rattle snake's skins. One is 4 feet 6 inches long. The others are a small kind. The darkies say they are very thick during the summer." A week later Pvt. James Martin in Co. I wrote his friend Harry in Vermont: "They have some of the darndest snakes in N.C. that you ever saw. I saw one the other day that was big as my leg. You had ought to see me run when I saw him it would have made you laugh." Captain Sherman was impressed with the quantity and variety of snakes in North Carolina: "Almost all kinds. Rattlesnakes, moccasins, King snakes, copperheads, Black, hoop, glass, green and alligators. Is that reptiles enough?"[142]

As the weather warmed up so did rebel activity. Late in March the Confederate War Department asked General Pickett to provide a plan of operations against some of the larger Federal outposts in North Carolina. Pickett's plan, submitted on April 6, was a detailed proposal for an attack on the garrison at Plymouth, some 60 miles as the crow flies, northeast of New Bern on the Roanoke River. The plan called for using Brigadier General James L. Kemper's and Brigadier General Matthew W. Ransom's brigades, and an unspecified third brigade, plus a sizable cavalry force and four light batteries. Within several days the War Department accepted the plan, but, as if to punish Pickett for his bungled attempt to capture New Bern in February, gave the mission to Brigadier General Hoke.[143]

Through some means, Colonel Ripley received intelligence that General Martin would move again against Newport Barracks, which information he passed on to Brigadier General Peck. The feared Confederate attack finally began on April 17, but not at Newport Barracks as Colonel Ripley feared. Hoke, with his brigade and those of Ransom and Kemper, attacked the Federal garrison at Plymouth. The garrison, under the command of Brigadier General Henry W. Wessells, was composed of four infantry regiments with some artillery and cavalry but was largely dependent on naval gunboats for support. The Confederate iron-clad *Albemarle* appeared on the Roanoke River on April 19 and sank the Union's *Smithfield*, disabled the *Miami*, and drove off the other Federal gunboats. Meanwhile, Hoke's units surrounded the town. At 10:00 A.M. on April 20, Wessells raised the white flag. The Federals lost 2,834 men, most of which were captured, and a large quantity of supplies. For this feat Hoke was promoted to major general. After the fall of Plymouth, the Federals evacuated their garrison at Washington, North Carolina, on April 27.[144]

Although Plymouth was 60 miles away, the rebel activity stirred up a lot of anxiety in the 9th Vermont's area. Captain Sherman noted:

A little excitement again in this district. It is currently reported that Plymouth, N.C. has been taken by the rebels and I fear it is true. You will know about it long before this reaches you. We expect an attack will be made upon New Berne and Gen. Peck is ready for it. Today all women etc. were ordered to leave the place. I am not sure either that *all* women are included but many went by here today enroute for Morehead City and Beaufort.[145]

On Saturday, April 23, official business as the provost marshal took Captain Sherman out to the house where Major Jarvis had died. Not one to pass up the opportunity to make time with a pretty girl, he noted in his diary, "Went to Sanders, where Maj. Jarvis died. Saw a pretty girl who agreed to give me her picture if she could get it taken."[146]

Brigadier General Innis N. Palmer replaced Brigadier General Peck as the commander of the District of North Carolina on April 24, and Colonel Ripley returned from Morehead City the next day, relieving Lieutenant Colonel Barney from command of the 9th Vermont.[147]

Palmer, a Regular Army officer from New York, graduated from the U.S. Military Academy in 1846. He served in the Mexican War, where he was wounded once and won two brevet promotions for bravery. He commanded the 1st U.S. Cavalry at the first battle of Bull Run and since that time he had commanded several other units.[148]

Captain Sam Kelley, with a detail of 20 men, was sent to Bogue Banks on Wednesday, April 27, to capture a group of Confederate soldiers. The rebels were using seines to gather fish for the Confederate commissary at Kinston. Acting on intelligence from local citizens, two 9th Vermont men had scouted the area several days before and confirmed the rebels were in fact there fishing. Kelley returned from his mission on the 29th with a rebel sergeant, three soldiers, a large seine, and two small boats. But before returning, Kelley had his prisoners continue fishing after they were captured and brought in about 400 pounds of nice sea trout which was distributed throughout the regiment.[149]

While Captain Kelley was out capturing the rebel fishermen, Colonel Ripley, with three companies of cavalry, went on a scouting expedition looking for rebels on April 28, but they did not find any. To cover Ripley an artillery piece was sent out from the barracks and Captain Edwin Kilbourne and his Co. G accompanied the artillery as support. Kilbourne wrote later:

Just after breakfast I was ordered to take my Co. and go to the front some 8 miles with a field piece (howitzer) and support the piece in case the enemy made an advance. I did so. Reached my destination about 11:30 A.M. Through [sic] out my pickets and videtts and waited there until after 8 in the evening at which time, acting upon orders, I fell back and arrived safely in camp about midnight. Marching through mud holes up to my knees and at one time came pretty near losing my boots in the mud![150]

On April 29, after Captain Kelley and his men got rid of their prisoners, they were sent back on another mission that evening. This time they were taken by boat to the White Oak River opposite Swansboro, where they debarked and lay in hiding. After dark they crossed the river and captured a rebel lieutenant, a sergeant and 17 enlisted men of the 7th North Carolina Cavalry with their horses, a 6-pounder howitzer and several sailboats. They also destroyed a large quantity of Confederate stores. Kelley returned the next day with his prisoners without the loss of a single man.[151]

Soon after the evacuation of the town of Washington by the Federals, Hoke decided to try to take New Bern again. By May 4, Hoke had driven in the Union pickets within eight miles of New Bern and had moved down the south side of the Trent River just below the town. The next day Hoke engaged the land and naval batteries at Newbern. During the artillery exchange, Brig. Gen. James Dearing's cavalry captured the blockhouse and fortifications at Brice's Creek that had earlier stopped General Barton. Just as Hoke was poised to assault the town he received an urgent message from his superior, General Pierre G.T. Beauregard, ordering him to cease operations immediately and return to Virginia with all possible haste. On May 4, Lee attacked Grant in the Wilderness and President Davis recalled as many units as possible to support Lee. Although greatly disappointed, Hoke did as ordered and was in Petersburg by May 10.[152]

The Vermonters at Newport Barracks could hear the cannon fire on the morning of Thursday, May 5, and were put on alert, but the enemy never appeared. The rebels did get close, though, as Captain Kilbourne related:

The enemy made their appearance at a point on the railroad about 20 miles above here on Thursday last and tore up the tracks and crossed over the Neuse River and planted batteries along the shore and opened fire upon our vessel in transit. The gunboats soon engaged the enemy and all day Thursday we heard very heavy firing and supposed it to be in from Newbern, believing the enemy to have surrounded and attacked that place with the intention of laying siege to it. But it proved to be the gunboats and shore batteries only and not any general attack upon Newbern. All the force at this place packed up their baggage and sent it down to Morehead City and prepared ourselves to give the enemy a warm reception. Fatigue parties were at work night and day throwing up an abatis in front of our rifle pits making the place as strong as we could. We were kept constantly on the qui vive expecting an attack every day and I assure you the excitement at times was not a little when we would hear that the enemy were 7,000 strong with 18 pieces of artillery and only 10 miles to the front and moving rapidly upon us. But it all blew over. We did not receive there [sic] compliments nor they ours.[153]

By May 8, the rebels were gone and Captain Kilbourne noted:

Yesterday the enemy having left, the [rail] road was repaired and a train came down and brought us a very large mail which had been accumulating for a number of days. They captured at Croatan (a few miles this side of Newbern) 1 Co. of the 5th R. Island Heavy Artillery, but not without, as I understand it, a determined resistance. This Dept. is about stripped of soldiers. For weeks they have been drawing away troops from Newbern and going to Va. to aid in the coming campaign up the peninsula. We were in hopes to go, but we have no orders yet.[154]

Unfortunately for the Vermonters, their time for leaving North Carolina had not come as Captain Kilbourne had hoped.

Thursday, May 5, while the rebels were attempting to take New Bern, Co. A, on picket at Canaday's Mills, had some excitement. Some Confederate soldiers, or bushwhackers, started taking potshots at the Green Mountain Boys on picket. During the brief engagement Pvt. Seymour Trowbridge, a 25-year-old farmer from Montgomery, was hit in the left hand. The bullet cut across the back of his hand, injuring the metacarpal bones and tendons. Trowbridge was taken to the U.S. Hospital in Morehead City and then evacuated to Governor Smith General Hospital in Brattleboro. After the wound healed the index, middle and ring fingers of his left hand were left in a permanent contraction. Without the use of his trigger finger, Trowbridge was no longer fit as an infantryman and was discharged from the army May 11, 1865, on a disability. In 1883 Trowbridge stated, "The hand has ever since been a source of suffering and in consequence it would have been better for me if it had been taken off when hurt." He continued to suffer with the hand until he died April 5, 1903.[155]

With the excitement of a rebel attack gone and camp life getting back to normal, one of the most unusual demotions that occurred in the 9th Vermont took place on Tuesday, May 10. Because of his lack of talent, or a lack of interest, 20-year-old Franklin L. Forbes, a farmer from Middlebury and a musician in Co. C, was reduced to the ranks "for inefficiency in his line of duty as a musician."[156]

Lee and Grant clashed in the Wilderness on May 5 and 6. In the two days of fighting Grant lost 17,000 killed and wounded. The First Vermont Brigade was in the thick of the fight and took fearful casualties, as Captain Kilbourne wrote to his wife:

Alas that Gen. Meade and Grant have "moved upon the enemy's works" across the Rapidan and fought 6 days, but with no immediate advantage. The contest still going on and the carnage awful! I see the Vt. Brigade was in it hard and done splendidly, but loosing [sic] severely. Oh the many stricken hearts at home the many widows and orphans. The suffering and sorrow it has carried to many hearts and homes in the green hills of Vt. Surely it is a great sacrifice, but not too dear for our country. No! Nothing can be too costly or precious to offer up upon her alter [sic] that she may live. My heart is sad today because of the suffering of my brothers in arms.[157]

One of the men to lay his life on the altar that Captain Kilbourne mentioned was Lieutenant Colonel Barney's brother, Colonel Elisha L. Barney, commander of the 6th Vermont Infantry. On the first day of the battle Colonel Barney was struck in the left temple by a partially spent minie ball. He survived the wound long enough to be evacuated to Fredericksburg, where he died on May 10. Valentine Barney learned of his brother's death on May 18 in a letter from his wife. The next day he wrote:

Yesterday your letter was received containing the sad intelligence of brother Elisha's death. I had seen in the New York Herald that he was wounded and had been in great anxiety for two days about him but I was not prepared to hear that it was a fatal wound and the news was almost crushing to me. I had not seen him for nearly two years, which made me feel coarse. This is the deepest affliction I have ever experienced.... I can hardly realize my *dear brother* is gone, but I know of course it must be so. I have read your letter over and over and oh! how my heart aches when I think I shall never see him never.... I thought yesterday I would immediately request a leave of absence and talked to Col. Ripley about it but he thinks that at the present time it would be useless to attempt to get away and fears that Gen. Butler might censure me for trying to get home when every thing looks so much like fighting.... A sadness pervades over the whole regiment and almost every one here has lost a brother or a dear friend.[158]

On May 21, Barney was still mourning the loss of his brother, as he expressed in another letter to his wife: "I can hardly look into the paper but I see something about my lost brother and on every such occasion the tears will start and as I peruse your letters they are wet with my tears."[159]

At about 8:00 P.M. on May 11,1864, Major Brooks had just gotten into bed and drifted off to sleep when he was awakened by the sound of a large body of men tramping around outside the tent that he shared with Lieutenant Colonel Barney. Then he heard someone halt the group and then there was a rapping on the pole in the front of his tent. Without getting out of bed he told the caller to come in. Private James C. Town, the regiment's wagoner, opened the tent flap and stepped in and asked for Lieutenant Colonel Barney. Brooks told Town that Lieutenant Colonel Barney was not there, but was probably at Colonel Ripley's quarters. Town backed out of the tent and turned to the group of 200 to 300 soldiers and said, "Boys, the colonel is not here, he is over to Colonel Ripley's quarters, shall we go?" The men shouted back, "Yes we'll go, we'll go!" Town gave the command to "march" and off they went into the darkness.[160]

Curiosity got the better of Major Brooks and he got up, threw on his uniform and followed the formation. When Brooks caught up with them the men were at the regiment's color line, near Colonel Ripley's quarters, where Town was trying to shape up the formation. Brooks asked Town what was going on, but Town was somewhat evasive at first. Finally, he told Brooks the men were going to see Lieutenant Colonel Barney about the man in Co. I that had been tied up for punishment for 12 hours for some misdeed and to tell Barney they wanted the man released. Brooks then ordered all the men back to their tents, which they did without much fuss. A short time later Town was arrested by the officer of the day and thrown into the guardhouse. Whether Town remained in the guardhouse or was released until his trial is unclear in his record, but he was not brought before a general court-martial until September 3, when he was charged with mutiny and conduct prejudicial to good order and military discipline. Town pleaded not guilty to both charges. The court agreed with him on the charge of mutiny, but found him guilty of the second charge. Although his court-martial in February 1863 was not mentioned in the transcript of his trial, he was sentenced to be confined at hard labor for the rest of his term of enlistment and to forfeit all his pay during his time of confinement, "excepting the just fees of the laundress." He was then incarcerated in the Carver Street jail in New Bern. For some unexplained reason a special order was cut by the War Department in Washington, D.C., on September 13 releasing Town and ordering him to return to his regiment.[161]

There is good reason to assume Town probably used his connections to get his release. On July 20, 1862, Colonel Stannard had assigned Town as a wagoner. He held that job until the regiment's capture at Harpers Ferry. At Camp Douglas he had been in charge of the regiment's adjutant's horse for a short time. Then on October 5 he was detailed to Brigadier General Tyler as an orderly and he traveled with the general to Cincinnati, Ohio, and Nashville, Tennessee. On April 7, 1863, Town was requested by then Brigadier General Stannard to serve as an enlisted aide, which post he held until April 2, 1864. During the jobs with these high ranking officers he must have curried some favors.[162]

By the end of May, Grant had fought the battles of the Wilderness and Spotsylvania and a number of smaller battles as he pushed on toward Richmond. On May 31, Lieutenant Colonel Barney seemed to be getting over the loss of his brother but had some doubts about the Federals' chance of success in the ongoing campaign, as he shared with his wife:

I hardly know what to think of our late battles and the future looks a little dark to me. I don't tell my thoughts and feelings to everybody, but to you I tell all. The great advantage which the rebels have over us is the better discipline of the troops but could we but have an army like the *Old Vermont Brigade* here, soon would rebeldom quake before it and unity be restored. I have and earnestly pray that Grant will give the rebellion its finishing blow this time and I don't doubt his ability as a general to do it. I don't think he would use as much strategy as some other Generals but work at and by dealing death blows to the Army of Lee with bullets and bayonets. But the great object can't be accomplished without the requisite numbers of men and I fear that he has not got them but I think the Lee numbers as many as he does.[163]

Toward the end of May, after being away from home for nearly two years, Captain Kilbourne poured out his feelings about the internal struggle he was having concerning the welfare of his family versus his duty to his country. To his wife he wrote:

The principle anxiety I've had since leaving home has been in relation to your sickness. At times since I've left you I have thought my duty lay in another direction. That it was my duty to remain in the army. When my family needed me at home or even my care and sympathy, if such aid would exercise a beneficial effect upon you, and in any degree assist in restoring you to health and strength again. But such thoughts were only momentary with me. Tis true, family ties are endearing and sacred. But it's a question whether a man is more bound to his family, to his wife and children, under any circumstances (either in sickness or in health) than to *his country* when that country in imperiled and in danger of being overthrown by a traitorous foe. My country is worth more to me than my interests at home. Worth more to succeeding than my even *my family*, or a dozen families! This is the *truth* in the *abstract*, but then "abstract truth" seldom governs our actions much in this world. The common and ruling instincts of our natures teach us to promise and provide for the welfare of our families to the sacrifice of all other considerations, yet we are so short sighted as to believe that we are doing so. When even the very foundation and ground work of our happiness, of the peace and quiet of our families is rested in the permanency of the government, of its free and glorious institutions being sacred to us, and we lend no helping hand to sustain and perpetuate such privileges and blessings (when in danger of being wrested from us), but sit quietly at *home* around our family hearth stones and talk of the duties we owe *first* to our wife and children, placing their present comfort and happiness infinitely above and paramount to the future good of the same and of the generations which are to follow. Alas! Our "*selfishness*" is a stronger motive power impelling us to do good or evil as best suits our convenience than any other power of the human mind yet developed. Do you not think so? Would it not be supreme selfishness in me to leave the army at such a time as this, when our government needs the help of every man that it can muster, upon the plea that my wife was sick and I ought to go home! My country needs me, needs every man. Is my *wife* more than *my country*? What say you? In my candid moments I've but one answer to that, and although I love my wife and child above measure, and my happiness is based upon them, yet I deem it wisdom to forgo present pleasure that a far higher and noble object may be attained, that of the preservation of my government, and with it the blessings which will naturally come from it to make happy my family and myself during the remainder of our lives.[164]

Brigadier General Palmer gave Colonel Jourdan the mission, on June 18, to assemble a force and destroy the railroad bridge that crossed the Cape Fear River near Wilmington. Five companies of the 9th Vermont were among the units selected to participate in the raid. Colonel Ripley, who had returned to the regiment on June 11, had three days' rations issued and at 5:00 P.M. Sunday, June 19, the Vermonters left on a train heading to New Bern. On a train behind them were the 158th New York Infantry, 23rd New York Cavalry Battalion, 12th New York Cavalry, and two howitzers. The trains stopped three or four miles south of New Bern at about 10:30 P.M. and the troops were unloaded. Here the command picked up four more artillery pieces and a wagon train. Once assembled, the column started for Evan's Mills arriving there around midnight where it rested for a few hours.[165]

The men ate breakfast early on Monday morning and before daylight were on the march again, arriving at Pollocksville at noon. Here they made coffee and ate their lunch. It was an extremely hot day so the march was not resumed until 4:00 P.M. The command reached Young's Cross Roads about 10:00 P.M. that night where they stopped in an open field, stacked arms and slept for two hours. Companies E, F and K of the 9th Vermont were loaded into wagons so they could keep up with the cavalry and left. The rest of the troops had to march. Leaving the 158th New York Infantry behind to build a bridge across the White Oak River, the column was off again at 3:00 A.M. Just after daybreak Jourdan and his men came to where the cavalry had a brush with rebel cavalry. Jourdan's cavalry had captured two rebels and killed another, but the rest of the gray-backs had escaped. The column pressed on to a crossroads two miles past Jacksonville, where they stopped to rest. According to Captain Kilbourne the rest was greatly needed:

That day was a hard march for us for we went so fast and the sun poured down so hot that sometimes it seemed as if we should melt and run into the road one mass of water, but the boys stood it first rate, not one giving out. In the late afternoon the troops were marched back to Jacksonville where they worked all night, tearing down an old barn and a blacksmith shop to repair the bridge across New [Neuse] River. Corporal Wandell remembered, "Jacksonville is a very pretty village on the banks of New [Neuse] river. There is a Courthouse, Jail, a hotel and five or six stores.[166]

While the other Vermonters were destroying the buildings to repair the bridge, Companies A and G was sent out on picket duty, as Captain Kilbourne explained:

Immediately after dinner my co. was called for with Co. A to go on picket. So I went on to the road leading to Swansboro and threw out my pickets almost like skirmishers, owing to the fact that the woods all around were full of bushwhackers and had already shot at 2 of our cavalry and wounding one in the leg. About an hour after posting my men and giving them thorough instructions what to do in any and all cases, bang went a gun right in the direction of a meeting house in the woods when I had just placed the pickets. Thinking the enemy would be likely to come up there and try to pick off our men if possible I immediately sent down Lt. Whitcher [John Witcher from Ryegate] and three men to find out what the firing meant and found that my man Private Stearns [Warren E. Stearns of Braintree] had seen two men crawling up and after halting them and not obeying him he fired upon them, but did not hit them as they were running for dear life at the time he fired. He changed position a little and waited for the enemy to come up again. At this time I sent down word to him not to halt any body with arms in their hands again if he was satisfied they were rebels or bushwhackers. Some 40 minutes after, bang went another gun in the same direction and this time to some effect for Mr. Grayback laid down his arms and came up and surrendered himself. He had on a rebel suit and was armed with a carbine. I immediately examined his piece to see if it had been fired that day and found it had not. So sent him to Hd. Qrts. Very soon there was a party of cavalrymen came back and we went down into the woods where he was shot at and beyond and found three nice horses and equipment, bridles, saddles and all. So Co. G captured so much that day. We were relieved at night and during that night the woods rung with the crack of guns. Bushwhacking back and forth. The enemy were in some force at Jacksonville, but hearing of our approach they fell back just as our cavalry charged through the town and all we captured there was a few stragglers. Destroyed some property belonging to the C.S.A. government and took a great many negroes back with us. They flocked to us all along the route and by the time we got in to our camp again we had a string of them, old, young and some almost white. There was one very pretty Creole. One white family joined us and came within our lines.[167]

When the five companies of the 9th Vermont left with Colonel Jourdan, Captain Kelley with about 100 Vermonters went to Morehead City, where they left on a steamer for Snead's Ferry. Kelley and his men landed down the coast toward Wilmington, at the mouth of the Neuse River, and seized a rebel picket post. Then the Green Mountain Boys went four miles up the river up to Snead's Ferry where they captured another rebel outpost. In all, Kelley captured one officer and fifteen men along with several horses, mules, and weapons. Captain Kelley found himself deep in enemy territory holding the back door through which the rebels were expected to retreat as Colonel Jourdan's force pushed them. Kelley had his men entrench and waited in ambush for any retreating rebels.

The 9th Vermont in marching formation in North Carolina (*Vermont General*).

On June 21, the 12th New York Cavalry was ordered to Snead's Ferry to see if Captain Kelley had been successful. The cavalrymen arrived just at dark. Not knowing the cavalry was coming, Kelley and his men thought the New Yorkers were rebels and fired on them. Without hesitation the cavalry returned fire. Colonel James W. Savage, commander of the 12th New York Cavalry, drew his revolver and fired at Kelley but missed.[168]

Seeing Savage fire at his commander, Corporal David Buffum of Co. B, from Pawlet, shot Colonel Savage's horse with his musket. He then drew a revolver, which he had taken from a rebel, and was about to shoot the colonel when another officer on horse came dashing forward toward him and Buffum shot his horse. He then shot another officer's horse and then again shot at Colonel Savage, but fortunately missed him. The colonel shot at Corporal Buffum several times, but missed him also. The

Colonel James W. Savage, commander of the 12th New York Cavalry, who was nearly shot by Corporal David Buffam, Co. B, 9th Vermont (U.S. Army Military History Institute).

firing went on for several minutes until one of the cavalry officers' wounded horses fell on him and for some reason he cried out who he was. It was then that the mistake was discovered by both sides and a cease-fire was called. Unfortunately, the cavalry had one sergeant and several horses killed and one man and six horses wounded.[169]

On June 21, Colonel Jourdan learned that the Confederates had found out about his expedition and were gathering forces to stop him. Jourdan decided he did not have enough troops to successfully confront the enemy and decided to return to Morehead City. The Federals were up early on Wednesday, June 22, and by daybreak were on the march north. Because of the heat they halted at noon and camped. The next day at sundown they reached the White Oak River, where they were reunited with the 158th New York. The New Yorkers had been left behind several days before to bridge the river, which saved the Vermonters at least nine miles of hard marching. After crossing the White Oak they marched until dark, when they were allowed to stop and cook supper. After supper they marched until midnight and camped at Pelletier's Mills.[170]

Jourdan had the men up early on Friday, June 24, and by noon had reached the Sanders house, where Major Jarvis had died. Here they were met by the sutler with two wagonloads of goodies. The men were allowed to rest and eat at the Sanders house until 4:00 P.M. before resuming the march. Needless to say, everyone were exhausted and out of sorts. As Corporal John Shono of Co. D was getting his squad into formation one of his men, Pvt. George Strong, a 31-year-old farmer from Cavendish, called Shono a "damned fool." Strong's little outburst got him a regimental court-martial a few days later and a $10.00 fine.[171]

The Vermonters reached Newport Barracks at 10:30 that night. They had marched over 100 miles in five days and everyone was tired and hungry. Captain Kilbourne remembered, "My feet for the last two days of the march were one complete blister and every step I took felt like stepping on hot coals of fire."[172]

Although most of the Green Mountain Boys were stiff and sore when they got up on Saturday, June 25, it turned out to be a great day. The paymaster arrived with back pay for the months of January, February and March. Unfortunately, the paymaster did not have enough money and most of the officers went without their back pay, as Lieutenant Colonel Barney complained to his wife: "The paymaster came and paid off the enlisted men of the Regt. last week but on account of shortness of funds did not pay many of the officers so I have now six months pay due (about $1000)."[173]

After three weeks of drill and easy duty in the pleasant camp at Newport Barracks, companies A, F, H and K, under the command of Major Brooks, were ordered to New Bern on July 11 to replace troops whose term of service had expired. Captain Sherman wrote, "A Battalion of four companies under Maj. Brooks are here at New Berne & expect to do duty in and about the city. We have an excellent place. Barracks just on the banks of the Neuse river & a pleasant lookout. If we remain here we shall do well." Sergeant Wandell remembered the move fondly: "We did not leave till seven O'clock this morning. We went to Newbern and went into good barracks close to the river near where the remains of the gunboat *Underwriter* lies. We had to go to work and build bunks. Went in swimming in the Neuse river; the water is quite fresh."[174]

Colonel Ripley was sent to Morehead City on July 14, for court-martial duty. As he wrote his mother he looked forward to the duty:

> I expect to be at Morehead City most of the time for sometime to come, as they have got a large General Court Martial ready to announce, and they say I am on as President.
> I don't object, as Mrs. Palmer is staying at Morehead now, and we have got to be excellent friends, and she is very beautiful, and very cultivated and charming, and I have been starving for ladies society to relieve the irksomeness of this life here.[175]

On July 20, Ripley wrote his mother again of his keeping company with Brig. Gen. Palmer's wife:

I have a carriage and two horses here, and find long rides every day in a comfortable shady top buggy with Mrs. Palmer a decided improvement on horseback riding in the hot sun at Newport. Sometimes we go over to the beach in sailboats, and enjoy sea bathing.[176]

How General Palmer felt about the young colonel squiring his wife around is not recorded, but apparently the general trusted Ripley and the two men remained good friends. Ripley wrote his brother on July 28:

Do send the nicest shirts, plain bosoms, you can find. Real elegant ones, Also the other things. I want, also, a couple of cases of the best whiskey you can get — one a Claret, a half dozen each of nice Irish or Scotch Whiskey and of Brandy, 2 cases of the best Champagne. I am much at General Palmer's, and if I keep house will have to entertain him and family, and I want to make a fair reputation in this direction.

Unfortunately, Edward Ripley would not receive the liquor he wanted until after the regiment left North Carolina.[177]

By July 26, the rest of the regiment was in New Bern and were stationed at various outposts within a 10 mile radius of the town. Colonel Ripley's headquarters was located in a beautiful spot on the south side of the Trent River, near Fort Spinola. Companies D and K were posted at Red House, Companies I and E at Rocky Run, Company A at Evans's Mill on Brice's Creek, Company H at Beechwood on the railroad, Company K on the Trent River near Fort Gaston, Company F in Fort Spinola and companies B and C at headquarters. On arrival at New Bern Dr. Carpenter was put in charge of the hospital there.[178]

Before the remainder of the regiment moved to New Bern, Lieutenant Colonel Barney had the regiment's graveyard spruced up:

We are fixing up a burying yard fence and putting up headboards for all our men who are buried here and by the labors of the chaplain we will have a very nice thing of it. The fence is made of cedar also the headboards which are nicely lettered so they will last for a number of years and when the war ends the friends can come and find them again.[179]

While on picket duty at Rocky Run, Benjamin C. Stone, a 32-year-old farmer from Strafford in Co. I, was shot in the left hand on August 1. The records differ as to how he was wounded. Some indicate it was an accident, but his discharge paper states he was shot by the enemy. Regardless of how it happened, Stone was badly injured. He was taken to the hospital in New Bern, where his middle finger was amputated. After the wound healed his ring and little fingers were left permanently contracted. From New Bern Stone was evacuated to the hospital at Fort Monroe, Virginia. After languishing there several months he wrote the secretary of war on December 8 requesting the Secretary's help in getting a discharge from the hospital. By January 3, 1865, Stone had not received a reply and he wrote the secretary the following letter:

I have the honor of addressing these few lines in regard to myself for a discharge, having lost the middle finger of my left hand at Newbern on the first day of August, 1864, and my hand in consequence being shriveled up so as to be perfectly useless, and having been shifted about from one hospital to another and getting neither satisfaction as to a furlough or discharge the doctor pronouncing me unfit for duty. I now take the liberty of writing you these few lines hoping that your honor will interest yourself in my behalf. I have written to your honor before on the 8th of December but for various reasons I have good cause to suspect that my letter was intercepted and fell into the hands of the doctor in charge here. Therefore I shall send this one by way of home to insure its receipt by your honor. I shall await your proceedings in my behalf hoping it will meet with your honor's approval. I should be happy to receive a few lines from your honor in regard to it.

Needless to say, the secretary of war did not intercede in Stone's case, and although Stone was finally transferred to the Governor Smith General Hospital in Brattleboro, he was not discharged until June 27, 1865.[180]

On Friday, August 12, a Massachusetts recruiting officer brought a North Carolina man

The Dixon-Stevenson house in New Bern, North Carolina, used as the 9th Vermont Hospital in 1864. The house was built by George W. Dixon in the 1830s (*Vermont General*).

named Michael Willisford, who wanted to enlist in the 9th Vermont, to Colonel Ripley's headquarters. The man said he was from Duplin County, North Carolina, and had been in the Confederate army but had come through Federal lines just that morning and taken the oath of allegiance to the United States. Whether he had been discharged from the army or was a deserter was not made clear. At first, Ripley denied the man's request, but gave in after the man begged him to be allowed to enlist. Ripley assigned him to Co. A. After completing the necessary paperwork Willisford was sent out to Co. A's picket post at Evan's Mill to join the company.[181]

The next morning Willisford was back at Ripley's headquarters with a note from Co. A's commander, Captain Linus Sherman, stating the men of the company did not want to serve with Willisford because he was a Negro. It seems that when the fortifications at Newport Barracks were being built, Willisford was one of the Negroes hired to help in the construction. Because the men of the 9th Vermont had been so good to him when he was working on the fortifications he wanted to join the regiment and indicated on his enlistment papers that he was of Portuguese descent. After doing a little investigative work, Ripley found an affidavit from a trial in which Willisford had been involved in the New Bern provost marshal's office that proved Willisford was, in fact, a Negro. Colonel Ripley had Willisford taken to the 132nd New York Infantry in the New Bern area so he could enlist in that unit. That was the end of that, or so Ripley thought.[182]

On Saturday morning, August 13, the 9th Vermont was up at 4:30 A.M. A little after 5 o'clock the men were ordered to fall in and were marched out of camp to witness the execution of Pvt. Thomas G. Baker of Co. F, 26th New York Infantry. Captain Kilbourne noted:

The poor fellow was a regular "bounty jumper" having enlisted 6 times and deserted every time and for the avowed purpose of making all the money he could. The fifth time upon being arrested he threatened and attempted to take the life of the officers making the arrest and said he would not have been caught then if it had not been for his wife and that if he got freed this time he would kill her. He was not far from 25 years of age I should judge.[183]

The Green Mountain Boys were marched about a quarter of a mile from their camp to the spot where the execution was to take place. There, along with a number of other units, they were formed into a hollow square. At 6:30 the procession marched in. Leading was the provost marshal followed by a band playing a funeral dirge. Behind the band came four men carrying a wooden coffin on their shoulders. Then came Private Baker accompanied by a chaplain, followed by a 10-man firing squad carrying loaded muskets with fixed bayonets. According to one of the Vermonters, Baker "looked very pale but walked with a firm step, his hands tied in front, he did not appear to realize his awful situation." Last in the column was a platoon of soldiers from the 15th Connecticut Infantry forming the provost guard. The prisoner was marched around the inside the hollow square so every man could see him and stopped near his newly dug grave. Then the coffin was placed on the ground about 10 feet in front of the grave. The chaplain read a portion of scripture and said a prayer. After that the chaplain and the provost marshal shook hands with Baker and bade him good-bye. Next, one of the guards tied a white handkerchief over Baker's eyes and seated him on the foot of his coffin facing the firing squad.[184]

The firing squad was marched forward to within 20 feet of Baker and halted. The provost marshal gave the order to six of the men in the firing squad — "Ready!" — and the men cocked their loaded muskets. Then he shouted, "Aim!" "Fire!" The men fired and six minie balls went through Baker, mostly in the center of his body. One passed through his neck and the others his stomach and lungs. He fell like a log on his coffin and within a minute or so was dead. After Dr. Carpenter pronounced Baker dead, the troops were marched past the corpse and then back to their camps. Several fainted at the sight of the bloody body as they filed past, as did two of the men who shot him.[185]

Apparently witnessing the scene had the desired effect. One Vermonter wrote later:

This, though sad in the extreme, is the manner prescribed for the punishment of deserters. Let those who have sneakingly deserted their brothers in arms ponder over the solemnity of such a scene! If the insane idea of deserting ever entered the head of one, after witnessing the terrible reality of an execution, it must vanish forever and forever! God grant it may never be the doom of a Vermonter![186]

As though Baker's execution was not enough, six more men were executed the next day across the river at Fort Totten. This time, though, the 9th Vermont did not have to witness the sight. Out of curiosity several of the 9th Vermont's officers did. The ceremony was carried out exactly like the day before until the order "Fire!" was issued. Lieutenant Colonel Barney described the grizzly scene that happened next: "Three of them were not killed dead so they were shot by one man each through the head."[187]

Captain Edwin Kilbourne, who had not witnessed the execution, wrote:

This morning six more were executed for the same offense within a mile of our camp. But our Regt were not obliged to be present and so but very few from this side of the river witnessed it. But we could hear the volleys of musketry from our camp. I have preferred charges and specifications of Clark J. Beede a private in my Co. for desertion and he is to be tried I suppose before long. But I hardly think the court will sentence him to be shot. But will punish him probably severely in some manner and make him serve out the time he lost by deserting, which would be very just. [About the execution the day before] I cannot put it out of my mind. The whole thing being so very solemn and unlike any thing I ever saw before. Could witness the killing of a thousand men in battle better than such a scene as this.[188]

The man Captain Kilbourne referred to was Pvt. Clark E. Beede of Co. G, who had deserted from Camp Douglas February 9, 1863, and gone home. After he got home Beede wrote to his commanding officer as to his whereabouts, but Capt. William J. Henderson had resigned. Soon afterward Beede became ill and reported by letter to the adjutant general of Vermont that he was at home sick, to which he got a reply on or about April 20, 1863. He stayed home until he was "called for to come back." He reported to the enrollment station in Vermont, where he was given a letter by the 9th Vermont's former adjutant, John C. Stearns, who had resigned and was now working in the Vermont adjutant general's office. Stearns attested to Beede's good character prior to his deserting and mentioned that Beede had a wife and five children who were very poor. In addition, Stearns asked that leniency be considered "for his family's sake" when Beede was court-martialed. Beede returned to the regiment with the large group of recruits arriving at Newport Barracks on January 27, 1864. He was promptly arrested and put in the guardhouse. On February 2, when Newport Barracks was overrun by Confederate forces, Beede and the other prisoners were let out of the guardhouse and told they were on their own. Not being familiar with the area, Beede and nine recruits hid in the woods until the Confederates left and then made their way to Beaufort where he reported to the commander of the 2nd Massachusetts Heavy Artillery. The next morning Beede was put on a boat and sent to join his regiment. At Morehead City he was given a musket and rejoined his company and performed his normal duties until arrested again on June 26 for his original charge of desertion. He was brought before a court-martial August 15 and found guilty of desertion. The court apparently believed his story and was lenient in his sentencing. Instead of being executed, his only punishment was forfeiture of pay for the time he was absent and he had to make up the time away after his normal term of enlistment.[189]

While making his rounds of the picket line near his headquarters on August 20, Colonel Ripley saw in the distance one of the pickets, lying on the ground. The man he spotted was Corp. Spencer Green of Co. B, a 42-year-old lawyer from Danby. Green had taken off his equipments to take a nap and had allowed one of his men to do the same. On hearing Ripley approach, Green tried to crawl into the bushes on his hands and knees, but Ripley had already identified him. For this act Green was reduced to the ranks three days later. Ripley was so incensed over this breach of discipline that he directed the order reducing Green to be read to each company at three successive evening dress parades so it would be understood that another offense of this kind would be punished to the full extent of military law.[190]

The dissatisfaction with Chaplain Dickinson never seemed to go away. Captain Edwin Kilbourne complained on August 24, "Last Sabbath evening I went over to the city in a sailboat with Captain Kelley, Lieutenant Peck and others to hear our chaplain preach, but he was not very interesting. In fact, never is!" Although the chaplain apparently was always boring, he probably did not have his mind on business the evening Captain Kilbourne complained about. Two days later he got approval for a 20 day leave to return home to Vermont.[191]

The 9th Vermont got an infusion of badly needed recruits on August 25. Captain Kilbourne commented, "On Thursday we received an accession of 27 to our Regt. New recruits from the So. portion of the state. Good, stout looking boys."[192]

There was a bit of excitement in the New Bern area on Monday, August 28, when a detachment of about 60 rebels tore out a section of railroad track in hopes of wrecking a train. Captain Edwin Kilbourne related the incident in a letter home:

The other day (Monday) the train was thrown off the track on its way from Morehead to this place by the rebels. They came upon the road early in the morning and tore up the track some little distance, causing a complete smash of the train. But the raiding party being small they immediately decamped and left for points unknown. My Co. was ordered out to go to the relief of the train as we understood the rebels had killed and wounded quite a number. I went down with the Co. about 15 miles on the road and found that the gray backs had all left but not until they had shot 2 negroes, killing one and wounding the other. They rifled through the pockets of the dead negro taking what little change he happened to have and dragged him out into the bushes and left him to his sad fate. Upon reaching the spot, I threw out my Co. as skirmishers and scoured the whole country about for miles on either side of the track. Staid there all night in hopes of finding some trace of them, but did not and consequently returned to camp the next morning.[193]

Company H was doing picket duty on the same railroad where the raid took place and was ordered to go after the rebels, as Horace described in one of his letters to the *Lamoille Newsdealer*:

Co. H was up and after them soon as the news arrived, but the weather being quite warm by the time we had marched four miles, some of them "played out." All who could march were deployed as skirmishers and the country was all hunted over for miles around. At length we found their trail which we followed for miles, coming in sight of them once. We learned where they landed, went and found their boat which was a fine yawl capable of carrying thirty men; probably once it was a boat belonging to some vessel.

It being near night, and all tired, hungry and wet, fourteen of us jumped on board and with a few poles we started. It was three or four miles to the river down through a narrow creek; but we worked along splendidly, until we met a small schooner going up the creek after turpentine. We informed the master of the trouble, when he immediately "about ship," took us in "tow," headed toward new Berne and when we got nearly opposite our camp we managed to get on shore and into camp, where we arrived at 10 o'clock P.M.[194]

Lieutenant Colonel Barney had the distasteful task of holding regimental court-martials on August 29 for several men who had committed various breaches of military discipline. One of the surviving records from that session is of Sgt. Dennis Cornin, a 29-year-old Irish immigrant from Alburgh, Vermont, in Co. A. Cornin had deserted the regiment at Camp Douglas December 3, 1862, and returned February 7, 1863. He was apparently one of the many who did not receive punishment during that troubling time. This time, however, was a different story. It seems Sergeant Cornin had a pass to visit New Bern on August 5. Cornin was charged with drunkenness and conduct prejudicial to good order and military discipline. One of Company A's musicians, George W. Spicer, related to the court what happened:

I saw him first at New Bern and he went down to the cars with me to Croatan and by the time we got there he was pretty drunk and kept drinking so that before we got to Evan's Mills he was unable to walk and I left him there and went on alone and got to camp about dark.

When asked if Cornin required assistance to get to camp, Spicer replied, "Yes sir, he was taken up on a hand car by some darkies."

Sergeant Cornin was found guilty of both charges and sentenced to be reduced to the ranks. Whether or not he was reduced does not appear in his compiled service record. He was, however, promoted to First Sergeant of Co. A on January 1, 1865.[195]

On August 31, Colonel Ripley finally received orders to move to Petersburg, Virginia. There they would be part of the XVIII Corps in the Army of the James under the command of Maj. Gen. Benjamin F. Butler. The move would take place as soon as the Vermonters could be replaced by another regiment.[196]

While the regiment was waiting for a ship to take them to Virginia, Pvt. John Kinsley, a 34-year-old farmer from Monkton in Co. C, committed suicide in the regimental hospital on the evening of September 8. He had done hardly any duty since joining the regiment because of an ailment which Colonel Ripley believed Kinsley had prior to enlisting and joined only to get his bounty and a disability discharge. Ripley was in the process of having Kinsley discharged for defrauding the government.[197]

The 9th Vermont was finally relieved by the 23rd and 25th Massachusetts Infantry regiments on September 11. The next day the Vermont camp was a beehive of activity, with the men marking and packing personal and unit equipment and loading it aboard the waiting ships. Ripley had his regiment up early on Tuesday, September 13. The men quickly had their breakfast and then marched aboard the vessels. Six companies of the regiment left in the late morning on the steamer *Escort* and the other four left later in the afternoon on the steamer *Winnona*.[198]

6

THE BATTLE OF FORT HARRISON

On April 2, 1864, Lt. Gen. Ulysses S. Grant ordered Maj. Gen Benjamin F. Butler, commander of the Department of Virginia and North Carolina, to organize his department as a field army to cooperate with Maj. Gen. George G. Meade's Army of the Potomac in an attack on Richmond. With that order, the Army of the James was born. The Army of the James consisted of the X and XVIII Corps and a cavalry division. Grant instructed Butler to seize City Point, move his command to the south side of the James River and then make a push to take Richmond.[1]

Benjamin Franklin Butler was born in Deerfield, New Hampshire, on November 5, 1818. He graduated from Maine's Colby College in 1838, was admitted to the Massachusetts bar in 1840 and became a highly successful criminal lawyer. He was elected to the Massachusetts House of Representatives in 1853 and the state senate in 1859. In 1860 Butler was a delegate at the Democratic convention in Charleston, South Carolina, and voted to nominate Jefferson Davis for U.S. president. Later he backed the extreme States' Rights candidate John C. Breckinridge, but when the southern states started to secede from the Union Butler became a War Democrat.[2]

At the outbreak of the Civil War, Butler was a brigadier general in the Massachusetts militia and was assigned as the commander of the District of Annapolis, Maryland, on April 27, 1861. Because the citizens of Baltimore attacked the 6th Massachusetts Infantry Regiment while it was en route to Washington, Butler occupied the city with Federal troops. Lincoln rewarded the Democrat by appointing him as the first major general of volunteers on May 16. Two weeks later he was assigned as the commander of Fort Monroe in Hampton, Virginia. Unfortunately, he was soundly defeated in the Civil War's first major land battle at Big Bethel, Virginia, June 10, 1861. As the commander of Fort Monroe, he was the first person to apply the term "contraband of war" to slaves who fled into the Union lines and, therefore, refused to return them to their former owners. Butler saved his military reputation with the successful amphibious assault of Forts Hatteras and Clark at Hatteras Inlet, North Carolina, 28–29 August 1861.[3]

On May 1, 1862, Butler became the military administrator of New Orleans, Louisiana, after its capture by the U.S. Navy. In this capacity he earned two onerous nicknames that would plague him the rest of his life. There were false stories of his confiscating silver from churches and homes in the city for which he was dubbed "Spoons Butler." In his capacity as the city's administrator, he had a New Orleans man hanged for tearing down an American flag. To add insult to injury, he issued his infamous "Women Order" that proclaimed that any woman insulting U.S. military personnel would be "regarded and held liable to be treated as a woman of the town plying her trade." These two acts, as well as others, earned him the nickname "Beast Butler" and made him one of the most hated men in the South. Although Butler had alienated the Southerners, he endeared himself to the northern abolitionists by creating Negro regiments in and around New Orleans. He was recalled from his post in New Orleans on December 16, 1862. Because Butler was so politically influential, President Lincoln could not dismiss him from the service, so he side tracked him until late 1863 when he was finally given command of the Department of Virginia and North Carolina headquartered at Fort Monroe.[4]

The Army of the Potomac moved south on May 4, 1864, and collided with Lee's army in the Wilderness the next day. In concert with the Army of the Potomac, Butler's X and XVIII Corps embarked on May 4 and sailed up the James River. By May 6, the two corps had disembarked and established a defensive line across the narrow neck of Bermuda Hundred. The line, about three miles long, was quickly entrenched.[5]

Bermuda Hundred is a peninsula formed by the James and Appomattox rivers. A hundred was a territorial division adopted in England by the Normans as an administrative district. In Virginia, hundreds were individual entities that were each led by a "governor." Between 1613 and 1619, settlers financed a huge tract of land from the city of Henricus south of the mouth of the Appomattox River. This parcel was named Bermuda Hundred by Governor Sir Thomas Gates to commemorate the time he had spent shipwrecked in Bermuda while en route to Virginia.[6]

Also on May 6, Butler's cavalry division departed Portsmouth on an expedition to cut the Petersburg and Weldon Railroad at Stony Creek, Rowanty Creek and the Nottoway River. After accomplishing its mission, which seriously hindered the transport of Confederate troops, the cavalry arrived at City Point on May 10.[7]

After several days of inactivity, Butler sent the majority of his two corps up the James River against the Confederate stronghold at Drewry's Bluff on May 12 and by the next day the rebels had been driven from their outer works into their main defensive line. Butler's main attack against Drewry's Bluff commenced on May 16 but ended in failure and the Army of the James returned to the safety of the Bermuda Hundred line. While Butler was trying to take Drewry's Bluff, his cavalry made another raid southwest of Petersburg, destroying stores, tracks and installations on the Richmond and Danville Railroad before returning to City Point on May 17.[8]

Butler made two additional attempts to take Petersburg in June. On June 9 he sent the X Corps to capture Petersburg, but the attack never materialized and the corps returned the same day. While Butler was bottled up at Bermuda Hundred, the Army of the Potomac was slowly closing in on Richmond, but not without horrendous losses. Since May 5, Grant had fought the battles of the Wilderness, Spotsylvania, and Cold Harbor, losing nearly 50,000 killed and wounded. Butler's XVIII Corps and portions of the X Corps, under the command of Maj. Gen. William F. Smith, had been detached from their position of safety at Bermuda Hundred, sent to join the Army of the Potomac and participated in the battle at Cold Harbor on June 1–3. On June 12 Grant sidestepped Lee and headed for the James River with Petersburg as his objective. Smith's corps was sent ahead by vessel, arriving at Bermuda Hundred on June 14. The XVIII Corps, along with Butler's cavalry division crossed the Appomattox the next day to capture Petersburg. Smith was to be supported by the II Corps of the Army of the Potomac, the first unit to cross the James River. Smith, however, was slow to move and then was deceived by the rebel defenders into thinking he was outnumbered. Even with the arrival of the II and V corps, Smith's reticence allowed Lee to rush troops south and save Petersburg. In light of this failure, Grant decided to lay siege to the town.[9]

After his failed attempts to take Petersburg and Richmond, Butler decided to busy himself with the construction of a canal. About two miles northeast of Bermuda Hundred was a place in the James River that formed an oxbow known as Trent's Reach. Union gunboats could not navigate past Trent's Reach because of a heavily fortified Confederate battery named Battery Dantzler on the south side of the river. The narrowest neck of the oxbow was 175 yards wide and called Dutch Gap after a Dutch engineer who had tried to construct a canal there a number of years before. Butler reasoned that if he could cut a canal across Dutch Gap, U.S. Navy gunboats could safely bypass Battery Dantzler and continue on upriver toward Richmond. Construction began on August 10. The Confederates were soon pounding Dutch Gap with artillery and mortars, making the labor dangerous. Most of the digging was performed by black troops and was kept up through fall and into winter.[10]

Lee and Grant had been lengthening their lines all summer and by fall they extended for more than 35 miles. The Confederate lines began north of the James River, ringed Richmond and then curved and twisted for almost eight miles to the north bank of the James River below the city. Just before the line reached the James River below Richmond, an offshoot ran south between the Osborne and New Market roads to Fort Gilmer, then curved down to the northern face of an entrenched camp on Chaffin's Bluff. The camp anchored the line as well as covered the water batteries on the bluff above the James River.[11]

On the south side of the James River was a four-mile stretch where Confederate artillery at Drury's Bluff barred the river approach to Richmond. Then, at the end of this stretch, the trenches, known as the Howlett Line, began and ran for five miles across Bermuda Hundred to the Appomattox River. At Petersburg they followed the battle lines that had been fixed the previous June, and led south and west almost to Hatcher's Run. The Confederate works were virtually impregnable from a frontal assault. They consisted of an outer line of earthworks connected by breastworks backed with logs with deep ditches in front. The front of the works was covered with lines of abatis and other obstructions. Forts for artillery were built at frequent intervals to sweep the approaches with a crossfire and in front were rifle pits to protect the pickets.[12]

At the beginning of September 1864, the Army of the James was organized as follows:

X Corps, Maj. Gen. David B. Birney:
1st Division, Maj. Gen. Alfred H. Terry
2nd Division, Brig. Gen. Robert S. Foster
3rd Division, Brig. Gen. William Birney

XVIII Corps, Maj. Gen. Edward O.C. Ord:
1st Division, Brig. Gen. George J. Stannard
2nd Division, Brig. Gen. Adelbert Ames (Brig. Gen. Charles H. Heckman would assume command September 19 while Ames was on leave)
3rd Division, Brig. Gen. Charles J. Paine

Cavalry Division, Brig. Gen. August V. Kautz.[13]

On September 16, Confederate scouts reported 2,500 head of Federal cattle in a guarded camp at Coggin's Point on the south side of the James River opposite Harrison's Landing. Confederate Maj. Gen. Wade Hampton quickly moved out to capture them. The 13th Pennsylvania Cavalry and the 1st District of Columbia Cavalry attempted to stop the rebels at Sycamore Church but were brushed aside. One rebel cavalry regiment held off the Federals while the others set the cattle free and herded them back to Confederate lines. The Federals sustained 400 casualties in the raid while the Confederates lost only 50.[14] Such was the situation around Petersburg prior to the arrival of the 9th Vermont.

The Vermonters experienced smooth passage from North Carolina to Virginia. Unbeknownst to them as they headed north, they passed a steamer heading to North Carolina with 170 recruits from Vermont for the regiment. After arrival in North Carolina, the new recruits were put aboard another vessel heading to Virginia and caught up with the regiment later.[15]

The 9th Vermont sailed up the James River and arrived at Bermuda Hundred on Thursday, September 15. As the regiment disembarked, Colonel Ripley noted, "We landed at Bermuda Hundred rather ominously (or, as I feel, rather the reverse) it being the anniversary of, and within twenty minutes of the hour of our surrender at Harper's Ferry." After getting their feet on dry

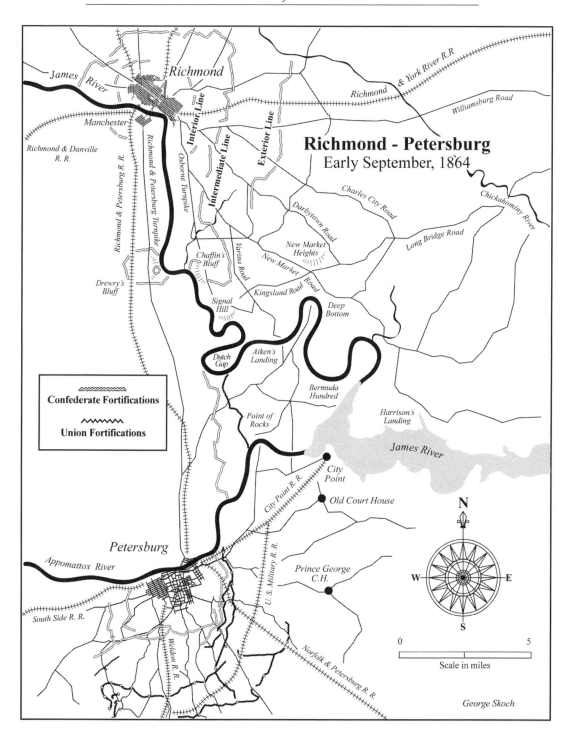

Richmond and Petersburg, September 1864

land, the Green Mountain Boys marched six miles to the west and bivouacked in the rear of the Union lines midway between the James and Appomattox rivers.[16]

As the men were getting their camp set up, Colonel Ripley reported to Maj. Gen. John Gibbon at XVIII Corps headquarters. (Gibbon was temporarily in command while Major General Ord was incapacitated with an illness. Ord would return to command September 22.) Ripley was told the 9th Vermont would be assigned to the XVIII Corps' 2nd Division. While having dinner with Gen. Gibbon, Colonel Ripley told him that the Ninth was Stannard's old regiment, and if possible he would like to be assigned to Stannard's division, also in the XVIII Corps. Gibbon immediately countermanded the order and assigned the Vermonters to Stannard, but within several hours Gibbon's staff realized that assigning the Vermonters to Stannard would leave the 2nd Division severely short of troops and the regiment was reassigned to Brig. Gen. Adelbert Ames' 2nd Division.[17]

Upon reporting to General Ames, Ripley was detached from his regiment and temporarily assigned as the commander of the 1st brigade of the 2nd Division. Ripley's brigade consisted of the 9th Vermont, 148th New York, 8th Maine, and 1st Battery of the 2nd Pennsylvania Artillery. (The 148th New York and the Pennsylvania artillery would soon be pulled from Ripley's brigade to bring up the strength of other brigades in the division.) Lieutenant Colonel Barney, of course, was left in command of the 9th Vermont. Ripley wrote home of his promotion:

> ... this but temporarily, as I have the largest Regiment in the XVIII Army Corps, and since the accession of 225 recruits within three weeks a very green one, and I shall have all I want to put it and keep it in a creditable position, without permitting a foolish ambition to attract my attention from my own proper and undeniable line of duty.[18]

The Vermonters' camp was on the left of the XVIII Corps' line very near the Confederate pickets. Ripley's boys were finally in the middle of the action, as Capt. Edwin Kilbourne noted: "We arrived here on Thursday P.M. and went into camp. Our camp is right behind breastworks, the pickets in front some 50 rods. Can look over the breastworks and see the Johnnie rebs very plainly."[19]

At the time, there was an unofficial truce between the combatants on this portion of the line, as Captain Kilbourne explained:

> In front of this Corps the pickets are very friendly. Standing a few rods of each other and talk back and forth, exchange newspapers and tobacco and crack jokes with one another. I went out onto the picket line this morn and saw the rebs very plainly up on our left, however they are not so friendly but greet you with a ball if you show yourself above the parapet. The canal Butler is digging is only a short distance from us and the rebel guns are playing upon it a good share of the time.[20]

Even the XVIII Corps' newest brigade commander was a willing participant in the truce, as Ripley noted two days after taking command:

> Today I am General and Field Officer of the Day for the 18th Army Corps. I found it a novel position to be riding along our picket lines on Grey Eagle too, with a staff officer and two orderlies within easy talking distance of the Rebel pickets; the distance between whom and myself was not in some places further than from the kitchen door to the iron gate; any one of whom were he to break the inviolable truce to picket firing that exists, could have shot me with a pistol. I enclose a Richmond paper I exchanged with one of them for a N.Y. Herald. Although talking together, trading tobacco for coffee, exchanging newspapers (except by the Officer of the Day) is expressly forbidden, yet it is constantly kept up, and quite a free and easy acquaintance is the result. Farther up the line opposite other Corps, the picket firing is deadly, so much so that it is a continual rattle, and no one dare put a finger in sight.[21]

The day after arriving at Bermuda Hundred, Lieutenant Jewett and Sergeant Charles F. Branch were detailed with 100 men to help defend Redoubt Dutton, an isolated, exposed earthwork on the Bermuda Hundred line. The redoubt was named for Col. Arthur H. Dutton of the

21st Connecticut Infantry, who had been killed on that spot several weeks before. Dutton had commanded the brigade the 9th Vermont was in for a while when it was in Suffolk in the spring of 1863. The location was quite exposed and was one of the most important positions on the line. In addition to the Vermonters' rifles, the position mounted a number of large howitzers. The redoubt stood on a bluff facing southward and was flanked by a deep ravine on the east and west. Northward, the ground sloped gently to a strong line of Confederate earthworks about 200 yards away. Behind the rebel earthworks were no less than nine artillery batteries. The Vermonters were quartered in bomb proofs, or "gopher holes" as the men called them, on the east side of the bluff to protect them from incoming mortar and artillery shells. The detachment would remain away from the regiment until November 28.[22]

On September 17, the 170 recruits who had been passed in the Atlantic by the 9th Vermont as it sailed to Virginia finally caught up with the regiment, bringing its aggregate strength up to 1,129, with over 700 men actually present for duty. The 9th Vermont's troop strength exceeded that of most of the brigades in the corps.[23]

The First and Second Brigades of the XVIII Corps' 2nd Division, along with three new Pennsylvania regiments, were temporarily detached and sent under the command of Colonel Ripley to a position near Coggin's Point on September 16. Ripley's mission was to support the Union cavalry which was in pursuit of the stolen cattle, and to construct a line of works near Coggin's Point to protect the army's supply base at City Point from a more daring Confederate raid. The men worked night and day for a week entrenching the position. Horace noted in one of his articles to the *Lamoille Newsdealer*:

> Once again the 9th Vermont has moved. We are now south of the Appomattox, near City Point, doing picket duty. The successful raid of the rebels upon the cattle herds near this place, stealing twenty five hundred head, has opened the eyes of some who now are anticipating an attack upon City Point, the base of supplies for the Army of the Potomac. Two brigades are now bivouacked near this place, under the command of Col. Ripley, of the 9th, and preparations are being made for defense. Perhaps it may be well enough to lock the doors after the horse is stolen, but for fear of no more danger of attack here than there is on Mount Mansfield.[24]

The morning after the two brigades left the Bermuda Hundred Line, Union artillery all along the line was fired in celebration of Maj. Gen. Philip Sheridan's victory at Winchester in Virginia's Shenandoah Valley on September 19. Captain Kilbourne, who had been left behind in charge of the sick and infirm members of the 9th Vermont, remembered:

> We fired a shotted salute in honor of Sheridan's victory the other morning, by order of Gen. Grant. The rebs flew to their breastworks expecting an attack. Our pickets sung out to them and told them of the victory and they hollered back, "Fresh Beef! Fresh Beef!" alluding to the capture of our cattle near City Point.[25]

Ripley unexpectedly received orders at 11:00 P.M. on September 26 to return his two brigades to Bermuda Hundred, leaving the three Pennsylvania regiments to man the new entrenchments. As he was directed to keep his movement secret, the troops were ordered into line of march at midnight and were marched rapidly through the black of night back toward Bermuda Hundred. Ripley described the ordeal as "a most cruel forced march" and the week's hard work on the entrenchments caused the men to straggle badly. It was daylight before the two brigades crossed the Appomattox and by the time they reached their former camp it was 10:00 A.M. Upon arriving, the men threw themselves on the ground and many slept in spite of the constant artillery firing. At 4:00 P.M., the XVIII Corps was aroused by orders to prepare for a review. Muskets were quickly cleaned and clothes brushed, but something seemed different from the normal review. The men's suspicions were confirmed after the review when 60 rounds of ammunition and three days' rations were issued. The Army of the James was about to go into battle.[26]

While the Vermonters had been working on the fortifications at Coggin's Point, Lieutenant General Grant, as part of his autumn offensive, decided to try a plan devised by Major General Butler to capture Richmond from the north side of the James River. Butler's Army of the James would attempt the breakthrough while Maj. Gen. George G. Meade's Army of the Potomac kept Lee's troops south of the James River at Petersburg too busy to reinforce the weaker force on the north side. Butler first had to reassemble his forces, which were spread out from Petersburg to Bermuda Hundred; this was not accomplished until 3:30 A.M. September 29. While the units were being assembled, Butler met with his commanders to issue orders for the next day. To accomplish his mission, Butler divided his army into two wings. The left wing, commanded by Major General Ord, consisted of George J. Stannard's 1st Division and Charles A. Heckman's 2nd Division of the XVIII Corps, making up a force of 8,000 men. The right wing, commanded by Maj. Gen. David B. Birney, consisted of the X Corps and Brig. Gen. Charles J. Paine's 3rd Division of the XVIII Corps, a force of about 12,400.[27]

Edward Otho Cresap Ord, born October 18, 1818, in Cumberland, Maryland, was a regular army officer who had graduated from West Point in 1839. He had combat experience in the Seminole War in Florida and fighting Indians on the western frontier. Even though he had held the equivalent of Corps command since 1862, wounds and illness had kept him out of all but two battles. In spite of this, Ord still retained General Grant's confidence.[28]

Unlike Ord, Charles A. Heckman, commanding the XVIII Corps' 2nd Division, was not a regular army officer. He was born in Easton, Pennsylvania, on December 3, 1822, and at the outbreak of the Mexican War he enlisted in the regular army as a private. He was discharged in 1848 as a sergeant. Between the Mexican War and the Civil War he worked as a conductor on the Central Railroad of New Jersey. He was mustered in the army again on October 8, 1861, this time however, not as a private, but as the lieutenant colonel of the 9th New Jersey Infantry Regiment. He had served with Burnside in the North Carolina Expedition and had been with him ever since. In Burnside's failed attack of Drewry's Bluff the previous May, Heckman had been captured and had just recently been exchanged and returned to command in early September. He was a lackluster officer who had been protected by Burnside.[29]

The move to attack Fort Harrison was to begin at 4:30 A.M. September 29 and the men were to go in light with only a single blanket rolled and carried over their shoulders, three days' rations in their haversacks, and sixty rounds of ammunition. Ord's mission was to cross the James River on a newly laid pontoon bridge at Aiken's Landing, march his corps men up the Varina Road and attack the rebels in their entrenched position on Chaffin's Farm and destroy the Confederate

Brigadier General Charles A. Heckman, commander of the 2nd Division of the XVIII Corps. (John Kuhl Collection, U.S. Army Military History Institute).

bridges across the James River at and above Chaffin's Bluff. Then he was to move up the Osborne Turnpike toward Richmond. Birney's mission was to move his X Corps north from Deep Bottom, capture New Market Heights, and move northwest on the New Market Road toward Richmond. With the way clear, Kautz's cavalry was to move from Deep Bottom to the Darbytown Road and into Richmond. The plan was sound, but the execution would not be easy.[30]

The XVIII Corps' primary target was Fort Harrison, a huge earthwork four miles north of Aiken's Landing. It was named for Lieutenant William Ellzey Harrison, the engineer who supervised its construction, and it crowned a hill on the Chaffin farm and commanded the approach to Richmond by the Varina Road. The fort mounted 16 heavy guns, one being an 8-inch Columbaid, and the others 64- and 32-pounders. Fort Harrison was the strongest fort on a line of earthworks that ran from Richmond south to the James River. An offshoot of the lower end of this line ran south between the Osborne and New Market roads to Fort Gilmer and then wound down to the northern face of an entrenched camp seven and one-half miles below the city.[31]

To lead the assault on Fort Harrison, General Ord selected his 1st Division, commanded by Brig. Gen. Stannard, with Heckman's 2nd Division in support. Heckman's Division consisted of the brigades of Col. James Jourdan, Col. Edward H. Ripley and Col. Harrison S. Fairchild. The XVIII Corps would make a surprise crossing of the James River at Aiken's Landing. Stannard was to lead the way along the Varina Road until reaching open ground near Fort Harrison. There he was to form up on the left of the road and assault the works. Heckman was to follow closely behind Stannard and push through the breach. The 9th Vermont was selected to lead the column of Heckman's division. Ripley's brigade, after entering the breach opened by Stannard, was to turn to the right and attack Fort Gilmer and the Laurel Hill batteries farther to the right from the rear as the X Corps hit them from the front.[32]

Years later, Stannard told Ripley that when he received his orders he went to Corps headquarters to protest, but was told that General Grant had personally chosen his division to lead the attack. Stannard then went to see General Grant, who at the time was located at Deep Bottom. He reportedly said to Grant, "I am told that I must lead this attack, and I have come to protest in behalf of the poor men of my division, who have led every assault of the XVIII Corps, from Cold Harbor until now, and are fought down to a skeleton of a division. I have not a word to say for myself—I will freely go wherever you send me; but it is inhuman to give my men so much more than their share of these forlorn hopes." General Grant replied, "General Stannard, we must carry Fort Harrison, and I know you will do it." Stannard, ever the consummate soldier, knew when to salute and execute, and he returned to his division to prepare his men for the next day's action.[33]

While the Confederate works were strong, they were grossly undermanned. Out of necessity Lee had stationed most of his forces around Petersburg, feeling the Chaffin's Bluff area was not seriously threatened. To further exacerbate the situation, the few troops that were in the area were divided between two independent commands. The 2,900 troops in and around Fort Harrison were under the command of Lt. Gen. Richard S. Ewell, commander of the Department of Richmond. The others were under the command of Brig. Gen. John Gregg, whose men manned the works from New Market Heights to Signal Hill, a little south of Fort Harrison. Additionally, Gregg took his orders from the Army of Northern Virginia, not Ewell. Together, the two commands amounted to only about 6,000 men.[34]

Butler's movement to the James River did not commence until after evening roll call and taps, in order to deceive the enemy pickets. The 9th Vermont left camp near midnight led by Major Books, as Lieutenant Colonel Barney had gone home on sick leave not long after arriving at Bermuda Hundred. At this time the regiment numbered about 700 officers and men. The Green Mountain Boys reached Aiken's Landing behind Stannard's division at 2:00 A.M. and waited while the engineers completed the pontoon bridge across the river. When the bridge was finished it stretched 1,320 feet from shore to shore. While waiting for the bridge to be completed, the 10th New Hampshire and 18th New York, of Stannard's division, exchanged their muzzle loading rifled muskets for new Spencer repeating rifles. About 3:00 A.M. Stannard's division began crossing the bridge. His skirmishers fanned out as soon as they cleared the bridge-head on the far shore, and headed up the Varina Road. Somehow the Federals made the crossing without being detected by the Confederates. This phase of the operation was a total success.[35]

By the time the 2nd Division completed crossing, near daylight, the 1st Division's skirmishers had made contact with the rebel's pickets. The scattered firing in front increased as the columns moved on through a pine woods. As Stannard's division emerged on the open ground near the fort rebel gunners opened fire on them. Here the Union commanders could see the terrain they would have to cross to take the fort. The distance between the head of the column and the fort was nearly 1,400 yards. In front was a swath of low ground covered with fallen brush. Next came a wide, open slope. Finally came the abatis and a deep ditch that protected the parapets of the fort.[36]

Stannard ordered Brigadier General Hiram Burnham's Second Brigade to assault the fort. Burnham would be supported by the other two brigades of the division. The blue wave started across the open plain with a cheer. When the Federals were in range the Goochland (Virginia) Artillery, manning the guns in the fort, opened fire with shell and double rounds of canister. Initially, the inexperienced Virginians overshot Stannard's men but soon got their range and started doing fearful damage. In addition to the rebel artillery, 200 Tennessee and Georgia infantrymen added their firepower to the defense of the fort. A third of the men in the division and about half of the actual storming party fell, but nothing could stop the rush of Stannard's men. They plunged through the ditch at the bottom of the wall of the fort, climbed the steep embankment, sprang inside the parapet, and captured a considerable portion of the regiment which defended the fort, along with the lieutenant colonel who commanded it. General Stannard rode at the side of his Third Brigade and entered the fort with his men. General Burnham was killed while helping some of his men turn one of the fort's cannons on the fleeing rebels. His successor, Colonel Aaron F. Stevens, soon after fell severely wounded. The rebels were then driven from two smaller works adjacent to the fort. The gray-backs who were not captured or killed fled to the second line of works a half a mile nearer Richmond.[37]

After taking Fort Harrison, Ord and Stannard tried to reorganize the 1st Division to charge down the line of earthworks toward the river to destroy the Confederate pontoon bridges, but the troops were too scattered and the units too mixed up to mount a charge. It was some time before the senior officers could sort the units out and start down the line. Unfortunately, when the charge got underway Ord personally led the men and paid the price with a very painful gunshot wound in his right thigh. He tried to retain command, but a doctor had him sent to the rear. This left Heckman in command of the XVIII Corps.[38]

As Stannard's Division entered the open ground in its charge on Fort Harrison, Colonel Ripley and Colonel Jourdan were deploying their brigades to the left of the Varina road to exploit the breakthrough as planned. Just as Ripley got his men into some woods for cover and Stannard's division entered the clearing in its charge on Fort Harrison, Heckman rode up to Colonel Ripley and, disobeying General Ord's orders, changed Ripley's orders. Instead of following behind Stannard's Division, as originally planned, Heckman ordered Ripley to move his brigade across the Varina road to the right of Stannard and assault a smaller fort designated as Battery No. 11. The other two brigades of Heckman's Division were to follow Ripley. As Ripley moved his brigade forward it passed through an area where a Federal battery was taking heavy fire from a cannon in Fort Harrison. The battery was in full view of the fort and was being mauled pretty badly. The 9th Vermont's Dr. Fairman described the scene: "As we passed through the woods on the turnpike, we found many of our artillery horses disemboweled, others with their heads shot off, by shot and shell from the Fort. Many of the carriages were stove into kindling wood."[39]

The road was on a narrow causeway with ditches on each side. Dead horses, along with a disabled gun, were blocking the way. The battery commander and his men were trying their best to clear the road by rolling the dead and wounded horses into the ditches. Colonel Ripley rode forward to assist the battery, commander in clearing the road so he could get his brigade through. As Ripley was talking to the battery commander another shell exploded in the midst of the battery wounding more men and horses. At the instant of the explosion Ripley was struck by a piece of shell on his right temple, stunning him and knocking off his horse. By the time he regained his senses Captain Samuel Kelley was by his side. Ripley looked at Kelly and said, "How bad is it, Sam?" "Where are you hit?" Kelley asked. With a strange look Ripley said, "Is my head not gone?" Kelley replied, "No, it seems alright." Ripley wrote later, "Slowly and timidly I put my hand up to what felt to be a cavity where my ear had been, and could hardly believe my senses that it felt all right to my hand. The piece of shell had clipped my hair and cap button."[40]

After getting the artillery cleared out of the way, Ripley got his brigade to the right of the road in the pines, where, Dr. Fairman said, "Now shot and shell went just over our heads and the limbs of the trees fell thick and fast all around us." The 9th Vermont deployed with its left on the road and the 8th Maine deployed on the Vermonters' right. Unfortunately, the Maine men got mired in a swamp and the Vermonters had to go it alone, but with mounting excitement when they heard the cheers of Stannard's Division as they closed on Fort Harrison. The other two brigades behind Ripley also got bogged down in the swamp.[41]

The Vermonters followed the Varina road, which took a sharp turn to the right within 600 yards of the front of Fort Harrison, but by this time the guns of the fort were in Stannard's hands. Eight hundred yards to the northeast, Battery No. 11 stood squarely across the road with its guns making a sweep of a quarter of a mile. As the regiment charged for the battery, companies B and K veered to the right to avoid felled timber and crowded into the road. Here the road ran through a cut five or six feet deep and quickly became clogged with men. Colonel Ripley could see in his mind's eye the slaughter of his troops if the guns in the battery opened up with canister. He tried desperately to keep his men from bunching up in the cut. By this time, however, adrenaline was pumping through the men's veins and they paid no attention to him. The cannons in the fort remained strangely quite, as though they were waiting for the Vermonters to get closer.[42]

As the mass of men poured out of the cut, company officers tried to form a line, but the men would not stop long enough. As the first group of men cleared the cut they let out a yell and ran toward the fort one half mile in the distance. It became an all-out race with the regiment's color sergeant, six-foot-two-inch, Felix Quinn, leading the way. As they neared the battery the Vermonters had to clear out a line of abatises. Here Pvt. Henry P. French, an 18-year-old farmer from Tunbridge in Co. A, fell or, in the rush to get through, was accidentally pushed into the abatis. The sharpened point of a tree limb stabbed him through the outside of his right shin. The wound was slow to heal, but he finally returned to his company several months later.[43]

Private Henry P. French, Co. A, wounded in the right shin by a sharpened tree limb on September 29, 1864 (National Archives).

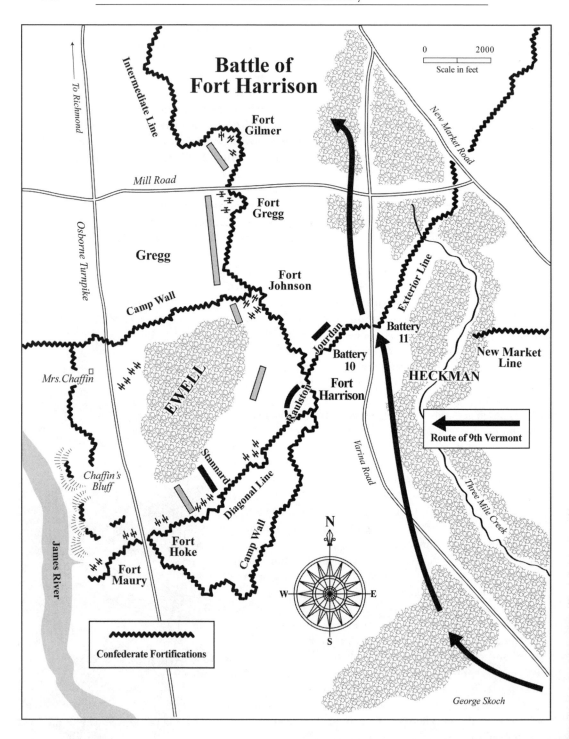

The Battle of Fort Harrison, September 29, 1864.

A few minutes earlier, the Virginia reserves in the vicinity of Battery No. 11 had fallen back after seeing the fall of Fort Harrison. In turn, the James City Artillery manning Battery No. 11 also retreated, leaving their cannons, as the Green Mountain Boys came charging toward them.[44]

After clearing the abatis, the fastest runners, among whom was Colonel Ripley, reached the fort's ramparts and scrambled over them. Colonel Ripley remembered: "I was over the works with 15 or 20 of my men and blazing away with my revolver, it was a dream, so great was the intoxication of the excitement." The only real defense put up by the Confederates was from the artillery's infantry support, who halted a short distance away and delivered a parting volley that knocked over nearly everyone inside the fort except for Colonel Ripley.[45]

One of the first men into the fort was the regiment's sergeant major, 21-year-old Henry D. Belden from Burlington, and he had the dubious honor of being the first man wounded. He received three gunshot wounds nearly simultaneously. One bullet hit the middle joint of his right index finger. The second bullet hit him in the left index finger at the first joint splitting the tendon and taking out several pieces of bone. Then a third bullet hit him in his upper left arm. Ignoring his wounds he seized the tail of a rebel cannon, which Ripley was trying to wheel around to fire at the retreating rebels. Belden shouted over the din of battle, "Go on, colonel, we wounded men will work these guns." After his wounds healed Belden's left index finger remained stiff and swollen. The bullet in his upper left arm was left in place, causing the arm to atrophy in later years. After the war he went back to school and became a doctor. Henry Belden died May 21, 1903, in St. Albans of what the doctor at the time called "cerebral softening."[46]

After Belden was hit, men started dropping like flies. A rebel minie ball hit Pvt. Allen J. Dearborn of Co. G on the inside of his left leg between the knee joint and the ankle, cutting straight through the leg without hitting the bone. The 25-year-old farmer and father of one, from Vershire, was first sent to the hospital at Point of Rocks the day after he was wounded. When the ball exited Dearborn's leg it took

Sergeant Major Henry D. Belden, wounded three times in the battle of Fort Harrison on September 29, 1864. Pictured here as a hospital steward (U.S. Army Military History Institute).

out a considerable amount of tissue. Later, more was cut out in the hospital due to gangrene. On October 26, 1864, Dearborn was transferred to Chesapeake General Hospital in Hampton and six months later to the Governor Smith Hospital in Brattleboro. Dearborn's wound finally healed in April and he returned to the regiment May 12, 1865. Unfortunately, during his hospitalization he contracted mumps, which affected his right testicle. When Dearborn returned home in June his right testicle was swollen to twice its original size. This condition, however, did not hinder him in fathering two more children. Allen J. Dearborn died March 7, 1915, in Concord, New Hampshire, of kidney disease.[47]

Private William Hatch Chamberlain of Co. G was knocked down by a minie ball through his left leg. The 19-year-old farmer from Strafford had only been in the regiment several days.

W. Hatch Chamberlain and family, in a photograph taken sometime between 1885 and 1890. Standing, from left to right, are Romero Chamberlain, Herbert Chamberlain, Edward Chamberlain and Emogene Chamberlain. Seated, from left to right, are Hatch's second wife, Myra Chamberlain, Hatch Chamberlain and Curtis Chamberlain (Pete Chamberlain).

He was taken to the Hamilton General Hospital where he recovered before being sent back to his company; however, his leg bothered him the rest of his life. Chamberlain family history has it that Hatch used to bounce his wife on his left knee to keep his leg from stiffening up. He died September 24, 1930, and is buried in Highland Cemetery, Chelsea, Vermont.[48]

Twenty-year-old Sgt. John Riley, an Irish immigrant from Rutland in Co. B., was dropped by a bullet in his left thigh that shattered his thigh bone. After the battle his left leg was amputated and he was shipped to Hamilton General Hospital at Fort Monroe, where died of his wound October 31.[49]

Hatch Chamberlain and great grandson Bill Chamberlain. Standing in the rear, left to right, are Harold Chamberlain and his father, Curtis Chamberlain (Pete Chamberlain).

Private Benjamin F. Stone of Co. I, a 24-year-old farmer from Roxbury, was wounded in the left foot by a minie ball that took out the 3rd and 4th metacarpal bones. He was evacuated to Chesapeake General Hospital in Hampton where his 4th toe was amputated, leaving him with a permanent limp. He received a disability discharge from the army at Sloan General Hospital in Montpelier on June 24, 1865. Stone had originally mustered into Co. I on July 9, 1862, but was discharged with pulmonary tuberculosis July 1, 1863. He recovered from his illness and enlisted for a second time in Co. I on December 8, 1863. Benjamin Stone died on December 2, 1897, in Dracus, Massachusetts, of heart disease. He is buried in Edson Cemetery in Lowell, Massachusetts.[50]

John L. Newton, a 19-year-old private in Co. F, was hit in his right thigh. The young carpenter from Burlington was evacuated to the Chesapeake General Hospital and then to McDougal General Hospital at Fort Schuyler in New York City, where he died of complications of his wound on October 27. He is buried in Cypress Hill National Cemetery in Brooklyn. Newton was a bachelor who had been the sole support of his mother. His father was a drunkard and had deserted the family. Mrs. Newton received a modest government pension in return for her son's life.[51]

Thirty-two-year-old Pvt. Horace H. Preston, a blacksmith from Charlotte in Co. I, had a rebel bullet go through his right hand, taking off most of his thumb. The remainder of his thumb was amputated the next day at the Point of Rocks Hospital. After the wound healed the index finger on his right hand was permanently extended. He received a disability discharge May 25, 1865. Preston's days of blacksmithing were over. He received an $8.00 a month pension from the government and did odd jobs for a living thereafter. Horace Preston died in Windham, Vermont, on September 17, 1873.[52]

Private Joseph Lafayette of Co. B was knocked over backwards by a bullet in his chest. He lingered in the hospital at Fort Monroe until he died on October 23. The 18-year-old wheelwright from Richmond, Vermont, had been in the regiment only a couple of weeks. He is buried in Hampton National Cemetery, Hampton, Virginia.[53]

Private Benjamin F. Stone, Co. I, displaying the wound to his left foot to the U.S. Pension Bureau. Stone was wounded September 29, 1864, in the attack at Battery No. 11 (National Archives).

Lieutenant George W. Gould saw Sgt. Sylvester C. Burlingame of Co. K dropped by a Confederate bullet in the left thigh. Gould ran to the 21-year-old farmer from Dummerston and quickly bandaged his leg to stop the bleeding. Luckily, the bullet had gone completely through Burlingame's thigh without hitting the femur. He was taken to Hamilton General Hospital at Fort Monroe and stayed for six days before being transferred to McDougal General Hospital, on October 11, where he stayed for 4 months. During his stay in the hospital he lost additional tissue from the area around the wound due to infection. Nerve damage left the leg weak and years after the war it started to atrophy. Additionally, he suffered from neuralgia. In 1865 he got a $10 a month government pension. He died December 13, 1903, in Meriden, Connecticut.[54]

Private Octave Bushy, a mechanic from Chittenden, in Co. H, should have been having a special day since it was his 19th birthday, but instead he was in the middle of a battle. After entering Battery No. 11 he was hit in the left arm by a rebel minie ball that passed through his

arm just above the elbow, shattering the humerus. Years later Bushy's descendants found a small note inside his framed discharge paper that he had sent home from the hospital. It read "Dear Mom and Dad be home from the war soon. Signed Octave." Bushy returned home several months later as promised. After the wound healed his elbow joint was paralyzed and he could no longer straighten his arm. He was discharged on a disability February 17, 1865. After the war Bushy lived in Burlington, where he died February 17, 1934, of arteriosclerosis. He is buried in the St. Francis Cemetery in Winooski.[55]

Nineteen-year-old Pvt. Nelson C. Roberts of Co. A was brought down by a rebel minie ball in his right leg. The ball entered about three inches below the right knee joint, fracturing the tibia and exiting out the back of his calf. After a few short stays in several army hospitals he was transferred to Sloan General Hospital in Montpelier. Not long after he arrived in Vermont he was given a furlough to go home to his father's farm in Sharon. While recuperating at home he fell ill and his family doctor was supposed to notify the general hospital that he was too sick to return before his furlough expired. Either the doctor forget to send a note to the hospital or it got lost, and a deputy sheriff was sent to arrest him. When the officer saw his condition he left him alone and Roberts returned to the hospital as soon as he was able to travel. He was

Private Octave Bushy, Co. H, wounded in the left arm during the attack of Battery No. 11 on September 29, 1864 (James J. Ticehurst).

discharged from the army June 24, 1865, with his wound not yet completely healed. Nelson C. Roberts died April 4, 1880, of tuberculosis.[56]

One noncombat-related injury occurred soon after Battery No. 11 was taken. After the run for the fort First Lt. Josiah O. Livingston, the regiment's adjutant, felt weak and his heart was beating irregularly. He went to the rear and found Dr. Fairman, who gave him some heart tonic and had him lie down for several hours. Livingston was promoted to captain and command of Co. G the next month. After mustering out of the army the following summer, Captain Livingston received a $12.75 monthly pension for intermittent fever and disease of the lungs. He tried to get his pension increased for heart trouble, but the pension bureau deemed it a preexisting condition. Josiah Livingston died July 23, 1917, at the Vermont Soldier's Home in Bennington, where he had been diagnosed as insane.[57]

At some time during the battle, one of Ripley's men came limping by and ask him where to go for medical help. Ripley asked him were he was hit and the man showed him a hole in his leg about two inches above his ankle. The bullet had traveled clear through the man's leg without hitting bone, nerves or tendons. Ripley said to the man, " Courage old fellow, I wish you could sell that little hole. I know you'd find a purchaser at five hundred dollars." Ripley wrote later, "It was what is called a sixty day wound, and one of the prettiest, not laming, maiming or hurting or preventing a fellow's having a good time at home for a couple of months this charming fall weather."[58]

After taking Battery No. 11, a number of the Green Mountain Boys pressed on and secured several smaller adjacent works, rounding up about 50 prisoners, two of whom were officers: one a lieutenant colonel and the other a major. Colonel Jourdan's brigade captured Battery No. 10 about the same time the 9th Vermont was taking Battery No. 11. By 10:00 A.M. all the Confederate works from Fort Harrison northeast to Battery No. 11 were securely in Federal hands.[59]

After his wound forced him off the field, Ord went to Deep Bottom to see Grant to get him to send forward more cannons, small arms ammunition and a new corps commander. Unfortunately, Grant left for the front just before Ord arrived. Not finding the general, Ord went on to the hospital for treatment of his wound.[60]

Grant first went to New Market Heights, which by that time had been cleared. He then proceeded on to Fort Harrison not long after Stannard captured it. By this time, of course, Ord had left to find Grant and part of the XVIII Corps had gotten somewhat reorganized and was pushing toward the river. Apparently Grant thought things were going well and sent a message to Birney to hurry from New Market Heights to reinforce the XVIII Corps. And with that, he returned to headquarters.[61]

Although somewhat altered from the original, the Federal plan seemed to be working until Major General Ord was wounded. Colonel Ripley complained later that Ord "had no business being there." With Ord out of action, Brigadier General Heckman assumed command of the XVIII Corps and, according to Ripley, "Heckman seemed to have become crazed when he lost the control of his Corps' commander, without which he was good for nothing."[62]

Soon after assuming command, Heckman rode up to Battery No. 11 and in great excitement said to Ripley, "Very good, Colonel, push right on, charge that fort." Heckman was pointing to Fort Gilmer, a fort even stronger than Fort Harrison. In the original plan, Ripley was to take Fort Gilmer from the rear as the X Corps hit it from the front, but the X Corps was still trying to take the works on New Market Heights. Ripley had only the 9th Vermont and a few troops from the 8th Maine who had managed to extract themselves from the swamp. Obeying Heckman's order, Ripley formed up his brigade with the Maine men moving ahead as skirmishers followed by the 9th Vermont in line of battle.[63]

Ripley and his men had not gone far before they were stopped by trees dropped by the Confederates sometime earlier. Then the guns from Forts Gregg and Gilmer got the New Englanders' range. Shells from the forts cut swaths through the regiment, with companies E and F taking the heaviest casualties.[64]

Private Daniel Dwyer, a 41-year-old farmer from Salem, Vermont, in Co. E, was standing up when a shell fragment hit him just above his wrist, taking off most of his right hand and then gouging out a hole in his right thigh. What was left of his hand was amputated in the hospital. Dwyer received a disability discharge from the army on July 30, 1865, and returned to Vermont. On August 2, he went to his family doctor in West Charleston about his thigh wound that would not heal. The doctor could not do much for him, but recommended he have a photograph taken of the wound, which he sent to the U.S. Pension Bureau along with a request to have his pension increased since he could not possibly work with an open wound of that size. In June 1866, his pension was increased to $20.00 a month. It was upped to $22.00 in 1890, and later to $30.00. There seemed to be little doctors could do for the wound, which was still oozing in 1884. In spite of his wound, Daniel Dwyer lived until July 19, 1907, aged 84.[65]

At almost the same time that Dwyer was hit, another Co. E soldier, Pvt. James Lunge, a 21-year-old farmer from Glover, had a piece of shell strike his cartridge box, tearing away flesh from his abdomen and right hip and knocking him senseless. He was evacuated to the hospital at Fort Monroe where he remained for two months before returning to his unit. By 1923 he was receiving $72.00 a month pension for his wound. James Lunge died January 23, 1926, in Burke.[66]

Wall and ditch of Fort Johnson located between Fort Harrison and Fort Gilmer. Forts Gilmer and Johnson being similar in construction, one can see why Colonel Ripley was reluctant to attack Fort Gilmer (Richmond National Battlefield Park).

Corporal George W. Davis of Co. E took a shell fragment in the right shoulder. His comrades managed to get him back to the regimental aid station, where his wound was treated. (Davis had been court-martialed November 24, 1863, for going to sleep on guard duty. He served his sentence of 30 days of hard labor and came back to the regiment and was a good soldier. He was promoted to corporal February 2, 1864.) After being treated at the regiment's aid station he was then taken to Point of Rocks Hospital where he died of complications of his wound October 8. Davis was the sole support of his mother, father, and his two younger brothers, one 16 and the other four-years old. His father was totally blind. His family received a small government pension after his death.[67]

Eighteen-year-old Pvt. Henry Sias, a farmer from Newport in Co. E, was hit in the right side of his face by a piece of shell and lay on the ground senseless all night in the rain. In addition to catching cold, he suffered injuries from the shell fragment, which knocked out his upper right bicuspid and lower right first molar and damaged several other teeth. Dirt from the explosion of the shell flew into his left eye, permanently blinding it. After the war the effects of his wounds grew worse and by 1874 he had headaches and was blind in his left eye and partially blind in the right one. In spite of his ailments he somehow managed to work as a logger. Henry Sias died October 10, 1897, at age 53, and is buried in the Willis Cemetery in Dummer, New Hampshire.[68]

Private Edward R. Cook, a laborer from Sunderland, Co. E, had his left arm mangled by a piece of shell. What remained of the 19-year-old's left arm was later amputated between shoulder and elbow. The same piece of shell that shattered his arm also struck the left side of his chest an inch below and to the left of the left nipple. A doctor wrote later, "Considerable

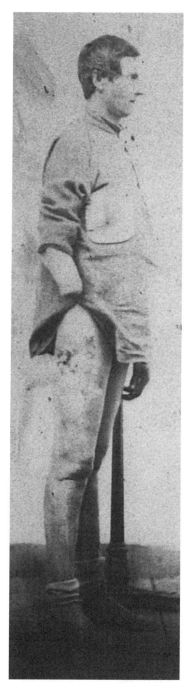

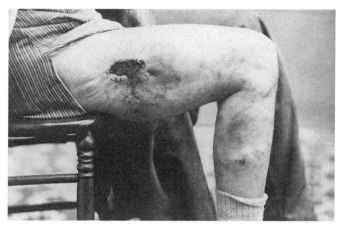

Left: Private Daniel Dwyer, Co. E, displaying the wounds he received, on September 29, 1864, for the U.S. Pension Bureau (National Archives). *Above:* Close-up photograph taken in August 1865 of Private Daniel Dwyer's wound on his right thigh. The back of the photograph reads, "Farmer Taylor, Portrait and Landscape Photographer, W. Charleston, Vt." (National Archives).

Above, left: Private Henry Sias, Co. E, wounded in the face on September 29, 1864. Sias family history indicates Henry always wore a beard and would seldom smile because of the scars on his face and his loss of teeth. Notice the slight depression on the right side of his face caused by a shell fragment (Donna Winauski). *Above, right:* Hattie L. Yates of Holland, Vermont, whom Henry Sias married on April 4, 1874 (Donna Winauski).

hemorrhage followed per the bronchial tube and mouth showing that the lung was injured, probably force of the blow rather that the actual contact of the shell as there were no symptoms denoting escape of air." On January 3, 1865, Cook wrote Vermont's Adjutant General Henry H. Baxter asking him to help him get transferred to the general hospital in Brattleboro. His request moved exceptionally fast through the bureaucracy and was approved by the War Department on January 17; Cook was transferred soon thereafter.[69]

Two men, Privates John Mickman of Co. E and John Nickerson of Co. F, were killed instantly by exploding shells.[70]

As the bombardment continued Pvt. George W. Patrick, a farmer from Hinesburgh in Co. F, was dropped by a shell fragment and died within minutes. Patrick's wife, Ellen S. Patrick, died one year and one day later, leaving four children ranging in age from four to ten years old. After their mother's death the children were taken in by Mrs. Patrick's parents. The children received a small government pension until each turned 16. One son, Elmer E. Patrick, applied for a dependent child pension in 1908. Elmer was retarded and had been living with a guardian since his grandparents' deaths. He had been working at odd jobs on different farms in the area, but his eyesight had gotten so bad he was unable to work. For several years the Pension Bureau questioned Elmer's ability to work, but finally was convinced that he was totally disabled and awarded him an $8.00 a month pension for the rest of his life.[71]

Private Leroy L. Bryant of Peru, Vermont, in Co. F, was killed by a shell. The 19-year-old private had been the sole support of his parents, his father being a disabled blacksmith. After his death they received Leroy's $30.00 bounty and a $12.00 a month government pension. Ironically, Leroy's brother George was living in Texas when the war broke out, and he joined the Confederate army.[72]

Although companies E and F took more casualties than the rest of the regiment, the other companies were also losing men to the barrage. Private Albert A. Niles of Co. H was standing within a few feet of his comrade, Pvt. Freeman Baker, when he saw Baker receive a direct hit from an incoming shell. Niles wrote later that Baker "was struck & blown to atoms by a shell from one of the guns in Fort Gilmer. After the fight we went in search of his body & found only one limb, which we buried. It was recognized by the new boot thereon; he having recd. a new pair from home only a few days previous." Baker's mother, Elisa Baker, whom he had supported, received an $8.00 a month pension in 1876 backdated to September 30, 1864. When she died February 16, 1883, his father, Arad Baker, who was disabled, applied for and received the $8.00 pension.[73]

It was plain to Ripley that it would be a "wicked" waste of life to advance or to stay where he was. He sent a staff officer back to tell Heckman to send up supports and to come personally to see the situation, but neither Heckman nor supporting troops arrived. At the same time he sent the staff officer to get Heckman, Ripley took it upon himself to get his men out of the rain of iron and ordered Major Brooks to have the command fall back to the cover of a cut several feet deep through which ran the Varina road. In the cut the men got some relief from the incoming artillery rounds, although the 9th Vermont continued to take a few more casualties.[74] For several hours Ripley's men lay in the cut with the white hot pieces of iron flying around overhead. Most closed their eyes and tried to imagine themselves somewhere else or cried or prayed to God to be spared.

Three privates in Co. K were hit while hunkered down in the cut. William Waters was wounded in the left thigh and Denny E. Mason was slightly injured when he was hit in the back. For his bravery in the attack Mason was promoted to corporal several days later. Thirty-four-year-old Albert E. Newton from Whitingham was killed outright by a shell.[75]

Private Oberon Payne, an 18-year-old Co. H soldier from North Hero, was hugging the earth trying to stay out of harm's way when the outside of his left leg was torn open by a jagged shell fragment. Payne was in the Sloan General Hospital in Montpelier when his wound finally healed. He was given the opportunity to serve in the V.R.C., but Payne was fed up with army life and wanted his discharge, which he received August 7, 1865. His wound healed, leaving a seven inch scar running down his leg from the knee joint. The large amount of scar tissue associated with the wound severely limited the movement of his leg. After the war he married Julia A. Tula in Wakeeney, Kansas, but they divorced May 21, 1881. He later married Anna E.

Zuckschwerst. Oberon Payne died August 12, 1919, of cancer of the face and is buried in Oak Lawn Cemetery, West Plains, Missouri.[76]

When the 9th Vermont moved back to the safety of the road, Colonel Ripley stayed forward for about 30 minutes studying the enemy positions with his field glass. After he gathered the intelligence he needed he returned to his brigade. On his way back he passed through the area where the 9th Vermont had been hit with the artillery barrage. There he saw what he recalled as "a most pitiable sight." Four Vermonters were lying in a pile, two dead and two wounded. One of the wounded was Corp. William Moranville, a 24-year-old, five-foot-nine-inch, Canadian-born farmer from Salem, Vermont. A fragment from an exploding shell had torn away the flesh on one side from his buttocks and down his thigh. Moranville was lying on one side, exposing a bloody mass of raw flesh with crushed bone protruding from it. He asked for water and Ripley knelt down and gave him a drink from his canteen. After taking a drink Moranville asked Ripley to leave for safety, as shells were still coming in. Ripley told him he would send a stretcher for him and his wounded comrade as soon as he got back to the brigade. Moranville told the colonel not to worry about them because they were going to die anyway. Captain Samuel Kelley and a party of Vermonters made several attempts during the day to recover the two men, but the artillery fire was too heavy. They finally got through to them after dark, but as Moranville predicted the two wounded men were dead. Moranville's widowed mother got a small pension from the government after his death. She went insane in 1900 and died in Derby on October 22, 1902.[77]

While the Vermont and Maine boys were lying down in the cut taking the shelling, Colonel Ripley had a horrible experience. He was standing with one foot down in the roadbed and the other one planted up on the side, looking through his field glass watching the enemy's movements. Major Brooks, Lieutenant Peck and two or three others were in a group around him. The shelling was noisy and the men were lying thickly near his feet. Almost under him was a private from a Massachusetts battery who had strayed into the ranks of the 9th Vermont. The man was frightened out of his senses by the explosions and at each one he would jump to his feet and stare

Private Oberon Payne displaying for the U.S. Pension Bureau the wound in his left leg that he received on September 29, 1864 (National Archives).

around as though he was crazy. Ripley told the man three or four times to keep down and finally pushed him down and put his foot on the back of the man's neck to keep him down and said, "There, damn you, will you lie still?" After several minutes he took his foot off the man and as soon as he did the man jumped again just as a shell exploded nearby. Ripley was instantly "dashed in the face with a streaming mass of something horrible, which closed my eyes, nose and mouth."[78]

Ripley had been hit with such force that he thought he had been wounded in the head. Captain Hart, of Heckman's staff, who had just come up to the group, helped him sit down.

Hart happened to have a towel in his pocket and cleaned the disgusting mass from Ripley's face. Ripley then opened his eyes, unbuckled his belt plate and threw open his blouse. From his blouse fell a mass of brains, skull, hair and blood. The headless body of the artilleryman lay between his feet with blood gurgling out of the man's neck with each pulse of his still beating heart.[79]

Lieutenant Theodore S. Peck of Co. H was hit in three places by a bursting shell. Fortunately, it was far enough away that the pieces had lost most of their force and did not penetrate his body. One piece hit him on the right arm, another on his belt plate and a third on the inside of his right calf. The worst injury was on the right leg just below the right knee, which was badly bruised, and formed a large knot. "I was unconscious for some time," he said "but upon regaining my senses requested the adjutant not place my name on the list of the wounded, because I did not wish my mother to hear such news, as she was an invalid." Major Brooks was also hit by a piece of the shell below the knee and like Lieutenant Peck chose not to have his name entered on the casualty list.[80]

While Ripley's command lay in the road absorbing artillery shells, Heckman found Fairchild's Third Brigade off the right side of the Varina road a little north of Battery No. 11, awaiting orders. Heckman ordered Fairchild to assault Fort Johnson. Instead of supporting him with Ripley's or Jourdan's brigade Heckman ordered Fairchild's brigade in alone. Fairchild did as ordered but unlike the token resistance experienced by Ripley in taking Battery No. 11, Fairchild ran into a beehive. By this time the Confederates had had time to reinforce their positions. What Fairchild ran into were two Georgia regiments and an artillery battery. Almost all were combat experienced troops under the able command of Col. Dudley M. DuBose. The outcome was predictable. Fairchild was soundly whipped and had to fall back.[81]

DuBose was not going to take the chance that Fairchild could reorganize and charge again or, worse yet, be reinforced. He sent his two Georgia regiments out of the works to hit the Third Brigade's unprotected right flank. The first inkling Fairchild's men had of the impending attack was the rebel yell the Georgians let loose as they charged. This was more than Fairchild's troops could handle and they fled south in disorder toward Battery No. 11.[82]

While the XVIII Corps had been busy capturing Fort Harrison, Birney's X Corps had been slugging it out with the Confederates on the New Market Line. The X Corps got off to a bit of a bad start. Because of the distance Birney's troops had to travel to assemble and then march to the heights, the corps had many stragglers. Instead of the 12,400 troops he started with, Birney had only about 10,300 extremely tired men to push the rebels off the New Market Heights. Confederate Brig. Gen. John Gregg had five infantry regiments from the Texas Brigade and dismounted cavalry from Virginia and South Carolina, along with the Rockbridge Artillery and the Richmond Howitzers. Although Gregg's force consisted of only 2,000 men, they were all hardened combat veterans and were protected by multilayered breastworks, fronted by a double line of abatises.[83]

The first X Corps units in the fight were the Negro regiments of Brig. Gen. Charles J. Paine's 3rd Division of the XVIII Corps. Unfortunately, in the early morning fog two of the regiments charged the heights not knowing the rest of the division had been delayed by swampy ground. Of course, the two lone regiments were slaughtered. After the sun rose and burned off the fog, approximately 7:00 A.M., Birney threw three more of the Negro regiments against the heights and cleared out Gregg's Butternuts. What was unknown to the Federal troops at the time was that, because of the fall of Fort Harrison, Gregg had already started withdrawing his units from their defensive positions before the Negro troops made their final assault. Gregg's troops fell back in good order and reinforced a portion of the Confederate line on Mill Road between Fort Johnson and Fort Gilmer.[84]

Around 1:30 P.M., and about the time Gregg's troops were firmly ensconced in the line between Forts Johnson and Gilmer, Birney arrived and attacked Fort Gilmer. After a valiant try the X Corps men were driven back with canister and rifle fire. Just as the defeated Federals were retreating, Maj. Gen. Charles W. Field, with the vanguard of troops sent by Lee from Petersburg, arrived to give the retreating bluecoats a final volley. Next, Birney threw several Negro units at Fort Gilmer; like the white troops before them, they fought bravely but were repulsed with severe losses. Those not killed or severely wounded came streaming back through the line of Ripley's brigade.[85]

In the late afternoon, not long after the X Corps' defeat at Fort Gilmer, the 9th Vermont was sent to the left of Fort Harrison to support part of Stannard's Division, which was still trying to push toward the James River. Here the regiment came under fire from the Confederate gunboats that had come down the James River from Richmond earlier in the morning. Colonel Ripley wrote years later, "As a group of Ninth Vermont officers were standing together chatting with me and watching what they facetiously called the great iron kettles come through the air perfectly visible to the naked eye through the whole of their flight, one which we were watching exploded over head and the large fragments came humming straight toward us. They were perfectly visible and easily dodged." Someone in the group yelled, "Look out for that!" and all the men jumped out of the way — everyone except Second Lt. Calvin M. Jenkins of Co. E. Ripley stated, "Jenkins ... appeared to be mesmerized by it, standing motionless with mouth and eyes gaping wide open until it struck him with a sickening squashing thud." The projectile cut off his right hand and buried itself out of sight in his right groin, making a frightful wound. He was rushed to Dr. Fairman's field hospital where Fairman removed the shell fragment from Jenkins' leg. The incident was so extraordinary that Dr. Fairman mentioned it in his memoirs. He stated that the fragment removed from Jenkins' leg weighed eight pounds and three ounces. Jenkins' leg was so mangled that Fairman had to amputate it at the hip. That night Jenkins was loaded aboard a hospital ship and evacuated to Chesapeake General Hospital in Hampton, but he died en route the next day. Second Lieutenant Calvin M. Jenkins is buried in the Hampton National Cemetery in Hampton, Virginia.[86]

Calvin M. Jenkins was born in Lyndon, Vermont, on October 1, 1828, but was raised in Canada. He married his wife, Adeline, on April 24, 1858, in Coatisook, Canada. They were living in Barnston, Canada, where Jenkins was farming, when the war broke out. He returned to Vermont and enlisted in the 9th Vermont Infantry on June 16, 1862. He rose through the ranks to second lieutenant in Co. E. on June 22, 1863. His transition from enlisted man to commissioned apparently was not very successful and he was brought before a board of examination in the late summer of 1864. His performance was found unacceptable and he was to be cashiered from the army but was mortally wounded before he was to be discharged. On February 4, 1865, the adjutant general's office in Washington, D.C., published Special Order No. 57 reinstating Lieutenant Jenkins. The order reads:

Second Lieutenant Calvin M. Jenkins, Co. E, mortally wounded September 29, 1864 (Vermont Historical Society).

3. So much of Special Orders, No. 432, Paragraph 18, December 16th, 1864, from this Office, as discharged, on the adverse report of a Board of Examination, 2d Lieutenant *Calvin M. Jenkins*, 9th

Vermont Volunteers, is hereby revoked, he having been killed in action whilst conducting himself with great bravery and devotion, prior to the promulgation of the order of discharge.[87]

At nightfall most of the hostilities ended and the 9th Vermont was moved to the south of Fort Harrison to form part of a line that had been extended from the fort to the river. The Green Mountain Boys were worn out from the loss of sleep, marching and combat stress. Ripley gives a glimpse of the hardship:

> The instant we halted, the men dropped in their tracks as though shot. In a few moments along would come the order "side step to the right and close a gap with such Brigade." We would kick, prick, and pound the almost insensible men up, and side-step, halt and drop. Then would come another order from the other direction, "side step to the left" or "march forward" or "backward" until at last we got the engineers satisfied and we thought we were going to sleep. Instead of that shovels and pickaxes were passed along, and we dug like beavers all night, until by morning for two miles or more we presented to the enemy a fairly strong breastwork with five redoubts in it manned by light batteries.[88]

While his men were digging Ripley left to find Stannard to congratulate him for capturing Fort Harrison. Upon his return to his brigade Ripley saw a group of horsemen riding toward him. Still angry after many years, Ripley remembered:

> I had not long rejoined my command lying on the grass chatting and dodging the pots and kettles when we saw a large cavalcade come dashing along the Varina road, up which we had come in the morning This was about 4 P.M. It was easily recognized as Major General Butler, the commander of the Army of the James which had been fighting since daylight and he had just ventured up to see what was going on. He came dashing toward us. No large shells had fallen since he had pushed out into the opening of the woods. The boys began to laugh and prepare to see him turn tail as soon as the gunboats opened again, and they prayed devoutly for them to do so quickly. At last the dull angry roar rolled up again from under the bluffs of the James, Butler pulled up his gallop to a trot. Another roar, and from his trot to a walk, another and from a walk to a halt. For a moment he sat with his arms akimbo on his hips, taking in the scene with a melodramatic air and, turning tail, he walked a little, trotted a little, and then broke into a gallop, and the Major General Commanding the Army of the James had fought the battle of Fort Harrison and all was over. Glittering staff and dashing escort all plunged out of sight from whence they came and we saw them no more.[89]

After the capture of Fort Harrison, the XVIII Corps medical director ordered the 9th Vermont's assistant surgeon, Erastus P. Fairman, along with four attendants, into the fort to set up an aid station. Dr. Fairman explained what happened next:

> Myself and hospital boys went thither, under a continuous fire from the rebel gunboats in the river, and sharp shooters, who had climbed into some tall pines nearly half a mile to our left from the Fort. None of us were harmed, but some of the missiles did strike in the grass, perilously close to us. I was the first surgeon in the Fort. In a hollow nearby I established a little operating hospital, and dressed the wounds, not only of the men in the Ninth, but other regiments, performing amputations and minor operations, until it became to dark to operate. All day shot and shell, from the rebel gunboats, were flying over our heads. As we were packing up our instruments, we heard quite a commotion a short distance from us, where a New York surgeon was dressing wounds. We walked over to see what the row was about. A Captain had received a wound of the main artery of his arm, and was bleeding profusely. The surgeon had been trying for some time to take up the artery, but had not succeeded in doing it. The Captains patience had become exhausted, and he was using language very much more forcible, than diplomatic, making fearful havoc of the Second Commandment. He ordered his surgeon to let him alone, and he would find a surgeon, that knew enough to take up the artery. The Surgeon looked as though he wished he had never been born. At this juncture I begged the privilege of making one trial. As good luck would have it, I seized the bleeding vessel the first attempt I made and tied it. I then dressed the wound, for he would not let his surgeon do it, and the Captain went on his way rejoicing.[90]
>
> From there myself and assistants went to a farm house, a short distance from the Fort. There we found the table set. The breakfast of that morning, evidently having been about half eaten, when upon the advent of our troops, the occupants had left without stopping to wash the dishes. In a little

hovel close by, we found a plenty of poultry, and a good fat hog. Having dressed the poultry and hog, we cooked our supper out of the family provision, and retired for the night. By making a liberal donation of pork and poultry to the Colonel's mess, there never was fault found, with our confiscating the same.[91]

Lee arrived on the field on the afternoon of September 29 and took charge of the situation. He quickly determined the Federals were too strong to attack with the troops he had on hand and decided to postpone a counterattack until the next afternoon. During the night and next morning Lee brought Hoke's division, four regiments from Pickett's division, and six artillery batteries to the north side of the James River.[92]

The Union troops dug furiously during the night preparing for the expected counterattack by the rebels the next morning. The only bright spot for the weary troops was receiving badly needed rations that were brought forward in the darkness. By the next morning the XVIII Corps was in no shape to renew the attack and contented itself with waiting for Lee to make his next move.[93]

Also during the evening of September 29, Butler sent Heckman back to his division and replaced him with Maj. Gen. Godfrey Weitzel. Godfrey Weitzel was born in Cincinnati, Ohio, of German immigrant parents on November 1, 1835. He graduated from West Point in 1855 with a commission in the Engineer Corps. His first four years after graduation were spent on the construction of fortifications guarding the approaches to New Orleans. After that he was posted at West Point, where he was an assistant professor of engineering. He accompanied Butler as his second in command in the occupation of New Orleans in the spring of 1862. In August 1862, he was promoted to brigadier general of volunteers. He commanded a division at the siege of Port Hudson in 1863 and afterward was assigned as Butler's chief engineer in the Army of the James. On November 1, 1864, Weitzel was promoted to Major General.[94]

Considering what the Vermonters had been through their casualties were fairly light. Out of the approximately 700 men who went into battle that morning, only seven were killed in action. Forty-two were wounded, of whom six died later. Of the 13 soldiers reported missing after the battle, only Pvt. Eli Sweeny of Co. F was never accounted for. Like Freeman Baker, he had probably been blown to bits. In total the Army of the James lost approximately 3,000 men in the operation.[95]

At daybreak on the morning of Friday, September 30, the anticipated rebel counterattack failed to materialize, giving Butler time to shift his units around and continue digging. By midmorning he had a strong line from Fort Harrison to the New Market Road. Around 11:00 A.M., Confederate artillery and gunboats commenced their opening bombardment of the Union lines in preparation of their counterattack.[96]

The anticipated Confederate counterattack was finally launched at 2:00 P.M. and was directed straight at Fort Harrison. The attacking force consisted of Hoke's and Field's Divisions. Hoke's attack position was about 200 yards west of Fort Harrison, while Field's was about 500 yards to the northwest. Because of this difference, Field's lead brigades were to get close to the fort and then lie down and wait until they could see Hoke's men advancing before hitting the Yankees with maximum force. Unfortunately the word did not get down to the regimental commanders in Field's brigades and they hit the fort before Hoke's men arrived, and were driven back in confusion. Hoke's brigades attacked at their prescribed time, but it was after Field's repulse and they hit the fort unsupported and suffered the same fate as Field. The fragmented Confederate attack was a lucky stroke of fate for Stannard, as the only artillery unit in the fort almost immediately ran out of ammunition and, with the aid of the new Spencers, he was able to hold off the butternuts with rifle fire.[97]

As Hoke's men fell back they were met by General Lee, who encouraged them to hit the fort again. With a cheer, they reformed and charged again but like the first charge, Stannard's riflemen were too much for them and they came scurrying back in disorder and with more casualties than in the first attack. It was during this charge that Brigadier General Stannard was wounded in the right arm while pacing back and forth on the fort's traverse (an inner wall to deflect artillery shells fired from Union gunboats on the James River) cheering on his men. The rebel bullet hit him just above the elbow, shattering the humerus, whirling him around and knocking him down. He was assisted to safety within the fort's interior where he fainted from shock. From the Vermonter's position they could see Stannard on the traverse as he went down. Ripley related later, "A shiver passed along the lines, as close upon the cheers of victory came the whispered word 'Stannard is killed.' Immediately after, triumphant cheers rang out and we knew he had been spared."[98]

This was Stannard's fifth and final wound of the war. He had first been wounded in the right thigh at the battle of Gettysburg July 3, 1863. He was wounded twice in the left thigh June 3, 1864, at the battle of Cold Harbor. In the middle of July 1864, he was accidentally wounded by a pistol shot from one of his subordinate officers and was on leave of absence from July 28 until September 15. The wound he had just received required amputating his right arm several inches below the shoulder. He would not recover from this wound until December 12. In March 1865 he was assigned to a commission to establish a hospital for disabled veterans and in February 1866 he was assigned as superintendent of Freedmen's Affairs in Maryland. General Stannard resigned from the army June 28, 1866.[99]

Keenly aware the fort was a key position in the defense of the Confederate capital, Lee had Hoke's men make a third charge that again failed and threw the men into near panic as they retreated. It was now nearly 3:00 P.M. and Lee realized it was a lost cause and called a halt to the slaughter. In all, Lee lost over 1,200 badly needed men trying to regain possession of the fort. Butler, on the other hand, had only 260 men killed or wounded.[100]

Just about the time the Confederates fell back, it started to rain and by 6:00 P.M. the rain changed to a downpour. The Federal soldiers had to suffer the wet and cold throughout the night. "We were without tents and were obliged to sleep upon the ground without any protection what ever except our blankets. Lived in storm and mud," remembered George W. Durkee, a 20-year-old farmer from Tunbridge in Co. D. Captain Sherman seconded Durkee's misery when he wrote, "It has rained all day long and night and we are wet to the skin. The men have to lay in the water and mud 6 inches deep." To make matters worse the men were forbidden to build fires for warmth or to cook a meal. The lucky ones, although they probably did not think so at the time, were the men required to keep digging in the trenches. At least they kept warm. By the next morning the Federal line ran from Signal Hill to just above the Darbytown Road. The 9th Vermont remained in the trenches just a little south of Fort Harrison toward the James River.[101]

During the night both sides had to endure the agonizing cries and moans of the Confederate wounded, as Horace noted: "Their wounded lay on the field all night uncared for, and their dead unburied. Their sharpshooters will neither allow our men nor theirs to bury the dead." The Confederate sharpshooters were

Postwar photograph of George W. Durkee (Euclid D. Farnham).

not the only problem. Every time the rebel stretcher bearers tried to rescue their wounded comrades they were fired on by Yankee sharpshooters. Consequently, many Southern boys had died by the time the sun rose the next morning.[102]

The next morning, Saturday, October 1, the Confederate commanders readied their soldiers for the inevitable attack they knew Lee would order, but for some unknown reason Lee called it off and rode off to Richmond. For the next several weeks the Vermonters' lives consisted of picket duty, digging trenches and dodging rebel mortar shells. Captain Sherman complained, "Continued shelling from the rebs. They have planted a mortar to rake the fort on our right." Colonel Ripley also hated the mortars:

> We have been almost constantly under mortar shelling, the most villainous kind, as they come straight down from the sky and its no use trying to get behind anything for protection as you do for other shells. I wish you could see the Woodchuck hole known as Headquarters 2d Brigade, 2d Division. It's a curiosity in its way. You would wonder how we could live in it.[103]

Sunday morning started off like Saturday had, with rain, mortar shells and picket firing, but by afternoon the sun came out and the men had a chance to dry out their clothes and blankets. That same day Grant called a temporary halt to offensive operations on the south side of the James.[104]

The 9th Vermont received 23 more recruits on October 7, bringing their aggregate strength up to 1,150 officers and men. First Lieutenant Alfred Ballard of Co. B reported home: "Our regiment being so large we are often called the 9th Vt. Brigade, and we have often supplied the place of a brigade during the present operations north of the James."[105]

The night of October 8 brought the year's first frost and the Vermonters were still without their tents. Captain Linus Sherman noted in his diary on the morning of October 9, "Another night of rest broken by a severe frost. Cold as you please"; and the same the next night, "Last night there was a hard frost. The men suffered severely without tents." Finally, the tents were brought forward on Wednesday, October 12.[106]

On Sunday, October 9, many of the men of the 9th Vermont, as usual, were hard at work in the trenches. Somehow 21-year-old Pvt. George W. Smith of Co. H, from Craftsbury, was accidentally struck in the hand with a pickaxe by one of his comrades. The wound was bad enough that he was evacuated to Hampton General Hospital. While his wound did not appear that serious, it became infected while he was in the hospital and caused Smith's death on December 16, 1864.[107]

After the failed attack to take back Fort Harrison, the rebels' morale started to deteriorate. Captain Linus Sherman wrote on October 10, "The rebels have given up all hope of taking back Fort Harrison which we took from them. Deserters flock in every day. They report that the rebels are sick and about ready to give up the contest." Colonel Ripley noted the same thing on October 1:

> In every night on the front occupied by this division, about twenty come in, and last night we were turned out by rapid fire in front of the forts by the Rebs, and in a few minutes in piled a Rebel Major, Captain and two lieutenants and about fifty men. Their own troops were shooting at them, and the most inexplicable thing is that a man who today fires on his comrades for going, will probably come in himself tonight.[108]

Colonel Ripley also noted on October 12 a cease-fire along the picket line and complained about the hygiene problem caused by living in the trenches:

> By common consent picket firing and sharpshooting is given up. I have today brought up my Headquarters tents and teams, and no longer play woodchuck, sitting on the edge of my hole to enjoy the sunlight, and scrambling in at the approach of a 13 [inch] mortar shall. 'Twas time to give it up, as after seeing Captain Deacon, my Senior Aide, and Mr. Roberts my A. A. G., hunt their clothes with much better success than Independence quail hunting, I took a notion that a peculiar feeling down

my neck could be explained beyond possibility. It was made, and the results exceeded my most sanguine expectations. Think of it, *Lousy*.[109]

"There was considerable fighting on our right yesterday," Capt. Linus Sherman wrote on October 13, "but I guess it did not amount to much. We had to move camp twice to take the place of troops that went out. It was all within distinct hearing." What the Vermonter's heard was a force that Butler sent out earlier that morning making contact with the enemy. Brigadier General Krautz, the Army of the James' cavalry commander, confirmed the Confederates were building a new defense line in advance of Richmond's intermediate line on October 12. Grant ordered Butler to attack the work party and halt the construction. Butler sent the 1st Division of the X Corps and Krautz's cavalry on October 13 to stop the digging. But as usual, the Federal force returned with its tail between its legs later in the evening after losing over 440 men.[110]

The same day as the cavalry advance, Pvt. Horatio N. Stoliker, a 22-year-old farmer from Monkton in Co. A, accidentally shot himself in the left foot while on picket duty on the Charles City road. His company commander, Capt. Linus Sherman, stated, "He was in no way responsible for the wound and was a faithful and brave soldier and always did his whole duty." Stoliker's big toe on his left foot had to be amputated. He returned to duty with his company April 14, 1865, where he served until he was mustered out June 13, 1865. Horatio Stoliker died March 17, 1911, in West Boylston, Massachusetts, from a skull fracture at age 70. He left a wife and five grown children.[111]

During the night of October 13, Pvt. Samuel Hartley of Co. C, an Irish-born brush maker from Middlebury, was captured while on picket. Exactly how he was captured remains a mystery. Hartley, one of the original members of the 9th Vermont, had a checkered career in the regiment. He had deserted the British army in Canada to enlist in the 9th Vermont on June 7, 1862. Because of demonstrated leadership abilities he was promoted to corporal December 1, 1862, while the regiment was in Chicago. In August 1863, while in Yorktown, he had forged an order with his company commander's signature to get liquor and was court-martialed and reduced to the ranks. He was again promoted to corporal January 30, 1863, and for some unexplained reason was reduced to the ranks again July 28, 1864. Samuel Hartley was exchanged by the Confederates on February 22, 1865, and returned to the regiment, where he served until he was mustered out June 29, 1865.[112]

Lieutenant Colonel Barney returned from leave the second week of October and wrote his wife on October 17:

> The Regt. encamped in their shelter tents close behind a line of earthworks which runs from Ft. Harrison to the James River being about ½ mile from the fort. The officers and most of the men are living in holes in the ground like a potato hole and cover it with a shelter tent on a few bushes. Hd. Qtrs. is without a tent but one of the queerest holes in existence.... The Rebel pickets are plainly seen from our parapet.[113]

On Friday, October 21, Barney reported home:

> The most exciting news we have is from Gen. Sheridan. Last night a shotted salute of one hundred guns fired from Ft. Harrison in honor of the great victory and cheering was kept along our lines for an hour. The rebs also cheered very heartily and we made up our minds that they had heard only the first part of the news from the Shenandoah and supposed their victory was complete. They only answered our fire by a few mortar shells which done no damage.[114]

The battle Barney wrote about was the battle of Cedar Creek, fought near Middletown in the Shenandoah Valley on October 19. The Confederates had launched a surprise attack on Maj. Gen. Philip H. Sheridan's Army of the Shenandoah in the wee hours of the morning on October 19 and had driven them back several miles. Sheridan, who had been summoned to Washington several days before, returned in the afternoon and rallied his troops. Sheridan counterattacked and defeated the Confederates, clearing them out of the Shenandoah for good.[115]

After the celebration of the battle of Cedar Creek, life around Fort Harrison relaxed somewhat. An unofficial cease-fire on the picket line was established and the Yankees and the rebels began trading newspapers, coffee and tobacco again, as Captain Sherman noted: "Exchanged papers with Johnny Reb and he gave me a plug of tobacco." Val Barney, now back in command of the 9th Vermont did likewise: "I went out day before yesterday and exchanged papers with a rebel major."[116]

Captain Sherman recorded on October 22:

> All quiet except a duel between our forts on the river and Reb. gunboats. One shell came into our camp but did not hurt anybody. I hardly think we shall move again soon. We have no baggage and no knapsacks. Cannot write much for I have to be up at 4½ A.M. We have to be up at 4½ A.M. each day to guard against an advance of the enemy.[117]

In addition to the more relaxed living conditions, the Vermonters got a welcome surprise on Sunday, October 23, with the arrival of the paymaster. As luck would have it, the 9th Vermont's sutler had just arrived from New Bern four days before, so the men had some place to spend their money.[118]

As the month wore on, the Vermonters still did not have their baggage and knapsacks and the nights started getting chilly. Lieutenant Colonel Barney complained to his wife:

> Since I arrived here there has been continual good weather and we are enjoying the sunshine very much. The nights are pretty cold, but the Maj., Adj., and I all sleep under the same blanket and so close together that we keep pretty warm in our little potato hole. I have not had my pants off nor my coat and boots but two or three times since I came, in fact pants not once.[119]

During the latter part of October, Grant decided to make another foray against the South Side Railroad, Petersburg's last supply link with the Deep South. To keep Lee from bringing reinforcements from the north side of the James River, Grant ordered Butler to make another demonstration against Richmond. Grant specifically ordered Butler to feel out to the right beyond his front and if possible to turn the enemy's left, but not to attack any entrenched positions. Butler's plan was to demonstrate with the X Corps on the enemy's front on the Darbytown and Charles City roads and simultaneously attempt to turn the Confederate left with Weitzel's XVIII Corps. Kautz's cavalry division (temporarily under the command of Col. Robert M. West, Kautz being down with malaria) would cover the XVIII Corps move around Terry's right flank.[120]

The X Corps moved out before dawn on October 27 to take up their blocking position. Weitzel had formed up his XVIII Corps the day before on the Cox farm near the James River where the troops had cooked three days' rations for the upcoming advance. His units consisted of Brig. Gen. Gilman Marston's 1st Division with Col. John R. Raulston's First Brigade, Col. Edgar M. Cullen's Second Brigade and Col. Joab N. Patterson's Third Brigade, Heckman's 2nd Division with Ripley's Second Brigade, Fairchild's Third Brigade and Col. Alonzo G. Draper's Third Brigade of the 3rd Division temporarily attached to Heckman. Rounding out the XVIII Corps task force were Col. John H. Holman's First Brigade of the 3rd Division as well as two four-gun batteries. Weitzel's force numbered approximately 8,000 men. The troops moved out on the Kingsland road on the cold rainy morning of October 27 at 5:00 A.M. From the Kingsland road they hit the New Market road heading north with the 1st Division in the lead followed by Heckman's division and Holman's brigade bringing up the rear. Later in they day the column took the Charles City road to the Williamsburg road leading to Fair Oaks.[121]

By the time the XVIII Corps reached Fair Oaks it had marched about 16 grueling miles. The march had been fast and many men had fallen out of the column. One of those was Pvt. Stephen B. Wing, a Troy resident in the 9th Vermont's Co. E. Wing was in his early forties and apparently the march was too much for him and he died from apoplexy (congestion or rupture of the vessels in the brain). Wing left a wife, Luthera Litchfield Wing, and five children. Wing family history has it that Private Charles Warboys, also in Co. E, dropped out of the ranks to bury Stephen Wing by the roadside and was reprimanded for doing so. Stephen Wing's parents had two other sons in the war. George K. Wing enlisted in the 7th Vermont Infantry and died of disease October 14, 1862. A third son, Reuben Wing, enlisted in the 9th Vermont June 23, 1862, and was discharged with a disability April 29, 1863. Stephen Wing also had a nephew, Private Seth Burgess Wing, in the 9th Vermont. Seth Wing had initially enlisted in the 29th Maine Infantry, but for some unknown reason, deserted after only one week. He enlisted in the 9th Vermont's Co. E as Seth Burgess on August 17, 1864, presumably changing his name to avoid being charged with desertion from the 29th Maine. Seth Wing survived the war and was mustered out December 1, 1865, and returned to Vermont, where he married Stephen Wing's widow, Luthera, and moved to Wisconsin where they had three children of their own. Luthera died in 1918 at age 64, and not long after her death Stephen married Emma Minday of Watertown, Wisconsin. Seth died May 10, 1928, of a stroke. He is buried in the Marcellon Cemetery in Pardeeville, Wisconsin. Years after his death one of Seth's relatives applied for a veteran's stone from the Veterans Administration. In order to get the stone it had to be inscribed as Seth Burgess rather than Seth B. Wing because of his desertion.[122]

The XVIII Corps arrived at Fair Oaks at about 2:00 P.M. with high hopes of success, since Weitzel had been led to believe the Confederate trenches were lightly manned with Brig. Gen. Martin W. Gary's dismounted cavalry. The Confederate works had in fact been manned with Gary's dismounted cavalry, but Field's division of combat hardened veterans had arrived just before Weitzel's appearance. The Confederate forces were under the able leadership of Lt. Gen. James Longstreet, who quickly realized Terry's movement was a feint and left Hoke's division to confront Terry and dispatched Field's division to Fair Oaks.[123]

Still believing the Confederate works were thinly manned, and against orders, Weitzel decided to attack. Where the Williamsburg road approached the Confederate entrenchments it ran through a stretch of woods for a little more than 800 feet and then through a large field before cutting through the rebel line. Just inside the tree line Weitzel deployed his units for the assault. Brig. Gen. Gilman Marston's division was posted on the right side of the Williamsburg road and Heckman's division on the left. Marston placed Cullen's brigade's left flank on the Williamsburg road with Raulston's brigade to the right of Cullen. Marston's Third Brigade was put behind the other two as support. Heckman shifted Fairchild's brigade forward and aligned on Cullen's left. Draper's brigade was put behind Fairchild's with its right flank resting on the Williamsburg road and was to attack with Cullen. Ripley's brigade was positioned with its right flank on the

Left, top: Private Stephen B. Wing, Co. E, died of a stroke on the march to the battle of Fair Oaks, October 27, 1864 (Barb Pahlow). *Left, bottom:* Private Charles N. Warboys, Co. E (Barb Pahlow).

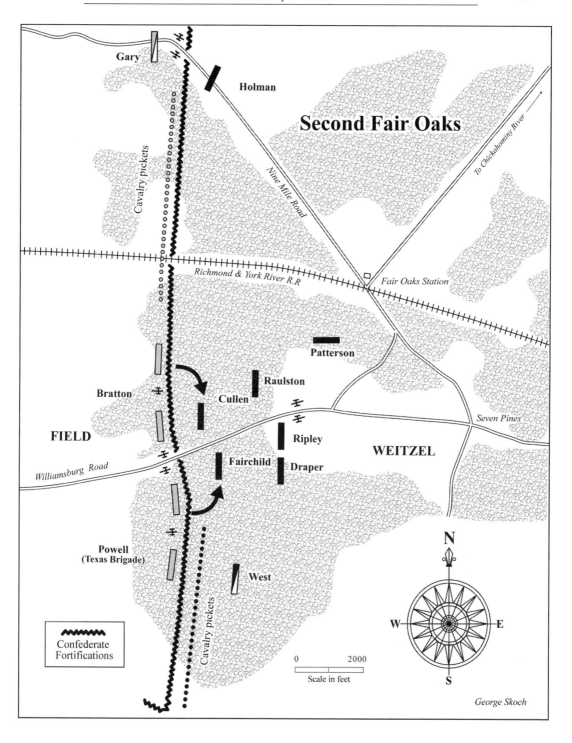

The Second Battle of Fair Oaks, October 27, 1864.

Williamsburg Road and Draper was to the left of Ripley. Weitzel sent a brigade of colored troops to the right across the York River Railroad to turn the Confederate left.[124]

Near 4:00 P.M. Cullen's and Fairchild's brigades left the safety of the woods and entered the field and immediately started taking heavy artillery and rifle fire. Cullen was facing Brig. Gen. John Bratton's South Carolina Brigade and Fairchild the Texas Brigade. The two Union brigades still had to cross an open space of about 1,500 feet before hitting the rebel fortifications. The supporting brigades entered the field and were ordered to lie down. The field, which had grown up in bushes, offered the supporting units some protection, but the attacking units were cut to pieces. Ripley provided a detachment of the 8th Maine as skirmishers for Fairchild. Of the 150 Maine men who went out only 75 returned unharmed. Dr. Fairman described the intensity of the combat:

> As the head of the column emerged into the open field, we were greeted with a shower of shot and shell. Solid shot tore through the tops of the trees, and others ploughed the ground. Limbs fell and dirt flew. Had the men stood up, they were literally in the jaws of death. All the regiments filed out into the bushes, and every man fell flat upon his face, and hugged the ground the best he knew how. As a rule the officers were no exception.[125]

As the attacking units advanced the men of the 9th Vermont hugged the ground. Pieces of exploding artillery shells and lead minie balls filled the air around them and occasionally hit among them. Private Alonzo R. Grover, a young farmer from Rupert in Co. K, was hit in the back of his head by one of the pieces of shell that were whizzing about. The shell fragment took off the back of his skull, killing him instantly. When his lieutenant attempted to inventory Grover's personal effects several days later, he found that Grover had nothing. Private Grover left a widow and two young children.[126]

The same shell fragment that killed Grover slammed into Pvt. Edward B. Bissell, also of Co. K, from Wardsboro. He was struck in the right arm several inches below the shoulder joint. Not only did the missile open up a nasty gash on his arm, but it impacted with such force it fractured the humerus up into the shoulder joint. Bissell was quickly taken to the rear on a stretcher where the 9th Vermont's assistant surgeon Fairman put Bissell under with ether and amputated the arm at the shoulder joint. Surprisingly, the wound was almost completely healed in about 10 weeks, but Bissell did not return to the regiment. He was discharged from the Central Park General Hospital in New York City on July 25, 1865.[127]

Private Joel Grout, Co. K, wounded in the left ankle on October 27, 1864, in the battle of Fair Oaks (Kent Young).

Private Peter Ladeau (also spelled Ladu and Ladoo) in Co. H was struck by a minie ball, although the records do not indicate where. He was eventually transferred to the Chesapeake General Hospital in Hampton where he died February 1, 1865. He is buried in the Hampton National Cemetery.[128]

Twenty-two-year-old Pvt. Joel Grout, a farmer from Stratton in Co. K, was lying low trying to stay out of harm's way when a rebel minie ball slammed into his left ankle. The ball went through the ankle joint, fracturing several bones before exiting. After being treated in the 9th Vermont's field hospital, he was taken to Chesapeake General Hospital in Hampton. Sometime later Grout was transferred to the Governor Smith General Hospital in Brattleboro where he received a disability discharge May

26, 1865. As a result of his wound he had a slight limp the rest of his life. He married Martha Jane Pike after his discharge and purchased a farm in Newfane, where he spent the rest of his life. Joel Grout died July 12, 1921.[129]

One of the luckier wounded men was Pvt. Alson N. Wheatley, an 18-year-old farmer from Brookfield in Co. C, who was hit on the big toe of his left foot by a spent minie ball. The ball took off the end of his big toe and the toenail. After the war he suffered from chronic diarrhea and rheumatism and had a limp from his wounded toe. Alson Wheatly died January 30, 1922, in East Brookfield of pneumonia and is buried in the East Brookfield Cemetery.[130]

As the bullets and shrapnel continued to whine and zing through the air, Pvt. Charles W. Stoddard of Co. K, who had been wounded the previous February at Newport Barracks, finally could not take any more and shot off the end of the middle finger of his right hand. Then, for some reason he did not leave the ranks. The next day he was sent to the Point of Rocks Hospital for chills and fever. At the hospital the doctors discovered his wounded finger and amputated more of it between the first and second knuckles. Stoddard was then sent to Annapolis Junction Hospital in Maryland, where he was kept until discharged from the army June 7, 1865. It appears Stoddard was never charged for intentionally wounding himself because he never returned to the regiment after going to the hospital. Years later a U.S. Pension Bureau examiner said Stoddard admitted to shooting off his own finger, but that Stoddard had not claimed the finger wound and was receiving an $8.00 a month pension for malaria.[131]

Private David M. Buffum in Co. B from Pawlet was wounded slightly in the head, but that was not mentioned when he applied for a pension after the war. His biggest ailment was that his right testicle was enlarged to 10½ inches in circumference from a varicocele (a backing up of blood in the veins to the testicle) contracted in Suffolk May 10, 1863. He received a small pension for his problem.[132]

First Lieutenant William A. Dodge, a 21-year-old clerk from Shrewsbury in Co. B, was wounded for the second time in a month. He had been slightly wounded at the battle of Fort Harrison and now was hit in the left thigh. This new wound was also slight, but while in the hospital gangrene set in, complicating his recovery. He survived his wound, but had to resign from the army. After the war he studied at the Eastman's Business College in Poughkeepsie, New York, and then engaged in the mercantile business in Thetford, Vermont, from 1873 to 1883, when his store burned. He then began farming in Thetford, which he continued until his death on November 15, 1903.[133]

Lieutenant Colonel Barney later related a close call he had during the attack: "Many pieces of shell and spherical case shot struck around me and one piece grazed my back just after I had dismounted and two men were hit within 3 feet of me but nothing came nearer than 6 inches of me and that a small piece of shell."[134]

Years later Surgeon Erastus Fairman recorded his part of the action:

> Myself and squad had followed the 9th into their boiling caldron of lead and iron. There I stood for an instant, wondering what I should do. Presently some General came to me and told me to go back to the rear, out of range of the enemies missils, where I could care for the wounded, as they were brought back to me. I never obeyed an order more cheerfully, or with greater alacrity in my life. As we passed back over the turnpike, the shot and shell followed us for a third of a mile. We did not double quick, but we made good time nevertheless. According to orders I made my way back to an old hovel, and there dressed the wounds of the 9th and those of other regiments until dark, when the corps received orders to fall back.[135]

By the time Cullen's and Fairchild's Brigades were 150 yards from the rebel entrenchments they had been cut to pieces. At about 5:00 P.M. several regiments of each of the two Confederate brigades swept out on the flanks of the Federal units and scooped up a great many prisoners, especially the 19th Wisconsin and the 148th New York in Fairchild's brigade. According to Ripley:

The 148th New York out of 225 came out with 75. The 19th Wisconsin lost every officer but the Major and a 2d Lieutenant, and over 75 percent of the men.... All the 1st Division Sharpshooters were captured. They were close up under the enemies works and could not get away, the enemy held them there, charged out and captured them all.[136]

In all, six Federal units lost their colors. Unable to extricate themselves under such an extremely heavy fire, Marston's and Heckman's troops had to wait until dark to back off the field. Holman's colored troops, who had been sent to the right, were at first successful. They initially captured the Confederate works between the Williamsburg and Nine Mile roads, but Gary's cavalry eventually pushed them back.[137]

Under cover of darkness, in a driving rain that continued all night, Weitzel pulled his units out and made his way to the Charles City road. The 9th Vermont, bringing up the rear, only got as far as the Darbytown Road before stopping. The march was horrible, as Dr. Fairman explained:

> On the retreat the 9th brought up the rear. I could not see the horse I rode. One can imagine what kind of a road the 9th had to pass over that night in that fearful down pour of rain, with corps of infantry, a regiment of cavalry, and forty or fifty pieces of artillery ahead of us, to cut up the road.[138]

The 9th Vermont stopped for the night at about 3:00 A.M. where Lieutenant Colonel Barney recalled, "Although the rain continued and we were all thoroughly soaked we slept 3 hours very nicely."[139]

While slogging through the mud in the darkness, Pvt. Edward Hawkins, Co. E, slipped and fell, straining his left testicle and causing a varicocele. In 1881 Hawkins was awarded a pension of $16.00 a month for rheumatism, heart disease and piles. In May 1891, he filed a claim for additional pension due to the varicocele, but was rejected because there was no record of his being treated in any military hospital. He did have affidavits from three of his army comrades, Henry O. Elliott, George Warboys, and Clement George, attesting to the injury. George stated, "He showed me his testicle not long afterwards and the knotted veins upon it." Elliott stated, "I tented with him and saw it often." The claim, however, was not accepted. The injury did not seem to affect his sexual functioning, as he fathered five children. Edward Hawkins died November 17, 1899, of hepatitis.[140]

Private Peter Brady, a 24-year-old Irish immigrant in Co. C, also fell behind and was captured. He was initially imprisoned in the Confederate prisoner of war camp at Salisbury, North Carolina. While being moved to another camp he escaped at Averysboro, North Carolina, March 5, 1865, and returned to Federal lines. He was furloughed home April 11, 1865, and then sent to Camp Parole, Maryland, on May 15 and was finally mustered out of service June 2, 1865.[141]

Another 9th Vermont straggler picked up by the Confederates was Pvt. Alvora M. Sargent of Co. A, a 25-year-old, five-foot five-inch farmer from Sharon. He was captured on the Williamsburg road and incarcerated in Castle Thunder in Richmond for 8 days before being sent to the prisoner of war camp in Salisbury, North Carolina. He survived the ordeal and was paroled February 24, 1865. Sargent was sent to the hospital at Camp Parole, Maryland, for about a week before he was sent home to Sharon. After being mustered out he received a $12.00 a month pension for a chronic ulcer on his right leg, and deafness, and it was several years before he could farm again. Sargent wrote later:

> In the prison I was starved and neglected so that I contracted scurvy, rheumatism, fever and ague and the deafness. Was treated in what they called No. 8 Hospital for my general condition. At that time I was in a terrible condition from the disease malnutrition. Seemed to me that I had had everything. I had taken a cold and sores were running in my head and discharging matter from my right ear. The other ear did not seem to be affected.[142]

The next morning the rain had stopped and Weitzel prepared his units to resume the offensive, but at about 10:00 A.M. Butler ordered him back to his old position at Fort Harrison. Lieutenant Colonel Barney gives a glimpse of what the 9th Vermont went through:

At 7 O'c. we formed line of battle to charge the works on that road but for some reason the idea was abandoned and we came to our old camp, getting here at 3 o'c. yesterday and our men and those who have been through all the battles of this summer say this was the hardest time they ever saw and all on account of the mud and rain and hard and rapid marching.[143]

The affair at Fair Oaks had cost the Army of the James about 1,600 casualties and accomplished nothing. Captain Sherman opined, "It was a poor specimen of war," but, he added, "We are by no means discouraged but ready for anything that is coming for us." Dr. Fairman wrote sarcastically, "The affair proved to [be] a perfect fizzle."[144]

After returning to their old camp near Fort Harrison, the Vermonters got back into the routine of fatigue and picket duty. Then at 9:00 P.M. Wednesday, November 2, the regiment got orders to prepare to deploy to some yet undisclosed location. Three days' rations were cooked and knapsacks, which had just recently arrived, were packed. At midnight the 9th Vermont, along with 15 other regiments, marched to Deep Bottom, where they arrived at 4:00 A.M.[145]

After standing around in the rain and mud all day and evening, the 9th Vermont was split up and loaded aboard the steamers *Constitution* and *General Wool* just before midnight. The vessels then sailed to Bermuda Hundred to wait for daylight before the trip down the James River to the Chesapeake Bay. As the vessels were moving to Bermuda Hundred, Private James Duggan of Co. B, a 29-year-old Irish-born laborer from Fairhaven, somehow fell overboard from the *General Wool*. The vessel's crew tried to rescue him, but before they could reach him, Duggan was run over by the steamer *Washington Irving*, which was following behind the *General Wool*, and drowned. His body was recovered

Private Alfred Avery, Co. H, died of chronic diarrhea at Point of Rocks Hospital on October 27, 1864 (Shane Gower).

several days later. In Duggan's compiled service record at the National Archives in Washington, D.C., is a report of the incident written by Duggan's company commander, Capt. Samuel Kelley. The last sentence of Kelley's report reads, "He was a good soldier." James Duggan is buried in the City Point National Cemetery in Hopewell, Virginia.[146]

The vessels with the Vermonters onboard set sail down the James River early in the morning hours of Friday, November 4, and arrived at Fort Monroe just after dark that evening. Upon arrival at Fort Monroe the Vermont men on the *General Wool* were transferred to the *John Romer*. The *John Romer* sailed early the next morning, but the *Constitution* had to steam across the Chesapeake Bay to Craney Island to take on coal. It was not until 9:00 that night that she set sail for her final destination. Once out in the Atlantic everyone was told where they were going and why. All 15 regiments were off to New York City to quell any riots that might ensue because of the presidential election on November 8.[147]

The government's concern about riots was well founded. There had been terrible riots in New York City when the military draft was instituted in July of 1863. When the first names for the draft were published in the newspapers mobs started gathering and on July 13 rioting began. The local government was unable to restore order. The mob, which soon numbered 50,000, burned a Negro church and orphanage and Negro men were hung from trees and lampposts.

The mob also sacked and burned armories, draft stations, the office of the New York *Tribune*, and the home of the provost marshal. In all, they did about $1,500,00 worth of property damage, and killed more than a dozen people. Working class Irishmen made up the majority of the mob and their main victims were Negroes, on whom they blamed the war. With the antiwar sentiment in New York City the government was afraid if Lincoln won the election rioting would begin again.[148]

The *Constitution* arrived in New York Harbor at 11:00 A.M., Sunday, November 6, and anchored off Staten Island near Fort Richmond. Companies G and K were taken ashore after dark that evening while the rest of the regiment remained aboard the vessel. Monday morning Co. K loaded aboard the steamer *Vanderbilt* along with the 98th New York Infantry and sailed up the Hudson to West Troy, where they were assigned to guard the Watervliet Arsenal. The rest of the Vermonters were transferred to two other vessels and stationed in the North and East rivers, ready to go ashore when and where needed.[149]

The weather was cold and rainy and the men had no opportunity to see friends or the sights of the city. The election passed off quietly on November 8, yet the Vermonters continued to stay aboard the cramped ships. Lieutenant Colonel Barney wrote on November 10:

> We have been laying here so long that it is getting rather tedious and I am getting anxious to get a shore. The men were quite jubilant when they first knew we were coming to N.Y. but now they all say they would prefer laying in the trenches before the enemy than brought here to be kept so confined. The rain has poured down ever since we started and the decks of our steamer are anything but pleasant to live on. On this boat however we took forcible possession of the after cabin much to the disgust of the Capt. and crew but as we out numbered them we done just about as we pleased and we (officers) have had a pleasant place to live for two days past.[150]

Company K got orders to leave Watervliet Arsenal at 10:00 A.M. Saturday, November 12, and rejoin the regiment in New York City, but transportation on the train could not be arranged until the next day. Before daylight on November 13 Co. K marched to East Troy and boarded a train for New York City, arriving there at 3:00 P.M. They stayed in the cars until nearly dark before they could get a steamer to rejoin the regiment.

When Co. K left Watervliet for New York City it left behind Privates Emery S. Wilder and Jesse C. Jones. The two men had gone AWOL to Vermont while on guard duty at the arsenal. Emery Wilder was a 21-year-old farmer from Jamaica, Vermont. Jesse Jones, age 31, was a farmer from Randolph. Both men returned to the regiment at Chaffin's Bluff of their own volition on December 3 and were thrown into the guardhouse.

Wilder was brought before a general court-martial December 24 and pleaded guilty to the charges of leaving his guard post and being AWOL. He had his first sergeant, J. Webster Stebbins, and his platoon leader, Second Lt. Joel C. Baker, testify to his spotless military record prior to his recent absence. Then, in his own defense he read a statement explaining why he had deserted. He indicated that he had been raised by his grandmother in Jamaica, Vermont, and loved her very much and that that because of a current illness and her advanced age, it might be his last chance to see her alive. He concluded by stating that he had always been a good soldier and intended to continue being one in the future. He apparently came across as sincere since the court was lenient in its sentence. Wilder lost $5.00 of his pay per month for the rest of his enlistment and was to be publicly reprimanded in front of his regiment by his commanding officer.

Jones was brought before the court on December 31 on the same charges as Wilder, and like Wilder, pleaded guilty. First Sergeant Stebbins was called as a witness and testified that Jones had been a good soldier and that his wife was very sick. Private Jason E. Goss was also called as a witness for the defense and testified that Jones had told him about his wife's illness. Jones said in a statement to the court that he had received a letter from his wife in Stratton stating that her doctor had said she wouldn't live to see his time in the service completed, without help. He then said, "I have always intended to be a good soldier and do my duty faithfully and I shall do the same hereafter." Although his sentence was stiffer than Wilder's, the court was again lenient. He was sentenced to be reprimanded in the presence of the regiment by his commanding officer and to be placed at hard labor for the period of 15 days, working from 6:00 A.M. to 6:00 P.M. with an intermission of three-fourths of an hour in the middle of the day. True to their words both Wilder and Jones served without incident until honorably discharged at the expiration of their service on June 13, 1865.[151]

The following April, Wilder was playing around and threw several signal rockets into a campfire. The rockets ignited and burned his eyes. After the war he got a pension for the damage to his eyes and malaria. He died June 5, 1916, of cirrhosis of the liver and kidney disease.[152]

Two other members of the 9th Vermont also went AWOL while in New York City, Major Brooks and John T. Bascom of Co. F. They were gone overnight, as Captain Sherman related: "When they came back Col. Barney put them under arrest. If charges are preferred against them Gen. Butler will very likely dismiss them from the service. It will serve them right." The two officers may have gotten verbal reprimands, but their records do not show any type of official punishment. It appears that rank always has its privileges.[153]

The 9th Vermont finally departed New York City aboard the steamer *John Rice* (one of the vessels that had taken part of the regiment to North Carolina) on Tuesday, November 15, and made Fort Monroe at sunrise on the 17th and started up the James River at 9:00 A.M. The regiment arrived at Jones Landing a little after dark and stayed aboard the *John Rice* until the next morning. The morning was rainy and cold as the Vermonters marched back to their old camp and put up their shelter tents.[154]

When the 9th Vermont had left Chaffin's Bluff for New York City, it left behind three detachments. One was the group at Redoubt Dutton. The second was the 140 men under the command of Lieutenant Jewett who caught up with the regiment in New York. Third was a 15-man picket under the supervision of Corp. Charles H. Sweeney, a 41-year-old carriage maker from Wolcott in Co. H. When the regiment left camp to deploy to New York, Sweeney and his men had not been called in and subsequently missed the embarkation. After returning from their tour on the picket line and realizing they had been left behind, Sweeney hailed a tugboat and had it take him and his men to City Point, where he reported to the provost marshal. The provost marshal thought Sweeney's story seemed suspicious and told him that he believed that Sweeney and his men were deserters and that he was going to put them in the guardhouse. Sweeney indignantly denied the charge and refused to go to the guardhouse.

This refusal, of course, infuriated the provost marshal, who ordered his men to "hand cuff this man and take him to the bull-pen." But Sweeney had more men with him than the provost marshal did and quickly ordered his men to fix bayonets. He posted 10 of his men to watch the provost marshal, with strict orders to let no one pass in or out, while he and the remainder of his men started for army headquarters. He made his way to General Grant's quarters, where he explained the situation to an orderly at the door of Grant's office. He was soon ushered in to talk with the army commander. Grant asked the corporal to be seated and asked what regiment he belonged to. Sweeney told him that he belonged to the 9th Vermont and related to Grant what had happened and how he had put the provost marshal under guard for threatening to put him in the guardhouse. Grant listened, probably with some amusement, and said, "We'll see about that" and sat down and wrote a note for Sweeney to give to the provost marshal. Sweeney returned to the provost marshal's office and handed him the note ordering the provost marshal to arrange transportation for the Vermonter to New York City. The provost marshal blanched when Sweeney informed him that he had a note from General Grant and his hand trembled as he took the note from the Vermonter. The provost marshal quickly dispatched one of his men to accompany the Green Mountain Boys to the commissary and, after procuring rations, Sweeney and his men were provided with transportation to New York City, where they rejoined their regiment.[155]

While the regiment was away in New York, the 9th Vermont's chief surgeon, Walter Carpenter, resigned. He had been temporarily assigned to the Chesapeake General Hospital in Hampton and had not been with the regiment for some time. He had been in the army since May of 1861 and was worn out. Carpenter returned to Burlington, where he became a successful physician. He remained a bachelor his whole life and died March 20, 1906, and is buried in Green Mount Cemetery in Burlington.[156]

Walter S. Vincent, one of the 9th Vermont's two assistant surgeons, was promoted on November 15 to replace Carpenter. Assistant Surgeon Fairman was upset with Vincent's promotion. Vincent had spent most of his time with the regiment at higher echelon hospitals and Fairman did not think Vincent was a very good doctor. It is not known if Vincent was as incompetent as Fairman thought, or if it was just professional jealously, but Fairman was still smarting over the promotion years after the war when he wrote in his recollections of the war:

On the 4th of November, Surgeon Carpenter resigned and on the 15th the vacancy was filled by the promotion of Assistant Surgeon Vincent, he having been in the service longer than I had. From that time until the close of the war, with the exception of two weeks in February, when I was sick with Jaundice, he never had any care whatever of the Regiment. With the exception named, the last seven months of his army life were spent wholly in playing checkers and backgammon, for which government paid him 200 dollars a month. Query, how many such men would it take, to put down the Rebellion? What would it cost? We had too many such parasites in the U.S. Service, who were depleting the government treasury, thereby aiding the Rebel cause. It made me mad to see men under the guise of patriots, and having a reputation as such, thus robbing their country.[157]

Once back in camp the Vermonters got back into life in the field. There was very little firing between the pickets so the only distasteful part of that duty was the rain that continued to come down for almost the entire first week. Captain Sherman noted in his diary on November 20, "We dug a hole yesterday for a 'Go for it.' It is full of water this A.M. and hence unhabitable." Lieutenant Colonel Barney also complained about the weather to his wife: "Today is Sunday and we got back on Friday since which time the rain has poured down without cessation and the weather is quite cold the wind from the north, mud in large quantities." On November 22 the temperature dropped and a little snow fell. Thankfully that same day the regiment drew overcoats.[158]

From about the time the 9th Vermont arrived in Virginia the detachment under Lieutenant Jewett remained at Redoubt Dutton and had some exciting times. On the night of September 30 they were called into the trenches to help repel a Confederate assault. During the next two months several attempts were made by the enemy to advance their lines to Redoubt Dutton and an attempt was made on the Union side to retake a portion of the line which the enemy had carried. After these efforts ceased, picket firing became routine, and as the lines were very near each other, picket duty was extremely dangerous. The firing between the pickets, however, subsided after a while, and hostilities in that vicinity were confined to frequent artillery duels. Fortunately, none of the Vermonters were injured. On November 21, Lieutenant Jewett resigned, leaving Sgt. Charles F. Branch in charge of the detachment. On November 28 the detachment was relieved and rejoined the regiment at Chapin's Farm.[159]

Not long after returning from New York, the 9th Vermont was given orders to start building winter quarters and everyone went to work in earnest, as the weather was rapidly getting colder. By the last week of November most of the log walls for the huts were up and tents were being put on top for roofs. Then, true to army form, orders were received for some of the men to move, as Capt. Sherman noted:

We have been building little log houses & covering them with tents. I have mine done and have built a mud and stick chimney so I can keep warm if only they will let me remain here. It is near where we were when we first came across the James Sep 29th/64. All is quiet along the lines as far as I know. As a example of the military I will state that soon after we came back we received orders to build huts to make us more comfortable. We worked with one night & [illegible] for several days. Even took Thanksgiving Day when there were no details from the Regt. for extra duty. Well! We go well along with our work many having completed their houses and built chimneys and ordered to move to another place about 200 rods from present one. Some cursed. Some made fun of the matter etc. etc. But after a while the order was modified so that only half of the of the men had to move.[160]

One 9th Vermont soldier, known only as "Sylvester," wrote a letter to the *Lamoille Newsdealer* describing how the men made fireplaces for their huts.:

We have very comfortable quarters indeed, although it was a very tedious job to build them. We hade to take our stockade timbers about two miles on our backs, but we feel amply rewarded for our labor by having a good fire place to sit by these cold winter nights. Perhaps it would be interesting to some to know how we build our fire places. Well I will tell you. We drive into the ground some stakes in the form of a half circle, or nearly so, then we drive another row outside of them in the same manner, then we fill up the space between the two rows with mortar which is already mixed, quite plenty in this part of the country. As the stakes burn the mortar becomes baked, and when thoroughly baked is very hard. In this manner we get a very comfortable fire place. Our chimneys are made of small sticks put up cob house fashion and well mortared out side and in.[161]

On November 30, another tragedy happened to one of the 9th Vermont boys that the others in the regiment never learned about. Private Nelson Stinehowe of Co. C, who had been captured at the battle of Newport Barracks and incarcerated at Andersonville, had been exchanged on November 19. He was put aboard the steamer *Baltic* for the trip to Camp Parole in Annapolis, Maryland. Unfortunately, he died en route of chronic diarrhea he had contracted while at Andersonville.[162]

On December 4 the X and XVIII Corps were disbanded and two new corps formed. The white units were assigned to the XXIV Corps and the Negro units were assigned to the XXV Corps. The XXIV Corps, commanded by Major General Edward O.C. Ord, consisted of three divisions: The 1st Division, commanded by Brig. Gen. Alfred H. Terry; the 2nd Division, commanded by Brig. Gen. Adelbert Ames, and the 3rd Division, commanded by Brig. Gen. Charles Devens. The 9th Vermont became a part of Col. Joseph H. Potter's Second Brigade of the 3rd Division. The other regiments of Potter's brigade were the X and 12th New Hampshire, 96th New York and 5th Maryland.[163]

In this shuffle Colonel Ripley returned to the command of the 9th Vermont. In a letter to his brother, Ripley, intentionally or not, seemed to question Lieutenant Colonel Barney's ability to command the regiment:

I am hard at work on my Regt., overhauling, inspecting and tightening things up. I get up nearly two hours before dawn every morning, and form line of battle on my color line, and wait til daylight, then through the day work like a trooper, attending Company kitchens and quarters, supertending [sic] Company and squad drill, and drill the Battalion two hours each P.M., overhaul books and newspapers, and by a great use of my own, try to infuse new life and vigor, more energy and interest into the regiment. The knocking about for the last three months had put our clothing, Arms, etc., in a bad way.[164]

At the time of the reorganization of the two Corps, the 9th Vermont was one of the largest infantry regiments in the army, with over 600 muskets present for duty.[165]

Longstreet made a push against the XXIV Corps lines on December 10 and 11. The 9th Vermont, along with the other regiments in the XXIV Corps, lay in line of battle for the better part of two days in mud whitened with snow. The Confederate demonstration did not amount to much and from that time on all the regiments in the XXIV Corps were required to fall in at 4:00 every morning and stand to arms until daylight in anticipation of a rebel attack.[166]

During the fall and winter of 1864 there were a number of personnel changes in the 9th Vermont. Adjutant Livingston was promoted to captain and given command of Co. G. He was succeeded as adjutant by Sgt. Maj. Henry D. Belden. Sergeant John W. Thomas of Co. F replaced Belden as the regiment's sergeant major. Quartermaster Francis O. Sawyer was promoted to be captain and moved up to brigade staff as the assistant quartermaster, and Commissary Sergeant Franklin E. Rice replaced Sawyer. First Lieutenant Abel E. Leavenworth of Co. K was promoted to captain and given command of his company. Second Lieutenant Edmund F. Cleveland was appointed first lieutenant of Co. A at the advice of First Lieutenant Jewett, who resigned. First Lieutenant William A. Dodge, Co. B, who was still in the hospital after being wounded at Fair Oaks, was honorably discharged on account of his wound and transferred to the Veteran Reserve Corps. First Lieutenant James F. Bolton of C, who had never recovered from the wound he received at Newport Barracks, was also transferred to the Veteran Reserve Corps, and First Sergt. Herbert H. Moore was promoted in his place. Second Lieutenant Joel C. Baker was promoted to first lieutenant of Co. K. Sergeant John S. Halbert was appointed second lieutenant in Co. A. Sergeant Arthur W. Hathaway was promoted to second lieutenant in Co. B. Sergeant George W. Sneden was promoted to second lieutenant in Co. C. Sergeant Richard F. Parker was promoted to second lieutenant in Co. E. Sergeant Charles F. Branch was promoted to second lieutenant of Co. H. Sergeant Sylvester C. Burlingame was promoted to second lieutenant in Co. K. Captain Leavenworth was detailed as assistant adjutant general of the brigade, Captain Kelley as assistant inspector general and Captain Viele as ordnance officer of the 3rd Division of the XXV Corps. Lieutenant Peck was chosen as an aide on the staff of the brigade commander.[167]

On Thursday, December 15, Colonel Ripley had a man brought to his tent by the provost marshal. It was none other than Michael Willisford, the Negro who had tried to enlist in the regiment the previous August in New Bern. When the 9th Vermont left New Bern, Willisford had been left with the 132nd New York Infantry, but had refused to join that regiment. For this he had been thrown into jail. After sitting in jail for several weeks he convinced someone that

Left: Second Lieutenant George W. Sneden, Co. C (Vermont Historical Society). *Right:* First Lieutenant Herbert H. Moore, Co. C (Vermont Historical Society).

Left: Second Lieutenant Richard F. Parker, Co. E (U.S. Army Military History Institute). *Right:* Second Lieutenant Charles F. Branch, Co. H (Vermont Historical Society).

he was a member of the 9th Vermont and he was sent to Chaffin's Farm to rejoin his regiment. Ripley sent Willisford to Butler's headquarters for reassignment with a note explaining the background of the situation, ending with, "As this Regt. is more than full of Vt. men I do not require or wish this man. I therefore respectfully return him to the office from which he came from." From Butler's headquarters Willisford was taken to the guardhouse and kept about four weeks. Finally, he was taken to the 38th U.S. Infantry Regiment (United States Colored Troops) to join that unit. Again, everyone in the chain of command thought the matter was settled.[168]

There was a bit of excitement at the morning inspection on December 18, 1864. Quartermaster Sgt. Edward D. Barber of Middlebury showed up drunk, and in front of the entire regiment Colonel Barney had him arrested. Barber was court-martialed on December 24, 1864, and was reduced to the ranks February 15, 1865. Private George C. Chamberlain of Bradford in Co. G was selected to replace him as the regiment's quartermaster sergeant in February.[169]

Second Lieutenant Sylvester C. Burlingame, Co. K (Vermont Historical Society).

At the same dress parade where Sergeant Barber made a spectacle of himself news of Union successes were publicly announced, as Lieutenant Colonel Barney mentioned to his wife:

> We had a "dress parade" last eve and their [sic] we first heard of the glorious news from Sherman and Thomas and some rousing cheers were given for our gallant officers and men.[170]

The next week more war news was passed out at dress parade. Again Lieutenant Colonel Barney:

> We were pleased to hear of the Christmas present to President Lincoln from Genl. Sherman and on the reception of the news our brigade formed line and gave three hearty cheers for Genl. Sherman and army, for a time we had some anxious fears regarding his safety but now we have another source of anxiety. The expedition of Genl. Butler to Wilmington has not been heard from and it is feared will be a total failure on account of the bad weather.[171]

The Union victories by Maj. Gen. William T. Sherman and Maj. Gen. George H. Thomas were certainly something to be celebrated. Sherman had completed his famous "March to the Sea." He had started from Atlanta, Georgia, on November 15 and entered Savannah, which he spared, on December 21. He had sent a telegram to President Lincoln stating he was giving him Savannah as a Christmas present. Thomas had taken Nashville, Tennessee, on December 16.[172]

As usual, Butler's expedition was not something to celebrate. Butler had been sent on December 8 to North Carolina with Ames and Paine's divisions to take Fort Fisher and close the port of Wilmington. Butler's last troop transport arrived on December 24 and a naval bombardment began on Fort Fisher the next day; but before dark it was apparent taking the fort would be extremely costly and the assault was called off and Butler's force sailed north with only 15 men wounded. The only good from the venture was Grant was finally able to get Lincoln's permission to relieve Butler, which he did on January 6, 1865.[173]

Private James Martin of Co. I probably summed up how most men the Army of the James felt about Butler when he wrote, "Gen. Butler and Duck Gap have plaid out. Butler has gone home and Gen. Ord has command of the army of the James. Gen. Butler was good to fight the women in new orleans but he couldn't take Fort Fisher."[174]

7

"RICHMOND IS OURS. THE WHOLE THING."*

The new year rolled in with the 9th Vermont in good shape and with high morale. January 1, 1865, showed an aggregate 1,136 officers and men, with 743 of them fit for duty and a sick list of 383. Combat operations were at a standstill and duty in camp was light. Rebel soldiers were deserting to the Union lines in droves and everyone knew the end of the war must be close at hand. "The rebs are getting sick of the war," wrote Pvt. James Martin of Co. I to a friend in Vermont. "There is some come in bout every night. They say that they don't have but seven hard tack for two days rations. We get ten hard tack for one days rations. The rebs say that they wont fight much more any way. Thare are a good many of them freese to death. They are half naked some of them." Captain Linus Sherman also wrote of the deserters:

Deserters come in from the enemy every night and all agree that the Johnnies are evacuating Richmond. These that came in on different parts of the line all agree. Tell the same story. Deserters come in *squads* almost every night. The last night I was on picket (8) eight came in on our Div. Front. A few nights ago a Lieut. Col. came in with quite a large number of non coms & privates.[1]

The entries in Pvt. George W. Durkee's diary were typical of the Green Mountain Boy's lives in camp during January and February of 1865:

January 4 — Been on detail chopped wood for Co. been up & saw Sergt M.F. Whitney [Durkee's cousin Milo F. Whitney, Co. D, from Tunbridge] he gave me some "whiskey" pretty good rations. I guess so.
January 5 — Still on picket. Charles [Durkee's brother] came and I fetched us some Breakfast. Whiskey ration about noon. pretty good time. I guess so.
January 7 — In camp drilling in the forenoon. doing nothing but eat slap jacks.
January 14 — In camp doing nothing but fatigue. been writing letters, etc.
January 19 — Came off guard this morning. pretty cold morning. have done nothing all day long. having inspection today.
January 21 — we have two drills today & one dress parade.
February 8 — forenoon have done nothing. Afternoon have been target shooting.
February 17 — Have been on inspection this morning. A very pleasant day so far. Been to Fort Harrison this afternoon.
February 27 — Been down to Dutch Gap today with Dood. A very nice Day. have had a good time Playing Ball.[2]

On January 17, Lieutenant Colonel Barney was pulled from the regiment to serve as the brigade commander replacing Colonel Potter who had been selected as chief of staff of the XXIV Corps. Major Brooks was left to run the regiment until Barney returned on February 6.[3]

Even though life in the Vermont camp seemed pretty good, not all of the men thought so. During the night of January 23, Privates John Baker and Louis Benway, both in Co. B, deserted

*Quote from Private George W. Durkee, U.S. Army

while on picket. Both men were new to the regiment, Baker being mustered in August 1864 and Benway in October. Their military records indicate they deserted to the enemy but with the condition everyone knew the Confederate army was in, that seems unlikely. The reason was probably the rashness of two young boys who were disenchanted with army life and just left. Baker was 19 years old and Benway a mere 14. What happened to John Baker after he deserted is lost to time, but Louis Benway is another story.[4]

Louis Benway was not his real name. He was born Louis Sebastian Belouin on October 27, 1849, in Trois Rivieres, Quebec, Canada. His parents were Francois Belouin and Marguerite Duquette. Louis had an older brother named John Henry. Not long after Louis' birth the family moved to Montreal. For some reason, probably to anglicize their surname, both John and Louis changed their last names from Belouin to Bellware. John enlisted in the 9th Vermont on December 22, 1863, under the name John Benway and was assigned to Co. H. Louis ran away about a year later to Vermont when he was 14 and was paid as a substitute for a Norman Dunham of Montgomery. He was mustered into the regiment October 12 and like his brother he enlisted under the name of Benway. Nothing is known of Louis Bellware after he deserted until six years afterward to the day when he married Cynthia Ann Trimble on January 23, 1871, in Frenchburg, Kentucky. Louis and Cynthia had two children, Mary Margaret born in 1872 and John Shirley born in 1876. Louis and Cynthia moved to Middletown, Ohio, for a short time just after the turn of the century, and then moved to Miamisburg, Ohio. Cynthia died in July 1932 and Louis followed her a year later in May 1933. They are both buried in Hill Grove Cemetery in Miamisburg.[5]

Louis N. and Cynthia Ann Bellware, circa 1900. Louis N. Bellware deserted from the 9th Vermont on January 23, 1865 (Daniel A. Bellware).

Confederate gunboats from Richmond sailed down the James River on January 24 in an attempt to reach City Point and destroy the Union depots there. They were driven back by Union batteries, leaving behind the ram *Drewry* which sank to the bottom. A demonstration by the Confederates on the north side of the river accompanied the river assault, but led to nothing more than having the Union troops standing in the cold muddy trenches for two days. The incident did not seem to impress the boys in the 9th Vermont. Corporal Nelson Wandell in Co. K noted in his diary, "A bad chilly day. There was firing all along the lines. The rebs threw a number of shells over our Camp." "Ordered into the Rifle Pits this morning with Sharpshooters. Stayed all day & came in under marching orders & one days rations," is all Pvt. George Durkee of Co. D jotted in his diary that night about the incident.[6]

Lieutenant Colonel Barney was ordered to have the 9th Vermont witness the execution of a Union soldier on February 9 who had been convicted of desertion. He described the event to his wife in one of his letters:

Yesterday my time was occupied more than usual on account of taking the regiment out to witness an execution. A deserter from the 12th N.H. was shot at 2 O'c P.M. and with the formation of troops and

John H. Bellware (center left) and Louis N. Bellware (center right) in Middletown, Ohio, circa 1910 (Daniel A. Bellware).

the usual delays on such occasions about three hours was occupied. These executions come off very frequently of late here. I think three or four are shot every week. It is sad to think of but it only brings the fact more fiercely to our minds that with war comes many evils and even should this one close immediately the evil effects will be felt for many years to come. I am almost astonished to know that I am alive and free from nearly of the evil habits of the army and I feel that the love for my dear wife has more than any thing else seemed to keep me from going far astray.

Then, in the same letter, his mood lightened as he confessed to his wife:

> You will no doubt wish to know what that "nearly" means. Well I have to acknowledge that I do occasionally utter an oath. I presume you know I used to sometimes before I came into the army. More from being so constantly being associated constantly with officers who are profane. I have got to using large words oftener than before. I often feel provoked at myself for it, but this seems to be the only way that the gas will escape when I am really provoked and provocations are very frequent in army life when one has many ignorant men to look after. [In response to a question from his wife and a cousin in a previous letter] It seems that she and you both have a very queer idea of the inhabitants of this part of Va. You should no doubt think that negro wenches are plenty here. Well I wish they were for my darky is a poor washer woman and if some of the softer sex were here my shirts would get better cleaned. Perhaps it will astonish you to tell you I have not had the exquisite pleasure of seeing a "female woman" since we came from New York. Not even a "Cullud one."[7]

Discharges for disability were a common thing in all Civil War regiments, but the 9th Vermont had a most unusual one occur on February 12. Private Thomas Flynn, a 21-year-old, five foot three and one-half inch boot maker from Rockingham in Co. E, had some time earlier been transferred to the Baxter General Hospital in Burlington for urinary incontinence. The surgeon at Baxter Hospital indicated on Flynn's disability certificate that Flynn had been afflicted with the problem since he was four years old. How Flynn had gotten into the army with his problem, or had been able to stay in the army for a year, is amazing. The doctor went on to say that Flynn was not even fit for service in the Veteran Reserve Corps and he was discharged with total disability.[8]

Lieutenant Colonel Barney noted on February 12 a division inspection the 9th Vermont participated in and the promotion of Colonel Ripley:

> I did not write yesterday [Feb 12]. Our division was reviewed by Genl. Ord and Gibbons and as we were obliged to appear without our coats and as the day was extremely cold we all suffered very much from it. It would not probably have been so had Genl. Ord known what the weather would have been. Our regiment was complimented by all the generals and when I was introduced to Genl. Ord he congratulated me on having the honor of commanding the finest appearing regiment in the division. Genl. Gibbons also spoke in very high terms of its marching & etc. In fact there was such a contrast between ours and other regiments that it was a source of general remarks. After the parade was over all the officers of the div. some two or three hundred in number were invited over to Genl. Devens Hd. Qrs. And there we had speeches from the other named generals and all who felt inclined to partake of whiskey done so and a few instances of intoxication occurred and in fact made the occasion quite disgusting in these particulars. I expect to have this regiment now entirely to myself as Col. Ripley has got news that he has been appointed by the President as Brevet Brigadier Genl. and he is feeling quite fine over it.[9]

Sometime during the week of February 13, Pvt. James Martin had a close call, as he related to his friend Harry in Vermont:

> I came pretty close getting hurt the other night. I was on picket the other day and it was very windy and cold. We made our fire & had to get it behind some brush that we put up to break off the wind and bout one o'clock at night thare was two of us laying down side of our fire telling what a good fire we had when pretty soon bang went some thing under our fire and throwed our fire in all directions. It didn't as much as leave us a coal. Come to find out thare was a shell in the ground whare we built our fire and we didn't see it. It was covered over with dirt and it got hot up. Bang went the shell and our fire went up. It happened lucky that we were laying down for if we had been standing up it would have bloud us all to pieces. We had quite a laugh over it when we found out we wasn't hurt. It was some time before I could stand up. I thought one of my legs was bloud off. But we come to get up looking around and we found every thing all wright but our fire and that had gone up. But soon we had another fire going as good as ever.[10]

Lieutenant Colonel Barney went to view the hanging execution of two Union deserters on Saturday, February 18, and reported home:

Day before yesterday I went out about a mile from camp and witnessed the hanging of two men who were caught while attempting to desert to the enemy and it was a sight which was impressive in the extreme. They were both hung at the same time, and side by side upon the scaffold. My curiosity only led me to go to see this execution as I had never before seen a person hung and I am now satisfied and never want to see any more.[11]

Private James Martin also wrote of the hanging, but he had a little different take on it than his lieutenant colonel: "Thare was two men hung Saturday for murdering a man. They are getting so that they shoot or hang some one bout every day. The rebs don't kill them fast enough."[12]

The 9th Vermont was in a division inspection on February 20 in which all the regiments were in competition with each other. The 9th Vermont was declared "the best in order" and was excused from picket duty and details for a week. Also during the day a 100-gun salute was fired in celebration of the news that Sherman had occupied Charleston and Columbia, South Carolina, and for Washington's birthday.[13]

Lieutenant Colonel Barney was quite pleased with the news from the south:

The news from Sherman is encouraging and it seems he is marching through S.C. with much ease as he did through Georgia. We got news through Reb sources yesterday that he was in possession of Columbia. I wonder how the people of S.C. feel about their times, probably not exactly as they did four years ago. It seems that the war must end this spring or summer as the rebel cause seems getting very desperate but they hang on with great tenacity.[14]

A letter in the *Lamoille Newsdealer* described the celebration of Washington's birthday in Co. H:

Washington's birthday was observed by a salute of one hundred guns from the left of Fort Harrison. We were also furnished with a little of the Irishman's riches. After all had imbibed Capt. Gorham proposed three cheers for our Bully Colonel E.H. Ripley which was given with a hearty good will and then came the tiger, and all retired to their respective places of abode.[15]

Not all the men in the regiment were that fond of Colonel Ripley. Company K's first sergeant, J. Webster Stebbins, complained, "Col. Ripley is very haughty and overbearing man. I am not one of his admirers at all. Think he will do some *tall showing* if he does not *tall fighting*. His pride makes him *brave*."[16]

On Thursday, February 27, Lieutenant Colonel Barney answered a very disturbing letter he had gotten from his wife concerning the remains of Pvt. Spencer Green, of Co. B from Danby, who had died of disease on December 27. Green's remains had been sent back to Vermont for burial and had arrived in a bad condition. Barney explained what had taken place in Virginia to get the body home:

Some time ago you wrote about the condition that the remains of Spencer Green were in when received at Danby and I have omitted to speak of it before. I will inform you that but very few soldiers who are killed or die up here at the front get as much as a rough box to be buried in and any one who has an idea of what a large army is will readily see how this is but there is no reason why Spencer's remains should not have been in the best of condition when sent home. He died over at Point of Rocks Hospital and Lt. Baker was appointed to look after the matter and if desired by the people of Danby to send his remains home and Col. Ripley paid 75 dollars for this purpose and we though not able to go over and see to the matter personally, supposed everything was attended to properly. I told Col. what you wrote and he is looking after the man who got the $75 for embalming & etc. and will make him smart if he finds him. I hope the people of Danby will not feel that the irregularity was from any neglect on our part for every thing was done that could be situated as we are and the Hospital out of our limits entirely when we cant go without many signatures of high officials.[17]

As the month of March rolled on it was becoming more and more obvious that the war was coming to an end, as Lieutenant Colonel Barney opined in a letter to his wife on March 2:

Deserters continue to come in abundance. Eight came in last night on our front and all report that preparations are being made for the evacuation of Richmond. That all heavy guns are being dismantled in our front. I don't think they will leave the city if they can by any means stop Sherman and thereby keep open their communications with the south. Perhaps you are not aware that we are in sight of Richmond here. Such is the case. Still only the church spires are visible, 4 in number. I was out on the picket line a few days since and looked at them through a glass. They are no more than five miles distant. It is one thing to see an object but another to get it.[18]

For the Vermonters, March turned out to be a great month. Colonel Ripley held true to his promise to "tighten up" the regiment and on March 6, the 9th Vermont was again chosen as the best regiment in the brigade. On March 10, the regiment was not only chosen as the best regiment in the brigade, but also the best in the division. Each win relieved the Vermonters from picket and fatigue duty for a week, for a total of three weeks.[19]

Colonel Ripley was so obsessed with having the best regiment in the Army of the James that even the regiment's assistant surgeon felt his wrath:

Now came the saddest day of my life, while in the army. One morning quite early, Colonel Ripley came to my quarters, and gave me a severe calling down, for having so many on the sick list. Said it made a bad showing for the Regiment, and by implication, of course, a bad showing of my ability as a Surgeon. Said he thought the sick report did not compare at all favorable with that of the other Regiments in the Brigade. The Colonel must have seen from my appearance that I felt the reprimand keenly, and I simply told him I had a large Regiment to care for, with no one but the hospital boys to assist me. Told him I had done the very best I could. Besides holding surgeons call every morning, I daily visited those that were the sickest, in their quarters, and worked faithfully to keep the Regiment in good fighting condition.

The Colonel left me. The tears ran down my cheeks, for I could not keep them back. I felt abused; for I did not believe I deserved any such reprimand. Up to that time I had supposed my ability and services compared favorably with those of other Surgeons in the Brigade or Corps for that matter. All day it rang in my ears, that I was the poorest Surgeon in the Army. I was tempted to throw up my commission, resign and go home. Early the next morning the Colonel called again. He said the day before he examined the health record of every regiment in the Brigade, and he had come to apologize, and beg my pardon, for what he said to me the day previous. Said he was very happy to inform me he found the health record of the Ninth the best of any Regiment in the Brigade. Considering the number of men in the regiment, he said I had a right to be proud of the record, and said he was proud of it; as he wanted the Ninth to have the best record, and make the best appearance, of any regiment in the Army. He was so proud, he would not be satisfied with anything short of that. He did his part by way of drill, as I will show presently, and expected every commissioned officer to do their part, towards making it the ideal Regiment. As a frail, weakly, sickly man cannot make a good appearance, as a soldier, it was my part and duty to keep as many of the regiment, as possible, presenting the appearance of strong, robust healthy men. His encomium only spurred me on, to do my best to keep the Regiment at the head of the brigade, which I did. My ability and faithfulness was never again called in question. In my official capacity, in the line of my duty, my word was ever afterward law in that Regiment.

While writing the previous passage Dr. Fairman was apparently reminded of Dr. Vincent's incompetence. Years later he was still bristling:

During my sickness in February, the Colonel noticed a good many men, that looked pretty well, were not on duty. He would inquire of them, by whom they were excused. By Surgeon Vincent, would be the reply. Very well he would say, if you will bring me an excuse from Surgeon Fairman all right, otherwise you will go on full duty. Some I excused, but there were more I did not. Under the circumstances, most men, of any spirit and self-respect would have resigned so quick, that their Colonel would never have had a chance to snub them a second time. About this time, or very soon after, Colonel Ripley put the Surgeon under guard for a whole week, for insubordination. Still he did not resign. Oh no. Government was paying him 200 dollars a month for wearing a Surgeons uniform and playing checkers. While I was off duty, sick with jaundice, one of the privates had his shoulder dislocated. I was sent for to set it. As I was off duty, I sent the messenger for the Surgeon, knowing very well, he could not reduce the dislocation. I wanted the Regiment to know it. This was my opportunity. After giving chloroform and taxing his skill to the utmost for two hours, with three or four men to help him pull it into place, he was obliged to acknowledge he could not set it. Considering his rank, it was pretty humiliating to be obliged to come after me to do what he has utterly failed to do. But he came to my quarters, and asked me if I was well enough, to go and set the shoulder. It was Just what I wanted. I was very glad of the chance, for I was able to be out about the camp. As I started to go with him, he says take some chloroform with you. Said he had to give it, and then he could not set it. I said I would go and see what kind of an injury he had got to deal with. The injury had got noised around, so that more than half of the Regiment was about the mans quarter when we got there. I went inside, set the man on a stool, he being already divested of his clothing. The Surgeon and a half dozen were anxious to know, what they should do to help me. Without any chloroform, and without any one else touching the patient, I reduced the dislocation in half the time I have been writing it. The head of the bone went into place with a snap heard by every one in the tent. I gave some directions, as how it should be cared for, and started back for my tent. The Surgeon followed me. As we left for our quarters, I would not have taken the Jibes, Sneers and hooting he did, for all the money government ever paid him. On our way back he wanted to know how in H-11 I set the shoulder so easy. Said I did it so quick, he could not see how it was done. I explained it to him, by saying it was all in knowing how.[20]

The XXIV Corps was reviewed by Lieutenant General Grant and Secretary of War Edwin Stanton on March 17, after which the troops celebrated Saint Patrick's Day with sports and games and probably with more than a little libation. There was another corps review on Sunday, March 26, which turned out to have quite a surprise, as Lieutenant Colonel Barney described to his wife:

I should have written yesterday but we were extremely busy all day. First came inspections then an order for review and the rumor was circulated that the *President* was to be present, so all were anxious to be out and get a sight of him. We formed line at 12 o'c noon and remained waiting for him until 4½ o'c when the long dark forms and honest Abe made their appearance on a fine horse and the cheers from regt. after regt. as he passed along the line were almost deafening and made many horses frantic with excitement much to the discomfort of their riders. The President rode along the line with his hat in his hand and bowing to all as he passed. He was accompanied by a host of officers, women and orderlies. The most prominent was Genl. Grant, Ord, and Gibbon. Mrs. Lincoln and other distinguished ladies were along and rode in ambulances. Old Abe looked very much careworn and emaciated. On the whole it was quite a grand affair.[21]

Colonel Ripley received orders on March 20 to assume command of the Third Brigade of the Independent Division of the XXIV Corps, but the order was almost immediately rescinded, leaving him without a job. Two days later he was given command of the First Brigade of the 3rd Division of the XXIV Corps, which he retained for the rest of the war. Ripley later recalled, "This A.M. an order came assigning me to the Command of this Brigade. It has six full regts. in it, and is the finest Brigade in the Army of the James. I hope this will be a permanent command, I am so tired of being knocked about." Ripley finally received his brevet promotion to brigadier general in March, which was back dated to August 4, 1864.[22]

On Tuesday, March 21, the 3rd Division got orders to move. In the 9th Vermont's camp, knapsacks were packed and tents struck and by 7:30 A.M. the troops were in formation ready to march. After standing in formation for several hours the order was countermanded and tents were pitched again. The next day, the order came again to move out at 10:00 A.M. and the Second Brigade marched down the Newmarket Road about three miles, where it stayed until dark and then returned to camp. Lieutenant Colonel Barney described the movement and guessed at its meaning:

Yesterday [March 22] we got orders at 8 o'c A.M. to fall in and get ready to march. We were in line immediately and with the rest of the brigade went about three miles to the rear and went into camp there. Got fairly fixed up in our shelter tents but just before dark orders came to return to our old camp and so here we are again. It is hard to tell what all these moves mean but this one in my opinion was for two purposes, to bewilder the enemy and to get our men in proper condition for any emergency. Orders have been issued by Genl. Ord to send all our baggage to the rear and today we are at work packing up and getting everything sent off that we do not actually need here.[23]

The last week of March saw the beginning of the end of the war. At 4:00 A.M. on March 25, Confederate Major General Gordon attacked and captured Fort Stedman on the outskirts of Petersburg. The objective was to pull Grant's units off the right of the Confederate line to facilitate the army's move south to link up with Johnston. After breaching the Federal lines, Confederate cavalry was to pour through and destroy Grant's supply base at City Point and possibly capture Grant himself. After the capture of the fort the Confederates captured two flanking batteries, but then the attack stalled out. Many of the starving rebel soldiers stopped to plunder the captured Federal bombproof, and the troops that continued the advance ran into the IX Corps reserve. As the attack ground to a halt the Confederates were caught in the crossfire from the Federal batteries on either side of the breached line. Realizing the attack had failed, Gordon withdrew, leaving almost 2,000 of his men in the hands of the Union. By 8:30 A.M. it was all over. Assuming Lee had weakened his right by pulling enough troops to make the attack on Fort Stedman, Grant counterattacked that afternoon, but made no significant gain.[24]

On the night of March 27, Major General Ord was ordered to move his 1st and 2nd divisions to the south side of the James River. By the next morning he had crossed the river and joined the Army of the Potomac. This left Devens' division and two divisions of colored troops of the XXV Corps under the command of General Weitzel. Devens' division had to extend out and hold the trenches vacated by the 1st and 2nd divisions and the 9th Vermont had to cover the area left by a brigade. To conceal the loss of troop strength, bands played reveille and tattoo in different parts of their bivouacs, as well as keeping fires lit in the abandoned camps.[25]

On March 31, Sheridan clashed with Pickett's infantry division and Confederate cavalry at Dinwiddie Court House, with Pickett gaining the upper hand. The next day, the two forces battled again at a strategic crossroads called Five Forks. Five Forks was crucial to Lee's ability to hold his last supply line into Petersburg — the South Side Railroad. Sheridan saw the opportunity to cut off and capture Pickett's division, but he would need infantry. Grant gave him the V Corps and ordered him, along with his Cavalry Corps, to attack the Confederate line. Sheridan attacked the Confederate forces at Five Forks at 4:00 P.M. on April 1. Pickett was routed, losing a number of his guns and about half of his force captured. The rest of his command, cut off from Petersburg, fled to the west and slipped away into the darkness. Lee's last supply line had been cut.[26]

On April 1, Grant ordered an all-out assault on the Confederate line around Petersburg the next day. At 4:00 A.M. the next morning the VI Corps, spearheaded by the Old Vermont Brigade, punched through the line as ordered and the siege of Petersburg was finally broken. Lee's Army of Northern Virginia did what it could to stem the blue tide that was rolling over it until an organized retreat could begin, which started that night.[27]

On Sunday, April 2, the picket line between the Varina and New Market roads was held by a detail of 135 men of the 9th Vermont and 50 from the 12th New Hampshire, under command of the 9th Vermont's Capt. Abel E. Leavenworth. With him were Lieutenants Joel C. Baker of company B, Burnham Cowdrey of company G of the 9th Vermont and a Lieutenant Monahan from the 12th New Hampshire. The picket line was facing Forts Gilmer, Gregg and Johnson, all of which were bristling with artillery and rifle muskets. Baker noted later, "The Rebels also, showed unusual bustle and activity. We could see them leveling glasses in our direction, and details using strenuous efforts to strengthen their works, especially at Fort Johnson, and northerly towards Fort Gilmer."[28]

At about 10:00 A.M. Col. Michael Donohoe, who had been commanding the Second Brigade since mid–February, came out to the picket line and informed Captain Leavenworth that he had received a telegram directing the XXIV Corps to get ready to assault the works to their front if the breakthrough at Petersburg was not successful. Leavenworth described his actions at the thought of an assault: "I quietly penciled a letter to my wife, thinking it might be my last message to loved ones at home, though I said nothing of the expected movement, and then addressed myself to the duties at hand." Fortunately, the breakthrough at Petersburg was successful and the impending assault never materialized.[29]

Earlier in the morning, as the Union breakthrough progressed, General Lee sent a telegram to the Confederate secretary of war stating, "I see no prospect of doing more than holding our position here until night. I am not certain I can do that. If I can I shall withdraw to-night north of the Appomattox, and, if possible, it will be better to withdraw the whole line to-night from James River. I advise that all preparations be made for leaving Richmond tonight. I will advise you later according to circumstances." Shortly after receiving Lee's telegram, it was passed on to Confederate President Jefferson Davis, who was attending Sunday services, and preparations were started to immediately evacuate the government from Richmond.[30]

Shortly after Lee was forced from his headquarters on Sunday afternoon, he sent his last telegram informing the Confederate authorities, "It is absolutely necessary that we abandon our position tonight, or run the risk of being cut off in the morning." Lee's immediate destination was Amelia Court House located 36 miles west of Petersburg.[31]

Under the cover of darkness Lee got his troops on the road. Near midnight Jefferson Davis and his cabinet left Richmond on a train, their destination Danville, Virginia. There Davis could stay in contact with both Lee's and Johnston's armies.[32]

By mid-afternoon the Confederate troops on the north side of the James had been ordered to prepare to join Lee's army in the retreat the next morning. To cover their preparations to pull out, the rebel bands played patriotic tunes, which were replied to by the Federal bands. But the band's music could not totally disguise the sounds of the rebel troops preparing to leave. From the Federal side it could not be determined if the enemy was getting ready to move out or were preparing to attack. Leavenworth was fearful the enemy had learned of the XXIV Corps units being pulled out and were preparing for an attack. As night fell, every Union picket was awake and peering into the darkness toward the Confederate fortifications.[33]

At about 2:00 A.M. on April 3, one of Leavenworth's pickets brought in a rebel deserter from a Virginia regiment. The deserter told Leavenworth the rebels were evacuating their fortifications. The man indicated he deserted because Lee would take his retreating army to North Carolina to join General Joseph E. Johnston, and he did not want to leave his home state. Leavenworth thought the man was telling the truth and sent him under guard to higher head-quarters. Not long afterwards, Devens sent out an order to move the whole picket line forward at daybreak, or sooner, if deemed wise to advance. Devens was somewhat cautious because the Confederates had mined the land between the opposing lines of earthworks. The mines were actually artillery shells planted vertically in the ground with fuses that would go off when stepped on. During the Civil War, mines, land or waterborne, were known as torpedoes.[34]

While the Union pickets were staring into the darkness, the Confederate troops were already in Richmond and marching across the bridges spanning the James River, heading west to join Lee. As the last units crossed, the rear guard set fire to the government warehouses and finally the bridges. Unfortunately, the fires were soon out of control and the city of Richmond was on fire.[35]

Daylight came slowly due to a low hanging fog, but as soon as it lifted, about 4:30 A.M., the picket line, led by the 9th Vermont's Major Brooks and Captain George A. Bruce of the 13th New Hampshire, started forward toward the Confederate fortifications. The pickets reached the fortifications, losing only one man (not a Vermonter) in the mine field. The retreating rebel soldiers had not taken the time to remove the little red flags which marked the torpedoes so their own men would not step on them. After determining the trenches were empty of rebels, the Union pickets moved on until they were two miles from where they had started and struck a bend in the James River, where they halted.[36]

As the pickets had moved from the trenches to the river they had passed several farmhouses where the women told them the Confederate rear guard was just beyond the tree line and they "would catch it" when they met them. While at the halt by the river, Colonel William W. Bamberger, the division field officer of the day, joined Captain Leavenworth and ordered him to deploy his men as skirmishers. Bamberger said he would follow with 75 of the remaining pickets as a reserve. Leavenworth did as ordered and extended his line to the left across the Osborn Turnpike. Lieutenant Baker was put in charge of the right of the line and Lieutenant Cowdrey the left. Leavenworth then started his line forward up the Osborne Turnpike until he hit a tree line near the junction with the Newmarket road, where he halted. Here the men were told to rest and fix their breakfasts while Leavenworth awaited further orders from Major Brooks. It was now about 5:30 A.M.[37]

As the men were fixing their breakfasts, Colonel Alonzo G. Draper, commander of the First Brigade of the 1st Division of the XXV Corp, with his staff and about 100 colored troops, came up and asked Leavenworth if the road in front was clear. Leavenworth remembered "I replied that I thought it was; that we were awaiting the report of the aforesaid officers [Brooks and Bruce] who had ridden on to make a reconnaissance. He demanded to be let through our line and pushed on. I at once gave the order to my line to 'rally on the centre' and said 'come on, boys, we will see who will lead.'" The Vermonters had just begun to eat their breakfast, but they did not intend to be beaten into Richmond. At Leavenworth's order, they were on their feet immediately. The Green Mountain Boys had not slept for 24 hours, had not had anything to eat for hours and were loaded down with 40 rounds of ammunition and three days' rations, but they were not going to be beaten to the prize. Led by Leavenworth, they took off on the run and overtook the colored troops, who were giving the Vermonters a run for their money.[38]

Captain Leavenworth continues his remembrance of the foot race:

> I had captured a sorry looking pony and placed upon him a man who seemed unable to walk and handed him my blanket and overcoat. We over took the colored troops just as we emerged from the woods. I gave the order to oblique to the right and take the double quick step. The colored lads had a swinging route step and were talking cheerily to each other. As we passed each file, the men would shout to those ahead to "hurry up." But their demonstrations were so noisy that their officers did not learn of our presence till we turned in ahead. Then their Captain gave them the order to double quick also. For more than a mile we raced it. I became so heated that I tore off my sword-belt and threw it with scabbard and revolver behind me, saying that if there were any that could not keep up they might, if they pleased, bring them along. My dress coat and vest soon followed, collar and necktie followed suit, and my panting breast was bared to the breeze. Soon our colored braves gave up the race and we entered the inner line of defence just as we came up to the aforesaid officers [Draper and staff] who had halted for their men to come up. We were ordered to halt. I repeated the order. It was obeyed to the loss of one or two steps. The commanding officer began to curse us for passing his men and sent his Adjutant ahead with the order to halt or he would "break" the officer in command. I gave the order to halt that I might hear what he had to say and then passed on. Soon Lieut. Col. Bamberger came up and said, "Captain, are you ready to go home?" I replied, "Yes, if going into Richmond in the lead is a crime." He then said, "You needn't halt again." Soon we came to a small stream, the bridge of which was torn up. We went down through it and up the opposite bank, getting our feet wet. As we passed on, Maj. Gen. Weitzel, accompanied by his staff, one of whom was Capt. Wheeler of Vermont, and his body of cavalry, galloped by us. We cheered and saluted. Soon we came to the New Market Road, and turned towards Rockett's. As we drew to a second hand store at the head of Main Street, a flag was thrust out of the scuttle window. As we saw the stars and stripes floating in Richmond, our weariness left us for the time and we went wild with huzzas. My hat went high in the air and I shouted myself hoarse and my comrades were not far behind me in enthusiasm. The scene before us was indescribably grand. "Confusion confounded" expresses it best. Before us were the lofty bridges, the navy yard and gunboats on fire. Magazine after magazine were being blown up. We turned up the street and halted on "Church Hill" for the rest of our line under the brigade and division officers of the day.

A private who had his overcoat belted on, came up to me and took it off and threw it around my shoulders, saying, "Captain, you will take cold." Soon my men who fell behind came in bringing my cast away property. I lost only my rubber blanket. I began to re-dress, but before I was in presentable shape Maj. Gen. Devens and staff rode up. Capt Kelley had caught up with us, and as he said to me, seeing that I was engaged, drew the men up in line and presented arms.[39]

General Devens described the scene from Church Hill:

Richmond lay before us. The heavy fog of the river, mingled with the dense clouds of smoke, hung over it like a pall, and relieve against the vapors came up the lurid flames from the burning arsenals and ware-houses which had been set on fire by some unaccountable madness of the rebel commander as he retreated from the here blazing bridges which had spanned the noble James, and from the gun-boats, once a formidable fleet on the river. Every moment the earth seemed to vibrate with the explosions of the magazines of the gunboats and the arsenals with which the city had been filled. It was a sight of terrible magnificence, and might well fill the heart of every Union soldier with enthusiasm. We knew that our work was done, fully and completely done, and that it was the Confederacy that was passing away in the fervent heats on which we gazed.[40]

Before long Devens' division arrived on Church Hill. One of Weitzel's staff officers rode up to Ripley and said, "You are in luck today, general. General Weitzel has given orders that you are to have the head of the column in the triumphal entry which we are about ready to make into the city." Ripley remembered, "I was of course elated at this, for it might have been possible that General Weitzel would have chosen to give it to the colored troops of his own corps the place of honor for the pageant."[41]

Ripley arranged his units in the following order prior to entering the city: General Devens and staff; Captain Leavenworth's skirmishers composed of the 9th Vermont, 10th and 12th New Hampshire, 10th Connecticut, 5th Maryland and the 96th and 118th New York. Then came the Ripley's First Brigade followed by the Second Brigade, then Third Brigade and finally the light artillery.[42]

With the bands playing patriotic Union tunes, the column marched into the burning city, snaking its way up Franklin Street to the Exchange Hotel, then across to Main Street and up Main to Capitol Square. The scene must have looked surreal to the Vermonters. The air was dark with thick black smoke and cinders which swept through the streets, and as the column marched deeper into the city the sounds of the bands were almost drowned out by the noise of collapsing buildings, the roaring flames and the exploding shells in the burning warehouses.[43]

The sides of the streets were packed with a surging mob of Confederate stragglers, scared Richmonders and jubilant Negroes. The black folks, realizing they were finally free, were down on their knees throwing their hands wildly in the air, while floods of tears poured down their faces. They shouted "Glory to God! Glory to God! The day of Jubilee hab come! Massa Linkum am here! Massa Linkum am here!"[44]

At the gate of Capitol Square, opposite the east entrance of the Confederate capitol, one of Weitzel's aides told Ripley to halt his column and report to General Weitzel at the eastern porch. On the broad landing at the head of the steps of the capitol were Generals Weitzel and Devens and their staffs, as well as the division commanders of the XXV Corps and their staffs. Also present were Joseph Mayo, the mayor of the city, and the other city officials. Mayo and his associates had earlier surrendered the city to the Union forces.[45]

Ripley dismounted from his horse at the bottom of the steps and quickly walked up and reported to General Weitzel. Weitzel told Ripley, "I have sent for you, general Ripley, to inform you that I have selected you to take command in this city, and your brigade as its garrison. I have no orders further to communicate except to say that I want this conflagration stopped and the city saved if it is in the bounds of human possibility, and you have carte blanche to do it in your own way." Ripley replied that he wanted the other troops, especially the colored troops, who could incite the white populace, withdrawn from the city. Weitzel agreed and ordered his

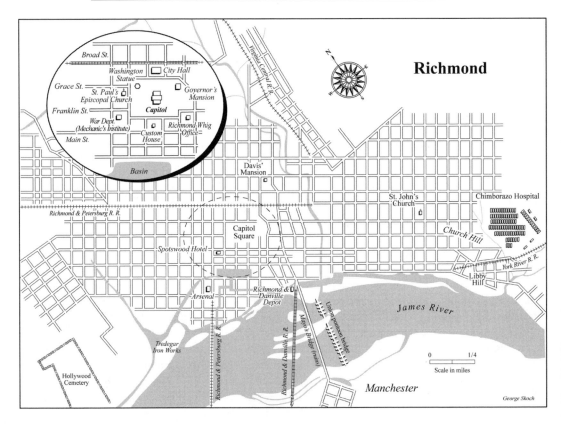

Richmond, April 1865.

division commanders to march their troops through the city and go into camp along the interior line of earthworks surrounding Richmond and to let no one enter.[46]

Leaving General Weitzel, Ripley quickly returned to the head of his brigade and led it to city hall, where he established his headquarters. He then dispatched his regimental commanders, under the guidance of the city officials, to select their headquarters at locations in the city where their units would be the most effective. He also dispatched other officers with members of the city fire department to get out the engines and hose carts, but found the rioters had disabled the fire engines and cut all the hoses.[47]

The troops were quickly marched to their assigned places and Ripley set up his headquarters in city hall. He had placards printed and posted throughout the city ordering the citizens to assist the military authorities in restoring order by remaining in their houses. The citizens faced arrest if found on the streets after dark. He directed his patrols to arrest the drunken mob of pillagers who were rioting and to bring all stolen property to the city hall. The property was then taken by an officer, receipted and stored away in the back rooms of the building, until an immense amount of property had been accumulated.[48]

Officers were quickly sent to Libby Prison to liberate the Union prisoners of war who being held there. The infamous prison was then used to confine some 7,000 Confederate stragglers. By the next morning the prison was so crowded rebel soldiers were actually sitting on the roof.[49]

The Union soldiers courageously battled the fire all day and by nightfall had it under control. Even with the fire under control, the horrible roar of the flames went on, as well as the crashing of falling walls and the detonations of ordnance, but the fire was stopped in its tracks and the troops were allowed to rest for the night. In all, 1,000 buildings were burned before the

Brigadier General Edward H. Ripley's staff camp on Libby Hill, Richmond, Virginia (The Library Company of Philadelphia).

fire was completely extinguished on April 4. The city was engulfed in smoke for weeks.[50]

The 9th Vermont went into camp on Fulton Hill. Lieutenant Colonel Barney wrote his wife that evening telling her of the day's activities:

Here we are and I am too much elated to write but will merely say that we came into the city about ten o'c this forenoon and are situated as you see by my date. The enemy evacuated their line

The last headquarters of Ripley's brigade, near Brock Road Race Course outside Richmond, Virginia, June 1865. (Left to right, seated) Captain Guffy, 13th New Hampshire; Captain Staniels, 13th New Hampshire; Brigadier General Ripley; Captain S. Vawn, chief of staff. (Standing center left to right) Captain Peck, aide-de-camp, 9th Vermont; Captain Foote, 10th Connecticut; Captain Curtis, 13th New Hampshire (*Vermont General*).

during the night and we started at daylight and came in at double quick time. The first infantry that entered the city were 9th Vt. skirmishers. We found the city all on fire and explosions are now heard every second in all directions. I have just rode through the city and visited the Capitol, Custom House and the Spotswood Hotel. There is intense excitement throughout. Streets thronged with homeless women and children. Col. Ripley is Provost Marshal Genl. of the city and I think we are to be the provost guard of the city. The main business part of the city is now on fire but the fires are being allayed and I think the greater part of the city will be preserved. We are about one mile from the capitol and my Hd. Qrs. are at a very fine and elegantly furnished dwelling. The people are from Massachusetts and have raised the stars and stripes over their house. I hear nothing from Grant yet but suppose he is in pursuit of Lee's flying mob. All looks favorable and we are enjoying ourselves hugely over our success and cheer after cheer are heard from every Regt.[51]

Private George W. Durkee simply noted in his diary, "Started from Signal Hill about 10 o'clock P.M. Arrived in Richmond about 1 A.M. Richmond is ours. The whole thing. Grand capture of artillery."[52]

The next day, Tuesday, April 4, the 9th Vermont moved its camp to Church Hill on the east side of the city near the Chimborazo Military Hospital and St. John's Episcopal Church where Patrick Henry made his "Give me liberty or give me death" speech. Lieutenant Colonel Barney informed his wife of the move on April 5:

We came over last eve and to day have been fixing up our camp and getting into proper condition for an approaching storm. I am making my headquarters at an elegant house where a family lives who are very fine people but pretty strong sesech.[53]

Also on April 4, the city of Richmond had two very important visitors—President Abraham Lincoln and his son, Tad. Lincoln had been at Grant's headquarters when the breakthrough occurred and after four years of war could not resist seeing the Confederate capital. He was brought upriver by ship and then to shore by a rowboat. His first destination was Jefferson Davis' house. Along the way the recently freed slaves were overjoyed at the sight of the president. One woman was reported to have said, "I know that I am free, for I have seen Father Abraham." After visiting Davis' mansion, Lincoln and his party were taken by carriage to the capitol and then they toured the burned district. He wanted to stay for the night, but the military authorities feared for his safety and he left in the late afternoon. He did, however, stay aboard a vessel in the James River opposite the city.[54]

In his nonchalant way, Co. D's Pvt. George W. Durkee noted in his diary on April 4, "On Guard last night. have done nothing today but loaf. have been down in the city and saw Old Abe there."[55]

By Wednesday, April 5, the men of the 9th Vermont were over their giddiness of capturing the Confederate capital and got back into a normal military routine, as Corp. Nelson L. Wandell noted: "We pitched our tents in regular order this morning. We drilled today in Co. drill. Pleasant."[56]

On Saturday, April 8, The 9th Vermont participated in a division review. Nelson L. Wandell wrote, "We were reviewed today in the City by Gen. Devens and Weitzel and marched through the principle streets of the City (Richmond) and were dismissed at the Libby prison. Oh, how sad the City looks. Nearly all the ladies are dressed in mourning for some loved one sacrificed." The next day the Union troops were notified of another piece of good news, as Corporal Wandell noted: "At twelve were woke up to hear the news of the Surrender of the army of Northern Virginia by Gen. R.E. Lee to Lieut. Gen. U.S. Grant. We screamed and yelled ourselves hoarse and then went to bed once more."[57]

On April 10, Lieutenant Colonel Barney led the 9th Vermont on a reconnaissance out Nine Mile Road toward the old battlefields of Cold Harbor and Gaines Mill. It rained continuously the entire day. The only thing accomplished was the capture of eight Confederate deserters and a couple of horses.[58]

With the war over in Virginia, it was difficult to keep the men in line. One example occurred on Tuesday, April 11. Corporal Charles H. Sweeney, the man who had gone to U.S. Grant trying to get his squad transportation to New York, stole some commissary whiskey and got drunk. To add insult to injury, he caused a disturbance in his company area and then used insulting language to his company commander. For this breech of discipline Sweeney was reduced to the ranks. In an attempt to curtail the lax discipline, Lieutenant Colonel Barney read the following statement to the regiment at dress parade: "Noncommissioned officers of this regiment are hereby notified that they *must* set proper examples to privates or not only will they receive the same punishment as Sergeant Sweeney — but be punished otherwise in proportion to their offense."[59]

After the war Sweeney returned home to Morrisville. Nine months later, on March 12, 1866, his wife, Augusta Grout Sweeney, had a baby boy, whom they named Carroll Francis Sweeney. Augusta died on May 27, 1867. Not long after his first wife's death, Charles Sweeney married a lady named Oliva, but she divorced Charles in December 1871 for desertion and got custody of Charles' son. Sweeney married for a third time, to Mary J. Hill in Morristown on November 17, 1888. He was 61 and she was 47. Charles Sweeney died in North Hyde Park on April 5, 1902, and was buried in the North Hyde Park Cemetery. The next year Mary applied for a widow's pension. On October 27, 1903, a lawyer named Charles L. Gleed wrote the following to the commissioner of Pensions in Washington, D.C., in support of Mary's pension claim:

> When I was a very small boy, which was a great many years ago, there lived in my father's house a cook who was a very good cook besides being very good to me regardless of my frequent turbulence. Her name was Mary Hill. One of my earliest and most vivid recollections of her was the event of her falling down stairs in a way that nearly cost her life. She has been falling down stairs ever since. In fact her falling down stairs began a good while before I was born. On the third of May, 1855, she married a plausible chap who was a stranger in the village and whose name was Simmons. Within a week of the date of her marriage officers of the law came from somewhere and arrested Simmons for bigamy. Mary Hill applied to my father for counsel and he advised her that inasmuch as Simmons was a bigamist she was not his wife. Mary never tried matrimony again until November 17, 1884, when she married Charles H. Sweeney who died April 5, 1903. Mary Hill Sweeney's pension claim is old law No. 782,722. This is one of the matters that I have consented to call to your personal attention and I respectfully request that you do whatever you consistently can to give Mary Hill Sweeney whatever is due her. My knowledge of the above facts is derived from a recollection of my Mother's recital of Mary Hill's story and statements to the same effect made to me this summer by ex-governor Hendee [George W. Hendee, governor of Vermont in 1870] and others in Morrisville, Lamoille County, Vermont. No one remembers to what place Simmons was taken by the officers who arrested him and it has been impossible to find any record of the case.[60]

Mary Hill Sweeney got her government pension.

The 9th Vermont got orders to relocate their camp on April 13. The next morning at 6:00 A.M. the regiment packed up and marched off Church Hill to downtown Richmond, where it joined the rest of the brigade on Main Street. The column then swung left and crossed over the James River on a pontoon bridge to Manchester. The Vermonters marched about three miles after crossing the river and set up camp. In this new location the Green Mountain Boys were responsible for guarding the Richmond & Danville Railroad. Two days later the camp was moved a short distance away, which pleased Lieutenant Colonel Barney: "When I last wrote you we were just about on the move and in less that an hour after I closed my letter we had got our camp pitched in this place which is about a half mile from the other and nearer the city and I would be pleased to have you see us in our fine position. It is the prettest camp we were ever in and I have got my headquarters situated in one of the most romantic spots I ever saw."[61]

As soon as the camp was established on April 14, First Lt. Charles W. Haskell, First Lt. Elias L Brownell and Second Lt. Charles F. Branch were detailed with 100 men to guard and protect the coal mines at Midlothian some 12 miles to the west. Coal had been discovered in the area in 1701 and was being mined by 1709. For the next 150 years the Richmond Coal Basin, most of which lies in Chesterfield County, produced more coal that any other area in the United States. While at the coal fields, Second Lieutenant Branch was quartered at Railey Hill, the home Mr. and Mrs. Edward Allen. Mr. Allen, from Strafford, England, was in the coal business in the area. While on duty at the coal fields, Branch became quite fond of, and often visited, a Miss Bettie Jewett, who lived near Railey Hill. Bettie Jewett's mother was a widow with 11 children who ran a store in the Midlothian area. Branch visited Bettie often and continued to do so even after the detachment left Midlothian on June 5. He saw her on the Fourth of July to watch fireworks and again on July 9 to attend church. On July 11, Lieutenant Branch went home to Vermont on leave and when he returned his unit had been transferred to Norfolk and he never saw Miss Jewett again. While at Railey Hill, Branch used a diamond in his ring to scratch the following into a parlor window pane: "Charles F. Branch/Lt. U.S. Army/Orwell, Vermont/April 1865." Branch's name and hometown remain in the window pane to this day.[62]

The same day the 9th Vermont moved to Manchester, President Lincoln was assassinated. Word of the assassination was apparently slow getting to the Vermonters. Corporal Wandell noted in his diary on April 16, "There is a rumor that President Lincoln was shot by an actor and that Secretary Seward was attacked and stab[b]ed in his bed." The official notification of the president's death did not arrive at the Vermont camp until April 17. Lieutenant Colonel Barney probably summed up everyone's feelings when he wrote:

> This morning we have received the most awful and appalling news ever heard. The assassination of our President!! I was almost struck dumb at the news and I can't imagine what the country is coming to. We cannot as a people place much confidence in our Vice President and I think something out of the regular line of proceeding must be done. My mind at once suggested Genl. Grant as dictator but perhaps this would be too fast and not advisable to go so far. It was expected that on the news being made public in the city here there would be an up rising of the people in the city and we sent part of our regiment in to guard against any trouble. The streets are fairly crowded with rebel soldiers who have been paroled by Genl. Grant and deserters from their army. Many officers are among them and it was thought that they were getting together to organize and liberate all the rebel soldiers in Libby Prison and many of them were arrested and placed in confinement.[63]

Several days later Barney revisited the president's death: "We are feeling a sense of sorrow to a great degree at the President's death. We all wear a piece of crepe on the left arm and our colors are draped in morning."[64]

The news of the president's death hit the army hard. Corporal Wandell penned in his diary on the night of April 17, "Guns are fired every half hour for the death of President Lincoln. He was shot by John Wilkes Booth last Friday night in the theatre. May his name be linked with that of Benedict Arnold."[65]

After the initial shock of Lincoln's death, life in the 9th Vermont went on. Private James Martin of Co. I related an incident to a friend of his in Vermont that happened to him while on guard duty in Richmond:

> I was on guard in the city yesterday. They was a reb Conl. thare. He was in a house of ill fame and thare was two or three of our boys in thare and they got up to a dispute about something and the reb Conl. said he could lick any son of a bitch of a yankee that was in the house when one of our boys shot him dead. It don't do for them to run over our boys to much for our boys havent any respect for them. We are across the river from Richmond. We have to go over the river to Richmond on guard bout every other day.[66]

On Sunday afternoon, April 30, the regiment was ordered out for drill. While First Sgt. John W. Roberts was getting his men in Co. H in formation, Pvt. Harry B. Thomas of Pomfret yelled from of his tent, "I'll be damned if I'll fall in." Thomas had just come in from duty in Richmond and felt he did not have to drill. Roberts told him again to get out of his tent and

Thomas again said that he would not. Roberts left and reported the situation to his company commander, Capt. Lewis H. Bisbee. Roberts returned and told Thomas the captain said he had to fall in. Thomas told Roberts he would go to the captain. As Thomas crawled out of his tent, Roberts grabbed him and threw him up against the tent, tearing Thomas's coat. Roberts then hit him in the side. Thomas finally got to Captain Bisbee and asked him if he had to fall in for drill and Bisbee told him that he did and that he had to obey orders. Captain Bisbee then told Corp. Albert S. Tobin to take Thomas down to the brook and have him fill his knapsack up with stones. While the rest of the company was at drill, Tobin drilled Thomas, who was wearing his stone-filled knapsack, by himself. After the company returned the captain told Thomas to get his equipments, haversack and musket. After Thomas returned he was drilled until almost dark. The next day, Thomas was drilled for an hour in the morning and afternoon wearing his stone filled knapsack and equipments.

First Sergeant John W. Roberts, Co. H (Vermont Historical Society).

Thomas was drilled on May 1 and on the morning of May 2 he was at it again in the company street. This time he was being drilled by Sgt. Frederick Gauthier. By now, Thomas was getting tired of the punishment and was moving as slowly as he thought he could get away with and had his head hanging down with his chin resting on his chest. Sergeant Gauthier kept telling Thomas to hold his head up, but Thomas ignored him. Finally, Gauthier got a piece of hardtack and put it on its edge under Thomas's chin and said, "God damn you, I will put this under your chin and make you hold up your head." Thomas yelled at Gauthier to keep his hands off him. By that time Gauthier had had it with Thomas and punched him. Thomas hit the sergeant back. By now the two had drawn a crowd. Gauthier grabbed Thomas's musket from him and handed it to one of the other men. In the process of taking the musket Gauthier got stabbed in the thumb by Thomas's bayonet. This incensed Gauthier and the two started fighting. First Sergeant Roberts came out of his tent to see what the commotion was and told Corp. Richard Wheeler to separate the two, but Pvt. George T. Chase got between the two combatants and stopped the fight before Wheeler could reach them.

Private Harry Thomas was brought before a general court-martial on May 15 and charged with disobeying an order, disobeying a superior officer and violating the 9th Article of War, which, in short, authorized the execution of any officer or soldier who would strike, draw or lift a weapon, or threaten violence to a superior officer. Thomas pleaded not guilty to all charges, but the court saw otherwise. Thomas was sentenced to serve three months at hard labor, one month of which he was to wear a ball and chain, and to forfeit his pay during his confinement. Although it is somewhat unclear, it appears Thomas did not have to serve his whole sentence, as his records show that he was mustered out of the army June 13, 1865.[67]

A tragic accident occurred at the Midlothian coal mines on Wednesday, May 10. The particulars of the incident are unclear, but apparently one of men of the 9th Vermont accidentally discharged a rifle, hitting 39-year-old Pvt. Joseph H. Larock of Co. C, from Panton, in the right shoulder. The minie ball entered the right pectoral muscle and passed through the shoulder joint, shattering the head of the humerus before exiting through the back of the shoulder. Larock was taken to the XXIV Corps Hospital where, on May 13, he underwent surgery on his shoulder. He was anesthetized with chloroform, and the remainder of the head of the humerus and about two inches of the shaft were removed. For a few days after the operation, Larock suffered from excessive pain and his general health began to decline, but with plenty of beef tea and milk punch he rallied, and the wound started healing.

After the wound had healed sufficiently he was transferred to Hamilton General Hospital at Fort Monroe and then to Sloan General Hospital in Montpelier, where he was discharged with a disability and a pension on November 30, 1865. At the time of his discharge, there was no appreciable difference in the length of his two arms and he still could make a firm grip with his right hand. He had enough mobility in his right arm to be able to raise it high enough to take off his cap. There was a slight depression over the right deltoid region indicating the loss of the head of the bone but the space was rapidly filling up with cartilage. By September 1873, however, his right arm had started to atrophy and during a medical examination, Larock's family doctor declared, "The right arm is useless."[68]

Wednesday, May 31, was a glorious day for most of the men in the 9th Vermont. That day they received word that the men who had been in the regiment for three years, and those who would be discharged before October 1, were going to be mustered out soon. Company commanders were ordered to begin filling out the mustering out paperwork. Captain Linus Sherman happily wrote home: "We have received an order in relation to our *muster out* which takes effect at once, but I hardly think that we shall get home in less than a month. If I am home to spend the 4th of July I shall feel satisfied.[69]

The detachment at the Midlothian coal fields returned to the regiment on June 5, just in time to get their mustering out paperwork completed. On June 13, those that were eligible, 633 officers and men altogether, were mustered out of the service. The next day they marched to Richmond where they were put aboard two steamers, along with the 118th New York. They reached Ft. Monroe at 10:00 P.M. where they anchored for the night. The steamers left Ft. Monroe at noon on Thursday, June 15, for Baltimore. The Vermonters reached Baltimore the next morning and were put aboard a train for Philadelphia. At Philadelphia the regiment was ferried across the river and loaded aboard a train for New York City. In New York City they were put on the steamer *Thomas P. Way* and sailed up the Hudson to Troy, New York, arriving there on the morning of Saturday, June 16. From Troy they boarded a train for Vermont. The regiment arrived in Rutland at 10:00 P.M. and had a chance to grab a bite to eat before boarding another train for Burlington. The weary veterans did not arrive in Burlington until almost 2:00 A.M. Monday, June 19. In spite of the late hour, there was a reception committee and a large number of citizens to greet them.[70]

The returning heroes were greeted with cheers, booming cannons and ringing church bells as they marched to city hall under command of Major Brooks. Lieutenant Colonel Seligson was sick and could not be present. At City Hall, speeches were made and then the tired men were ushered inside for coffee, sandwiches, cold meats, pies and cakes. After they had eaten their fill, the regiment marched to Sloan General Hospital where they were quartered.[71]

At 7:30 P.M. the next evening the men were formed up again at city hall and were inspected by Governor John G. Smith, Major General Stannard, Major William Austine, military commandant of the State of Vermont, Adjutant and Inspector General Peter T. Washburn, Quartermaster General Perely P. Pitkin and Surgeon General Samuel W. Thayer. After the men were inspected, they passed in review around the city square. Then, the Governor gave a short speech, followed by the regiment being exercised in the manual of arms, after which they were marched back to their quarters.[72]

On Wednesday, June 21, Companies A, B, C, D, E, F, and G were paid off and sent home. Companies H, I and K were paid off the next day. With that, the 9th Vermont ceased to exist as a regiment.[73]

After the original members of the 9th Vermont went home, there were only 408 officers and men left. With so few men remaining, the 10 companies were merged into four, all under the command of Captain Seligson, who was promoted to lieutenant colonel July 20. The unit was officially known as the 9th Vermont Battalion. Captain Charles F. Branch commanded Co. A, Capt. Patrick Hobon commanded Co. B, Capt. Elias L. Brownell commanded Co. C, and Captain Burnham Cowdrey Co. D. The lieutenants were Elijah W. Bird, John Gray, John W. Thomas, John E. McGinnis, Edson B. Palmer, Gordon N. Briggs, Harrison K. Bacon and George C. Chamberlin.[74]

The men knew in their heads that they had to serve out their obligation, but in their hearts they wanted to go home and morale and discipline deteriorated rapidly. Two examples of the decay of military order were experienced by First Lieutenant Elias L. Brownell, who was temporarily in command of Co. D. On Friday, June 16, Co. D was ordered to fall in for the men to be detailed for guard and fatigue duty. Pvt. Albert A Davis, who had been a member of Co. G and was still smarting from the transfer to Co. D, was selected for guard duty, but said, "I will not go until my company commander details me." He then told the other men, from what had been Co. G, that they also should not obey orders from officers

Second Lieutenant Harrison K. Bacon, Co. C (**Vermont Historical Society**).

and noncommissioned officers if they were not from Co. G. Then Davis started walking out of camp. First Lieutenant Elias L. Brownell yelled for Davis to come back, to which Davis replied, "I'll see about it" and kept on walking. Brownell yelled again to him to return and Davis yelled back, "I'll be back there when I come back." Brownell had several men physically restrain Davis and put him in the guardhouse. He was charged with encouraging mutiny, disobeying an order, and contempt and disrespect toward his commanding officer.[75]

On Monday morning, June 19, Pvt. James Houghtalin of Rockingham left camp without permission and did not return until the next day. When brought before Brownell, Houghtalin was very insolent. When Brownell asked Houghtalin where he had been and who had given him permission to leave he replied, "I have been to town. What of it? Any harm done?" Then Brownell told him to stand at attention and Houghtalin said, "I stand well enough." By this time Brownell had had enough and ordered a detail of men to take Houghtalin to the guardhouse. Houghtalin did not physically resist, but kept running his mouth. As he was leaving the room he said to Brownell, "Going to put me in the guardhouse are you? Well go ahead. I shall always be a soldier. I'll get even with you." Brownell told him to shut up, to which Houghtalin replied in a threatening way that he would be out of the army soon and so would Brownell. Houghtalin was charged with being AWOL and contempt and disrespect towards his commanding officer.[76]

Houghtalin was tried before a general court-martial on June 27 and on Davis June 28. Both pleaded guilty to all charges and both were sentenced to six months confinement and forfeiture of their pay. For some unexplained reason, on July 7, both Davis' and Houghtalin's sentences were reduced to one month confinement with the loss of one month's pay.[77]

The decline in military discipline was not confined to the men in the ranks. In the late afternoon of July 9, First Lt. John Gray of Co. D, and a native of Hardwick, rode through the back gate of the house on the corner of Jefferson and Main streets. He tied up his horse and went into the house uninvited and asked the owner, Mrs. William Smoot, for a room to rent for a lady friend of his from Norfolk, Virginia. Mrs. Smoot's house was known by the soldiers as a house of ill fame. Mrs. Smoot told Gray that she did not have any rooms to rent. Gray, who was under the influence of alcohol, started arguing with her. As the argument continued Gray's language got more offensive and Mrs. Smoot retreated upstairs and asked one of her tenants, Mr. Collier, a broker from New York, to make Lieutenant Gray leave. Collier asked Gray to leave, but Gray said he would shoot any man that touched him. Gray remained in the house about an hour arguing for a room. In the meantime Mrs. Smoot sent one of her servants for the officer of the guard.[78]

When the officer of the guard, First Lt. O.H. Nealy of the 11th U.S. Infantry, arrived he found Gray in Mrs. Smoot's basement. Mr. Collier and the others told Nealy that Gray had been creating a disturbance and abusing them. Nealy asked Gray for his name, rank and regiment. Gray replied that he was Lieutenant Ward of the 9th Vermont. Nealy then asked him to pledge his word of honor to quietly follow him to General Turner's headquarters. Gray agreed to go peacefully and the two mounted their horses and left. Not long after departing Gray tried to escape, but Nealy stopped him. Some time later Gray broke away again and when Nealy tried to stop him Gray told him he would shoot him, and made good his escape.[79]

Gray was arrested in camp later and charged with conduct unbecoming an officer and a gentleman, conduct prejudicial to good order and military discipline [being drunk], and breach of arrest. He was brought before a general court-martial on Wednesday August 16, where he pleaded not guilty to all charges.[80] The court found Gray guilty of conduct unbecoming and breach of arrest, but not guilty of being drunk. He was sentenced to be cashiered from the army. On August 28, 1865, John Gray left Richmond in disgrace for Vermont.[81]

The last serious breach of discipline in the 9th Vermont Battalion occurred at about 6:00 P.M. on June 20. While passing through the company barracks, Pvt. George Pierson, a Scottish immigrant in Co. C, saw one of his comrades tied up for punishment. He stated, loud enough for his company commander to hear, "I would like to see the man that would tie me up that way." His company commander, Captain Elais L. Brownell, yelled out Pierson's name to stop him, to which Pierson yelled back, "That's my name!" and kept on going. In fact, he left camp without permission and did not return until 6:00 the next morning. After returning to camp, Pierson was arrested and thrown into the guardhouse, where he behavior only worsened.[82]

On June 24 he used "provoking and threatening" language toward First Lt. John W. Thomas of Co. B, who was the officer of the day, yelling, "You are a God damned Son of a Bitch" and other equally insulting epitaphs. The next day he tried to hit Lieutenant Thomas with his fists, but was restrained. Then he threw two cups of coffee at him. To make matters worse, a little later that day he tried to pick up a piece of wood to hit Thomas, saying, "Let me reach that club till I knock the God Damned Son of a Bitch." In the process of being restrained, he yelled at Thomas, "I'll dig your grave and follow you till I put you in it!"[83]

Private George Pierson was brought before a court-martial on July 13 and charged with conduct prejudicial to good order and military discipline, contemptuous and distrustful conduct toward his commanding officer, absence without leave, and violating the 9th Article of War (striking or threatening to strike a superior officer). He pleaded guilty of all charges and offered in his defense the following statement: "I was outrageous with liquor and did not know what I did. I have been punished severely and imprisoned at least five weeks and supposed it was for the offenses. I have never been punished before since I was with the regiment." Pierson did not call any witnesses in his defense and neither did the judge advocate in his prosecution of the case. The judge advocate merely submitted the charges to the court. To be sure, the court found Pierson guilty of all charges, but in view of the time he had served it sentenced him to only two months' hard labor and loss of his pay during that time. This was a fairly light sentence considering violation of the 9th Article of War could be punishable by execution.[84]

For some reason Pierson's earlier transgressions did not come up in his court-martial. George Pierson enlisted in the 9th Vermont on October 12, 1864, as a substitute for George B. Powers of Westford. On October 31 he arrived at Camp Distribution in Alexandria, Virginia, en route to join the regiment below Richmond. Pierson and another recruit for the 9th Vermont, Michael Foley, deserted November 4 and headed for Washington, D.C. Foley had written to a friend in Washington and arranged for him to meet them on the bank of the Potomac River opposite Georgetown, with civilian clothes and a boat. The two met up with Foley's friend as arranged, changed clothes and were rowed across the river. Pierson and Foley "Went about Washington, D.C., drinking and seeing the city." On November 8 Pierson decided to go to New York City. He bought a train ticket and was just stepping onto a passenger car when he was arrested for desertion. He was court-martialed and confined in the Military Prison in Washington. He was admitted to the First Division Hospital in Alexandria on December 6 for a fever and again on January 2, 1865, for epilepsy. He was released from prison in late February, joined the regiment in early March and was mustered out of service on October 18, 1865.[85]

The 9th Vermont Battalion was sent to Norfolk to guard government stores on August 4. While in Norfolk, Lieutenant Colonel Seligson was sent on detached duty as the assistant provost marshal of the 3rd Division of the XXIV Corps, leaving Capt. Patrick Hobon in command. A week later the battalion was sent by steamer to Drummondtown (renamed Accomac in 1893) on Virginia's Eastern Shore to guard the jail and telegraph office located there. The week the battalion was in Drummondtown there was a bit of excitement.[86]

Somehow Capt. Patrick Hobon got word that Capt. Richard B. Winder was in the area. Winder had been the quartermaster of the infamous Confederate prisoner of war camp in Andersonville, Georgia, where so many of the 9th Vermont men captured on February 2, 1864, had died; he was wanted by the Federal authorities. Winder was being sought to testify at the trial of Capt. Henry Wirz, who had been the commandant of the prisoner of war camp at Andersonville and was being tried for war crimes.[87]

Hoban sent for Capt. Burnham Cowdrey, commanding Co. D, and told him to take as many men as he needed and scour the area for Winder. Hobon could not give Cowdry any idea where Winder might be or what he looked like. Cowdrey took only Second Lt. George C. Chamberlin with him, thinking a large group would scare off Winder if they were lucky enough to run across him.[88]

The two young officers took off hoping they could get some information on Winder from the local populace. They rode back and forth across the countryside for some time before coming upon a group of Negroes who said they knew Winder. They told them where he might be found, and after riding a short time they came upon a Negro man who said he had seen Winder earlier that day at the house of the local doctor and he told them where the doctor's house was. Cowdrey and Chamberlin quickly rode in the direction the man pointed out.[89]

Finding the house, Cowdrey asked if the doctor was home. The servants told him that the doctor and Winder had ridden off earlier in a carriage, but they did not know where the men had gone. Cowdrey felt they could not be too far off, and he and Chamberlin spurred their horses off down the road. Because the land is so flat on the Eastern Shore they knew they could spot a carriage easily. At about 5:00 P.M. they spotted a carriage off in the distance. Cowdrey turned to Chamberlin and said, "There is our man. Come on," and put the spurs to his horse, leaving Chamberlin in his dust. He soon overtook the carriage, wheeled about and ordered it to halt. He then yelled as though he knew Winder was in the carriage, "Richard B. Winder, I want you. Get out of that carriage." Surprisingly, the man who was not driving jumped to the ground with a surprised look on his face. Now knowing which one was Winder, Cowdrey told him to get back in the carriage. About this time Chamberlin rode up, for which Cowdrey was thankful because Chamberlin had a pistol with him. Cowdrey left so quickly on the mission he had forgotten to strap on his pistol. Without any resistance, the doctor turned the carriage around and started off to Drummondtown as directed.[90]

As soon as Cowdrey and Chamberlin and their captives arrived in Drummondtown, Hobon handcuffed Winder, put him in jail, and telegraphed Fort Monroe of his capture. Word was soon telegraphed back to have Winder at the steamboat landing at 6:00 the next morning for transport to Washington, D.C. The doctor was allowed to leave as soon as Winder was handcuffed. Winder was picked up the next morning and taken to Washington. Winder did in fact testify at the Wirtz trial. Wirtz was found guilty of mistreatment of Union prisoners of war and hanged November 10, 1865.[91]

During the last week of August the battalion was transferred to Portsmouth. Captain Hobon was transferred to Norfolk and put in charge of the military prison that had been established there. Captain Brownell was made the provost marshal in Suffolk, leaving Captain Branch in command of the battalion. For the men, the duty was easy and their quarters quite comfortable, and the summer and autumn passed by pleasantly.[92] Sadly, the battalion lost their last man of the war on November 10, when First Lt. Lieutenant John E. McGinnis of company C died of disease.[93]

On November 25, Captain Branch received an order they all had been waiting for. He was to start filling out the paperwork to muster out the battalion. On December 1, the Green Mountain Boys, comprising 265 officers and men, embarked for Baltimore. They arrived in Burlington on the evening of December 6 under the command of Brevet Major Charles F. Branch. Lieutenant Colonel Seligson had somehow been accidentally left in New York. Except for the 7th Vermont, which was still on duty in Texas, they were the last group of veterans to return to Vermont. The battalion was met at the rail depot and escorted to the city hall by a committee of citizens and was received by the mayor and a delegation of city officials. After the speeches, the boys gave the mayor three cheers, as well as three cheers for Major George G. Benedict, who also gave a short speech, and then they gave three cheers and a tiger to the Green Mountain State. They were then taken into city hall for a delightful meal before being marched to Sloan General Hospital for the night. The next day the men were paid off and left for home.[94]

In the three years and a half years the 9th Vermont existed it had a total of 1,878 officers and men in its ranks. This aggregate included 34 officers and 885 men mustered in July 9, 1862. The 9th Vermont received 953 recruits and six transfers from other units.

Of the 1,878, thirteen enlisted men were killed in action and two officers and 8 enlisted men died of wounds. Thirty-six enlisted men died in Confederate prisoner of war camps. Five men died from accidents and two from suicide. Three officers and 229 enlisted men died of disease for a total of 298 deaths.[95]

Thirty-two officers resigned and 247 enlisted men were honorably discharged. Three officers and eight enlisted men were promoted to other units. One officer and nine enlisted men were dishonorably discharged. One hundred and fifteen enlisted men deserted and four were unaccounted for. One hundred and seventy-nine were transferred to the V. R. C. making losses other than death a total of 598.[96]

Epilogue

The author has tried in the previous chapters to tell the story of the men after the war as they were wounded or resigned. There are four key regimental members, however, that survived the war and the following are their stories after they returned home.

After the war George J. Stannard's star continued to rise—for a while. He returned to Vermont in 1866, and using his friendship with General Grant and Secretary of War Stanton, he was appointed by President Andrew Johnson as the collector of customs for the District of Vermont, based in Burlington. In the six years he was the collector of customs, Stannard made some wise investments and became quite wealthy. Unfortunately, in April 1872, his world fell apart when a Treasurer Department audit found his office short by $36,000.00. Stannard immediately resigned and within days had made up the discrepancy. Unfortunately, he was forced to file bankruptcy and was financially devastated. He tried several business ventures between 1872 and 1881, none of which worked out. Through his connections with army veterans, Stannard managed to secure the position as the assistant doorkeeper of the U.S. House of Representatives in Washington, D.C., which he kept until his death on June 1, 1886. He was buried in Burlington's Lake View Cemetery.[1]

During the first few years after the war, Edward H. Ripley worked for his father in the family marble business in Rutland. In the 1870s he moved to New York City, where he married Amelia Dykeman Van Doren on May 28, 1875. Over the next 20 years he was involved in the construction business and was the president of a shipping line. He died in Mendon, Vermont, on September 14, 1915, of pyelonephritis (chronic kidney infection). He is buried in Evergreen Cemetery in Rutland.[2]

Valentine G. Barney joined his father in the marble business in Swanton when he came back from the war. In the fall of 1869, he moved his family to Minneapolis, Minnesota, where he went into the real estate business. In July 1872, the Barney family moved to Charles City, Iowa, where he engaged in several different business ventures. His wife, Maria, died February 25, 1884. He married again on January 31, 1885, to Francis McKallor. Valentine Barney was troubled with fevers and lung problems resulting from his army service the rest of his life. He died June 14, 1889.[3]

Linus Elias Sherman, an 1861 graduate of Middlebury College, returned to Vermont to become the principal of Black River Academy in 1866. That same year he married Jennie C. Galer of Dunham, Canada, on May 16. In 1867, Linus Sherman became a pharmacist. In 1876, Jennie was diagnosed with tuberculosis. Her doctor recommended Linus and Jennie move to Colorado to take advantage of the dry, high-desert air. Leaving their two daughters with Jennie's family, Linus and Jennie, along with their young son, Clarence, moved to Colorado Springs. In Colorado Springs, Linus first worked in a dry goods store and then as a pharmacist. Unfortunately, the Colorado air did not help Jennie and she died November 17, 1877. On January 20, 1881, Linus married Louise B. Gould of Salem, Massachusetts. Linus and Louise continued to live in Colorado Springs, where Linus became a prominent attorney. Linus Sherman died February 17, 1912, and was buried in Evergreen Cemetery, Colorado Springs.[4]

At the close of the war, Charles F. Branch returned home to continue his education. His parents, however, requested he remain on the farm, which he did until 1875. During that year he entered the University of Vermont Medical College, from which he graduated with honors. After graduation, he first established a practice in Coventry but moved to Newport in 1887, where he became a leading physician in the town. He was also a United States pension examiner for several years and a professor of medicine and hygiene at the University of Vermont. For several years he was surgeon to the 1st Regiment of the Vermont National Guard and was the surgeon general of the State of Vermont from 1886 to 1888. He was a very active member of the Grand Army of the Republic and a member of the Military Order of the Loyal Legion.[5]

Doctor Branch married Emma Cook in Orwell in March 1868 and had three children before she died in September 1876. He then married Ida H. Burbank, with whom he had one daughter. Ida died in February 1888. His last marriage was to Martha J. Stewart in October 1891 in Derby. Charles F. Branch died in 1907 and is buried in Coventry.[6]

After the war the veterans tried to get on with their lives, but, as has been illustrated by this work, that was sometimes difficult for many because of physical or mental disabilities. To memorialize what they had accomplished and to provide an association in which common tragic wartime experiences could be shared with others who understood what they had gone through, the veterans of the U.S. armies organized a fraternal order named the Grand Army of the Republic (GAR), which was similar to today's Veterans of Foreign Wars organization. Virtually every city, town and village across the northern states had a post. Vermont had 116 GAR posts where the old veterans could meet and reminisce about the war and, as they grew older, complain about their aches and pains. Grand Army of the Republic Post No. 41 in Tunbridge, Vermont, was dominated by the Whitneys and Durkees of the 9th Vermont's Co. D and, according to Euclid D. Farnham, town historian of Tunbridge and a descendent of both the Whitneys and Durkees, they pretty much ran it as they saw fit. In fact, Post 41 was named for the 9th Vermont's Orlando

Whitney, who died of disease in West Point, Virginia, July 3, 1863. The last surviving member of the Whitney Post was George W. Durkee, who died August 13, 1931.[7]

The patriarch of the Whitneys and Durkees, Able Whitney, sent 13 grandsons off to the Civil War. They were Albert Whitney, Co. E, 2nd Vermont; James H. Whitney, Co. E, 4th Vermont; Charles Durkee, George W. Durkee, Rosewel Durkee, Able D. Whitney, John S. Whitney, Lewis Whitney, Milo F. Whitney, Orlando Whitney, Orson Whitney, Ransome Whitney, Co. D, 9th Vermont; and John Ordway, 1st Wisconsin Cavalry. Able Whitney planted a sugar maple to honor each of his grandsons along New Brighton Road leading to his house on Whitney Hill in Tunbridge. Most of the trees survive today.[8]

Homer Hoyt, a private from Tunbridge in the 9th Vermont's Co. D, moved to Massachusetts after the war to work in the mills there and became somewhat wealthy. He promised his hometown he would leave money in his will to have a monument built to com-

Postwar photograph of Lewis Whitney (Euclid D. Farnham).

Top left: Privates Orlando and Milo Whitney, Co. D (Euclid D. Farnham). *Bottom left:* The 1924 dedication of the Tunbridge Civil War monument in the Hoyt Memorial Park at the entrance of the village cemetery. From left to right are Edson "Bert" B. Osborn (Co. H, 2nd U.S. Sharpshooters), Elihu Tuller (Co. E, 2nd Vt. Inf.), Charles. B. Smith (Co. D, 12th Vt. Inf.), George W. Durkee (Co. D, 9th Vt. Inf.), and Charles Durkee (Co. D, 9th Vt. Inf.) (Euclid Farnham). *Top below:* Private Homer Hoyt, Co. D (Euclid D. Farnham). *Bottom below:* Postwar photograph of Homer Hoyt (Euclid D. Farnham).

memorate the Tunbridge boys' service during the war. Although Homer did not die until 1923, he held good his promise and left the town $5,000.00 for the monument. Only four Tunbridge Civil War veterans were still alive when the monument was dedicated on July 4, 1924. The monument is located just below the village cemetery and to this day is known as Hoyt Memorial Park.[9]

The 9th Vermont's last surviving veteran was George A. Coburn of Co. F, who died in Minturn, Colorado, at age 100 on April 1, 1946. Coburn enlisted in the 9th Vermont on January 5, 1865, and by the time he was mustered out on December 1, 1865, he had been promoted to sergeant.[10]

APPENDIX A:
ACRONYMS AND ABBREVIATIONS

Adj.— Adjutant
AWOL — Absent without leave
Brig. Gen.— Brigadier General
Bvt.— Brevet
Co.— Company
Col.— Colonel
Corp.— Corporal
Capt.— Captain
G.C.M.— General courts martial
GAR — Grand Army of the Republic
KIA — Killed in action
Lt.— Lieutenant
Lt. Col.— Lieutenant Colonel
Lt. Gen.— Lieutenant General

Maj.— Major
Maj. Gen.— Major General
MIA — Missing in action
NCO — Noncommissioned officer
N.F.R.— no further record
POW — Prisoner of war
Pvt.— Private
QM.— Quartermaster
QM. Sgt.— Quartermaster Sergeant
Sgt. Maj.— Sergeant Major
Sgt.— Sergeant
USAMHI — U.S. Military History Institute
U.S.C.T — United States Colored Troops
V.R.C.— Veteran Reserve Corps

Appendix B:
Ninth Vermont Infantry
Regiment Roster

This roster is extracted from the *Revised Roster of Vermont Volunteers and Lists of Vermonters Who Served in the Army and Navy of the United States During the War of the Rebellion*, Theodore S. Peck, Montpelier: Watchman Co., 1892, pages 344–377. Where possible, information has been updated or corrected from the individuals' military service records, military pension records, and court-martial records at the National Archives, Washington, DC. Most of the information on the soldiers' deaths and places of burial came from the Vermont in the Civil War Web page's cemetery project at http://www.vermontcivilwar. org/cem.

The regiment was mustered into service of the United States on July 9, 1862. Original members and recruits, whose term of service would expire prior to October 1, 1865, were mustered out of service June 13, 1864. Remaining officers and men were consolidated into a battalion of four companies, but their record is completed in their original companies. The battalion was mustered out December 1, 1865.

Field and Staff

Colonels

Stannard, George J. Residence: St. Albans. Commission Date: May 21, 62. Issue Date: May 21, 62. Lt. Col. 2nd Vt.; Promoted Brig. Gen. U.S. Volunteers Mar 11, 63; Bvt. Maj. Gen. Oct 28, 64, for gallant and meritorious service at Ft. Harrison, Va.; Wounded Jul 3, 63, Jun 15, 64, and Sep 30, 64; Resigned Jun 28, 66; Died Jun 1, 1886, and buried in Lakeview Cemetery, Burlington, Vt.

Andross, Dudley K. Residence: Bradford. Commission Date: Mar 20, 63. Issue Date: Mar 20, 63. Lt. Col.; Resigned May 22, 63; Died Nov 28 in Bridport.

Ripley, Edward H. Residence: Rutland. Commission Date: May 22, 63. Issue Date: Jun 12, 63. Capt. Co. B; Promoted to Maj. Mar 20, 63; to Lt. Col. May 16, 63; to Bvt. Brig. Gen. Aug 1, 64; Wounded Sep 29, 64; Mustered out Jun 13, 65; Died Sep 14, 1915, and buried in Evergreen Cemetery, Rutland, Vt.

Lieutenant Colonels

Andross, Dudley K. Residence: Bradford. Commission Date: May 26, 62. Issue Date: May 26, 62. *See* Col.

Stowell, Edwin S. Residence: Cornwall. Commission Date: Mar 20, 63. Issue Date: Mar 20, 63. Capt. Co. F. 5th Vt.; Promoted to Maj. 9th Vt. Jun 21, 62; Resigned May 11, 63; Died Sep 11, 1880, and buried in Central Cemetery, Cornwall, Vt.

Ripley, Edward H. Residence: Rutland. Commission Date: May 16, 63. Issue Date: May 22, 63. *See* Col.

Barney, Valentine G. Residence: Swanton. Commission Date: May 24, 63. Issue Date: Jun 19, 63. Capt. Co. A; Mustered out Jun 13, 65; Died Jun 14, 1889.

Seligson, Herman. Residence: Burlington. Commission Date: Jul 20, 65. Issue Date: Jul 20, 65. First. Lt. Co. C; Promoted to Capt. Co. C Jan 1, 63; Transferred to Co. A Jun 13, 65; Mustered out Dec 1, 65; Died Aug 18, 1891 in Baltimore, Md. and buried in Arlington National Cemetery, Arlington, Va.

Majors

Stowell, Edwin S. Residence: Cornwall. Commission Date: Jun 21, 62. Issue Date: Jun 21, 62. *See* Lt. Col.

Ripley, Edward H. Residence: Rutland. Commission Date: Mar 20, 63. Issue Date: Mar 20, 63. *See* Col.

Jarvis, Charles. Residence: Weathersfield. Commission Date: May 24, 63. Issue Date: Jun 19, 63. Capt. Co. D; Died Dec 1, 63, of wounds received same day.

Bartlett, Amasa. Residence: Irasburgh. Commission Date: Dec 21, 63. Issue Date: Dec 22, 63. Capt. Co. E; Died Mar. 16, 64, of disease and buried in Center Cemetery, Coventry, Vt.

Brooks, Joseph C. Residence: Westminster. Commission Date: Mar 20, 64. Issue Date: Apr 21, 64. First Lt. Co. K; Promoted Capt. Co. F Nov 17, 62; Wounded Sep 29, 64; Mustered out Jun 13, 65.

Adjutants

Stearns, John C. Residence: Bradford. Commission Date: Jun 30, 62. Issue Date: Jun 30, 62. Resigned May 31, 63; Died Jul 2, 1914, in Bradford.

Livingston, Josiah O. Residence: Marshfield. Commission Date: Jun 4, 63. Issue Date: Jun 12, 63. *See* Capt. Co. G.

Belden, Henry D. Residence: Burlington. Commission Date: Oct 19, 64. Issue Date: Nov 19, 64. First Sgt. Co. F; Promoted to Hospital Steward Aug 10, 62; to Sgt. Maj. Mar 13, 63; Wounded Sep 29, 64; Resigned Apr 25, 65, Died May 21, 1903, and buried in Greenwood Cemetery, St. Albans, Vt.

Gould, George W. Residence: Brattleboro. Commission Date: May 2, 65. Issue Date: May 15, 65. Musician Co. K; Transferred to Co. F and promoted to Sgt. Jun 1, 64; to Sgt. Maj. Apr 10, 65; Mustered out Jun 13, 65; Died Mar 4, 1901, at Winchester, N.H.

Quartermasters

Sawyer, Francis O. Residence: Burlington. Commission Date: Jun 10, 62. Issue Date: Jun 10, 62. Promoted Capt. and Asst. QM of U.S. Volunteers Jun 30, 64; Mustered out May 31, 66.

Rice, Franklin E. Residence: Isle La Mott. Commission Date: Oct 19, 64. Issue Date: Dec 20, 64. Pvt. Co. F; Promoted to Commissary Sgt. Nov 20, 62; Mustered out Jun 13, 65.

Surgeons

Carpenter, Walter B. Residence: Burlington. Commission Date: Jun 21, 62. Issue Date: Jun 21, 62. Asst. Surgeon 2nd Vt.; Resigned Nov 4, 64; Died Mar 20, 1906, and in buried Green Mountain Cemetery, Burlington, Vt.

Vincent, Walter S. Residence: Plainfield. Commission Date: Nov 15, 64. Issue Date: Nov 25, 64. Asst. Surgeon; Mustered out Jun 13, 65; Died Nov 10, 1921, and buried in Lakeview Cemetery, Burlington, Vt.

Assistant Surgeons

Hall, Horace P. Residence: St. Albans. Commission Date: Jun 30, 62. Issue Date: Jun 30, 62. Resigned Mar 13, 63; Died Mar 12, 1883, and buried in Greenwood Cemetery, St. Albans, Vt.

Goss, Story N. Residence: Georgia. Commission Date: Sep 26, 62. Issue Date: Oct 7, 62. Resigned Oct 15, 63; Died Apr 27, 1905, and buried in Highland Cemetery, Chelsea, Vt.

Vincent, Walter S. Residence: Plainfield. Commission Date: Apr 20, 63. Issue Date: Apr 20, 63. *See* Surgeon.

Fairman, Erastus, P. Residence: Wolcott. Commission Date: Apr 9, 64. Issue Date: Apr 21, 64. Pvt. Co. C 17th Vt.; Mustered out Jun 13, 65; Died Apr 6, 1904, and buried in Fairmont Cemetery, Wolcott, Vt.

Chaplains

Dickinson, Lucius C. Residence: Cavendish. Commission Date: Jul 2, 62. Issue Date: Jul 2, 62. Mustered out Jun 13, 65; Died Dec 3, 1887, and buried in St. Johnsbury Center Cemetery, St. Johnsbury, Vt.

Noncommissioned Officer Staff

Sergeants Major

Gorham, James T. Residence: Ludlow. Enlistment Date: Jun 21, 62. Muster Date: Jul 9, 62. *See* Capt. Co. H.

Belden, Henry D. Residence: Burlington. Enlistment Date: Jun 2, 62. Muster Date: Jul 9, 62. *See* Adjutant.

Thomas, John W. Residence: Burlington. Enlistment Date: Jul 21, 63. Muster Date: Jul 27, 63. *See* First Lt. Co. B.

Gould, George W. Residence: Brattleboro. Enlistment Date: Jun 16, 62. Muster Date: Jul 9, 62. *See* Adjutant.

Church, Andrew J. Residence: Washington. Enlistment Date: Jul 10, 62. Muster Date: Jul 10, 62. Pvt. Co. G; Promoted to Corp.; to Sgt. Dec 18, 64; to Sgt. Maj. May 20, 65; Mustered out Jun 13, 65.

Newell, Oliver W. Residence: Burke. Enlistment Date: Dec 10, 63. Muster Date: Dec 23, 63. *See* Second Lt. Co. D.

Jefferds, John G. Residence: Washington. Enlistment Date: Jan 4, 64. Muster Date: Jan 9, 64. Pvt. Co. I; Promoted to Corp. Nov 27, 64; to Sgt. Jun 19, 65; Transferred to Co. D Jun 13, 65; to Sgt. Maj. Nov 1, 65; Mustered out Dec 1, 65; Died Apr 26, 1927, and buried in Swan Point Cemetery, Providence, R.I.

Quartermaster Sergeants

Peck, Theodore S. Residence: Burlington. Enlistment Date: Jun 27, 62. Muster Date: Jul 9, 62. *See* First Lt. Co. H.

Barber, Edward D. Residence: Middlebury. Enlistment Date: Jun 24, 62. Muster Date: Jul 13, 62. *See* Pvt. Co. C.

Chamberlin, George C. Residence: Bradford. Enlistment Date: Feb 27, 64. Muster Date: Mar 8, 64. *See* First Lt. Co. D.

Leyden, Thomas. Residence: Jamaica. Enlistment Date: Feb 17, 65. Muster Date: Feb 17, 65. Pvt. Co. C; Transferred to Co. A Jun 13, 65; Promoted to QM Sgt. Nov 1, 65; Mustered out Dec 1, 65.

Commissary Sergeants

Pattee, David J. Residence: Georgia. Enlistment Date: Jun 9, 62. Muster Date: Jul 9, 62. Discharged Nov 20, 62, for disability.

Rice, Franklin E. Residence: Isle La Mott. Enlistment Date: Jun 17, 62. Muster Date: Jul 9, 62. *See* Quartermaster.

Musk, Henry A. Residence: Derby. Enlistment Date: Jun 25, 62. Muster Date: Jul 62. Pvt. Co. E.; Promoted to Commissary Sgt. Jan 1, 65; Mustered out Jun 13, 65.

Page, William, Jr. Residence: Corinth. Enlistment Date: Dec 17, 63. Muster Date: Dec 31, 63. Pvt. Co. F; Transferred to Co. B Jun 13, 65; Promoted to Sgt. Jun 19, 65; to Commissary Sgt. Aug 18, 65; Mustered out Dec 1, 65; Died Feb 26, 1910, and buried in Old East Corinth Cemetery, Corinth, Vt.

Hospital Steward

Belden, Henry D. Residence: Burlington. Enlistment Date: Jun 2, 62. Muster Date: Jul 9, 62. *See* Adjutant.

Squier, Algernon M. Residence: Weathersfield. Enlistment Date: Jun 2, 62. Muster Date: Jul 9, 62. Pvt. Co. D; Promoted to Corp. Jul 23, 62; Reduced Aug 11, 62; Promoted to Hospital Steward Apr 12, 63; Discharged for appointment as Hospital Steward in the Regular Army.

French, Heman R. Residence: Waitsfield. Enlistment Date: Jun 23, 62. Muster Date: Jul 9, 62. Pvt. Co. I; Promoted to Hospital Steward Feb 4, 65; Mustered out Jun 13, 65.

Flanders, Royal C. Residence: Orange. Enlistment Date: Dec 31, 63. Muster Date: Jan 6, 64. Pvt. Co. I; Transferred to Co. D Jun 13, 65; Promoted to Corp. Jun 19, 65; to Hospital Steward Aug 18, 65; Mustered out Dec 1, 65; Died Aug 30, 1866, and buried in Orange Cemetery, Orange, Vt.

Drum Major

Hardie, Robert G. Residence: Brattleboro. Enlistment Date: Jun 25, 62. Muster Date: Jul 9, 62. Discharged Mar 31, 63, by special order of the War Department; Died Oct 26, 1890, and buried in Prospect Hill Cemetery, Brattleboro, Vt.

Principal Musicians

Edgerton, Edward M. Residence: Clarendon. Enlistment Date: Jun 18, 62. Muster Date: Jul 9, 62. Musician Co. B; Promoted to Sgt. May 28, 63; Reduced May 12, 64; Promoted to Sgt. Oct 19, 64; to Principal Musician Dec 26, 64; Mustered out Jun 13, 65.

Morse, Richard H. Residence: Wolcott. Enlistment Date: Jun 26, 62. Muster Date: Jul 9, 62. Pvt. Co. H; Promoted to Principal Musician Dec 26, 64; Mustered out Jun 13, 65; Died May 4, 1883, and buried in the village cemetery, Bradford, Vt.

Company A

Captains

Barney, Valentine G. Residence: Swanton. Commission Date: Jun 14, 62. Issue Date: Jun 14, 62. *See* Lt. Col.

Sherman, Linus E. Residence: Montgomery. Commission Date: May 24, 63. Issue Date: Jun 24, 63. First Lt. Co. A; Taken prisoner Sep 3, 62; Paroled Sep 28, 62; Mustered out Jun 13, 65; Died Feb 17, 1912, and buried in Evergreen Cemetery, Colorado Springs, Colo.

Seligson, Herman. Residence: Burlington. Commission Date: Jan 1, 63. Issue Date: Jan 14, 63. *See* Lt. Col.

Branch, Charles F. Residence: Orwell. Commission Date: Jul 3, 65. Issue Date: Jul 20, 65. Corp. Co. C; Promoted to Sgt. Jan 27, 64; to First Sgt. Feb 1, 65; to Second Lt. Co. H Mar 6, 65; to First Lt. Co. C May 20, 65; Transferred to Co. A Jun 13, 65; Mustered out Dec 1, 65.

First Lieutenants

Sherman, Linus E. Residence: Montgomery. Commission Date: Jun 14, 62. Issue Date: Jun 14, 62. *See* Capt. Co. A.

Jewett, Erastus W. Residence: St. Albans. Commission Date: May 24, 63. Issue Date: Jun 24, 63. Second Lt. Co. A.; Taken prisoner Sep 3, 62; Paroled Sep 28, 62; Resigned Nov 21, 64; Died Feb 20, 1906, and buried in Church Street Cemetery, Swanton, Vt.

Cleveland, Edmund F. Residence: Richford. Commission Date: Nov 28, 64. Issue Date: Dec 21, 64. Corp. Co. A; Promoted to Sgt. Mar 14, 63; to First Sgt. May 28, 63; to Second Lt. May 24, 63; Mustered out Jun 13, 65.

Branch, Charles F. Residence: Orwell. Commission Date: May 20, 65. Issue Date: May 20, 65. *See* Capt. Co. A.

Bird, Elijah W. Residence: New Haven. Commission Date: Jul 3, 65. Issue Date: Jul 20, 65. Pvt. Co. C; Promoted to Corp. Oct 25, 64; to Sgt. Jun 14, 65; Transferred to Co. A Jun 13, 65; Mustered out Dec 1, 65; Died Mar 18, 1905, and buried in Evergreen Cemetery, New Haven, Vt.

Second Lieutenants

Jewett, Erastus W. Residence: St. Albans. Commission Date: Jun 14, 62. Issue Date: Jun 14, 62. *See* First Lt. Co. A.

Cleveland, Edmund F. Residence: Richford. Commission Date: May 24, 63. Issue Date: Jun 24, 63. *See* First Lt. Co. A.

Halbert, John S. Residence: Fairfax. Commission Date: Nov 28, 64. Issue Date: Dec 21, 64. Sgt. Co. A; Promoted First Sgt. Jul 1, 63; Mustered out Jun 13, 65; Died Jun 8, 1899, and buried in Plains Cemetery, Fairfax, Vt.

Palmer, Edson B. Residence: New Haven. Commission Date: Jul 3, 65. Issue Date: Jul 20, 65. Pvt. Co. C; Promoted to Corp. Jun 15, 64; to Sgt. Jun 14, 65; Transferred to Co. Co. A Jun 13, 65; Mustered out Dec 1, 65; Died Mar 1, 1923, and buried in Greenwood Cemetery, Bristol, Vt.

Sergeants

Whitmore, Orange S. Residence: Bakersfield. Enlistment Date: Jun 9, 62. Muster Date: Jul 9, 62. Discharged March 15, 63, for disability.

Halbert, John S. Residence: Fairfax. Enlistment Date: May 29, 62. Muster Date: Jul 9, 62. *See* Second Lt. Co. A.

Bowditch, Josiah B. Residence: Fairfax. Enlistment Date: May 29, 62. Muster Date: Jul 9, 62. Deserted Jan 11, 63; Returned Feb 6, 63; Reduced Aug 1, 64; Mustered out Jun 13, 65; Died Mar 29, 1918, and buried in Herrick Cemetery, North Fairfield, Vt.

Smith, Levi T. Residence: Montgomery. Enlistment Date: Jun 5, 62. Muster Date: Jul 9, 62. Discharged Apr 27, 63, for disability.

Meigs, Harrison S. Residence: Swanton. Enlistment Date: Jun 9, 62. Muster Date: Jul 9, 62. Mustered out May 13, 65; Died May 22, 1885, and buried in Church St. Cemetery, Swanton, Vt.

Corporals

Cummins, Jed W. Residence: Georgia. Enlistment Date: Jun 5, 62. Muster Date: Jul 9, 62. Promoted to Sgt. Aug 1, 64; Mustered out Jun 13, 65.

Cleveland, Edmund F. Residence: Richford. Enlistment Date: Jun 4, 62. Muster Date: Jul 9, 62. *See* First Lt. Co. A.

White, Abner B. Residence: South Hero. Enlistment Date: Jun 7, 62. Muster Date: Jul 9, 62. Discharged Oct 18, 62, for accidental wound; Died Jan 14, 1902.

Williams, Wesley C. Residence: Bakersfield. Enlistment Date: Jun 2, 62. Muster Date: Jul 9, 62. Mustered out Jun 22, 65.

Johnson, Daniel, Jr. Residence: Berkshire. Enlistment Date: Jun 10, 62. Muster Date: Jul 9, 62. Reduced; Died Feb 4, 64, of disease.

Lamondy, Joseph G. Residence: Bakersfield. Enlistment Date: Jun 3, 62. Muster Date: Jul 9, 62. Died Aug 20, 62, of disease.

Perkins, James C. Residence: Bakersfield. Enlistment Date: Jun 2, 62. Muster Date: Jul 9, 62. Reduced Jun 5, 65; Mustered out Jun 13, 65.

Wright, Daniel E. Residence: Montgomery. Enlistment Date: Jun 3, 62. Muster Date: Jul 9, 62. Reduced May 18, 63; Transferred to Co. B; Back to Co. A Sep 1, 64; Mustered out Jun 13, 65. Died May 15, 1918, and buried in New Protestant Cemetery, Montgomery Center, Vt.

Musicians

Bushnell, Augustus T. Residence: Georgia. Enlistment Date: Jun 9, 62. Muster Date: Jul 9, 62. Discharged May 28, 63, for disability; Died 1910, and buried in Georgia Plains Cemetery, Georgia, Vt.

Bundy, Aaron W. Residence: Montgomery. Enlistment Date: May 30, 62. Muster Date: Jul 9, 62. Mustered out Jun 13, 65; Died Mar 28, 1882, and buried in Montgomery Center Cemetery, Montgomery, Vt.

Wagoner

Walker, Charles W. Residence: Swanton. Enlistment Date: Jun 17, 62. Muster Date: Jul 9, 62. Deserted Oct 4, 62.

Privates

Adams, Calvin S. Residence: Norwich. Enlistment Date: Dec 30, 63. Muster Date: Jan 7, 64. Discharged Feb 25, 64, for fraudulent enlistment.

Arrel, Ami. Residence: Enosburgh. Enlistment Date: Mar 7, 65. Muster Date: Mar 7, 65. Mustered out Dec 1, 65.

Baker, Elias W. Residence: Bakersfield. Enlistment Date: Jun 16, 62. Muster Date: Jul 9, 62. Deserted Oct 21, 62.

Barnard, William. Residence: Montgomery. Enlistment Date: Jun 2, 62. Muster Date: Jul 9, 62. Mustered out Jun 13, 65.

Barry, Charles E. Residence: Richford. Enlistment Date: Jun 2, 62. Muster Date: Jul 9, 62. Died Nov 1, 63.

Bartlett, Joseph J. Residence: St. Albans. Enlistment Date: Dec 31, 63. Muster Date: Jan 4, 64. Mustered out Jul 16, 65.

Bartram, Daniel P. Residence: Bakersfield. Enlistment Date: Jun 9, 62. Muster Date: Jul 9, 62. Deserted Feb 12, 63.

Bashaw, Trifley. Residence: Montgomery. Enlistment Date: Jun 14, 62. Muster Date: Jul 9, 62. Promoted to Corp. Dec 19, 64; Mustered out Jun 13, 65.

Belrose, Franklin. Residence: Swanton. Enlistment Date: Jun 12, 62. Muster Date: Jul 9, 62. Mustered out Jun 13, 65.

Belvel, Edward. Residence: Bakersfield. Enlistment Date: Jun 16, 62. Muster Date: Jul 9, 62. Mustered out Jun 13, 65; Died Dec 23, 1900, and buried in the village cemetery, Worcester, Vt.

Benjamin, Henry. Residence: Pownal. Enlistment Date: Dec 21, 63. Muster Date: Dec 30, 63. Mustered out Dec 1, 65; Died Dec 27, 1920, and buried in Park Lawn Cemetery, Bennington, Vt.

Bessey, Edgar F. Residence: Fairfield. Enlistment Date: Aug 11, 64. Muster Date: Aug 11, 64. Mustered out Jun 13, 65.

Billcock, John. Residence: Grand Isle. Enlistment Date: Jun 17, 62. Muster Date: Jul 9, 62. Mustered out Jun 13, 65.

Blake, Benjamin M. Residence: Fairfax. Enlistment Date: May 29, 62. Muster Date: Jul 9, 62. Discharged

Oct 17, 62, for disability; Died Feb 14, 1895, and buried in West Topsham Cemetery, West Topsham, Vt.

Blanchard, Merritt. Pownal. Enlistment Date: Dec 16, 63. Muster Date: Dec 30, 63. Mustered out Dec 1, 65.

Blodah, Theophilus. Residence: Enosburgh. Enlistment Date: Dec 18, 63. Muster Date: Dec 30, 63. Mustered out Dec 1, 65; Died Aug 7, 1880, and buried in Richford, Vt.

Bostwick, Homer. Residence: Monkton. Enlistment Date: Aug 29, 64. Muster Date: Aug 29, 64. Mustered out Jun 13, 65; Died Apr 15, 1905, and buried in Greenwood Cemetery, Bristol, Vt.

Bradley, Charles D. Residence: Highgate. Enlistment Date: Jul 11, 62. Muster Date: Jul 11, 62. Deserted Jan 25, 63.

Bridge, George S. Residence: Royalton. Enlistment Date: Sep 19, 64. Muster Date: Sep 19, 64. Mustered out Jun 13, 65; Died Oct 20, 1922, Ludlow Cemetery, Ludlow, Vt.

Briggs, Isaac. Residence: Monkton. Enlistment Date: Aug 25, 64. Muster Date: Aug 25, 64. Transferred to Co. C, 5th Vt. Jan 20, 65.

Bridge, Rodolphus. Residence: Jamaica. Enlistment Date: Sep 14, 64. Muster Date: Sep 14, 64. Transferred to Co. C, 6th Vt. Jan 20, 65; Died Nov 27, 1920, and buried in Riverside Cemetery, West Woodstock, Vt.

Browelette, Joseph. Residence: Acton, Can. Enlistment Date: Jul 11, 62. Muster Date: Jul 11, 62. Mustered out Jun 13, 65.

Bruce, Harry, Jr. Residence: Sharon. Enlistment Date: Dec 7, 63. Muster Date: Dec 7, 63. Discharged May 17, 65, for disability; Died Feb 16, 1869, and buried in Pine Hill Cemetery, Sharon, Vt.

Burroughs, Alfred. Residence: Belvidere. Enlistment Date: May 30, 62. Muster Date: Jul 9, 62. Died Dec 7, 62, of disease; Buried in Rosehill Cemetery, Chicago, Ill.; Memorial stone in Burroughs Cemetery, Belvidere, Vt.

Campbell, Warren O. Residence: Georgia. Enlistment Date: Sep 10, 64. Muster Date: Sep 10, 64. Transferred to Co. A., 5th Vt. Jan 20, 65; Died Apr 29, 1879, and buried in Old Cemetery, Montgomery, Vt.

Carner, Michael. Residence: Sheldon. Enlistment Date: Jun 5, 62. Muster Date: Jul 9, 62. Deserted Dec 3, 62.

Castor, Lewis. Residence: Highgate. Enlistment Date: Jun 23, 62. Muster Date: Jul 9, 62. Mustered out Jun 13, 65.

Clary, Cornelius C. Residence: Georgia. Enlistment Date: Dec 4, 63. Muster Date: Dec 11, 63. Mustered out Jul 7, 65.

Clary, Edward D. Residence: Georgia. Enlistment Date: Jun 5, 62. Muster Date: Jul 9, 62. Died Oct 3, 64, of yellow fever; Buried in New Bern National Cemetery, New Bern, N.C.

Clary, Orrin A. Residence: Georgia. Enlistment Date: Jun 27, 64. Muster Date: Jun 27, 64. Drafted; Transferred to Co. C, 5th Vt. Jan 20, 65; Died 1896, and buried in Hope Cemetery, Georgia, Vt.

Clary, Silas S. Residence: Georgia. Enlistment Date: Aug 14, 62. Muster Date: Sep 15, 62. Mustered out Jun 13, 65.

Clough, Burchard. Residence: Norwich. Enlistment Date: Jan 4, 64. Muster Date: Jan 7, 64. Taken prisoner Feb 2, 64, and died in Andersonville Jun 30, 64; Buried in Andersonville National Cemetery, Andersonville, Ga.

Comstock, Calvin. Residence: Monkton. Enlistment Date: Aug 25, 64. Muster Date: Aug 25, 64. Transferred to Co. C, 4th Vt. Jan 20, 65.

Connor, Charles. Residence: Strafford. Enlistment Date: Dec 22, 63. Muster Date: Jan 6, 64. Promoted to Corp. Mar 1, 65; to Sgt. Jun 5, 65; Mustered out Dec 1, 65.

Cooney, William I. Residence: Highgate. Enlistment Date: Jun 10, 62. Muster Date: Jul 9, 62. Mustered out Jun 13, 65.

Cronin, Dennis. Residence: Alburgh. Enlistment Date: Jun 9, 62. Muster Date: Jul 9, 62. Deserted Dec 3, 62; Returned Feb 7, 63; Promoted to Corp. May 28, 63; to Sgt. Jul 1, 63; to First Sgt. Jan 1, 65; Mustered out Jun 13, 65.

Crook, Charles K. Residence: Montgomery. Enlistment Date: Jun 3, 62. Muster Date: Jul 9, 62. Died Oct 15, 62, of disease; Buried in Rosehill Cemetery, Chicago, Il.

Cullin, Charles. Residence: Alburgh. Enlistment Date: Jun 12, 62. Muster Date: Jul 9, 62. Deserted Nov 12, 62.

Cunliffe, Thomas. Residence: Alburgh. Enlistment Date: Jun 9, 62. Muster Date: Jul 9, 62. Deserted Dec 16, 62.

Currier, George. Residence: Norwich. Enlistment Date: Dec 26, 63. Muster Date: Jan 7, 64. Died Nov 4, 64, of disease; Buried in Hampton National Cemetery, Hampton, Va.

Curtis, Francis. Residence: Sheldon. Enlistment Date: Jun 21, 62. Muster Date: Jul 9, 62. Discharged Oct 17, 62, for disability.

Daily, Edmund. Residence: Strafford. Enlistment Date: Dec 27, 63. Muster Date: Jan 6, 64. Mustered out Jul 17, 65; Died Apr 12, 1906, and buried in Evergreen Cemetery, Strafford, Vt.

Davis, Edwin L. Residence: Cambridge. Enlistment Date: Jun 2, 62. Muster Date: Jul 9, 62. Promoted to Corp. Oct 14, 64; Reduced March 1, 65; Mustered out Jun 13, 65.

Davis, Edward N. Residence: Montgomery. Enlistment Date: May 30, 62. Muster Date: Jul 9, 62. Mustered out Jun 13, 65.

Davis, Oscar F. Residence: Norwich. Enlistment Date: Dec 26, 63. Muster Date: Jan 7, 64. Taken prisoner Feb 2, 64, and died at Andersonville, Ga., Sep 9, 64; Buried in Andersonville National Cemetery, Andersonville, Ga.

Davis, Samuel. Residence: Montgomery. Enlistment Date: Sep 19, 64. Muster Date: Sep 19, 64. Transferred to Co. A, 5th Vt. Jan 20, 65; Died Jul 1, 1871, and buried in Cutler Cemetery, East Montpelier, Vt.

Davis, Sylvanus A. Residence: Montgomery. Enlistment Date: Jan 1, 64. Muster Date: Jan 5, 64. Mustered out Dec 1, 65.

Dearborn, Abial C. Residence: Starksboro. Enlistment Date: Aug 3, 64. Muster Date: Aug 3, 64. Mustered out Jun 13, 65.

Dimick, Marshall A. Residence: Bridgewater. Enlistment Date: Aug 9, 64. Muster Date: Aug 9, 64. Mustered out Jun 13, 65.

Dow, Francis R. Residence: Strafford. Enlistment Date: Dec 19, 63. Muster Date: Dec 19, 63. Mustered out Sep 1, 65.

Dow, Henry C. Residence: Strafford. Enlistment Date: Dec 22, 63. Muster Date: Jan 6, 64. Promoted to Corp. Feb 1, 64; To Sgt. Jun 5, 65; Reduced Sep 5, 65; Died Oct 11, 65, of disease; Buried in Evergreen Cemetery, Strafford, Vt.

Downing, Robert. Residence: ——. Enlistment Date: ——. Muster Date: ——. No descriptive list; Discharged Sep 26, 64, by General Palmer.

Dwyer, John. Residence: Alburgh. Enlistment Date: Jun 12, 62. Muster Date: Jul 9, 62. Deserted Jan 6, 63.

Dynan, Michael. Residence: Sheldon. Enlistment Date: Jun 5, 62. Muster Date: Jul 9, 62. Deserted Dec 3, 62.

Eaton, Edgar L. Residence: St. Albans. Enlistment Date: Jun 2, 62. Muster Date: Jul 9, 62. Discharged Nov 6, 62, for disability.

Eldred, Warren. Residence: Fairfield. Enlistment Date: Jun 20, 62. Muster Date: Jul 9, 62. Deserted Oct —, 62.

Fairbanks, Artemas P. Residence: Townshend. Enlistment Date: Dec 16, 63. Muster Date: Jan 2, 64. Mustered out Dec 1, 65; Died Jun 10, 1886, and buried in the village cemetery, Grafton, Vt.

Fay, Luther C. Residence: Sharon. Enlistment Date: Dec 9, 63. Muster Date: Dec 9, 63. Mustered out Jul 17, 65.

Fitch, Luther E. Residence: Bakersfield. Enlistment Date: Jun 4, 62. Muster Date: Jul 9, 62. Deserted Oct —, 62; Returned May 5, 65; Dishonorably discharged Jun 12, 65; Died Jun 28, 1929, and buried in Chester Arthur Cemetery, North Fairfield, Vt.

Franklin, Benjamin. Residence: Onslow Co., N.C. Enlistment Date: Dec 4, 63. Muster Date: Dec 4, 63. Colored under cook; Discharged Aug 21, 65, by special order of the War Department.

French, Henry P. Residence: Tunbridge. Enlistment Date: Dec 26, 63. Muster Date: Jan 7, 64. Discharged Jun 13, 65, for wounds received Sep 29, 64; Died Aug 16, 1909, and buried in Branchview Cemetery, Royalton, Vt.

Frink, Luman. Residence: Pownal. Enlistment Date: Dec 22, 63. Muster Date: Dec 30, 63. Died Nov 22, 64, of disease.

Gilman, James K. Residence: Strafford. Enlistment Date: Aug, 15, 64. Muster Date: Aug 15, 64. Mustered out Jun 13, 65; Died May 24, 1910, and buried in Evergreen Cemetery, Strafford, Vt.

Girouard, Raymond. Residence: Acton, Can. Enlistment Date: Jul 11, 62. Muster Date: Jul 11, 62. Discharged Jan 22, 63, to enlist in the Regular Army.

Hagan, George. Residence: Bakersfield. Enlistment Date: May 30, 62. Muster Date: Jul 9, 62. Deserted Dec 16, 62.

Hair, William C. Residence: Montgomery. Enlistment Date: Jan 2, 64. Muster Date: Jan 5, 64. Mustered out Dec 1, 65.

Haley, Josiah. Residence: Pownal. Enlistment Date: Aug 18, 64. Muster Date: Aug 18, 64. Transferred to Co. I, 5th Vt. Jan 20, 65.

Hebard, Abel C. Residence: Norwich. Enlistment Date: Dec 26, 63. Muster Date: Jan 7, 64. Promoted to Corp Jun 5, 65; Mustered out Dec 1, 65; Died Nov 13, 1917, and buried in Hillside Cemetery, Norwich, Vt.

Ingles, Monroe. Residence: Montgomery. Enlistment Date: May 31, 62. Muster Date: Jul 9, 62. Mustered out Jun 13, 65.

Jackson, Heber A. Residence: Enosburgh. Enlistment Date: Sep 10, 64. Muster Date: Sep 10, 64. Transferred to Co. G, 5th Vt. Jan 20, 65.

James, Edward H. Residence: Starksboro. Enlistment Date: Sep 6, 64. Muster Date: Sep 6, 64. Mustered out Jun 13, 65.

Jones, John G. Residence: St. Johnsbury. Enlistment Date: Nov 23, 63. Muster Date: Dec 1, 63. Taken prisoner Oct 27, 64, and died in Richmond, Va., Dec 19, 64.

Judd, Levi. Residence: Richford. Enlistment Date: Jun 8, 62. Muster Date: Jul 9, 62. Deserted Oct 4, 62; Returned Apr 21, 65, under Presidential proclamation; Died Jun 18, 65; Buried in Richmond National Cemetery, Richmond, Va.

Kendall, George H. Residence: Sharon. Enlistment Date: Dec 12, 63. Muster Date: Dec 12, 63. Discharged Apr 9, 65, for disability.

Kendall, Oramel. Residence: Sharon. Enlistment Date: Dec 12, 63. Muster Date: Dec 12, 63. Died Sep 8, 65, of disease; Buried in Richmond National Cemetery, Richmond, Va.

Kennedy, Austin. Residence: Richford. Enlistment Date: Jun 9, 62. Muster Date: Jul 9, 62. Died Oct 27, 63, of disease; Buried in Hampton National Cemetery, Hampton, Va.

Kimball, Daniel. Residence: Norwich. Enlistment Date: Dec 29, 63. Muster Date: Jan 7, 64. Mustered out Oct 19, 65.

King, Mitchell, Jr. Residence: Westford. Enlistment Date: Jun 12, 62. Muster Date: Jul 9, 62. Deserted Oct 13, 62; Apprehended Sep 29, 63; Deserted Sep 30, 63; Died Nov 5, 1930, and buried in the village cemetery, Essex Junction, Vt.

Laflure, Priest. Residence: Montgomery. Enlistment Date: May 31, 62. Muster Date: Jul 9, 62. Mustered out Jun 13, 65.

Lambert, Joseph. Residence: Cambridge. Enlistment Date: Jun 5, 62. Muster Date: Jul 9, 62. Mustered out Jun 13, 65.

Lamondy, Moses. Residence: Bakersfield. Enlistment Date: Jun 3, 62. Muster Date: Jul 9, 62. Mustered out Jun 19, 65.

Lamson, Anderson E. Residence: Monkton. Enlistment Date: Aug 29, 64. Muster Date: Aug 29, 64. Mustered out Jun 13, 65; Died Jun 19, 1930, and buried in East Cemetery, Williston, Vt.

Laraba, Moses. Residence: Enosburgh. Enlistment Date: Jun 14, 62. Muster Date: Jul 9, 62. Deserted Dec 3, 62.

Lario, Leander. Residence: St. Albans. Enlistment Date: Jun 6, 62. Muster Date: Jul 9, 62. Promoted to Corp. Feb 1, 64; To Sgt. Jan 1, 65; Mustered out Jun 13, 65; Died Jun 27, 1922, in Snohomish Co., Wash., and buried in the Grand Army of the Potomac Cemetery in Snohomish, Wash.

Leach, Lucius W. Residence: Fairfield. Enlistment Date: May 31, 62. Muster Date: Jul 9, 62. Mustered out Jun 13, 65; Died Dec 12, 1868, and buried in Maple Grove Cemetery, Bakersfield, Vt.

Laplant, James. Residence: Enosburgh. Enlistment Date: Jun 12, 62. Muster Date: Jul 9, 62. Discharged Jan 14, 64, for disability; Died May 12, 1920, and buried in Pleasant View Cemetery, Morrisville, Vt.

Loud, George W. Residence: Hartford. Enlistment Date: Dec 29, 63. Muster Date: Dec 30, 63. Taken prisoner Feb 2, 64, and died at Andersonville, Ga., Jul 1, 64; Buried in Andersonville National Cemetery, Andersonville, Ga.

Marco, Joseph. Residence: Sheldon. Enlistment Date: Jun 17, 62. Muster Date: Jul 9, 62. Deserted Jan 11, 63.

Martin, John. Residence: Highgate. Enlistment Date: Jun 2, 62. Muster Date: Jul 9, 62. Mustered out Jun 13, 65; Died Jan 16, 1914, and buried in Saint Mary's Cemetery, Springfield, Vt.

Massi, Isaiah. Residence: St. Albans. Enlistment Date: Jun 4, 62. Muster Date: Jul 9, 62. Discharged Oct 3, 62, for disability.

Massi, John. Residence: St. Albans. Enlistment Date: Jun 4, 62. Muster Date: Jul 9, 62. Deserted Oct 13, 62; Returned Mar 20, 65; Sentenced by G.C.M. to be dishonorably discharged and confined three years at hard labor at Norfolk, Va.

Maynard, Samuel M. Residence: Enosburgh. Enlistment Date: Dec 16, 63. Muster Date: Dec 30, 63. Wounded Sep 29, 64; Mustered out Jun 2, 65.

McGrath, George H. Residence: Georgia. Enlistment Date: Jun 4, 62. Muster Date: Jul 9, 62. Discharged Oct 17, 62, for disability.

Merrill, John. Residence: Ryegate. Enlistment Date: Jan 2, 64. Muster Date: Jan 12, 64. Died Nov 2, 64, of disease; Buried in Hampton National Cemetery, Hampton, Va.

Mincen, William J. Residence: Montgomery. Enlistment Date: Jun 4, 62. Muster Date: Jul 9, 62. Deserted Dec 30, 62.

Minckler, Edgar. Residence: Grand Isle. Enlistment Date: Jun 17, 62. Muster Date: Jul 9, 62. Mustered out Jun 13, 65; Died Jun 12, 1902, and buried in Methodist Cemetery, Trowbridge, Minn.

Moore, Isaac S. Residence: Barnet. Enlistment Date: Sep 9, 64. Muster Date: Sep 9, 64. Mustered out Jun 13, 65.

Morgan, Charles. Residence: Milton. Enlistment Date: Jun 6, 62. Muster Date: Jul 9, 62. Wounded accidentally while in line of duty; Transferred to V.R.C. Oct 18, 64; Mustered out Jun 29, 65.

Morits, John. Residence: Highgate. Enlistment Date: Jun 23, 62. Muster Date: Jul 9, 62. Discharged Oct 3, 63, by special order of the War Department; Died Mar 18, 1910, and buried in Saint Mary's Cemetery, Swanton, Vt.

Morse, Ira E. Residence: Benson. Enlistment Date: Sep 7, 64. Muster Date: Sep 7, 64. Transferred to Co. D, 4th Vt. Jan 20, 65.

Murphy, John. Residence: Strafford. Enlistment Date: Dec 30, 63. Muster Date: Jan 6, 64. Mustered out Dec 1, 65.

Murray, Joseph. Residence: Sheldon. Enlistment Date: Jun 3, 62. Muster Date: Jul 9, 62. Deserted Jan 28, 63.

Nary, John. Residence: St. Albans. Enlistment Date: May 30, 62. Muster Date: Jul 9, 62. Deserted Dec 30, 62.

Neal, James K. Residence: Norwich. Enlistment Date: Aug 18, 64. Muster Date: Aug 18, 64. Transferred to Co. B, 4th Vt. Jan 20, 65.

North, James A. Residence: Pownal. Enlistment Date: Mar 14, 64. Muster Date: Mar 14, 64. Promoted to Corp. Sep 5, 65; Mustered out Dec 1, 65; Died May 4, 1913, and buried in North Pownal Cemetery, North Pownal, Vt.

Nye, George W. Residence: Norwich. Enlistment Date: Dec 26, 63. Muster Date: Jan 7, 64. Mustered out Aug 7, 65; Died Jan 30, 1870, and buried in Fairview Cemetery, Norwich, Vt.

O'Regan, Thomas. Residence: Bakersfield. Enlistment Date: Jun 20, 62. Muster Date: Jul 9, 62. Promoted to Corp. Aug 1, 64; Reduced Dec 19, 64; Discharged Sep 16, 65.

Paine, David. Residence: Strafford. Enlistment Date: Dec 22, 63. Jan 6, 64. Promoted to Corp. Jun 5, 65; to Sgt. Sep 5, 65; Mustered out Dec 1, 65; Died Apr 5, 1905, and buried in Hartford Cemetery, Hartford, Vt.

Papaw, George. Residence: Enosburgh. Enlistment Date: Dec 26, 63. Muster Date: Dec 30, 63. Discharged Oct 24, 65, for disability.

Paranto, Francis. Residence: Enosburgh. Enlistment Date: Mar 14, 65. Muster Date: Mar 14, 65. Mustered out Dec 1, 65.

Parent, Joseph. Residence: Alburgh. Enlistment Date: Jun 23, 62. Muster Date: Jul 9, 62. Discharged Jan 22, 63, for enlistment in the Regular Army.

Parker, Emery S. Residence: Franklin. Enlistment Date: Jun 12, 62. Muster Date: Jul 9, 62. Wounded Sep 29, 64; Discharged May 29, 65.

Parker, John E. Residence: Thetford. Enlistment Date: Dec 19, 63. Muster Date: Dec 19, 63. Mustered out Jun 22, 65.

Parker, William O. Residence: Montgomery. Enlistment Date: Sep 19, 64. Muster Date: Sep 19, 64. Mustered out Jun 13, 65.

Peckham, Braddock, Jr. Residence: Pownal. Enlistment Date: Dec 21, 63. Muster Date: Dec 30, 63. Mustered out Dec 1, 65.

Pelkey, Peter. Residence: Sheldon. Enlistment Date: Jun 6, 62. Muster Date: Jul 9, 62. Deserted Jan 28, 63.

Perkins, Henry W. Residence: Bakersfield. Enlistment Date: Dec 14, 63. Muster Date: Dec 30, 63. Died Mar 10, 65, of disease; Buried in City Point National Cemetery, Hopewell, Va.

Pixley, Richard B. Residence: Strafford. Enlistment Date: Sep 2, 64. Muster Date: Sep 2, 64. Mustered out Jun 13, 65; Died Sep 30, 1920, and buried in Hillside Cemetery, Norwich, Vt.

Potter, Charles E. Residence: Montgomery. Enlistment Date: Jun 3, 62. Muster Date: Jul 9, 62. Discharged Jan 8, 64, for disability.

Potter, Martin V. Residence: Pownal. Enlistment Date: Aug 10, 64. Muster Date: Aug 16, 64. Transferred to Co. I, 5th Vt. Jan 20, 65.

Powers, Harvey, S. Residence: Barnet. Enlistment Date: Sep 9, 64. Muster Date: Sep 9, 64. Mustered out Jun 13, 65.

Proud, Austin. Residence: Pownal. Enlistment Date: Aug 15, 64. Muster Date: Aug 15, 64. Mustered out Jun 13, 65.

Proud, Zara P. Residence: Bennington. Enlistment Date: Dec 14, 63. Muster Date: Dec 30, 63. Taken prisoner Feb 2, 64, and died in a POW camp in Savannah, Ga., Oct 1, 64; Buried in Richmond National Cemetery, Richmond, Va.

Puffer, Luman P. Residence: Bakersfield. Enlistment Date: Jun 9, 62. Muster Date: Jul 9, 62. Discharged Jan 22, 63, for enlistment in the Regular Army.

Ray, Edwin R. Residence: Norwich. Enlistment Date: Dec 26, 63. Muster Date: Jan 7, 64. Died Mar 7, 64.

Richardson, George. Residence: Strafford. Enlistment Date: Dec 30, 63. Muster Date: Jan 6, 64. Mustered out May 13, 65.

Robbins, George W. Residence: Bridgewater. Enlistment Date: Aug 9, 64. Muster Date: Aug 9, 64. Wounded Sep 29, 64; Mustered out Jun 13, 65; Died in Nelson, N.H., Apr 4, 1914.

Roberts, Franklin B. Residence: Sharon. Enlistment Date: Dec 10, 63. Muster Date: Dec 10, 63. Mustered out Jun 22, 65; Died Aug 18, 1897, and buried in Pine Hill Cemetery, Sharon, Vt.

Roberts, Nelson C. Residence: Sharon. Enlistment Date: Dec 10, 63. Muster Date: Dec 10, 63. Wounded Sep 29, 64; Discharged Jun 25, 65; Died Apr 4, 1880.

Russell, Hiram C. Residence: Starksboro. Enlistment Date: Sep 6, 64. Muster Date: Sep 6, 64. Mustered out Jun 13, 65.

Russell, Simon H. Residence: Montgomery. Enlistment Date: Jun 2, 62. Muster Date: Jul 9, 62. Died May 19, 63, of disease and buried in Old Cemetery, Montgomery Center, Vt.

Rutherford, Wallace E. Residence: Rutland. Enlistment Date: Jan 12, 65. Muster Date: Jan 12, 65. Discharged Oct 24, 65, for disability.

Sabbeville (Sabberville), John. Residence: Alburgh. Enlistment Date: Jun 19, 62. Muster Date: Jul 9, 62. Real name John B. Sabre; Also went by John Barney; Deserted Jan 10, 63; G.C.M Feb 9, 63, and confined to seven days hard labor; Deserted Mar 4, 63; and enlisted in the 2nd N.Y. Inf.; Died Apr 24, 1909, in Cornwell, Mass., and buried in Chazy, N.Y.

Sargent, Alvora M. Residence: Sharon. Enlistment Date: Dec 8, 63. Muster Date: Dec 8, 63. Taken prisoner Oct 27, 64; Paroled Feb 24, 65; Mustered out May 15, 65; Died Jun 12, 1909, and buried in Pine Hill Cemetery, Sharon, Vt.

Sartwell, William. Residence: Highgate. Enlistment Date: May 30, 62. Muster Date: Jul 9, 62. Mustered out Jun 13, 65; Died Mar 29, 1912, and buried in the village cemetery, Albany, Vt.

Service, John W. Residence: Bennington. Enlistment Date: Dec 14, 63. Muster Date: Dec 30, 63. Transferred to U.S. Navy Jun 30, 64; Discharged Aug 8, 65; Died Jul 28, 1903, and buried in Oak Hill Cemetery, Pownal, Vt.

Shaw, Alexander. Residence: Highgate. Enlistment Date: Jun 9, 62. Muster Date: Jul 9, 62. Deserted Jul 17, 62.

Sheehe, Patrick. Residence: Hartford. Enlistment Date: Dec 29, 63. Muster Date: Dec 29, 63. Deserted Mar 12, 65; Returned Apr 18, 65, under Presidential Proclamation; Mustered out Dec 1, 65.

Shelley, William. Residence: St. Albans. Enlistment Date: Jun 11, 62. Muster Date: Jul 9, 62. Deserted Jan 11, 63.

Sherman, Joseph J. Residence: Pownal. Enlistment Date: Aug 2, 64. Muster Date: Aug 2, 64. Mustered out Jun 13, 65; Died Mar 12, 1879, and buried in Towsley Cemetery, Pownal Center, Vt.

Simonds, Henry M. Residence: Sharon. Enlistment Date: Dec 5, 63. Muster Date: Dec 5, 63. Mustered out Dec 1, 65; Died Mar 30, 1866, and buried in Beaver Meadow Cemetery, West Norwich, Vt.

Smith, Harlow C. Residence: Enosburgh. Enlistment Date: Dec 22, 63. Muster Date: Dec 30, 63. Taken prisoner Feb 2, 64, and died at Andersonville, Ga., Aug 16, 64; Buried in Andersonville National Cemetery, Andersonville, Ga.

Smith, James E. Residence: Montgomery. Enlistment Date: May 30, 62. Muster Date: Jul 9, 62. Mustered out Jun 13, 65; Died Jul 25, 1926, and buried in the village cemetery, Montgomery, Vt.

Smith, Jason. Residence: Hartford. Enlistment Date: Dec 31, 63. Muster Date: Jan 2, 64. Mustered out Dec 1, 65.

Smithson, George. Residence: St. Johnsbury. Enlistment Date: Mar 20, 65. Muster Date: Mar 30, 65. Died Jul 14, 65; Buried in Hollywood Cemetery, Richmond, Va.; Removed to Richmond National Cemetery, Richmond, Va.

Spicer, Edwin. Residence: Enosburgh. Enlistment Date: Dec 17, 63. Muster Date: Dec 30, 63. Died Jan 25, 65.

Spicer, George W. Residence: Enosburgh. Enlistment Date: Dec 19, 63. Dec 30, 63. Musician; Mustered out Dec 1, 65; Died Apr 2, 1905, and buried in Methodist Cemetery, Enosburg, Vt.

Stanhope, Obed. Residence: Hartford. Enlistment Date: Dec 31, 63. Muster Date: Jan 2, 64. Mustered out Jul 18, 65.

Stanley, Caleb A. Residence: Berkshire. Enlistment Date: Jun 10, 62. Muster Date: Jul 9, 62. Deserted Oct —, 62.

Stanley, Eleazer. Residence: Bakersfield. Enlistment Date: Jun 20, 62. Muster Date: Jul 9, 62. Promoted to Corp. Feb 10, 64; Reduced Oct 1, 64; Discharged Oct 31, 64, by special order of the War Department.

Stevens, Newell. Residence: Jamaica. Enlistment Date: Sep 14, 64. Muster Date: Sep 14, 64. Transferred to Co. C, 6th Vt., Jan 20, 65.

Stoliker, Charles E. Residence: Sheldon. Enlistment Date: Jun 9, 62. Muster Date: Jul 9, 62. Deserted Feb 12, 63.

Stoliker, Horatio. Residence: Sheldon. Enlistment Date: Jun 9, 62. Muster Date: Jul 9, 62. Promoted to Corp. Jul 1, 63; Mustered out Jun 13, 65.

Stone, Frank. Residence: Monkton. Enlistment Date: Dec 21, 63. Muster Date: Jan 2, 64. Mustered out Dec 1, 65.

Sullivan, John. Residence: Sheldon. Enlistment Date: Jun 5, 62. Muster Date: Jul 9, 62. Taken prisoner Sep 15, 62; Paroled Oct 1, 62; Deserted Dec 26, 62.

Thomas, Sylvester. Residence: Montgomery. Enlistment Date: Jun 3, 62. Muster Date: Jul 9, 62. Taken Prisoner Sep 15, 62; Paroled Oct 1, 62; Deserted Dec 26, 62.

Touchet, Lewis. Residence: St. Albans. Enlistment Date: Dec 29, 63. Muster Date: Jan 4, 64. Deserted Dec 29, 64; Died Dec 13, 1914, and buried in Catholic Cemetery, Montgomery, Vt.

Trowbridge, Seymour. Residence: Montgomery. Enlistment Date: Jun 3, 62. Muster Date: Jul 9, 62. Transferred to Co. B; Transferred back to Co. A Sep 1, 64; Discharged May 11, 65, for disability; Died Apr 4, 1903, and buried in Newport Center Cemetery, Newport Center, Vt.

Trudell, Lewis M. Residence: Enosburgh. Enlistment Date: Mar 7, 65. Muster Date: Mar 7, 65. Mustered out Dec 1, 65.

Turner, Theodore E. Residence: Bakersfield. Enlistment Date: Jul 1, 62. Muster Date: Jul 9, 62. Mustered out Jun 10, 65.

Tuttle, Tyler. Residence: Georgia. Enlistment Date: Aug 13, 62. Muster Date: Sep 15, 62. Died Sep 26, 63, of disease.

Van Ornum, Roger W. Residence: Fairfax. Enlistment Date: May 29, 62. Muster Date: Jul 9, 62. Promoted to Corp. Aug 26, 62; to Sgt. Feb 18, 64; Mustered out Jun 12, 65.

Vincent, Edmund. Residence: Enosburgh. Enlistment Date: Dec 7, 63. Muster Date: Dec 30, 63. Furloughed from General Hospital, Point of Rocks, Va., Nov 3, 64; N.F.R.

Vincent, Hiram. Residence: Littleton, N.H. Enlistment Date: Jul 9, 62. Muster Date: Jul 9, 62. Deserted Dec 16, 62.

Waterman, Dexter P. Residence: Hartford. Enlistment Date: Dec 31, 63. Muster Date: Jan 2, 64. Mustered out Dec 7, 65; Died Jul 8, 1866, and buried in Branchview Cemetery, Royalton, Vt.

Webster, Birchard E. Residence: Sheldon. Enlistment Date: Jun 2, 62. Muster Date: Jul 9, 62. Promoted to Corp. Jan 1, 65; Mustered out Jun 13, 65.

Wellman, Henry. Residence: Manchester. Enlistment Date: Jan 16, 65. Muster Date: Jan 16, 65. Mustered out Dec 1, 65.

Wellman, Norman A. Residence: Manchester. Enlistment Date: Jan 16, 65. Muster Date: Jan 16, 65. Promoted to Corp. Aug 15, 65; Mustered out Dec 1, 65.

Westover, Henry. Residence: Swanton. Enlistment Date: May 29, 62. Muster Date: Jul 9, 62. Discharged Dec 20, 62.

Wilcox, Julius. Residence: Fairfield. Enlistment Date: Aug 11, 64. Muster Date: Aug 11, 64. Mustered out Jun 13, 65; Died Apr 3, 1914, and buried in the village cemetery, Newport Center, Vt.

Wilcox, Manley H. Residence: Westford. Enlistment Date: Jun 4, 62. Muster Date: Jul 9, 62. Mustered out Jun 13, 65.

Willey, George W. Residence: Sharon. Enlistment Date: Dec 18, 63. Muster Date: Dec 18, 63. Discharged Aug 14, 65, for disability.

Wright, Alexis B. Residence: Norwich. Enlistment Date: Dec 29, 63. Muster Date: Jan 7, 64. Died Mar 25, 65, of disease.

Yarrington, Merrill E. Residence: Norwich. Enlistment Date: Jan 2, 64. Muster Date: Jan 7, 64. Promoted to Corp. Jun 5, 65; Mustered out Dec 1, 65; Died Dec 12, 1908, and buried in South View Cemetery, Randolph, Vt.

Yarrington, William P. Residence: Norwich. Enlistment Date: Jan 4, 64. Muster Date: Jan 7, 64. Promoted to Corp. Feb 4, 64; Mustered out Jun 22, 65; Died Dec 19, 1877, and buried in Union Village Cemetery, Norwich, Vt.

Young, Flavey. Residence: Franklin. Enlistment Date: Jun 12, 62. Muster Date: Jul 9, 62. Discharged Dec 14, 62, for enlistment in the 14th U.S. Infantry.

Company B

Captains

Ripley, Edward H. Residence: Rutland. Commission Date: Jun 20, 62. Issue Date: Jun 20, 62. *See* Col.

Kelley, Samuel H. Residence: Clarendon. Commission Date: May 1, 63. Issue Date: May 1, 63. First Lt. Co. B; Mustered out Jun 13, 65; Died Feb 2, 1922, in Salisbury, Vt.

Hobon, Patrick. Residence: Brandon. Commission Date: Mar 13, 65. Issue Date: Apr 6, 65. *See* Capt. Co. F.

First Lieutenants

Kelley, Samuel H. Residence: Clarendon. Commission Date: Jun 20, 62. Issue Date: Jun 20, 62. *See* Capt. Co. B.

Ballard, Alfred C. Residence: Tinmouth. Commission Date: May 1, 63. Issue Date: May 20, 63. Second Lt. Co. B; Resigned Jun 27, 64; Died Nov 28, 1874, and buried in Green Mountain Cemetery, Burlington, Vt.

Dodge, William A. Residence: Shrewsbury. Commission Date: Oct 19, 64. Issue Date: Nov 19, 64. Sgt. Co. B; Promoted to Second Lt. Co. B Apr 7, 64; Wounded Sep 29, 64 and Oct 27, 64; Resigned Jun 7, 65; Died Jan 31, 1918, and buried in Oakwood Cemetery, Chicago, Ill.

Thomas, John W. Residence: Burlington. Commission Date: Jul 3, 65. Issue Date: Jul 20, 65. Pvt. Co. F; Promoted to Sgt. Aug 9, 63; to Sgt. Maj. Jan 1, 65; to Second Lt. Co. F Mar 13, 65; Transferred to Co. B Jun 13, 65; Mustered out Dec 1, 65.

Second Lieutenants

Ballard, Alfred C. Residence: Tinmouth. Commission Date: Jun 20, 62. Issue Date: Jun 20, 62. *See* First Lt. Co. B.

Kelley, Edward L. Residence: Clarendon. Commission Date: May 1, 63. Issue Date: May 20, 63. *See* Capt. Co. E.

Dodge, William A. Residence: Shrewsbury. Commission Date: Apr 7, 64. Issue Date: May 5, 64. *See* First Lt. Co. B.

Hathaway, Arthur W. Residence: Tinmouth. Commission Date: Oct 19, 64. Issue Date: Nov 19, 64. Sgt. Co. B; Promoted to First Sgt. Feb 10, 64; Mustered out Jun 13, 65.

Thomas, John W. Residence: Burlington. Commission Date: Mar 13, 65. Issue Date: Apr 6, 65. *See* First Lt. Co. B.

Briggs, Gordon N. Residence: Whiting. Commission Date: Jul 3, 65. Issue Date: Jul 20, 65. Pvt. Co. F; Transferred to Co. B Jun 13, 65; Mustered out Dec 1, 65.

Sergeants

Kelley, Edward L. Residence: Clarendon. Enlistment Date: Jun 18, 62. Muster Date: Jul 9, 62. *See* Capt. Co. E.

Dodge, William A. Residence: Shrewsbury. Enlistment Date: May 29, 62. Muster Date: Jul 9, 62. *See* First Lt. Co. B.

Baker, Joel C. Residence: Danby. Enlistment Date: May 27, 62. Muster Date: Jul 9, 62. *See* First Lt. Co. K.

Hathaway, Arthur W. Residence: Tinmouth. Enlistment Date: May 31, 62. Muster Date: Jul 9, 62. *See* Second Lt. Co. B.

Slason, James L. Residence: Sudbury. Enlistment Date: Jun 9, 62. Muster Date: Jul 9, 62. Mustered out Jun 13, 65.

Corporals

Sisco, Willard J. Residence: West Haven. Enlistment Date: Jun 3, 62. Muster Date: Jul 9, 62. Promoted to Sgt. Feb 10, 64; Mustered out Jun 13, 65; Died Oct 27, 1894, and buried in Pleasant View Cemetery, Middletown Springs, Vt.

Phillips, Ephraim. Residence: Tinmouth. Enlistment Date: Jun 2, 62. Muster Date: Jul 9, 62. Discharged Feb 23, 64, for disability.

Monroe, Lester E. Residence: Poultney. Enlistment Date: Jun 2, 62. Muster Date: Jul 9, 62. Deserted Oct 27, 62; Returned Apr 21, 63; Died Sep 26, 63, of disease.

Edson, Amos W. Residence: Mendon. Enlistment Date: Jun 18, 62. Muster Date: Jul 9, 62. Reduced May 15, 64; Transferred to V.R.C. Jul 20, 64; Discharged Jul 8, 65.

Metcalf, Edwin S. Residence: Rutland. Enlistment Date: May 30, 62. Muster Date: Jul 9, 62. Reduced Dec 21, 63; Transferred to V.R.C. Mar 31, 64; Mustered out Jul 11, 65.

Graham, Joseph B. Residence: Rutland. Enlistment Date: May 28, 62. Muster Date: Jul 9, 62. Discharged Jan 16, 63, for enlistment in the Regular Army.

Dorsett, Edwin H. Residence: Clarendon. Enlistment Date: Jun 16, 62. Muster Date: Jul 9, 62. Discharged Oct 23, 62, for disability.

O'Brien, Thomas. Residence: Pittsford. Enlistment Date: Jun 11, 62. Muster Date: Jul 9, 62. Discharged Jan 16, 63, for enlistment in the Regular Army.

Musicians

Edgerton, Edward M. Residence: Clarendon. Enlistment Date: Jun 18, 62. Muster Date: Jul 9, 62. *See* Principal Musician; Died Jul 31, 1891, and buried in Evergreen Cemetery, Rutland, Vt.

Metcalf, William H. Residence: Brandon. Enlistment Date: Jul 7, 62. Muster Date: Jul 9, 62. Died Jul 5, 63, of disease.

Wagoner

Streeter, Lemuel. Residence: Castleton. Enlistment Date: Jun 21, 62. Muster Date: Jul 9, 62. Appointed wagoner Aug 23, 62.

Privates

Aldrich, George F. Residence: Clarendon. Enlistment Date: Aug 23, 64. Muster Date: Aug 23, 64. Mustered out Jun 13, 65; Died Nov 7, 1908, and buried in Mt. Holly Cemetery, Mt. Holly, Vt.

Alexander, Samuel C. Residence: Goshen. Enlistment Date: Aug 13, 64. Muster Date: Aug 13, 64. Transferred to Co. D., 4th Vt. Jan 20, 65.

Allen, Otis J. Residence: Wallingford. Enlistment Date: May 30, 62. Muster Date: Jul 9, 62. Deserted Oct 7, 62.

Archer, Lawson E. Residence: Mt. Holly. Enlistment Date: Aug 23, 64. Muster Date: Aug 23, 64. Transferred to Co. I, 5th Vt. Jan 20, 65; Died Sep 22, 1910, and buried in Maple Grove Cemetery, East Wallingford, Vt.

Baird, Oran E. Residence: Chittenden. Enlistment Date: Jun 11, 62. Muster Date: Jul 9, 62. Discharged Jan 16, 63, for enlistment in the Regular Army.

Baird, Walcott, Jr. Residence: Chittenden. Enlistment Date: Dec 3, 63. Muster Date: Dec 20, 63. Transferred to Co. C Jun 13, 65; Mustered out Dec 1, 65; Died Jun 10, 1899, and buried in Goshen Cemetery, Goshen, Vt.

Baker, Holden D. Residence: Danby. Enlistment Date: Jun 2, 62. Muster Date: Jul 9, 62. Promoted to Corp. Jun 13, 64; Wounded Sep 29, 64; Discharged May 17, 65, for wounds; Died Feb 13, 1932, in Hudson Falls, N.Y. and buried in Union Cemetery.

Baker, John. Residence: Rutland. Enlistment Date: Aug 22, 64. Muster Date: Aug 22, 64. Deserted to the enemy Jan 23, 65.

Barrass, George. Residence: Brandon. Enlistment Date: Jun 5, 62. Muster Date: Jul 9, 62. Promoted to Corp. Feb 24, 63; to Sgt. Jun 18, 64; Reduced May 9, 65; Mustered out Jun 13, 65.

Barrett, Oliver. Residence: Shrewsbury. Enlistment Date: Jun 7, 62. Muster Date: Jul 9, 62. Deserted Oct 27, 62.

Barden, Herbert. Residence: Wells. Enlistment Date: Jun 2, 62. Muster Date: Jul 9, 62. Mustered out Jun 13, 65 by special order of the War Department; Died Jun 23, 1922, and buried in Morningside Cemetery, Brattleboro, Vt.

Barton, Jacob V. Residence: Starksboro. Enlistment Date: Feb 1, 65. Muster Date: Feb 1, 65. Transferred to Co. C Jun 13, 65; Mustered out Dec 1, 65; Died Oct 29, 1917, and buried in Lamoille View Cemetery, Johnson, Vt.

Batise, George W. Residence: Tinmouth. Enlistment Date: Jun 7, 62. Muster Date: Jul 9, 62. Died Dec 9, 62, of disease; Buried in Rosehill Cemetery, Chicago, Ill.

Beaudry, Alexander. Residence: St. Hilaire, Can. Enlistment Date: Jun 7, 62. Muster Date: Jul 9, 62. Deserted Apr 12, 63.

Bellany, Francis. Residence: Shrewsbury. Enlistment Date: Aug 20, 64. Muster Date: Aug 20, 64. Mustered out Jun 13, 65; Died Jul 1894, and buried in St. Joseph Cemetery, Rutland, Vt.

Bellany, Joseph. Residence: Shrewsbury. Enlistment Date: Jun 7, 62. Muster Date: Jul 9, 62. Mustered out Jun 13, 65; Died Jan 22, 1911, and buried in St. Joseph Cemetery, Rutland, Vt.

Benway (Bellware), Louis N. Residence: Montreal, Can. Oct 12, 64. Muster Date: Oct 12, 64. Substitute for Norman Dunham, Montgomery; Deserted to the enemy Jan 23, 65; Died May 1933, and buried in Holly Grove Cemetery, Miamisburg, Ohio.

Brannan, Malachi. Residence: Bridport. Enlistment Date: Aug 27, 64. Muster Date: Aug 27, 64. Detained by civil authority in New York Nov 13, 64; N.F.R.

Breed, Augustus L. Residence: Pittsford. Enlistment Date: Dec 18, 63. Muster Date: Dec 26, 63. Transferred to Co. C Jun 13, 65; Mustered out Dec 1, 65; Died Mar 31, 1905, and buried in Pine Hill Cemetery, Brandon, Vt.

Brewer, Samuel R., Jr. Residence: Rutland. Enlistment Date: Jun 18, 62. Muster Date: Jul 9, 62. Died Dec 19, 63, of disease; Buried in New Bern National Cemetery, New Bern, N.C.

Brezette, Frederick. Residence: Grand Isle. Enlistment Date: Dec 17, 63. Muster Date: Dec 22, 63. Transferred to Co. C Jun 13, 65; Mustered out Dec 1, 65.

Briggs, George W. Residence: Mt. Holly. Enlistment Date: Jun 7, 62. Muster Date: Jul 9, 62. Mustered out Jun 28, 65.

Broe, Nelson. Residence: Mt. Holly. Enlistment Date: Jun 12, 62. Muster Date: Jul 9, 62. Discharged Jan 16, 63, for enlistment in the Regular Army.

Brown, Josiah, Jr. Residence: Mendon. Enlistment Date: Jun 28, 62. Muster Date: Jul 9, 62. Deserted Dec 10, 62, and enlisted in Co. B, 55th Penn. Vols. under the name of Daniel Bennett; Returned under Presidential Proclamation and mustered out Jun 7, 65; Died Jan 14, 1901, and buried in Ludlow Cemetery, Ludlow, Vt.

Bryant, John P. Residence: Weston. Enlistment Date: Dec 26, 63. Muster Date: Jan 2, 64. Died Feb 20, 65; Buried in City Point National Cemetery, Hopewell, Va.

Buck, Edward M. Residence: Grand Isle. Enlistment Date: Dec 17, 63. Muster Date: Dec 22, 63. Mustered out May 22, 65.

Buffum, David. Residence: Pawlet. Enlistment Date: Jun 7, 62. Muster Date: Jul 9, 62. Promoted to Corp. Jun 19, 62; to Sgt May 9, 65; Wounded Oct 27, 64; Mustered out Jun 13, 65.

Buffum, Leonard C. Residence: Poultney. Enlistment Date: Aug 26, 64. Muster Date: Aug 26, 64. Mustered out Jun 13, 65.

Butler, James A. Residence: Poultney. Enlistment Date: May 30, 62. Muster Date: Jul 9, 62. Deserted Oct 26, 62; Returned Apr 20, 63; Transferred to V.R.C. Feb 8, 64; Discharged Nov 28, 65; Died Aug 29, 1915, and buried in Center Cemetery, Highgate, Vt.

Butler, James D. Residence: Pittsford. Enlistment Date: Jun 9, 62. Muster Date: Jul 9, 62. Discharged Apr 2, 63, for disability.

Butler, William O. Residence: Poultney. Enlistment Date: Jun 3, 62. Muster Date: Jul 9, 62. Deserted Dec 10, 62; Returned Feb 7, 63; Died Oct 6, 63, of disease.

Carpenter, Harry I. Residence: Middlebury. Enlistment Date: May 31, 62. Muster Date: Jul 9, 62. Discharged Jan 16, 63, for enlistment in the Regular Army.

Caswell, Franklin. Residence: St. Johnsbury. Enlistment Date: Dec 30, 63. Muster Date: Jan 4, 64. Taken prisoner Feb 2, 64, and died at Andersonville, Ga., Jun 30, 64; Buried in Andersonville National Cemetery, Andersonville, Ga.

Chamberlin, Solon T. Residence: Goshen. Enlistment Date: Aug 13, 64. Muster Date: Aug 13, 64. Mustered out Jun 13, 65.

Clark, Francis E. Residence: Rutland. Enlistment Date: Aug 15, 64. Muster Date: Aug 15, 64. Transferred to Co. D, 4th Vt. Jan 20, 65.

Clark, Paul. Residence: Mendon. Enlistment Date: Aug 10, 64. Muster Date: Aug 10, 64. Mustered out Jun 13, 65.

Clines, James. Residence: Sudbury. Enlistment Date: Feb 14, 65. Muster Date: Feb 14, 65. Transferred to Co. C Jun 13, 65; Died Oct 27, 65 of disease; Buried in Richmond National Cemetery, Richmond, Va., under the name E.P. Clines, Co. K, 9th Vermont Inf.

Coleman, Royal L. Residence: Middletown. Enlistment Date: Jun 9, 62. Muster Date: Jul 9, 62. Died Oct 3, 63, of disease and buried in Oak Ridge Cemetery, Sandwich, Ill.

Conlin, James. Residence: Rutland. Enlistment Date: Dec 25, 63. Muster Date: Dec 26, 63. Promoted to Corp. Jun 18, 64; Reduced Sep 8, 64; Promoted to Sgt. Jun 27, 65; Transferred to Co. C Jun 13, 65; Mustered out Dec 1, 65.

Cook, Francis F. Residence: Vernon. Enlistment Date: Aug 2, 64. Muster Date: Aug 2, 64. Discharged Jan 4, 65, for disability; Died Oct 4, 1899, and buried in Christ Church Cemetery, Guilford, Vt.

Cook, Orin B. Residence: Shrewsbury. Enlistment Date: Aug 29, 64. Muster Date: Aug 29, 64. Mustered out Jun 13, 65.

Cooley, Charles W. Residence: Granville. Enlistment Date: Jun 18, 62. Muster Date: Jul 9, 62. Died Oct 5, 63, of disease; Buried in Hampton National Cemetery, Hampton, Va.

Culver, Eliphalet. Residence: Wallingford. Enlistment Date: Jun 5, 62. Muster Date: Jul 9, 62. Discharged Nov 6, 62, for disability; Died Mar 1, 1905, and buried in Old Public Green Cemetery, Wallingford, Vt.

Danforth, George. Residence: Lunenburg. Enlistment Date: Dec 8, 63. Muster Date: Dec 30, 63. Transferred to Co. C Jun 13, 65; Mustered out Dec 1, 65; Died Mar 28, 1895, and buried in Old Protestant Cemetery, Island Pond, Vt.

DeForge, Nathan. Residence: Shrewsbury. Enlistment Date: Jul 1, 62. Muster Date: Jul 9, 62. Wounded Feb 2, 64; Transferred to the V. R. C. Oct 11, 64; Discharged Jul 7, 65; Died Sep 13, 1894, and buried in Vermont Veteran's Home Cemetery, Bennington, Vt.

Doty, Deforest T. Residence: Tinmouth. Enlistment Date: Dec 14, 63. Muster Date: Dec 22, 63. Transferred to Co. C Jun 13, 65; Promoted to Corp. Nov 15, 65; Mustered out Dec 1, 65; Died Feb 21, 1912, and buried in the village cemetery, Tinmouth, Vt.

Duggan, James. Residence: Fairhaven. Enlistment Date: Dec 28, 63. Muster Date: Dec 30, 63. Drowned Nov 6, 64; Buried in City Point National Cemetery, Hopewell, Va.

Duncan, George J. Residence: Burlington. Enlistment Date: Dec 10, 63. Muster Date: Dec 23, 63. Promoted to Corp. Dec 26, 64; Transferred to Co. C Jun 13, 65; Promoted to Sgt. Jul 25, 65; Reduced Sep 21, 65; Mustered out Dec 1, 65.

Durkee, George F. Residence: Chittenden. Enlistment Date: Dec 3, 63. Muster Date: Dec 26, 63. Wounded Feb 2, 64; Transferred to the V.R.C. Dec 14, 64; Discharged Sep. 14, 65, for disability; Died Feb 29, 1892, in Jewell, Kan.

Dutcher, Edwin. Residence: Tinmouth. Enlistment Date: Aug 26, 64. Muster Date: Aug 26, 64. Mustered out Jun 13, 65; Died Jun 9, 1922, and buried in Athol, Mass.

Dwyer, Philip, 3rd. Residence: Starksboro. Enlistment Date: Dec 21, 63. Muster Date: Jan 13, 64. Transferred to Co. C Jun 13, 65; Mustered out Dec 26, 65.

Edwards, William. Residence: West Haven. Enlistment Date: Jun 5, 62. Muster Date: Jul 9, 62. Deserted Dec 24, 62.

Elliott, Alden J. Residence: Starksboro. Enlistment Date: Dec 19, 63. Muster Date: Jan 6, 64. Transferred to Co. C Jun 13, 65; Mustered out Dec 1, 65; Died Apr 3, 1905, and buried in Jerusalem Cemetery, Starksboro, Vt.

Fay, Loomis C. Residence: Pittsford. Enlistment Date: Jun 2, 62. Muster Date: Jul 9, 62. Deserted Oct 7, 62; Returned Jul 1, 64; Deserted from arrest Aug __, 64.

Flagg, Henry. Residence: Ira. Enlistment Date: Jun 9, 62. Muster Date: Jul 9, 62. Discharged Jan 16, 63, for enlistment in the Regular Army.

Flanders, Stanislaus. Residence: Pittsfield. Enlistment Date: Dec 10, 63. Muster Date: Dec 22, 63. Died Mar 5, 65, of disease; Buried in City Point Cemetery, Hopewell, Va.

Fletcher, Henry W. Residence: Mt. Holly. Enlistment Date: Jun 7, 62. Muster Date: Jul 9, 62. Taken prisoner Feb 2, 64; Paroled Dec 13, 64; Mustered out Jun 13, 65; Died Sep 17, 1921, and buried in Hortonville Cemetery, Mt. Holly, Vt.

Freeman, James C. Residence: Pittsfield. Enlistment Date: Jun 13, 62. Muster Date: Jul 9, 62. Died Oct 13, 63, of disease.

Frisbie, John N. Residence: Pawlet. Enlistment Date: Jun 2, 62. Muster Date: Jul 9, 62. Deserted Oct 27, 62; Returned Sep 1, 63; Mustered out Jun 13, 65; Died Oct 29, 1902, and buried in Mettowee Cemetery, Pawlett, Vt.

Gee, Edward B. Residence: Clarendon. Enlistment Date: Aug 2, 64. Muster Date: Aug 2, 64. Transferred to Co. I, 5th Vt., Jan 20, 65.

Gerard, Jesse. Residence: Pittsford. Enlistment Date: May 29, 62. Muster Date: Jul 9, 62. Discharged Sep 2, 63, for disability.

Gero, Henry. Residence: Lunenburgh. Enlistment Date: Dec 8, 63. Muster Date: Dec 31, 63. Transferred to Co. C Jun 13, 65; Mustered out Dec 1, 65.

Gibson, Dascomb E. Residence: Leicester. Enlistment Date: Sep 2, 64. Muster Date: Sep 2, 64. Mustered out Jun 13, 65; Died Apr 19, 1911, and buried in West Salisbury Cemetery, Salisbury, Vt.

Gingras, Charles. Residence: Brandon. Enlistment Date: Jun 24, 62. Muster Date: Jul 9, 62. Mustered out Jun 13, 65.

Goodnough, William. Residence: Barnet. Enlistment Date: Dec 11, 63. Muster Date: Jan 4, 64. Died Oct 24, 64, of yellow fever; Buried in New Bern National Cemetery, New Bern, N.C.

Goodrich, Prosper. Residence: Can. Enlistment Date: May 31, 62. Muster Date: Jul 9, 62. Discharged Jan 16, 63, for enlistment in the Regular Army.

Gorman, George. Residence: Rockingham. Enlistment Date: Dec 16, 63. Muster Date: Dec 16, 63. Transferred to Co. C. Jun 13, 65; Mustered out Dec 1, 65.

Grant, John. Residence: West Haven. Enlistment Date: Dec 28, 63. Muster Date: Dec 30, 63. Taken prisoner Feb 2, 64; Paroled Feb 24, 65; Furloughed from Camp Parole Mar 4, 65; N.F.R.

Graves, Corwin. Residence: Mt. Holly. Enlistment Date: Jul 9, 62. Muster Date: Jul 9, 62. Promoted to Corp. Sep 25, 64; Mustered out Jun 13, 65; Died Feb 23, 1923, and buried in Laurel Glenn Cemetery, Shrewsbury, Vt.

Graves, Edmund B. Residence: Mt. Holly. Enlistment Date: Jul 9, 62. Muster Date: Jul 9, 62. Transferred to the V.R.C. Mar 25, 64; Mustered out Jul 9, 65.

Graves, Lucius D. Residence: Rutland. Enlistment Date: Aug 15, 64. Muster Date: Aug 15, 64. Mustered out Jun 13, 65; Died Jun 7, 1907, and buried in Mechanicsville Cemetery, Mt. Holly, Vt.

Graves, Stephen A. Residence: Mt. Holly. Enlistment Date: Jul 9, 62. Muster Date: Jul 9, 62. Discharged Nov 1, 62, for disability; Died Nov 25, 1908, and buried in the village cemetery, Weston, Vt.

Graves, Willard R. Residence: Rupert. Enlistment Date: Aug 29, 64. Muster Date: Aug 29, 64. Mustered out Jun 13, 65; Died Apr 19, 1888, and buried in Maple Grove Cemetery, East Wallingford, Vt.

Green, Spencer. Residence: Danby. Enlistment Date: Dec 3, 63. Muster Date: Dec 26, 63. Promoted to Corp. Mar 28, 64; Reduced Aug 23, 64; Died Dec 27, 64, of disease.

Griffith, George W. Residence: Starksboro. Enlistment Date: Sep 1, 64. Muster Date: Sep 1, 64. Transferred to Co. F, 4th Vt., Jan 20, 65.

Grover, Joel. Residence: Wallingford. Enlistment Date: Jun 17, 62. Muster Date: Jul 9, 62. Discharged Nov 1, 62, for disability.

Haskins, Joseph. Residence: Starksboro. Enlistment Date: Sep 2, 64. Muster Date: Sep 2, 64. Transferred to Co. C, 4th Vt. Jan 20, 65; Died Apr 18, 1909, and buried in Maple Cemetery, Lincoln, Vt.

Higgins, Orlin H. Residence: Benson. Enlistment Date: Jun 9, 62. Muster Date: Jul 9, 62. Died Nov 6, 62, of disease; Buried in Rosehill Cemetery, Chicago, Ill.

Hill, David N. Residence: Mt. Holly. Enlistment Date: Jun 16, 62. Muster Date: Jul 9, 62. Deserted Dec 24, 62; Returned Feb 7, 63; Died Oct 6, 63, of disease and buried in Mechanicsville Cemetery, Mt. Holly, Vt.

Holbrook, Edward Z. Residence: Mendon. Enlistment Date: Aug 10, 64. Muster Date: Aug 10, 64. Mustered out Jun 13, 65.

Holt, Nathan. Residence: Weston. Enlistment Date: Dec 21, 63. Muster Date: Jan 2, 64. Discharged May 31, 65, for disability; Died Oct 2, 1891, and buried in the village cemetery, Weston, Vt.

Holt, Sidney Z. Residence: Weston. Enlistment Date: Dec 26, 63. Muster Date: Jan 2, 64. Transferred to Co. C Jun 13, 65; Mustered out Dec 13, 65.

Horton, Henry N. Residence: Mt. Holly. Enlistment Date: Jun 2, 62. Muster Date: Jul 9, 62. Mustered out Jun 29, 65; Died Apr 8, 1871, and buried in Hortonville Cemetery, Mt. Holly, Vt.

Houghtaling, James. Residence: Rockingham. Enlistment Date: Dec 16, 63. Muster Date: Dec 16, 63. Transferred to Co. C Jun 13, 65; Mustered out Dec 1, 65.

Hubbard, Medad. Residence: Tinmouth. Enlistment Date: Dec 16, 63. Muster Date: Dec 22, 63. Died Aug 27, 64, of disease; Buried in New Bern National Cemetery, New Bern, N.C.

Ives, Franklin. Residence: Clarendon. Enlistment Date: Dec 24, 63. Muster Date: Jan 4, 64. Taken prisoner Feb 2, 64, and died May 30, 64, at Salisbury, N.C.

Jackson, Wendell W. Residence: Grand Isle. Enlistment Date: Jan 11, 64. Muster Date: Jan 13, 64. Mustered out Jun 22, 65.

Jenks, William B. Residence: Manchester. Enlistment Date: Jun 23, 62. Muster Date: Jul 9, 62. In hospital Oct 62; Returned Sep 1, 63; Taken prisoner Feb 2, 64; Paroled Nov 29, 64; Returned Apr 26, 65; Mustered out Jun 13, 65.

Jones, Oliver. Residence: Poultney. Enlistment Date: Jun 4, 62. Muster Date: Jul 9, 62. Mustered out Jun 13, 65.

Kavanaugh, James. Residence: Plymouth. Enlistment Date: Jun 2, 62. Muster Date: Jul 9, 62. Discharged Nov 6, 62, for disability.

Kean, James. Residence: ——. Enlistment Date: Jul 27, 64. Muster Date: Jul 27, 64. Substitute for Levi Allen, Rockingham; Transferred to Co. C, 11th Vt., Jan 20, 65.

Kellogg, Daniel E. Residence: Rutland. Enlistment Date: Jun 20, 62. Muster Date: Jul 9, 62. Mustered out Jun 19, 65.

Labor, Francis W. Residence: Starksboro. Enlistment Date: Dec 22, 63. Muster Date: Jan 6, 64. Discharged May 31, 64, for disability; Died Apr 25, 1912, and buried in Greenwood Cemetery, Bristol, Vt.

Lafayette, Joseph. Residence: Richmond. Enlistment Date: Aug 8, 64. Muster Date: Aug 8, 64. Died October 23, 64, of wounds received Sep 29, 64; Buried in Hampton National Cemetery, Hampton, Va.

Lapine, Dennis. Residence: Brandon. Enlistment Date: May 30, 62. Muster Date: Jul 9, 62. Mustered out Jun 13, 65; Died Jul 25, 1902, and buried in Calvary Cemetery, Rutland, Vt.

Leonard, William. Residence: Chittenden. Enlistment Date: Aug 22, 64. Muster Date: Aug 22, 64. Mustered out Jun 13, 65; Died Oct 9, 1917, and buried in the Vermont Veteran's Home Cemetery, Bennington, Vt.

Lewis, Israel W. Residence: Wallingford. Enlistment Date: Aug 18, 64. Muster Date: Aug 18, 64. Mustered out Jun 13, 65.

Liberty, Levi. Residence: Starksboro. Enlistment Date: Jul 26, 64. Muster Date: Jul 26, 64. Mustered out Jun 13, 65; Died Dec 26, 1878, and buried in Jerusalem Cemetery, Starksboro, Vt.

Little, Nelson. Residence: Leicester. Enlistment Date: Jun 23, 62. Muster Date: Jul 9, 62. Mustered out Jun 13, 65.

Lozelle, John. Residence: Clarendon. Enlistment Date: Jul 8, 62. Muster Date: Jul 9, 62. Deserted Oct 27, 62.

Madeline, Peter. Residence: Shrewsbury. Enlistment Date: Jun 14, 62. Muster Date: Jul 9, 62. Mustered out Jun 13, 65.

Mann, Benjamin, Jr. Residence: Ira. Enlistment Date: Jun 4, 62. Muster Date: Jul 9, 62. Died Oct 13, 62, of disease.

Marshall, Eber N. Residence: Orange. Enlistment Date: Jan 2, 64. Muster Date: Jan 6, 64. Transferred to Co. C Jun 13, 65; Mustered out Sep 7, 65.

Martin, Joel R. Residence: Rutland. Enlistment Date: Aug 15, 64. Muster Date: Aug 15, 64. Transferred to Co. I, 5th Vt. Jan 20, 65; Died Mar 26, 1905, and buried in Maple Grove Cemetery, East Wallingford, Vt.

Martin, Lewis A. Residence: Mendon. Enlistment Date: Aug 10, 64. Muster Date: Aug 10, 64. Died Nov 21, 64, of disease; Buried in City Point National Cemetery, Hopewell, Va.

Martin, Wesley E. Residence: Rutland. Enlistment Date: Aug 15, 64. Muster Date: Aug 15, 64. Mustered out Jun 15, 65; Died Oct 11, 1928, and buried in the village cemetery, Cuttingsville, Vt.

Mason, George W. Residence: St. Johnsbury. Enlistment Date: Dec 3, 63. Muster Date: Dec 26, 63. Transferred to Co. C Jun 15, 65; Mustered out Aug 2, 65; Died Jul 10, 1905, and buried in Old Protestant Cemetery, Island Pond, Vt.

Mason, Joseph. Residence: Greensboro. Enlistment Date: Aug 30, 64. Muster Date: Aug 30, 64. Transferred to Co. C, 3rd Vt. Jan 20, 65.

Maxham, Chauncey. Residence: Rutland. Enlistment Date: Dec 15, 63. Muster Date: Dec 22, 63. Promoted to Corp. Feb 18, 64; Transferred to Co. C Jun 13, 65; Reduced Sep 1, 65; Mustered out Dec 1, 65.

McGill, John. Residence: Barnet . Enlistment Date: Dec 14, 63. Muster Date: Jan 4, 64. Transferred to Co. C Jun 13, 65; Mustered out Dec 1, 65.

McGlinnis, John E. Residence: Rutland. Enlistment Date: Dec 16, 63. Muster Date: Jan 2, 64. *See* First Lt. Co. C.

Moore, Charles. Residence: Whitingham. Enlistment Date: Jun 23, 64. Muster Date: Jun 23, 64. Died Nov 30, 64.

Morrison, John. Residence: Barnet. Enlistment Date: Dec 12, 63. Muster Date: Jan 4, 64. Transferred to Co. C Jun 13, 65; Mustered out Dec 1, 65; Died Apr 8, 1869, and buried in West Cemetery, Middlebury, Vt.

Morse, Isaac A. Residence: Stockbridge. Enlistment Date: Aug 26, 64. Muster Date: Aug 26, 64. Mustered out Jun 10, 65; Died May 28, 1891, and buried in Town Cemetery, Pittsfield, Vt.

Morse, Warren. Residence: Stockbridge. Enlistment Date: Aug 26, 64. Muster Date: Aug 26, 64. Mustered out Jun 13, 65.

Mudge, Harry H. Residence: Mt. Holly. Enlistment Date: Jun 7, 62. Muster Date: Jul 9, 62. Discharged Jan 16, 63, for enlistment in the Regular Army.

Murray, John H. Residence: Lincoln. Enlistment Date: Sept 2, 64. Muster Date: Sep 2, 64. Transferred to Co. C, 5th Vt. Jan 20, 65; Died Apr 16, 1889, and buried in Lee Cemetery, Lincoln, Vt.

Newton, Charles W. Residence: Mt. Holly. Enlistment Date: Jun 16, 62. Muster Date: Jul 9, 62. Died Apr 3, 63, of accidental gunshot wound.

Nicholson, Rufus. Residence: Tinmouth. Enlistment Date: Jun 5, 62. Muster Date: Jul 9, 62. Deserted Oct 7, 62; Returned Oct 16, 63; Transferred to Co. C Jun 13, 65; Deserted Aug 1, 65.

Nye, Edward. Residence: Pawlet. Enlistment Date: Jun 2, 62. Muster Date: Jul 9, 62. Deserted Aug 25, 62; Returned Jan 12, 64; Died Mar 30, 64, of disease; Buried in New Bern National Cemetery, New Bern, N.C.

O'Brien, Charles. Residence: Rutland. Enlistment Date: Dec 19, 63. Muster Date: Dec 26, 63. Transferred to Co. C Jun 13, 65; Mustered out Dec 1, 65.

Overing, Robert J. Residence: Wallingford. Enlistment Date: Aug 18, 64. Muster Date: Aug 18, 64. Mustered out May 26, 65.

Parker, Daniel C. Residence: Mt. Holly. Enlistment Date: Jul 9, 62. Muster Date: Jul 9, 62. Died Mar 6, 64, of disease.

Pease, James T. Residence: Weston. Enlistment Date: Dec 26, 63. Muster Date: Jan 2, 64. Transferred to Co. C Jun 13, 65; Promoted to Corp. Sep 11, 65; Mustered out Dec 1, 65.

Poacher, Peter. Residence: Shrewsbury. Enlistment Date: Jun 10, 62. Muster Date: Jul 9, 62. Deserted Oct 27, 62.

Potter, George W. Residence: Shaftsbury. Enlistment Date: Dec 31, 63. Muster Date: Dec 31, 63. Transferred to Co. C Jun 13, 65; Mustered out Aug 3, 65; Died Mar 15, 1914, and buried in the Vermont Veteran's Home Cemetery, Bennington, Vt.

Powers, Thomas. Residence: Sudbury. Enlistment Date: Feb 14, 65. Muster Date: Feb 14, 65. Transferred to Co. C Jun 13, 65; Mustered out Dec 1, 65.

Randall, John M. Residence: Barnet. Enlistment Date: Jan 5, 64. Muster Date: Jan 5, 64. Promoted to Corp. May 15, 64; to Sgt. Jun 15, 65; Transferred to Co. C Jun 13, 65; Mustered out Dec 1, 65; Died Jan 10, 1916, and buried in Passumpsic Cemetery, Waterford, Vt.

Riley, John. Residence: Rutland. Enlistment Date: Dec 16, 63. Muster Date: Dec 26, 63. Died Oct 31, 64, of wounds received Sep 29, 64; Buried in Hampton National Cemetery, Hampton, Va.

Ripley, Thomas. Residence: Shrewsbury. Enlistment Date: Jun 10, 62. Muster Date: Jul 9, 62. Taken prisoner Sep 3, 62; Paroled Oct 3, 62; Taken prisoner Feb 2, 64; Died at Andersonville, Ga., Sep 13, 64; Buried in Andersonville National Cemetery, Andersonville, Ga.

Rivers, Joseph. Residence: West Haven. Enlistment Date: Sep 1, 64. Muster Date: Sep 1, 64. Mustered out Jun 13, 65.

Roberts, William S. Residence: Mt. Holly. Enlistment Date: Jul 14, 62. Muster Date: Jul 14, 62. Discharged Apr 22, 63, for disability; Died Apr 14, 1891, and buried in Tarbellville Cemetery, Mt. Holly, Vt.

Rogers, Elias J. Residence: Orwell. Enlistment Date: Jun 9, 62. Muster Date: Jul 9, 62. Mustered out Jun 13, 65.

Rudd, Thomas. Residence: Fairhaven. Enlistment Date: Dec 28, 63. Muster Date: Dec 30, 63. Taken prisoner Feb 2, 64; Paroled Dec 16, 64; Died Jan 10, 65, of disease and buried in Green Mountain Cemetery, Burlington, Vt.

Sawyer, Elijah L. Residence: Starksboro. Enlistment Date: Dec 21, 63. Muster Date: Jan 6, 64. Transferred to Co. C Jun 13, 65; Mustered out Dec 1, 65.

Sharrow, John. Residence: Mt. Holly. Enlistment Date: Jun 16, 62. Muster Date: Jul 9, 62. Discharged Jan 16, 63, for enlistment in the Regular Army.

Shedd, Charles D. Residence: Sherburne. Enlistment Date: Aug 25, 64. Muster Date: Aug 25, 64. Mustered out Jun 13, 65.

Shurtleff, Nathan H. Residence: Starksboro. Enlistment Date: Jan 4, 64. Muster Date: Jan 13, 64. Promoted to Corp. Sep 5, 64; to Sgt. Dec 26, 64; Reduced Jun 26, 65; Transferred to Co. C Jun 13, 65; Mustered out Jul 7, 65; Died May 1, 1903, and buried in Lyndon Center Cemetery, Lyndon, Vt.

Slason, George F. Residence: Mendon. Enlistment Date: Aug 3, 64. Muster Date: Aug 3, 64. Mustered out Jun 13, 65.

Slason, John C. Residence: Sudbury. Enlistment Date: Jun 19, 62. Muster Date: Jul 9, 62. Discharged Nov 6, 62, for disability.

Slason, John C. Residence: Springfield. Enlistment Date: Aug 2, 64. Muster Date: Aug 2, 64. Transferred to Co. B, 11th Vt. Jan 20, 65.

Slason, William E. Residence: Springfield. Enlistment Date: Aug 20, 64. Muster Date: Aug 20, 64. Mustered out Jun 13, 65.

Smith, Charles. Residence: —. Enlistment Date: Sep 1, 64. Muster Date: Sep 1, 64. Substitute for Gilman Warren, Guilford; Transferred to Co. C, 11th Vt. Jan 20, 65.

Smith, Edward C. Residence: Castleton. Enlistment Date: Jun 5, 62. Muster Date: Jul 9, 62. Deserted Dec 22, 62; Returned Mar 8, 63; Promoted to Corp. Feb 18, 64; Reduced Sep 18, 64; Mustered out Jun 13, 65.

Smith, George H. Residence: Enfield, N.H. Enlistment Date: Jun 3, 62. Muster Date: Jul 9, 62. Taken prisoner Sep 3, 62; Paroled Sep 11, 62; Mustered out Jun 13, 65.

Smith, William P. Residence: Poultney. Enlistment Date: May 30, 62. Muster Date: Jul 9, 62. Deserted Oct 28, 62; Returned Apr 21, 63; Wounded Feb 2, 64; Transferred to V. R. C. Dec 20, 64; Discharged Mar 9, 65; Died Jun 15, 1901, and buried in Hillside Cemetery, Castleton, Vt.

Spaulding, Nathan. Residence: Tinmouth. Enlistment Date: Jun 7, 62. Muster Date: Jul 9, 62. Discharged Apr 25, 63, for disability.

Sprague, Orick. Residence: Mendon. Enlistment Date: Aug 10, 64. Muster Date: Aug 10, 64. Wounded Sep 29, 64; Mustered out Jun 17, 65; Died Aug 30, 1881, and buried in Baird Cemetery, Chittenden, Vt.

Stewart, Martin V. Residence: Rutland. Enlistment Date: Aug 15, 64. Muster Date: Aug 15, 64. Mustered out Jun 13, 65; Died Jan 3, 1915, and buried in Northam Cemetery, Shrewsbury, Vt.

Stewart, Warren F. Residence: Rutland. Enlistment Date: Aug 15, 64. Muster Date: Aug 15, 64. Mustered out Jun 13, 65.

Stickney, Edward E. Residence: Fairfax. Enlistment Date: Dec 17, 63. Muster Date: Dec 29, 63. Transferred to Co. C Jun 13, 65; Mustered out Aug 2, 65; Died Mar 11, 1919, and buried in Edmond, Kan.

Sullivan, Daniel P. Residence: Rutland. Enlistment Date: Jun 10, 62. Muster Date: Jul 9, 62. Deserted Dec 12, 62; Enlisted in Co. K, 14th Ill. Cav. Dec 12, 62.

Sweet, John. Residence: Starksboro. Enlistment Date: Sep 1, 64. Muster Date: Sep 1, 64. Transferred to Co. C, 5th Vt. Jan 20, 65; Died Apr 3, 1905, and buried in the village cemetery, Jay, Vt.

Swinyer, John. Residence: Starksboro. Enlistment date: Jan 4, 64. Muster Date: Jan 13, 64. Transferred to Co. C Jun 13, 65; Mustered out Dec 1, 65.

Tarte, Ambrose. Residence: Starksboro. Enlistment Date: Dec 19, 63. Muster Date: Jan 6, 64. Mustered out Jun 19, 65.

Taylor, George F. Residence: Danby. Enlistment Date: May 30, 62. Muster Date: Jul 9, 62. Discharged Feb 5, 63, for disability.

Taylor, John. Residence: Sherburne. Enlistment Date: Jun 17, 62. Muster Date: Jul 9, 62. Promoted to Corp. Sep 9, 62; Reduced May 15, 64; Transferred to V.R.C. Jul 1, 64; Discharged Jul 6, 65; Died Jul 9, 1879, and buried in Parker Cemetery, Mendon, Vt.

Thompson, William P. Residence: Starksboro. Enlistment Date: Sep 1, 64. Muster Date: Sep 1, 64. Mustered out Jun 13, 65; Died Jan 3, 1905, and buried in Jerusalem Cemetery, Starksboro, Vt.

Tobias, James B. Residence: Grand Isle. Enlistment Date: Dec 17, 63. Muster Date: Dec 22, 63. Transferred to Co. C Jun 13, 65; Promoted to Corp. Sep 21, 65; Mustered out Dec 1, 65; Died Apr 13, 1885, and buried in the village cemetery, Grand Isle, Vt.

Trask, Converse T. Residence: Shrewsbury. Enlistment Date: Aug 31, 64. Muster Date: Aug 31, 64. Mustered out Jun 13, 65.

Travers, John. Residence: Sandgate. Enlistment Date: Sep 5, 64. Muster Date: Sep 5, 64. Transferred to Co. C, 4th Vt. Jan 20, 65; Died Sep 13, 1906, and buried in Calvary Cemetery, Rutland, Vt.

Turner, William. Residence: Can. Enlistment Date: Sep 17, 64. Muster Date: Sep 17, 64. Substitute for Henry M. Brown, Jericho; Transferred to Co. C Jun 13, 65; Mustered out Dec 1, 65; Died Mar 29, 1885, and buried in East Side Cemetery, Sandgate, Vt.

Wainwright, Harry, A. Residence: Leicester. Enlistment Date: Aug 30, 64. Muster Date: Aug 30, 64. Mustered out Jun 13, 65; Died Aug 31, 1903, and buried in the village cemetery, Salisbury, Vt.

Watkins, Charles. Residence: Grand Isle. Enlistment Date: Dec 28, 63. Muster Date: Dec 30, 63. Mustered out May 22, 65.

Welch, Michael. Residence: Vergennes. Enlistment Date: Aug 23, 64. Muster Date: Aug 23, 64. Mustered out Jun 13, 65; Died Dec 11, 1903, and buried in St. Mary's Cemetery, Brandon, Vt.

Weller, David. Residence: Clarendon. Enlistment Date: Jun 12, 62. Muster Date: Jul 9, 62. Taken prisoner Feb 2, 64, and died at Andersonville, Ga. Jul 11, 64; Buried in Andersonville National Cemetery, Andersonville, Ga.

Wells, Edward B. Residence: Rutland. Enlistment Date: Aug 15, 64. Muster Date: Aug 15, 64. Transferred to Co. K.

Wheeler, Ellery G. Residence: Sutton. Enlistment Date: Sep 8, 64. Muster Date: Sep 8, 64. Mustered out Jun 13, 65.

White, Alphonso E. Residence: Huntington. Enlistment Date: Aug 7, 64. Muster Date: Aug 7, 64. Mustered out Jun 13, 65.

White, Calvin. Residence: Mt. Tabor. Enlistment Date: Jun 18, 62. Muster Date: Jul 9, 62. Discharged Nov 6, 62, for disability.

White, Mason L. Residence: Wallingford. Enlistment Date: Jun 16, 62. Muster Date: Jul 9, 62. Mustered out Jun 13, 65.

Wilder, Daniel. Residence: Wallingford. Enlistment Date: Jun 16, 62. Muster Date: Jul 9, 62. Promoted to Corp. Feb 18, 64; Reduced Oct 16, 64; Mustered out Jun 13, 65; Died Jun 11, 1935, and buried in the villager cemetery Surry, N.H.

Wilkinson, Jay. Residence: Weston. Enlistment Date: Dec 25, 63. Muster Date: Jan 2, 64. Mustered out Jun 28, 65; Died Nov 20, 1922, and buried in the village cemetery, Weston, Vt.

Williams, Francis E. Residence: Brandon. Enlistment Date: Jun 3, 62. Muster Date: Jul 9, 62. Deserted Dec 22, 62.

Williams, William, Jr. Residence: Castleton. Enlistment Date: Jun 7, 62. Muster Date: Jul 9, 62. Promoted to Corp. Oct 19, 64; Reduced Apr 4, 65; Mustered out Jun 13, 65.

Winter, Wallace S. Residence: Granville, N.Y. Enlistment Date: Jun 14, 62. Muster Date: Jul 9, 62. Deserted Oct 29, 62.

Wood, Hiram. Residence: Wells. Enlistment Date: Jun 2, 62. Muster Date: Jul 9, 62. Deserted Jan 27, 63; Returned Sep 1, 63; Dishonorably discharged Jun 13, 65, by G.C.M.; Died Dec 22, 1926, and buried in the village Cemetery, East Clarendon, Vt.

Woodard, Edmund A. Residence: Mt. Holly. Enlistment Date: Jun 5, 62. Muster Date: Jul 9, 62. Died Oct 12, 63, of disease.

York, Henry L. Residence: Shrewsbury. Enlistment Date: Aug 19, 64. Muster Date: Aug 19, 64. Mustered out Jun 13, 65.

Young, John M. Residence: Poultney. Enlistment Date: Aug 26, 64. Muster Date: Aug 26, 64. Mustered out Jun 13, 65.

Young, Mancer W. Residence: Ira. Enlistment Date: Jun 5, 62. Muster Date: Jul 9, 62. Discharged Feb 10, 63.

Company C

Captains

Sabin, Albert R. Residence: Rockingham. Commission Date: Jun 24, 62. Issue Date: Jun 24, 62. Resigned Dec 24, 62; Died Jan 29, 1914, and buried in Rosehill Cemetery, Chicago, Ill.

Seligson, Herman. Residence: Burlington. Commission Date: Jan 1, 63. Issue Date: Jan 14, 63. *See* Lt. Col.

Brownell, Elias L. Residence: Essex. Commission Date: Jul 3, 65. Issue Date: Jul 20, 65. Corp. Co. F; Promoted to Sgt. Dec 1, 62; to First Sgt. Jan 23, 64; to Second Lt. Co. F Dec 22, 63; to First Lt. Co. F Mar 13, 65; Transferred to Co. C Jun 13, 65; Mustered out Dec 1, 65.

First Lieutenants

Seligson, Herman. Residence: Burlington. Commission Date: Jun 24, 62. Issue Date: Jun 24, 62. *See* Lt. Col.

Bolton, James F. Residence: Middlebury. Commission Date: Jan 1, 63. Issue Date: Jan 14, 63. First Sgt. Co. C; Discharged Nov 22, 64 for wounds received Feb 2, 64.

Moore, Herbert H. Residence: Middlebury. Commission Date: Nov 28, 64. Issue Date: Dec 21, 64. Corp. Co. C; Promoted to Sgt. Jul 11, 63; to First Sgt. Mar 17, 64; to Second Lt. Co. C Jun 10, 64; Discharged May 9, 65.

Branch, Charles F. Residence: Orwell. Commission Date: May 20, 65. Issue Date: May 31, 65. *See* Capt. Co. A.

Brownell, Elias L. Residence: Essex. Commission Date: Mar 13, 65. Issue Date: Apr 6, 65. *See* Capt. Co. C.

McGinnis, John E. Residence: Rutland. Commission Date: Jul 5, 65. Issue Date: Jul 20, 65. Pvt. Co. B; Promoted to Corp. Sep 26, 64; to First Sgt. Jun 15, 65; Transferred to Co. C Jun 13, 65; Died Nov 10, 65, and buried in Calvary Cemetery in Rutland, Vt.

Bacon, Harrison K. Residence: Dummerston. Commission Date: Nov 17, 65. Issue Date: Nov 27, 65. Pvt. Co. K; Promoted to Corp. Jun 15, 65; Transferred to Co. C Jun 13, 65; Promoted to Second Lt. Jul 3, 65; Wounded Sep 29, 64; Mustered out as Second Lt. Dec 1, 65; Died Jul 22, 1866, and buried in Greenwood Cemetery, Dummerston, Vt.

Second Lieutenants

Sherman, Elijah B. Residence: Brandon. Commission Date: Jun 24, 62. Issue Date: Jun 24, 62. Resigned Jan 7, 63; Died May 1, 1910, Chicago, Il., and is buried in Rosehill Cemetery, Chicago, Ill.

Peck, Theodore S. Residence: Burlington. Commission Date: Jan 8, 63. Issue Date: Jan 14, 63. *See* First Lt. Co. H.

Moore, Herbert H. Residence: Middlebury. Commission Date: Jun 10, 64. Issue Date: Aug 3, 64. *See* First Lt. Co. C.

Sneden, George W. Residence: New Haven. Commission Date: Nov 28, 64. Issue Date: Dec 21, 64. Corp. Co. C; Promoted to Sgt. Jul 11, 63; to First Sgt. Aug 20, 64; Discharged May 4, 65.

Smith, Luman. Residence: Addison. Commission Date: May 20, 65. Issue Date: May 31, 65. Pvt. Co. K; Promoted to Corp.; to Sgt. Mar 21, 64; to First Sgt. Mar 24, 65; Mustered out as First Sgt. Jun 13, 65; Died Jul 7, 1921, and buried in Greenwood Cemetery, Bristol, Vt.

Bacon, Harrison K. Residence: Dummerston. Commission Date: Jul 3, 65. Issue Date: Jul 20, 65. *See* First Lt. Co. C.

Vancor, James Henry. Residence: Jericho. Commission Date: Nov 17, 65. Issue Date: Nov 27, 65. Pvt. Co. H; Promoted to Corp. Mar 3, 65; to Sgt. Jun 15, 65; to First Sgt. Aug 8, 65; Transferred to Co. C Jun 13, 65; Mustered out as First Sgt. Dec 1, 65; Died Aug 9, 1896, and buried in Lakeview Cemetery, Burlington, Vt.

Sergeants

Bolton, James F. Residence: Middlebury. Enlistment Date: May 30, 62. Muster Date: Jul 9, 62. *See* First Lt. Co. C.

Hayes, Nathan C. Residence: Weybridge. Enlistment Date: Jun 17, 62. Muster Date: Jul 9, 62. Reduced; Mustered out Jun 13, 65; Died Jan 17, 1917, and buried in Greenwood Cemetery, St. Albans, Vt.

Ward, Franklin. Residence: New Haven. Enlistment Date: Jun 18, 62. Muster Date: Jul 9, 62. Promoted to First Sgt. Jul 11, 63; Reduced Mar 19, 64; Transferred to V. R. C. Mar 8, 64; Mustered out Jul 9, 65; Died Nov 5, 1910, and buried in Greenwood Cemetery, Bristol, Vt.

Sanderson, William H. Residence: Brandon. Enlistment Date: Jun 2, 62. Muster Date: Jul 9, 62. Discharged Jan 16, 63, for enlistment in the Regular Army; Died Dec 4, 1911, and buried in Pine Hill Cemetery, Brandon, Vt.

Carr, Anthony. Residence: Middlebury. Enlistment Date: Jun 2, 62. Muster Date: Jul 9, 62. To First Sgt. Jan 21, 63; Reduced Jun 27, 63; Mustered out Jun 13, 65; Died Jul 2, 1918, and buried in Vermont Veteran's Home Cemetery, Bennington, Vt.

Corporals

Hurlburt, Oliver L. Residence: Weybridge. Enlistment Date: Jun 17, 62. Muster Date: Jul 9, 62. Deserted Dec 16, 62.

Hobon, Patrick. Residence: Brandon. Enlistment Date: Jun 4, 62. Muster Date: Jul 9, 62. *See* Capt. Co. F.

Meyers, Charles R. Residence: Bristol. Enlistment Date: Jun 9, 62. Muster Date: Jul 9, 62. Reduced Dec 5, 62; Mustered out Jun 13, 65.

Moore, Herbert H. Residence: Middlebury. Enlistment Date: Jun 7, 62. Muster Date: Jul 9, 62. *See* First Lt. Co. C.

Norton, Charles O. Residence: Middlebury. Enlistment Date: Jun 10, 62. Muster Date: Jul 9, 62. Discharged May 5, 63, for disability.

Branch, Charles F. Residence: Orwell. Enlistment Date: Jun 23, 62. Muster Date: Jul 9, 62. *See* Capt. Co. A.

Rock, James. Residence: Vergennes. Enlistment Date: Jun 7, 62. Muster Date: Jul 9, 62. Deserted Dec 10, 62; Returned Feb 14, 63; Discharged Feb 6, 63, for disability.

Sneden, George W. Residence: New Haven. Enlistment Date: Jun 21, 62. Muster Date: Jul 9, 62. *See* Second Lt. Co. C.

Musicians

Forbes, Franklin L. Residence: Middlebury. Enlistment Date: Jun 14, 62. Muster Date: Jul 9, 62. Transferred to the ranks May 1, 64; Promoted to Corp. Nov 30, 64; Mustered out Jun 13, 65.

Taylor, Charles H. Residence: Bridport. Enlistment Date: Jun 9, 62. Muster Date: Jul 9, 62. Deserted Jan 23, 63; Returned Apr 1, 63; Mustered out Jun 13, 65.

Wagoner

Green, Stephen. Residence: Vergennes. Enlistment Date: Jun 7, 62. Muster Date: Jul 9, 62. Mustered out Jun 13, 65.

Privates

Abbot, Collamer P. Residence: Pomfret. Enlistment Date: Aug 30, 64. Muster Date: Aug 30, 64. Mustered out Jun 13, 65; Died Dec 15, 1913, and buried in Riverview Cemetery, Royalton, Vt.

Abbott, Ira A. Residence: Pomfret. Enlistment Date: Aug 31, 64. Muster Date: Aug 31, 64. Mustered out Jun 13, 65.

Acome, Franklin. Residence: Wells. Enlistment Date: Dec 30, 63. Muster Date: Jan 5, 64. Transferred to Co. A Jun 13, 65; Mustered out Dec 14, 65.

Albee, Calvin. Residence: New Haven. Enlistment Date: Jul 19, 64. Muster Date: Jul 19, 64. Mustered out May 27, 65.

Alden, Edward. Residence: Vergennes. Enlistment Date: Jun 5, 62. Muster Date: Jul 9, 62. Deserted Dec 20, 62.

Aldrich, Lyman. Residence: Ripton. Enlistment Date: Jun 27, 62. Muster Date: Jul 9, 62. Discharged Feb 24, 63, for disability.

Ainsworth, Charles. Residence: Boston. Enlistment Date: Jun 23, 62. Muster Date: Jul 9, 62. Promoted to Sgt. Jul 11, 63; Reduced Nov 30, 64; Mustered out Jun 10, 65; Died Sep 7, 1916, and buried in Hinsdillville Cemetery, North Bennington, Vt.

Atkins, Alson D. Residence: Lincoln. Enlistment Date: Aug 20, 64. Muster Date: Aug 20, 64. Mustered out Jun 13, 65; Died Oct 29, 1909, and buried in Greenwood Cemetery, Bristol, Vt.

Atkins, George A. Residence: Lincoln. Enlistment Date: Dec 28, 63. Muster Date: Jan 6, 64. Mustered out May 13, 65; Died Apr 5, 1910, and buried in Maple Cemetery, Lincoln, Vt.

Austin, Abraham. Residence: Hartford. Enlistment Date: Dec 29, 63. Muster Date: Dec 30, 63. Died Apr 20, 65; Buried in Hampton National Cemetery, Hampton, Virginia.

Austin, Ira B. Residence: Ferrisburgh. Enlistment Date: Jun 20, 62. Muster Date: Jul 9, 62. Discharged Jan 1, 65, for disability.

Austin, Julius T. Residence: Hancock. Enlistment Date: Jun 5, 62. Muster Date: Jul 9, 62. Discharged Nov 23, 62, for disability; Died Jan 13, 1912, and buried in Hope Cemetery, Barre, Vt.

Ayers, George. Residence: Vergennes. Enlistment Date: Jun 4, 62. Muster Date: Jul 9, 62. Transferred to the V. R. C. Sep 1, 63; Discharged Aug 11, 64; Died May 25, 1900, and buried in Morningside Cemetery, Brattleboro, Vt.

Baker, Edward. Residence: New Haven. Enlistment Date: Jun 24, 62. Muster Date: Jul 9, 62. Deserted Jan 22, 63; Died Aug 10, 1935, and buried in Green Mount Cemetery, Montpelier, Vt.

Baker, Solomon. Residence: Waltham. Enlistment Date: Jun 9, 62. Muster Date: Jul 9, 62. Mustered out Jun 13, 65.

Baker, William. Residence: Bridport. Enlistment Date: Jul 5, 64. Muster Date: Jul 5, 64. Transferred to Co. A Jun 13, 65; Deserted Aug 5, 65.

Baldwin, Jay N. Residence: Monkton. Enlistment Date: Dec 19, 63. Muster Date: Dec 24, 63. Transferred to Co. A Jun 13, 65; Mustered out Dec 1, 65; Died Aug 6, 1917, and buried in Monkton Cemetery, Lincoln, Vt.

Bannister, John. Residence: Brookfield. Enlistment Date: Dec 28, 63. Muster Date: Jan 6, 64. Transferred to Co. A Jun 13, 64; Mustered out Dec 7, 65; Died Dec 21, 1916, and buried in East Roxbury Cemetery, Roxbury, Vt.

Bannister, William. Residence: Brookfield. Enlistment Date: Dec 28, 63. Muster Date: Jan 6, 64. Transferred to Co. A Jun 13, 65; Mustered out Jul 24, 65.

Barber, Edward D. Residence: Middlebury. Enlistment Date: Jun 24, 62. Muster Date: Jul 9, 62. Promoted to QM Sgt. Jan 8, 63; Reduced Feb 15, 65; Mustered out Jun 15, 65.

Barry, Edward. Residence: Bridport. Enlistment Date: Jun 21, 62. Muster Date: Jul 9, 62. Deserted Dec 1, 63.

Barrows, Dustin. Residence: Addison. Enlistment Date: Jul 11, 62. Muster Date: Jul 11, 62. Mustered out Jun 13, 65; Died Sep 9, 1920, and buried in Prospect Hill Cemetery, Vergennes, Vt.

Barrows, Peter. Residence: Addison. Enlistment Date: Jul 7, 62. Muster Date: Jul 9, 62. Discharged Dec 22, 62, for disability; Died Jun 16, 1887, and buried in Perkinsville Plain Cemetery, Weathersfield, Vt.

Barton, Peter. Residence: Vergennes. Enlistment Date: May 28, 62. Muster Date: Jul 9, 62. Deserted Sep 28, 62; Returned Apr 7, 63; Taken prisoner Feb 2, 64 and died at Salisbury, N.C. Apr 20, 64; Buried in Salisbury National Cemetery, Salisbury, N.C.

Barton, John M. Residence: Pomfret. Enlistment Date: Sep 6, 64. Muster Date: Sep 6, 64. Transferred to Co. H; Mustered out Jun 13, 65.

Bates, Hiram P. Residence: Lincoln. Enlistment Date: Feb 25, 65. Muster Date: Feb 25, 65. Transferred to Co. A Jun 13, 65; Discharged Sep 8, 65; Died Aug 22, 1913, and buried in Greenwood Cemetery, Bristol, Vt.

Bates, Levi W. Residence: Shaftsbury. Enlistment Date: Dec 28, 63. Muster Date: Dec 28, 63. Transferred to Co. A Jun 13, 65; Died Jun 20, 65, and buried in Greenwood Cemetery, Bristol, Vt.

Beach, Levi S. Residence: Ferrisburgh. Enlistment Date: Dec 28, 63. Muster Date: Dec 31, 63. Transferred to Co. A Jun 13, 65; Mustered out Dec 1, 65; Died Jun 23, 1919, and buried in Hollow Road Cemetery, North Ferrisburg, Vt.

Beedle, Henry A. Residence: Brookfield. Enlistment Date: Dec 26, 63. Muster Date: Jan 6, 64. Taken prisoner Feb 2, 64, and died at Andersonville, Ga., Jul 29, 64; Buried in Andersonville National Cemetery, Andersonville, Ga.

Been, Andrew M. Residence: New Haven. Enlistment Date: Jun 21, 62. Muster Date: Jul 9, 62. Discharged Oct 23, 62, for disability.

Benson, George S. Residence: Orwell. Enlistment Date: Jun 23, 62. Muster Date: Jul 9, 62. Promoted to Corp.; to Sgt. Feb 1, 65; Mustered out Jun 13, 65.

Benson, Hamden W. Residence: Royalton. Enlistment Date: Sep 8, 64. Muster Date: Sep 8, 64. Died Dec 19, 64; Buried in City Point National Cemetery, Hopewell, Va.

Bird, Elijah W. Residence: New Haven. Enlistment Date: Dec 14, 63. Muster Date: Jan 6, 64. *See* First Lt. Co. A.

Bisbee, George W. Residence: New Haven. Enlistment Date: Jun 2, 62. Muster Date: Jul 9, 62. Promoted to Sgt. Aug 18, 63; Died Oct 30, 1863, of diarrhea and buried in Evergreen Cemetery, New Haven, Vt.

Blayes, Joseph. Residence: Waltham. Enlistment Date: Jun 9, 62. Muster Date: Jul 9, 62. Died Aug 17, 63; Buried in Yorktown National Cemetery, Yorktown, Va.

Brady, Peter. Residence: Middlebury. Enlistment Date: Jun 7, 62. Muster Date: Jul 9, 62. Deserted Nov 28, 62; Returned Apr 1, 63; Taken prisoner Oct 27, 64; Escaped Mar 28, 65; Mustered Out Jun 2, 65.

Braley, Alson H. Residence: Berlin. Enlistment Date: Aug 15, 64. Muster Date: Aug 15, 64. Mustered out Jun 13, 65.

Brown, Sidney B. Residence: Starksboro. Enlistment Date: Aug 31, 64. Muster Date: Aug 31, 64. Mustered out Jun 13, 65.

Brown, Wickliffe L. Residence: New Haven. Enlistment Date: Nov 30, 63. Muster Date: Dec 24, 63. Died Feb 20, 65 and buried in Evergreen Cemetery, New Haven, Vt.

Bruen, James. Residence: Orwell. Enlistment Date: Jun 26, 62. Muster Date: Jul 9, 62. Promoted to Aug 20, 64; Mustered out Jun 13, 65.

Bruckhardt, Franz. Residence: Bridgewater. Enlistment Date: Sep 14, 64. Muster Date: Sep 14, 64. Mustered out Jun 13, 64.

Bush, Charles. Residence: New Haven. Enlistment Date: Jun 11, 62. Muster Date: Jul 9, 62. Deserted Sep 28, 62; Returned Apr 14, 63; Mustered out Jun 13, 65.

Carl, Joseph. Residence: Starksboro. Enlistment Date: Dec 23, 63. Muster Date: Jan 6, 64. Captured Feb 21, 64; Paroled Mar 21, 64; Discharged Jun 13, 65.

Carpenter, David, Jr. Residence: Bridport. Enlistment Date: Jun 7, 62. Muster Date: Jul 9, 62. Deserted Jan 20, 63.

Carpenter, Joel V. Residence: Starksboro. Enlistment Date: Sep 1, 64. Muster Date: Sep 1, 64. Transferred to Co. D, 4th Vt. Jan 20, 65; Died May 6, 1907, and buried in Greenwood Cemetery, Bristol, Vt.

Chase, Erastus D. Residence: Bristol. Enlistment Date: Jun 9, 62. Muster Date: Jul 9, 62. Discharged May 25, 63, for disability.

Cilley, Don B. Residence: Berlin. Enlistment Date: Aug 10, 64. Muster Date: Aug 16, 64. Mustered out Jun 13, 65.

Clapper, Joseph. Residence: New Haven. Enlistment Date: Dec 14, 63. Muster Date: Dec 31, 63. Transferred to Co. A Jun 13, 65; Promoted to Corp. Oct 21, 65; Mustered out Dec 1, 65.

Clark, Joseph. Residence: Lincoln. Enlistment Date: Jun 10, 62. Muster Date: Jul 9, 62. Deserted Sep 28, 62; Returned under Presidential Proclamation May 4, 65; Transferred to Co. A Jun 13, 65; Mustered out Dec 1, 65.

Clinton, James M. Residence: Bridport. Enlistment Date: Jul 3, 62. Muster Date: Jul 9, 62. Taken prisoner Aug 8, 61; Paroled Aug 6, 62; Deserted Aug 11, 62.

Cobb, George W. Residence: Starksboro. Enlistment Date: Dec 22, 63. Muster Date: Jan 6, 64. Discharged Mar 18, 65, for disability.

Colby, Joseph. Residence: Starksboro. Enlistment Date: Aug 31, 64. Muster Date: Aug 31, 64. Mustered out Jul 23, 65.

Collins, Edmond T. Residence: Monkton. Enlistment Date: Dec 21, 63. Muster Date: Dec 31, 63. Mustered out May 13, 65.

Collins, Ezra S. Residence: Monkton. Enlistment Date: Dec 21, 63. Muster Date: Dec 31, 63. Transferred to Co. A Jun 13, 65; Mustered out Dec 14, 65.

Colomb, Francis, Jr. Residence: Waltham. Enlistment Date: Dec 18, 63. Muster Date: Dec 24, 63. Real name Frank Daniels; Transferred to Co. A Jun 13, 65; Mustered out Aug 25, 65.

Cummings, John. Residence: Middlebury. Enlistment Date: Jun 7, 62. Muster Date: Jul 9, 62. Deserted Nov 21, 62; Died Jan 12, 1919, and buried in Pine Hill Cemetery, Bridport, Vt.

Cunningham, Patrick. Residence: Ferrisburg. Enlistment Date: Aug 30, 64. Muster Date: Aug 30, 64. Mustered out Jun 13, 65.

Daniels, Frank. Residence: Waltham. Enlistment Date: Dec 18, 63. Muster Date: Dec 24, 63. *See* Colomb, Francis Jr.

Day, David S. Residence: Addison. Enlistment Date: Dec 23, 63. Muster Date: Dec 31, 63. Transferred to Co. A Jun 13, 65; Mustered out Jul 26, 65; Died Dec 9, 1918, and buried in Greenwood Cemetery, Bristol, Vt.

Denno, Tuffeil. Residence: Orwell. Enlistment Date: Aug 22, 64. Muster Date: Aug 22, 64. Mustered out Jun 13, 65.

Depra, Joseph. Residence: Ferrisburgh. Enlistment Date: Jan 1, 64. Muster Date: Jan 6, 64. Mustered out May 13, 65.

Diggles, Samuel W. Residence: Ferrisburgh. Enlistment Date: Dec 23, 63. Muster Date: Jan 6, 64. Transferred to Co. A Jun 13, 65; Discharged Aug 8, 65.

Douglass, Joseph. Residence: Vergennes. Enlistment Date: Aug 27, 64. Muster Date: Aug 17, 64. Mustered out Jun 13, 65; Died Jan 22, 1911, and buried in St. Joseph Cemetery, Rutland, Vt.

Downing, Jesse W. Residence: Brookfield. Enlistment Date: Dec 28, 63. Muster Date: Jan 2, 64. Transferred to Co. A Jun 13, 65; Promoted to Corp. Aug 15, 65; Mustered out Dec 1, 65.

Dower, James N. Residence: Starksboro. Enlistment Date: Dec 21, 63. Muster Date: Jan 6, 64. Taken pris oner Feb 2, 64; Paroled Nov 24, 64; Transferred to Co. A Jun 13, 65; Mustered out Dec 1, 65; Died Apr 4. 1904, and buried in St. Mary's Cemetery, Richmond, Vt.

Duffy, Frank W. Residence: New Haven. Enlistment Date: Aug 13, 64. Muster Date: Aug 16, 64. Mustered out Jun 13, 65.

Durkee, Sidney. Residence: Brookfield. Enlistment Date: Dec 29, 63. Muster Date: Jan 6, 64. Died Mar 7, 64.

Dwyer, Francis M. Residence: Bristol. Enlistment Date: Jul 29, 64. Muster Date: Jul 29, 64. Died Jul 1, 65 of disease; Buried in Ft. Harrison National Cemetery, Richmond, Va.

Eno, Frank. Residence: Waltham. Enlistment Date: Dec 16, 63. Muster Date: Dec 24, 63. Transferred to Co. A Jun 13, 65; Mustered out Aug 25, 65; Died Jun 12, 1889, and buried in Oak Hill Cemetery, Bellows Falls, Vt.

Farmer, George W. Residence: Ripton. Enlistment Date: Jun 27, 62. Muster Date: Jul 9, 62. Discharged Jan 16, 65, for enlistment in the 17th U.S. Infantry; Died Oct 10, 1926, and buried in Holom Cemetery, Salisbury, Vt.

Farrell, John. Residence: Ferrisburgh. Enlistment Date: Dec 28, 63. Muster Date: Dec 31, 63. Transferred to Co. A Jun 13, 65; Promoted to Corp. Sep 3, 65; Mustered out Dec 1, 65.

Finch, Loyal C. Residence: Bristol. Enlistment Date: Aug 5, 64. Muster Date: Aug 5, 64. Mustered out Jun 13, 65.

Flannery, Timothy. Residence: Randolph. Enlistment Date: Jan 4, 64. Muster Date: Jan 6, 64. Transferred to Co. A Jun 13, 65; Mustered out Aug 29, 65.

Foster, Evelyn J. Residence: New Haven. Enlistment Date: Dec 14, 63. Muster Date: Dec 21, 63. Transferred to Co. A Jun 13, 65; Mustered out Dec 1, 65.

Freeman, Henry J. Residence: Monkton. Enlistment Date: Aug 2, 64. Muster Date: Aug 2, 64. Mustered out Jun 13, 65; Died Aug 26, 1919, and buried in Vermont Veteran's Home Cemetery, Bennington, Vt.

Freeman, John. Residence: Whitingham. Enlistment Date: Sep 16, 64. Muster Date: Sep 16, 64. Transferred to Co. A, 5th Vt., Jan 20, 65.

Fuller, Joseph H. Residence: Newbury. Enlistment Date: Dec 28, 63. Muster Date: Jan 6, 64. Mustered out May 13, 65; Died Sep 30, 1917, and buried in Town House Cemetery, Newbury, Vt.

Gilligan, Matthew. Residence: Middlebury. Enlistment Date: Jun 11, 62. Muster Date: Jul 9, 62. Discharged Jan 16, 63, for enlistment in the 17th U.S. Infantry.

Gilman, Lewis E. Residence: Middlebury. Enlistment Date: Jun 21, 62. Muster Date: Jul 9, 62. Discharged Apr 9, 63, for disability.

Good, Edward Z. Residence: Hubbardton. Enlistment Date: Jun 19, 62. Muster Date: Jul 9, 62. Deserted Jan 29, 63; Returned Mar 21, 63; Promoted to Corp.; to Sgt. Aug 20, 64; Mustered out Jun 13, 65.

Grace, James H. Residence: Starksboro. Enlistment Date: Dec 28, 63. Muster Date: Jan 6, 64. Captured Feb 21, 64; Paroled Mar 21, 64; Dishonorably discharged Jun 12, 65; Charges of desertion from Feb 21, 64, dropped Aug 1873, as he had enlisted in the 14th U.S. Inf.; Died Feb 11, 1917, and buried in Quaker Cemetery, Starksboro, Vt.

Graham, William W. Residence: Rutland. Enlistment Date: Jun 9, 62. Muster Date: Jul 9, 62. Promoted to Corp. Jan 27, 64; Mustered out Jun 13, 65; Buried in Mobile National Military Cemetery, Mobile, Ala.

Green, George W. Residence: Bristol. Enlistment Date: Jul 30, 64. Muster Date: Jul 30, 64. Mustered out Jun 13, 65; Died Jun 15, 1919, and buried in Lee Cemetery, Lincoln, Vt.

Greeno, John, III. Residence: Monkton. Enlistment Date: Aug 2, 64. Muster Date: Aug 2, 64. Mustered out Jun 13, 65.

Grover, Lucius. Residence: Tinmouth. Enlistment Date: Aug 26, 64. Muster Date: Aug 26, 64. Transferred to Co. E, 5th Vt., Jan 20, 65; Died Mar 17, 1907, and buried in Public Cemetery, Tinmouth, Vt.

Hall, Charles E. Residence: Ferrisburgh. Enlistment Date: Jun 20, 62. Muster Date: Jul 9, 62. Discharged Oct 23, 62, for disability.

Halpin, Patrick. Residence: New Haven. Enlistment Date: Jun 24, 62. Muster Date: Jul 9, 62. Mustered out Jun 13, 65; Died Mar 26, 1918, and buried in St. Mary's Cemetery, Middlebury, Vt.

Hannagan, Patrick. Residence: Highgate. Enlistment Date: Jun 23, 62. Muster Date: Jul 9, 62. Died Mar 2, 65.

Harper, Zeb. Residence: Brandon. Enlistment Date: Jun 27, 62. Muster Date: Jul 9, 62. Discharged Jan 16, 63, for enlistment in the 17th U.S. Infantry.

Hart, Julius. Residence: Tinmouth. Enlistment Date: Aug 27, 64. Muster Date: Aug 27, 64. Transferred to Co. E, 5th Vt., Jan 20, 65; Oct 30, 1873, and buried in Public Cemetery, Tinmouth, Vt.

Hartley, Samuel. Residence: Middlebury. Enlistment Date: Jun 7, 62. Muster Date: Jul 9, 62. Promoted to Corp.1, 62; reduced Sep 1, 63; to Corp. Jan 30, 64; Reduced Jul 28, 64; Taken prisoner Oct 13, 64; Paroled Feb 23, 65; Mustered out Jun 29, 65.

Hayes, Elmer. Residence: Bridport. Enlistment Date: Dec 3, 63. Muster Date: Jan 2, 64. Transferred to Co. A Jun 13, 65; Mustered out Dec 1, 65.

Hebert, Nelson. Residence: Bridport. Enlistment Date: Jun 18, 62. Muster Date: Jul 9, 62. Deserted Nov 21, 62.

Hill, Hiland D. Residence: Huntington. Enlistment Date: Mar 21, 64. Muster Date: Mar 21, 64. Transferred to Co. A Jun 13, 65; Discharged Oct 24, 65, for disability.

Hinman, William H. Residence: New Haven. Enlistment Date: Dec 14, 63. Muster Date: Jan 7, 64. Promoted to Corp. Mar 1, 65; Transferred to Co. A Jun 13, 65; Promoted to Sgt. Sep, 65; Mustered out Dec 1, 65; Died May 8, 1914, and buried in Evergreen Cemetery, Fairhaven, Vt.

Hodges, George. Residence: Cornwall. Enlistment Date: Jun 24, 62. Muster Date: Jul 9, 62. Discharged Jan 16, 63, for enlistment in the 17th U.S. Infantry; Died Jul 5, 1924, and buried in Saint Mary's Cemetery, Middlebury, Vt.

Hubbell, Jacob O. Residence: New Haven. Enlistment Date: Jun 20, 62. Muster Date: Jul 9, 62. Deserted Feb 1, 64.

Hutchins, Orrin B. Residence: Monkton. Enlistment Date: Dec 19, 63. Muster Date: Dec 24, 63. Transferred to Co. A Jun 13, 65; Mustered out Dec 1, 65; Died Dec 22, 1877, and buried in Monkton Boro Cemetery, Monkton, Vt.

Isabell, Joseph. Residence: Middlebury. Enlistment Date: Jun 21, 62. Muster Date: Jul 9, 62. Deserted Jan 16, 65.

Jillson, Elba L. Residence: Pomfret. Enlistment Date: Aug 31, 64. Muster Date: Aug 31, 64. Mustered out Jun 13, 65.

Kemp, Henry. Residence: Hancock. Enlistment Date: Jul 7, 62. Muster Date: Jul 9, 62. Discharged Nov 6, 62, for disability.

Keyes, James W. Residence: Rutland. Enlistment Date: Jun 6, 62. Muster Date: Jul 9, 62. Discharged Sep 2, 63, for disability; Died Jan 7, 1865, and buried in Evergreen Cemetery, Rutland, Vt.

Kinsley, John. Residence: Monkton. Enlistment Date: Dec 10, 63. Muster Date: Dec 24, 63. Committed suicide Sep 8, 64; Buried in New Bern National Cemetery, New Bern, N.C.

Kirkpatrick, James. Residence: Hancock. Enlistment Date: Jun 11, 62. Muster Date: Jul 9, 62. Promoted to Corp. Jan 30, 64; to Sgt. Nov 30, 64; Mustered out Jun 13, 65.

Knights, Sidney. Residence: Addison. Enlistment Date: Dec 10, 63. Muster Date: Dec 24, 63. Transferred to Co. A Jun 13, 65; Mustered out Dec 1, 65.

Lafountain, Joseph. Residence: Vergennes. Enlistment Date: Aug 27, 64. Muster Date: Aug 27, 64. Mustered out Jun 13, 65.

Lamson, James. Residence: Monkton. Enlistment Date: Dec 16, 63. Muster Date: Dec 24, 63. Promoted to Corp. Jun 14, 65; Transferred to Co. A Jun 13, 65; Reduced Oct 21, 65; Mustered out Dec 1, 65; Died Jul 31, 1911, and buried in Oakland Cemetery, Springfield, Vt.

Larabee, Chauncey C. Residence: Orwell. Enlistment Date: Jun 26, 62. Muster Date: Jul 9, 62. Died Dec 4, 62.

Larock, Joseph H. Residence: Panton. Enlistment Date: Dec 1, 63. Muster Date: Dec 24, 63. Transferred to Co. A Jun 13, 65; Discharged Dec 1, 65, by reason of accidental wound.

Larrow, Francis. Residence: Ferrisburgh. Enlistment Date: Jan 1, 64. Muster Date: Jan 6, 64. Deserted Dec 13, 64.

Laverty, John. Residence: Bridport. Enlistment Date: Jun 10, 62. Muster Date: Jul 9, 62. Discharged Jan 16, 63, for enlistment into the 7th U.S. Infantry.

Lyden, Thomas. Residence: Jamaica. Enlistment Date: Feb 17, 65. Muster Date: Feb 17, 65. *See* QM Sgt.

Lilly, Calvin R. Residence: Orwell. Enlistment Date: Aug 22, 64. Muster Date: Aug 22, 64. Mustered out Jun 13, 65; Died Aug 22, 1913, and is buried in Mountainview Cemetery Orwell, Vt.

Lovejoy, Daniel W. Residence: Royalton. Enlistment Date: Sep 5, 64. Muster Date: Sep 5, 64. Mustered out Jun 13, 65; Died Jul 18, 1880, and buried in Broadbrook Cemetery, Sharon, Vt.

Maney, John. Residence: Middlebury. Enlistment Date: Jun 16, 62. Muster Date: Jul 9, 62. Transferred to V. R. C. Apr 20, 64; Mustered out Jul 9, 65; Died Jun 26, 1929, and buried in Prospect Cemetery, West Middlebury, Vt.

Mardin, Riley H. Residence: Randolph. Enlistment Date: Dec 22, 63. Muster Date: Jan 6, 64. Promoted to Second Lieutenant in the U.S.C.T. Mar 24, 65.

Martin, Joseph L. Residence: Bridport. Enlistment Date: Jun 10, 62. Muster Date: Jul 9, 62. Deserted Jan 16, 63.

Maxham, Edwin B. Residence: Pomfret. Enlistment Date: Aug 31, 64. Muster Date: Oct 7, 64. Transferred to Co. A Jun 13, 65; Mustered out Oct 8, 65; Died Apr 22, 1839, and buried in the village cemetery, Hartland, Vt.

McGill, John S. Residence: Starksboro. Enlistment Date: Jun 27, 62. Muster Date: Jul 9, 62. Deserted Jul 10, 63.

McMurray, William. Residence: Burlington. Enlistment Date: Jun 19, 62. Muster Date: Jul 9, 62. Promoted to Corp. Mar 21, 64; to Sgt. Mar 24, 65; Mustered out Jun 13, 65.

Mignault, John W. Residence: Ferrisburg. Enlistment Date: Jun 25, 62. Muster Date: Jul 9, 62. Mustered out Jun 13, 65.

Miller, Isaac. Residence: Vergennes. Enlistment Date: Sep 6, 64. Muster Date: Sep 6, 64. Mustered out Jun 13, 65; Died Apr 20, 1930, and buried in St. Peter's Cemetery, Vergennes, Vt.

Miner, Nelson. Residence: Lincoln. Enlistment Date: Jun 10, 62. Muster Date: Jul 9, 62. Discharged Jan 16, 63, for enlistment in the 17th U.S. Infantry; Died Jun 5, 1914, and buried in Lee Cemetery, Lincoln, Vt.

Murray, Louis. Residence: Addison. Enlistment Date: Jul 7, 62. Muster Date: Jul 9, 62. Discharged Nov 28, 62 for disability.

Myers, Harvey C. Residence: Bristol. Enlistment Date: Aug 25, 64. Muster Date: Aug 25, 64. Mustered out Jun 13, 65.

Myrick, Charles B. Residence: Bridport. Enlistment Date: Jun 21, 62. Muster Date: Jul 9, 62. Deserted Feb 10, 63.

Noirel, Charles. Residence: Middlebury. Enlistment Date: Jun 27, 62. Muster Date: Jul 9, 62. Promoted to Corp. Oct 15, 63; Reduced Jun 18, 64; Taken prisoner Oct 27, 64; Paroled__; Mustered out Jun 13, 65.

Noirel, Francis C. Residence: Albany, N.Y. Enlistment Date: Jun 7, 62. Muster Date: Jul 9, 62. Transferred to Co. A Jun 13, 65; Mustered out Dec 1, 65.

Obin, John. Residence: Waltham. Enlistment Date: Jun 9, 62. Muster Date: Jul 9, 62. Deserted Oct 20, 62.

Osier, Joseph. Residence: Monkton. Enlistment Date: Dec 23, 63. Muster Date: Dec 31, 63. KIA Feb 2, 64; Buried in New Bern National Cemetery, New Bern, N.C.

Osier, Peter. Residence: Monkton. Enlistment Date: Dec 21, 63. Muster Date: Dec 31, 63. Wounded and taken prisoner Feb 2, 64; Paroled Dec 6, 64; Died Dec 15, 64, of wounds; Buried in Annapolis National, Annapolis, Md.

Owens, Benjamin. Residence: Middlebury. Enlistment Date: Jun 4, 62. Muster Date: Jul 9, 62. Deserted Jan 29, 63; Returned Feb 26, 63; Mustered out Jun 13, 65; Died Feb 9, 1893, and buried in West Cemetery, Middlebury, Vt.

Palmer, Edson B. Residence: New Haven. Enlistment Date: Nov 30, 63. Muster Date: Dec 24, 63. *See* Second Lt. Co. A.

Palmer, Joseph. Residence: New Haven. Enlistment Date: Jun 24, 62. Muster Date: Jul 9, 62. Deserted Jan 13, 63.

Palmer, William H. Residence: Ferrisburgh. Enlistment Date: Dec 26, 63. Muster Date: Jan 6, 64. Transferred to Co. A Jun 13, 65; Mustered out Dec 1, 65.

Parker, Philo F. Residence: Brandon. Enlistment Date: Jun 2, 62. Muster Date: Jul 9, 62. Discharged for enlistment in the 17th U.S. Infantry.

Peterson, Charles L. Residence: Benson. Enlistment Date: Jun 27, 62. Muster Date: Jul 9, 62. Discharged Jan 22, 64, for disability; Died Jul 22, 1918, and buried in Lower Waterford Cemetery, Waterford, Vt.

Pollens, Julius J. Residence: Switzerland. Enlistment Date: Oct 11, 64. Muster Date: Oct 11, 64. Substitute for O. N. Kelton, Montgomery; Transferred to Co. C 4th Vt. Jan 20, 65.

Preston, Henry E. Residence: Berlin. Enlistment Date: Aug 16, 64. Muster Date: Aug 16, 64. Mustered out Jun 13, 65; Died 1925, and buried in the village cemetery, Brownington, Vt.

Preston, Russell N. Residence: Ferrisburgh. Enlistment Date: Dec 21, 63. Muster Date: Jan 6, 64. Promoted to Corp. Mar 21, 65; Transferred to Co. A Jun 13, 65; Promoted to First Sgt. Sep 5, 65; Mustered Dec 1, 65.

Richardson, William. T. Residence: Bristol. Enlistment Date: Dec 12, 63. Muster Date: Dec 31, 63. Transferred to Co. A Jun 13, 65; Mustered out Jul 17, 65; Died Jun 7, 1900, and buried in Riverside Cemetery, New Haven, Vt.

Robinson, Edgar W. Residence: Burlington. Enlistment Date: Jun 19, 62. Muster Date: Jul 9, 62. Transferred to V.R.C. Sep 1, 63; Discharged Jul 9, 65.

Samson, Hilen. Residence: Cornwall. Enlistment Date: Jun 23, 62. Muster Date: Jul 9, 62. Discharged Jan 16, 63, for enlistment in the 17th U. S. Infantry.

Sears, Casper H. Residence: Monkton. Enlistment Date: Jun 12, 62. Muster Date: Jul 9, 62. Mustered out Jun 13, 65; Died Jun 27, 1865, and buried in Barnumtown Cemetery, Monkton, Vt.

Sears, Cassius C. Residence: Monkton. Enlistment Date: Jun 12, 62. Muster Date: Jul 9, 62. Mustered out Jun 13, 65; Died Dec 20, 1927, and buried in Barnumtown Cemetery, Monkton, Vt.

Sherman, Elbert. Residence: Danby. Enlistment Date: Aug 25, 64. Muster Date: Aug 25, 64. Transferred to Co. K. 5th Vt. Jan 20, 65; Died Jan 13, 1925, and buried in Public Cemetery, Tinmouth, Vt.

Shina, Leander. Residence: New Haven, Conn. Enlistment Date: Oct 10, 64. Muster Date: Oct 10, 64. Substitute for Alfred Combs, Montgomery; Transferred to Co. A, 5th Vt. Jan 20, 65; Died Aug 3, 1912, and buried in Village Cemetery, Montgomery, Vt.

Smith, Carlos. Residence: Starksboro. Enlistment Date: Sep 1, 64. Muster Date: Sep 1, 64. Mustered out Jun 13, 65; Died Feb 24, 1909, and buried in Green Mount Cemetery, Starksboro, Vt.

Smith, John M. Residence: Starksboro. Enlistment Date: Dec 26, 63. Muster Date: Jan 6, 64. Mustered out May 13, 65.

Smith, Luman. Residence: Addison. Enlistment Date: Jul 7, 62. Muster Date: Jul 9, 62. *See* Second Lt. Co. C.

Smith, Royal. Residence: New Haven. Enlistment Date: Jun 24, 62. Muster Date: Jul 9, 62. Discharged Nov 6, 62, for disability; Died Sep 21, 1908, and buried in Grand View Cemetery, Addison, Vt.

Sproul, John. Residence: Bridport. Enlistment Date: Dec 31, 63. Muster Date: Jan 5, 64. Promoted to Corp. Jul 28, 64; Reduced Oct 25, 64; Transferred to Co. A Jun 13, 65; Mustered out Dec 1, 65.

Squires, Andrew G. Residence: New Haven. Enlistment Date: Dec 14, 63. Muster Date: Dec 31, 63. Transferred to Co. A Jun 13, 65; Mustered out Dec 1, 65; Died Oct 3, 1903, and buried in Evergreen Cemetery, New Haven, Vt.

Stanlew, George. Residence: Ferrisburg. Enlistment Date: Dec 23, 63. Muster Date: Dec 31, 63. Transferred to Co. A Jun 13, 65; Mustered out Dec 1, 65.

Steele, David. Residence: Weybridge. Enlistment Date: Jun 13, 62. Muster Date: Jul 9, 62. Discharged Jan 17, 63 for enlistment in the 17th U.S. Infantry; Deserted Feb 8, 64; Discharged for disability Dec 18, 63; Died January 29, 1892.

Stinehowe, Nelson. Residence: Ferrisburgh. Enlistment Date: Dec 31, 63. Muster Date: Jan 6, 64. Taken prisoner Feb 2, 64; Paroled Nov 19, 64; Died Nov 30, 64, of disease on board the transport *Baltic.*

Stokes, Benjamin E. Residence: Starksboro. Enlistment Date: Dec 21, 63. Muster Date: Jan 6, 64. Captured Feb 21, 64; Paroled Mar 21, 64; Dishonorably discharged Jun 12, 65; Died May 9, 1914, and buried in Mason Hill Cemetery, Starksboro, Vt.

Strait, Frank. Residence: Bristol. Enlistment Date: Aug 5, 64. Muster Date: Aug 5, 64. Died Dec 30, 64, of disease; Buried in Hampton National Cemetery, Hampton, Va.

Strickland, Frank B. Residence: Vergennes. Enlistment Date: Jun 21, 62. Muster Date: Jul 9, 62. Discharged Jan 8, 64, for disability.

Sullivan, Daniel. Residence: New Haven. Enlistment Date: Aug 13, 64. Muster Date: Aug 13, 64. Mustered out Aug 19, 65; Died Nov 1, 1882, and buried in St. Mary's Cemetery, Middlebury, Vt.

Sweet, Henry C. Residence: Monkton. Enlistment Date: Dec 16, 63. Muster Date: Dec 24, 63. Mustered out Jun 27, 65; Died Jul 16, 1906, and buried in Monkton Boro Cemetery, Monkton, Vt.

Taylor, George C. Residence: Middlebury. Enlistment Date: Jun 10, 62. Muster Date: Jul 9, 62. Transferred to V.R.C. Mar 25, 64; Discharged Jun 20, 65.

Teyvaw, Alexander. Residence: Berkshire. Enlistment Date: Oct 10, 64. Muster Date: Oct 10, 64. Substitute for Charles W. Jones, Montgomery; Transferred to Co. A 5th Vt. Jan 20, 65.

Theim, Carl. Residence: Bridgewater. Enlistment Date: Sep 14, 64. Muster Date: Sep 14, 64. Mustered out Jun 13, 65.

Thomas, Henry C. Residence: Orwell. Enlistment Date: Jun 24, 62. Muster Date: Jul 9, 62. Died Oct 11, 62; Buried in Annapolis National Cemetery, Annapolis, Md.

Tucker, Byron. Residence: Starksboro. Enlistment Date: Dec 22, 63. Muster Date: Jan 6, 64. Died Dec 8, 64.

Towle, Henry. Residence: Bridport. Enlistment Date: Jun 21, 62. Muster Date: Jul 9, 62. Died Dec 8, 64, of disease; Buried in Hampton National Cemetery, Hampton, Va.

Utly, Hiram S. Residence: Tinmouth. Enlistment Date: Aug 15, 64. Muster Date: Aug 15, 64. Transferred to Co. E 5th Vt. Jan 20, 65.

Van Steenburg, Charles. Residence: Monkton. Enlistment Date: Dec 19, 63. Muster Date: Dec 24, 63. Wounded Feb 2, 64; Transferred to the V. R. C. Jun 15, 64; Mustered out Aug 5, 65; Died Dec 29, 1917, and buried in Lakeview Cemetery, Burlington, Vt.

Varney, Frederick. Residence: New Haven. Enlistment Date: Nov 24, 63. Muster Date: Dec 3, 63. Promoted to Corp. Feb 1, 65; to Sgt. Jun 14, 65; Transferred to Co. A Jun 13, 65; Mustered out Dec 1, 65.

Vere, Joseph. Residence: Waltham. Enlistment Date: Dec 16, 63. Muster Date: Dec 24, 63. Transferred to Co. A Jun 13, 65; Mustered out Dec 1, 65.

Weaver, Lyman. Residence: Bristol. Enlistment Date: Jul 26, 64. Muster Date: Jul 26, 64. Mustered out Jun 13, 65; Died 1924, and buried in Glendale Cemetery, Vernon, Colo.

Wheatley, Alson N. Residence: Brookfield. Enlistment Date: Dec 26, 63. Muster Date: Jan 6, 64. Wounded Oct 27, 64; Transferred to Co. A Jun 13, 65; Promoted to Corp. Sep 5, 65; Mustered out Dec 1, 65; Died Jan 30, 1922, and buried in East Brookfield Cemetery, East Brookfield, Vt.

Williams, Joshua. Residence: Lincoln. Enlistment Date: Jun 16, 62. Muster Date: Jul 9, 62. Died Jan 27, 64.

Wolcott, Louis N. Residence: Orwell. Enlistment Date: Aug 25, 64. Muster Date: Aug 25, 64. Mustered out Jun 13, 65.

Wright, Charles. Residence: Middlebury. Enlistment Date: Jun 7, 62. Muster Date: Jul 9, 62. Deserted Nov 28, 62.

York, George. Residence: Randolph. Enlistment Date: Jan 4, 64. Muster Date: Jan 6, 64. Died Feb 14, 64; Buried in New Bern National Cemetery, New Bern, N.C.

Company D

Captains

Jarvis, Charles. Residence: Weathersfield. Commission Date: Jun 25, 62. Issue Date: Jun 25, 62. *See* Maj.

Clark, Asaph. Residence: Cavendish. Commission Date: May 25, 63. Issue Date: Jun 26, 63. First Lt. Co. D; Mustered out Jun 13, 65; Died Jan 8, 1886, and buried in Togus National Cemetery, Veterans Administration Medical and Regional Office Center, Togus, Me.

Cowdrey, Burnham. Residence: Bradford. Commission Date: Sep 7, 65. Issue Date: Sep 15, 65. Sgt. Co. G; Promoted to First Sgt. ; to Second Lt. Feb 4, 65; Transferred to Co. D Jun 13, 65; Promoted to First Lt. July 3, 65; Mustered out Dec 1, 65; Died Jan 22, 1914, and buried in the village cemetery, Bradford, Vt.

First Lieutenants

Clark, Asaph. Residence: Cavendish. Commission Date: Jun 25, 62. Issue Date: Jun 25, 62. *See* Capt. Co. D.

Haskell, Charles W. Residence: Weathersfield. Commission Date: May 25, 63. Issue Date: Jun 26, 63. First Sgt. Co. D; Promoted to Second Lt. Nov 17, 62; Mustered out Jun 13, 65; Died Sep 10, 1915, in Newton, Mass. and is buried in Evergreen Cemetery, Brighton, Mass.

Gray, John. Residence: Hardwick. Commission Date: May 2, 65. Issue Date: May 15, 65. Sgt. Co. I; Promoted to First Sgt. Jan 1, 63; to Second Lt. Co. I May 8, 64; to First Lt. Co. K May 2, 65; Transferred to Co. D Jun 13, 65; cashiered and dismissed from the service by C.G.M. Aug 28, 65.

Cowdrey, Burnham. Residence: Bradford. Commission Date: Jul 3, 65. Issue Date: Jul 20, 65. *See* Capt. Co. D.

Chamberlin, George C. Residence: Bradford. Commission Date: Sep 7, 65. Issue Date: Sep 15, 65. Private Co. G; Promoted to QM. Sgt. Feb 24, 65; to Second Lt. Co. D Jul 3, 65; Mustered out Dec 1, 65; Died Nov 8, 1896, and buried in the village cemetery, Bradford, Vt.

Second Lieutenants

Dartt, Justus. Residence: Weathersfield. Commission Date: Jun 25, 62. Issue Date: Jun 25, 62. Taken prisoner Sep. 3, 62; Paroled Sep 15, 62; Resigned Nov 13, 62; Died Jul 1, 1912, and buried in Summer Hill Cemetery, Springfield, Vt.

Haskell, Charles W. Residence: Weathersfield. Commission Date: Nov 17, 62. Issue Date: Nov 17, 62. *See* First Lt. Co. D

Snow, Asa H. Residence: Pomfret. Commission Date: May 25, 65. Issue Date: Jun 26, 65. Corp. Co. D; Promoted to Sgt. Dec 4, 62; Discharged Dec 11, 64; Buried in Los Angeles National Cemetery, Los Angeles, Calif.

Carpenter, George N. Residence: Marshfield. Commission Date: Feb 5, 65. Issue Date: Mar 6, 65. *See* First Lt. Co. I.

Cowdrey, Burnham. Residence: Bradford. Commission Date: Feb 4, 65. Issue Date: Feb 20, 65. *See* Capt. Co. D.

Bagley, Frank M. Residence: Topsham. Commission Date: Jun 21, 65. Issue Date: Jul 10, 65. Sgt. Co. G; Promoted to First Sgt. Mar 1, 65; Mustered out as First Sgt. Co. G Jun 13, 65.

Chamberlin, George C. Residence: Bradford. Commission Date: Jul 3, 65. Issue Date: Jul 20, 65. *See* First Lt. Co. D.

Newell, Oliver W. Residence: Burke. Commission Date: Sep 17, 65. Issue Date: Oct 2, 65. Pvt. Co. E; Transferred to Co. B Jun 13, 65; Promoted to Sgt. Jun 19, 65; to Sgt. Maj. Jul 1, 65; Mustered out Dec 1, 65.

Sergeants

Haskell, Charles W. Weathersfield. Enlistment Date: May 27, 62. Muster Date: Jul 9, 62. *See* First Lt. Co. D.

Russell, Albert F. Residence: Claremont, N.H. Enlistment Date: Jun 10, 62. Muster Date: Jul 9, 62. Reduced Jul 22, 63; Mustered out Jun 13, 65.

Bennett, John W. Residence: Weathersfield. Enlistment Date: Jun 9, 62. Muster Date: Jul 9, 62. Taken prisoner Sep 3, 62; Paroled Oct 1, 62; Reduced Dec 4, 62; Mustered out Jun 13, 65; Died Dec 1, 1904, and buried in the National Military Home Cemetery, Leavenworth, Kan.

Russell, Lysander W. Residence: Peru. Enlistment Date: Jun 24, 62. Muster Date: Jul 9, 62. Promoted to First Sgt. ; Discharged Sep 2, 63 for disability; Died Mar 24, 1909, and buried in Vermont Veteran's Home Cemetery, Bennington, Vt.

Corporals

Dodge, William L. Residence: Springfield. Enlistment Date: Jun 2, 62. Muster Date: Jul 9, 62. Promoted to Sgt. Jul 23, 62; Reduced Nov 20, 62; Promoted to Corp. Jul 21, 63; to Sgt. Feb 18, 64; Mustered out Jun 13, 65.

Nichols, George W. Residence: Weathersfield. Enlistment Date: Jun 2, 62. Muster Date: Jul 9, 62. Promoted to Sgt. Dec 4, 62; Died Apr 21, 63; Buried in Hampton National Cemetery, Hampton, Va.

Taylor, Charles B. Residence: Andover. Enlistment Date: Jun 5, 62. Muster Date: Jul 9, 62. Promoted to Sgt.; Discharged Jun 10, 62, for disability.

Snow, Asa H. Residence: Pomfret. Enlistment Date: Jun 17, 62. Muster Date: Jul 9, 62. *See* Second Lt. Co. D.

Howe, Charles W. Residence: Sharon. Enlistment Date: May 28, 62. Muster Date: Jul 9, 62. Discharged Jul 27, 63, for disability.

Weston, James. Residence: Weathersfield. Enlistment Date: Jun 2, 62. Muster Date: Jul 9, 62. Reduced; Mustered out Jun 13, 62; Died Mar 26, 1905, and buried in Ascutney Cemetery, Weathersfield, Vt.

Whitney, Milo F. Residence: Tunbridge. Enlistment Date: Jun 19, 62. Muster Date: Jul 9, 62. Promoted to Sgt. Jul 11, 63; Reduced Nov 10, 65; Promoted to Sgt. Feb 18, 64; Reduced Feb 7, 65; Mustered out Jun 13, 65; Died Apr 30, 1915, and buried in Whitney Hill Cemetery, Tunbridge, Vt.

Sawyer, Joseph S. Residence: Plymouth. Enlistment Date: Jun 2, 62. Muster Date: Jul 9, 62. Discharged Nov 6, 62, for disability; Died Jun 25, 1927, and buried in Plymouth Cemetery, Plymouth, Vt.

Musician

Thomas, Edward G. Residence: Montgomery. Enlistment Date: Jun 2, 62. Muster Date: Jul 9, 62. Deserted Jan 1, 63.

Wagoner

Smith, David D. Residence: Weathersfield. Enlistment Date: Jun 2, 62. Muster Date: Jul 9, 62. Discharged Oct 15, 62, for disability; Died Dec 14, 1886, and buried in Perkinsville Plain Cemetery, Weathersfield, Vt.

Privates

Adams, Thomas. Residence: West Windsor. Enlistment Date: Dec 25, 63. Muster Date: Jan 5, 64. Died Jun 19, 64; Buried in New Bern National Cemetery, New Bern, N.C.

Alexander, Hazen C. Residence: Tunbridge. Enlistment Date: Dec 23, 63. Muster Date: Jan 2, 64. Died Jan 21, 65, of disease and buried in Strafford Rd. Cemetery, Tunbridge, Vt.

Allard, Joshua. Residence: Pomfret. Enlistment Date: Jun 17, 62. Muster Date: Jul 9, 62. Promoted to Corp. Dec 4, 62; Reduced Jul 11, 64; Mustered out Jun 13, 65.

Archer, Alfred. Residence: Plymouth. Enlistment Date: May 30, 62. Muster Date: Jul 9, 62. Mustered out Jun 13, 65; Buried in Vermont Veteran's Home, Bennington, Vt.

Avery, Gideon H. Residence: Strafford. Enlistment Date: Jun 9, 62. Muster Date: Jul 9, 62. Discharged Jan 15, 63, for enlistment in the Regular Army.

Avery, John W. Residence: Strafford. Enlistment Date: May 29, 62. Muster Date: Jul 9, 62. Discharged Nov 6, 62, for disability; Died May 14, 1895, and buried in Evergreen Cemetery, Strafford, Vt.

Ball, Homer E. Residence: Athens. Enlistment Date: Aug 23, 64. Muster Date: Aug 23, 64. Mustered out May 13, 65; Died Jun 5, 1871, and buried in Summer Hill Cemetery, Springfield, Vt.

Beal, Andrew J. Residence: Woodstock. Enlistment Date: Jun 18, 62. Muster Date: Jul 9, 62. Promoted to Corp. Jan 23, 65; Mustered out Jun 13, 65.

Bemis, John L. Residence: Chester. Enlistment Date: Jun 9, 62. Muster Date: Jul 9, 62. Mustered out Jun 13, 65; Died Jan 12, 1910, and buried in Smokeshire Cemetery, Chester, Vt.

Bennett, Francis J. Residence: Weathersfield. Enlistment Date: Jun 9, 62. Muster Date: Jul 9, 62. Taken prisoner Sep 3, 62; Paroled Sep 15, 62; Died Apr 23, 63, of small pox.

Benson, Rodney L. Residence: Chester. Enlistment Date: Aug 13, 64. Muster Date: Aug 13, 64. Died Oct 28, 64, of disease; Buried in Hampton National Cemetery, Hampton, Va.

Bent, Charles E. Residence: Sharon. Enlistment Date: Sep 7, 64. Muster Date: Sep 7, 64. Mustered out Jun 13, 65.

Blanchard, Hiram K. Residence: Sharon. Enlistment Date: May 28, 62. Muster Date: Jul 9, 62. Discharged Nov 12, 62, for disability; Died May 29, 1876, and buried in Beaver Meadows Cemetery, Norwich, Vt.

Blanchard, Seth. Residence: West Windsor. Enlistment Date: Dec 7, 63. Muster Date: Jan 2, 64. Died Feb 2, 64; Buried in Brownsville Cemetery, West Windsor, Vt.

Bridges, Charles W. Residence: Chester. Enlistment Date: Jul 2, 62. Muster Date: Jul 9, 62. Promoted to Corp. Feb 18, 64; Reduced Dec 5, 64; Mustered out Jun 13, 65; Died Jul 27, 1928, and buried in Oakland Cemetery, Springfield, Vt.

Brown, Henry. Residence: Warren. Enlistment Date: Jun 5, 62. Muster Date: Jul 9, 62. Mustered out Jun 8, 65.

Butler, Omar D. Residence: Plymouth. Enlistment Date: Jun 2, 62. Muster Date: Jul 9, 62. Died Oct 20, 62; Buried in Rosehill Cemetery, Chicago, Ill.

Campbell, Edwin R. Residence: Barnard. Enlistment Date: Aug 25, 64. Muster Date: Aug 25, 64. Mustered out Jun 13, 65; Died Oct 11, 1894.

Campbell, Oscar F. Residence: Barnard. Enlistment Date: Aug 25, 64. Muster Date: Aug 25, 64. Mustered out Jun 13, 65; Died Apr 6, 1921, and buried in Branchview Cemetery, Royalton, Vt.

Carpenter, Henry D. Residence: Plymouth. Enlistment Date: Jun 2, 62. Muster Date: Jul 9, 62. Transferred to the V. R. C. Jan 9, 64; Discharged Aug 23, 64.

Carlisle, Ara M. Residence: Chester. Enlistment Date: Jun 3, 62. Muster Date: Jul 9, 62. Taken prisoner Aug 2, 62; Paroled Aug 16, 62; Discharged Oct 17, 62, for disability; Died Mar 23, 1894, and buried in Chester, Vt.

Cass, Laton M. Residence: Springfield. Enlistment Date: Dec 2, 63. Muster Date: Jan 2, 64. Promoted to Corp. Jan 20, 65; Mustered out Dec 1, 65.

Chamberlin, Charles L. Residence: Chelsea. Enlistment Date: Jun 9, 62. Muster Date: Jul 9, 62. Discharged Jan 15, 63, for enlistment in the Regular Army; Died Sep 9, 1865, and buried in Elmwood Cemetery, Barre, Vt.

Chaplin, Ira. Residence: Chittenden. Enlistment Date: Dec 3, 63. Muster Date: Dec 26, 63. Mustered out Jun 19, 65.

Chehin, Daniel. Residence: Wardsboro. Enlistment Date: Jan 5, 64. Muster Date: Jan 7, 64. Transferred to Co. B Jun 13, 65; Mustered out Dec 1, 65.

Cilley, Charles S. Residence: Bridgewater. Enlistment Date: Jun 9, 62. Muster Date: Jul 9, 62. Promoted to Corp. Dec 4, 62; Reduced Mar 25, 64; Died Oct 18, 64, of disease; Buried in Hampton National Cemetery, Hampton, Va.

Clapp, George. Residence: Pomfret. Enlistment Date: Jun 16, 62. Muster Date: Jul 9, 62. Died Dec 6, 62; Buried in Rosehill Cemetery, Chicago, Ill.

Cozen, John. Residence: Weathersfield. Enlistment Date: Jun 23, 62. Muster Date: Jul 9, 62. Deserted Oct 28, 62.

Currier, Henry A. Residence: Chester. Enlistment Date: Aug 9, 64. Muster Date: Aug 19, 64. Transferred to Co. M, 11th Vt., Jan 20, 65; Died Aug 26, 1913, and buried in Evergreen Cemetery, Cornwall, Vt.

Darling, Gilbert A. Residence: Tunbridge. Enlistment Date: Jun 20, 62. Muster Date: Jul 9, 62. Mustered out Jun 13, 65.

Dartt, George. Residence: Weathersfield. Enlistment Date: Jun 4, 62. Muster Date: Jul 9, 62. Died Oct 3, 63, of disease; Buried in Perkinsville Plain Cemetery, Weathersford, Vt.

Davis, Edward W. Residence: Woodstock. Enlistment Date: Jun 6, 62. Muster Date: Jul 9, 62. Mustered out Jun 13, 65.

Davis, George W. 1st. Residence: Poultney. Enlistment Date: Sep 3, 64. Muster Date: Sep 3, 64. Mustered out Jun 13, 65.

Davis, George W. 2nd. Residence: Claremont, N.H. Enlistment Date: Jun 10, 62. Muster Date: Jul 9, 62. Mustered out Jun 13, 65.

Davis, Herbert W. Residence: Springfield. Enlistment Date: Aug 8, 64. Muster Date: Aug 8, 64. Mustered out Jul 18, 65.

Davis, John. Residence: Woodstock. Enlistment Date: Jun 2, 62. Muster Date: Jul 9, 62. Promoted to Corp. Mar 28, 64; Died Jan 13, 65, of disease; Buried in Hampton National Cemetery, Hampton, Va.

Davis, Lewis. Residence: Barton. Enlistment Date: Nov 23, 63. Muster Date: Dec 17, 63. Discharged Jun 12, 65; Died Apr 10, 1898, and buried in the village cemetery, Barton, Vt.

Diggins, Azro B. Residence: Andover. Enlistment Date: Jun 21, 62. Muster Date: Jul 9, 62. Mustered out Jun 13, 65; Died Apr 8, 1914, and buried in Perkinsville Plain Cemetery, Weathersfield, Vt.

Dockham, Henry O. Residence: Strafford. Enlistment Date: Nov 28, 63, . Muster Date: Dec 31, 63. Mustered out May 25, 65; Died Aug 16, 1892, and buried in North Kingston Cemetery, Kingston, Ill.

Dodge, Charles H. Residence: Chelsea. Enlistment Date: Sep 5, 64. Muster Date: Sep 5, 64. Mustered out Jun 13, 65; Died Jun 14, 1876, and buried in Highland Cemetery, Chelsea, Vt.

Duquez, John. Residence: Bridgewater. Enlistment Date: May 29, 62. Muster Date: Jul 9, 62. Discharged Aug 26, 63, for disability; Died May 30, 1893, and buried in Quechee Lower Cemetery, Hartford, Vt.

Duphiney, Philip. Residence: Reading. Enlistment Date: Dec 23, 63. Muster Date: Dec 23, 63. Taken prisoner Feb 2, 64; Paroled Apr 28, 65; Mustered out May 23, 65.

Durkee, Charles. Residence: Tunbridge. Enlistment Date: Dec 30, 63. Muster Date: Jan 2, 63. Mustered out Dec 7, 65; Died Mar 4, 1931, and buried in Durkee Cemetery, Tunbridge, Vt.

Durkee, George W. Residence: Tunbridge. Enlistment Date: Aug 27, 64. Muster Date: Aug 27, 64. Mustered out Jun 13, 65; Died Aug 13, 1931, and buried in Hunt Cemetery, Tunbridge, Vt.

Edwards, Norris E. Residence: Springfield. Enlistment Date: May 31, 62. Muster Date: Jul 9, 62. Promoted to Corp. Feb 18, 64; Wounded Sep 29, 64; mustered out May 13, 65; Died Sep 19, 1906, and buried in Oakland Cemetery, Springfield, Vt.

Emery, Harrison S. Residence: Barnard. Enlistment Date: Aug 25, 64. Muster Date: Aug 25, 64. Died Dec 8, 64, of disease; Buried in Alexandria National Cemetery, Alexandria, Va.

Fairbanks, Hiram C. Residence: Springfield. Enlistment Date: Dec 15, 63. Muster Date: Jan 2, 64. Died Dec 8, 64, and buried in Summer Hill Cemetery, Springfield, Vt.

Fallan, James. Residence: Hartland. Enlistment Date: Jun 2, 62. Muster Date: Jul 9, 62. Died Apr 23, 63; Buried in Hampton National Cemetery, Hampton, Va.

Farnsworth, George H. Residence: Springfield. Enlistment Date: Aug 4, 64. Muster Date: Aug 4, 64. Mustered out Jun 13, 65; Died Oct 30, 1911, and buried in East Cemetery, Williston, Vt.

Field, Levi W. Residence: Weathersfield. Enlistment Date: Jun 6, 62. Muster Date: Jul 9, 62. Mustered out Jun 13, 65; Died Sep 25, 1887, and buried in Ascutney Cemetery, Weathersfield, Vt.

Finchon, John. Residence: Tunbridge. Enlistment Date: May 30, 62. Muster Date: Jul 9, 62. Mustered out Jun 13, 65.

Fletcher, Otis F. Residence: Chester. Enlistment Date: Aug 18, 62. Muster Date: Nov 21, 62. Mustered out Nov 21, 65; Died Apr 26, 1898, and buried in Summer Hill Cemetery, Springfield, Vt.

Forbes, Darwin A. Residence: West Haven. Enlistment Date: Dec 15, 63. Muster Date: Dec 19, 63. Transferred to Co. B Jun 13, 65; Mustered out Dec 1, 65.

Foss, Elijah D. Residence: Tunbridge. Enlistment Date: Aug 5, 64. Muster Date: Aug 5, 64. Mustered out Jun 13, 65; Died Jul 10, 1901, and buried in Hunt Cemetery, Tunbridge, Vt.

French, John. Residence: Andover. Enlistment Date: Jun 6, 62. Muster Date: Jul 9, 62. Discharged Dec 5, 62, for disability.

Fuller, David W. Residence: Mt. Holly. Enlistment Date: Jun 25, 62. Muster Date: Jul 9, 62. Discharged Nov 6, 62, for disability; Died Jan 8, 1912, and buried in the village cemetery, Weston, Vt.

Gallup, William W. Residence: Tunbridge. Enlistment Date: Sep 2, 64. Muster Date: Sep 2, 64. Mustered out Jun 13, 65; Died May 27, 1905, and buried in the village cemetery, South Royalton, Vt.

Gard, William. Residence: Springfield. Enlistment Date: Dec 16, 63. Muster Date: Jan 2, 64. Mustered out Dec 1, 65.

Garry, Thomas P. Residence: Weathersfield. Enlistment Date: Jun 9, 62. Muster Date: Jul 9, 62. Wounded Feb 2, 64; Discharged Feb 27, 65.

Gifford, Collins F. Residence: Royalton. Enlistment Date: Jun 14, 62. Muster Date: Jul 9, 62. Discharged Jan 15, 63, for enlistment in the Regular Army.

Glynn, Henry. Residence: Mt. Holly. Enlistment Date: Aug 18, 64. Muster Date: Aug 18, 64. Mustered out Jun 13, 65; Died Oct 24, 1907, and buried in Pine Hill Cemetery, North Springfield, Vt.

Glynn, Justinian C. Residence: Chester. Enlistment Date: Jul 2, 62. Muster Date: Jul 9, 62. Mustered out Jun 13, 65; Died Nov 2, 1919, and buried in Pine Grove Cemetery, North Springfield, Vt.

Gould, Elbert M. Residence: Ludlow. Enlistment Date: Jun 27, 62. Muster Date: Jul 9, 62. Discharged Jan 15, 63, for enlistment in the Regular Army.

Grennell, Abel H. Residence: Springfield. Enlistment Date: Dec 19, 63. Muster Date: Jan 5, 64. Transferred to Co. B Jun 13, 65; Mustered out Aug 3, 65.

Griswold, Thomas. Residence: Springfield. Enlistment Date: Dec 3, 63. Muster Date: Jan 2, 64. Taken prisoner Feb 2, 64; Paroled Apr 21, 65; Mustered out May 18, 65; Died Mar 10, 1905, and buried in Summer Hill Cemetery, Springfield, Vt.

Grover, James C. Residence: Mt. Holly. Enlistment Date: Jun 25, 62. Muster Date: Jul 9, 62. Discharged Nov 18, 62, for disability.

Hamilton, Charles. Residence: Springfield. Enlistment Date: Aug 6, 64. Muster Date: Aug 6, 64. Mustered out Jun 13, 65; Died Jun 5, 1872, and buried in the village cemetery, Bridport, Vt.

Harrington, Daniel. Residence: Bridgewater. Enlistment Date: Jun 26, 62. Muster Date: Jul 9, 62. Discharged Aug 2, 63, for disability.

Harrington, John R. Residence: Windham. Enlistment Date: Jun 23, 62. Muster Date: Jul 9, 62. Discharged Oct 2, 62, for disability.

Haskell, Eben S. Residence: Weathersfield. Enlistment Date: Jul 28, 64. Muster Date: Aug 2, 64. Wounded Sep 29, 64; Mustered out May 13, 65; Died Mar 18, 1924, and buried in Glenwood Cemetery, Scytheville, N.H.

Hathaway, Timothy. Residence: Can. Enlistment Date: Aug 9, 64. Muster Date: Aug 9, 64. Substitute for Buel H. Day, Jericho; Transferred to Co. I, 5th Vt. Jan 20, 65.

Hearren, James. Residence: St. Albans. Enlistment Date: Jan 2, 64. Muster Date: Jan 5, 64. Transferred to Co. B Jun 13, 65; Mustered out Dec 1, 65.

Heath, William K. Residence: Woodstock. Enlistment Date: Jun 18, 62. Muster Date: Jul 9, 62. Promoted to Corp. Nov 10, 63, to Sgt. Feb 18, 64, to First Sgt. Aug 11, 64, to Second Lt. Co. Dec 21, 64, but commission not accepted; mustered out Jun 13, 65; Died Feb 7, 1905, and buried in Fish Cemetery, Washington, Vt.

Hesselton, Homer. Residence: Andover. Enlistment Date: May 31, 62. Muster Date: Jul 9, 62. Deserted; Returned Mar 5, 63; Died Apr 12, 63.

Hobson, William L. Residence: Weathersfield. Enlistment Date: Jun 17, 62. Muster Date: Jul 9, 62. Died Sep 26, 62.

Hopkins, William. Residence: Royalton. Enlistment Date: May 31, 62. Muster Date: Jul 9, 62. Discharged Jan 17, 63, for enlistment in the Regular Army; Died Feb 7, 1905, and buried in Fish Cemetery, Washington, Vt.

Hoyt, George H. Residence: Clarendon. Enlistment Date: Jan 4, 64. Muster Date: Jan 7, 64. Transferred to Co. B Jun 13, 65; Discharged Aug 31, 65; Died May 24, 1902, and buried in South View Cemetery, Randolph, Vt.

Hoyt, Homer. Residence: Tunbridge. Enlistment Date: Dec 30, 63. Muster Date: Jan 2, 64. Mustered out Dec 1, 65.

Hubbard, George W. Residence: Sharon. Enlistment Date: Jun 23, 62. Muster Date: Jul 9, 62. Died Oct 16, 63, of disease.

Hurlburt, Jeremiah. Residence: Strafford. Enlistment Date: Dec 22, 63. Muster Date: Jan 7, 64. Transferred to Co. B Jun 13, 65; Mustered out Dec 1, 65; Died Sep 26, 1904, and buried in the village cemetery, Worcester, Vt.

Jacobs, James. Residence: Brookfield. Enlistment Date: Jun 23, 62. Muster Date: Jul 9, 62. Died Dec 11, 62.

Jeffs, George. Residence: Mt. Holly. Enlistment Date: Aug 27, 64. Muster Date: Aug 27, 64. Transferred to Co. M, 11th Vt. Jan 20, 65.

Johnson, David S. Residence: Plymouth. Enlistment Date: Jun 7, 62. Muster Date: Jul 9, 62. Discharged Jan 17, 63, for enlistment in the Regular Army.

Kendrick, Benjamin S. Residence: Springfield. Enlistment Date: Dec 30, 63. Muster Date: Jan 2, 64. Mustered out Dec 1, 65; Died Jul 13, 1868, and buried in Summer Hill Cemetery, Springfield, Vt.

Kenyon, John S. Residence: Cornish, N.H. Enlistment Date: May 31, 62. Muster Date: Jul 9, 62. Discharged Apr 16, 63, for disability.

Keyes, Lysander J. Residence: Weathersfield. Enlistment Date: Jun 9, 62. Muster Date: Jul 9, 62. Discharged Oct 15, 62, for disability.

Kibbie, Milton M. Residence: Tunbridge. Enlistment Date: Dec 29, 63. Muster Date: Jan 2, 64. Mustered out Dec 1, 65; Died Mar 30, 1906, and buried in the village cemetery, Tunbridge, Vt.

Kneeland, William A. Residence: Sharon. Enlistment Date: Jul 5, 62. Muster Date: Jul 9, 62. Discharged Nov 18, 62, for disability. Buried in Forefather's Cemetery, Chelmsford Centre, Mass.

Knight, Nelson D. Residence: Plymouth. Enlistment Date: Aug 22, 64. Muster Date: Aug 24, 64. Transferred to Co. C, 4th Vt. Jan 20, 65; Died Jan 22, 1865, and buried in City Point National Cemetery, Hopewell, Va.

Ladd, Corin. Residence: Springfield. Enlistment Date: Dec 19, 63. Muster Date: Jan 2, 64. Mustered out Dec 1, 65.

Ladd, Jefferson M. Residence: Sharon. Enlistment Date: Jun 27, 62. Muster Date: Jul 9, 62. Deserted; Returned Mar 3, 63; Discharged Jul 21, 63, for disability; Charge of desertion dropped Nov 26, 1886; Died Mar 7, 1895, and buried in Kibling Cemetery, Strafford, Vt.

Lee, James H. Residence: Tunbridge. Enlistment Date: Dec 14, 63. Muster Date: Jan 2, 64. Mustered out Dec 1, 65; Died Jun 21, 1877, and buried in Drew Cemetery, Tunbridge, Vt.

Lemrise, Obert. Residence: Peacham. Enlistment Date: Mar 30, 65. Muster Date: Mar 30, 65. Mustered out Dec 1, 65.

Lewis, John T. Residence: Springfield. Enlistment Date: Aug 23, 64. Muster Date: Aug 23, 64. Transferred to Co. M, 11th Vt. Jan 20, 65; Died Jul 6, 1882, and buried in Brookside Cemetery, Chester, Vt.

Lewis, William A. Residence: Springfield. Enlistment Date: Aug 9, 64. Muster Date: Aug 9, 64. Mustered out Jun 13, 65; Died May 24, 1898, and buried in Summer Hill Cemetery, Springfield, Vt.

Lieber, John W. Residence: Tunbridge. Enlistment Date: Dec 28, 63. Muster Date: Jan 2, 64. Mustered out Jun 13, 65.

Lovejoy, Daniel W. Residence: Royalton. Enlistment Date: Jan 4, 64. Muster Date: Jan 6, 64. Died Sep 23, 64.

Luce, Charles A. Residence: Royalton. Enlistment Date: Jun 13, 62. Muster Date: Jul 9, 62. Killed by train Sep 28, 62.

Lynch, Patrick H. Residence: Mt. Holly. Enlistment Date: Jun 9, 62. Muster Date: Jul 9, 62. Mustered out Jun 10, 65; Died Jul 14, 1868, and buried in Ludlow Cemetery, Ludlow, Vt.

Manion, Patrick. Residence: Rutland. Enlistment Date: Dec 29, 63. Muster Date: Jan 5, 64. Taken prisoner Feb 2, 64, and died in Andersonville, Ga., Jun 24, 64; Buried in Andersonville National Cemetery, Andersonville, Ga.

Marcy, George L. Residence: Weathersfield. Enlistment Date: May 30, 62. Muster Date: Jul 9, 62. Discharged Nov 1, 62, for disability; Died May 22, 1916, and buried in Oakland Cemetery, Springfield, Vt.

Marsh, Henry E. Residence: W. Windsor. Enlistment Date: Dec 21, 63. Muster Date: Jan 2, 64. Died Sep 29, 64; Buried in New Bern National Cemetery, New Bern, N.C.

Marston, Jeremiah W. Residence: Tunbridge. Enlistment Date: Feb 4, 65. Muster Date: Feb 4, 65. Mustered out Dec 1, 65; Died Aug 12, 1914, and buried in the village cemetery, Plainfield, Vt.

Marston, William B. Residence: Chelsea. Enlistment Date: Aug 18, 64. Muster Date: Aug 18, 64. Mustered out Jun 13, 65; Died Sep 26, 1893, and buried in Highland Cemetery, Chelsea, Vt.

McKennan, James. Residence: Substitute. Enlistment Date: Aug 16, 64. Muster Date: Aug 16, 64. Substitute for Azro Kent, St. Albans; Mustered out Dec 13, 65.

Menard, Franc. Residence: Windsor. Enlistment Date: Jun 7, 62. Muster Date: Jul 9, 62. Mustered out Jun 13, 65.

Monahan, Thomas. Residence: Guilford. Enlistment Date: Dec 25, 63. Muster Date: Dec 26, 63. Died Jun 11, 64, of disease; Buried in New Bern National Cemetery, New Bern, N.C.

Moore, Franklin A. Residence: Mt. Holly. Enlistment Date: Aug 5, 64. Muster Date: Aug 5, 64. Died Dec 14, 64, of disease.

Morse, Charles. Residence: Springfield. Enlistment Date: Feb 14, 65. Muster Date: Feb 14, 65. Mustered out Dec 1, 65.

Morse, Charles H. Residence: Plymouth. Enlistment Date: Jun 2, 62. Muster Date: Jul 9, 62. Mustered out Jun 13, 65.

Moxley, Azro G. Residence: Tunbridge. Enlistment Date: Dec 26, 63. Muster Date: Jan 2, 64. Promoted to Corp. Jul 11, 64, to Sgt. Feb 7, 65, to First Sgt. Jul 1, 65; Mustered out Dec 7, 65; Died Mar 6, 1877, and buried in Spring Road Cemetery, Tunbridge, Vt.

Olney, George. Residence: Poultney. Enlistment Date: Sep 3, 64. Muster Date: Sep 3, 64. Mustered out Jun 13, 65; Died Jan 11, 1922, and buried in Pine Grove Cemetery, North Springfield, Vt.

Ormes, Doran H. Residence: West Haven. Enlistment Date: Dec 12, 63. Muster Date: Dec 19, 63. Transferred to Co. B Jun 13, 65; Mustered out Dec 1, 65.

Pangburn, James K. Residence: Barnard. Enlistment Date: Aug 25, 64. Muster Date: Aug 25, 64. Mustered out Jun 13, 65.

Parmelee, Albert E. Residence: Claremont, N.H. Enlistment Date: Jun 10, 62. Muster Date: Jul 9, 62. Taken prisoner and pardoned at Winchester, Va., in 1862; Discharged Oct 31, 62, for disability.

Partridge, James A. Residence: Springfield. Enlistment Date: Aug 5, 64. Muster Date: Aug 5, 64. Mustered out Jun 13, 65.

Patch, Daniel. Residence: Hartland. Enlistment Date: Jul 11, 62. Muster Date: Jul 11, 62. Discharged Nov 21, 62, for disability.

Pearsons, George H. Residence: Brookfield. Enlistment Date: Dec 17, 63. Muster Date: Jan 2, 64. Taken prisoner Feb 2, 64, and died at Salisbury, N.C., Apr 4, 64; Buried in Salisbury National Cemetery, Salisbury, N.C.

Perham, Henry. Residence: Springfield. Enlistment Date: Dec 19, 63. Muster Date: Jan 2, 64. Transferred to Co. B Jun 13, 65; Died Oct 8, 65; Buried in Hampton National Cemetery, Hampton, Va.

Piper, William. Residence: Weathersfield. Enlistment Date: Jun 18, 62. Muster Date: Jul 9, 62. Promoted to Sgt. Jul 4, 63; Killed in action Feb 2, 64; Buried in New Bern National Cemetery, New Bern, N.C.

Poole, Edward P. Residence: Tunbridge. Enlistment Date: Jun 18, 62. Muster Date: Jul 9, 62. Mustered out Jun 13, 65.

Powers, Samuel C. Residence: Springfield. Enlistment Date: Dec 25, 63. Muster Date: Jan 5, 64. Mustered out Dec 1, 65; Buried in Togus National Cemetery Veterans Administration Medical and Regional Office Center, Togus, Me.

Pratt, Charles P. Residence: Woodstock. Enlistment Date: Jun 19, 62. Muster Date: Jul 9, 62. Discharged Jan 15, 63, for enlistment in the Regular Army.

Putnam, Rufus. Residence: Putney. Enlistment Date: Jul 3, 62. Muster Date: Jul 9, 62. Promoted to Corp. Feb 18, 64; Reduced Jan 25, 65; Mustered out Jun 13, 65.

Quirk, Jeremiah. Residence: Springfield. Enlistment Date: Dec 15, 63. Muster Date: Jan 2, 64. Promoted to Corp. Dec 5, 64; Mustered out Dec 1, 65.

Quirk, Michael M. Residence: Shaftsbury. Enlistment Date: Dec 31, 63. Muster Date: Dec 31, 63. Mustered out Dec 1, 65.

Reed, Joseph U. Residence: Ludlow. Enlistment Date: May 26, 62. Muster Date: Jul 9, 62. Discharged Jul 31, 64, for disability.

Rice, Alonzo H. Residence: Chester. Enlistment Date: Jun 27, 62. Muster Date: Jul 9, 62. Discharged Nov 18, 62, for disability.

Roby, James F. Residence: Springfield. Enlistment Date: Aug 9, 64. Muster Date: Aug 9, 64. Mustered out Jun 13, 65; Died 1927 and buried in Summer Hill Cemetery, Springfield, Vt.

Rounsevel, Elbridge G. Residence: Unity, N.H. Enlistment Date: Jun 11, 62. Muster Date: Jul 9, 62. Taken prisoner Feb 2, 64, and died at Andersonville, Ga., Jan 25, 65; Buried in Andersonville National Cemetery, Andersonville, Ga.

Rumrill, Luman C. Residence: Springfield. Enlistment Date: Dec 17, 63. Muster Date: Jan 2, 64. Transferred to Co. B Jun 13, 65; Mustered out Dec 1, 65; Died Mar 2, 1905, and buried in Pine Grove cemetery, Springfield, Vt.

Russell, Richard K. Residence: Springfield. Enlistment Date: Aug 10, 64. Muster Date: Aug 10, 64. Transferred to Co. C, 4th Vt., Jan 20, 65; Died Mar 30, 1873, and buried in Summer Hill Cemetery, Springfield, Vt.

Scott, Daniel S. Residence: Charlestown, N.H. Jun 19, 62. Muster Date: Jul 9, 62. Died Nov 7, 62.

Shono, John. Residence: Milton. Enlistment Date: Jun 9, 62. Muster Date: Jul 9, 62. Promoted to Corp. Mar 28, 64; Mustered out Jun 13, 65.

Simonds, Frank P. Residence: Peru. Enlistment Date: Jun 24, 62. Muster Date: Jul 9, 62. Musician; Taken prisoner Sep 3, 62; Paroled Oct 1, 62; Discharged Apr 29, 63, for disability.

Smith, Nathan C. Residence: Brookfield. Enlistment Date: Dec 23, 63. Muster Date: Jan 2, 64. Killed in action Feb 2, 64; Buried in New Bern National Cemetery, New Bern, N.C.

Smith, Oscar C. Residence: Leicester. Enlistment Date: Feb 27, 65. Muster Date: Feb 27, 65. Transferred to Co. B Jun 13, 65; Promoted to Corp. Jun 19, 65; Mustered out Dec 1, 65.

Smith, Royal C. Residence: Randolph. Enlistment Date: Dec 31, 63. Muster Date: Jan 6, 64. Promoted to Corp. Feb 7, 65; Mustered out Dec 1, 65; Died Jun 12, 1910, and buried in Durkee Cemetery, Tunbridge, Vt.

Smith, Theodore R. Residence: W. Haven. Enlistment Date: Dec 17, 63. Muster Date: Dec 19, 63. Promoted to Sgt. Feb 18, 64; Mustered out Dec 1, 65; Died Oct 22, 1892, and buried in Victor, Iowa.

Snell, William H. Residence: Cavendish. Enlistment Date: Jun 3, 62. Muster Date: Jul 9, 62. Promoted to Corp., to Sgt. Aug 11, 64; Reduced Sep 23, 64; Promoted to Sgt. Jan 20, 65; Mustered out Jun 13, 65.

Spafford, John W. Residence: Shelburne. Enlistment Date: Jun 9, 62. Muster Date: Jul 9, 62. Committed suicide Sep 5, 62.

Spafford, Wesley H. Residence: Springfield. Enlistment Date: Jun 23, 62. Muster Date: Jul 9, 62. Discharged Nov 6, 62, for disability.

Spaulding, George W. Residence: Claremont, N.H. Enlistment Date: Jun 29, 62. Muster Date: Jul 9, 62. Mustered out Jun 13, 65.

Spaulding, William W. Residence: Cavendish. Enlistment Date: Jun 9, 62. Muster Date: Jul 9, 62. Discharged Jan 17, 63, for enlistment in the Regular Army.

Spring, John O. Residence: Springfield. Enlistment Date: Aug 9, 64. Muster Date: Aug 9, 64. Mustered out Jun 13, 65; Died Aug 4, 1925, and buried in Summer Hill Cemetery, Springfield, Vt.

Spring, Osman A. Residence: Springfield. Enlistment Date: Aug 4, 64. Muster Date: Aug 4, 64. Mustered out Jun 13, 65; Died Sep 28, 1878, and buried in Summer Hill Cemetery, Springfield. Vt.

Squier, Algernon M. Residence: Weathersfield. Enlistment Date: Jun 2, 62. Muster Date: Jul 9, 62. *See* Hospital Steward.

Squires, David. Residence: Cornish, N.H. Enlistment Date: May 31, 62. Muster Date: Jul 9, 62. Discharged May 26, 63, for disability.

Staples, Daniel W. Residence: Springfield. Enlistment Date: Dec 2, 63. Muster Date: Jan 2, 64. Promoted to Corp. Feb 18, 64; Mustered out Dec 1, 65; Died Oct 26, 1896, and buried in Summer Hill Cemetery, Springfield, Vt.

Stearns, Myron. Residence: Lincoln. Enlistment Date: Feb 25, 65. Muster Date: Feb 25, 65. Transferred to Co. B June 13, 65; Mustered out Sep 1, 65; Died Oct 29, 1922, and buried in Evergreen Cemetery, Rutland, Vt.

Stevens, Leonard M. Residence: Claremont, N.H. Enlistment Date: Jun 23, 62. Muster Date: Jul 9, 62. Mustered out Jun 13, 65.

Stevens, William L. Residence: Barnard. Enlistment Date: Aug 25, 64. Muster Date: Aug 25, 64. Discharged June 24, 65; Died Jul 10, 1865, and buried in the village cemetery, Barnard, Vt.

Strong, George. Residence: Cavendish. Enlistment Date: Jun 3, 62. Muster Date: Jul 9, 62. Deserted Apr 8, 63; Returned May 3, 63; Mustered out Jun 13, 65; Died Feb 19, 1905, and buried in Tyson Cemetery, Plymouth, Vt.

Taft, William H. Residence: Rutland. Enlistment Date: Jan 13, 65. Muster Date: Jan 13, 65. Transferred to Co. B Jun 13, 65; Mustered out Dec 1, 65.

Taylor, Matthew. Residence: Can. Enlistment Date: Sep 24, 64. Muster Date: Sep 24, 64. Substitute for Madison J. Black, Newport; Transferred to Co. A, 5th Vt. Jan 20, 65; Died Jan 13, 1879, and buried in West Hill Cemetery, Ryegate, Vt.

Taylor, Oscar E. Residence: Springfield. Enlistment Date: Jun 6, 62. Muster Date: Jul 9, 62. Deserted Jul 15, 62; Died 1908, and buried in Summer Hill Cemetery, Springfield, Vt.

Thompson, Eugene A. Residence: Chester. Enlistment Date: Nov 19, 63. Muster Date: Nov 19, 63. Died Jan 9, 65; Buried in City Point National Cemetery, Hopewell, Va.

Thompson, Putnam J. Residence: Chester. Enlistment Date: Aug 9, 64. Muster Date: Aug 9, 64. Mustered out Jun 13, 65; Died Dec 5, 1875, and buried in Brookside Cemetery, Chester, Vt.

Thompson, Ransom T. Residence: Springfield. Enlistment Date: Jun 4, 62. Muster Date: Jul 9, 62. Promoted to Corp. Dec 4, 62; to Sgt. Nov 10, 63; to First Sgt. Feb 18, 64; Died Jun 15, 64.

Tucker, Rufus B. Residence: Bridgewater. Enlistment Date: Jun 24, 62. Muster Date: Jul 9, 62. Died Aug 9, 62, of diphtheria.

Turner, George. Residence: Springfield. Enlistment Date: Dec 16, 63. Muster Date: Jan 2, 64. Transferred to Co. B Jun 13, 65; Mustered out Dec 1, 65.

Walker, Guy B. Residence: Rockingham. Enlistment Date: Dec 10, 63. Muster Date: Dec 11, 63. Wounded Feb 2, 65; Mustered out Dec 1, 65; Died Sep 18, 1868, and buried in Walker Cemetery, Springfield, Vt.

Walker, Ward C. Residence: West Windsor. Enlistment Date: Dec 8, 63. Muster Date: Jan 2, 64. Mustered out Dec 1, 65.

Ward, Henry H. Residence: Castleton. Enlistment Date: Dec 10, 63. Muster Date: Dec 15, 63. Discharged May 27, 65, for disability; Died Dec 10, 1912, and buried in Evergreen Cemetery, New Haven, Vt.

Wells, Lester F. Residence: Strafford. Enlistment Date: May 29, 62. Muster Date: Jul 9, 62. Discharged Jan 15, 63, for enlistment in the Regular Army.

Whipple, Henry R. Residence: Unity, N.H. Enlistment Date: Jun 5, 62. Muster Date: Jul 9, 62. Discharged Oct 15, 63, for disability.

Whipple, William M. Residence: Unity, N.H. Enlistment Date: Jun 5, 62. Muster Date: Jul 9, 62. Discharged Jan 15, 63, for enlistment in the Regular Army.

Whitney, Abel D. Residence: Tunbridge. Enlistment Date: Dec 30, 63. Muster Date: Jan 2, 64. Taken prisoner Feb 2, 64, and died at Andersonville, Ga., Aug 8, 64; Buried in Andersonville National Cemetery, Andersonville, Ga.

Whitney, John S. Residence: Tunbridge. Enlistment Date: Dec 26, 63. Muster Date: Jan 2, 64. Promoted to Corp. Aug 11, 64; Mustered out Dec 1, 65.

Whitney, Lewis. Residence: Tunbridge. Enlistment Date: Aug 4, 64. Muster Date: Aug 4, 64. Mustered out Jun 13, 65.

Whitney, Orlando. Residence: Tunbridge. Enlistment Date: Jul 7, 62. Muster Date: Jul 9, 62. Died Jul 3,

63, of disease at West Point, Va.; Buried in Yorktown National Cemetery, Yorktown, Va.; Memorial stone in Whitney Hill Cemetery, Tunbridge, Vt.

Whitney, Orson. Residence: Tunbridge. Enlistment Date: Aug 27, 64. Muster Date: Aug 27, 64. Mustered out Jun 13, 65; Died Jul 25, 1915, and buried in Durkee Cemetery, Tunbridge, Vt.

Whitney, Ransom. Residence: Tunbridge. Enlistment Date: Aug 27, 64. Muster Date: Aug 27, 64. Transferred to Co. C, 2nd Vt. Jan 20, 65.

White, Josiah G. Residence: Barnard. Enlistment Date: Jan 5, 64. Muster Date: Jan 5, 64. Mustered out Dec 1, 65; Died Aug 8, 1926, and buried in North Saint Cemetery, Chester, Vt.

Wilcox, Edward T. Residence: Springfield. Enlistment Date: Jun 21, 62. Muster Date: Jul 9, 62. Mustered out Jun 13, 65.

Winslow, Joseph J. Residence: Barnard. Enlistment Date: Aug 25, 64. Muster Date: Aug 25, 64. Mustered out Jun 13, 65.

Company E

Captains

Bartlett, Amasa. Residence: Irasburg. Commission Date: Jun 25, 62. Issue Date: Jun 25, 62. *See* Maj.

Quimby, Elisha M. Residence: Charleston. Commission Date: Dec 22, 63. Issue Date: Feb 1, 64. First Lt. Co. E; Resigned May 11, 65.

Kelley, Edward L. Residence: Claredon. Commission Date: May 20, 65. Issue Date: May 31, 65. First Sgt. Co. B; Promoted to Second Lt. Co. B May 1, 63; to First Lt. Co. E Dec 22, 63; Mustered out Jun 13, 65.

First Lieutenants

Quimby, Elisha M. Residence: Charleston. Commission Date: Jun 25, 62. Issue Date: Jun 25, 62. *See* Capt. Co. E.

Kelley, Edward L. Residence: Claredon. Commission Date: Dec 22, 63. Issue Date: Feb 1, 64. *See* Capt. Co. E.

Parker, Richard F. Residence: Coventry. Commission Date: May 20, 65. Issue Date: May 31, 65. Sgt. Co. E; Promoted to First Sgt. Jan 20, 63; to Second Lt. Co. E Oct 19, 64; Mustered out Jun 13, 65; Died Dec 13, 1914, and buried in Pine Grove Cemetery, Derby, Vt.

Second Lieutenants

Hibbard, Curtis A. Residence: Troy. Commission Date: Jun 25, 62. Issue Date: Jun 25, 62. Resigned May 16, 63; Died Dec 6, 1908, and buried in Lakeview Cemetery, Burlington, Vt.

Jenkins, Calvin M. Residence: Barnston, Can. Commission Date: Jun 22, 63. Issue Date: Jun 26, 63. Pvt. Co. E; Promoted to Sgt. Mar 17, 63; Died Sep 30, 64, of wounds received Sep 29, 64; Buried in Hampton National Cemetery, Hampton, Va.

Parker, Richard F. Residence: Coventry. Commission Date: Oct 19, 64. Issue Date: Nov 19, 64. *See* First Lt. Co. E.

Sleeper, Asa C. Residence: Newport. Commission Date: May 20, 65. Issue Date: May 31, 65. Corp. Co. E; Promoted to Sgt. Aug 8, 62; to First Sgt. Nov 28, 64; Mustered out Jun 13, 65; Died Jul 25, 1926, and buried in Newport Center Cemetery, Newport Center, Vt.

Sergeants

Bisbee, Lewis H. Residence: Derby. Enlistment Date: Jun 10, 62. Muster Date: Jul 9, 62. *See* Capt. Co. H.

Parker, Richard F. Residence: Coventry. Enlistment Date: Jun 3, 62. Muster Date: Jul 9, 62. *See* First Lt. Co. E.

Bowley, Abner G. Residence: Coventry. Enlistment Date: Jun 5, 62. Muster Date: Jul 9, 62. Discharged Nov 17, 62, for disability.

Lund, Leonard A. Residence: Brownington. Enlistment Date: Jun 16, 62. Muster Date: Jul 9, 62. Reduced Aug 8, 62; Promoted to Corp. Feb 17, 63; to Sgt. Mar 17, 63; Mustered out Jun 13, 65; Died Feb 23, 1923, and buried in Brownington Cemetery, Brownington, Vt.

Kilburn, Marcellus D. Residence: Barnston, Can. Enlistment Date: Jun 9, 62. Muster Date: Jul 9, 62. Discharged Mar 14, 63, for disability.

Corporals

Sleeper, Asa C. Residence: Newport. Enlistment Date: Jun 9, 62. Muster Date: Jul 9, 62. *See* Second Lt. Co. E.

Wadleigh, John G. Residence: Brownington. Enlistment Date: Jun 16, 62. Muster Date: Jul 9, 62. Reduced; Transferred to Co. I Jun 1, 64; Mustered out Jun 19, 65; Died Feb 22, 1902, and buried in the village cemetery, Weston, Vt.

Barnard, William. Residence: Charleston. Enlistment Date: Jun 6, 62. Muster Date: Jul 9, 62. Reduced Feb 7, 63; Died Aug 12, 63; Buried in Yorktown National Cemetery, Yorktown, Va.

Hamblet, Edson L. Residence: Salem. Enlistment Date: Jun 6, 62. Muster Date: Jul 9, 62. Promoted to Sgt. Nov 20, 62; Deserted Feb 13, 63; Returned Mar 27, 63; Reduced Feb 20, 63; Promoted to Corp. Feb 2, 64; to Sgt. Nov 28, 64; Mustered out Jun 13, 65; Died Nov 24, 1871, and buried in Gore Cemetery, Morgan, Vt.

Cutts, Loren. Residence: Newport. Enlistment Date: Jun 9, 62. Muster Date: Jul 9, 62. Died Jan 10, 63; Buried in Annapolis National Cemetery, Annapolis, Md.

Tucker, Willard. Residence: Albany. Enlistment Date: Jun 7, 62. Muster Date: Jul 9, 62. Mustered out Jun 13, 65.

Blake, Joseph. Residence: Troy. Enlistment Date: Jun 18, 62. Muster Date: Jul 9, 62. Discharged Jan 16, 63, to enlist in the Regular Army.

Morrill, Alvah J. Residence: Derby. Enlistment Date: Jun 9, 62. Muster Date: Jul 9, 62. Promoted to Sgt. Feb 2, 64; Mustered out Jun 13, 65.

Musician

Wing, Reuben B. Residence: Troy. Enlistment Date: Jun 23, 62. Muster Date: Jul 9, 62. Discharged Apr 29, 63, for disability; Died Oct 31, 1897, and buried in the village cemetery, North Troy Cemetery, North Troy, Vt.

Wagoner

Freeman, Charles W. Residence: Albany. Enlistment Date: Jun 5, 62. Muster Date: Jul 9, 62. Mustered out Jun 13, 65.

Privates

Adams, Alvin W. Residence: Troy. Enlistment Date: Jun 14, 62. Muster Date: Jul 9, 62. Promoted to Corp. Dec 1, 63; to Sgt. Feb 2, 64; Mustered out Jun 28, 65; Died Jun 22, 1918, and buried in Mount Pleasant Cemetery, St. Johnsbury, Vt.

Adams, Orrin J. Residence: Newport. Enlistment Date: Jun 14, 62. Muster Date: Jul 9, 62. Deserted Jan 30, 63; Returned May 4, 64; Mustered out Jun 13, 65.

Ash, David. Residence: Barton. Enlistment Date: Sep 5, 64. Muster Date: Sep 5, 64. Mustered out Jun 19, 65.

Ash, Thomas. Residence: Bristol. Enlistment Date: Feb 23, 65. Muster Date: Feb 23, 65. Transferred to Co. B Jun 13, 65; Mustered out Dec 1, 65.

Ashley, Jerry. Residence: Brattleboro. Enlistment Date: Aug 5, 63. Muster Date: Aug 5, 63. Drummer; Transferred to V. R. C. Mar 31, 64; Deserted Nov 30, 64.

Batchelder, Charles M. Residence: Troy. Enlistment Date: May 31, 62. Muster Date: Jul 9, 62. Discharged Feb 4, 63, for disability; Died Dec 24, 1910, and buried in Pine Grove Cemetery, Newport, Vt.

Balch, Joseph A. Residence: Newport. Enlistment Date: Aug 10, 64. Muster Date: Aug 10, 64. Transferred to Co. F, 11th Vt. Jan 20, 65.

Balch, Samuel A. Residence: Newport. Enlistment Date: Sep 23, 64. Muster Date: Sep 23, 64. Transferred to Co. F, 11th Vt. Jan 20, 65.

Barry, Charles A. Residence: Troy. Enlistment Date: Jun 14, 62. Muster Date: Jul 9, 62. Mustered out Jun 11, 65.

Bassett, John. Residence: Coventry. Enlistment Date: Jun 2, 62. Muster Date: Jul 9, 62. Deserted Jan 7, 64; Died Mar 30, 1918, and buried in St. Mary's Cemetery, Swanton, Vt.

Beach, Edwin B. Residence: Brunswick. Enlistment Date: Jan 1, 64. Muster Date: Jan 7, 64. Transferred to Co. B Jun 13, 65; Promoted to Corp. Jul 26, 65; Mustered out Dec 1, 65.

Belding, Heman. Residence: Bridgewater. Enlistment Date: Dec 18, 63. Muster Date: Dec 18, 63. Died Mar 11, 64, and buried in Jay Cemetery, Jay, Vt.

Belknap, Fenelon A. Residence: Barton. Enlistment Date: Sep 3, 64. Muster Date: Sep 3, 64. Mustered out Jun 13, 65; Died Jan 22, 1889, and buried in Welcome Brown Cemetery, Barton, Vt.

Bemis, George N. Residence: Irasburg. Enlistment Date: Jun 14, 62. Muster Date: Jul 9, 62. Deserted Oct 21, 62.

Bigelow, George M. Residence: Stanstead, Can. Enlistment Date: Jun 12, 62. Muster Date: Jul 9, 62. Discharged Jan 17, 63, by special order of the War Department; Died Mar 11, 1914, and buried in Lyndon Center Cemetery, Lyndon, Vt.

Blake, Nye O. Residence: Wells. Enlistment Date: Dec 25, 63. Muster Date: Dec 25, 63. Transferred to Co. B Jun 13, 65; Mustered out Dec 1, 65.

Blanchard, Daniel. Residence: Sunderland. Enlistment Date: Dec 11, 63. Muster Date: Dec 24, 63. Taken prisoner Oct 28, 64, and died at Salisbury, N.C., Feb. 9, 65; Buried in Salisbury National Cemetery, Salisbury, N.C.

Blanchard, Francis. Residence: Derby. Enlistment Date: Jun 11, 62. Muster Date: Jul 9, 62. Deserted Dec 19, 62; Returned March 30, 63; Promoted to Corp. Feb 2, 64; Mustered out Jun 13, 65; Died Feb 8, 1917, and buried in Catholic Cemetery, Newport, Vt.

Bolton, John. Residence: Danville. Enlistment Date: Jul 14, 62. Muster Date: Jul 14, 62. Discharged Apr 29, 63, for disability; Died Feb 14, 1905, and buried in Danville Green Cemetery, Danville, Vt.

Bowman, Edward E. Residence: Sunderland. Enlistment Date: Dec 4, 63. Muster Date: Dec 24, 63. Transferred to Co. B Jun 13, 65; Mustered out Dec 1, 65; Died May 5, 1905, and buried in Evergreen Cemetery, Rutland, Vt.

Brainard, Charles F. Residence: Bridgewater. Enlistment Date: Dec 17, 63. Muster Date: Dec 17, 63. Mustered out Jun 19, 65.

Brainard, Lorenzo F. Residence: Bridgewater. Enlistment Date: Dec 17, 63. Muster Date: Dec 17, 63. Mustered out Jun 22, 65.

Brown, Byron D. Residence: Jay. Enlistment Date: Jun 25, 62. Muster Date: Jul 9, 62. Promoted to Corp. Feb 11, 65; Mustered out Jun 13, 65; Died Dec 12, 1900, and buried in Lower Waterford Cemetery, Waterford, Vt.

Brown, Calvin C. Residence: Derby. Enlistment Date: Jun 9, 62. Muster Date: Jul 9, 62. Promoted to Corp. Aug 5, 62; to Sgt. Mar 17, 63; Discharged Jan 18, 64, for disability.

Brown, Horace W. Residence: Troy. Enlistment Date: Jun 9, 62. Muster Date: Jul 9, 62. Promoted to Corp. Aug 4, 62; Discharged Oct 17, 62, for disability.

Brown, Stillman A. Residence: Craftsbury. Enlistment Date: Feb 28, 65. Muster Date: Feb 28, 65. Transferred to Co. B Jun 13, 65; Discharged Oct 24, 65, for disability; Died Mar 8, 1866, and buried in South Troy Cemetery, South Troy, Vt.

Burdett, James. Residence: Hartford. Enlistment Date: Dec 25, 63. Muster Date: Dec 25, 63. Transferred to Co. B Jun 13, 65; Mustered out Dec 1, 65.

Burgess, Seth. Residence: Randolph. Enlistment Date: Aug 17, 64. Muster Date: Aug 17, 64. Transferred to Co. B Jun 13, 65; Mustered out Dec 1, 65.

Buzzell, Henry A. Residence: Newport. Enlistment Date: Jun 16, 62. Muster Date: Jul 9, 62. Mustered out Jun 13, 65; Died Aug 11, 1919, and buried in Lake Road Cemetery, Newport Center, Vt.

Buzzell, Sheldon A. Residence: Enosburgh. Enlistment Date: Sep 2, 64. Muster Date: Sep 2, 64. Died Nov 22, 64; Buried in City Point National Cemetery, Hopewell, Va.

Caswell, Freeman A. Residence: Sutton. Enlistment Date: Jun 11, 62. Muster Date: Jul 9, 62. Mustered out Jun 13, 65.

Chase, Henry C. Residence: Derby. Enlistment Date: Jun 25, 62. Muster Date: Jul 9, 62. Discharged Jan 19, 63, for disability.

Church, Allen. Residence: Georgia. Enlistment Date: Jan 4, 64. Muster Date: Jan 5, 64. Transferred to Co. B Jun 13, 65; Promoted to Corp. Oct 13, 65; Mustered out Dec 1, 65.

Church, Joseph P. Residence: Georgia. Enlistment Date: Jan 4, 64. Muster Date: Jan 5, 64. Died Sep 9, 64; Buried in the New Bern National Cemetery, New Bern, N.C.

Church, Sullivan R. Residence: Salem. Enlistment Date: Jul 7, 62. Muster Date: Jul 9, 62. Mustered out Jun 13, 65; Died Sep 2, 1881.

Clark, Frederick H. Residence: Glover. Enlistment Date: Jun 5, 62. Muster Date: Jul 9, 62. Mustered out Jun 13, 65.

Clark, George T. Residence: Bridgewater. Enlistment Date: Dec 18, 63. Muster Date: Dec 18, 63. Mustered out Jun 22, 65.

Clark, Marvin T. Residence: Bridgewater. Enlistment Date: Dec 18, 63. Muster Date: Dec 18, 63. Transferred to Co. B Jun 13, 65; Mustered out Dec 1, 65.

Connal, James. Residence: Troy. Enlistment Date: Jun 7, 62. Muster Date: Jul 9, 62. Discharged Jan 14, 63, for enlistment in the Regular Army.

Cook, Edward R. Residence: Sunderland. Enlistment Date: Dec 14, 63. Muster Date: Dec 24, 63. Wounded Sep 29, 64; Discharged Jun 21, 65; Died Feb 8, 1918, and buried in Cutting Cemetery, Wilmington, Vt.

Crandall, William H. Residence: Brownington. Enlistment Date: Jun 24, 62. Muster Date: Jul 9, 62. Deserted Sep 2, 62; Died Oct 26, 1864, and buried in the village cemetery, Brownington, Vt.

Crawford, George. Residence: Wilmington. Enlistment Date: Jan 5, 64. Muster Date: Jan 5, 64. Mustered out May 25, 65; Died Jan 16, 1901, and buried in Newport Center Cemetery, Newport Center, Vt.

Cronk, Chauncey. Residence: Pomfret. Enlistment Date: Dec 26, 63. Muster Date: Dec 29, 63. Transferred to Co. B Jun 13, 65; Mustered out Dec 1, 65.

Cutts, Allen E. Residence: Barre. Enlistment Date: Aug 8, 64. Muster Date: Aug 8, 64. Wounded Sep 29, 64; Mustered out Jun 13, 65; Died Mar 28, 1933, and buried in Elmwood Cemetery, Barre, Vt.

Cutts, Frank E. Residence: Barre. Enlistment Date: Aug 17, 64. Muster Date: Aug 17, 64. Mustered out Jun 13, 65; Died Aug 26, 1907, and buried in Elmwood Cemetery, Barre, Vt.

Davis, George W. Residence: Derby. Enlistment Date: Jun 7, 62. Muster Date: Jul 9, 62. Promoted to Corp. Feb 2, 64; Died Oct 8, 64, of wounds received Sep 29, 64.

Dewey, Byron E. Residence: Greensboro. Enlistment Date: Aug 27, 64. Muster Date: Aug 27, 64. Mustered out Jun 13, 65.

Dix, Mahlon C. Residence: Albany. Enlistment Date: Aug 13, 64. Muster Date: Aug 13, 64. Mustered out Jun 13, 65; Died Feb 26, 1905, and buried in Westmoro Cemetery, Barton, Vt.

Donaldson, Nathan. Residence: Alburgh. Enlistment Date: Sep 3, 64. Muster Date: Sep 3, 64. Mustered out Jun 13, 65.

Douvalle, Joseph F. Residence: Burke. Enlistment Date: Feb 13, 65. Muster Date: Feb 13, 65. Transferred to Co. B Jun 13, 65; Mustered out Dec 1, 65; Died Jan 18, 1879, and buried in Burke Hollow Cemetery, Burke Vt.

Drown, Erastus. Residence: Greensboro. Enlistment Date: Jun 6, 62. Muster Date: Jul 9, 62. Discharged Jan 14, 63, for enlistment in the Regular Army.

Drown, Hiram. Residence: Newport. Enlistment Date: Mar 4, 65. Muster Date: Mar 4, 65. Transferred to Co. B Jun 13, 65; Mustered out Dec 1, 65.

Dwyer, Amasa. Residence: Salem. Enlistment Date: Jun 16, 62. Muster Date: Jul 9, 62. Promoted to Corp. Dec 28, 64; Mustered out Jun 13, 65.

Dwyer, Daniel. Residence: Salem. Enlistment Date: Jun 16, 62. Muster Date: Jul 9, 62. Discharged Jul 20, 65, for wounds received Sep 29, 64; Died Jul 20, 1907, and buried in Westlook Cemetery, Glover, Vt.

Dwyer, Jonathan. Residence: Westminster. Enlistment Date: Dec 25, 63. Muster Date: Dec 25, 63. Died Jan 25, 65; Buried in City Point National Cemetery, Hopewell, Va.

Eggleston, Henry C. Residence: Burke. Enlistment Date: Aug 15, 64. Muster Date: Aug 15, 64. Died Jan 5, 65.

Eggleston, Royal A. Residence: Burke. Enlistment Date: Aug 4, 64. Muster Date: Aug 4, 64. Mustered out Jun 13, 65; Died Feb, 20, 1930, and buried in East Burke Cemetery, Burke, Vt.

Elliott, Henry O. Residence: Enosburgh. Enlistment Date: Sep 5, 64. Muster Date: Sep 5, 64. Mustered out Jun 13, 65; Died Apr 1, 1931, and buried in the village cemetery, Waterbury, Vt.

Elmer, Alva W. Residence: Sutton. Enlistment Date: Jun 11, 62. Muster Date: Jul 9, 62. Deserted Oct 23, 62; Returned Aug 31, 63; Deserted Nov 25, 63.

Estell, Vercil L. Residence: Moretown. Enlistment Date: Dec 14, 63. Muster Date: Jan 2, 64. Transferred to Co. B Jun 13, 65; Mustered out Dec 1, 65.

Exford, David S. Residence: Pownal. Enlistment Date: Jan 2, 64. Muster Date: Jan 7, 64. Transferred to Co. B Jun 13, 65; Mustered out Dec 1, 65; Died Aug 13, 1891, and buried in Oak Hill Cemetery, Pownal, Vt.

Ferguson, Alexander. Residence: Peacham. Enlistment Date: Jun 7, 62. Muster Date: Jul 9, 62. Promoted to Corp. Feb 2, 64; Mustered out Jun 13, 65.

Flanders, Luther. Residence: Wilmington. Enlistment Date: Jan 5, 64. Muster Date: Jan 5, 64. Transferred to Co. I Jun 13, 65; Mustered out Dec 1, 65; Died Apr 13, 1906, and buried in Newport Center Cemetery, Newport Center, Vt.

Flynn, Thomas. Residence: Rockingham. Enlistment Date: Dec 21, 63. Muster Date: Dec 22, 63. Discharged Feb 12, 65, for disability.

Fox, Dennis H. Residence: Westminster. Enlistment Date: Dec 17, 63. Muster Date: Dec 17, 63. Transferred to Co. B Jun 13, 65; Mustered out Dec 1, 65; Died Jan 23, 1903, and buried in Brownington Center Cemetery, Brownington, Vt.

Freeto, Harvey M. Residence: Burke. Enlistment Date: Dec 10, 63. Muster Date: Dec 23, 63. Transferred to Co. B Jun 13, 65; Mustered out Jul 15, 65; Died Jun 18, 1910, and buried in East Burke Cemetery, Burke, Vt.

Fuller, Dana. Residence: Pomfret. Enlistment Date: Dec 18, 63. Muster Date: Dec 30, 63. Transferred to Co. B Jun 13, 65; Promoted to Corp. Oct 13, 65; Mustered out Dec 1, 65; Died Nov 23, 1923, and buried in South Troy Cemetery, South Troy, Vt.

Gardner, William H. Residence: Dover. Enlistment Date: Jan 2, 64. Muster Date: Jan 2, 64. Deserted Mar 5, 65.

George, Clement D. Residence: Derby. Enlistment Date: Jun 23, 62. Muster Date: Jul 9, 62. Deserted Dec 20, 62; Returned Feb 7, 63; Mustered out Jun 13, 65.

Gorham, James G. Residence: Coventry. Enlistment Date: Nov 28, 63. Muster Date: Dec 16, 63. Transferred to Co. B Jun 13, 65; Promoted to Corp. Oct 13, 65; Mustered out Dec 1, 65.

Hawkins, Edward. Residence: Salem. Enlistment Date: Jun 16, 62. Muster Date: Jul 9, 62. Wounded Sep 29, 64; Mustered out Jun 13, 65; Died Nov 17, 1899, and buried in the village cemetery, West Charleston, Vt.

Hon, David. Residence: Shaftsbury. Enlistment Date: Dec 10, 63. Muster Date: Dec 24, 63. Transferred to Co. B Jun 13, 65; Mustered out Aug 2, 65.

Hoyt, Hollis K. Residence: Bridgewater. Enlistment Date: Dec 17, 63. Muster Date: Dec 17, 63. Transferred to Co. B Jun 13, 65; Mustered out Dec 1, 65.

Hoyt, William B. Residence: Hartford. Enlistment Date: Dec 17, 63. Muster Date: Dec 17, 63. Transferred to Co. B Jun 13, 65; Mustered out Dec 1, 65; Died Mar 23, 1905, and buried in Newport Center Cemetery, Newport, Vt.

Hunter, Elias C. Residence: Westminster. Enlistment Date: Dec 18, 63. Muster Date: Dec 18, 63. Mustered out Jun 22, 65, Died Sep 1, 1881, and buried in South Troy Cemetery, South Troy, Vt.

Huntoon, John. Residence: Barnston, Can. Enlistment Date: Jun 16, 62. Muster Date: Jul 9, 62. Deserted Jan 23, 63.

Ingerson, John W. Residence: Wilmington. Enlistment Date: Jan 5, 64. Muster Date: Jan 5, 64. Mustered out Jun 10, 65.

Isham, Charles H. Residence: Derby. Enlistment Date: Jun 21, 62. Muster Date: Jul 9, 62. Died Oct 11, 63, of disease; Buried in Centerville Cemetery, Hyde Park, Vt.

Jenkins, Calvin M. Residence: Barnston, Can. Enlistment Date: Jun 16, 62. Muster Date: Jul 9, 62. *See* Second Lt. Co. E.

Johnson, David. Residence: Salem. Enlistment Date: Jun 9, 62. Muster Date: Jul 9, 62. Mustered out Jun 13, 65.

Johnson, William H. Residence: Salem. Enlistment Date: Jun 28, 62. Muster Date: Jul 9, 62. Promoted to Corp. Jan 20, 63; Reduced Jun 5, 63; Discharged Mar 22, 64, for disability.

Jones, Charles. Residence: Rockingham. Enlistment Date: Dec 10, 63. Muster Date: Dec 11, 63. Transferred to Co. B Jun 13, 65; Mustered out Dec 1, 65.

Joslyn, Sylvester A. Residence: Newport. Enlistment Date: Jun 7, 62. Muster Date: Jul 9, 62. Died Oct 2, 63.

Keating, John. Residence: Barton. Enlistment Date: Sep 5, 64. Muster Date: Sep 5, 64. Wounded Sep 29, 64; Transferred to Co. C, 4th Vt. Jan 20, 65; Died Nov 23, 1918.

Kennon, Marshall T. Residence: Alburgh. Enlistment Date: Sep 5, 64. Muster Date: Sep 5, 64. Mustered out Jun 13, 65.

Kilburn, Charles A. Residence: Enosburgh. Enlistment Date: Sep 1, 64. Muster Date: Sep 1, 64. Transferred to Co. A, 4th Vt. Jan 20, 65; Died Jan 2, 1882, and buried in East Craftsbury Cemetery, East Craftsbury, Vt.

Kittredge, Chandler. Residence: Derby. Enlistment Date: Jun 7, 62. Muster Date: Jul 9, 62. Discharged Jan 8, 64, for disability.

Ladd, John W. Residence: Barnston, Can. Enlistment Date: Jun 16, 62. Muster Date: Jul 9, 62. Deserted Jul 13, 62.

Lane, Edward H. Residence: Newport. Enlistment Date: Jun 21, 62. Muster Date: Jul 9, 62. Discharged Oct 17, 62, for disability.

Lane, Edward H. Residence: West Windsor. Enlistment Date: Dec 21, 63. Muster Date: Dec 25, 63. Transferred to Co. B Jun 13, 65; Mustered out Dec 1, 65; Died Jan 13, 1895, and buried in Lake Road Cemetery, Newport Center, Vt.

Lane, George M. Residence: West Windsor. Enlistment Date: Dec 21, 63. Muster Date: Dec 25, 63. Promoted to Corp. Jun 19, 65; Transferred to Co. B Jun 13, 65; Reduced Oct 13, 65; Mustered out Dec 1, 65.

Lathe, Robert R. Residence: Newport. Enlistment Date: Jun 7, 62. Muster Date: Jul 9, 62. Mustered out Jun 13, 65; Died Nov 11, 1891, and buried in Newport Center Cemetery, Newport Center, Vt.

Lawrence, Joseph. Residence: Newport. Enlistment Date: Jun 12, 62. Muster Date: Jul 9, 62. Died Jul 26, 62, from falling off a train car.

Lee, Emerson F. Residence: Pownal. Enlistment Date: Dec 10, 63. Muster Date: Dec 24, 63. Died Jul 19, 64; Buried in New Bern National Cemetery, New Bern, N.C.

Lee, John W. Residence: Pownal. Enlistment Date: Dec 10, 63. Muster Date: Dec 24, 63. Transferred to Co. B Jun 13, 65; Mustered out Dec 1, 65.

Leon, Joseph. Residence: Peacham. Enlistment Date: Mar 30, 65. Muster Date: Mar 30, 65. Transferred to Co. B Jun 13, 65; Mustered out Dec 1, 65.

Lunge, James. Residence: Glover. Enlistment Date: Aug 23, 64. Muster Date: Aug 23, 64. Wounded Sep 29, 64; Mustered out Jun 13, 65; Died Jan 16, 1926, and buried in East Burke Cemetery, East Burke, Vt.

McClellan, Samuel T. Residence: Jamaica. Enlistment Date: Sep 15, 64. Muster Date: Sep 15, 64. Transferred to Co. D, 11th Vt. Jan 20, 65.

McGuire, James H. Residence: Albany. Enlistment Date: Aug 16, 64. Muster Date: Aug 16, 64. Mustered out Jun 13, 65; Died Dec 29, 1907, and buried in the village cemetery, Albany, Vt.

Merrill, Lewis W. Residence: Reading. Enlistment Date: Dec 31, 63. Muster Date: Jan 5, 64. Transferred to Co. B Jun 13, 65; Mustered out Dec 1, 65.

Merrill, William L. Residence: Newport. Enlistment Date: Jun 9, 62. Muster Date: Jul 9, 62. Discharged Dec 5, 62, for disability.

Mickman, John. Residence: Charleston. Enlistment Date: Jun 9, 62. Muster Date: Jul 9, 62. Promoted to Corp. Jan 17, 63; KIA Sep 29, 64.

Moranville, Simon. Residence: Salem. Enlistment Date: Jul 7, 62. Muster Date: Jul 9, 62. Promoted to Corp. Feb 2, 64; Reduced Feb 11, 65; Mustered out 13 Jun, 65; Died Jun 13, 1910, and buried in Pine Grove Cemetery, Newport, Vt.

Moranville, Wallace. Residence: Salem. Enlistment Date: Jun 18, 62. Muster Date: Jul 9, 62. Musician, Mustered out Jun 13, 65.

Moranville, William. Residence: Salem. Enlistment Date: Jun 19, 62. Muster Date: Jul 9, 62. Promoted to Corp. Feb 17, 63; KIA Sep 29, 64; Buried in Pine Hill Cemetery, Derby, Vt.

Moses, Alonzo D. Residence: Hartford. Enlistment Date: Dec 17, 63. Muster Date: Dec 17, 63. Died Sep 17, 64; Buried in New Bern National Cemetery, New Bern, N.C.

Mott, Langdon. Residence: Irasburgh. Enlistment Date: Jun 23, 62. Muster Date: Jul 9, 62. Discharged Jan 15, 63, for enlistment in the Regular Army.

Moulton, Charles S. Residence: Newport. Enlistment Date: Sep 23, 64. Muster Date: Sep 23, 64. Mustered out Jun 13, 65.

Moulton, Joel C. Residence: Newport. Enlistment Date: Jun 19, 62. Muster Date: Jul 9, 62. Promoted to Corp. Nov 28, 64; Mustered out Jun 13, 65.

Murphy, Edward F. Residence: Barnston, Can. Enlistment Date: Jun 19, 62. Muster Date: Jul 9, 62. Promoted to Corp. Jan 12, 63; Discharged Apr 9, 63, for disability; Died Mar 28, 1908, and buried in State Soldier's Home, Orting, Wash.

Musk, Henry A. Residence: Derby. Enlistment Date: Jun 25, 62. Muster Date: Jul 9, 62. *See* Commissary Sgt.

Newell, Oliver W. Residence: Burke. Enlistment Date: Dec 10, 63. Muster Date: Dec 23, 63. *See* Second Lt. Co. D.

Niles, Asa. Residence: Albany. Enlistment Date: Jun 9, 62. Muster Date: Jul 9, 62. Deserted Jan 27, 63.

Norris, Ward J. Residence: Albany. Enlistment Date: Aug 22, 64. Muster Date: Aug 22, 64. Transferred to Co. C, 2nd Vt. Jan 20, 65.

Nye, Lorenzo D. Residence: Coventry. Enlistment Date: Jun 2, 62. Muster Date: Jul 9, 62. Died Oct 26, 62; and buried in Rosehill Cemetery, Chicago, Ill.

Ord, John. Residence: Can. Enlistment Date: Jun 17, 62. Muster Date: Jul 9, 62. Mustered out Jun 13, 65.

Paine, Henry H. Residence: Albany. Enlistment Date: Aug 13, 64. Muster Date: Aug 13, 64. Mustered out Jun 13, 65; Died Jul 25, 1909, and buried in Underhill Flats Cemetery, Underhill, Vt.

Perkins, Jonathan. Residence: Newbury. Enlistment Date: Dec 30, 63. Muster Date: Dec 31, 63. Transferred to Co. B Jun 13, 65; Promoted to Corp. Jul 26, 65; Mustered out Dec 1, 65; Died Dec 31, 1889, and buried in the village cemetery, Weston, Vt.

Pettengill, Nathaniel B. Residence: Bridgewater. Enlistment Date: Dec 18, 63. Muster Date: Dec 18, 63. Discharged May 20, 65, for disability.

Phillips, Charles. Residence: Burke. Enlistment Date: Aug 4, 64. Muster Date: Aug 4, 64. Wounded Sep 29, 64; Mustered out Jun 13, 65; Died Dec 9, 1900, in East Burke.

Phippen, Myron A. Residence: Dover. Enlistment Date: Jan 4, 64. Muster Date: Jan 7, 64. Died Sep 17, 64; Buried in New Bern National Cemetery, New Bern, N.C.

Powers, Charles. Residence: Barton. Enlistment Date: Sep 6, 64. Muster Date: Sep 6, 64; Mustered out Jun 13, 65.

Putney, John H. Residence: Barton. Enlistment Date: Jun 19, 62. Muster Date: Jul 9, 62. Deserted Jan 30, 63; Returned May 4, 64; Mustered out Jun 13, 65; Died Oct 6, 1907, and buried in the village cemetery, Brownington, Vt.

Rice, Rodney N. Residence: Newport. Enlistment Date: Jun 10, 62. Muster Date: Jul 9, 62. Mustered out Jun 13, 65.

Riley, Peter. Residence: Norwich. Enlistment Date: Sep 7, 64. Muster Date: Sep 7, 64. Transferred to Co. D, 11th Vt. Jan 20, 65.

Robbins, John E. Residence: Brownington. Enlistment Date: Jun 16, 62. Muster Date: Jul 9, 62. Discharged May 8, 63, for disability.

Roby, Fredric. Residence: Brunswick. Enlistment Date: Jan 1, 64. Muster Date: Jan 7, 64. Transferred to Co. B Jun 13, 65; Promoted to Corp. Jun 19, 65; Mustered out Dec 1, 65.

Rockwell, William T. Residence: Newport. Enlistment Date: Mar 13, 65. Muster Date: Mar 13, 65. Transferred to Co. B Jun 13, 65; Mustered out Dec 1, 65.

Rogers, Peter. Residence: Greensboro. Enlistment Date: Jun 9, 62. Muster Date: Jul 9, 62. Mustered out Jun 13, 65.

Rogers, Robert. Residence: Greensboro. Enlistment Date: Jun 2, 62. Muster Date: Jul 9, 62. Discharged Nov 6, 62, for disability.

Rollins, William H. Residence: Bethel. Enlistment Date: Dec 31, 63. Muster Date: Dec 31, 63. Transferred to Co. B Jun 13, 65; Mustered out Jul 7, 65.

Rush, George. Residence: Holland. Enlistment Date: Jun 10, 62. Muster Date: Jul 9, 62. Transferred to Co. I Jun 9, 64; Mustered out Jun 13, 65.

Ryder, Ziba E. Residence: Coventry. Enlistment Date: Jun 20, 62. Muster Date: Jul 9, 62. Deserted Jul 15, 62.

Shannon, Patrick. Residence: Charleston. Enlistment Date: Jun 13, 62. Muster Date: Jul 9, 62. Died Sep 14, 63; Buried in Yorktown National Cemetery, Yorktown, Va.

Shaw, Lowell. Residence: Albany. Enlistment Date: Aug 17, 64. Muster Date: Aug 17, 64. Mustered out Jun 13, 65.

Sias, Henry. Residence: Newport. Enlistment Date: Jun 13, 62. Muster Date: Jul 9, 62. Wounded Sep 29, 64; Mustered out Jun 13, 65; Died Oct 10, 1897, and buried in Dummer Cemetery, Dummer, N.H.

Spencer, Curtis. Residence: Salem. Enlistment Date: Jun 25, 62. Muster Date: Jul 9, 62. Died Oct 14, 63, of disease; Buried in Hampton National Cemetery, Hampton, Va.

Spencer, George A. Residence: Brownington. Enlistment Date: Jun 23, 62. Muster Date: Jul 9, 62. Discharged Jan 14, 63, for enlistment in the 14th U.S. Inf.; Died Jun 6, 1908, and buried in Lakeview Cemetery, Westmore, Vt.

Spencer, Horace. Residence: Salem. Enlistment Date: Jun 24, 62. Muster Date: Jul 9, 62. Mustered out Jun 13, 65.

Stone, Samuel A. Residence: Irasburgh. Enlistment Date: Jun 6, 62. Muster Date: Jul 9, 62. Mustered out Jun 13, 65; Died Apr 6, 1914, and buried in Eden Cemetery, Eden, Vt.

Stow, Sidney. Residence: Troy. Enlistment Date: Jun 5, 62. Muster Date: Jul 9, 62. Died Sep 27, 63.

Toushet, Andrew. Residence: Enosburgh. Enlistment Date: Jun 12, 62. Muster Date: Jul 9, 62. Deserted Dec 4, 62; Died Feb 27, 1898, and buried in New Catholic Cemetery, Enosburg, Vt.

Turner, Henry S. Residence: Derby. Enlistment Date: Jun 10, 62. Muster Date: Jul 9, 62. Promoted to Corp. Jun 5, 63; Discharged Jan 8, 64, for disability; Died May 9, 1864, and buried in Derby Center Cemetery, Derby, Vt.

Underwood, William C. Residence: Coventry. Enlistment Date: Jun 16, 62. Muster Date: Jul 9, 62. Discharged Nov 6, 62, for disability; Died May 19, 1884, and buried in Pleasant View Cemetery, Orleans, Vt.

Vandooer, Samuel. Residence: Pownal. Enlistment Date: Jan 4, 64. Muster Date: Jan 7, 64. Transferred to Co. B Jun 13, 65; Mustered out Dec 1, 65.

Walker, Gilbert D. Residence: Vershire. Enlistment Date: Jan 5, 64. Muster Date: Jan 5, 64. Discharged Jun 12, 65, for disability; Died Apr 1, 1895, and buried in the village cemetery, Albany, Vt.

Warboys, Charles N. Residence: Charleston. Enlistment Date: Jun 16, 62. Muster Date: Jul 9, 62. Mustered out Jun 13, 65; Died Oct 7, 1905, and buried in the village cemetery, West Charleston, Vt.

Warboys, Henry. Residence: Charleston. Enlistment Date: Jun 6, 62. Muster Date: Jul 9, 62. Promoted to Corp. Feb 2, 64; Wounded Sep 29, 64; Mustered out Jun 13, 65.

Ward, James O. Residence: Brownington. Enlistment Date: Jun 23, 62. Muster Date: Jul 9, 62. Died Sep 27, 63.

Ward, Joseph. Residence: Pomfret. Enlistment Date: Dec 19, 63. Muster Date: Dec 30, 63. Transferred to Co. B Jun 13, 65; Died Sep 4, 65, buried in North Troy Cemetery, North Troy, Vt.

Warner, William, Jr. Residence: Moretown. Enlistment Date: Dec 14, 63. Muster Date: Jan 2, 64. Discharged Nov 19, 64, by special order of the War Department.

Wells, George. Residence: Guilford. Enlistment Date: Dec 30, 63. Muster Date: Dec 30, 63. Transferred to Co. B Jun 13, 65; Died Nov 5, 65, of disease.

Whipple, Samuel N. Residence: Barton. Enlistment Date: Sep 3, 64. Muster Date: Sep 3, 64. Mustered out Jun 13, 65.

Whipple, Simon O. Residence: Enosburgh. Enlistment Date: Sep 1, 64. Muster Date: Sep 1, 64. Mustered out Jun 13, 65; Died Oct 12, 1907, and buried in Newport Center Cemetery, Newport Center, Vt.

White, Moses W. Residence: Irasburgh. Enlistment Date: Jun 25, 62. Muster Date: Jul 9, 62. Wounded Sep 29, 64; Mustered out Jun 13, 65; Died Jun 12, 1910, in Irasburg and buried there.

Whitman, Thomas H. Residence: Sunderland. Enlistment Date: Dec 14, 63. Muster Date: Dec 24, 63. Mustered out May 22, 65; Died Sep 13, 1927, and buried in Evergreen Cemetery, Arlington, Vt.

Wiggins, James A. Residence: Barton. Enlistment Date: Jun 19, 62. Muster Date: Jul 9, 62. Discharged May 11, 63, for disability.

Wilkerson, Rosell. Residence: Sunderland. Enlistment Date: Dec 11, 63. Muster Date: Dec 24, 63. Transferred to Co. B Jun 13, 65; Mustered out Jun 13, 65.

Wilson, Alvin W. Residence: Lyndon. Enlistment Date: Dec 25, 63. Muster Date: Dec 30, 63. Transferred to Co. B Jun 13, 65; Mustered out Aug 8, 65; Died Jan 31, 1927, and buried in Lyndon Center Cemetery, Lyndon, Vt.

Wilson, Calvin. Residence: Salem. Enlistment Date: Jun 16, 62. Muster Date: Jul 9, 62. Promoted to Corp. Oct 1, 64; Wounded Sep 29, 64; Mustered out Jun 13, 65; Died Dec 28, 1921, and buried in the village cemetery, West Charleston, Vt.

Wing, Stephen B. Residence: Wilmington. Enlistment Date: Jan 5, 64. Muster Date: Jan 5, 64. Died Oct 27, 64, of exhaustion.

Woodward, John S. Residence: Enosburgh. Enlistment Date: Sep 1, 64. Muster Date: Sep 1, 64. Transferred to Co. F, 11th Vt. Jan 20, 65.

Company F

Captains

Beebe, George A. Residence: Burlington. Commission Date: Jun 25, 62. Issue Date: Jun 25, 62. Died Aug 10, 62, of disease, and buried in North Gore Cemetery, Highgate, Vt.

Brooks, Joseph C. Residence: Westminster. Commission Date: Nov 17, 62. Issue Date: Nov 17, 62. *See* Maj.

Bascom, John T. Residence: Milton. Commission Date: May 8, 64. Issue Date: May 30, 64. Pvt. Co. C 2nd Vt.; promoted to Second Lt. Co. F 9th Vt.; Jun 25, 62; to First Lt. Co. F Dec 22, 63; Mustered out Mar 9, 65; Died Apr 30, 1880, and buried in the village cemetery, Milton, Vt.

Hobon, Patrick. Residence: Brandon. Commission Date: Mar 13, 65. Issue Date: Apr 6, 65. Corp. Co. C; Promoted to Sgt.; to First Sgt.; to Second Lt. Co. 1 Jun 22, 63; to First Lt. Co. F May 8, 64; Transferred to Co. B Jun 13, 65; Mustered out Dec 1, 65.

First Lieutenants

Viele, Eugene. Residence: Hinesburgh. Commission Date: Jun 25, 62. Issue Date: Jun 25, 62. *See* Capt. Co. I.

Bascom, John T. Residence: Milton. Commission Date: Dec 22, 63. Issue Date: Feb 1, 64. *See* Capt. Co. F.

Hobon, Patrick. Residence: Brandon. Commission Date: May 8, 64. Issue Date: May 30, 64. *See* Capt. Co. F.

Brownell, Elias L. Residence: Essex. Commission Date: Mar 13, 65. Issue Date: Apr 6, 65. *See* Capt. Co. C.

Second Lieutenants

Bascom, John T. Residence: Milton. Commission Date: Jun 25, 62. Issue Date: Jun 25, 62. *See* Capt. Co. F.

Brownell, Elias L. Residence: Essex. Commission Date: Dec 22, 63. Issue Date: Feb 1, 64. *See* Capt. Co. C.

Thomas, John W. Residence: Burlington. Commission Date: Mar 13, 65. Issue Date: Apr 6, 65. *See* First Lt. Co. B.

Sergeants

Belden, Henry D. Residence: Burlington. Enlistment Date: Jun 2, 62. Muster Date: Jul 9, 62. *See* Adj.

Barker, Jared. Residence: Hinesburgh. Enlistment Date: Jun 1, 62. Muster Date: Jul 9, 62. Discharged Oct 25, 62.

Russell, Edward B. Residence: Jericho. Enlistment Date: Jun 4, 62. Muster Date: Jul 9, 62. Deserted Nov 30, 62.

Williams, Nathan A. Residence: Essex. Enlistment Date: Jun 9, 62. Muster Date: Jul 9, 62. Reduced ; Transferred to V. R. C. Feb 15, 64; Discharged May 21, 64.

Corporals

Parks, Clark L. Residence: Charlotte. Enlistment Date: May 29, 62. Muster Date: Jul 9, 62. Promoted to Sgt.; to First Sgt. Dec 1, 62; Reduced to Fourth Sgt. Jan 23, 63; Promoted to First Sgt. Feb 12, 64; Mustered out Jun 13, 65.

Brownell, Elias L. Residence: Essex. Enlistment Date: Jun 11, 62. Muster Date: Jul 9, 62. *See* Capt. Co. C.

Shedd, Lorenzo W. Residence: Richmond. Enlistment Date: Jun 23, 62. Muster Date: Jul 9, 62. Promoted to Sgt.; Discharged Nov 10, 63, for promotion in U. S. C. T; Died Sep 24, 1910, and buried in Green Mount Cemetery, Montpelier, Vt.

Lord, George E. Residence: Burlington. Enlistment Date: Jun 2, 62. Muster Date: Jul 9, 62. Promoted to Sgt. Feb 12, 64; Died Mar 7, 64, of disease in Sloan General Hospital and buried in Elmwood Ave. Cemetery, Burlington, Vt.

Newton, John L. Residence: Burlington. Enlistment Date: Jun 2, 62. Muster Date: Jul 9, 62. Deserted Jan 4, 63; Returned Feb 23, 63; Died Oct 27, 64, of wounds received Sep 29, 64; Buried in Cypress Hills National Cemetery, Brooklyn, N.Y.

Clark, John. Residence: Huntington. Enlistment Date: Jun 19, 62. Muster Date: Jul 9, 62. Deserted Oct 5, 62.

Stearns, Alonzo B. Residence: Charlotte. Enlistment Date: Jun 2, 62. Muster Date: Jul 9, 62. Discharged Oct 23, 62; Died Apr 17, 1905, and buried in Morningside Cemetery, East Charlotte, Vt.

Blake, Alson H. Residence: Milton. Enlistment Date: May 29, 62. Muster Date: Jul 9, 62. Taken prisoner Feb 2, 64; Paroled Apr 28, 65; Mustered out May 23, 65.

Musician

Walker, Loren S. Residence: Hinesburgh. Enlistment Date: Jun 1, 62. Muster Date: Jul 9, 62. Discharged Mar 18, 63; Died Jul 31, 1888, and buried in Briggs Hill Cemetery, Bristol, Vt.

Wagoner

Witherby, Leonard S. Residence: Essex. Enlistment Date: Jun 2, 62. Muster Date: Jul 9,62. Discharged Oct 23, 62; Jan 12, 1891, and buried in the village cemetery, Essex Junction, Vt.

Privates

Adams, Everett E. Residence: Manchester. Enlistment Date: Jan 4, 64. Muster Date: Jan 5, 64. Mustered out May 25, 65.

Adams, Lucius C. Residence: Wilmington. Enlistment Date: Jan 5, 64. Muster Date: Jan 5, 64. Transferred to Co. B Jun 13, 65; Died Dec 11, 65.

Allen, Warren. Residence: Newfane. Enlistment Date: Aug 23, 64. Muster Date: Aug 23, 64. Mustered out Jun 13, 65.

Ash, Samuel B. Residence: Hinesburgh. Enlistment Date: Jun 9, 62. Muster Date: Jul 9, 62. Deserted Jan 4, 63.

Atkins, Almon. Residence: Richmond. Enlistment Date: Jun 17, 62. Muster Date: Jul 9, 62. Died Sep 2, 62, of disease.

Austin, John. Residence: Hinesburgh. Enlistment Date: Jun 9, 62. Muster Date: Jul 9, 62. Deserted Dec 20, 62; Returned Feb 7, 63; Mustered out Jun 13, 65.

Baisnor, Carlos. Residence: Hinesburgh. Enlistment Date: Aug 17, 64. Muster Date: Aug 17, 64. Mustered out Jun 13, 65; Died Mar 17, 1905, and buried in the village cemetery, Hinesburg, Vt.

Ball, Daniel S. Residence: Charlotte. Enlistment Date: Jun 2, 62. Muster Date: Jul 9, 62. Died Nov 23, 63, of disease and buried in Hollow Road Cemetery, Lunenburg, Vt.

Barker, Jared. Residence: Hinesburgh. Enlistment Date: Dec 31, 63. Muster Date: Jan 4, 64. Transferred to Co. B Jun 13, 65; Mustered out Dec 1, 65; Died Dec 10, 1893, and buried in Barker Cemetery, Hinesburg, Vt.

Barnes, Edward P. Residence: Bethel. Enlistment Date: Aug 23, 64. Muster Date: Aug 23, 64. Mustered out Jun 13, 65; Died Apr 24, 1904, and buried in South View Cemetery, Randolph, Vt.

Beauchine, John. Residence: Montreal, Can. Enlistment Date: Jun 21, 62. Muster Date: Jul 9, 62. Deserted Dec 11, 62.

Belden, Zachary T. Residence: Waterford. Enlistment Date: Sep 2, 64. Muster Date: Sep 2, 64. Mustered out Jun 13, 65.

Bennett, Charles. Residence: Hinesburgh. Enlistment Date: Jun 9, 62. Muster Date: Jul 9, 62. Taken prisoner Feb 2, 64, and died at Andersonville, Ga., Dec 15, 64; Buried in Andersonville National Cemetery, Andersonville, Ga.; Memorial stone in Barker Cemetery, Hinesburg, Vt.

Bissonette, Lewis. Residence: Hinesburgh. Enlistment Date: Dec 17, 63. Muster Date: Jan 4, 64. Transferred to V.R.C. Apr 26, 65; Mustered out Nov 18, 65.

Bixby, William H. Residence: Underhill. Enlistment Date: Jun 18, 62. Muster Date: Jul 9, 62. Promoted to Corp. Jun 9, 64; Mustered out Jun 13, 65.

Blair, Lewis. Residence: Pomfret. Enlistment Date: Aug 1, 64. Muster Date: Aug 9, 64. Died Nov 30, 64, of wounds received Sep 29, 64; Buried in Hampton National Cemetery, Hampton, Va.

Blanchard, Edward. Residence: Windsor. Enlistment Date: Jul 26, 64. Muster Date: Aug 2, 64. Taken prisoner Oct 27, 64, and died at Salisbury, N.C., Dec 24, 64; Buried in Salisbury National Cemetery, Salisbury, N.C.

Bowen, Azro B. Residence: Bethel. Enlistment Date: Aug 30, 64. Muster Date: Aug 30, 64. Mustered out Jun 13, 65; Died Aug 3, 1933, and buried in South View Cemetery, Randolph, Vt.

Bowen, James F. Residence: Royalton. Enlistment Date: Jul 12, 62. Muster Date: Jul 12, 62. Died Oct 10, 63, of disease.

Bradley, Henry S. Residence: Essex. Enlistment Date: Jun 14, 62. Muster Date: Jul 9, 62. Died Oct 1, 62, of disease.

Bradley, Michael. Residence: New York City, N.Y. Enlistment Date: Jun 25, 62. Muster Date: Jul 9, 62. Promoted to Corp. Feb 12, 64; Reduced Mar 16, 64; Mustered out Jun 13, 65.

Briggs, Gordon N. Residence: Whiting. Enlistment Date: Feb 25, 65. Muster Date: Feb 25, 65. *See* Second Lt. Co. B.

Brown, Charles T. Residence: Winhall. Enlistment Date: Nov 30, 63. Muster Date: Dec 17, 63. Transferred to Co. B Jun 13, 65; Mustered out Dec 1, 65.

Bruce, David R. Residence: Granby. Enlistment Date: Jan 2, 64. Muster Date: Jan 7, 64. Died Mar 4, 64, of disease.

Bryant, Calvin R. Residence: Peru. Enlistment Date: Aug 4, 64. Muster Date: Aug 4, 64. Mustered out Jun 13, 65.

Bryant, Leroy L. Residence: Wardsboro. Enlistment Date: Jan 5, 64. Muster Date: Jan 21, 64. KIA Sep 29, 64; Buried in Fort Harrison National Cemetery, Richmond, Va.

Burley, John. Residence: Hinesburgh. Enlistment Date: Aug 25, 64. Muster Date: Aug 25, 64. Mustered out Jun 13, 65; Died Jul 29, 1934, and buried in Hinesburg Cemetery, Hinesburg, Vt.

Burtch, William A. Residence: Westford. Enlistment Date: Jun 3, 62. Muster Date: Jul 9, 62. Promoted to Sgt.; Discharged Apr 10, 63.

Buzier, Antoine. Residence: Hinesburgh. Enlistment Date: Jun 2, 62. Muster Date: Jul 9, 62. Deserted Sep 18, 62.

Buzier, John. Residence: Hinesburgh. Enlistment Date: Jun 2, 62. Muster Date: Jul 9, 62. Deserted Dec 11, 62.

Callaghan, James. Residence: Hinesburgh. Enlistment Date: Jun 5, 62. Muster Date: Jul 9, 62. Promoted to Corp. Jun 9, 64; Reduced Jul 5, 64; Mustered out Jun 13, 65.

Callaghan, Thomas. Residence: Underhill. Enlistment Date: Jun 24, 62. Muster Date: Jul 9, 62. Promoted to Corp. Feb 17, 64; Reduced Aug 25, 64; Mustered out Jun 13, 65.

Campbell, Joseph. Residence: Isle La Mott. Enlistment Date: Jun 24, 62. Muster Date: Jul 9, 62. Deserted Dec 20, 62; Returned Feb 7, 63; Mustered out Jun 13, 65; Died Mar 30, 1883, and buried in Holy Cross Cemetery, St. Albans, Vt.

Caples, Thomas. Residence: Westfield. Enlistment Date: Aug 18, 64. Muster Date: Aug 18, 64. Died Nov 1, 64, of disease; Buried in Hampton National Cemetery, Hampton, Va.

Carpenter, James M. Residence: Hinesburgh. Enlistment Date: Jun 14, 62. Muster Date: Jul 9, 62. Promoted to Corp. Dec 1, 62; Reduced Jan 7, 64; Mustered out Jun 13, 65; Died Feb 11, 1917, and buried in Maplewood Cemetery, Huntington, Vt.

Carr, Anson K. Residence: Rutland. Enlistment Date: Aug 16, 64. Muster Date: Aug 16, 64. Mustered out Jun 13, 65; Died Apr 19, 1915, and buried in West Cemetery, Middlebury, Vt.

Carr, Columbus N. Residence: Georgia. Enlistment Date: Jun 20, 62. Muster Date: Jul 9, 62. Died Nov 29, 62, of disease.

Carr, Nelson H. Residence: Georgia. Enlistment Date: Jun 23, 62. Muster Date: Jul 9, 62. Deserted Jan 4,

63; Returned under Presidential proclamation Apr 15, 65; Transferred to Co. B Jun 13, 65; Mustered out Dec 1, 65; Died 1911, and buried in Georgia Plains Cemetery, Georgia, Vt.

Caswell, Homer B. Residence: Milton. Enlistment Date: Dec 28, 63. Muster Date: Jan 6, 64. Transferred to Co. B Jun 13, 65; Mustered out Dec 1, 65; Died Oct 15, 1935, and buried in Evergreen Ledge Cemetery, Johnson, Vt.

Chase, Kinsman P. Residence: Bolton. Enlistment Date: Aug 13, 64. Muster Date: Aug 13, 64. Mustered out Jun 13, 65; Died Jul 6, 1866, and buried in West Bolton Cemetery, West Bolton, Vt.

Clapper, Clufus. Residence: Milton. Enlistment Date: Jul 4, 62. Muster Date: Jul 9, 62. Deserted Oct 6, 62.

Clark, John K. Residence: Shaftsbury. Enlistment Date: Dec 12, 63. Muster Date: Dec 24, 63. Taken prisoner Feb 2, 64; Paroled Nov 24, 64; Transferred to V. R. C. Mar 1, 65; Mustered out Jul 25, 65.

Clinton, Charles. Residence: Rutland. Enlistment Date: Aug 30, 64. Muster Date: Aug 30, 64. Transferred to Co. B Jun 13, 65; Deserted Aug 18, 65.

Cobb, Edson R. Residence: Huntington. Enlistment Date: Jun 21, 62. Muster Date: Jul 9, 62. Died Nov 10, 63, of disease.

Cobb, George W. Residence: Huntington. Enlistment Date: Jun 21, 62. Muster Date: Jul 9, 62. Discharged Oct 14, 62, for disability.

Coburn, George A. Residence: Wilmington. Enlistment Date: Jan 5, 64. Muster Date: Jan 5, 64. Promoted to Corp. Aug 8, 64; to Sgt. Apr 27, 65; Transferred to Co. B Jun 13, 65; Mustered out Dec 1, 65.

Curavoo, Antoine. Residence: Hinesburgh. Enlistment Date: Jun 13, 62. Muster Date: Jul 9, 62. Mustered out Jun 13, 65; Died Apr 18, 1911, and buried in the village cemetery, Hinesburg, Vt.

Dapo, Henry. Residence: Essex. Enlistment Date: Aug 25, 64. Muster Date: Aug 25, 64. Mustered out Jun 13, 65.

Davis, Daniel. Residence: Underhill. Enlistment Date: Aug 17, 64. Muster Date: Aug 17, 64. Mustered out Jun 13, 65; Died Nov 23, 1930, and buried in West Bolton Cemetery, West Bolton, Vt.

Emerson, Hollis M. Residence: Lyndon. Enlistment Date: Dec 16, 63. Muster Date: Dec 23, 63. Mustered out May 13, 65.

Emerson, Moses. Residence: Burke. Enlistment Date: Dec 14, 63. Muster Date: Dec 23, 63. Discharged May 26, 65, for disability; Died Jan 12, 1881, and buried in Woodmont Cemetery, Burke, Vt.

Faneuf, Dostie, Jr. Residence: Hartford. Enlistment Date: Aug 10, 64. Muster Date: Aug 12, 64. Mustered out Jun 13, 65; Died Dec 26, 1896, and buried in the village cemetery, Royalton, Vt.

Fifield, Freeman. Residence: Bethel. Enlistment Date: Nov 23, 63. Muster Date: Nov 23, 63. Transferred to Co. B Jun 13, 65; Discharged Oct 24, 65, for disability.

Fletcher, William W. Residence: Colchester. Enlistment Date: Jun 17, 62. Muster Date: Jul 9, 62. Promoted to Corp. Feb 12, 64; to Sgt. Jan 1, 65; Mustered out Jun 13, 65.

Foss, Daniel A. Residence: Hinesburgh. Enlistment Date: Jun 23, 62. Muster Date: Jul 9, 62. Transferred to V.R.C. Apr 20, 64; Mustered out Sep 5, 65; Died Apr 3, 1898, and buried in Barnes Cemetery, Hyde Park, Vt.

Fox, James S. Residence: Ira. Enlistment Date: Aug 15, 64. Muster Date: Aug 15, 64. Mustered out Jun 13, 65.

Fry, William T. Residence: Wells. Enlistment Date: Jan 1, 64. Muster Date: Jan 1, 64. Promoted to Corp. Oct 26, 64; Transferred to Co. B Jun 13, 65; Mustered out Dec 1, 65.

Furlong, Patrick. Residence: Hinesburgh. Enlistment Date: Dec 18, 63. Muster Date: Jan 4, 64. Transferred to Co. B Jun 13, 65; Mustered out Dec 1, 65.

Gall, John. Residence: Hinesburgh. Enlistment Date: Aug 4, 64. Muster Date: Aug 4, 64. Transferred to Co. B Jun 13, 65; Mustered out Dec 1, 65.

Gorton, Amos O. Residence: Huntington. Enlistment Date: Jun 21, 62. Muster Date: Jul 9, 62. Discharged Oct 3, 62.

Hawley, Thomas. Residence: Milton. Enlistment Date: Dec 29, 63. Muster Date: Jan 6, 64. Died Oct 21, 64, of disease; Buried in New Bern National Cemetery, New Bern, N.C.

Hemery, Peter. Residence: Norwich. Enlistment Date: Dec 21, 63. Muster Date: Jan 7, 64. Transferred to Co. B Jun 13, 65; Mustered out Dec 1, 65.

Hoffman, Henry F. Residence: Burke. Enlistment Date: Dec 11, 63. Muster Date: Dec 23, 63. Transferred to Co. B Jun 13, 65; Mustered out Dec 1, 65; Died Oct 16, 1881, and buried in Pleasant View Cemetery, Newark, Vt.

Hood, Charles. Residence: Albany. Enlistment Date: Aug 17, 64. Muster Date: Aug 17, 64. Transferred to Co. C, 2nd Vt., Jan 20, 65; Died Feb 27, 1901, and buried in East Albany Cemetery, Albany, Vt.

Hosford, Orwell J. Residence: Barre. Enlistment Date: Aug 19, 64. Muster Date: Aug 19, 64. Mustered out Jun 13, 65; Died Mar 2, 1921, and buried in West Bolton Cemetery, West Bolton, Vt.

Hudson, George L. Residence: Lyndon. Enlistment Date: Dec 7, 63. Muster Date: Dec 23, 63. Mustered out Jun 22, 65; Died Feb 26, 1904, and buried in Westlook Cemetery, Glover, Vt.

Humphrey, Charles P. Residence: Burke. Enlistment Date: Nov 30, 63. Muster Date: Dec 23, 63. Transferred to Co. B Jun 13, 65; Promoted to Corp. Jul 26, 65; to Sgt. Oct 13, 65; Mustered out Dec 1, 65.

Humphrey, George W. Residence: Burke. Enlistment Date: Aug 4, 64. Muster Date: Aug 4, 64. Mustered out Jun 13, 65; Died Jan 3, 1908, and buried in East Burke Cemetery, East Burke, Vt.

Jones, John E. Residence: Randolph. Enlistment Date: Aug 30, 64. Muster Date: Aug 30, 64. Wounded Sep 29, 64; Transferred to Co. C, 2nd Vt., Jan 20, 65.

Kelley, William. Residence: St. Johns, Canada. Enlistment Date: Jun 23, 62. Muster Date: Jul 9, 62. Promoted to Corp.; Deserted Mar 24, 63.

Kimball, William W. Residence: Huntington. Enlistment Date: Jun 18, 62. Muster Date: Jul 9, 62. Discharged Apr 10, 63.

King, John. Residence: Milton. Enlistment Date: Jun 23, 62. Muster Date: Jul 9, 62. Promoted to Corp. Sep 2, 63; to Sgt. Feb 12, 64; Reduced Mar 16, 65; Mustered out Jun 13, 65.

Laddy, William. Residence: Shelburne. Enlistment Date: Dec 30, 63. Muster Date: Jan 4, 64. Transferred to Co. B Jun 13, 65; Mustered out Dec 1, 65; Died Dec 22, 1934, and buried in Grand View Cemetery, Addison, Vt.

Ladoue, John. Residence: Milton. Enlistment Date: Jun 12, 62. Muster Date: Jul 9, 62. Died Apr 17, 63, of disease; Buried in Hampton National Cemetery, Hampton, Va.

Lakin, Thomas J. Residence: Peru. Enlistment Date: Dec 9, 63. Muster Date: Dec 17, 63. Discharged May 20, 65, for disability.

Lawrence, Morris S. Residence: Hinesburgh. Enlistment Date: Dec 18, 63. Muster Date: Dec 31, 63. Mustered out Jun 22, 65.

Lincoln, Clarence B. Residence: Peru. Enlistment Date: Dec 9, 63. Muster Date: Dec 17, 63. Died Oct 3, 64, of disease; Buried in New Bern National Cemetery, New Bern, N.C.

Luce, Jabez. Residence: Chelsea. Enlistment Date: Aug 20, 64. Muster Date: Aug 20, 64. Transferred to Co. C, 4th Vt., Jan 20, 65; Died Jan 4, 1894, and buried in Highland Cemetery, Chelsea, Vt.

Mansfield, Seth A. Residence: Essex. Enlistment Date: Dec 4, 63. Muster Date: Dec 16, 63. Promoted to Corp. Aug 27, 64; Transferred to Co. B Jun 13, 65; Promoted to Sgt. Jul 1, 65; Mustered out Dec 1, 65.

Marshall, Henry C. Residence: Windham. Enlistment Date: Dec 16, 63. Muster Date: Dec 22, 63. Transferred to Co. B Jun 13, 65; Mustered out Dec 1, 65.

Martin, Frank. Residence: Pomfret. Enlistment Date: Aug 1, 64. Muster Date: Aug 9, 64. Mustered out Jun 13, 65.

Massey, Jerry. Residence: Underhill. Enlistment Date: Jun 17, 62. Muster Date: Jul 9, 62. Promoted to Corp. Oct 26, 64; Mustered out Jun 13, 65; Died Dec 10, 1895, and buried in St. Ann Cemetery, Milton, Vt.

Mayville, Peter. Residence: Milton. Enlistment Date: Jul 4, 62. Muster Date: Jul 9, 62. Deserted Oct 6, 62.

Melcher, William. Residence: Burke. Enlistment Date: Dec 7, 63. Muster Date: Dec 23, 63. Wounded and taken prisoner Feb 2, 64, and died at Andersonville, Ga. Aug 30, 64; Buried in Andersonville National Cemetery, Andersonville, Ga.

Monger, Simon F. Residence: Colchester. Enlistment Date: Jun 23, 62. Muster Date: Jul 9, 62. Discharged May 26, 64, for disability.

Morey, George. Residence: Norwich. Enlistment Date: Dec 25, 63. Muster Date: Jan 7, 64. Transferred to Co. B Jun 13, 65; Mustered out Dec 1, 65.

Morey, Robert R. Residence: Norwich. Enlistment Date: Dec 19, 63. Muster Date: Jan 7, 64. Transferred to Co. B Jun 13, 65; Mustered out Dec 1, 65.

Moultroup, Obadiah. Residence: Burke. Enlistment Date: Dec 7, 63. Muster Date: Dec 23, 63. Transferred to Co. B Jun 13, 65; Mustered out Dec 1, 65.

Moynan, Thomas. Residence: Can. Enlistment Date: Sep 13, 64. Muster Date: Sep 13, 64. Substitute for C.H. Simpson, Castleton; Mustered out Jun 13, 65; Died Oct 27, 64; Buried in Cypress Hills National Cemetery, Brooklyn, N.Y.

Nichols, Silas. Residence: Hinesburgh. Enlistment Date: Jun 9, 62. Muster Date: Jul 9, 62. Died Oct 9, 63, of disease; Buried in Hampton National Cemetery, Hampton, Va.

Nickerson, John. Residence: Montreal, Can. Enlistment Date: Jun 28, 62. Muster Date: Jul 9, 62. Deserted Oct 6, 62; Returned Mar 27, 63; KIA Sep 29, 64; Buried in Fort Harrison National Cemetery, Richmond, Va.

Norris, George E. Residence: Burke. Enlistment Date: Feb 20, 65. Muster Date: Feb 20, 65. Transferred to Co. B Jun 13, 65; Died Sep 9, 65, of disease.

Otis, William A. Residence: Au Sable Forks, N.Y. Enlistment Date: Jun 7, 62. Muster Date: Jul 9, 62. Deserted Jan 1, 63.

Owen, Harry W. Residence: Wilmington, N.Y. Enlistment Date: Jun 14, 62. Muster Date: Jul 9, 62. Promoted to Corp. Feb 12, 64; Reduced Oct 26, 64; Mustered out Jun 13, 65.

Packard, Wright. Residence: Georgia. Enlistment Date: Jun 23, 62. Muster Date: Jul 9, 62. Died Feb 18, 63, of disease; Buried in Rosehill Cemetery, Chicago, Ill.

Page, William, Jr. Residence: Corinth. Enlistment Date: Dec 17, 63. Muster Date: Dec 31, 63. *See* Commissary Sgt.

Parker, Stephen. Residence: Hinesburgh. Enlistment Date: June 23, 62. Muster Date: Jul 9, 62. Died Aug 10, 62, of disease.

Parkhurst, Lyman D. Residence: Barre. Enlistment Date: Aug 23, 64. Muster Date: Aug 23, 64. Transferred to Co. G, 5th Vt. Jan 20, 65; Died Oct 5, 1929, and buried in Highland Cemetery, Chelsea, Vt.

Patridge, Cyrus. Residence: Wilmington. Enlistment Date: Jun 21, 62. Muster Date: Jul 9, 62. Died Dec 9, 62, of disease.

Patrick, George W. Residence: Hinesburg. Enlistment Date: Jun 16, 62. Muster Date: Jul 9, 62. Deserted Jan 4, 63; Returned Jan 31, 63; KIA Sep 29, 64; Buried in Hinesburg Cemetery, Hinesburg, Vt.

Penfield, John W. Residence: Peru. Enlistment Date: Aug 4, 64. Muster Date: Aug 4, 64. Mustered out Jun 13, 65.

Penfield, William A. Residence: Peru. Enlistment Date: Aug 4, 64. Muster Date: Aug 4, 64. Mustered out Jun 13, 65.

Peppin, Joseph. Residence: Essex. Enlistment Date: Jun 6, 62. Muster Date: Jul 9, 62. Promoted to Corp. Jan 1, 65; Mustered out Jun 13, 65; Died Jan 8, 1914, and buried in Mountain View Cemetery, Essex Center, Vt.

Perry, Charles H. Residence: Orange. Enlistment Date: Jan 2, 64. Muster Date: Jan 6, 64. Promoted to Corp. Jun 29, 64; to Sgt. Mar 17, 65; to First Sgt. June 19, 65; Transferred to Co. B Jun 13, 65; Mustered out Dec 1, 65.

Perry, Leander. Residence: Barre. Enlistment Date: Aug 4, 64. Muster Date: Aug 4, 64. Died May 16, 65, of disease; Buried in Richmond National Cemetery, Richmond, Va.

Phillips, David C. Residence: Hinesburgh. Enlistment Date: Jun 5, 62. Muster Date: Jul 9, 62. Taken prisoner Sep 3, 62; Paroled Oct 2, 62; Mustered out Jun 13, 65.

Prentice, Clark. Residence: Colchester. Enlistment Date: Jan 1, 64. Muster Date: Jan 4, 64. Mustered out May 13, 65.

Prescott, Freedom D. Residence: Lyndon. Enlistment Date: Dec 21, 63. Muster Date: Dec 30, 63. Transferred to Co. B Jun 13, 65; Mustered out Dec 1, 65.

Preston, James M. Residence: Bethel. Enlistment Date: Aug 1, 64. Muster Date: Aug 1, 64. Mustered out Jun 13, 65.

Quackenbush, John P. Residence: Peru. Enlistment Date: Dec 8, 63. Muster Date: Jan 5, 64. Died Apr 29, 65, of disease; Buried in City Point National Cemetery, Hopewell, Va.

Radford, James. Residence: Montreal, Can. Enlistment Date: Jun 16, 62. Muster Date: Jul 9, 62. Deserted Dec 20, 62.

Rawson, Julius. Residence: Burlington. Enlistment Date: Jun 7, 62. Muster Date: Jul 9, 62. Promoted to Corp. Apr 27, 65; Mustered out Jun 13, 65.

Raymond, Joseph. Residence: Bolton. Enlistment Date: Jun 14, 62. Muster Date: Jul 9, 62. Discharged Nov 25, 62; Died Feb 5, 1913, and buried in Catholic Cemetery, Randolph, Vt.

Reynolds, Herbert G. Residence: Milton. Enlistment Date: May 29, 62. Muster Date: Jul 9, 62. Discharged Mar 31, 63.

Rice, Franklin E. Residence: Isle La Mott. Enlistment Date: Jun 17, 62. Muster Date: Jul 9, 62. *See* Quartermaster.

Robbins, James P. Residence: Hinesburgh. Enlistment Date: Jun 5, 62. Muster Date: Jul 9, 62. Promoted to Corp. Apr 7, 65; Mustered out Jun 13, 65; Died Feb 21, 1905, and buried in West Cemetery, New Haven, Vt.

Rogers, Albert E. Residence: Richford. Enlistment Date: Jun 30, 62. Muster Date: Jul 9, 62. Mustered out Jun 13, 65.

Rogers, William B. Residence: Westford. Enlistment Date: Dec 29, 63. Muster Date: Jan 4, 64. Died Mar 4, 64, of disease and buried in Brookside Cemetery, Westford, Vt.

Sadlier, John. Residence: Hinesburgh. Enlistment Date: Aug 8, 64. Muster Date: Aug 8, 64. Mustered out Jun 13, 65.

Salter, Alonzo L. Residence: Windham. Enlistment Date: Dec 19, 63. Muster Date: Dec 22, 63. Transferred to Co. B Jun 13, 65; Mustered out Nov 15, 65.

Sawyer, Alfred F. Residence: Essex. Enlistment Date: Jun 9, 62. Muster Date: Jul 9, 62. Died Aug 30, 62, of disease.

Sawyer, Henry O. Residence: Milton. Enlistment Date: Jun 30, 62. Muster Date: Jul 9, 62. Deserted Dec 23, 62.

Scott, James. Residence: Pomfret. Enlistment Date: Aug 4, 64. Muster Date: Aug 9, 64. Mustered out Jun 13, 65; Died Aug 31, 1919, and buried in Danville Green Cemetery, Danville, Vt.

Sears, Edward. Residence: Monkton. Enlistment Date: Aug 25, 64. Muster Date: Aug 25, 64. Mustered out Jun 13, 65.

Sears, Francis. Residence: Hinesburgh. Enlistment Date: Aug 27, 64. Muster Date: Aug 27, 64. Mustered out Jun 13, 65; Died Sep 10, 1876, and buried in Morningside Cemetery, East Charlotte, Vt.

Sears, George. Residence: Shelburne. Enlistment Date: Sep 1, 64. Muster Date: Sep 1, 64. Transferred to Co. D, 4th Vt. Jan 20, 65.

Sibley, J. Nelson. Residence: Westford. Enlistment Date: Jun 7, 62. Muster Date: Jul 9, 62. Promoted to Sgt. Dec 1, 62; Reduced Sep 12, 64; Mustered out May 13, 65; Died Jan 4, 1880, and buried in Green Mountain Cemetery, Burlington, Vt.

Simeno, Godefroi. Residence: St. Hugar, Can. Enlistment Date: Jun 21, 62. Muster Date: Jul 9, 62. Mustered out Jun 13, 65.

Simonds, Albert J. Residence: Peru. Enlistment Date: Dec 9, 63. Muster Date: Dec 17, 63. Transferred to Co. B Jun 13, 65; Mustered out Dec 1, 65; Died Jul 26, 1924, and buried in the village cemetery, Peru, Vt.

Sleeper, John H. Residence: Chelsea. Enlistment Date: Aug 16, 64. Muster Date: Aug 16, 64. Transferred to Co. C, 2nd Vt. Jan 20, 65.

Smith, Oglander. Residence: Lyndon. Enlistment Date: Nov 30, 63. Muster Date: Dec 30, 63. Transferred to Co. B Jun 13, 65; Mustered out Dec 1, 65; Died Sep 22, 1897, and buried in Woodmount Cemetery, Burke, Vt.

Steady, Eugene. Residence: Monkton. Enlistment Date: Dec 29, 63. Muster Date: Dec 31, 63. Transferred to Co. B Jun 13, 65; Mustered out Dec 1, 65; Died May 28, 1902, and buried in Lakeview Cemetery, Burlington, Vt.

Steady, Henry. Residence: Hinesburgh. Enlistment Date: Dec 12, 63. Muster Date: Dec 23, 63. Promoted to Corp. Jul 6, 64; to Sgt. Jun 26, 65; Wounded Sep 29, 64; Transferred to Co. B Jun 13, 65; Mustered out Dec 1, 65; Died May 3, 1912.

Steady, Lewis. Residence: Bristol. Enlistment Date: Aug 17, 64. Muster Date: Aug 17, 64. Mustered out Jun 13, 65; Died Dec 1879, and buried in Lakeview Cemetery, Burlington, Vt.

Steady, Lewis, Jr. Residence: Bristol. Enlistment Date: Dec 4, 63. Muster Date: Dec 31, 63. Transferred to Co. B Jun 13, 65; Mustered out Nov 15, 65.

Steady, Muty. Residence: Hinesburgh. Enlistment Date: Aug 17, 64. Muster Date: Aug 17, 64. Mustered out Jun 13, 65; Died May 5, 1902, and buried in Mountain View Cemetery, Essex Center, Vt.

Steady, Timothy. Residence: Hinesburgh. Enlistment Date: Jun 10, 62. Muster Date: Jul 9, 62. Deserted; Returned Jan 15, 63; Mustered out Jun 13, 65; Died Sep 11, 1899, and buried in Lakeview Cemetery, Burlington, Vt.

Stone, William. Residence: Strafford. Enlistment Date: Aug 31, 64. Muster Date: Aug 31, 64. Transferred to Co. C, 4th Vt. Jan 20, 65; Died Apr 2, 1915, and buried in Elmwood Cemetery, Northfield, Vt.

Sweeny, Eli. Residence: Hinesburgh. Enlistment Date: Aug 18, 64. Muster Date: Aug 18, 64. MIA Sep 29, 64.

Taft, Benoni. Residence: Richmond. Enlistment Date: Jun 14, 62. Muster Date: Jul 9, 62. Died May 23, 64, of disease.

Taft, Sanborn. Residence: Starksboro. Enlistment Date: Jun 10, 62. Muster Date: Jul 9, 62. Discharged Oct 22, 62.

Tatro, Alfred. Residence: Charlotte. Enlistment Date: Dec 29, 63. Muster Date: Dec 31, 63. Wounded and taken prisoner Feb 2, 64, and died at Andersonville, Ga., Aug 16, 64; Buried in Andersonville National Cemetery, Andersonville, Ga.

Tatro, Andrew. Residence: Underhill. Enlistment Date: Jun 17, 62. Muster Date: Jul 9, 62. Transferred to V.R.C. Feb 15, 64; Discharged Apr 13, 65; Died Apr 2, 1889, and buried in Pascoage, R.I.

Tatro, Edward. Residence: Bethel. Enlistment Date: Aug 23, 64. Muster Date: Aug 23, 64. Transferred to Co. D, 11th Vt. Jan 20, 65.

Thomas, John W. Residence: Burlington. Enlistment Date: Jul 21, 63. Muster Date: Jul 27, 63. *See* First Lt. Co. B.

Thompson, Columbus. Residence: Colchester. Enlistment Date: Jun 10, 62. Muster Date: Jul 9, 62. Discharged Apr 10, 63; Died Jun 24, 1881, and buried in United Cemetery, Colchester, Vt.

Thurber, Stephen L. Residence: Burke. Enlistment Date: Dec 17, 63. Muster Date: Dec 23, 63. Transferred to Co. B Jun 13, 65; Mustered out Jul 11, 65; Died Oct 8, 1910, and buried in East Burke Cemetery, East Burke, Vt.

Turner, Andrew W. Residence: Bethel. Enlistment Date: Jul 12, 62. Muster Date: Jul 12, 62. Promoted to Sgt. Apr 4, 64; Mustered out Jun 13, 65.

Turner, Lewis W. Residence: Bethel. Enlistment Date: Aug 30, 64. Muster Date: Aug 30, 64. Mustered out Jun 13, 65; Died Apr 18, 1917, and buried in Mt. Pleasant Cemetery, St. Johnsbury, Vt.

Waller, Edgar G. Residence: Newfane. Enlistment Date: Aug 18, 64. Muster Date: Aug 18, 64. Transferred to Co. D, 4th Vt. Jan 20, 65.

Walston, Amos. Residence: Williston. Enlistment Date: Dec 12, 63. Muster Date: Jan 4, 64. Transferred to Co. B Jun 13, 65; Mustered out Dec 1, 65; Died Mar 11, 1905, and buried in East Cemetery, Williston, Vt.

Warner, Zenas A. Residence: Sunderland. Enlistment Date: Dec 4, 63. Muster Date: Dec 24, 63. Mustered out Jun 22, 65; Died Dec 1, 1895, and buried in Evergreen Cemetery, Arlington, Vt.

Warren, Addison. Residence: Bolton. Enlistment Date: Jun 10, 62. Muster Date: Jul 9, 62. Died Aug 12, 62, of disease.

Waterman, Warren. Residence: Newport. Enlistment Date: May 30, 62. Muster Date: Jul 9, 62. Died Jan 20, 63, of disease; Buried in Rosehill Cemetery, Chicago, Ill.

Wells, Lewis J. Residence: Jericho. Enlistment Date: Jun 27, 62. Muster Date: Jul 9, 62. Discharged Oct 31, 62, for disability.

West, William C. Residence: Montreal, Can. Enlistment Date: Jun 28, 62. Muster Date: Jul 9, 62. Deserted Dec 20, 62.

Wetherby, Leonard S. Residence: Essex. Enlistment Date: Dec 18, 63. Muster Date: Dec 23, 63. Transferred to Co. B Jun 13, 65; Mustered out Dec 1, 65.

Wheeler, Horace H. Residence: Ira. Enlistment Date: Aug 12, 64. Muster Date: Aug 12, 64. Mustered out Jun 13, 65.

White, Ransome C. Residence: Hartland. Enlistment Date: Dec 22, 63. Muster Date: Dec 23, 63. Transferred to Co. B Jun 13, 65; Mustered out Sep 4, 65.

White, Wallace. Residence: Huntington. Enlistment Date: Jun 23, 62. Muster Date: Jul 9, 62. Promoted to Corp. Dec 1, 62; Reduced Jun 7, 64; Mustered out Jun 13, 65; Died Aug 1, 1878, and buried in Maplewood Cemetery, Huntington, Vt.

Wilcox, Lewis. Residence: Hinesburgh. Enlistment Date: Jun 19, 62. Muster Date: Jul 9, 62. Discharged Oct 23, 62; Died Jun 30, 1907, and buried in Rhode Island Corner Cemetery, Hinesburg, Vt.

Willey, Charles. Residence: Barre. Enlistment Date: Aug 29, 64. Muster Date: Aug 29, 64. Mustered out Jun 13, 65.

Williams, Henry. Residence: Herford, Can. Enlistment Date: Sep 16, 64. Muster Date: Sep 16, 64. Substitute for Albert M. Prouty, Marlboro; Transferred to Co. B Jun 13, 65; Mustered out Dec 1, 65.

Wilson, Robert. Residence: Bethel. Enlistment Date: Aug 1, 63. Muster Date: Aug 17, 63. Transferred to Co. B Jun 13, 65; Mustered out Dec 1, 65; Died Jan 8, 1904, and buried in the village cemetery, East Rupert, Vt.

Witherell, William A. Residence: Moretown. Enlistment Date: Jun 24, 62. Muster Date: Jul 9, 62. Discharged Jan 31, 63.

Wright, Allen S. Residence: Williston. Enlistment Date: Jun 23, 62. Muster Date: Jul 9, 62. Promoted to Corp. Dec 1, 62; Reduced May 7, 64; Mustered out Jun 13, 65; Died Jun 13, 1911, and buried in Green Mountain Cemetery, Burlington, Vt.

Company G

Captains

Henderson, William J. Residence: Rygate. Commission Date: Jun 26, 62. Issue Date: Jun 26, 62. Resigned Feb 17, 63; Died Apr 30, 1904, in Ryegate.

Kilbourne, Edwin A. Residence: Bradford. Commission Date: Mar 12, 63. Issue Date: Mar 20, 63. First Lt. Co. G; Resigned Sep 27, 64; Died Feb 27, 1890, in the Northern Insane Hospital, Oconto County, Wis., and buried in Bluff City Cemetery Elgin, Ill.

Livingston, Josiah O. Residence: Marshfield. Commission Date: Oct 19, 64. Issue Date: Nov 19, 64. First Lt. Co. I; Promoted to Adj. Jun 4, 63; Wounded Feb 2, 64; Mustered out Jun 13, 65; Died Jul 23, 1917, at the Vermont Soldier's Home, Bennington, Vt.

First Lieutenants

Kilbourne, Edwin A. Residence: Bradford. Commission Date: Jul 1, 62. Issue Date: Jul 1, 62. *See* Capt. Co. G.

Holman, William C. Residence: Braintree. Commission Date: Mar 12, 63. Issue Date: Mar 20, 63. Second Lt. Co. G; Taken prisoner Feb 2, 64; Exchanged May 6, 65; Mustered out Jun 13, 65.

Second Lieutenants

Holman, William C. Residence: Braintree. Commission Date: Jul 1, 62. Issue Date: Jul 1, 62. *See* First Lt. Co. G.

Witcher, John. Residence: Rygate. Commission Date: Mar 12, 63. Issue Date: Mar 20, 63. First Sgt. Co. G; Resigned Jan 29, 65; Died Oct 18, 1873, and buried in Boltonville Cemetery, Newbury, Vt.

Cowdrey, Burnham. Residence: Bradford. Commission Date: Feb 4, 65. Issue Date: Feb 20, 65. *See* Capt. Co. D.

Sergeants

Witcher, John. Residence: Rygate. Enlistment Date: Jun 3, 62. Muster Date: Jul 9, 62. *See* Second Lt. Co. G.

Cowdery, Burnham. Residence: Bradford. Enlistment Date: Jun 9, 62. Muster Date: Jul 9, 62. *See* Capt. Co. D.

Bagley, Frank M. Residence: Topsham. Enlistment Date: Jun 3, 62. Muster Date: Jul 9, 62. *See* Second Lt. Co. D.

Dearborn, George M. Residence: Corinth. Enlistment Date: Jun 4, 62. Muster Date: Jul 9, 62. Reduced Dec 18, 64; Mustered out Jun 13, 65.

Learned, Benjamin F. Residence: Newbury. Enlistment Date: Jun 6, 62. Muster Date: Jul 9, 62. Discharged Mar 14, 63, for disability.

Corporals

Mattoon, Lyman D. Residence: Vershire. Enlistment Date: Jun 2, 62. Muster Date: Jul 9, 62. Promoted to Sgt. Mar 26, 63; Mustered out Jun 13, 65.

McFarland, Andrew J. Residence: Bradford. Enlistment Date: Jun 18, 62. Muster Date: Jul 9, 62. Promoted to Sgt. Mar 26, 63; Mustered out Jun 13, 65.

Church, Freeman L. Residence: Vershire. Enlistment Date: Jun 18, 62. Muster Date: Jul 9, 62. Deserted Jan 22, 63.

Sweatt, Greenlief. Residence: Thetford. Enlistment Date: Jun 19, 62. Muster Date: Jul 9, 62. Reduced to the ranks Nov 8, 62; Discharged Jan 14, 63, for enlistment in the 17th U.S. Inf.

Stearns, Warren E. Residence: Braintree. Enlistment Date: Jun 6, 62. Muster Date: Jul 9, 62. Reduced Jun 17, 64; Promoted to Corp. Apr 1, 65; Mustered out Jun 13, 65.

Vance, David E. Residence: Rygate. Enlistment Date: Jun 17, 62. Muster Date: Jul 9, 62. Promoted to Sgt. May 19, 65; Mustered out Jun 13, 65.

Brown, Robert J. Residence: Chelsea. Enlistment Date: May 31, 62. Muster Date: Jul 9, 62. Discharged Sep 3, 64, for promotion as Second Lt. in the 14th U. S. C. T.

Coleman, Chester W. Residence: Orange. Enlistment Date: Jun 25, 62. Muster Date: Jul 9, 62. Discharged Nov 27, 62, for disability.

Musicians

Wilson, Harrison A. Residence: Corinth. Enlistment Date: Jun 12, 62. Muster Date: Jul 9, 62. Mustered out Jun 13, 65.

Cook, Charles O. Residence: Corinth. Enlistment Date: Jun 16, 62. Muster Date: Jul 9, 62. Mustered out Jun 27, 65; Died Apr 4, 1899, and buried in Center Cemetery, Corinth, Vt.

Wagoner

McLure, James T.H. Residence: Rygate. Enlistment Date: Jun 17, 62. Muster Date: Jul 9, 62. Mustered out Jun 6, 65.

Privates

Aldrich, George S. Residence: Strafford. Enlistment Date: Aug 17, 62. Muster Date: Sep 22, 62. Mustered out Jun 13, 65.

Ames, Richard P. Residence: Strafford. Enlistment Date: Aug 11, 62. Muster Date: Sep 22, 62. Promoted to Corp. Jun 18, 63; Reduced Jun 17, 64; Mustered out Jun 13, 65.

Angell, Rufus M. Residence: Randolph. Enlistment Date: Aug 11, 62. Muster Date: Sep 22, 62. Mustered out Jun 13, 65.

Arnold, Robert. Residence: Bradford. Enlistment Date: Jun 25, 62. Muster Date: Jul 9, 62. Mustered out Jun 13, 65.

Ash, Francis. Residence: Randolph. Enlistment Date: Sep 20, 62. Muster Date: Sep 22, 62. Discharged Jul 15, 63, for disability.

Avery, Cortic. Residence: Corinth. Enlistment Date: Dec 21, 63. Muster Date: Jan 6, 64. Mustered out Jun 17, 65; Died Feb 3, 1912, and buried in Center Cemetery, Corinth, Vt.

Avery, George S. Residence: Corinth. Enlistment Date: Dec 21, 63. Muster Date: Dec 24, 63. Transferred to Co. D Jun 13, 65; Mustered out Dec 7, 65; Died Nov 25, 1867, and buried in Meadow Meetinghouse Cemetery, Corinth, Vt.

Avery, John H. Residence: Orange. Enlistment Date: Aug 10, 64. Muster Date: Aug 10, 64. Mustered out Jun 13, 65.

Bacon, Olcott M. Residence: Strafford. Enlistment Date: Nov 24, 63. Muster Date: Jan 6, 64. Taken prisoner Feb 2, 64, and died at Andersonville, Ga. Aug 14, 64; Buried in Andersonville National Cemetery, Andersonville, Ga.

Bagley, Charles. Residence: Topsham. Enlistment Date: Jun 21, 62. Muster Date: Jul 9, 62. Died Mar 13, 63, of disease; Buried in Hampton National Cemetery, Hampton, Va.

Bagley, Charles. Residence: Topsham. Enlistment Date: Jan 1, 64. Muster Date: Jan 1, 64. Died Apr 11, 64, of disease and buried in Highland Cemetery, Chelsea, Vt. (Either this or the previous entry is in error)

Bailey, Hibbard H. Residence: Newbury. Enlistment Date: Jun 17, 62. Muster Date: Jul 9, 62. Deserted Jan 13, 63.

Bailey, William L. Residence: Haverhill, N.H. Enlistment Date: Jul 10, 62. Muster Date: Jul 10, 62. Died Aug 19, 62, of disease.

Barker, Alexander L. Residence: Corinth. Enlistment Date: Jun 11, 62. Muster Date: Jul 9, 62. Mustered out Jun 13, 65.

Bartholomew, John N. Residence: Vershire. Enlistment Date: Aug 15, 64. Muster Date: Aug 15, 64. Mustered out Jun 13, 65.

Batchelder, Alfred H. Residence: Bradford. Enlistment Date: Jun 18, 62. Muster Date: Jul 9, 62. Transferred to Co. I Jun 1, 64; Mustered out Jun 13, 65; Died Sep 23, 1930, and buried in the village cemetery, Bradford, Vt.

Beede, Clark J. Residence: Orange. Enlistment Date: Jun 5, 62. Muster Date: Jul 9, 62. Deserted Feb 9, 63; Returned Jan 27, 64; G. C. M. Jul 30, 64; Mustered out Jun 13, 65; Died Mar 24, 1888, and buried in West Corinth Upper Cemetery, Corinth, Vt.

Bixby, Cyren. Residence: Topsham. Enlistment Date: Jan 2, 64. Muster Date: Jan 2, 64. Transferred to Co. D Jun 13, 65; Mustered out Jun 22, 65.

Blay, Charles A. Residence: Braintree. Enlistment Date: Jun 2, 62. Muster Date: Jul 9, 62. Discharged Jan 14, 63, for enlistment in the Regular Army.

Bolton, Carlos E. Residence: Newbury. Enlistment Date: Jun 17, 62. Muster Date: Jul 9, 62. Mustered out Jun 13, 65.

Bond, William W. Residence: Strafford. Enlistment Date: Aug 12, 62. Muster Date: Sep 9, 62. Mustered out Jun 13, 65; Died Oct 20, 1919, and buried in North Thetford Cemetery, Thetford, Vt.

Brock, Andrew. Residence: Newbury. Enlistment Date: Jul 1, 62. Muster Date: Jul 9, 62. Discharged Mar 14, 63, for disability; Died may 14, 1888, and buried in Togus National Cemetery, Veterans Administration Medical and Regional Office Center, Togus, Me.

Brown, Portus L. Residence: Corinth. Enlistment Date: Dec 17, 63. Muster Date: Dec 31, 63. Transferred to Co. D Jun 13, 65; Mustered out Jun 22, 65.

Burrill, George C. Residence: Braintree. Enlistment Date: Jun 18, 62. Muster Date: Jul 9, 62. Discharged Feb 13, 63, for disability.

Burroughs, Henry. Residence: Tunbridge. Enlistment Date: Jul 23, 62. Muster Date: Sep 22, 62. Died Dec 14, 63, of disease; Buried in Alexandria National Cemetery, Alexandria, Va.

Burroughs, John. Residence: Strafford. Enlistment Date: Aug 11, 62. Muster Date: Sep 22, 62. Mustered out Jun 13, 65.

Burroughs, William. Residence: Strafford. Enlistment Date: Jul 9, 62. Muster Date: Jul 9, 62. Died Mar 25, 65, of disease; Buried in City Point National Cemetery, Hopewell, Va.

Carlton, John C. Residence: Vershire. Enlistment Date: Jun 7, 62. Muster Date: Jul 9, 62. Mustered out Jun 13, 65; Died Dec 11, 1900, and buried in the village cemetery, Vershire, Vt.

Caswell, Willard S. Residence: Barnard. Enlistment Date: Jul 11, 62. Muster Date: Jul 11, 62. Deserted Sep 22, 62.

Chamberlin, Amos J. Residence: Newbury. Enlistment Date: Jun 12, 62. Muster Date: Jul 9, 62. Mustered out Jun 13, 65; Died Dec 21, 1919, and buried in Boltonville Cemetery, Newbury, Vt.

Chamberlin, George C. Residence: Bradford. Enlistment Date: Feb 26, 64. Muster Date: Mar 8, 64. *See* First Lt. Co. D.

Chamberlin, William Hatch. Residence: Strafford. Enlistment Date: Sep 2, 64. Muster Date: Sep 2, 64. Wounded Sep 29, 64; Transferred to Co. B, 4th Vt. Jan 20, 65; Died Sep 24, 1930, and buried in Highland Cemetery, Chelsea, Vt.

Church, Andrew J. Residence: Washington. Enlistment Date: Jul 10, 62. Muster Date: Jul 10, 62. *See* Sgt. Maj.

Clemont, Almon. Residence: Orange. Enlistment Date: Aug 17, 64. Muster Date: Aug 17, 64. Transferred to Co. H.

Clifford, Charles W. Residence: St. Johnsbury. Enlistment Date: Jun 3, 62. Muster Date: Jul 9, 62. Mustered out May 21, 65.

Clogston, Henry H. Residence: Strafford. Enlistment Date: Aug 12, 62. Muster Date: Sep 22, 62. Discharged Mar 15, 64, for disability.

Codey, Peter. Residence: Strafford. Enlistment Date: Aug 12, 62. Muster Date: Sep 22, 62. Mustered out Jun 13, 65.

Coffrin, James H. Residence: Topsham. Enlistment Date: Dec 26, 63. Muster Date: Dec 26, 63. Mustered out May 13, 65.

Coleman, Chester W. Residence: Orange. Enlistment Date: Jan 2, 64. Muster Date: Jan 6, 64. Mustered out Jun 27, 65.

Coleman, Philander. Residence: Orange. Enlistment Date: Jun 18, 62. Muster Date: Jul 9, 62. Mustered out Jun 22, 65.

Cook, Jesse M. Residence: Thetford. Enlistment Date: Aug 14, 62. Muster Date: Sep 22, 64. Mustered out Jun 13, 65; Dec 25, 1921, and buried in Pine Hill Cemetery, Sharon, Vt.

Copeland, Charles. Residence: Braintree. Enlistment Date: Nov 28, 63. Muster Date: Dec 3, 63. Died Jul 3, 64, of disease; Buried in New Bern National Cemetery, New Bern, N.C.

Copp, George. Residence: Bradford. Enlistment Date: Jun 17, 62. Muster Date: Jul 9, 62. Taken prisoner Sep 2, 62; Paroled Sep 30, 62, and never returned to his company.

Copp, John. Residence: Bradford. Enlistment Date: Jun 17, 62. Muster Date: Jul 9, 62. Deserted Sep 16, 62.

Davenport, Norman B. Residence: Brookfield. Enlistment Date: Jun 10, 62. Muster Date: Jul 9, 62. Mustered out Jun 13, 65; Died Apr 21, 1926, and buried in Highland Cemetery, Chelsea, Vt.

Davis, Albert A. Residence: Topsham. Enlistment Date: Jan 2, 64. Muster Date: Jan 2, 64. Transferred to Co. D Jun 13, 65; Mustered out Dec 1, 65.

Day, John H. Residence: Washington. Enlistment Date: Jun 10, 62. Muster Date: Jul 9, 62. Discharged Apr 17, 63, for disability; Died Dec 18, 1916, and buried in the village cemetery Bradford, Vt.

Dearborn, Allen J. Residence: Vershire. Enlistment Date: Aug 20, 64. Muster Date: Aug 20, 64. Wounded Sep 29, 64; Mustered out Jun 13, 65; Died Mar 7, 1915, in Concord, N.H., and buried in Meadow Meeting House Cemetery, Corinth, Vt.

Dexter, Lewis. Residence: Topsham. Enlistment Date: Aug 31, 64. Muster Date: Aug 31, 64. Transferred to Co. H; Mustered out Jun 13, 65.

Douglas, Franklin J. Residence: West Fairlee. Enlistment Date: Jun 20, 62. Muster Date: Jul 9, 62. Discharged Nov 6, 62, for disability.

Dow, Daniel S. Residence: Vershire. Enlistment Date: Jun 23, 62. Muster Date: Jul 9, 62. Discharged Aug 22, 63, for disability.

Dow, Daniel S. Residence: Vershire. Enlistment Date: Aug 15, 64. Muster Date: Aug 15, 64. Mustered out Jun 13, 65.

Drew, George F. Residence: Vershire. Enlistment Date: Aug 16, 64. Muster Date: Aug 16, 64. Mustered out Jun 13, 65.

Dwyer, John. Residence: Barton. Enlistment Date: Jan 24, 65. Muster Date: Jan 24, 65. Transferred to Co. D Jun 13, 65; Discharged Dec 6, 65.

Eastman, Oscar D. Residence: Bradford. Enlistment Date: Jun 3, 62. Muster Date: Jul 9, 62. Discharged Aug 21, 62, for disability.

Fisk, George W. Residence: Bradford. Enlistment Date: Jun 26, 62. Muster Date: Jul 9, 62. Promoted to Corp. Feb 3, 63; Mustered out Jun 13, 65.

Fisk, Orin J. Residence: Randolph. Enlistment Date: Aug 11, 62. Muster Date: Sep 22, 62. Discharged Mar 7, 64; Died May 27, 64, of disease in Randolph, Vt., and buried in South View Cemetery, Randolph, Vt.

Flagg, Watson O. Residence: Braintree. Enlistment Date: Jun 9, 62. Muster Date: Jul 9, 62. Promoted to

Corp. Dec 18, 64; Mustered out Jun 13, 65; Died Mar 25, 1891, and buried in South View Cemetery, Randolph, Vt.

Flanders, Abner. Residence: Newbury. Enlistment Date: Jun 6, 62. Muster Date: Jul 9, 62. Discharged Jan 15, 63, for enlistment in the Regular Army; Died Apr 8, 1872, and buried in Ludlow Cemetery, Ludlow, Vt.

Flanders, Charles A. (Real name Albert K. Sammons). Residence: Corinth. Enlistment Date: Jun 18, 62. Muster Date: Jul 9, 62. Discharged Dec 24, 64, at Insane Asylum, Washington, D.C.; Drowned Oct 27, 1896, while trying to escape from Maine Insane Asylum, Augusta, Me.

Flanders, Daniel H. Residence: Bradford. Enlistment Date: Nov 30, 63. Muster Date: Nov 30, 63. Promoted to Corp. Jun 19, 65; Transferred to Jun 13, 65; Mustered out Dec 1, 65.

Flanders, George A. Residence: Vershire. Enlistment Date: Aug 20, 64. Muster Date: Aug 20, 64. Mustered out Jun 13, 65; Died Apr 9, 1905, and buried in Center Cemetery, Hardwick, Vt.

George, Roswell F. Residence: Topsham. Enlistment Date: Dec 30, 63. Muster Date: Dec 30, 63. Mustered out Jun 22, 65; Died Jan 16, 1910, and buried in Old East Corinth Cemetery, Corinth, Vt.

Getchell, Gailon. Residence: Sandgate. Enlistment Date: Feb 27, 64. Muster Date: Mar 4, 64. Transferred to Co. D Jun 13, 65; Mustered out Dec 1, 65.

Goodale, Wheatley. Residence: Randolph. Enlistment Date: Jul 18, 62. Muster Date: Jul 15, 62. Died Nov 22, 62, of disease; Buried in Rosehill Cemetery, Chicago, Ill.

Green, Orrin. Residence: Topsham. Enlistment Date: Jun 2, 64. Muster Date: Jan 5, 64. Transferred to Co. D Jun 13, 65; Mustered out Dec 7, 65.

Hartshorn, John F. Residence: Guildhall. Enlistment Date: Aug 27, 64. Muster Date: Aug 27, 64. Transferred to Co. H; Mustered out Jun 13, 65.

Hayward, George W. Residence: Rygate. Enlistment Date: Jun 13, 62. Muster Date: Jul 9, 62. Mustered out Jun 13, 65; Died Jul 6, 1909, and buried in Branchview Cemetery, Royalton, Vt.

Heath, Abel A. Residence: Vershire. Enlistment Date: Aug 31, 64. Muster Date: Aug 31, 64. Transferred to Co. I, 10th Vt. Jan 20, 65.

Heath, Daniel, Jr. Residence: Topsham. Enlistment Date: Jun 4, 62. Muster Date: Jul 9, 62. Deserted Jan 8, 63; Returned Feb 14, 63; Discharged Mar 7, 64; Died Jul 20, 1864, and buried in the village cemetery, Groton, Vt.

Heath, Henry B. Residence: Topsham. Enlistment Date: Dec 30, 63. Muster Date: Dec 30, 63. Transferred to Co. D Jun 13, 65; Died Oct 16, 65; Buried in Hampton National Cemetery, Hampton, Va.

Hildreth, Albert G. Residence: Thetford. Enlistment Date: Aug 14, 62. Muster Date: Sep 22, 62. Mustered out Jun 13, 65.

Hix, Stephen, Jr. Residence: Bradford. Enlistment Date: Jun 28, 62. Muster Date: Jul 9, 62. Mustered out Jun 13, 65; Died Jan 9, 1895, and buried in Oxbow Cemetery Newbury, Vt.

Hooper, Joseph A. Residence: Topsham. Enlistment Date: Jan 1, 64. Muster Date: Jan 1, 64. Transferred to Co. D Jun 13, 65; Mustered out Dec 1, 65; Died Mar 19, 1900, and buried in the village cemetery, Groton, Vt.

Howard, James R. Residence: Braintree. Enlistment Date: Jun 2, 62. Muster Date: Jul 9, 62. Mustered out May 23, 65.

Jackson, Albert P. Residence: Orange. Enlistment Date: Jun 6, 62. Muster Date: Jul 9, 62. Discharged Feb 16, 63, for disability.

Jackson, Lyman R. Residence: Topsham. Enlistment Date: Dec 31, 63. Muster Date: Dec 31, 63. Mustered out Jun 10, 65.

Johnson, Charles L. Residence: Thetford. Enlistment Date: Jun 23, 62. Muster Date: Jul 9, 62. Mustered out Jun 13, 65.

Johnson, Peter. Residence: Braintree. Enlistment Date: Dec 24, 63. Muster Date: Jan 6, 64. Transferred to Co. D Jun 13, 65; Mustered out Dec 1, 65.

Johnston, Erastus C. Residence: Newbury. Enlistment Date: Nov 30, 63. Muster Date: Nov 30, 63. Promoted to Corp. May —, 64; Reduced Dec 18, 64; Mustered out Jun 19, 65.

Kent, George F. Residence: Strafford. Enlistment Date: Dec 17, 63. Muster Date: Jan 6, 64. Transferred to Co. D Jun 13, 65; Mustered out Aug 28, 65.

Kirkby, Thomas. Residence: Bradford. Enlistment Date: Jun 6, 62. Muster Date: Jul 9, 62. Died of disease Jan 8, 64, and buried in the village cemetery, Bradford, Vt.

King, David W. Residence: Burke. Enlistment Date: Feb 13, 65. Muster Date: Feb 13, 65. Transferred to Co. D Jun 13, 65; Mustered out Dec 1, 65.

Knight, Edwin S. Residence: Thetford. Enlistment Date: Aug 16, 62. Muster Date: Sep 22, 62. Promoted to Corp. Jun 19, 64; Mustered out Jun 13, 65.

Kriege, George A. Residence: Burke. Enlistment Date: Feb 20, 65. Muster Date: Feb 20, 65. Transferred to Co. D Jun 13, 65; Mustered out Dec 1, 65.

Laird, Joseph F. Residence: Topsham. Enlistment Date: Dec 30, 63. Muster Date: Dec 30, 63. Mustered out Jun 22, 65.

Lavoie, Joseph. Residence: Bradford. Enlistment Date: Jun 20, 62. Muster Date: Jul 9, 62. Promoted to Corp. Feb 3, 63; Mustered out Jun 13, 65.

Learned, Selden F. Residence: Newbury. Enlistment Date: Jun 6, 62. Muster Date: Jul 9, 62. Mustered out Jun 13, 65; Died Jun 22, 1934, and buried in Wells River Cemetery, Newbury, Vt.

Learned, William A. Residence: Newbury. Enlistment Date: Jun 6, 62. Muster Date: Jul 9, 62. Died Jun 21, 63, of disease; Buried in Hampton National Cemetery, Hampton, Va.

Lillie, Elhanan T. Residence: Randolph. Enlistment Date: Dec 30, 63. Muster Date: Jan 6, 64. Transferred to Co. D Jun 13, 65; Mustered out Dec 1, 65; Died Mar 13, 1907, and buried in South View Cemetery, Randolph, Vt.

Loverin, George H. Residence: Topsham. Enlistment Date: Jan 2, 64. Muster Date: Jan 2, 64. Transferred to Co. D Jun 13, 65; Mustered out Dec 1, 65.

Luce, Albert S. Residence: Braintree. Enlistment Date: Jun 2, 62. Muster Date: Jul 9, 62. Discharged Jan 14, 63, for disability.

McFarland, William. Residence: Bradford. Enlistment Date: Nov 20, 63. Muster Date: Dec 10, 63. Transferred to Co. D Jun 13, 65; Mustered out Dec 1, 65.

McMannis, Patrick. Residence: Montpelier. Enlistment Date: Jun 5, 62. Muster Date: Jul 9, 62. Taken prisoner Sep 3, 62; Paroled Sep 21, 62; Discharged Nov 16, 62, for disability; Died Aug 9, 1883, and buried in Catholic Cemetery, Montpelier, Vt.

Miller, John H. Residence: Topsham. Enlistment Date: Jan 4, 64. Muster Date: Jan 4, 64. Transferred to Co. D Jun 13, 65; Mustered out Dec 1, 65.

Minard, David B. Residence: Orange. Enlistment Date: Jun 9, 62. Muster Date: Jul 9, 62. Mustered out Jun 13, 65.

Minard, George B. Residence: Orange. Enlistment Date: Jun 9, 62. Muster Date: Jul 9, 62. Promoted to Corp.; Died Mar 12, 63, of disease.

Morse, Henry E. Residence: Rygate. Enlistment Date: Aug 25, 62. Muster Date: Sep 22, 62. Shot and killed Sep 23, 63; Buried in Yorktown National Cemetery, Yorktown, Va.

Mudgett, George E. Residence: Washington. Enlistment Date: Jun 25, 62. Muster Date: Jul 9, 62. Mustered out Jun 13, 65.

Muzzey, George M. Residence: Newbury. Enlistment Date: Jun 12, 62. Muster Date: Jul 9, 62. Mustered out Jun 13, 65.

Noyes, John B. Residence: Braintree. Enlistment Date: Jun 2, 62. Muster Date: Jul 9, 62. Deserted Jan 10, 63; Returned Jan 30, 63; Mustered out Jun 13, 65.

Page, Charles, II. Residence: Corinth. Enlistment Date: Dec 18, 63. Muster Date: Dec 31, 63. Died Mar 17, 64, of disease; Buried in New Bern National Cemetery, New Bern, N.C.

Parker, Cyrus H. Residence: Corinth. Enlistment Date: Jun 11, 62. Muster Date: Jul 9, 62. Discharged Jan 15, 63.

Parker, George L. Residence: Corinth. Enlistment Date: Aug 22, 64. Muster Date: Aug 22, 64. Died Nov 18, 64, of disease; Buried in City Point National Cemetery, Hopewell, Va.

Parker, Lewis E. Residence: Corinth. Enlistment Date: Dec 18, 63. Muster Date: Jan 14, 64. Transferred to Co. D Jun 13, 65; Mustered out Dec 1, 65; Died Jan 21, 1921, and buried in East Orange Cemetery, East Orange, Vt.

Parkhurst, Charles. Residence: Barre. Enlistment Date: Aug 15, 64. Muster Date: Aug 15, 64. Transferred to Co. G 5th Vt. Jan 20, 65.

Peake, Harry. Residence: Orange. Enlistment Date: Jun 9, 62. Muster Date: Jul 9, 62. Discharged Aug 11, 63, for disability; Died Aug 20, 1892, and buried in Vermont Veteran's Home Cemetery, Bennington, Vt.

Perkins, George W.T. Residence: Haverhill, N.H. Enlistment Date: Jul 12, 62. Muster Date: Jul 12, 62. Mustered out Jun 13, 65.

Plunkett, James. Residence: Milton. Enlistment Date: Jul 7, 62. Muster Date: Jul 9, 62. Deserted Aug 8, 62; Returned May 9, 65; Discharged Jun 12, 65.

Porter, Carlos S. Residence: Hartford. Enlistment Date: Aug 11, 64. Muster Date: Aug 11, 64. Mustered out Jun 13, 65.

Porter, William B. Residence: Hartford. Enlistment Date: Aug 22, 64. Muster Date: Aug 22, 64. Mustered out Jun 13, 65.

Pratt, Birney J. Residence: Bethel. Enlistment Date: Aug 24, 64. Muster Date: Aug 24, 64. Transferred to Co. H; Mustered out Jun 13, 65.

Prescott, Dexter S. Residence: Corinth. Enlistment Date: Jun 25, 62. Muster Date: Jul 9, 62. Mustered out May 13, 65.

Prescott, George. Residence: Corinth. Enlistment Date: Jan 4, 64. Muster Date: Jan 13, 64. Transferred to Co. D Jun 13, 65; Promoted to Sgt. Jun 19, 65; Mustered out Dec 1, 65.

Raymore, Lewis. Residence: Braintree. Enlistment Date: Dec 24, 63. Muster Date: Jan 6, 64. Taken prisoner Feb 2, 64, and died at Andersonville Sep 21, 64; Buried in Andersonville National Cemetery, Andersonville, Ga.

Reynolds, Charles C. Residence: Strafford. Enlistment Date: Aug 15, 62. Muster Date: Sep 22, 62. Mustered out Jun 13, 65.

Reynolds, William A. Residence: Strafford. Enlistment Date: Nov 28, 63. Muster Date: Jan 6, 64. Transferred to Co. D Jun 13, 65; Mustered out Dec 1, 65.

Rice, George H. Residence: Topsham. Enlistment Date: Jan 2, 64. Muster Date: Jan 2, 64. Mustered out Jun 10, 65.

Riley, Matthew. Residence: Randolph. Enlistment Date: Aug 11, 62. Muster Date: Sep 22, 62. Died Feb 6, 64, of wounds received Feb 2, 64; Buried in New Bern National Cemetery, New Bern, N.C.

Rindge, Nehemiah W. Residence: Bethel. Enlistment Date: Dec 23, 63. Muster Date: Jan 2, 64. Mustered out Jun 13, 65; Died Dec 25, 1898, and buried in South View Cemetery, Randolph, Vt.

Robinson, Winfield S. Residence: Woodstock. Enlistment Date: Aug 2, 64. Muster Date: Aug 2, 64. Mustered out Jun 13, 65.

Rogers, Albert. Residence: Barre. Enlistment Date: Aug 6, 64. Muster Date: Aug 6, 64. Mustered out May 13, 65.

Rogers, William. Residence: Strafford. Enlistment Date: Aug 11, 62. Muster Date: Sep 22, 62. Mustered out Jun 13, 65.

Sanborn, Edmund M. Residence: Strafford. Enlistment Date: Aug, 62. Muster Date: Sep 22, 62. Promoted to Corp. Apr 1, 64; to Sgt. Mar 1, 65; Mustered out Jun 13, 65.

Sanborn, Lyman W. Residence: Topsham. Enlistment Date: Jun 16, 62. Muster Date: Jul 9, 62. Died Nov 12, 63, of disease; Buried in Hampton National Cemetery, Hampton, Va.

Sanborn, Ophir S. Residence: Topsham. Enlistment Date: Jun 10, 62. Muster Date: Jul 9, 62. Mustered out Jun 13, 65; Died Jul 8, 1908, and buried in New Cemetery, West Topsham, Vt.

Sargent, Chauncey D. Residence: Strafford. Enlistment Date: Aug 11, 62. Muster Date: Sep 22, 62. Mustered out Jun 13, 65; Died Nov 6, 1917, and buried in Locust Ridge Cemetery, Brattleboro, Vt.

Slack, Royal P. Residence: Chelsea. Enlistment Date: Jun 18, 62. Muster Date: Jul 9, 62. Mustered out Jun 13, 65; Died Dec 12, 1895, and buried in Randolph Center Cemetery, Randolph, Vt.

Sleeper, Calvin N. Residence: Strafford. Enlistment Date: Aug 29, 64. Muster Date: Aug 29, 64. Transferred to Co. H; Mustered out Jun 13, 65; Died Mar 7, 1875, and buried in Blaisdell Cemetery, Chelsea, Vt.

Sleeper, Samuel F. Residence: Strafford. Enlistment Date: Aug 11, 62. Muster Date: Sep 22, 62. Mustered out Jun 13, 65; Died Aug 24, 1881, and buried in South View Cemetery, Randolph, Vt.

Smith, David L. Residence: Washington. Enlistment Date: Jun 25, 62. Muster Date: Jul 9, 62. Promoted to Corp. Dec 18, 64; Mustered out Jun 13, 65.

Smith, Lorenzo D. Residence: Randolph. Enlistment Date: Dec 30, 63. Muster Date: Jan 6, 64. Mustered out Jun 22, 65.

Stevens, George W. II. Residence: Corinth. Enlistment Date: Dec 17, 63. Muster Date: Dec 31, 63. Transferred to Co. D Jun 13, 65; Promoted to Sgt. Jul 1, 65; Mustered out Dec 1, 65; Died Jul 13, 1891, and buried in Old East Corinth Cemetery, Corinth, Vt.

Thurston, Wilbur N. Residence: Braintree. Enlistment Date: Jun 2, 62. Muster Date: Jul 9, 62. Discharged Jan 14, 63, for enlistment in the Regular Army; Died Nov 27, 1901, and buried in the village cemetery, Royalton, Vt.

Titus, Carlo. Residence: Vershire. Enlistment Date: Aug 27, 64. Muster Date: Aug 27, 64. Transferred to Co. C, 2nd Vt. Jan 20, 65; Died Nov 1, 1893, and buried in Highland Cemetery, Chelsea, Vt.

Titus, Freeman. Residence: Vershire. Enlistment Date: Jun 21, 62. Muster Date: Jul 9, 62. Mustered out Jun 13, 65; Died Jun 17, 1916, and buried in Forestdale Cemetery, Brandon, Vt.

Towle, Franklin. Residence: Thetford. Enlistment Date: Jul 1, 62. Muster Date: Jul 9, 62. Discharged Jan 14, 63, for enlistment in the Regular Army; Died Mar 20, 1925, and buried in Orange Cemetery, Thetford, Vt.

Tucker, Milo. Residence: Strafford. Enlistment Date: Dec 19, 63. Muster Date: Jan 6, 64. Taken prisoner Feb 2, 64, and died at Andersonville Aug 24, 64; Buried in Andersonville National Cemetery, Andersonville, Ga.

Tucker, Silas H. Residence: Stowe. Enlistment Date: Jun 11, 62. Muster Date: Jul 9, 62. Promoted to Corp. Apr 1, 64; Mustered out Jun 13, 65; Died Sep 9, 1900, and buried in Sanborn Cemetery, Hardwick, Vt.

West, Daniel G. Residence: Strafford. Enlistment Date: Jun 21, 62. Muster Date: Jul 9, 62. Mustered out Jun 13, 65; Died Sep 31, 1888, and buried in West Cemetery, Middlebury, Vt.

West, Elliott. Residence: Strafford. Enlistment Date: Sep 2, 64. Muster Date: Sep 2, 64. Transferred to Co. H; Mustered out May 16, 65.

Wheeler, Harvey. Residence: Rygate. Enlistment Date: Jun 6, 62. Muster Date: Jul 9, 62. Died Nov 26, 63, of disease; Buried in New Bern National Cemetery, New Bern, N.C.

Whitney, Chester C. Residence: Fairlee. Enlistment Date: Jun 4, 62. Muster Date: Jul 9, 62. Died Aug 15, 62, of disease.

Whitney, George P. Residence: Braintree. Enlistment Date: Jun 2, 62. Muster Date: Jul 9, 62. Discharged Aug 21, 62, for disability.

Wiggins, Edwin D. Residence: Chelsea. Enlistment Date: Jun 26, 62. Muster Date: Jul 9, 62. Died Dec 18, 62, of disease.

Willey, Charles H. Residence: Topsham. Enlistment Date: Jan 2, 64. Muster Date: Jan 2, 64. Died Apr 1, 65, of disease.

Willey, Harvey. Residence: Barre. Enlistment Date: Aug 15, 64. Muster Date: Aug 15, 64. Mustered out Jun 13, 65; Died Mar 11, 1905, and buried in Oxbow Cemetery, Newbury, Vt.

Willey, Oramel D. Residence: Topsham. Enlistment Date: Jan 2, 64. Muster Date: Jan 2, 64. Transferred to Co. D Jun 13, 65; Mustered out Dec 1, 65; Died Jul 13, 1922, and buried in New Cemetery, Topsham, Vt.

Williams, John R. Residence: Braintree. Enlistment Date: Jun 2, 62. Muster Date: Jul 9, 62. Discharged Jul 5, 63, for disability; Died Jan 18, 1911, and buried in Lower Branch Cemetery, Braintree, Vt.

Williams, Theodore J. Residence: Braintree. Enlistment Date: Jun 2, 62. Muster Date: Jul 9, 62. Discharged Dec 10, 62, for disability.

Wilson, Calvin O. Residence: Plainfield. Enlistment Date: Jun 21, 62. Muster Date: Jul 9, 62. Died Feb 23, 65, of disease; Buried in City Point National Cemetery, Hopewell, Va.

Woodard, Silas. Residence: Bradford. Enlistment Date: Jun 12, 62. Muster Date: Jul 9, 62. Died Oct 10, 64, of disease.

Woodward, William A. Residence: Randolph. Enlistment Date: Jun 16, 62. Muster Date: Jul 9, 62. Discharged Mar 14, 63.

Woodward, William O. Residence: Randolph. Enlistment Date: Jun 16, 62. Muster Date: Jul 9, 62. Discharged Apr 18, 63, for disability due to accidental gunshot in right hand.

Wright, William T. Residence: Newbury. Enlistment Date: Jun 6, 62. Muster Date: Jul 9, 62. Transferred to V.R.C. Nov 1, 63; Mustered out Jul 1, 65; Died Jun 30, 1887, and buried in Haverhill, N.H.

Company H

Captains

Slayton, Abial H. Residence: Stowe. Commission Date: Jun 27, 62. Issue Date: Jun 27, 62. Resigned Dec 8, 62; Died Jan 14, 1917, and buried in Riverbank Cemetery, Stowe, Vt.

Guyer, Guy H. Residence: Morristown. Commission Date: Jan 6, 63. Issue Date: Jan 14, 63. First Lt. Co. H; Resigned Feb 13, 63; Died Jun 17, 1864, and buried in Riverside Cemetery, Morrisville, Vt.

Bisbee, Lewis H. Residence: Derby. Commission Date: Mar 13, 63. Issue Date: Mar 20, 63. First Sgt. Co. E; Promoted to First Lt. Co. H Jan 6, 63; Resigned Jun 3, 63; Died Jul 19, 1900.

Gorham, James T. Residence: Ludlow. Commission Date: Jun 4, 63. Issue Date: Jun 24, 63. Sgt. Maj.; Promoted to First Lt. Co. H Mar 13, 63; Mustered out Jun 13, 65; Died Sep 2, 1922.

First Lieutenants

Guyer, Guy H. Residence: Morristown. Commission Date: Jun 27, 62. Issue Date: Jun 27, 62. *See* Capt. Co. H.

Bisbee, Lewis H. Residence: Derby. Commission Date: Jan 6, 63. Issue Date: Jan 14, 63. *See* Capt. Co. H.

Gorham, James T. Residence: Ludlow. Commission Date: Mar 13, 63. Issue Date: Mar 20, 63. *See* Capt. Co. H.

Stone, Stillman. Residence: Eden. Commission Date: Jun 4, 63. Issue Date: Jun 24, 63. First Sgt. Co. H; Promoted to Second Lt. Co. H Mar 13, 63; Resigned Oct 19, 63.

Peck, Theodore S. Residence: Burlington. Commission Date: Jun 10, 64. Issue Date: Aug 3, 64. Promoted from Pvt. Co. K, 1st Vt. Cav. to Quartermaster Sgt. 9th Vt.; Promoted to Second Lt. Co. C Jan 8, 63; Wounded Sep 29, 64; Promoted to Capt. and Assistant Quartermaster U.S. Volunteers Mar 11, 65, but not mustered; declined commission on account of the end of the war; mustered out Jun 23, 65; Died Mar 15, 1918, and buried in Lakeview Cemetery, Burlington, Vt.

Second Lieutenants

Loveland, Calvin R. Residence: Hyde Park. Commission Date: Jun 27, 62. Issue Date: Jun 27, 62. Resigned Mar 5, 63.

Stone, Stillman. Residence: Eden. Commission Date: Mar 13, 63. Issue Date: Mar 20, 63. *See* First Lt. Co. H.

Hodge, Charles H. Residence: Stowe. Commission Date: Jun 4, 63. Issue Date: Jun 24, 63. Private Co. H; Promoted to Sgt.; Resigned Dec 18, 64; Died Dec 8, 1908, and buried in Motley, Minn.

Branch, Charles F. Residence: Orwell. Commission Date: Dec 21, 64. Issue Date: Mar 6, 65. *See* Capt. Co. A.

Roberts, John W. Residence: Montgomery. Commission Date: Jun 21, 65. Issue Date: Jul 10, 65. Pvt. Co. H; Promoted to Corp. Jan 1, 64; to Sgt. Mar 1, 65; to First Sgt. Apr 12, 65; Mustered out as First Sgt. Jun 13, 65.

Sergeants

Stone, Stillman. Residence: Eden. Enlistment Date: May 29, 62. Muster Date: Jul 9, 62. *See* First Lt. Co. H.

Barnes, David P. Residence: Elmore. Enlistment Date: May 29, 62. Muster Date: Jul 9, 62. Died Mar 17, 63, of smallpox.

Smith, Truman B. Residence: Stowe. Enlistment Date: Jun 25, 62. Muster Date: Jul 9, 62. Discharged Aug 22, 62, for disability; Died Dec 18, 1914, and buried in Riverbank Cemetery, Stowe, Vt.

McElroy, James P. Residence: Waterville. Enlistment Date: Jun 23, 62. Muster Date: Jul 9, 62. Taken prisoner Sep 3, 62; Paroled Oct 6, 62; Promoted to First Sgt. Aug 1, 63; Reduced Mar 2, 65; Mustered out Jun 13, 65.

Titus, David K. Residence: Wolcott. Enlistment Date: May 12, 62. Muster Date: Jul 9, 62. Died Dec 12, 62, of disease.

Corporals

Keeler, Samuel E. Residence: Hyde Park. Enlistment Date: May 26, 62. Muster Date: Jul 9, 62. Promoted to Sgt.; Discharged Jan 17, 65, for promotion in U. S. C. T.

Clark, Seth L. Residence: Elmore. Enlistment Date: May 27, 62. Muster Date: Jul 9, 62. Discharged Jun 13, 63, for disability.

Graves, James A. Residence: Wolcott. Enlistment Date: Jun 23, 62. Muster Date: Jul 9, 62. Promoted to Sgt. Feb 1, 64; Reduced Mar 2, 65; Mustered out Jun 13, 65; Died Jan 5, 1888, and buried in Fairmont Cemetery, Wolcott, Vt.

Netting, Harrison S. Residence: Stowe. Enlistment Date: May 29, 62. Muster Date: Jul 9, 62. Discharged Apr 11, 63, for disability; Died Feb 6, 1917, and buried in West Branch Cemetery, Stowe, Vt.

Tinker, Eugene C. Residence: Hyde Park. Enlistment Date: Jun 16, 62. Muster Date: Jul 9, 62. Died Apr 18, 63, of disease; Buried in Rosehill Cemetery, Chicago, Ill.

Beard, William H. Residence: Waterville. Enlistment Date: Jun 9, 62. Muster Date: Jul 9, 62. Discharged Nov 5, 62, for disability.

Griswold, Leroy S. Residence: Eden. Enlistment Date: Jun 16, 62. Muster Date: Jul 9, 62. Discharged Jul 22, 63, for disability.

Reynolds, Sanford M. Residence: Belvidere. Enlistment Date: Jun 5, 62. Muster Date: Jul 9, 62. Taken prisoner Jul 2, 64; Paroled Nov 20, 64; Died at Camp Parole, Annapolis, Md., Jan 25, 65; Buried in the Annapolis National Cemetery, Annapolis, Md.

Musician

Bagley, George W. Residence: Craftsbury. Enlistment Date: Jul 7, 62. Muster Date: Jul 9, 62. Mustered out Jun 13, 65; Died Sep 3, 1904, and buried in West Topsham Cemetery, Topsham, Vt.

Parcher, Willis H. Residence: Stowe. Enlistment Date: Jun 2, 62. Muster Date: Jul 9, 62. Mustered out Jun 13, 65.

Wagoner

Town, James C. Residence: Stowe. Enlistment Date: Jun 12, 62. Muster Date: Jul 9, 62. Mustered out Jun 13, 65.

Privates

Adams, Arba N. Residence: Hyde Park. Enlistment Date: Jun 3, 62. Muster Date: Jul 9, 62. Discharged Sep 12, 63, for disability.

Allen, William H. H. Residence: Peacham. Enlistment Date: Mar 15, 65. Muster Date: Mar 15, 65. Transferred to Co. C Jun 13, 65; Mustered out Dec 1, 65.

Allen, William J. Residence: Winhall. Enlistment Date: Aug 20, 64. Muster Date: Aug 20, 64. Mustered out Jun 13, 65; Died Mar 19, 1901, and buried in Sunderland Hill Cemetery, Sunderland, Vt.

Atkins, Enos H. Residence: Stowe. Enlistment Date: Jul 1, 62. Muster Date: Jul 9, 62. Transferred to V. R. C. Feb 8, 64; Discharged Oct 2, 64.

Avery, Alfred C. Residence: Hardwick. Enlistment Date: Dec 18, 63. Muster Date: Dec 30, 63. Died Oct 27, 64; Buried in City Point National Cemetery, Hopewell, Va.

Axtell, Loren S. Residence: Jamaica. Enlistment Date: Dec 26, 63. Muster Date: Dec 31, 63. Promoted to Corp. Dec 28, 64; Transferred to Co. C Jun 13, 65; Promoted to Sgt. Oct. 18, 65; Mustered out Dec 1, 65; Died Dec 17, 1926, and buried in Windham Center Cemetery, Windham, Vt.

Baker, Freeman. Residence: Morristown. Enlistment Date: Jun 2, 62. Muster Date: Jul 9, 62. KIA Sep 29, 64.

Ballou, Adin. Residence: Eden. Enlistment Date: Jun 9, 62. Muster Date: Jul 9, 62. Deserted Nov 23, 62; Returned Feb 23, 63; Promoted to Sgt. Mar 6, 63; Reduced Nov 12, 63; Mustered out Jun 13, 65.

Barber, David. Residence: Hartland. Enlistment Date: Dec 9, 63. Muster Date: Dec 30, 63. Transferred to Co. C Jun 13, 65; Mustered out Dec 1, 65.

Barber, William. Residence: Bakersfield. Enlistment Date: Jun 23, 62. Muster Date: Jul 9, 62. Discharged Feb 10, 63, for disability.

Barlow, Frederick H. Residence: Ludlow. Enlistment Date: Aug 22, 64. Muster Date: Aug 22, 64. Mustered out Jun 13, 65; Died Nov 12, 1928, and buried in New South Cemetery, Springfield, Vt.

Barron, John M. Residence: Pomfret. Enlistment Date: Sep 6, 64. Muster Date: Sep 6, 64. Transferred to Co. C; Mustered out Jun 13, 65; Died Mar 20, 1905, and buried in River Street Cemetery, Woodstock, Vt.

Bell, Samuel. Residence: Ludlow. Enlistment Date: Aug 10, 64. Muster Date: Aug 10, 64. Transferred to Co. B 11th Vt. Jan 20, 65.

Benway, John. Residence: Jericho. Enlistment Date: Dec 22, 63. Muster Date: Dec 30, 63. Mustered out Jun 19, 65.

Bessette, Edward. Residence: Richmond. Enlistment Date: Dec 10, 63. Muster Date: Dec 18, 63. Transferred to Co. C Jun 13, 65; Mustered out Dec 1, 65; Died Mar 11, 1905, and buried in St. Mary Cemetery, Richmond, Vt.

Bishop, Jeremiah. Residence: Waterford. Enlistment Date: Aug 31, 64. Muster Date: Aug 31, 64. Wounded Sep 29, 64; Mustered out Jun 13, 65.

Bostwick, Charles. Residence: Richmond. Enlistment Date: Aug 25, 64. Muster Date: Aug 25, 64. Mustered out Jun 13, 65.

Burrows, Stephen. Residence: Wardsboro. Enlistment Date: Jan 2, 64. Muster Date: Jan 11, 64. Wounded Feb 2, 64; Discharged Dec 16, 64; Died May 16, 1904, and buried in Brownington Cemetery, Brownington, Vt.

Bushey, Octave. Residence: Chittenden. Enlistment Date: Jul 11, 64. Muster Date: Jul 11, 64. Discharged Feb 17, 65, for wounds received Sep 29, 64; Died 1938 and buried in St. Francis Xavier Cemetery, Winooski, Vt.

Butler, Andrew H. Residence: Orange. Enlistment Date: Dec 31, 63. Muster Date: Jan 6, 64. Transferred to Co. C Jun 13, 65; Mustered out Dec 1, 65; Died Mar 3, 1887, and buried in Seven Hills Cemetery, Enosburgh, Vt.

Cammel, Joseph. Residence: Jericho. Enlistment Date: Dec 26, 63. Muster Date: Dec 31, 63. Died Nov 22, 64, of disease; Buried in Cypress Hills National Cemetery, Brooklyn, N.Y.

Castle, William H. Residence: Jamaica. Enlistment Date: Dec 25, 63. Muster Date: Dec 30, 63. Transferred to Co. C Jun 13, 65; Mustered out Dec 1, 65.

Chamberlin, Franklin. Residence: Stowe. Enlistment Date: Jul 3, 62. Muster Date: Jul 9, 62. Discharged Oct 20, 62.

Chase, George T. Residence: Jamaica. Enlistment Date: Dec 17, 63. Muster Date: Dec 30, 63. Transferred to Co. C Jun 13, 65; Mustered out Dec 1, 65.

Chase, Henry P. Residence: Jamaica. Enlistment Date: Dec 17, 63. Muster Date: Dec 30, 63. Taken prisoner Feb 3, 64; Paroled Feb 26, 65; Mustered out Jun 5, 65.

Clark, Lucius L. Residence: Charlotte. Enlistment Date: Aug 18, 64. Muster Date: Aug 18, 64. Mustered out Jun 13, 65.

Clement, Almon. Residence: Orange. Enlistment Date: Aug 17, 64. Muster Date: Aug 17, 64. Transferred from Co. G; Mustered out Jun 13, 65.

Clifford, Ampilus B. Residence: Windsor. Enlistment Date: Jul 27, 64. Muster Date: Jul 27, 64. Substitute for Orville D. Sanborn, Orange; Transferred to Co. E 5th Vt. Jan 20, 65.

Cobb, Chandler L. Residence: Jamaica. Enlistment Date: Sep 13, 64. Muster Date: Sep 13, 64. Mustered out Jun 19, 65.

Coburn, Ransom. Residence: Topsham. Enlistment Date: Aug 20, 64. Muster Date: Aug 20, 64. Mustered out Jun 13, 65.

Corkron, Thomas. Residence: Lyndon. Enlistment Date: Sep 1, 64. Muster Date: Sep 1, 64. Mustered out Jun 13, 65.

Codding, George W. Residence: Hyde Park. Enlistment Date: Jun 23, 62. Muster Date: Jul 9, 62. Died Oct 7, 62.

Cole, Alvin H. Residence: Hyde Park. Enlistment Date: Jun 26, 62. Muster Date: Jul 9, 62. Taken prisoner Feb 2, 64, and died at Andersonville, Ga., Jul 15, 64; Buried in Andersonville National Cemetery, Andersonville, Ga.

Corey, John. Residence: Huntington. Enlistment Date: Dec 10, 63. Muster Date: Dec 18, 63. Transferred to Co. C Jun 13, 65; Mustered out Dec 1, 65.

Covey, Joseph N. Residence: Londonderry. Enlistment Date: Dec 1, 63. Muster Date: Jan 5, 64. Transferred to Co. C Jun 13, 65; Mustered out Dec 1, 65; Died Oct 12, 1892, and buried in the village cemetery, Newfane, Vt.

Currier, Israel, Jr. Residence: Wolcott. Enlistment Date: Aug 15, 64. Muster Date: Aug 15, 64. Transferred to Co. A 4th Vt. Jan 20, 65; Died Nov 15, 1878, and buried in Fairmont (upper) Cemetery, Wolcott, Vt.

Cushing, George W. Residence: Montgomery. Enlistment Date: Sep 19, 64. Muster Date: Sep 19, 64. Drafted; Mustered out Jun 13, 65; Died August 16, 1921, and buried in the village cemetery, Montgomery, Vt.

Dexter, Lewis. Residence: Topsham. Enlistment Date: Aug 31, 64. Muster Date: Aug 31, 64. Transferred from Co. G; Mustered out Jun 13, 65.

Divoll, John H. Residence: Jamaica. Enlistment Date: Sep 5, 64. Muster Date: Sep 5, 64. Transferred to Co. B 11th Vt. Jan 20, 65.

Douglas, Joseph. Residence: Stowe. Enlistment Date: Jun 23, 62. Muster Date: Jul 9, 62. Discharged Apr 10, 63, for disability.

Douglas, Joseph, Jr. Residence: Stowe. Enlistment Date: Jun 23, 62. Muster Date: Jul 9, 62. Transferred to V. R. C.; Discharged Nov 28, 65; Died Mar 5, 1912.

Eastman, Allen. Residence: Hyde Park. Enlistment Date: Jun 28, 62. Muster Date: Jul 9, 62. Died Nov 4, 62.

Emerson, John S. Residence: Hyde Park. Enlistment Date: Jun 4, 62. Muster Date: Jul 9, 62. Died Dec 27, 62 of disease; Buried in Rosehill Cemetery, Chicago, Ill.

Farnham, Joseph, Jr. Residence: Johnson. Enlistment Date: Jun 3, 62. Muster Date: Jul 9, 62. Mustered out Jun 13, 65.

Farrar, Jerome S. Residence: Waterville. Enlistment Date: Jun 23, 62. Muster Date: Jul 9, 62. Deserted Jan 9, 63; Returned Mar 28, 63; Mustered out May 13, 65; Died Dec 28, 1893, and buried in Riverton Cemetery, West Berlin, Vt.

Fletcher, Elias J. Residence: Waterville. Enlistment Date: Jun 18, 62. Muster Date: Jul 9. 62. Discharged Apr 17, 64, for disability.

Finegan, John D. Residence: Fairfield. Enlistment Date: Jun 21, 62. Muster Date: Jul 9, 62. Taken prisoner Feb 2, 64; Paroled Nov 20, 64; Promoted to Corp. Apr 12, 65; Mustered out Jun 13, 65.

Finegan, Michael P. Residence: Hyde Park. Enlistment Date: Jun 21, 62. Muster Date: Jul 9, 62. Deserted Oct 18, 62.

Finegan, Patrick. Residence: Eden. Enlistment Date: Sep 10, 64. Muster Date: Sep 10, 64. Transferred to Co. C Jun 13, 65; Mustered out Dec 1, 65.

Fisher, Jonas G. Residence: Morristown. Enlistment Date: Jun 4, 62. Muster Date: Jul 9, 62. Discharged Mar 20, 63, for disability.

Fisk, Granville C. Residence: Eden. Enlistment Date: Jun 5, 62. Muster Date: Jul 9, 62. Promoted to Corp. Jan 27, 63; Reduced Jan 17, 64; to Sgt. Mar 2, 65; Mustered out Jun 13, 65.

Flowers, William J. Residence: Jericho. Enlistment Date: Dec 3, 63. Muster Date: Dec 30, 63. Died Oct 1, 64, of yellow fever.

Flynn, James. Residence: Jericho. Enlistment Date: Dec 4, 63. Muster Date: Dec 30, 63. Transferred to Co. C Jun 13, 65; Mustered out Dec 1, 65; Died Mar 30, 1905, and buried in St. Joseph Cemetery, Burlington, Vt.

Fontaine, Louis. Residence: Morristown. Enlistment Date: Jun 21, 62. Muster Date: Jul 9, 62. Deserted Jan 11, 63.

Frazier, George W. Residence: Hyde Park. Enlistment Date: Jun 2, 62. Muster Date: Jul 9, 62. Discharged Apr 25, 63, for disability; Died Apr 14, 1876, and buried in the village cemetery, Lowell, Vt.

Frazier, Victor M. Residence: Hyde Park. Enlistment Date: Jun 2, 62. Muster Date: Jul 9, 62. Died Mar 20, 63; and is buried in the village cemetery Lowell, Vt.

Freeman, Charles E. Residence: Wolcott. Enlistment Date: Jun 26, 62. Muster Date: Jul 9, 62. Taken prisoner Feb 2, 64, and died at Andersonville, Ga., Jul 17, 64; Buried in Andersonville National Cemetery, Andersonville, Ga.

Fullington, Charles B. Residence: ——. Enlistment Date: Sep 28, 64. Muster Date: Sep 28, 64. Substitute for Lafayette Buck, Newport; Promoted to Corp. Mar 7, 65; Discharged May 2, 65, for promotion in U.S.C.T.

Fulton, Horatio P. Residence: Fletcher. Enlistment Date: Jun 10, 62. Muster Date: Jul 9, 62. Died Nov 2, 62, of disease; Buried in Rosehill Cemetery, Chicago, Ill.

Gallup, Edwin A. Residence: Cambridge. Enlistment Date: Jun 16, 62. Muster Date: Jul 9, 62. Discharged Mar 13, 63, for disability; Died Jan 1923, and buried in North Hyde Park Cemetery, Hyde Park, Vt.

Gallup, Robert S. Residence: Cambridge. Enlistment Date: Jun 16, 62. Muster Date: Jul 9, 62. Discharged Jan 22, 63, for enlistment in the Regular Army.

Gardner, James K. Residence: Craftsbury. Enlistment Date: Aug 23, 64. Muster Date: Aug 23, 64. Mustered out Jun 13, 65; Died Dec 27, 1908, and buried in Oak Land Cemetery, Rush City, Minn.

Gardner, Levi C. Residence: Craftsbury. Enlistment Date: Aug 30, 64. Muster Date: Aug 30, 64. Mustered out Jun 13, 65; Died Sep 22, 1920, buried in Oak Land Cemetery, Rush City, Minn.

Gauthier, Frederick. Residence: Hyde Park. Enlistment Date: Jun 9, 62. Muster Date: Jul 9, 62. Promoted to Corp. Jan 31, 64; to Sgt. Apr 12, 65; Mustered out Jun 13, 65; Died Mar 21, 1905, and buried in St. Theresa Cemetery, Hyde Park, Vt.

Gilley, Elbridge. Residence: Fairfield. Enlistment Date: Jan 2, 64. Muster Date: Jan 5, 64. Died Oct 20, 64.

Gilley, George A. Residence: Fairfield. Enlistment Date: Dec 2, 63. Muster Date: Jan 5, 64. Transferred to Co. C Jun 13, 65; Mustered out Dec 1, 65; Died Aug 13, 1921, and buried in Maplewood Cemetery, Huntington, Vt.

Glongie, Maguire. Residence: Cambridge. Enlistment Date: Jun 23, 62. Muster Date: Jul 9, 62. Deserted Dec 5, 62.

Goodale, George F. Residence: Jamaica. Enlistment Date: Sep 13, 64. Muster Date: Sep 13, 64. Mustered out Jun 13, 65.

Graves, Thaddeus O. Residence: Craftsbury. Enlistment Date: Sep 2, 64. Muster Date: Sep 2, 64. Promoted to Corp. Mar 2, 65; Mustered out Jun 13, 65; Died Apr 6, 1882, and buried in Fairmont (lower) Cemetery, Wolcott, Vt.

Griffin, Patrick. Residence: Waterford. Enlistment Date: Sep 5, 64. Muster Date: Sep 5, 64. Mustered out Jun 13, 65.

Hardie, Lyman H. Residence: Waterville. Enlistment Date: Jun 23, 62. Muster Date: Jul 9, 62. Discharged Nov 5, 62, for disability.

Hartshorn, John F. Residence: Guildhall. Enlistment Date: Aug 27, 64. Muster Date: Aug 27, 64. Transferred from Co. G; Mustered out Jun 13, 65.

Haskins, Adorno S. Residence: Hyde Park. Enlistment Date: Jun 22, 62. Muster Date: Jul 9, 62. Deserted Nov 9, 62; Returned Jul 31, 65; Discharged Sep 13, 65.

Havens, Edwin W. Residence: Stowe. Enlistment Date: May 30, 62. Muster Date: Jul 9, 62. Taken prisoner Feb 2, 64, and died at Andersonville, Ga., Aug 24, 64; Buried in Andersonville National Cemetery, Andersonville, Ga.

Hayes, John. Residence: Bakersfield. Enlistment Date: Dec 14, 63. Muster Date: Dec 30, 63. Transferred to Co. C Jun 13, 65; Died Jul 8, 65, of disease; Buried in Richmond National Cemetery, Richmond, Va.

Hazen, Dan. Residence: North Hero. Enlistment Date: Jan 4, 64. Muster Date: Jan 5, 64. Transferred to Co. C Jun 13, 65; Mustered out Aug 25, 65; Died Jan 15, 1939, and buried in Pine Grove Cemetery, Ansonia, Conn.

Hazen, A. Wayne. Residence: North Hero. Enlistment Date: Jan 4, 64. Muster Date: Jan 5, 64. Taken prisoner Feb 2, 64, and died at Andersonville, Ga., Aug 31, 64; Buried in Andersonville National Cemetery, Andersonville, Ga.

Hinch, Richard. Residence: Waterford. Enlistment Date: Aug 31, 64. Muster Date: Aug 31, 64. Mustered out Jun 13, 65.

Hodge, Charles H. Residence: Stowe. Enlistment Date: Jun 20, 62. Muster Date: Jul 9, 62. *See* Second Lt. Co. H.

Holman, Alonzo. Residence: Topsham. Enlistment Date: Aug 18, 64. Muster Date: Aug 18, 64. Died Dec 3, 64, and buried in City Point National Cemetery, Hopewell, Va.

Holland, Ebenezer. Residence: Wardsboro. Enlistment Date: Dec 30, 63. Muster Date: Jan 6, 64. Died Nov 3, 64, and buried in Hampton National Cemetery, Hampton, Va.

Holland, Leroy. Residence: Wardsboro. Enlistment Date: Jan 4, 64. Muster Date: Jan 8, 64. Died Dec 29, 64, and buried in the village cemetery, Jamaica, Vt.

Hull, Zura J. Residence: Morristown. Enlistment Date: Jun 2, 62. Muster Date: Jul 9, 62. Died Oct 28, 63, of disease and buried in Hampton National Cemetery, Hampton, Vt.

Humphrey, James. Residence: Wardsboro. Enlistment Date: Jan 2, 64. Muster Date: Jan 12, 64. Died Jan 2, 65, of disease; Buried in Hampton National Cemetery, Hampton, Va.

Humphrey, John O. Residence: Pawlet. Enlistment Date: Jan 2, 64. Muster Date: Jan 2, 64. Transferred to Co. C Jun 13, 65; Mustered out Dec 1, 65; Died 1925 and buried in Brownington Center Cemetery, Brownington, Vt.

Huntington, Charles. Residence: Orange. Enlistment Date: Dec 17, 63. Muster Date: Jan 6, 64. Died Dec 23, 64, and buried in Orange Cemetery, Orange, Vt.

Huse, William. Residence: Bethel. Enlistment Date: Dec 31, 63. Muster Date: Jan 2, 64. Mustered out May 26, 65.

Jackson, Henry. Residence: North Hero. Enlistment Date: Jan 4, 64. Muster Date: Jan 5, 64. Taken prisoner Feb 2, 64; Paroled Apr 28, 65; Mustered out Jun 9, 65.

Johnson, John. Residence: Waterford. Enlistment Date: Aug 30, 64. Muster Date: Aug 30, 64. Mustered out Jun 13, 65.

Kellam, Charles R. J. Residence: St. Johnsbury. Enlistment Date: Dec 7, 63. Muster Date: Dec 12, 63. Promoted to Corp. May1, 64; Discharged Dec 3, 64, for promotion as hospital steward in the Regular Army.

Kenney, Luke. Residence: Wolcott. Enlistment Date: Jun 23, 62. Muster Date: Jul 9, 62. Died Sep 27, 63.

Kidder, Thomas. Residence: St. Johnsbury. Enlistment Date: Nov 20, 63. Muster Date: Dec 12, 63. Died Nov 29, 64.

Kieley, Patrick. Residence: Georgia. Enlistment Date: Jan 1, 64. Muster Date: Jan 5, 64. Transferred to Co. C Jun 13, 65; Mustered out Dec 1, 65.

Kingsbury, Daniel O. Residence: Winhall. Enlistment Date: Sep 1, 64. Muster Date: Sep 1, 64. Mustered out Jun 13, 65.

Kingsbury, Ezra B. Residence: Winhall. Enlistment Date: Sep 1, 64. Muster Date: Sep 1, 64. Mustered out Jun 13, 65.

Kingsbury, Martin H. Residence: Winhall. Enlistment Date: Sep 1, 64. Muster Date: Sep 1, 64. Mustered out Jun 13, 65.

Kingsbury, Loren. Residence: Londonderry. Enlistment Date: Aug 31, 64. Muster Date: Aug 31, 64. Mustered out Jun 13, 65.

Knight, Alson R. Residence: Hyde Park. Enlistment Date: May 28, 62. Muster Date: Jul 9, 62. Discharged Oct 20, 62, for disability; Died Nov 1, 1862, and buried in the village cemetery, Covington, Vt.

Ladu, Marshall. Residence: Richmond. Enlistment Date: Jun 23, 62. Muster Date: Jul 9, 62. Discharged Mar 20, 63, for disability.

Ladu, Peter, Jr. Residence: Morristown. Enlistment Date: Jun 21, 62. Muster Date: Jul 9, 62. Promoted to Corp. Jan 31, 64; Reduced May 1, 64, by his own request; Wounded Oct 27, 64; Died Feb 1, 65, of wounds; Buried in City Point National Cemetery, Hopewell, Va.

Lapoint, Henry. Residence: Morristown. Enlistment Date: Dec 11, 63. Muster Date: Jan 2, 64. Transferred to Co. C Jun 13, 65; Mustered out Dec 1, 65.

Lapoint, William. Residence: Lowell. Enlistment Date: Dec 25, 63. Muster Date: Dec 30, 63. Transferred to Co. C Jun 13, 65; Promoted to Corp. Sep 11, 65; Mustered out Dec 1, 65; Died Nov 22, 1907, and buried in Center Cemetery, St. Johnsbury, Vt.

Lee, Henry B. Residence: Fletcher. Enlistment Date: Jul 7, 62. Muster Date: Jul 9, 62. Died Dec 5, 62, and buried in Old Cemetery, Waterbury, Vt.

LePage, Joseph, Jr. Residence: Hyde Park. Enlistment Date: Jun 6, 62. Muster Date: Jul 9, 62. Discharged Oct 7, 62, for disability.

Levally, George. Residence: Chittenden. Enlistment Date: Jul 19, 64. Muster Date: Jul 19, 64. Transferred Co. C Jun 13, 65; Mustered out Dec 1, 65.

Loverin, Austin. Residence: Dummerston. Enlistment Date: Jan 5, 64. Muster Date: Jan 5, 64. Discharged Jun 12, 65, for disability.

Lowell, Harrison. Residence: Fairfax. Enlistment Date: Jul 8, 62. Muster Date: Jul 9, 62. Discharged May 19, 63.

Luce, George W. Residence: Stowe. Enlistment Date: Jun 21, 62. Muster Date: Jul 9, 62. Died Mar 12, 65.

McGoven, Patrick. Residence: Jericho. Enlistment Date: Dec 4, 63. Muster Date: Dec 30, 64. Taken prisoner Feb 2, 64; paroled Nov 26, 64; Transferred to Co. C Jun 13, 65; Promoted to Corp. Oct 28, 65; Mustered out Dec 1, 65.

McManiman, William. Residence: Waterville. Enlistment Date: Jun 9, 62. Muster Date: Jul 9, 62. Discharged Oct 20, 62, for disability; Died Dec 14, 1893, and buried in Mount View Cemetery, Waterville, Vt.

Messier, Mitchell. Residence: Enosburg. Enlistment Date: Dec 23, 63. Muster Date: Jan 2, 64. Transferred to Co. C Jun 13, 65; Mustered out Dec 1, 65.

Metcalf, Wallace. Residence: Johnson. Enlistment Date: Jun 22, 62. Muster Date: Jul 9, 62. Deserted Jan 9, 63.

Miller, Edmund G. Residence: Jamaica. Enlistment Date: Sep 2, 64. Muster Date: Sep 2, 64. Mustered out Jun 13, 65.

Mills, Charles S. Residence: Johnson. Enlistment Date: Jun 15, 62. Muster Date: Jul 9, 62. Died Sep 17, 64, of disease; Buried in New Bern National Cemetery, New Bern, N.C.

Mills, John C. Residence: Johnson. Enlistment Date: Jun 15, 62. Muster Date: Jul 9, 62. Discharged Aug 12, 63, for disability.

Mitchell, George W. Residence: Hartland. Enlistment Date: Dec 29, 63. Muster Date: Dec 29, 63. Mustered out Jun 22, 65.

Moody, Sadona C. Residence: Stowe. Enlistment Date: Jul 1, 62. Muster Date: Jul 9, 62. Died Apr 22, 63, of disease; Buried in Rosehill Cemetery, Chicago, Ill.

Morse, Richard H. Residence: Wolcott. Enlistment Date: Jun 26, 62. Muster Date: Jul 9, 62. *See* Principal Musician.

Niles, Albert A. Residence: Morristown. Enlistment Date: Jun 1, 62. Muster Date: Jul 9, 62. Promoted to Corp. Jan 27, 63; to Sgt. Feb 1, 64; Reduced Mar 2, 65; Mustered out Jun 22, 65; Died April 1, 1922, and buried in Pleasant View Cemetery, Morrisville, Vt.

Niles, Porter S. Residence: Morristown. Enlistment Date: Jun 20, 62. Muster Date: Jul 9, 62. Died Oct 17, 63, of disease; Buried in Hampton National Cemetery, Hampton, Va.

Ober, Ingals K. Residence: Elmore. Enlistment Date: May 28, 62. Muster Date: Jul 9, 62. Mustered out May 15, 65.

Olena, Albert L. Residence: Alburgh. Enlistment Date: Dec 29, 63. Muster Date: Jan 5, 64. Taken prisoner Jun 21, 64; Paroled Apr 28, 65; Mustered out Jun 21, 65.

Palmer, Thomas H. Residence: Jericho. Enlistment Date: Dec 18, 63. Muster Date: Dec 30, 63. Transferred to Co. C. Jun 13, 65; Mustered out Dec 1, 65; Died Jun 19, 1884, and buried in East Cemetery, Williston, Vt.

Partlow, Charles H. Residence: Alburgh. Enlistment Date: Jan 1, 64. Muster Date: Jan 5, 64. Deserted before muster; Returned under presidential proclamation; Mustered out Jun 13, 65.

Payne, Oberon. Residence: North Hero. Enlistment Date: Jan 2, 64. Muster Date: Jan 5, 64. Wounded Sep 29, 64; Transferred to Co. C Jun 13, 65; Discharged Aug 7, 65 for wounds.

Perkins, Edwin C. Residence: Johnson. Enlistment Date: Jun 5, 62. Muster Date: Jul 9, 62. Promoted Corp. Jan 31, 64; Reduced Dec 28, 64; Mustered out Jun 13, 65.

Pettit, Thomas H. Residence: North Hero. Enlistment Date: Dec 31, 63. Muster Date: Jan 5, 64. Taken prisoner Feb 2, 64, and died in Millen, Ga., Nov 10, 64.

Phelps, Eugene. Residence: Jamaica. Enlistment Date: Dec 18, 63. Muster Date: Dec 31, 63. Transferred to Co. C Jun 13, 65; mustered out Dec 1, 65.

Phelps, Herman W. Residence: North Hero. Enlistment Date: Jan 4, 64. Muster Date: Jan 5, 64. Taken prisoner Feb 2, 64, and died at Andersonville, Ga., Aug 9, 64; Buried in Andersonville National Cemetery, Andersonville, Ga.

Potter, Herbert M. Residence: Waterville. Enlistment Date: Jun 3, 62. Muster Date: Jul 9, 62. Discharged Jan 22, 63, to enlist in the Regular Army.

Potter, Luke. Residence: Waterville. Enlistment Date: Jun 7, 62. Muster Date: Jul 9, 62. Deserted Oct —, 62; Returned Feb 23, 63; Transferred to V.R.C. May 30, 64; Discharged Jul 7, 65.

Pratt, Birney J. Residence: Bethel. Enlistment Date: Aug 24, 64. Muster Date: Aug 24, 64. Transferred from Co. G; Mustered out Jun 13, 65.

Pulsifier, Abel N. Residence: Charlotte. Enlistment Date: Sep 2, 64. Muster Date: Sep 2, 64. Mustered out Jun 13, 65.

Rawson, Chandler D. Residence: Jamaica. Enlistment Date: Sep 2, 64. Muster Date: Sep 2, 64. Mustered out Jun 13, 65.

Rawson, Chandler P. Residence: Poultney. Enlistment Date: Sep 2, 64. Muster Date: Sep 2, 64. Mustered out Jun 13, 65.

Rawson, Judson L. Residence: Winhall. Enlistment Date: Sep 1, 64. Muster Date: Sep 1, 64. Mustered out Jun 13, 65.

Rawson, Webster L. Residence: Jamaica. Enlistment Date: Sep 2, 64. Muster Date: Sep 2, 64. Mustered out Jun 13, 65.

Ravey, James. Residence: Whittingham. Enlistment Date: Dec 28, 63. Muster Date: Jan 7, 64. Died Jun 8, 65.

Revor, Peter. Residence: Chittenden. Enlistment Date: Jul 11, 64. Muster Date: Jul 11, 64. Transferred to Co. C Jun 13, 65; Mustered out Dec 1, 65.

Reynolds, Urial R. Residence: Belvidere. Enlistment Date: Jun 5, 62. Muster Date: Jul 9, 62. Taken prisoner Sep 3, 62; Paroled Oct 7, 62; Died Dec 31, 62.

Robbins, Jacob J. Residence: Wolcott. Enlistment Date: Jun 26, 62. Muster Date: Jul 9, 62. Discharged May 5, 63.

Roberts, John W. Residence: Montgomery. Enlistment Date: Jun 8, 62. Muster Date: Jul 9, 62. *See* Second Lt. Co. H.

Robinson, Judson A. Residence: Johnson. Enlistment Date: Jun 3, 62. Muster Date: Jul 9, 62. Died Mar. 14, 63, and buried in Johnson Plot Cemetery, Johnson, Vt.

Robinson, William. Residence: Jamaica. Enlistment Date: Dec 17, 63. Muster Date: Dec 31, 63. Transferred to Co. C Jun 13, 65; Mustered out Dec 1, 65.

Rugg, Argalus R. Residence: Jamaica. Enlistment Date: Dec 17, 63. Muster Date: Dec 31, 63. Transferred to Co. C Jun 13, 65; Promoted to Corp. Oct 28, 65; Mustered out Dec 1, 65; Died May 12, 1909, and buried in Westminster West Cemetery, Westminster, Vt.

Ryan, Michael. Residence: Georgia. Enlistment Date: Aug 18, 64. Muster Date: Aug 18, 64. Mustered out Jun 13, 65; Died Oct 23, 1907, and buried in Georgia Plains Cemetery, Georgia, Vt.

Sanborn, Ira C. Residence: Wolcott. Enlistment Date: Jun 24, 62. Muster Date: Jul 9, 62. Promoted to Corp. May 1, 64; Mustered out Jun 13, 65; Died Jun 2, 1885, and buried in Fairmont Cemetery, Wolcott, Vt.

Sanborn, John H. Residence: Wolcott. Enlistment Date: Aug 15, 64. Muster Date: Aug 15, 64. Transferred to Co. D 4th Vt., Jan 20, 65; Died Mar 17, 1905, and buried in Fairmont Cemetery, Wolcott, Vt.

Sanders, Harrison. Residence: Jamaica. Enlistment Date: Dec 20, 63. Muster Date: Dec 31, 63. Died Dec 12, 64, of disease; Buried in Hampton National Cemetery, Hampton, Va.

Sanders, Horace W. Residence: Jamaica. Enlistment Date: Dec 28, 63. Muster Date: Dec 31, 63. Transferred to Co. C Jun 13, 65; Mustered out Dec 1, 65; Died Dec 2, 1922, and buried in the village cemetery, Jamaica, Vt.

Scott, William. Residence: Wardsboro. Enlistment Date: Jan 2, 64. Muster Date: Jan 11, 64. Deserted Mar 1, 65.

Shambo, Joseph. Residence: Cambridge. Enlistment Date: Jun 7, 62. Muster Date: Jul 9, 62. Promoted to Corp. Jan 31, 64; to Sgt. Mar 2, 65; Mustered out Jun 13, 65.

Sherman, George D. Residence: Jericho. Enlistment Date: Sep 2, 64. Muster Date: Sep 2, 64. Mustered out Jun 13, 65.

Slade, George F. Residence: Winhall. Enlistment Date: Aug 27, 64. Muster Date: Aug 27, 64. Mustered out Jun 13, 65; Died Oct 4, 1912, and buried in Bondville Cemetery, Winhall, Vt.

Slade, Ora, Jr. Residence: Winhall. Enlistment Date: Aug 20, 64. Muster Date: Aug 20, 64. Mustered out Jun 13, 65.

Sleeper, Calvin N. Residence: Strafford. Enlistment Date: Aug 29, 64. Muster Date: Aug 29, 64. Transferred from Co. G; Mustered out Jun 13, 65; Died Mar 7, 1875, and buried in Blaidsdell Cemetery, Chelsea, Vt.

Smith, Benjamin M. Residence: Lowell. Enlistment Date: Dec 15, 63. Muster Date: Dec 30, 63. Taken prisoner Feb 2, 64, and died at Andersonville, Ga., Sep 12, 64; Buried in Andersonville National Cemetery, Andersonville, Ga.

Smith, George W. Residence: Craftsbury. Enlistment Date: Aug 17, 64. Muster Date: Aug 17, 64. Died Dec 16, 64, from accident; Buried in Hampton National Cemetery, Hampton, Va.

Smith, William. Residence: Orange. Enlistment Date: Jan 4, 64. Muster Date: Jan 6, 64. Transferred to Co. C Jun 13, 65; Mustered out Jul 21, 65.

Southwick, Frederick A. Residence: Duxbury. Enlistment Date: Dec 17, 63. Muster Date: Jan 7, 64. Promoted to Corp. Oct 30, 64; Transferred to Co. C Jun 13, 65; Reported sick in hospital on muster out roll; N. F. R.

Spikes, Miles. Residence: ——. Enlistment Date: Dec 6, 63. Muster Date: ——. Colored cook; Deserted Dec 11, 63.

Spooner, Alexander. Residence: Chittenden. Enlistment Date: Jul 16, 64. Muster Date: Jul 16, 64. Transferred to Co. C Jun 13, 65; Mustered out Dec 1, 65.

Snyder, Charles. Residence: Fairfax. Enlistment Date: Sep 16, 64. Muster Date: Sep 16, 64. Mustered out Jun 13, 65.

Steen, James R. Residence: Wolcott. Enlistment Date: Jun 25, 62. Muster Date: Jul 9, 62. Discharged May 20, 63, for disability; Died Oct 5, 1917, and buried in Pleasant View Cemetery, Morrisville, Vt.

Stewart, Henry C. Residence: Hyde Park. Enlistment Date: Jun 9, 62. Muster Date: Jul 9, 62. Died Oct 21, 62.

Stone, John B. Residence: Johnson. Enlistment Date: Jun 10, 62. Muster Date: Jul 9, 62. Discharged Mar 22, 63.

Stowell, Ezre. Residence: Hyde Park. Enlistment Date: Jun 20, 62. Muster Date: Jul 9, 62. Transferred to V. R. C. Feb 15, 64; Mustered out Jul 2, 65.

Strong, Simeon S. C. Residence: Orange. Enlistment Date: Jan 2, 64. Muster Date: Jan 6, 64. Mustered out Jun 19, 65.

Sweeney, Charles H. Residence: Wolcott. Enlistment Date: May 31, 62. Muster Date: Jul 9, 62. Promoted to Corp. Mar 6, 63; to First Sgt. Mar 1, 65; Reduced Apr 11, 65; Mustered out Jun 13, 65; Died Apr 5, 1903, and buried in North Hyde Park Cemetery, Hyde Park, Vt.

Thomas, Harry B. Residence: Pomfret. Enlistment Date: Jul 30, 64. Muster Date: Jul 30, 64. Mustered out Jun 13, 65; Died Sep 18, 1915, and buried in Oak Hill Cemetery, Rockingham, Vt.

Tobin, Albert S. Residence: Waterville. Enlistment Date: Jun 23, 62. Muster Date: Jul 9, 62. Promoted to Corp. Jan 7, 63; to Sgt. May 18, 63; to First Sgt. May 1, 64; Reduced to Sgt. Dec 28, 64; Mustered out Jun 13, 65.

Trefren, Niel. Residence: Georgia. Enlistment Date: Aug 17, 64. Muster Date: Aug 17, 64. Transferred to Co. B 11th Vt. Jan 20, 65.

Vancor, James H. Residence: Jericho. Enlistment Date: Dec 18, 63. Muster Date: Dec 30, 63. *See* Second Lt. Co. C.

Vosburgh, Jason. Residence: Alburgh. Enlistment Date: Dec 29, 63. Muster Date: Jan 5, 64. Taken prisoner Feb 2, 64; Paroled Nov 26, 64; Deserted Feb 20, 65; Returned May 9, 65; Dishonorably discharged Jun 12, 65.

Wells, Alpheus. Residence: Huntington. Enlistment Date: Aug 12, 64. Muster Date: Aug 12, 64. Mustered out Jun 13, 65.

West, Elliott. Residence: Strafford. Enlistment Date: Sep 2, 64. Muster Date: Sep 2, 64. Transferred from Co. G; Mustered out May 16, 65.

Wetherell, Ephraim B. Residence: Waterville. Enlistment Date: Jun 16, 62. Muster Date: Jul 9, 62. Taken prisoner Sep 3, 62; Paroled Sep 21, 62; Discharged Dec 30, 62, for disability; Died Aug 9, 1923, and buried in Mount View Cemetery, Waterville, Vt.

Wetherell, William. Residence: Waterville. Enlistment Date: Jun 16, 62. Muster Date: Jul 9, 62. Taken prisoner Sep 3, 62; Paroled Sep 21, 62; Discharged Dec 30, 62, for disability.

Wetherell, William V. Residence: Waterville. Enlistment Date: Jun 16, 62. Muster Date: Jul 9, 62. Taken prisoner Sep 3, 62; Paroled Sep 21, 62; Discharged Dec 30, 62, for disability; Died Sep 30, 1908, and buried in Mount View Cemetery, Waterville, Vt.

Wetherell, Wyman. Residence: Waterville. Enlistment Date: Jun 16, 62. Muster Date: Jul 9, 62. Discharged Oct 20, 62, for disability; Died Dec 5, 1895, and buried in Mount View Cemetery, Waterville, Vt.

Wheeler, Richard. Residence: Hartland. Enlistment Date: Aug 6, 64. Muster Date: Aug 6, 64. Promoted to Corp. Mar 2, 65; Mustered out Jun 13, 65; Died May 26, 1986, and buried in Lake View Cemetery, Burlington, Vt.

White, Austin D. Residence: Jamaica. Enlistment Date: Dec 17, 63. Muster Date: Dec 31, 63. Mustered out Jun 22, 65.

Whitcomb, Lucius S. Residence: Jericho. Enlistment Date: Dec 28, 63. Muster Date: Dec 30, 63. Transferred to Co. C Jun 13, 65, Mustered out Sep 11, 65.

Wood, Edward H. Residence: Cambridge. Enlistment Date: Jun 28, 62. Muster Date: Jul 9, 62. Discharged Oct 23, 62, for disability.

Wood, Gideon. Residence: Fletcher. Enlistment Date: Jun 5, 62. Muster Date: Jul 9, 62. Discharged Jul 27, 63, for disability.

Company I

Captains

Mower, Albion J. Residence: Calais. Commission Date: Jun 30, 62. Issue Date: Jun 30, 62. Resigned Jul 8, 63; Died Jun 16, 1906, and buried in Robinson Cemetery, Calais, Vt.

Viele, Eugene. Residence: Hinesburgh. Commission Date: Dec 22, 63. Issue Date: Feb 1, 64. First Lt. Co. F; Mustered out Jun 13, 65.

First Lieutenants

Livingston, Josiah O. Residence: Marshfield. Commission Date: Jun 30, 62. Issue Date: Jun 30, 62. *See* Capt. Co. G.

Vaughan, Alvan P. Residence: Woodbury. Commission Date: Jun 4, 63. Issue Date: Jun 12, 63. First Sgt. Co. I; Promoted to Second Lt. Co. I Jan 6, 63; Discharged May 2, 65.

Carpenter, George N. Residence: Marshfield. Commission Date: Jun 21, 65. Issue Date: Jul 10, 65. Sgt. Co. I; Promoted to First Sgt. Jul 1, 64; to Second Lt. Co. D Feb 5, 65; Mustered out as Second Lt. Co. D Jun 13, 65; Died Aug 9, 1906, and buried in Durant Cemetery, Cabot, Vt.

Second Lieutenants

Campbell, Oliver C. Residence: Waitsfield. Commission Date: Jun 30, 62. Issue Date: Jun 30, 62. Resigned Dec 20, 62; Enlisted in the V. R. C. Jul 6, 63; Discharged Nov 15, 65.

Vaughan, Alvan P. Residence: Woodbury. Commission Date: Jan 6, 63. Issue Date: Jan 14, 63. *See* First Lt. Co. I.

Hobon, Patrick. Residence: Brandon. Commission Date: Jun 22, 63. Issue Date: Jul 2, 63. *See* Capt. Co. F.

Gray, John. Residence: Hardwick. Commission Date: May 8, 64. Issue Date: May 30, 64. *See* First Lt. Co. D.

Stebbins, J. Webster. Residence: Brookline. Commission Date: May 2, 65. Issue Date: May 15, 65. Corp. Co. K; Promoted to Sgt. Apr 1, 63; to First Sgt. Dec 15, 64; Mustered out as First Sgt. Co. K Jun 13, 65; Died Apr 20, 1932.

Sergeants

Vaughan, Alvan P. Residence: Woodbury. Enlistment Date: Jun 18, 62. Muster Date: Jul 9, 62. *See* First Lt. Co. I.

Quigley, John H. Residence: Waitsfield. Enlistment Date: Jun 19, 62. Muster Date: Jul 9, 62. Promoted to First Sgt. Jan 1, 63; Reduced Jun 1, 63; Mustered out Jun 13, 65.

Minor, Asahel. Residence: Warren. Enlistment Date: Jun 24, 62. Muster Date: Jul 9, 62. Reduced Nov 11, 63; Discharged Feb 6, 65, for disability.

Gray, John. Residence: Hardwick. Enlistment Date: Jun 21, 62. Muster Date: Jul 9, 62. *See* First Lt. Co. I.

Carpenter, George N. Residence: Marshfield. Enlistment Date: Jun 11, 62. Muster Date: Jul 9, 62. *See* First Lt. Co. I.

Corporals

Quinn, Felix. Residence: Roxbury. Enlistment Date: Jun 20, 62. Muster Date: Jul 9, 62. Promoted to Sgt. May 26, 64; Mustered out Jun 13, 65.

Whitcher, D. G. Residence: Hardwick. Enlistment Date: Jun 27, 62. Muster Date: Jul 9, 62. Discharged Oct. 21, 62, for disability.

Hopkins, William, J. Residence: Cabot. Enlistment Date: May 29, 62. Muster Date: Jul 9, 62. Discharged Oct. 22, 62, for disability.

Hooker, Sanford O. Residence: Cabot. Enlistment Date: Jun 9, 62. Muster Date: Jul 9, 62. Promoted to Sgt. Nov 11, 63; Died Mar 12, 64.

Porter, Freeman J. Residence: Calais. Enlistment Date: Jun 4, 62. Muster Date: Jul 9, 62. Died Nov 19, 62, of disease.

Sanders, Thomas. Residence: Waitsfield. Enlistment Date: Jun 19, 62. Muster Date: Jul 9, 62. Reduced Mar 4, 64, Mustered out Jun 13, 65.

Phelps, Edward N. Residence: Waterbury. Enlistment Date: Jun 7, 62. Muster Date: Jul 9, 62. Reduced Mar 4, 64, Transferred To V.R.C. Mar 25, 64; Mustered out Jul 9, 65.

Brudenell, Thomas. Residence: Waterbury. Enlistment Date: May 29, 62. Muster Date: Jul 9, 62. Reduced May 10, 64; Mustered out Jun 13, 65.

Musician

Mann, Albert N. E. Residence: Montpelier. Enlistment Date: May 31, 62. Muster Date: Jul 9, 62. Discharged Nov 5, 62, for disability.

Jacobs, Don L. Residence: Montpelier. Enlistment Date: May 31, 62. Muster Date: Jul 9, 62. Transferred to V. R. C. Mar 25, 64 Mustered out Jul 8, 65.

Wagoner

Sprout, George W. Residence: Northfield. Enlistment Date: Jun 4, 62. Muster Date: Jul 9, 62. Discharged Aug 4, 63, for disability.

Privates

Ainsworth, Eugene. Residence: Woodbury. Enlistment Date: Jul 2, 62. Muster Date: Jul 9, 62. Discharged Nov 17, 62, for disability.

Ainsworth, Harrison E. Residence: Peacham. Enlistment Date: Aug 29, 64. Muster Date: Aug 29, 64. Mustered out Jun 13, 65.

Ainsworth, Henry A. Residence: Cabot. Enlistment Date: Jun 16, 62. Muster Date: Jul 9, 62. Promoted to Corp. Jul 15, 64; Mustered out 13, 65.

Ainsworth, William W. Residence: Hardwick. Enlistment Date: Dec 18, 63. Muster Date: Dec 30, 63. Transferred to Co. D Jun 13, 65; Mustered out Dec 7, 65.

Ashley, Eli. Residence: Waterbury. Enlistment Date: Jun 20, 62. Muster Date: Jul 9, 62. Mustered out Jun 22, 65.

Averill, Charles. Residence: Northfield. Enlistment Date: Jun 20, 62. Muster Date: Jul 9, 62. Promoted to Corp. Apr 3, 64; Reduced Jul 12, 64; Mustered out Jun 13, 65.

Averill, Franklin. Residence: Northfield. Enlistment Date: Jun 12, 62. Muster Date: Jun 9, 62. Taken Prisoner Feb 2, 64, and died at Andersonville, Ga., Jul 25, 64; Buried in Andersonville National Cemetery, Andersonville, Ga.

Bailey, Richard M. Residence: Hardwick. Enlistment Date: Dec 11, 63. Muster Date: Dec 30, 63. Mustered out May 31, 65.

Balaw, Edward. Residence: Peacham. Enlistment Date: Jun 9, 62. Muster Date: Jul 9, 62. Mustered out Jun 13, 65.

Baird, Alexander. Residence: Waitsfield. Enlistment Date: Jun 20, 62. Muster Date: Jul 9, 62. Promoted to Corp. Mar 16, 65; Mustered out Jun 13, 65; Buried in Hot Springs National Cemetery, Veterans Administration Medical Center, Hot Springs, S.D.

Ball, Henry L.C. Residence: Plainfield. Enlistment Date: Jun 16, 62. Muster Date: Jul 9, 62. Deserted Dec 25, 62.

Barrington, Henry M. Residence: Roxbury. Enlistment Date: Jun 20, 62. Muster Date: Jul 9, 62. Died Oct 6, 62.

Batchelder, Alfred H. Residence: Bradford. Enlistment Date: Jun 18, 62. Muster Date: Jul 9, 62. Transferred from Co. G; Mustered out Jun 13, 65.

Beede, John C. Residence: Orange. Enlistment Date: Aug 27, 64. Muster Date: Aug 27, 64. Discharged Jun 12, 65, for disability.

Beede, Washington C. Residence: Washington. Enlistment Date: Dec 23, 63. Muster Date: Jan 9, 64. Taken prisoner Feb 2, 64, and died at Andersonville, Ga. Sep 6, 64; Buried in Anderson National Cemetery, Andersonville, Ga.

Bemis, Warren L. Residence: Rutland. Enlistment Date: Sep 2, 64. Muster Date: Sep 2, 64. Mustered out Jun 13, 65; Died Jul 6, 1906, and buried in Smokeshire Cemetery, Chester, Vt.

Biette, Edward. Residence: — —. Enlistment Date: Sep 23, 64. Muster Date: Sep 23, 64. Substitute for John Allen, Westford; Transferred to Co. D, 5th Vt. Jan 20, 65.

Bill, Silas. Residence: Woodbury. Enlistment Date: Jul 1, 62. Muster Date: Jul 9, 62. Transferred to V.R.C. Mar 15, 64; Discharged Jul 28, 64; Died May 31, 1889, and buried in Harvey Cemetery, Woodbury, Vt.

Blanchard, Isaac N. Residence: Hardwick. Enlistment Date: Dec 14, 63. Muster Date: Dec 30, 63. Died Dec 16, 64; Buried in City Point National Cemetery, Hopewell, Va.

Bliss, Zenas. Residence: Calais. Enlistment Date: Jun 24, 62. Muster Date: Jul 9, 62. Promoted to Sgt. Discharged Sep 18, 64, for promotion to Capt. Co. K, 28th U.S.C.T.

Bohonan, Alba F. Residence: Corinth. Enlistment Date: Dec 16, 63. Muster Date: Dec 16, 63. Promoted to Corp. Mar 16, 65; Transferred to Co. D Jun 13, 65; Promoted to Sgt. Nov 1, 65; Mustered out Dec 1, 65.

Bohonan, Alvah. Residence: Washington. Enlistment Date: Jan 4, 64. Muster Date: Jan 9, 64. Deserted Nov 22, 64.

Bohonan, Fifield, Jr. Residence: Washington. Enlistment Date: Aug 13, 64. Muster Date: Aug 14, 64. Mustered out Jun 13, 65; Died May 1, 1876, and buried in Highland Cemetery, Chelsea, Vt.

Bohonan, Harris. Residence: Washington. Enlistment Date: Dec 30, 63. Muster Date: Jan 9, 64. Died Nov 25, 64, and buried in Cheney Cemetery, Washington, Vt.

Bohonan, Joseph. Residence: Washington. Enlistment Date: Dec 21, 63. Muster Date: Dec 26, 63. Taken prisoner Feb 2, 64, and died at Andersonville, Ga., Oct 24, 64; Buried in Andersonville National Cemetery, Andersonville, Ga.

Bohonan, Silas B. Residence: Chelsea. Enlistment Date: Aug 6, 64. Muster Date: Aug 6, 64. Mustered out Jun 13, 64; Died Jul 21, 1895, and buried in the village cemetery, Williamstown, Vt,

Bradish, Azro D. Residence: Chester. Enlistment Date: Sep 3, 64. Muster Date: Sep 3, 64. Mustered out Jun 13, 65.

Brown, Stephen. Residence: Montpelier. Enlistment Date: Jun 25, 62. Muster Date: Jul 9, 62. Discharged Mar 20, 63, for disability; Died Nov 7, 1877, and buried in the village cemetery, Elmore, Vt.

Bugbee, Alvah N. Residence: Orange. Enlistment Date: Sep 4, 64. Muster Date: Sep 4, 64. Mustered out Jun 13, 65.

Burgin, John W. Residence: Washington. Enlistment Date: Jan 4, 64. Muster Date: Jan 9, 64. Transferred to Co. D Jun 13, 65; Mustered out Dec 1, 65; Died Jul 20, 1920, and buried in Maple Hill Cemetery, Washington, Vt.

Burnell, Franklin J. Residence: Craftsbury. Enlistment Date: Aug 29, 64. Muster Date: Aug 29, 64. Mustered out Jun 13, 65; Died Aug 13, 1903, and buried in Fairmont Cemetery, Wolcott, Vt.

Burnham, Melville V. Residence: Calais. Enlistment Date: Jun 16, 62. Muster Date: Jul 9, 62. Died Mar 11, 63.

Button, Amasa G., 2nd. Residence: Washington. Enlistment Date: Jan 1, 64. Muster Date: Jan 9, 64. Transferred to Co. D Jun 13, 65; Mustered out Dec 1, 65; Died Sep 3, 1903, and buried in Maple Hill Cemetery, Washington, Vt.

Carr, George W. Residence: Corinth. Enlistment Date: Dec 14, 63. Muster Date: Dec 24, 63. Transferred to Co. D Jun 13, 65; Mustered out Dec 1, 65; Died Feb 6, 1888, and buried in Highland Cemetery, Chelsea, Vt.

Carr, Harlow. Residence: Woodbury. Enlistment Date: May 30, 62. Muster Date: Jul 9, 62. Discharged Mar 20, 63, for disability.

Carr, Samuel. Residence: Corinth. Enlistment Date: Dec 15, 63. Muster Date: Dec 24, 63. Transferred to Co. D Jun 13, 65; Mustered out Aug 4, 65; Died May 25, 1872, and buried in Danville Green Cemetery, Danville, Vt.

Cartier, Dolce. Residence: Enosburgh. Enlistment Date: Nov 21, 64. Muster Date: Nov 21, 64. Deserted to the enemy Jan 22, 65.

Chandler, Adoniram J. Residence: Chester. Enlistment Date: Aug 9, 64. Muster Date: Aug 9, 64. Mustered out Jun 13, 65.

Chappell, Edson K. Residence: Glover. Enlistment Date: Aug 24, 64. Muster Date: Aug 24, 64. Mustered out Jun 13, 65; Died Dec 31, 1920, and buried in Westmore Cemetery, Westmore, Vt.

Cheney, Carlos Z. Residence: Washington. Enlistment Date: Aug 13, 64. Muster Date: Aug 13, 64. Mustered out Jun 13, 65.

Clark, Walter C. Residence: Barnard. Enlistment Date: Jan 2, 64. Muster Date: Jan 5, 64. Mustered out Jun 22, 65.

Cobb, Henry. Residence: Washington. Enlistment Date: Jan 5, 64. Muster Date: Jan 9, 64. Taken prisoner Feb 2, 64; Paroled Dec 6, 64; Transferred to Co. D Jun 13, 65; Mustered out Dec 1, 65; Died Oct 14, 1913, and buried in Togus National Cemetery, Veterans Administration Medical and Regional Office Center, Togus, Me.

Courtney, Patrick. Residence: Chelsea. Enlistment Date: Dec 26, 63. Muster Date: Jan 6, 64. Died Jun 12, 65, and buried in Old Cemetery, Chelsea, Vt.

Craig, James M. Residence: Glover. Enlistment Date: Aug 24, 64. Muster Date: Aug 24, 64. Mustered out Jun 13, 65.

Cram, Horatio N. Residence: Northfield. Enlistment Date: Jun 12, 62. Muster Date: Jul 9, 62. Promoted to Corp. Mar 26, 64; Mustered out Jun 13, 65; Died Apr 12, 1898, and buried in Pleasant View Cemetery, Morrisville, Vt.

Derocher, Antoine. Residence: ——. Enlistment Date: Sep 29, 64. Muster Date: Sep 29, 64. Substitute for E.G. Rosebrook, Guildhall; Transferred to Co. D Jun 13, 65; Deserted Nov 10, 65.

Dickey, Orrin. Residence: Orange. Enlistment Date: Nov 6, 63. Muster Date: Nov 6, 63. Died Mar 15, 64.

Desilets, Carlos. Residence: Cabot. Enlistment Date: May 29, 62. Muster Date: Jul 9, 62. Died Oct 18, 62.

Downs, John H. Residence: Plainfield. Enlistment Date: Jun 12, 62. Muster Date: Jul 9, 62. Mustered out Jun 13, 65.

Downs, Thomas. Residence: Burlington. Enlistment Date: Jun 29, 63. Muster Date: Jul 7, 63. Died Nov 17, 63; Buried in Cypress Hills National Cemetery, Brooklyn, N.Y.

Durkee, Alba B. Residence: Waitsfield. Enlistment Date: Dec 21, 63. Muster Date: Jan 6, 64. Died Sep 25, 64; Buried in New Bern National Cemetery, New Bern, N.C.

Durkee, John A. Residence: Duxbury. Enlistment Date: Dec 19, 63. Muster Date: Jan 5, 64. Transferred to Co. D Jun 13, 65; Mustered out Dec 1, 65; Died Apr 5, 1902, and buried in North Duxbury Cemetery, Duxbury, Vt.

Eastman, John D. Residence: Washington. Enlistment Date: Aug 13, 64. Muster Date: Aug 13, 64. Mustered out Jun 13, 65; Died Aug 30, 1907, and buried in Fish Cemetery, Washington, Vt.

Eaton, Arthur G. Residence: Calais. Enlistment Date: Jun 20, 62. Muster Date: Jul 9, 62. Died Nov 9, 62.

Elliott, Isaac H. Residence: Waitsfield. Enlistment Date: Jun 26, 62. Muster Date: Jul 9, 62. Discharged Sep. 25, 62; Died Jul 29, 1915, and buried in the village cemetery, Waterbury, Vt.

Evans, Wright H. Residence: Corinth. Enlistment Date: Nov 10, 63. Muster Date: Nov 10, 63. Transferred to Co. D Jun 13, 65; Discharged Nov 7, 65, for disability; Died Dec 31, 1865, and buried in West Corinth Upper Cemetery, Corinth, Vt.

Flanders, Luther. Residence: Wilmington. Enlistment Date: Jan 5, 64. Muster Date: Jan 5, 64. Transferred from Co. E; Mustered out Jun 19, 65.

Flanders, Royal C. Residence: Orange. Enlistment Date: Dec 31, 63. Muster Date: Jan 6, 64. *See* Hospital Steward.

Fletcher, Gideon E. Residence: Roxbury. Enlistment Date: Jun 24, 62. Muster Date: Jul 9, 62. Deserted Jul 20, 62.

Flynn, John D. Residence: Calais. Enlistment Date: May 30, 62. Muster Date: Jul 9, 62. Promoted to Corp. Dec 1, 63; to Sgt. Sep 16, 64; Mustered out Jun 13, 65.

Forhen, James. Residence: Moretown. Enlistment Date: Jun 19, 62. Muster Date: Jul 9, 62. Deserted Dec 22, 62.

Foster, Henry M. Residence: Orange. Enlistment Date: Dec 11, 63. Muster Date: Jan 6, 64. Transferred to Co. D Jun 13, 65; Mustered out Dec 1, 65; Died Jun 1, 1897, and buried in Hope Cemetery, Barre, Vt.

Franklin, Elisha D. Residence: Greensboro. Enlistment Date: Sep 9, 64. Muster Date: Sep 9, 64. Transferred to Co. D Jun 13, 65; Mustered out Dec 1, 65; Died May 8, 1907, and buried in Fairmont Upper Cemetery, Wolcott, Vt.

French, Heman R. Residence: Waitsfield. Enlistment Date: Jun 23, 62. Muster Date: Jul 9, 62. *See* Hospital Steward.

Frizell, Amos H. Residence: Corinth. Enlistment Date: Dec 12, 63. Muster Date: Dec 31, 63. Transferred to Co. D Jun 13, 65; Promoted to Corp. Nov 1, 65; Mustered out Dec 1, 65.

Gates, Calvin K. Residence: Ryegate. Enlistment Date: Jun 9, 62. Muster Date: Jul 9, 62. Promoted to Sgt.; Reduced; Died Oct 14, 64, of disease.

George, Charles S. Residence: Corinth. Enlistment Date: Dec 14, 63. Muster Date: Dec 24, 63. Taken prisoner Feb 2, 64; Paroled Nov 19, 64; Transferred to Co. D Jun 13, 65; Mustered out Dec 1, 65.

Glines, William P. Residence: Topsham. Enlistment Date: Aug 18, 64. Muster Date: Aug 18, 64. Died May 25, 65.

Goodwin, George W. Residence: Barnard. Enlistment Date: Jul 11, 62. Muster Date: Jul 11, 62. Discharged Jan 15, 63, for enlistment in the Regular Army.

Greenslit, William H.H. Residence: Waitsfield. Enlistment Date: Jun 20, 62. Muster Date: Jul 11, 62. Committed suicide Aug 21, 62.

Grover, James C. Residence: New Haven. Enlistment Date: Sep 5, 64. Muster Date: Sep 5, 64. Mustered out Jun 13, 65.

Hall, George B. Residence: Waitsfield. Enlistment Date: Jun 25, 62. Muster Date: Jul 9, 62. Discharged Jan 15, 63, for enlistment in the Regular Army; Died Jun 13, 1914, and buried in Roxbury Cemetery, Roxbury, Vt.

Hall, Henry. Residence: Randolph. Enlistment Date: Aug 17, 64. Muster Date: Aug 17, 64. Transferred to Co. D 5th Vt. Jan 20, 65.

Hall, Hiram A. Residence: Calais. Enlistment Date: Jun 24, 62. Muster Date: Jul 9, 62. Promoted to Corp. Nov 27, 64; Mustered out Jun 13, 65.

Hanson, Frederick A. Residence: Corinth. Enlistment Date: Dec 13, 63. Muster Date: Dec 24, 63. Promoted to Corp Apr 3, 64; Reduced Jul 12, 64; to Corp. Nov 27, 64; Discharged for employment as a civilian Jun 9, 65 by Special Order of the War Department.

Harlow, Charles W. Residence: Pomfret. Enlistment Date: Aug 8, 64. Muster Date: Aug 8, 64. Transferred to Co. D 4th Vt. Jan 20, 65.

Hill, David. Residence: Plainfield. Enlistment Date: May 31, 62. Muster Date: Jul 9, 62. Discharged Mar 17, 63, for disability.

Hobon, Anthony J. Residence: Waltham. Enlistment Date: Aug 12, 64. Muster Date: Aug 12, 64. Mustered out Jun 13, 65.

Hoffman, Philip. Residence: Waitsfield. Enlistment Date: Jun 20, 62. Muster Date: Jul 9, 62. Promoted to Corp. Jan 15, 63; to Sgt. Jul 1, 64; Mustered out Jun 13, 65; Died Sep 4, 1883, and buried in Irasville Cemetery, Waitsfield, Vt.

Hogan, Henry. Residence: Middlesex. Enlistment Date: Jun 18, 62. Muster Date: Jul 9, 62. Promoted to Corp. Jan 15, 63; to Sgt. Mar 16, 65; Mustered out Jun 13, 65; Died Sep 14, 1930, and buried in Calvary Cemetery, Northfield, Vt.

Holt, Charles. Residence: Norwich. Enlistment Date: Dec 21, 63. Muster Date: Jan 7, 64. Transferred to Co. D Jun 13, 65; Mustered out Dec 1, 65.

Holt, Franklin. Residence: Hartford. Enlistment Date: Aug 15, 64. Muster Date: Aug 15, 64. Mustered out Jun 13, 65.

Hull, George D. Residence: Washington. Enlistment Date: Aug 26, 64. Muster Date: Aug 26, 64. Transferred to Co. D 5th Vt. Jan 20, 65; Died Apr 30, 1922, and buried in Maple Hill Cemetery, Washington, Vt.

Hunkins, John H. Residence: Washington. Enlistment Date: Jan 1, 64. Muster Date: Jan 9, 64. Transferred to Co. D Jun 13, 65; Mustered out Dec 1, 65.

Huntington, Benjamin F. Residence: Marshfield. Enlistment Date: Jun 16, 62. Muster Date: Jul 9, 62. Discharged Nov 5, 62, for disability; Died Jul 6, 1909, and buried in Nasmith Cemetery, Marshfield, Vt.

Jefferds, John G. Residence: Washington. Enlistment Date: Jan 4, 64. Muster Date: Jan 9, 64. *See* Sergeant Major; Died Apr 26, 1927, and buried in Swan Point, Providence, R. I.

Jenks, John E. Residence: Norwich. Enlistment Date: Sep 3, 64. Muster Date: Sep 3, 64. Transferred to Co. D 5th Vt. Jan 20, 65.

Kibbie, Albert N. Residence: Hartford. Enlistment Date: Aug 10, 64. Muster Date: Aug 10, 64. Mustered out Jun 13, 65.

Lapine, Joseph. Residence: Sheffeld. Enlistment Date: Aug 7, 64. Muster Date: Aug 16, 64. Transferred to Co. D 5th Vt. Jan 20, 65; Died Nov 6, 1916, and buried in Ascutney Cemetery, Windsor, Vt.

Lapine, Peter. Residence: Sheffeld. Enlistment Date: Aug 18, 64. Muster Date: Aug 18, 64. Transferred to Co. D 5th Vt. Jan 20, 65.

Lezer, Joseph. Residence: Plainfield. Enlistment Date: Jun 23, 62. Muster Date: Jul 9, 62. Deserted Sep 28, 62.

Lilley, Patrick. Residence: Woodbury. Enlistment Date: Jul 1, 62. Muster Date: Jul 9, 62. Discharged Apr, 25, 63, for disability; Died Oct 6, 1904, and buried in the Catholic cemetery, Montpelier, Vt.

Little, Philip. Residence: Whiting. Enlistment Date: Mar 3, 65. Muster Date: Mar 3, 65. Transferred to Co. D Jun 13, 65; Mustered out Dec 1, 65; Died Mar 5, 1869, and buried in Highland Cemetery, Chelsea, Vt.

Little, Triffly. Residence: Whiting. Enlistment Date: Mar 3, 65. Muster Date: Mar 3, 65. Transferred to Co. D Jun 13, 65; Mustered out Dec 1, 65.

Lockwood, Leander C. Residence: Springfield. Enlistment Date: Aug 6, 64. Muster Date: Aug 6, 64. Mustered out Jun 10, 65; Died Sep 9 1923, and buried in Pine Grove Cemetery, North Springfield, Vt.

Lovejoy, Albert J. Residence: Warren. Enlistment Date: Jun 27, 62. Muster Date: Jul 9, 62. Discharged Aug 4, 63, for disability.

Mack, Justus W. Residence: Woodbury. Enlistment Date: Jun 26, 62. Muster Date: Jul 9, 62. Died Oct 29, 62; Buried in Rosehill Cemetery, Chicago, Ill.

Madigan, James. Residence: Waterbury. Enlistment Date: Jun 3, 62. Muster Date: Jul 9, 62. Deserted Jan 10, 62.

Magett, Robert. Residence: Washington. Enlistment Date: Aug 13, 64. Muster Date: Aug 13, 64. Transferred to Co. D 5th Vt. Jan 20, 65; Died Feb 5, 1901, and buried in Fish Cemetery, Washington, Vt.

Marston, Orvis K. Residence: Williamstown. Enlistment Date: Dec 29, 63. Muster Date: Jan 6, 64. Transferred to Co. D Jun 13, 65; Mustered out Dec 11, 65; Died Apr 1885, and buried in Newport Center Cemetery, Newport Center, Vt.

Marston, William L. Residence: Williamstown. Enlistment Date: Jun 24, 62. Muster Date: Jul 9, 62. Wounded Sep 29, 64; Mustered out Jun 13, 65; Died Sep 26, 1893, and buried in Highland Cemetery, Chelsea, Vt.

Martin, David. Residence: Royalton. Enlistment Date: Aug 12, 64. Muster Date: Aug 12, 64. Mustered out Jun 13, 65.

Martin, James. Residence: Calais. Enlistment Date: Jun 18, 62. Muster Date: Jul 9, 62. Promoted to Corp. Jul 15, 64; Mustered out Jun 13, 65; Died Sep 23, 1899, and buried in West Church Cemetery, Calais, Vt.

Moore, Henry H. Residence: Randolph. Enlistment Date: Jan 2, 64. Muster Date: Jan 6, 64. Transferred to Co. D Jun 13, 65; Promoted to Corp. Jul 1, 65; Mustered out Dec 1, 65; Died Jul 20, 1908, and buried in Warren Cemetery, Warren, Vt.

Morse, John O. Residence: Marshfield. Enlistment Date: Dec 11, 63. Muster Date: Dec 31, 63. Died Nov 27, 64.

Moxley, Harvey C. Residence: Chelsea. Enlistment Date: Dec 17, 63. Muster Date: Dec 30, 63. Transferred to Co. D Jun 13, 65; Mustered out Dec 1, 65.

Newman, Martin L. Residence: Washington. Enlistment Date: Aug 13, 64. Muster Date: Aug 13, 64. Died Feb 27, 65; Buried in City Point National Cemetery, Hopewell, Va.

Norris, Leroy S. Residence: Williamstown. Enlistment Date: Jan 4, 64. Muster Date: Jan 4, 64. Mustered out May 13, 65; Died Mar 30, 1905, and buried in East Hill Cemetery, Williamstown, Vt.

O'Brien, Felix. Residence: Ireland. Enlistment Date: Sep 21, 64. Muster Date: Sep 21, 64. Substitute for Francis C. Adams, Marlboro; Transferred to Co. D 5th Vt. Jan 20, 65.

Paige, Francis A. Residence: Hardwick. Enlistment Date: Jun 23, 62. Muster Date: Jul 9, 62. Mustered out Jun 13, 65.

Parker, Joel G. Residence: Hardwick. Enlistment Date: Jun 18, 62. Muster Date: Jul 9, 62. Transferred to the V. R. C. Feb 15, 64; Mustered out Jul 2, 65.

Petty, Charles W. Residence: Bethel. Enlistment Date: Sep 1, 64. Muster Date: Sep 1, 64. Discharged Jul 4, 65, for disability; Died Jul 6, 1865, and buried in Rice Cemetery, Mendon, Vt.

Phelps, Charles C. Residence: Hardwick. Enlistment Date: Dec 18, 63. Muster Date: Dec 30, 63. Transferred to the U.S. Navy Jun 27, 64; Discharged Jul 9, 66.

Phelps, George W. Residence: Barre. Enlistment Date: Jun 23, 62. Muster Date: Jul 9, 62. Mustered out Jun 13, 65; Died Nov 17, 1905, and buried in Waits River Cemetery, Topsham, Vt.

Pitkin, Charles E. Residence: Pomfret. Enlistment Date: Aug 8, 64. Muster Date: Aug 8, 64. Mustered out Jun 13, 65.

Pitkin, Levi C. Residence: Hartford. Enlistment Date: Aug 10, 64. Muster Date: Aug 10, 64. Transferred to Co. C 3rd Vt. Jun 20, 65.

Plant, Charles. Residence: Montpelier. Enlistment Date: May 26, 62. Muster Date: Jul 9, 62. Deserted Jul 17, 62.

Poor, James H. Residence: Randolph. Enlistment Date: Jun 16, 62. Muster Date: Jul 9, 62. Taken prisoner Sep 3, 62; Paroled Sep 13, 62; Mustered out Jun 13, 65.

Preston, Asa L. Residence: Montpelier. Enlistment Date: Jun 16, 62. Muster Date: Jul 9, 62. Transferred to V.R.C. Apr 20, 64; Discharged Jul 6, 65.

Preston, Horacr H. Residence: Charlotte. Enlistment Date: Jan 4, 64. Muster Date: Jan 4, 64. Wounded Sep 29, 64; Mustered out May 22, 65; Died Sep 17, 1873, and buried in Center Cemetery, Windham, Vt.

Putnam, John C. Residence: Newbury. Enlistment Date: Aug 13, 64. Muster Date: Aug 13, 64. Mustered out Aug 3, 65.

Putnam, Stephen, Jr. Residence: Ryegate. Enlistment Date: Dec 30, 63. Muster Date: Jan 4, 64. Transferred to Co. D Jun 13, 65; Mustered out Dec 1, 65.

Quilty, George A. Residence: Waltham. Enlistment Date: Aug 12, 64. Muster Date: Aug 12, 64. Musician; Mustered out Jun 13, 65; Died Dec 4, 1865, and buried in Calvary Cemetery, Rutland, Vt.

Richardson, George W. Residence: Corinth. Enlistment Date: Dec 18, 63. Muster Date: Dec 24, 63. Transferred to Co. D Jun 13, 65; Mustered out Dec 1, 65.

Rush, George. Residence: Holland. Enlistment Date: Jun 10, 62. Muster Date: Jul 9, 65. Transferred from Co. E; Mustered out Jun 13, 65.

Russ, Daniel. Residence: Moretown. Enlistment Date: Jun 23, 62. Muster Date: Jul 9, 62. Promoted to Sgt. Jul 1, 64; to First Sgt. Mar 16, 65; Discharged May 29, 65; Died Oct 19, 1934, and buried in the village cemetery, Waterbury, Vt.

Sargent, Harlan P. Residence: Berlin. Enlistment Date: Jun 18, 62. Muster Date: Jul 9, 62. Died Nov 30, 63, of disease; Buried in Hampton National Cemetery, Hampton, Va.

Sears, Alexander. Residence: Can. Enlistment Date: Sep 24, 64. Muster Date: Sep 24, 64. Substitute for Benjamin R. McLarry, Newport; Transferred to Co. D Jun 13, 65; Mustered out Dec 1, 65; Died Dec 1, 1918, and buried in St. Jerome Cemetery, Dorset, Vt.

Seymour, Isaac. E. Residence: Montpelier. Enlistment Date: Jun 23, 62. Muster Date: Jul 9, 62. Discharged Feb 20, 63, for disability; Died Feb 3, 1984, and buried in the Catholic cemetery, Montpelier, Vt.

Smith, Cyrus H. Residence: Washington. Enlistment Date: Aug 13, 64. Muster Date: Aug 13, 64. Mustered out Jun 13, 65; Died Aug 9, 1905, and buried in Maple Hill Cemetery, Washington, Vt.

Smith, Daniel P, 2nd. Residence: Washington. Enlistment Date: Jan 4, 64. Muster Date: Jan 9, 64. Transferred to Co. D Jun 13, 65; Mustered out Dec 1, 65; Died Mar 31, 1919, and buried in Maple Hill Cemetery, Washington, Vt.

Smith, Otis B. Residence: Montpelier. Enlistment Date: Jun 23, 62. Muster Date: Jul 9, 62. Discharged Nov 5, 62, for disability; Died Mar 23, 1925, in Washington, Vt.

Smith, Vilas. Residence: Marshfield. Enlistment Date: Jun 28, 62. Muster Date: Jul 9, 62. Drowned Oct, 63; Hampton National Cemetery, Hampton, Va.

Smith, William P. Residence: Middlesex. Enlistment Date: Jun 30, 62. Muster Date: Jul 9, 62. Died Oct 12, 62; Buried in Rosehill Cemetery, Chicago, Ill.

Southwick, Elmer G. Residence: Corinth. Enlistment Date: Jan 4, 64. Muster Date: Jan 13, 64. Died Sep 12, 64, of yellow fever; Buried in New Bern National Cemetery, New Bern, N.C.

Southwick, Jehu M. Residence: Corinth. Enlistment Date: Dec 15, 63. Muster Date: Dec 24, 63. Transferred to Co. D Jun 13, 65; Mustered out Dec 1, 65.

Spiller, Alden. Residence: Chelsea. Enlistment Date: Dec 17, 63. Muster Date: Dec 30, 63. Died Jan 6, 65, of disease; Buried in Hampton National Cemetery, Hampton, Va.

Stone, Benjamin C. Residence: Strafford. Enlistment Date: Dec 12, 63. Muster Date: Jan 2, 64. Wounded Sep 29, 64; Transferred to Co. D Jun 13, 65; Discharged Jun 27, 65.

Stone, Benjamin F. Residence: Roxbury. Enlistment Date: Jun 24, 62. Muster Date: Jul 9, 62. Discharged Jul 1, 63, for disability.

Stone, Benjamin F. Residence: Chelsea. Enlistment Date: Dec 8, 63. Muster Date: Dec 30, 63. Discharged Jun 24, 65, for wounds received Sep 29, 64.

Stone, Francis. Residence: Barnard. Enlistment Date: Jul 11, 62. Muster Date: Jul 11, 62. Died Dec 5, 62; Buried in Rosehill Cemetery, Chicago, Il.

Stuart, Ernest B. Residence: Bethel. Enlistment Date: Jun 16, 62. Muster Date: Jul 9, 62. Transferred to V.R.C. Feb 15, 64; Mustered out Jul 2, 65.

Sylvester, Frank. Residence: Montpelier. Enlistment Date: May 29, 62. Muster Date: Jul 9, 62. Deserted Dec 1, 62.

Thomson, Joseph B. Residence: Barre. Enlistment Date: Jun 7, 62. Muster Date: Jul 9, 62. Promoted to Corp. Jul 15, 64; Mustered out Jun 13, 65.

Thurber, Thomas F. S. Residence: Washington. Enlistment Date: Sep 5, 64. Muster Date: Sep 5, 64. Mustered out Jun 13, 65; Died Sep 28, 1893, and buried in Maple Hill Cemetery, Washington, Vt.

Thurstin, George R. Residence: Brookfield. Enlistment Date: Dec 29, 63. Muster Date: Jan 6, 64. Transferred to Co. D Jun 13, 65; Discharged Jun 15, 65.

Wadleigh, John G. Residence: Brownington. Enlistment Date: Jun 16, 62. Muster Date: Jul 9, 62. Transferred from Co. E; Mustered out Jun 19, 65; Died Feb 22, 1902, and buried in the village cemetery, Weston, Vt.

Ward, Franklin A. Residence: Corinth. Enlistment Date: Dec 12, 63. Muster Date: Dec 24, 63. Died Nov 24, 64, and buried in Center Cemetery, Corinth, Vt.

Warren, Charles. Residence: Hardwick. Enlistment Date: Jun 21, 62. Muster Date: Jul 9, 62. Promoted to Corp; Reduced Jun 2, 64; Died Sep 23, 64; Buried in New Bern National Cemetery, New Bern, N.C.

Warren, Wallace B. Residence: Hartford. Enlistment Date: Aug 10, 64. Muster Date: Aug 10, 64. Mustered out Jun 13, 65; Died Jun 6, 1919, and buried in West Hartford Cemetery, Hartford, Vt.

Waterman, Stillman. Residence: Roxbury. Enlistment Date: Jun 20, 62. Muster Date: Jul 9, 62. Discharged Jun 15, 63, for enlistment in the Regular Army.

Wells, Joseph. Residence: Northfield. Enlistment Date: May 31, 62. Muster Date: Jul 9, 62. Mustered out Jun 13, 65; Died Aug 31, 1904, and buried in St. Monica Cemetery, Barre, Vt.

Wheeler, Edwin H. Residence: Ludlow. Enlistment Date: Aug 13, 64. Muster Date: Aug 13, 64. Transferred to Co. B 4th Vt. Jan 20, 65.

Wheelock, Oliver. Residence: Worcester. Enlistment Date: Jun 27, 62. Muster Date: Jul 9, 62. Mustered out Jun 13, 65; Died Jan 17, 1907, and buried in Green Mount Cemetery, Montpelier, Vt.

Whitney, George H. Residence: Bethel. Enlistment Date: Aug 24, 64. Muster Date: Aug 4, 64. Transferred to Co. D 4th Vt. Jan 20, 65.

Wilkey, William H. Residence: Derby. Enlistment Date: Jun 26, 62. Muster Date: Jul 9, 62. Deserted Mar 24, 63.

Wilkins, William G. Residence: Fayston. Enlistment Date: Jun 16, 62. Muster Date: Jul 9, 62. Discharged Jan 15, 63, for enlistment in the Regular Army.

Williams, Charles A. Residence: Springfield. Enlistment Date: Aug 10, 64. Muster Date: Aug 10, 64. Mustered out Jun 13, 65.

Witham, Aaron. Residence: Calais. Enlistment Date: May 28, 62. Muster Date: Jul 9, 62. Mustered out Jun 13, 65.

Witham, Moses. Residence: Woodbury. Enlistment Date: Jun 18, 62. Muster Date: Jul 9, 62. Deserted Jan 13, 63.

Withington, John. Residence: Ludlow. Enlistment Date: Aug 22, 64. Muster Date: Aug 22, 64. Mustered out Jun 13, 65.

Company K

Captains

Lewis, David W. Residence: Brattleboro. Commission Date: Jul 3, 62. Issue Date: Jul 3, 62. Taken prisoner Sep 3, 62; Paroled Sep 28, 62; Discharged Sep 2, 64, for disability.

Leavenworth, Abel E. Residence: Brattleboro. Commission Date: Dec 1, 64. Issue Date: Dec 21, 64. First

Sgt. Co. K; Promoted to First Lt. Co. K Nov 17, 62; Appointed Provost Marshall Apr 5, 65; Mustered out Jun 13, 65; Died Jun 3, 1901, and buried in Hillside Cemetery, Castleton, Vt.

First Lieutenants

Brooks, Joseph C. Residence: Westminster. Commission Date: Jul 3, 62. Issue Date: Jul 3, 62. *See* Maj.

Leavenworth, Abel E. Residence: Brattleboro. Commission Date: Nov 17, 62. Issue Date: Nov 17, 62. *See* Capt. Co. K.

Baker, Joel C. Residence: Danby. Commission Date: Dec 1, 64. Issue Date: Dec 21, 64. Sgt. Co. B; Promoted to First Sgt. May 28, 63; to Second Lt. Co. K Dec 22, 63; Resigned April 16, 65; Died Jun 6, 1904, and buried in Evergreen Cemetery, Rutland, Vt.

Gray, John. Residence: Hardwick. Commission Date: May 2, 65. Issue Date: May 15, 65. *See* First Lt. Co. D.

Second Lieutenants

Rice, Henry H. Residence: Brattleboro. Commission Date: Jul 3, 62. Issue Date: Jul 9, 62. Resigned Jun 1, 63.

Baker, Joel C. Residence: Danby. Commission Date: Dec 22, 63. Issue Date: Feb 1, 64. *See* First Lt. Co. K.

Burlingame, Sylvester C. Residence: Dummerston. Commission Date: Dec 30, 64. Issue Date: Jan 31, 65. Sgt. Co. K; Reduced Jun 23, 63; Promoted to Sgt. Aug 1, 63; Wounded Sep 29, 64; Mustered out Jun 13, 65; Died Dec 16, 1903, and buried in Prospect Hill Cemetery, Brattleboro, Vt.

Sergeants

Leavenworth, Abel E. Residence: Brattleboro. Enlistment Date: May 24, 62. Muster Date: Jul 9, 62. *See* Capt. Co. K.

Stebbins, Elijah, Jr. Residence: Vernon. Enlistment Date: Jun 2, 62. Muster Date: Jul 9, 62. Promoted to First Sgt. Dec 6, 62; Reduced Dec 15, 64; Mustered out May 13, 65.

Jackson, Charles. Residence: Vernon. Enlistment Date: May 27, 62. Muster Date: Jul 9, 62. Mustered out Jun 13, 65.

Burlingame, Sylvester C. Residence: Dummerston. Enlistment Date: May 27, 62. Muster Date: Jul 9, 62. *See* Second Lt. Co. K.

Gray, Adelbert E. Residence: Townshend. Enlistment Date: May 31, 62. Muster Date: Jul 9, 62. Discharged Mar 18, 63, for disability.

Corporals

Grout, James. Residence: Stratton. Enlistment Date: Jun 13, 62. Muster Date: Jul 9, 62. Died Mar 2, 63, of disease and buried in Pike Hollow Cemetery, Stratton, Vt.

Weymouth, Edward H. Residence: Westminster. Enlistment Date: Jun 6, 62. Muster Date: Jul 9, 62. Reduced Dec 6, 62; promoted to Corp. Mar —, 64; Mustered out Jun 13, 65.

Jones, Myron W. Residence: Dover. Enlistment Date: Jun 6, 62. Muster Date: Jul 9, 62. Died Sep 27, 62, of disease.

Newton, James H. Residence: Newfane. Enlistment Date: Jun 9, 62. Muster Date: Jul 9, 62. Promoted to Sgt. Dec 6, 62; Discharged May 20, 63, for disability.

Cutting, Asa. Residence: Whitingham. Enlistment Date: May 29, 62. Muster Date: Jul 9, 62. Reduced Jan 23, 63; Mustered out Jun 13, 65.

Smith, Edwin R. Residence: Wardsboro. Enlistment Date: May 29, 62. Muster Date: Jul 9, 62. Died Oct 6, 64, of wounds received Sep 29, 64.

Mann, Warren W. Residence: Wilmington. Enlistment Date: May 28, 62. Muster Date: Jul 9, 62. Reduced Dec 6, 62; Mustered out Jun 13, 65.

Stebbins, J. Webster. Residence: Brookline. Enlistment Date: May 31, 62. Muster Date: Jul 9, 62. *See* Second Lt. Co. I.

Musician

Baker, Herbert C. Residence: Guilford. Enlistment Date: Jun 30, 62. Muster Date: Jul 9, 62. Mustered out Jun 13, 65; Died Jan 17, 1919, and buried in Baker Cemetery, Guilford, Vt.

Gould, George W. Residence: Brattleboro. Enlistment Date: Jun 16, 62. Muster Date: Jul 9, 62. *See* Adj.

Wagoner

Chase, George A. Residence: Whitingham. Enlistment Date: Jun 2, 62. Muster Date: Jul 9, 62. Reduced Sep 8, 62; Mustered out Jun 13, 65; Died Jan 6, 1903, and buried in the village cemetery, Whitingham, Vt.

Privates

Aiken, William D. Residence: Dummerston. Enlistment Date: Jan 2, 64. Muster Date: Jan 7, 64. Transferred to Co. C Jun 13, 65; Promoted to Corp. Jul 22, 65; Mustered out Dec 1, 65.

Allard, Albert J. Residence: Jamaica. Enlistment Date: Jul 8, 62. Muster Date: Jul 10, 62. Discharged Jan 15, 63, for enlistment in the Regular Army.

Allard, Chauncey M. Residence: Brownington. Enlistment Date: Jul 7, 62. Muster Date: Jul 10, 62. Discharged Jan 15, 63, for enlistment in the Regular Army; Died Mar 30, 1910, and buried in Somerville, Maine.

Allard, Kingsley G. Residence: Brownington. Enlistment Date: Jul 10, 62. Muster Date: Jul 10, 62. Taken prisoner Sep 2, 62; paroled; Died Oct 13, 63, of disease.

Atherton, Galen W. Residence: Vershire. Enlistment Date: Sep 13, 64. Muster Date: Sep 13, 64. Wounded Sep 29, 64; Mustered out Jun 13, 65.

Austigan, Alexander. Residence: Rutland. Enlistment Date: Sep 2, 64. Muster Date: Sep 2, 64. Mustered out Jun 13, 65.

Bacon, Harrison K. Residence: Dummerston. Enlistment Date: Jan 2, 64. Muster Date: Jan 7, 64. *See* First Lt. Co. C.

Baker, Charles E. Residence: Brattleboro. Enlistment Date: Jun 24, 62. Muster Date: Jul 9, 62. Mustered out Jun 13, 65.

Baker, David G. Residence: Guilford. Enlistment Date: Jun 30, 62. Muster Date: Jul 9, 62. Mustered out Jun 13, 65; Died Apr 2, 1905, and buried in Baker Cemetery, Guilford, Vt.

Balch, John C. Residence: Chester. Enlistment Date: Jul 10, 62. Muster Date: Jul 10, 62. Deserted Jul 24, 62.

Barnes, Darius. Residence: Montgomery. Enlistment Date: Sep 19, 64. Muster Date: Sep 19, 64. Drafted; Transferred to Co. A, 5th Vt. Jan 20, 65; Died Oct 10, 1928, and buried in New Protestant Cemetery, Montgomery Center, Vt.

Barrett, John S. Residence: Brookline. Enlistment Date: Aug 26, 64. Muster Date: Aug 26, 64. Mustered out Jun 13, 65; Died Jan 20, 1868, and buried in Riverside Cemetery, Brookline, Vt.

Beardow, Thomas. Residence: Rutland. Enlistment Date: Sep 2, 64. Muster Date: Sep 2, 64. Mustered out Jun 13, 64.

Bissell, Albert W. Residence: Wardsboro. Enlistment Date: Jun 12, 62. Muster Date: Jul 9, 62. Promoted to Corp. Dec 6, 62; Reduced Jul 27, 63; Promoted to Corp. Feb 9, 64; to Sgt. Feb 17, 65; Mustered out Jun 13, 65.

Bissell, Edward B. Residence: Wardsboro. Enlistment Date: Dec 8, 63. Muster Date: Dec 31, 63. Wounded Oct 27, 64; Transferred to Co. C Jun 13, 65; Discharged Jul 25, 65, for disability; Died Jan 17, 1928, and buried in Morningside Cemetery, Brattleboro, Vt.

Buck, William. Residence: Marlboro. Enlistment Date: Jan 5, 64. Muster Date: Jan 5, 64. Died Feb 4, 65; Buried in City Point National Cemetery, Hopewell, Va.

Burt, George E. Residence: Brattleboro. Enlistment Date: May 27, 62. Muster Date: Jul 9, 62. Transferred to Co. F Jul 15, 62; Discharged Nov. 17, 62.

Bush, Lorenzo W. Residence: Brookline. Enlistment Date: Aug 24, 64. Muster Date: Aug 24, 64. Mustered out Jun 13, 65; Died Nov 30, 1925, and buried in Riverside Cemetery, Brookline, Vt.

Butler, Charles P. Residence: Brattleboro. Enlistment Date: Jun 23, 62. Muster Date: Jul 9, 62. Discharged Jan 15, 63, to enlist in the Regular Army.

Butler, William G. Residence: Brattleboro. Enlistment Date: Jun 26, 62. Muster Date: Jul 9, 62. Mustered out Jun 13, 65.

Butterfield, William H. Residence: Brattleboro. Enlistment Date: Dec 12, 63. Muster Date: Jan 4, 64. Transferred to Co. C Jun 13, 65; Mustered out Dec 1, 65; Died Jul 9, 1916, and buried in Baptist Church Cemetery, West Dummerston, Vt.

Carroll, William M. Residence: Dover. Enlistment Date: Jun 6, 62. Muster Date: Jul 9, 62. Mustered out Jun 13, 65.

Carey, Theodore M. Residence: Montgomery. Enlistment Date: Jan 2, 64. Muster Date: Jan 5, 64. Died Dec 23, 64, of diarrhea; Buried in the Hampton National Cemetery, Hampton, Va.

Chates, William. Residence: Underhill. Enlistment Date: Aug 17, 64. Muster Date: Aug 17, 64. Died of pneumonia Apr 4, 65, in Chesapeake General Hospital, Hampton, Va.; Buried in Hampton National Cemetery, Hampton, Va.

Church, Carlos. Residence: Georgia. Enlistment Date: Jan 4, 64. Muster Date: Jan 5, 64. Transferred to Co. C Jun 13, 65; Mustered out Dec 1, 65; Died May 5, 1921, and buried in Minneapolis, Minn.

Clough, Alonzo P. Residence: Jamaica. Enlistment Date: Jun 18, 62. Muster Date: Jul 9, 62. Mustered out Jun 13, 65.

Coby, Jacob. Residence: Substitute. Enlistment Date: Sep 16, 64. Muster Date: Sep 16, 64. Substitute for George M. Brooks, Vernon; Transferred to Co. C Jun 13, 65; Mustered out Dec 1, 65.

Copeland, Edgar F. Residence: Dover. Enlistment Date: Jul 8, 62. Muster Date: Jul 9, 62. Mustered out Jun 13, 65.

Corbett, Myron L. Residence: Guilford. Enlistment Date: Jul 1, 62. Muster Date: Jul 9, 62. Promoted to Corp. Mar 1, 64; to Sgt. Mar 3, 65; Mustered out Jun 13, 65.

Covey, Andes B. Residence: Windham. Enlistment Date: Jun 3, 62. Muster Date: Jul 9, 62. Mustered out May 13, 65; Died Dec 30, 1928, and buried in Springhill Cemetery, Vermilion City, Ill.

Crane, Thomas S. Residence: Brookline. Enlistment Date: Aug 24. 64. Muster Date: Aug 24, 64. Mustered out May 25, 65; Died Apr 19, 1909, and buried in Oak Grove Cemetery, Townshend, Vt.

Cummings, Wm. H.H. Residence: Shrewsbury. Enlistment Date: Aug 18, 64. Muster Date: Aug 18, 64. Transferred to Co. E, 5th Vt. Jan 20, 65.

Curtis, Stephen H. Residence: Alburgh. Enlistment Date: Feb 21, 65. Muster Date: Feb 21, 65. Transferred to Co. C Jun 13, 65; Mustered out Jul 20, 65; Died Jun 17, 1920, and buried in Baptist Cemetery, Can.

Dawson, Lovell A. Residence: Clarendon. Enlistment Date: Aug 27, 64. Muster Date: Aug 27, 64. Died Feb 7, 65; Buried in City Point National Cemetery, Hopewell, Va.

Dodge, Charles L. Residence: Dummerston. Enlistment Date: Dec 14, 63. Muster Date: Jan 7, 64. Died Dec 5, 64, and buried in Greenwood Cemetery, Dummerston, Vt.

Dumas, Peter. Residence: Rutland. Enlistment Date: Sep 2, 64. Muster Date: Sep 2, 64. Mustered out Jun 13, 65; Died Mar 21, 1905, and buried in Pine Hill Cemetery, Brandon, Vt.

Eager, George E. Residence: Stratton. Enlistment Date: Jun 28, 62. Muster Date: Jul 9, 62. Mustered out Jun 13, 65.

Estey, Charles C. Residence: Readsboro. Enlistment Date: May 30, 62. Muster Date: Jul 9, 62. Mustered out Jun 13, 65; Died Apr 24, 1915, and buried in Vermont Veteran's Home Cemetery, Bennington, Vt.

Estey, Henry W. Residence: Whitingham. Enlistment Date: Sep 1, 64. Muster Date: Sep 1, 64. Mustered out Jun 27, 65.

Fairbanks, Edwin. Residence: Whitingham. Enlistment Date: May 27, 62. Muster Date: Jul 9, 62. Mustered out Jun 13, 65.

Fairbanks, Sanford S. Residence: Halifax. Enlistment Date: May 27, 62. Muster Date: Jul 9, 62. Died Oct 31, 64, of disease; Buried in Hampton National Cemetery, Hampton, Va.

Field, George A. Residence: Vernon. Enlistment Date: Jun 23, 62. Muster Date: Jul 9, 62. Mustered out Jun 13, 65.

Fish, Horace L. Residence: Halifax. Enlistment Date: Sep 12, 64. Muster Date: Sep 12, 64. Mustered out Jun 13, 65; Died Feb 25, 1923, and buried in Bell Cemetery, Halifax, Vt.

Flanders, Joshua A. Residence: Fletcher. Enlistment Date: Aug 20, 64. Muster Date: Aug 20, 64. Mustered out Jun 13, 65; Died Dec 26, 1897, and buried in Barrows Cemetery, East Fairfield, Vt.

Fletcher, Leslie C. Residence: Shelburne. Enlistment Date: Jan 5, 65. Muster Date: Jan 5, 65. Transferred to Co. C Jun 13, 65; Mustered out Dec 1, 65.

Goss, Jason E. Residence: Stratton. Enlistment Date: Jun 6, 62. Muster Date: Jul 9, 62. Mustered out Jun 13, 65.

Gould, George H. Residence: Marlboro. Enlistment Date: Jul 1, 62. Muster Date: Jul 9, 62. Discharged Jan 15, 63, for enlistment in the Regular Army.

Green, Richard. Residence: Peru. Enlistment Date: Sep 23, 64. Muster Date: Sep 23, 64. Mustered out Jun 13, 65.

Grout, Joel. Residence: Stratton. Enlistment Date: Jun 13, 62. Muster Date: Jul 9, 62. Discharged May 26, 65, for wounds received Oct 27, 64; Died Jul 12, 1921, and buried in Woodlawn Cemetery, Newfane, Vt.

Grout, Pliny F. Residence: Stratton. Enlistment Date: Jun 15, 62. Muster Date: Jul 9, 62. Died Feb 11, 63, of disease; Buried in Rosehill Cemetery, Chicago, Ill.

Grover, Alonzo R. Residence: Rupert. Enlistment Date: Aug 29, 64. Muster Date: Aug 29, 64. KIA Oct 27, 64.

Grover, Patrick M. Residence: Rutland. Enlistment Date: Aug 27, 64. Muster Date: Aug 27, 64. Mustered out Jun 13, 65; Died Apr 4, 1904, and buried in Cavendish Cemetery, Cavendish, Vt.

Hall, Joshua R. Residence: Holland. Enlistment Date: Jun 4, 62. Muster Date: — —. Dropped as an un-mustered recruit by special order HQ 9th Vt. Sep 4, 64.

Hannon, Thomas. Residence: Guilford. Enlistment Date: Jun 24, 62. Muster Date: Jul 9, 62. Promoted to Corp. Apr 11, 63; to Sgt. Dec 15, 64; Mustered out Jun 13, 65; Died Dec 3, 1928, and buried in Prospect Cemetery, Brattleboro, Vt.

Holden, Adelbert D. Residence: Townshend. Enlistment Date: Jun 17, 62. Muster Date: Jul 9, 62. Died May 1, 63, of small pox; Buried in Hampton National Cemetery, Hampton, Va.

Holden, George S. Residence: Westminster. Enlistment Date: Aug 27, 64. Muster Date: Aug 27, 64. Trans-ferred to Co. C, 3rd Vt. Jan 20, 65.

Holton, Chester O. Residence: Vernon. Enlistment Date: Aug 2, 64. Muster Date: Aug 2, 64. Mustered out Jun 13, 65.

Holton, Marshall B. Residence: Dummerston. Enlistment Date: Jan 2, 64. Muster Date: Jan 7, 64. Trans-ferred to Co. C Jun 13, 65; Promoted to Corp. Aug 24, 65; Died Nov 13, 65, of disease; Buried in Green-wood Cemetery, Dummerston, Vt.

Howard, Milton L. Residence: Wardsboro. Enlistment Date: Jun 2, 62. Muster Date: Jul 9, 62. Promoted to Corp. Dec 15, 64; Mustered out Jun 13, 65; Died Jan 4, 1915, and buried in the village cemetery, Jamaica, Vt.

Jones, Jesse C. Residence: Stratton. Enlistment Date: Jun 16, 62. Muster Date: Aug 16, 62. Mustered out Aug 13, 65; Died Jun 4, 1918, and buried in Ball Cemetery, Stratton, Vt.

Jones, Erastus H. Residence: Wardsboro. Enlistment Date: Jun 16, 62. Muster Date: Jul 9, 62. Died Dec 24, 62, of disease; Buried in Rosehill Cemetery, Chicago, Il.

Jones, Robert G. Residence: Brattleboro. Enlistment Date: Jul 9, 62. Muster Date: Jul 9, 62. Mustered out Jun 19, 65.

Kelsey, Morrill. Residence: Hardwick. Enlistment Date: Sep 1, 64. Muster Date: Sep 1, 64. Discharged Jul 9, 65.

Knowlton, John O. Residence: Springfield. Enlistment Date: Dec 27, 63. Muster Date: Jan 5, 64. Trans-ferred to Co. C Jun 13, 65; Promoted to Corp Jun 15, 65; Reduced Aug 24, 65; Mustered out Dec 1, 65.

Labare, William. Residence: Enosburgh. Enlistment Date: Dec 25, 63. Muster Date: Dec 30, 63. Trans-ferred to Co. C Jun 13, 65; Mustered out Dec 1, 65.

Lawson, Alfred N. Residence: Vernon. Enlistment Date: Aug 9, 64. Muster Date: Aug 9, 64. Mustered out Aug 3, 65.

Lucas, William J. Residence: Barton. Enlistment Date: Jul 5, 62. Muster Date: Jul 9, 62. Discharged Jan 15, 63, for enlistment in the Regular Army.

Lynch, John. Residence: Jamaica. Enlistment Date: Jun 17, 62. Muster Date: Jul 9, 62. Discharged Jan 27, 63, for disability.

Malloy, Patrick. Residence: Arlington. Enlistment Date: Jan 13, 65. Muster Date: Jan 13, 65. Transferred to Co. C Jun 13, 65; Mustered out Dec 1, 65.

Mansfield, Charles W. Residence: Dummerston. Enlistment Date: May 28, 62. Muster Date: Jul 9, 62. Died Apr 30, 64; Buried in New Bern National Cemetery, New Bern, N.C.

Marcy, Thomas E. Residence: Brattleboro. Enlistment Date: Jun 30, 62. Muster Date: Jul 9, 62. Deserted Jan 11, 63; Returned Mar 31, 63; Promoted to Corp. Sep 4, 64; Wounded Feb 2, 64; Mustered out Jun 13, 65.

Marsh, Evander G. Residence: Vernon. Enlistment Date: Jun 17, 62. Muster Date: Jul 9, 62. Promoted to Corp. Dec 6, 62; Reduced Jul 1, 64; Discharged Dec 9, 64; Died Jul 19, 1885, and buried in Whithed Cemetery, Vernon, Vt.

Martin, William H. Residence: Brattleboro. Enlistment Date: Jun 19, 62. Muster Date: Jul 9, 62. Deserted Dec 19, 62; Died May 18, 1864, and buried in West Hill Cemetery, Williamstown, Vt.

Mason, Denny E. Residence: Brookline. Enlistment Date: Jun 16, 62. Muster Date: Jul 9, 62. Wounded Sep 29, 64; Promoted to Corp. Oct 20, 64; Mustered out Jun 13, 65.

Mason, William H. Residence: Westminster. Enlistment Date: Aug 5, 64. Muster Date: Aug 5, 64. Mus-tered out Jun 13, 65.

McAllister, Talma H. Residence: Montgomery. Enlistment Date: Sep 19, 64. Muster Date: Sep 19, 64. Drafted; Transferred to Co. A, 5th Vt. Jan 20, 65; Died Jan 8, 1898, and buried in the village cemetery, Montgomery, Vt.

McLeoud, Daniel. Residence: Boston, Mass. Enlistment Date: Jul 8, 62. Muster Date: Jul 9, 62. Discharged Jan 15, 63, for enlistment in the Regular Army.

Miller, John. Residence: Dummerston. Enlistment Date: Jan 2, 64. Muster Date: Jan 7, 64. Transferred to Co. C Jun 13, 65; Promoted to Corp. Jul 22, 65; to Sgt. Sep 21, 65; Mustered out Dec 1, 65; Died Feb 21, 1899, and buried in Greenwood Cemetery, Dummerston, Vt.

Miller, Roswell. Residence: Westminster. Enlistment Date: Jun 17, 62. Muster Date: Jul 9, 62. Taken prisoner Sep 3, 62; Paroled Sep 28, 62; Mustered out Jun 13, 65; Died Jan 24, 1869, and buried in Westminster West Cemetery, Westminster, Vt.

Monta, Charles. Residence: Pownal. Enlistment Date: Dec 19, 63. Muster Date: Dec 31, 63. Transferred to Co. C Jun 13, 65; Mustered out Aug 7, 65; Died Jan 19, 1866, and buried in Gardener Cemetery, Pownal, Vt.

Morgan, Hiram H. Residence: Montgomery. Enlistment Date: Sep 19, 64. Muster Date: Sep 19, 64. Drafted; Transferred to Co. A, 5th Vt. Jan 20, 65; Died Aug 9, 1912, and buried in Center Cemetery, Highgate, Vt.

Morgan, John. Residence: Can. Enlistment Date: Jul 10, 62. Muster Date: Jul 10, 62. Discharged Nov 7, 62.

Murray, John, Jr. Residence: Rutland. Enlistment Date: Sep 2, 64. Muster Date: Sep 2, 64. Mustered out Jun 13, 65.

Murray, Joseph. Residence: Rutland. Enlistment Date: Sep 2, 64. Muster Date: Sep 2, 64. Mustered out Jun 13, 65.

Needham, Warren N. Residence: Wardsboro. Enlistment Date: Jun 6, 62. Muster Date: Jul 9, 62. Died Oct 23, 63, of disease.

Newton, Albert E. Residence: Whitingham. Enlistment Date: Jun 26, 62. Muster Date: Jul 9, 62. KIA Sep 29, 64.

Ovitt, Loyal S. Residence: Montgomery. Enlistment Date: Nov 23, 63. Muster Date: Dec 1, 63. Died Nov 5, 64; Buried in New Bern National Cemetery, New Bern, N.C.

Patch, Daniel. Residence: Shrewsbury. Enlistment Date: Aug 18, 64. Muster Date: Aug 18, 64. Mustered out Jun 13, 65.

Peeler, Albert S. Residence: Vernon. Enlistment Date: Sep 2, 64. Muster Date: Sep 2, 64. Mustered out Jun 13, 65.

Peck, Fordyce A. Residence: Ferrisburg. Enlistment Date: Dec 26, 63. Muster Date: Jan 7, 64. Transferred to Co. C Jun 13, 65; Discharged Oct 11, 65, for disability; Died Jul 14, 1866, and buried in Carter Cemetery, Monkton, Vt.

Penniman, Charles C. Residence: Athens. Enlistment Date: May 27, 62. Muster Date: Jul 9, 62. Deserted Dec 19, 62; Returned Jan 9, 64; Deserted Oct 1, 64.

Perham, Alanson E. Residence: Jamaica. Enlistment Date: Jul 12, 62. Muster Date: Jul 12, 62. Deserted Aug 16, 62; Died Nov 24, 1901, and buried in Factory Point Cemetery, Manchester, Vt.

Perry, Rollin. Residence: Weston. Enlistment Date: Nov 28, 63. Muster Date: Jan 2, 64. Transferred to Co. C Jun 13, 65; Mustered out Dec 1, 65; Died Jan 22, 1918, and buried in Evergreen Cemetery, Arlington, Vt.

Pettee, Aurelius. Residence: Dummerston. Enlistment Date: Dec 17, 63. Muster Date: Jan 7, 64. Transferred to Co. C Jun 13, 65; Mustered out Dec 1, 65.

Pierece, Alfred. Residence: Windsor. Enlistment Date: Aug 8, 64. Muster Date: Aug 8, 64. Mustered out Jun 13, 65.

Piersons, George. Residence: Scotland. Enlistment Date: Oct 12, 64. Muster Date: Oct 12, 64. Substitute for George B. Powers, Westford; Transferred to Co. C Jun 13, 65; Mustered out Dec 1, 65.

Potter, George H. Residence: Halifax. Enlistment Date: May 27, 62. Muster Date: Jul 9, 62. Deserted Sep 16, 62; Returned Apr 20, 63; Died Feb 11, 65.

Potter, John C. Residence: Brattleboro. Enlistment Date: Jul 7, 62. Muster Date: Jul 9, 62. Deserted Nov 22, 62.

Powers, Martin K. Residence: Brattleboro. Enlistment Date: Jun 6, 62. Muster Date: Jul 9, 62. Promoted to Corp. Dec 6, 62; Reduced Apr 10, 63; Mustered out Jun 13, 65.

Powers, William. Residence: Rutland. Enlistment Date: Sep 2, 64. Muster Date: Sep 2, 64. Mustered out Jun 13, 65.

Randall, James M. Residence: Pownal. Enlistment Date: Dec 19, 63. Muster Date: Dec 31, 63. Transferred to Co. C Jun 13, 65; Mustered out Sep 6, 65.

Randall, James P. B. Residence: Brattleboro. Enlistment Date: Jun 6, 62. Muster Date: Jul 9, 62. Promoted to Corp. Feb 17, 65; Mustered out Jun 13, 65; Died Oct 27, 1923, and buried in Burnett Cemetery, Dummerston, Vt.

Randall, Thomas J. Residence: Pownal. Enlistment Date: Dec 19, 63. Muster Date: Dec 31, 63. Discharged Feb 14, 65; Died Dec 14, 1881, and buried in Bowen's Corners Cemetery, Adams, Mass.

Rice, Cyren O. Residence: Wilmington. Enlistment Date: Jun 5, 62. Muster Date: Jul 9, 62. Died Mar 20, 64, of disease.

Riley, Thomas. Residence: Bennington. Enlistment Date: Jul 10, 62. Muster Date: Jul 10, 62. Deserted Jul 16, 62.

Robbins, Chauncey B. Residence: Winhall. Enlistment Date: Jun 3, 62. Muster Date: Jul 9, 62. Mustered out Jun 13, 65; Died May 24, 1926, and buried in Rawsonville Cemetery, Jamaica, Vt.

Rockwell, Atremas. Residence: Montgomery. Enlistment Date: Sep 19, 64. Muster Date: Sep 19, 64. Drafted; Transferred to Co. A, 5th Vt. Jan 20, 65.

Rogers, Frank. Residence: Halifax. Enlistment Date: May 28, 62. Muster Date: Jul 9, 62. Mustered out May 25, 65.

Rood, Stephen W. Residence: Townshend. Enlistment Date: Jun 10, 62. Muster Date: Jul 9, 62. Discharged Jan 15, 63, for enlistment in the Regular Army.

Roundy, Ralph W. Residence: Rockingham. Enlistment Date: Jul 4, 62. Muster Date: Jul 9, 62. Mustered out Jun 13, 65.

Ruiter, Henry W. Residence: Burke. Enlistment Date: Jul 11, 62. Muster Date: Jul 11, 62. Died Feb 2, 63, of disease.

Sawtell, John H. Residence: Vernon. Enlistment Date: Jun 18, 62. Muster Date: Jul 9, 62. Died Feb 18, 63, of disease.

Sears, Michael. Residence: Brattleboro. Enlistment Date: Jun 23, 62. Muster Date: Jul 9, 62. Promoted to Corp. Feb —, 64; Mustered out Jun 13, 65.

Scott, Bradford T. Residence: Wardsboro. Enlistment Date: Jun 6, 62. Muster Date: Jul 9, 62. Promoted to Corp. Dec 6, 62; to Sgt. May 30, 63; Reduced Mar 3, 65; Mustered out Jun 11, 65.

Sherlow, Miles. Residence: Westfield. Enlistment Date: Aug 18, 64. Aug 18, 64. Mustered out Jun 65; Died Mar 31, 1905, and buried in Newport Center Cemetery, Newport Center, Vt.

Smith, Everett W. Residence: Brookline. Enlistment Date: Aug 15, 64. Muster Date: Aug 15, 64. Mustered out Jun 13, 65.

Smith, George H. Residence: Brattleboro. Enlistment Date: Jul 7, 62. Muster Date: Jul 9, 62. Promoted to Corp. Apr 10, 63; Reduced Sep 2, 64; Promoted to Corp. Mar 3, 65; Mustered out Jun 13, 65.

Smith, Waldo J. Residence: Windham. Enlistment Date: Sep 3, 64. Muster Date: Sep 3, 64. Mustered out Jun 13, 65.

Stanclift, Josiah W. Residence: Halifax. Enlistment Date: Sep 8, 64. Muster Date: Sep 8, 64. Transferred to Co. C, 4th Vt. Jan 20, 65.

Stanley, Chauncey. Residence: Rutland. Enlistment Date: Sep 3, 64. Muster Date: Sep 3, 64. Mustered out Jun 13, 65.

Stoddard, Charles W. Residence: Dover. Enlistment Date: Dec 21, 63. Muster Date: Dec 31, 63. Wounded Feb 2, 64; Mustered out Jun 7, 65.

Stoddard, Levi A. Residence: Vernon. Enlistment Date: Jul 2, 62. Muster Date: Jul 9, 62. Discharged Dec 14, 64.

Streeter, Esmond. Residence: Vernon. Enlistment Date: May 29, 62. Muster Date: Jul 9, 62. Mustered out Jun 13, 65.

Stygles, Minard. Residence: Brattleboro. Enlistment Date: Jun 24, 62. Muster Date: Jul 9, 62. Mustered out Jun 13, 65.

Sumner, Eben S. Residence: Halifax. Enlistment Date: Sep 5, 64. Muster Date: Sep 5, 64. Mustered out Jun 13, 65.

Taylor, Henry. Residence: Norwich. Enlistment Date: Sep 7, 64. Muster Date: Sep 7, 64. Deserted Oct 15, 64.

Taylor, Seneca W. Residence: Plymouth. Enlistment Date: Jul 11, 62. Muster Date: Jul 11, 62. Wounded Sep 14, 62; Mustered out Jun 13, 65; Died Jun 30, 1926, in Iuka, Kan.

Wandell, Nelson. Residence: Brattleboro. Enlistment Date: Jun 4, 62. Muster Date: Jul 9, 62. Promoted to Corp. Sep 1, 63; Mustered out Jun 13, 65.

Ward, Gilbert M. Residence: Brattleboro. Enlistment Date: Jun 7, 62. Muster Date: Jul 9, 62. Promoted to Corp. Dec 6, 62; Reduced Jun 23, 63; Mustered out Jun 13, 65.

Waters, William. Residence: Montgomery. Enlistment Date: Jan 2, 64. Muster Date: Jan 5, 64. Wounded Sep 29, 64; Deserted Mar 9, 65.

Wells, Edward B. Residence: Rutland. Enlistment Date: Aug 15, 64. Muster Date: Aug 15, 64. Transferred from Co. B; Mustered out Jun 13, 65; Died Jul 18, 1923, and buried in Maple Grove Cemetery, Wallingford, Vt.

White, Charles C. Residence: Jamaica. Enlistment Date: Jun 19, 62. Muster Date: Jul 9, 62. Died Mar 5, 64.

Whitney, George T. Residence: Dummerston. Enlistment Date: Sep 2, 64. Muster Date: Sep 2, 64. Died Dec 11, 64; Buried in West Dummerston Cemetery, Dummerston, Vt.

Whitney, Orlin M. Residence: Westminster. Enlistment Date: Aug 5, 64. Muster Date: Aug 5, 64. Mustered out May 31, 65; Died Dec 29, 1913, and buried in Riverside Cemetery, Brookline, Vt.

Whitney, William L. G. Residence: Dummerston. Enlistment Date: Dec 14, 63. Muster Date: Jan 7, 64. Died Dec 11, 64; Buried in Upper West Dummerston Cemetery, Dummerston, Vt.

Wilder, Emery S. Residence: Jamaica. Enlistment Date: Jun 28, 62. Muster Date: Jul 9, 62. Taken prisoner

Sep 3, 62; Paroled Sep 15, 62; Mustered out Jun 13, 65; Died Jun 5, 1916, and buried in the village cemetery, Jamaica, Vt.

Willard, Earl F. Dummerston. Enlistment Date: Aug 23, 64. Muster Date: Aug 23, 64. Mustered out May
22, 65; Died Nov 12, 1904, and buried in West Dummerston Cemetery, Dummerston, Vt.

Willard, John L. Residence: Dummerston. Enlistment Date: Jan 2, 64. Jan 7, 64. Transferred to Co. C Jun
13, 65; Mustered out Dec 1, 65; Died Mar 12, 1910, and buried in West Dummerston Cemetery, Dummerston, Vt.

Williams, Alden L. Residence: Halifax. Enlistment Date: Sep 12, 64. Muster Date: Sep 12, 64. Mustered
out Jun 7, 65.

Williams, Ormando M. Residence: Jamaica. Enlistment Date: Jun 28, 62. Muster Date: Jul 9, 62. Discharged Nov 28, 62, for disability.

Wood, Otis W. Residence: Halifax. Enlistment Date: Sep 12, 64. Muster Date: Sep 12, 64. Mustered out
Jun 13, 65.

Wright, Edwin S. Residence: Brattleboro. Enlistment Date: Jun 18, 62. Muster Date: Jul 9, 62. Mustered
out Jun 13, 65; Died Feb 6, 1922, and buried in Weybridge Cemetery, Weybridge, Vt.

CHAPTER NOTES

Chapter 1

1. George G. Benedict, *Vermont in the Civil War. A History of the Part Taken by the Vermont Soldiers and Sailors in the War for the Union, 1861–5*, 2 vols. (Burlington, Vt.: The Free Press Association, 1886), vol. 2, pp. 182, hereinafter cited as Benedict and all references are to vol. 2 unless otherwise stated; *Vermont Phoenix*, 29 May 1862.

2. Benedict, vol. 1, pp. 28, 235–236; vol. 2, pp. 1–181, 533–534, 697–719.

3. Benedict, pp. 183–184.

4. *Lamoille Newsdealer*, 30 May 1862.

5. Ibid.

6. Paul G. Zeller, *The Second Vermont Volunteer Infantry Regiment, 1861–1865* (Jefferson, N.C.: McFarland & Co., Inc., Publisher, 2002), pp. 11, 29, hereinafter cited as Zeller.

7. *Lamoille Newsdealer*, 27 Jun 1862.

8. *Lamoille Newsdealer*, 4 Jul 1862; Theodore S. Peck, *Revised Roster of Vermont Volunteers and Lists of Vermonters who Served in the Army and Navy of the United States During the War of the Rebellion, 1861–66* (Montpelier, Vt.: Watchman Co., 1892), pp. 368–369, hereinafter cited as Peck; Bell Irvin Wiley, *The Life of Billy Yank, the common soldier of the Union.* (Baton Rouge: Louisiana State University Press, 1986), p. 24.

9. *Lamoille Newsdealer*, 4 Jul, 1862.

10. Benedict, p. 64; George J. Stannard's compiled service record, Records of the Adjutant General's Office, 1780–1917, Record Group 94, National Archives Building, Washington, DC., hereinafter cited as the individuals name and compiled service record; Peck, pp. 30, 344, hereinafter cited as Peck; Hiram Carlton, *Genealogical and Family History* of the *State of Vermont.* 2 vols. (New York: The Lewis Publishing Co., 1903), Vol. 1 pp. 150–151, hereinafter cited as Carlton; Abby Maria Hemenway, *The Vermont Historical Gazetteer: a magazine, embracing a history of each town, civil, ecclesiastical, biographical and military.* 5 vols. (Burlington, Vt.: Tuttle Co., 1923), vol. 2, pp. 385–387, hereinafter cited as *The Vermont Historical Gazetteer.*

11. United States War Department, *Revised Regulations for the Army of the United States, 1861*. 1861, reprint (Harrisburg,: National Historical Society, 1980), pp. 36, 519, hereinafter cited as *Revised Regulations for the Army of the United States, 1861.*

12. Benedict, p. 184; Peck, pp. 15, 344, Dudley K. Andross' compiled service and military pension records, Records of the Office of the Secretary of the Interior, Record Group 48, National Archives Building, Washington, DC., hereinafter cited as the individual's name and type of record; Jacob G. Ullery, compiler, *Men of Ver-*

mont: An illustrated Biographical History of Vermonters and Sons of Vermont (Brattleboro, Vt.: Transcript Publishing Company, 1894), p. 7, hereinafter cited as Ullery.

13. Benedict, p. 184; Peck, pp. 162, 344; William Arba Ellis ed., *Norwich University, 1819–1911; her history, her graduates, her roll of honor, published by Major-General Grenville M. Dodge, compiled and edited by William Arba Ellis in three volumes* (Montpelier: The Capitol City Press, 1911), p. 521, hereinafter cited as *Norwich University.*; Edwin S. Stowell's military pension record; John R. Witherell, *The Civil War Service of Edwin S. Stowell, 1861–1863* (n.p., n.d.), Antietam National Battlefield, Sharpsburg, Md., hereinafter cited as Edwin S. Stowell letter; *Lamoille Newsdealer*, 15 Aug 1862.

14. Benedict, p. 184; Peck, pp. 10, 16, 344; John C. Stearns' compiled service and military pension records; Ullery, part 2, p. 375.

15. Benedict, p. 184; Peck, pp. 10, 16, 344.

16. Benedict, p. 102, 184; Peck, pp. 31, 344; , *The Vermont Historical Gazetteer*, vol. 4, p. 632; Zeller, pp. 13, 35, 77, 86; *Vermont Phoenix*, 29 May and 3 Jul 1862.

17. Benedict, p. 184; Peck, p. 345.

18. Benedict, p. 184; Peck, p. 345; Lucius Dickinson's compiled service record.

19. Peck, p. 345.

20. Peck, p. 345.

21. Peck, p. 345.

22. Peck, pp. 22, 345, 363; Henry D. Belden's military pension record.

23. Peck, p. 345.

24. Mark M. Boatner, *Military Customs and Traditions* (Westport, Conn.: Greenwood Press, 1956; repr., New York: D. McKay Co., 1976), p. 88; *Revised Regulations for the Army of the United States, 1861*, p. 519.

25. Benedict, p. 183.

26. *Vermont Phoenix*, 17 Jul 1862,

27. Benedict, p. 183; Francis A. Lord, *Civil War Collector's Encyclopedia* (New York: Castle Books, 1965), pp. 295, 297, 301, 315, hereinafter cited as Lord; Valentine G. Barney, Civil War letters, Vermont Historical Society, Barre, Vt., hereinafter cited as Valentine G. Barney letters; Valentine G. Barney's service record; *Burlington Daily Free Press*, 18 Jul, 1862. Barney was named after Capt. Valentine Goodrich who had commanded a Swanton company in the War of 1812 and fell at the battle of Lundy's Lane, Benedict, vol. 1, p. 224.

28. Lord, p. 119.

29. Lord, pp. 119–121.

30. Lord, p. 310.

31. Benedict, p. 183; *Rutland Herald*, 28 Jun and 14 Jul 1862; Howard Coffin, *Full Duty: Vermonters in the Civil War* (Woodstock, Vt.: The Countryman Press, Inc., 1993),

p. 68, hereinafter cited as *Full Duty*; *Lamoille Newsdealer* 18 Jul 1862

32. Benedict, p. 183.

33. Valentine G. Barney letters.

34. Benedict, pp. 183–184; Nelson L Wandell, Civil War diaries, 1862–1865, Brooks Memorial Library, Brattleboro, Vt., hereinafter cited as Nelson L. Wandell diaries; *Rutland Herald*, 28 Jun 1862.

35. Donald H. Wickman, *Letters to Vermont From Her Civil War Soldier Correspondents to the Home Press* (Bennington, Vt.: Images from the Past, Inc., 1998), vol. 2, pp. 61–62.

36. *Rutland Herald*, 1 Jul 1862.

37. *Rutland Herald*, 1 Jul 1862.

38. Benedict, pp. 184–185; Nelson L. Wandell diaries; *Lamoille Newsdealer*, 18 Jul 62; *Vermont Phoenix*, 10 Jul 1863.

39. *Lamoille Newsdealer*, 18 Jul 62

40. Benedict, pp. 18, 24.

41. Benedict, p. 185; Nelson L. Wandell diaries; *Rutland Herald*, 26 Jul 1862; Valentine G. Barney letters; Linus E. Sherman letters; Linus E. Sherman, Civil War diaries January 1, 1862–November 31 and March 18, 1864–December 28, 1864, hereinafter cited as Linus E. Sherman diaries; Vermont Historical Society, Barre, Vermont. *Lamoille Newsdealer*, 25 Jul 1862; *Vermont Phoenix*, 17 Jul 1862; Edwin A. Kilbourne, Civil War letters, in the possession of Robert E. Kilbourne, hereinafter cited as Edwin A. Kilbourne letters.

42. Benedict, p. 185; Linus E. Sherman letters; *Lamoille Newsdealer*, 25 Jul 62; *Burlington Daily Free Press, 18 Jul, 1862*; Edwin A. Kilbourne letters.

43. Benedict, p. 186; Nelson L. Wandell diaries; *Rutland Herald*, 22 Jul 1862; Mark M. Boatner III, *The Civil War Dictionary* (rev. ed. New York: Vintage Books, 1991), p. 354, hereinafter cited as *The Civil War Dictionary*, pp. 354, 816; *Lamoille Newsdealer*, 25 Jul 62; *Burlington Daily Free Press*, 18 Jul, 1862; Edwin A. Kilbourne letters.

44. Benedict, p. 186; Alfred H. Guernsey and Henry M. Alden, *Harper's Pictorial History of the Civil War*, 2 vols., (New York: The Fairfax Press, 1866), vol. 1, p.86, hereinafter cited as *Harper's Pictorial History of the Civil War*; Margaret Leech, *Reveille in Washington 1860–1865* (New York: Harper & Brothers Publishers, 1941), pp.60–61, hereinafter cited as *Reveille in Washington*; Sherry H. Olson, *Baltimore* (Baltimore: The Johns Hopkins University Press, 1980), pp. 107, 226; Peck 338; Edwin A. Kilbourne letters.

45. Peck, 338; *Lamoille Newsdealer*, 25 Jul 1862; *Burlington Daily Free Press*, 18 Jul, 1862; Edwin A. Kilbourne letters.

46. Benedict, p. 186; Nelson L. Wandell diaries; *Rutland Herald*, 22 Jul 1862; Otto Eisenschiml, *Vermont General: The Unusual War Experiences of Edward Hastings Ripley (1862–1865)* (N.Y.: The Devin-Adair Company, Publishers, 1960), p. 9, hereinafter cited as Eisenschiml; Linus E. Sherman diaries.

47. Lord, pp. 242–243; William B. Edwards, *Civil War Guns* (Harrisburg: The Stackpole Company, 1962),p. 13, hereinafter cited as *Civil War Guns*; Bell Irvin Wiley and Hirst D. Milhollen, *They Who Fought Here* (New York: Bonanza Books, 1959), pp. 104, hereinafter cited as *They Who Fought Here*.

48. Lord, p. 17; *Civil War Guns*, pp. 13, 17–19; Harold L. Peterson, ed., *Encyclopedia of Firearms* (New York: E. P. Dutton and Company, Inc., 1964), pp. 72, 219; *They Who Fought Here*, p. 114; William M. Wallace, *Soul of the Lion* (Gettysburg: Stan Clark Military books, 1960; reprint, 1995), p. 133.

49. Charles E. Heller and William A. Stoft, *America's First Battles, 1776–1965* (Lawrence, Kans.: University Press of Kansas, 1986, p. 86; *Soul of the Lion*, p. 133; Grady McWhitney and Perry D. Jamieson, *Attack and Die* (University, Ala.: The University of Alabama Press, 1982), pp. 50, 82, hereinafter cited as *Attack and Die*; *The Life of Billy Yank*, pp. 187–189.

50. Bruce, Catton, *The Army of the Potomac: Mr. Lincoln's Army*. Garden City (N.Y.: Doubleday & Company, Inc., 1952), p. 28; *The Civil War Dictionary*, p. 101; Robert U. Johnson and Clarence C. Buel, eds., *Battles and Leaders of the Civil War, Being for the most part contributions by Union and Confederate officers* 4 vols. (New York: Century, 1887–1888), vol. 1, p.458, hereinafter cited as *Battles and Leaders*.

51. Benedict, p. 68; Margaret Leech, *Reveille in Washington*, pp.76, 86; Linus E. Sherman letters; Valentine G. Barney letters.

52. Charles A. Flanders' compiled service and military pension files.

53. Benedict, p. 186; *The Civil War Dictionary*, p. 816; Linus E. Sherman diaries,

54. Benedict, pp. 186–187; Nelson L. Wandell diaries; *Rutland Herald*, 26 Jul 1862; Eisenschiml , pp. 8–9; Charles F. Branch, History of the Ninth Vermont Inf. Vols. Vermont Historical Society, Barre, Vermont, hereinafter cited as The History of the Ninth Vermont Inf. Vols.

55. Benedict, pp. 186–187; Nelson L. Wandell diaries; *Rutland Herald*, 26 Jul 1862; Eisenschiml , p. 9; *Lamoille Newsdealer*, 8 Aug 1862; Edwin A. Kilbourne letters; Linus E. Sherman diaries.

56. Benedict, p. 186; *Rutland Herald*, 22 Jul 1862; Eisenschiml, p. 9; Valentine G. Barney letters.

57. Linus E. Sherman letters; *Lamoille Newsdealer*, 8 Aug 1862.

58. *Mr. Lincoln's Army*, p. 181; *The Life of Billy Yank*, p. 237.

59. *Mr. Lincoln's Army*, pp. 181–182; *The Life of Billy Yank*, p. 239.

60. *Mr. Lincoln's Army*, p. 182; *The Life of Billy Yank*, pp. 240–241.

61. *Rutland Herald*, 22 Jul 1862.

62. Benedict, p. 187; Eisenschiml, p. 10.

63. Benedict, p. 187; Nelson L. Wandell diaries; Wyman Wetherell's military pension record and compiled service record.

64. Benedict, p. 187; Nelson L. Wandell diaries; Eisenschiml, p. 10.

65. United States War Department, *War of the Rebellion: A Compilation of the Official Records of the Union and Confederate Armies*, 128 volumes (Washington: Government Printing Office, 1902), series 1, vol. 12, part 3, page 501, hereinafter cited as OR. All references will be to series 1, part 1 unless otherwise stated.

66. *Lamoille Newsdealer*, 8 Aug 1862.

67. Peck, pp. 361, 366; Joseph Lawrence's pension record; *Lamoille Newsdealer*, 8 Aug 1862; Alfred H. Batchelder compiled service record.

68. Eisenschiml, p. 10.

69. *Lamoille Newsdealer*, 8 Aug 1862; Edwin A. Kilbourne letters.

70. Valentine G. Barney letters; Ephraim Wetherell's compiled service and military pension records.

71. Benedict, p. 187; Eisenschiml, p. 11; *The Civil War Dictionary*, p. 651; Chester G. Hearn, *Six Years of Hell: Harpers Ferry During the Civil War* (Baton Rouge: Louisiana State University Press, 1996), p. 54, hereinafter cited as *Six Years of Hell*; Paul R .Teetor, *A Matter of*

Hours: Treason at Harper's Ferry (Fairleigh Dickenson, 1982, pp. 53–54, hereinafter cited as Teetor; *Lamoille Newasdealer*, 22 Aug 1862; Ezra J. Warner, *Generals in Blue: Lives of the Union Commanders* (Baton Rouge: Louisiana State University Press, 1964), p. 557, hereinafter cited as *Generals in Blue*.

72. George E. Pond, *The Shenandoah Valley in 1864.* 1885. (Wilmington, N.C.: Broadfoot Publishing Company, 1989), pp. 2–8; Bruce Catton, *The Army of the Potomac: A Stillness at Appomattox* (Garden City, N.Y.: Doubleday & Company, Inc., 1953), p. 275; Thomas A. *The Guns of Cedar Creek* (Strasburg, Va.: Heritage Associates, 1988) p. 5.

73. Chris Fordney, "A Town Embattled." *Civil War Times Illustrated*, vol. 34, no. 6 (February 1996), p. 32, hereinafter cited as Fordney.

74. Eisenschiml, p. 11; *Lamoille Newsdealer*, 15, 22 Aug 1862; Valentine G. Barney letters.

75. History of the Ninth Vermont Inf. Vols.

76. Fordney, p. 33; Eisenschiml, p. 11.

77. Zenas H. Bliss, Civil War Letter. In the possession of Daniel T. Hebert, hereinafter cited as Zenas H. Bliss letter, Co. I Descriptive List, Vermont Public Records Division of the Department of Buildings and General Services, Middlesex, Vermont; Zenas H. Bliss' compiled service record.

78. Eisenschiml, pp. 17–18, 21.

79. Eisenschiml, p. 12.

80. *Lamoille Newsdealer*, 8 Aug 1862.

81. Valentine G. Barney letters.

82. *The Civil War Dictionary*, p. 76; Ruth Scarborough, *Belle, Boyd, Siren of the South* (Macon, Ga.: Mercer University Press, 1983), p. 63; Louis A. Sigaud, *Belle Boyd, Confederate Spy* (Richmond, Va.: The Dietz Press, 1944), pp. 59–60; Valentine G. Barney letters; Eisenschiml, p. 12.

83. *Lamoille Newsdealer*, 8 Aug 1862.

84. Valentine G. Barney letters; Augustus T. Bushnell's compiled service record.

85. Valentine G. Barney letters; Peck, p. 346; Abner B. White's military pension record.

86. James Grout, Civil War letters, Russell Collection of Vermontiana at the Martha Canfield Library, Arlington, Vermont, hereinafter cited as James Grout letters; D. K. Young, *Echoes in the Forest, The Family History Supplement to the History Of Stratton, Vermont* (Published by the Town of Stratton, Vt., 2000), p. 186, here in after cited as D. K. Young.

87. Valentine G. Barney letters.

88. James Grout letters; Joseph Douglass' complied service record.; William V. Wetherell's compiled service and military pension records; Horace W. Brown's complied service record.

89. Rufus B. Tucker Civil War letters. In the possession of Pat and Jim Geary; Rufus Tucker's compiled service and military pension records; Peck, p. 359.

90. Rufus Tucker's military pension record.

91. Peck, p. 364; Stephen Parker's compiled service record.

92. Benedict, p. 187; Peck, pp. 359, 362; *Rutland Herald*, 16 Aug 1862; George A. Beebe's compiled service record; Edwin A. Kilbourne letters; Eisenschiml, p. 14.

93. Benedict, p. 187; *Rutland Herald*, 16 Aug 1862; *Burlington Daily Free Press*, 14 Aug, 1862.

94. Eisenschiml, p. 14; *Rutland Herald*, 16 Aug 1862.

95. Linus E. Sherman diaries.

96. Eisenschiml, p. 17.

97. Eisenschiml, p. 19.

98. Linus E. Sherman letters.

99. Valentine G. Barney letters.

100. James Grout letters.

101. Benedict, p. 187; Nelson L. Wandell, Civil War diaries 1862–1865, Nelson L. Wandell diaries; Edwin A. Kilbourne letters.

102. Edwin A. Kilbourne letters; Edwin R. Smith's military pension file.

103. Benedict, p. 187; Nelson L. Wandell diaries; Edwin R. Smith's military pension record.

104. Benedict, p. 187; Nelson L. Wandell diaries; James Grout letters.

105. James Grout letters.

106. *Rutland Herald*, 30 Aug 1862; *Lamoille Newsdealer*, 5 Sep 1862; Peck, P. 373; Valentine G. Barney letters; Co. I Descriptive List, Vermont Public Records Division of the Department of Buildings and General Services, Middlesex, Vermont; William H. H. Greenslit's compiled service record.

107. George Baylor, *Bull Run to Bull Run; or Four Years in the Army of Northern Virginia. Containing a detailed account of the career and adventures of the Baylor Light Horse, Company B, Twelfth Virginia Cavalry, C. S. A., with leaves from my scrapbook* (Richmond, Va.: D. F. Johnson Publishing Company, 1900), pp. 55–67; Eisenschiml, p. 17; Zenas H. Bliss letter.

108. Benedict, p. 187.

109. *The Civil War Dictionary*, p. 101; Douglas S. Freeman, *R. E. Lee: A Biography* (New York: Charles Scribner's Sons, 1936), vol. 2, pp. 225, 229, 256, hereinafter cited as *R. E. Lee*.

110. *The Civil War Dictionary*, p. 108; *R. E. Lee*, vol. 2, pp. 257–258.

111. The Civil War Dictionary, p. 102; Robert U. Johnson and Clarence C. Buel, eds., *Battles and Leaders*, vol. 2, p. 459; *R. E. Lee*, vol. 2, pp. 261–266, 271–272.

112. *The Civil War Dictionary*, p. 102; *R. E. Lee*, vol. 2, pp. 277–288, 300.

113. *The Civil War Dictionary*, pp. 102–103; *R. E. Lee*, vol. 2, pp. 292–316.

114. *The Civil War Dictionary*, pp. 102–104; *R. E. Lee*, vol. 2, pp. 312–316.

115. Benedict, p. 317.

116. Benedict, p. 317; *R. E. Lee*, vol. 2, pp. 350–354; Timothy J. Reese, *Sealed With Their Lives: The Battle for Crampton's Gap, Burkittsville, Maryland, September 14, 1862* (Baltimore: Butternut and Blue, 1998), pp. 2–7, hereinafter cited as Reese; *The Civil War Dictionary*, p. 17; Stephen, W. Sears, *Landscape Turned Red: The Battle of Antietam* (Boston: Houghton Mifflin Company, 1983) pp. 64–66, hereinafter cited as Sears.

117. *R. E. Lee*, vol. 2, p. 359; Sears, p. 66.

118. *R. E. Lee*, vol. 2, p. 360.

119. Valentine G. Barney letters.

120. Peck, p. 355; David Steele's compiled service and military pension records.

121. Benedict, p. 188; Eisenschiml, p. 21; Nelson L. Wandell diaries; *Rutland Herald*, 17 Sep 1862; Edwin A. Kilbourne letters.

122. Eisenschiml, p. 21.

123. Benedict, p. 189; *Lamoille Newsdealer*, 12 Sep 1862; Edwin A. Kilbourne letters; Valentine G. Barney letters; Fordney, p. 35.

124. Benedict, p. 189; Eisenschiml, p. 21; William Wetherell's compiled service record.

125. OR, vol. 19, p. 139; OR, series 1, vol. 19, part 2, pp. 594, 603; Fordney, p. 35.

Chapter 2

1. Benedict, vol. 2, p. 189; Eisenschiml, p. 21.
2. Benedict, vol. 2, p. 189; Nelson L. Wandell diaries; Emery S. Wilder's military pension record; Peck, p. 377.
3. Benedict, vol. 2, p. 189; Nelson L. Wandell diaries.
4. Edwin A. Kilbourne letters.
5. Benedict, p. 189; William J. Henderson's compiled service record.
6. Benedict, p. 189; Nelson L. Wandell diaries; Valentine G. Barney letters; Edwin A. Kilbourne letters.
7. Valentine G. Barney letters; *Lamoille Newsdealer*, 12 Sep, 1862.
8. Benedict, vol. 2, p. 190; R. E. Lee, p. 361; Hearn, pp. 7–33, 293–294; Dennis E. Frye, "Through God's Blessing," *North & South* 5, vol. 7 (October 2002). pp. 68, hereinafter cited as Frye.
9. Hearn, pp. 109–110; Teetor, pp. 13–14, 32, 34; OR, Series 1, vol. 2, 374–376, 426, 438–439.
10. Benedict, vol. 2, p. 189; Hearn, pp. 111–112; Teetor, p. 39; OR, series 1, vol. 12, part 3, p. 394.
11. Hearn, pp. 103–10; Teetor, pp. 41–42; Frye, p. 69; OR, vol. 19, pp. 548, 577.
12. Benedict, vol. 2, p. 189; Hearn, pp. 111–112; Teetor, p. 39; OR, series 1, vol. 12, part 3, p. 394.
13. Benedict, vol. 2, p. 190, Hearn, pp. 127–128; Teetor, pp. 55–56.
14. Teetor, p. 47; OR, vol. 19, p. 522; Stephen W. Sears, *Landscape Turned Red: The Battle of Antietam* (Boston: Houghton Mifflin Company, 1983), p. 90, hereinafter cited as Sears.
15. Valentine G. Barney letters; Peck, p. 359; John W. Spafford's compiled service record; John J. Duffy, Samuel B. Hand, Ralph H. Orth , *The Vermont Encyclopedia* (Hanover, N.H.: University Press of New England, 2003), p. 177, hereinafter cited as *The Vermont Encyclopedia*.
16. Benedict, vol. 2, p. 190; Hearn, pp. 129–134; OR, vol. 19, p. 533.
17. Hearn, p. 130.
18. Benedict, vol. 2, pp. 200–201; Hearn, p. 131; Teetor, p. 63; Edwin S. Stowell letter.
19. Hearn, pp. 135, Teetor, pp. 70–73; OR, vol. 19, p. 778.
20. Frye, p. 70.
21. OR, vol. 19, pp. 519, 739; Hearn, p. 135; Teetor, p. 72.
22. Hearn, pp. 141–142; Teetor, p. 89; OR, vol. 19, pp. 737–738.
23. Hearn, p. 142; Teetor, pp. 89–90, OR, vol. 19, pp. 738–739, 797.
24. Benedict, vol. 2, p. 192; OR, vol. 19, p. 520; Eisenschiml, p. 27.
25. Hearn, pp. 135–136; Teetor, p. 72; OR, vol. 19, pp. 519, 535, 788–789, 793.
26. Benedict, vol. 2, p. 201; Eisenschiml, p. 28; John Esten Cooke, *Wearing of the Gray: Being personal portraits, scenes, and adventures of the war* (1867; Reprint, Baton Rouge: Louisiana State University Press, 1977).
27. Benedict, vol. 2, p. 192; Nelson L. Wandell diaries; *Lamoille Newsdealer*, 29 Aug 1862; Edwin A. Kilbourne letters.
28. Benedict, vol. 2, p. 192; Nelson L. Wandell diaries; *Lamoille Newsdealer*, 29.
28. Eisenschiml, p. 25.
30. Elijah B. Sherman's compiled service record.
31. Edwin A. Kilbourne letters.
32. OR, series 1, vol. 19, part 2, pp. 603–604; *R. E. Lee*, p. 359; Sears, pp. 91–92; Frye, pp. 67–68.
33. OR, series 1, vol. 19, part 2, pp. 603–604; Sears, pp. 90–91.

34. OR, series 1, vol. 19, part 2, p. 604.
35. Hearn, p. 143; Teetor, pp. 96–98.
36. Benedict, vol. 2, p. 193; Hearn, pp. 145–146; Teetor, pp. 96–97; OR, vol. 19, pp. 524, 525.
37. Benedict, vol. 2, pp. 192–193; Teetor, pp. 99–100, 103; OR, vol. 19, pp. 536, 691, 707.
38. Teetor, p. 100, Hearn, p. 145; OR, vol. 19, pp. 536, 542, 691, 819.
39. Benedict, p. 192; Teetor, p. 101; Hearn, pp. 149–150; OR, vol. 19, p. 536.
40. Benedict, p. 193; Hearn, pp. 145–146; Teetor, pp. 107–108; OR, vol. 19, pp. 524, 525.
41. Benedict, p. 201; Teetor, p. 166; OR, vol. 19, pp. 632–633.
42. OR, vol. 19, p. 525, 775, 792, 797.
43. Benedict, p. 192; Teetor, pp. 116, 123–135; Hearn, pp. 157–159; Frye, p. 71.
44. Teetor, pp. 132–135; Hearn, p. 160; Frye, p. 71;
45. Teetor, p. 135, 136.
46. Hearn, p. 163, Frye, pp. 71, 73; OR, vol. 19, p. 537.
47. Hearn, p. 163, Frye, p. 71; OR, vol. 19, p. 537.
48. Benedict, p. 193; Teetor, p. 146; Hearn, p. 167.
49. Louis Murray's compiled service record.
50. *R. E. Lee*, vol. 2, pp. 363; Hearn, pp. 169–170; Teetor, pp. 147–148.
51. OR, vol. 19, p. 720.
52. Ibid., p. 785.
53. Benedict, vol. 2, p. 319; *Mr. Lincoln's Army*, p. 221; OR, vol. 19, p. 45.
54. OR, vol. 19, pp. 45–46.
55. OR, vol. 19, pp. 370, 374, 380; Sears, pp. 145–146.
56. Robert U. Johnson and Clarence C. Buel, eds. *Battles and Leaders of the Civil War. Being for the most part contributions by Union and Confederate officers*. 4 vols. (New York: Century, 1887–1888), vol. 2, p. 609, hereinafter cited as *Battles and Leaders*; OR, vol. 19, p. 958; Teetor, p. 159, Hearn, 172.
57. *Battles and Leaders*, vol. 2, pp. 609–610; OR, vol. 19, p. 958; Teetor, pp. 159–160; Hearn, pp. 172–173.
58. Benedict, p. 194.
59. Ibid., p. 194.
60. OR, vol. 19, p. 538.
61. Benedict, p. 193; Eisenschiml, p. 30.
62. Benedict, p. 195; Hearn, p. 175; OR, vol. 19, pp. 742, 745.
63. OR, vol. 19, p. 954.
64. Benedict, p. 195; OR, vol. 19, pp. 954, 980.
65. Benedict, p. 195; Hearn, pp. 174, 176; Edwin S. Stowell letter.
66. James Grout letters.
67. Peck, p. 377; Seneca W. Taylor's military pension record; William E. Connelley, *A Standard History of Kansas and Kansans* (Chicago: Lewis Publishing Co., 1919), pp. 2430–2431, hereinafter cited as Connelley.
68. Nelson L. Wandell diary; Peck, p. 377; Nelson L. Wandell's compiled service record.
69. Benedict, p. 193.
70. OR, vol. 19, pp. 527, 1004; Hearn, p. 176.
71. Hearn, p. 176.
72. Benedict, p. 195; OR, vol. 19, p. 980.
73. OR, vol. 19, p. 951; Teetor, p. 172.
74. Benedict, p. 323; Sears, p. 149; OR, vol. 19, p. 408.
75. Hearn, p. 177; Teetor, p. 173; Sears, p. 151.
76. Hearn, pp. 177–178; Teetor, pp. 173–175; Sears, pp. 151–152; OR, Vol. 19, pp. 583–584.
77. Hearn, pp. 178–179; Teetor, pp. 175–176; Sears, p. 152.
78. Benedict, p. 201.

79. Benedict, p. 196; OR, Vol. 19, p. 797; Edwin S. Stowell letter.

80. Benedict, p. 196.

81. Edwin S. Stowell letter.

82. James Grout letters.

83. Kent D. Young, *Echoes in the Forest, The Family History of Stratton, Vermont* (Stratton, Vt.: Published by the Town of Stratton, 2000), pp. 186–190, hereinafter cited as *Echoes in the Forest.*

84. Peck, pp. 344, 365; Josiah O. Livingston's military pension record.

85. Edwin A. Kilbourne letters.

86. Edwin S. Stowell letter.

87. Benedict, pp. 196–197.

88. Valentine G. Barney letters.

89. OR, vol. 19 p. 951.

90. Benedict, pp. 199; OR, vol. 19, p. 540; Hearn, p. 188; Noel A. Blakeman, ed. *Personal Recollections of the War of the Rebellion: Addresses Delivered Before the Commandery of the State of New York, Military Order of the Loyal Legion of the United States.* Fourth series (New York: G. P. Putnam's Sons, The Knickerbocker Press, 1912), pp. 157–158.

91. Hearn, p. 188.

92. Benedict, p. 199; OR, vol. 19, p. 540; Teetor, pp. 14, 211; Hearn, p. 188.

93. Benedict, pp. 197–198; Eisenschiml, p. 33.

94. OR, series 1 vol. 19, pp. 529–530, 980–981.

95. OR, vol. 19, pp. 549, 951, 981; Frye, p. 74.

96. Gerald J. Prokopowicz, "Word Of Honor: The Parole System in the Civil War," *North & South* 6, no. 4 (May 2003), pp. 24–26, hereinafter cited as Prokopowicz.

97. Prokopowicz, pp. 27–26; Boatner, p. 270, 619–620.

98. Benedict, p. 205.

99. Benedict, pp. 197–198; Co. I Descriptive List, Vermont Public Records Division of the Department of Buildings and General Services, Middlesex, Vermont, hereinafter cited as Co. I descriptive list.

100. Benedict, pp. 198, 205.

101. Valentine G. Barney letters.

102. Benedict, pp. 197–198; Eisenschiml, p. 33.

103. Benedict, p. 198; Nelson L. Wandell Diary.

104. Benedict, pp. 202–203.

105. Edwin S. Stowell letter.

106. Benedict, p. 198.

107. Valentine G. Barney letters; Edwin S. Stowell letter.

108. Benedict, p. 206; Nelson L. Wandell diary; Eisenschiml, p. 34; Peck, p. 350; Jesse Gerard's compiled service record; Jesse Gerard's pension record. Gerard's name was sometimes spelled Girard. The confusion with the spelling of his name came from the fact that he could not write, so the spelling was at the mercy of who ever wrote it. He signed his name with an X.

109. Lucius C. Dickinson, Civil War letters, in the possession of Steve Wakefield, hereinafter cited as Lucius C. Dickinson letters.

110. Benedict, pp. 205, 207; Nelson L. Wandell diary.

111. Benedict, p. 207; Nelson L. Wandell diary; Boatner, p. 21.

112. Benedict, p. 207; Nelson L. Wandell diary.

113. Eisenschiml, p. 36.

114. Nelson L. Wandell diary; William J. Henderson's compiled service record.

115. Nelson L. Wandell diary; Edwin A. Kilbourne letters.

116. Edward N. Phelps letters, Special Collections Library, Bailey/Howe Library, University of Vermont, Bur-

lington, Vermont, hereinafter cited as Edward N. Phelps letters; Co. I Descriptive List.

117. James Grout letters.

118. Eisenschiml, p. 40.

119. OR, vol. 19, p. 798.

120. OR, vol. 19, p. 799.

Chapter 3

1. James Grout letters; Edward N. Phelps letters.

2. Eisenschiml, p. 40.

3. Benedict, p. 207; Nelson L. Wandell diary; Eisenschiml, p. 45.

4. Nelson L. Wandell diary; *Rutland Herald*, 3 Oct 1862; Peck, p. 358; Charles A. Luce's compiled service record.

5. Benedict, pp. 207–208; Nelson L. Wandell diary; *Rutland Herald*, 9 Oct, 1862.

6. Benedict, pp. 207–208; Nelson L. Wandell diary; *Rutland Herald*, 9 Oct, 1862; *Lamoille Newsdealer*, 17 Oct 1862; Eisenschiml, p. 46; Valentine G. Barney letters; The History of the Ninth Vermont Inf. Vols.

7. Peck, p. 352; *Rutland Herald*, 25 Oct, 1862; Nathan Spaulding's military pension record and compiled service record.

8. George Levy, *To die in Chicago: Confederate prisoners at Camp Douglas, 1862–1865* (Evanston, Il.: Evanston Publishing, Inc., 1994), pp. 8, 9, hereinafter cited as Levy; *Full Duty*, pp. 43–49.

9. Levy, p. 12.

10. Ibid., p. 11.

11. Ibid., p. 11.

12. Ibid., p. 12.

13. Levy, p. 90; *Lamoille Newsdealer*, 17 Oct 1862.

14. The Civil War Dictionary, p. 855; Levy, p. 90; Stewart Sifakis, *Who was who in the Civil War* (New York: Facts on File Publications, 1988), p. 665, hereinafter cited as Sifakis; *Generals in blue*, p. 514.

15. Benedict, p. 208; Nelson L. Wandell diary; *Rutland Herald*, 9 Oct, 1862.

16. Valentine G. Barney letters.

17. *Lamoille Newsdealer*, 17 Oct 1862.

18. Eisenschiml, p. 46; OR, series 2, vol. 4, pp. 546–547.

19. *Rutland Herald*, 9 Oct 1862.

20. OR, series 2, vol. 4, p. 596.

21. *Burlington Daily Free Press*, 4 Oct, 1862.

22. Valentine G. Barney letters.

23. OR, series 2, vol. 4, p. 600.

24. Benedict, pp. 207, 208, Levy, p. 92.

25. Benedict, p. 208; Valentine G. Barney letters; Eisenschiml, p. 49.

26. Valentine G. Barney letters; Elijah B. Sherman, Civil War letters, Vermont Historical Society, Barre, Vermont, hereinafter cited as Elijah B. Sherman letters.

27. *Lamoille Newsdealer*, 17 Oct 1862.

28. Peck, p. 349; 9th Vermont regimental order book.

29. Peck, p. 375; 9th Vermont regimental order book.

30. Eisenschiml, p. 53; *Rutland Herald*, 9 Oct, 1862.

31. Benedict, p. *Lamoille Newsdealer*, 17 Oct 1862; Valentine G. Barney letters.

32. Peck, p. 361; Edward H. Lane's military pension record.

33. Peck, p. 361; Edward H. Lane's military pension record.

34. Peck, p. 357, Ara M. Carlisle's military pension record; Ara M. Carlisle's compiled service record.

35. Peck, p. 368; Lucius C. Dickinson letters; *The Civil War Dictionary*, p. 870.

36. Peck, p. 351; Benjamin Mann, Jr.'s compiled service record; *Rutland Herald*, 25 Oct, 1862.

37. Peck, p. 348; George H. McGrath's compiled service record.

38. *Lamoille Newsdealer*, 17 Oct 1862.

39. Benedict, p. 209; Eisenschiml, p. 55; *Rutland Herald*, 25 Oct, 1862.

40. Eisenschiml, p. 56.

41. Ibid., p. 56.

42. 9th Vermont regimental book; Peter Brady's compiled service record.

43. Benedict, p. 209; Eisenschiml, p. 58.

44. Eisenschiml, p. 64; Elijah B. Sherman letters.

45. Peck, p. 361; 9th Vt. regimental order book.

46. Peck, p. 360; John Bolton's compiled service record.

47. Peck, p. 374; 9th Vt. regimental order book.

48. Eisenschiml, p. 64.

49. Peck, p. 374; Otis B. Smith's compiled service record.

50. Peck, pp. 356, 357, 359; 9th Vt. regimental order book.

51. Levy, p. 94, 95; *The Civil War Dictionary*, p. 115; OR, series 2, p. 130.

52. Benedict, p. 209; Nelson L. Wandell diary; Elijah B. Sherman letters.

53. Benedict, pp. 209–210; *Revised Regulations for the Army of the United States,1861.* 1861, p. 503.

54. Eisenschiml, p. 68.

55. William A. Otis' court-martial record.

56. Ibid.

57. Peck, pp. 346–377; Eisenschiml, p. 68.

58. Valentine G. Barney letters.

59. *Vermont General.* p. 69, Lucius M. Dickinson letters.

60. Valentine G. Barney letters; Edwin A. Kilbourne letters.

61. Peck, 351; Thomas B. Ripley's compiled service record; 9th Vermont regimental order book.

62. Peck, p. 352; William Williams, Jr.'s compiled service record.

63. Benedict, p. 209.

64. Benedict, p. 210; *The Civil War Dictionary*, p. 12; Generals in Blue, pp. 6–7.

65. Eisenschiml, p. 72; *Rutland Herald*, Jan 10, 63; *The Civil War Dictionary,* p. 175.

66. Benedict, p. 211; Co. I Descriptive List, Vermont Public Records Division of the Department of Buildings and General Services, Middlesex, Vermont; William J. Henderson's compiled service record; *Lamoille Newsdealer*, 5 Feb 1863.

67. Elijah B. Sherman letters.

68. Ullery, Part 3, p. 140; Elijah B. Sherman's compiled service record.

69. Valentine G. Barney letters.

70. Peck, 356, 359; National Archives Record Group 153, Records of the Judge Adjutant General's Office (Army), entry 15, Court-martial Case File, file NN12, folder 1a.

71. Peck, 358; National Archives Record Group 153, Records of the Judge Adjutant General's Office (Army), entry 15, Court-martial Case File, file NN12, folder 1a.

72. National Archives Record Group 153, Records of the Judge Adjutant General's Office (Army), entry 15, Court-martial Case File, file NN12, folder 1a.

73. Zenas H. Bliss letters; J. Webster Stebbins, Civil War letters, In the possession of David Prentiss, hereinafter cited as J. Webster Stebbins letters; Benedict, p. 210; Nelson L. Wandell diary; Eisenschiml, p. 74.

74. Peck, p. 375; 9th Vermont regimental order book.

75. J. Webster Stebbins letters.

76. Edwin A. Kilbourne letters.

77. Benedict, pp. 210–211; Nelson L. Wandell Diary; Valentine G. Barney letters.

78. Edwin A. Kilbourne letters.

79. Robert G. Steele, *With pen and sword, lives and times of the remarkable Rutland Ripleys* (New York: Vantage Press, Inc., 1979), pp. 143–144, hereinafter cited as Steele; Eisenschiml, p. 70.

80. *Rutland Herald*, 10 Feb, 1863.

81. J. Webster Stebbins letters; Eisenschiml, p. 73; Edwin A. Kilbourne letters; *Rutland Herald*, 10 Feb, 1863; Valentine G. Barney letters. Rosehill Cemetery is located at 5800 N. Ravenswood Avenue, Chicago, Illinois.

82. OR, series 1, vol. 5, p. 588.

83. National Archives Record Group 153, Records of the Judge Adjutant General's Office (Army), entry 15, Court-martial Case File, file LL144; *Revised Regulations for the Army of the United States,1861*, pp. 503, 506; John Sabbeville's compiled service record; John Sabbeville's military pension record.

84. John Sabbeville's compiled service record; John Sabbeville's military pension record.

85. National Archives Record Group 153, Records of the Judge Adjutant General's Office (Army), entry 15, court-martial case file LL144; John C. Town's compiled service record.

86. Peck, P. 369; National Archives Record Group 153, Records of the Judge Adjutant General's Office (Army), entry 15, court-martial case file LL144.

87. Charles H. Hodge, Civil War letter, Special Collections, Bailey/Howe Library, University of Vermont, Burlington, Vermont.

88. Peck, p. 366; Clark J. Beede's compiled service record; National Archives Record Group 153, Records of the Judge Adjutant General's Office (Army), entry 15, Court-martial Case File, file. NN2434.

89. Valentine G. Barney letters.

90. Peck, p. 375; *Echoes in the Forest,* pp. 186–190; James Grout's military pension record; James Grout's compiled service record

91. Joel Grout, Civil War letter, Special Collections, Bailey/Howe Library, University of Vermont, Burlington, Vermont.

92. *Echoes in the Forest,* pp. 186–190.

93. J. Webster Stebbins letters.

94. Peck, p. 362; John E. Robbins' compiled service and military pension records.

95. Valentine G. Barney letters; *Rutland Herald*, 19, Mar, 1862; Edwin A. Kilbourne letters.

96. Benedict, pp. 397, 418–429; *The Civil War Dictionary*, p. 571.

97. Benedict, p. 212; *Rutland Herald*, 19 March 63.

98. Benedict, p. 212; *Rutland Herald*, 4 Apr 63.

99. Benedict p. 212; Peck, pp. 344, 349.

100. *Rutland Herald*, 4 April 1863.

101. Valentine G. Barney letters.

102. Edwin A. Kilbourne letters.

103. *Rutland Herald*, 4 April, 63.

104. Charles W. Newton's compiled service record; Peck, p. 351.

105. Benedict, pp. 212–213; *Rutland Herald*, 4 Apr, 63; Valentine G. Barney letters.

106. Benedict, p. 213; *Rutland Herald*, 13 Apr, 63; Linus E. Sherman letters.

107. Linus E. Sherman letters.

108. Ibid.

109. Ibid.

110. Nelson L. Wandell Diary.

111. *Vermont Journal*, 18 Apr, 63.

112. Peck, p. 369; Joseph Douglass, Jr.'s military pension record; Joseph Douglass, Jr.'s compiled service record

113. *Rutland Herald*, 13 April, 63.

114. Benedict, p. 213.

115. *Vermont Journal*, May 9, 63

Chapter 4

1. Benedict, p. 213; Steven A. Cormier, *The siege of Suffolk: the Forgotten Campaign, April 11–May 4, 1863* (Lynchburg, Va.: H. E. Howard, Inc., 1989), p. 2, hereinafter cited as *The Siege of Suffolk*; Stephen W. Sears, *Chancellorsville* (Boston: Houghton Mifflin Company, 1996), pp. 19–20, 58, hereinafter cited as *Chancellorsville*.

2. Benedict, p. 214; *The Siege of Suffolk*, pp. 4–6; *Chancellorsville*, pp. 28–35; R. E. Lee, p. 483.

3. *The Siege of Suffolk*, pp. 6–8; *Chancellorsville*, pp. 35–36.

4. *The Siege of Suffolk*, pp. 7–12, 297; *R. E. Lee*, p. 483.

5. *The Siege of Suffolk*, pp. 13–15; Edward G. Longacre, *Leader of the Charge: A Biography of General George E. Pickett, C.S.A.* (Shippensburg, PA: White Mane Publishing Company, Inc., 1998), p. 100, hereinafter cited as *Leader of the Charge*.

6. *Leader of the Charge*, pp. 102–103.

7. *The Siege of Suffolk*, pp. 52, 54–55; *Leader of the Charge*, p. 103.

8. *The Siege of Suffolk*, pp. 55–56; *Leader of the Charge*, pp. 103–104.

9. *The Siege of Suffolk*, pp. 65–66, 69; *Leader of the Charge*, pp. 103–104.

10. James Hagemann, *The Heritage of Virginia: the story of place names in the Old Dominion* (West Chester, Pa.: Whitford Press, 1988), p. 238, hereinafter cited as *The Heritage of Virginia*.

11. *The Siege of Suffolk*, pp. 19, 20, 22.

12. Ibid., pp. 27–28.

13. *The Siege of Suffolk*, pp. 30, 34; *The Civil War Dictionary*, p. 629; *Generals in Blue*, p. 364.

14. Benedict, p. 214; *The Siege of Suffolk*, pp. 35–37.

15. *The Siege of Suffolk*, pp. 37–38.

16. Ibid., pp. 76–77, 81.

17. *The Siege of Suffolk*, p. 89; OR, vol. 18, p. 271.

18. *The Siege of Suffolk*, p. 95; OR vol. 18, p. 271.

19. *The Siege of Suffolk*, pp. 127–128, 145.

20. Ibid., pp. 121, 304.

21. Benedict, p. 214; Nelson L. Wandell Diary; *Vermont Journal*, 9 May 1863; *Rutland Herald*, 22 April 1863; Valentine G. Barney letters

22. Benedict, p. 214; *The Siege of Suffolk*, pp. 76, 121, 313.

23. Benedict, pp. 214–215; Nelson L. Wandell diary; *Rutland Herald*; Lord, p. 279; OR, vol. 18, pp. 272, 317; *Lamoille Newsdealer*, 14 May 1863.

24. *Vermont Journal*, May 9, 1863; *Rutland Herald*, 22 April 1863.

25. Eisenschiml, p. 103.

26. Benedict, p. 215; Valentine G. Barney letters.

27. *The Siege of Suffolk*, pp. 131–133.

28. *The Siege of Suffolk*, pp. 35, 302–304, 327; Jeffery D. Wert, *General James Longstreet: The Confederacy's Most Controversial Soldier: A Biography* (New York: Simon & Shuster, 1994), pp. 235–236, hereinafter cited as *Longstreet*.

29. *The Siege of Suffolk*, pp. 140–143, 305.

30. Ibid., pp. 144, 148.

31. *The Siege of Suffolk*, p. 148; OR, vol. 18, p. 304.

32. *The Siege of Suffolk*, p. 149; OR, vol. 18, p. 304.

33. *The Siege of Suffolk*, p. 150; OR, vol. 18, p. 304.

34. *The Siege of Suffolk*, p. 147, 152; OR, vol. 18, p. 304; *Longstreet*, pp. 235–236.

35. Benedict, p. 215; *The Siege of Suffolk*, p. 166; *Vermont Journal*, 9 May 1863; OR, vol. 18, p. 304.

36. Benedict, p. 215; *The Siege of Suffolk*, pp. 166–168; OR, vol. 18, pp. 305, 318.

37. *The Siege of Suffolk*, pp. 159–161; *Longstreet*, pp. 235–236.

38. Eisenschiml, pp. 102, 106.

39. Valentine G. Barney letters.

40. Benedict, p. 215; OR, vol. 18, p. 299.

41. *The Siege of Suffolk*, p. 226.

42. *The Siege of Suffolk*, pp. 230–231; Eisenschiml, p. 105; Valentine G. Barney letters; Linus E. Sherman letters.

43. *The Siege of Suffolk*, pp. 231–236; Eisenschiml, pp. 103–106.

44. Benedict, pp. 215–216; *Rutland Herald*, 15 May 1863; *Lamoille Newsdealer*, 14 May 1863; Peck, pp. 344, 345, Story N. Goss' compiled service record; Ullery, part 2, p. 161; Walter S. Vincent's compiled and pension records.

45. J. Webster Stebbins letters; George W. Bisbee diary.

46. Charles H. Hodges letters; Nelson Wandell diary; George W. Bisbee diary; OR, vol. 18, p. 320; *Lamoille Newsdealer*, 14 May 1863.

47. Valentine G. Barney letters; J. Webster Stebbins letters.

48. J. Webster Stebbins letters.

49. Benedict, p. 216; *The Siege of Suffolk*, pp. 246–249; *Longstreet*, p. 238.

50. *The Siege of Suffolk*, pp. 284–286; *Longstreet*, pp. 237–238; Warren Wilkinson and Steven E. Woodworth, *A Scythe of Fire: A Civil War Story of the Eighth Georgia Infantry Regiment* (New York: William Morrow, 2002). p. 211.

51. Morristown Grand Army of the Republic Book, Morristown Historical Society, Morristown, Vermont, p. 314.

52. Charles H. Hodge letters; *The Siege of Suffolk*, p. 284.

53. Benedict, p. 216; Nelson L. Wandell diary; Eisenschiml, p. 112; *Lamoille Newsdealer*, 14 May 1863.

54. Benedict, p. 216; Nelson L. Wandell diary; George W. Bisbee diary; Valentine G. Barney letters.

55. Benedict, pp. 216–217, Peck, p. 344; Valentine G. Barney letters; Eisenschiml, p. 116.

56. Eisenschiml, pp. 104, 116.

57. *Rutland Herald*, 1 Jun 1863; Dudley K. Andross' compiled service record.

58. Edwin S. Stowell's military pension record.

59. Benedict, p. 216; Linus E. Sherman letters; James Martin, Civil War letters, in the possession of Daniel T. Hebert, hereinafter cited as James Martin letters; George W. Bisbee diary.

60. Benedict, p. 216; Linus E. Sherman letters; *The Civil War Dictionary*, p. 944; *Lamoille Newsdealer*, 28 May 1863; Sifakis, p. 727; OR, vol. 27, part 3, p. 453; OR, vol. 29, part 2, p. 143; Isaac J. Wistar, *The Autobiography of General Isaac J. Wistar* (Philadelphia: The Wistar Institute of Anatomy and Biology, 1937), pp. 366, 380, 381, 407, 408; *Generals in Blue*, p. 568; The History of the Ninth Vermont Inf. Vols.

61. Benedict, p. 216; Linus E. Sherman letters; James Martin, Civil War letters, in the possession of Daniel T. Hebert, hereinafter cited as James Martin letters; George W. Bisbee diary.

62. Benedict, p. 217; Peck, p. 344; Ullery, part 2, p. 7; Dudley K. Andross' complied service record.

63. Benedict, p. 217, Peck, p. 344, OR, vol. 18, p. 359.

64. Peck, p. 217; Nelson L. Wandell diary; *Rutland Herald*, 1 Jun 1863; Edward N. Phelps letters; J. Webster Stebbins letters; Valentine G. Barney letters.

65. Peck, p. 217; Nelson L. Wandell diary; *Rutland Herald*, 1 Jun 1863; Edward N. Phelps letters; J. Webster Stebbins letters; Valentine G. Barney letters.

66. *Attack and Die*, pp. 41–42

67. *Rutland Herald*, 1 Jun18 63; Edward N. Phelps letters; J. Webster Stebbins letters.

68. *Rutland Herald*, 1 Jun 1863.

69. J. Webster Stebbins letters; Valentine G. Barney letters.

70. *Rutland Herald*, 1 Jun 63; Valentine G. Barney letters.

71. Valentine G. Barney letters; Linus E. Sherman letters.

72. Nelson L. Wandell diary; *Rutland Herald*, 1 Jun 1863; Edward N. Phelps letters; J. Webster Stebbins letters; Valentine G. Barney letters.

73. Edward N. Phelps letters.

74. Eisenschiml, pp. 130–131.

75. Valentine G. Barney letters; Peck, p. 346.

76. Linus E. Sherman letters; Valentine G. Barney letters.

77. Valentine G. Barney letters.

78. Edwin A. Kilbourne letters.

79. Valentine G. Barney letters.

80. Ibid.

81. Ibid.

82. Eisenschiml, p. 126.

83. Edward H. Ripley's compiled service and pension records; Eisenschiml, p. ; Steele, Robert G. *With Pen and Sword, Lives and Times of the Remarkable Rutland Ripleys*. New York: Vantage Press, Inc., 1979, pp. 22–71; 99–114; 211–228.

84. Eisenschiml, p. 126.

85. Benedict, p. 218; Peck, p. 344; John C. Stearns' compiled service record.

86. Peck, p. 225; Lewis C. Aldrich, *History of Windsor County, Vermont* (Syracuse, NY: D. Mason & Co., Publishers, 1888), p. 992, hereinafter cited as *History of Windsor County*; John L. Hurd, *Weathersfield: Century Two*, vol. 2, (Canaan, N. H.: Phoenix Publishing, 1978), p. 15, hereinafter cited as Hurd; Charles Jarvis' compiled service record.

87. *Rutland Herald*, 12 June 63.

88. Valentine G. Barney letters.

89. Benedict, p. 219; *The Civil War Dictionary*, pp. 332, 779; OR, vol. 18, p. 820; John F. Marszalek, "Second Union Misfire on the Peninsula." *America's Civil War*, (July 2001), pp. 54, 57, hereinafter cited as Marszalek.

90. *The Civil War Dictionary*, p. 779; OR, vol. 18, p. 820; Marszalek, p. 57.

91. Benedict, pp. 218–219; Nelson L. Wandell Diary; Edwin A. Kilbourne letters; *Rutland Herald*, 24 June 1863; Valentine G. Barney letters; OR, vol. 18, p. 820; *Lamoille Newsdealer*, 2 Jul 1863; Wistar, p. 417.

92. Wistar, pp. 417–418

93. *The Civil War Dictionary* pp. 458, 463; Sifakis, pp. 361–361, 364–365; *Generals in Blue*, pp. 264, 269–270, 403.

94. *The Heritage of Virginia*, pp. 279–277; Zeller, p. 62.

95. Edwin A. Kilbourne letters, The Union cemetery was just to the rear of the 9thVermont's camp according to Charles H. Hodge, *Lamoille Newsdealer*, 2 Jul 1863.

96. Linus E. Sherman letters.

97. Edwin A. Kilbourne letters.

98. Edwin A. Kilbourne letters.

99. Peck, pp. 127, 375; 9th Vt. Regimental order book.

100. Benedict, p. 219; Nelson L. Wandell diary; Edwin A. Kilbourne letters; *Lamoille Newsdealer*, 9 Jul 1863.

101. Hageman, p. 265.

102. Edwin A. Kilbourne letters.

103. Benedict, p. 219; Nelson L. Wandell diary; *Lamoille Newsdealer*, 9 Jul 1863.

104. *Lamoille Newsdealer*, 9 Jul 1863.

105. Eisenschiml, p. 134.

106. Ibid., p. 135.

107. Benedict, p. 220; Eisenschiml, p. 137.

108. Benedict, pp. 448–477; George J. Stannard's military pension record.

109. OR, vol. 18, pp. 820–821; *The Civil War Dictionary*, pp. 80–81, 478, 779; Marszalek, p. 58.

110. OR, vol. 18, pp. 821–822; *The Civil War Dictionary*, p. 779; Marszalek, p. 58.

111. Benedict, p. 219; OR, vol. 18, p. 823; *The Civil War Dictionary* p. 779; Marszalek, pp. 58–60.

112. Nelson L. Wandell diary; Edwin A. Kilbourne letters; Peck, pp. 359; Orlando Whitney's military pension record and compiled service record; *Lamoille Newsdealer*, 23 Jul 1863.

113. Nelson L. Wandell diary; Edwin A. Kilbourne letters; Eisenschiml, p. 137; *Lamoille Newsdealer*, 23 Jul 1863.

114. Nelson L. Wandell diary; Edwin A. Kilbourne letters; Eisenschiml, pp. 138–139; Valentine G. Barney letters; *Lamoille Newsdealer*, 20 Aug, 1863.

115. Eisenschiml, pp. 138–139.

116. Edwin A. Kilbourne letters.

117. *The Cavalier*, 14 Jul, 1863; *The Civil War Dictionary*, pp. 458, 463, 944; Sifakis, pp. 362, 727.

118. Benedict, p. 220; Valentine G. Barney letters; *Rutland Herald*, 11 August 1863; *The Cavalier*, Jul 14, 1863; Wistar, pp. 418–419.

119. Benedict, p. 220; Valentine G. Barney letters; *Rutland Herald*, 11 August 1863.

120. Wistar, p. 418; Valentine G. Barney letters.

121. Edwin A. Kilbourne letters.

122. Peck, p. 365; National Archives Record Group 153, Records of the Judge Adjutant General's Office (Army), entry 15, Court-martial Case File, file NN491; Timothy Steady's compiled service record.

123. National Archives Record Group 153, Records of the Judge Adjutant General's Office (Army), entry 15, Court-martial Case File, file NN491.

124. Eisenschiml, p. 145.

125. Benedict, p. 220; OR, vol. 27, p. 978.

126. Benedict, p. 220; OR, vol. 27, pp. 978–979; *Lamoille Newsdealer*, 6 Aug 63.

127. *The Heritage of Virginia*, p. 38; *Burlington Free Press*, 4 Aug 63.

128. Valentine G. Barney letters; *Burlington Free Press*, 4 Aug 63.

129. Valentine G. Barney letters.

130. *Burlington Free Press*, 4 Aug 63; *Lamoille Newsdealer*, 6 Aug 63.

131. Valentine G. Barney letters; *Burlington Free Press*, 4 Aug 63.

132. National Archives Record Group 153, Records of the Judge Adjutant General's Office (Army), entry 15, Court-martial Case File, file NN491; John Finchon's compiled service record.

133. Nelson L. Wandell diary.

134. Valentine G. Barnet letters.

135. Linus E. Sherman Letters.

136. Ibid.

137. *The Cavalier*, Aug 3, 1863

138. Linus E. Sherman letters.

139. Valentine G. Barney letters.

140. Edwin A, Kilbourne letters.

141. Edwin A, Kilbourne letters; *Lamoille Newsdealer*, 20 Aug 63.

142. Edwin A, Kilbourne letters; Valentine G. Barney letters.

143. Benedict, p. 220; Edwin A. Kilbourne letters

144. Peck, p. 354; Samuel Hartley's compiled service record.

145. Benedict, p. 221.Valentine G. Barney letters.

146. Peck, p. 350; Jesse Gerard's compiled service record; Jesse Gerard's pension record.

147. National Archives Record Group 153, Records of the Judge Adjutant General's Office (Army), entry 15, Court-martial Case File, file NN 497; Hiram Wood's compiled service record.

148. Peck, p. 350; National Archives Record Group 153, Records of the Judge Adjutant General's Office (Army), entry 15, Court-martial Case File, file NN497.

149. Peck, p. 350; National Archives Record Group 153, Records of the Judge Adjutant General's Office (Army), entry 15, Court-martial Case File, file NN497.

150. National Archives Record Group 153, Records of the Judge Adjutant General's Office (Army), entry 15, Court-martial Case File, file NN497.

151. Edwin A. Kilbourne letters; Nelson L. Wandell Diary; *Rutland Herald*, 14 October 63.

152. Edwin A. Kilbourne letters.

153. Peck, p. 367; Henry E. Morse's compiled service record; Edwin A. Kilbourne letters, *The Cavalier*, 28 Sep, 1863.

154. Henry E. Morse's pension record.

155. Peck, p. 361; 9th Vt. regimental order book; John Mickman's compiled service record.

156. Peck, p. 360; George W. Davis Jr.'s compiled service and military pension records.

157. Benedict, p. 221; Valentine G. Barney letters.

158. Edwin A. Kilbourne letters; *Rutland Herald*, 19 October 63.

159. Peck, 345, Story N. Goss' compiled service record; Ullery, part 2, p. 161.

160. Valentine G. Barney letters.

161. Edwin A. Kilbourne letters.

162. J. Webster Stebbins letters.

163. *Rutland Herald*, 19 October 1863.

164. Morristown Grand Army of the Republic Book, Morristown Historical Society, Morristown, Vermont, pp. 162, 314, 371.

165. *Lamoille Newsdealer*, 25 Nov 1863.

166. Nelson L. Wandell Diary; *Rutland Herald*, 29 October 63; Eisenschiml, pp. 158–159.

167. Peck, p. 367; Orin J. Fisk's compiled service record; Joe Kittel and Marie Kittel, "A Randolph Civil War Mystery" (paper presented to the Randolph University Club, Randolph, Vt., March 15, 1999), herein after cited as Kittel.

168. Kittel.

169. Nelson L. Wandell Diary; *Rutland Herald*, 29 October 1863.

Chapter 5

1. Benedict, pp. 221–222; Nelson L. Wandell diary; Valentine G. Barney letters; Edwin A. Kilbourne letters; *Rutland Herald*, 9 Nov 1863; Lamoille Newsdealer, 25 Nov 1863.

2. Benedict, p. 222; Nelson L. Wandell diary; Valentine G. Barney letters; Edwin A. Kilbourne letters; Linus E. Sherman letters; *Rutland Herald*, 9 Nov 1863.

3. Benedict, p. 222; Valentine G. Barney letters; Peck, p. 374; Vilas Smith's compiled service record.

4. *Lamoille Newsdealer*, 25 Nov 1863.

5. Benedict p. 222; Edwin A. Kilbourne letters; Valentine G. Barney letters.

6. Benedict, p. 222; Eisenschiml, p. 163.

7. Benedict, p. 223; Eisenschiml, pp. 163, 164.

8. Edwin A. Kilbourne letters.

9. Linus E. Sherman letters.

10. Benedict, p. 222; Valentine G. Barney letters; OR, vol. 33, p. 485; William L. Pohoresky, *The True Story: Newport North Carolina during the Civil War* (Havelock, N.C.: The Print Shop, 1978), p, 10, hereinafter cites as Pohoresky; J. Madison Drake, *The History of the Ninth New Jersey Veteran Vols., A Record of its Service from Sept. 13th, 1861, to July 12th, 1865, With a Complete Official Roster, and Sketches of prominent Members* (Elizabeth, N. J.: Journal Printing House, 1889), p. 85.

11. Pohoresky, pp. 4–5; Benedict, p. 223; Valentine G. Barney letters.

12. Pohoresky, p. 7.

13. Benedict, p. 223; Eisenschiml, p. 168.

14. Benedict p. 224; Eisenschiml, p. 169.

15. Valentine G. Barney letters; Eisenschiml, p. 168.

16. Edwin A. Kilbourne letters.

17. Eisenschiml, pp. 167, 170.

18. *Lamoille Newsdealer*, 9 Dec 1863.

19. Nelson L. Wandell diary.

20. Benedict, p. 223; Valentine G. Barney letters; Linus E. Sherman letters; *Vermont Phoenix*, 7 Dec 1863; Charles Jarvis's compiled service record.

21. Benedict, pp. 223–224; Valentine G. Barney letters; Linus E. Sherman letters; *Vermont Phoenix*, 7 Dec 1863; *History of Windsor County*, vol. 2, p. 992; Hurd, p. 16.

22. Benedict, pp. 223–224; Valentine G. Barney letters; Linus E. Sherman letters; *Vermont Phoenix*, 7 Dec 1863; *History of Windsor County*, vol. 2, p. 992.

23. Benedict, p. 224; Linus E. Sherman letters; Valentine G. Barney letters.

24. Benedict, p. 224; *History of Windsor County*, vol. 2, p. 16.

25. Benedict, p. 224; *Revised Regulations for the Army of the United States, 1861*, p. 45; *Vermont Phoenix*, 7 Dec 1863; *Lamoille Newsdealer*, 16 Dec 1863.

26. Peck, p. 347; Benjamin Franklin's compiled service record.

27. Peck, pp. 355, 365; Katharine F. DuClos, *The History of Braintree, Vermont*, vol. 2 (Published by the History Book Committee of Braintree, 1976), pp. 201–202, hereinafter cited as *The History of Braintree*.

28. *The History of Braintree*, p. 202.

29. Ibid.

30. Eisenschiml, pp. 172–173.

31. John W. Bennett, Civil War letters, in the possession of Doris King, hereinafter cited as John W. Bennett letters.

32. National Archives Record Group 153, Records of the Judge Adjutant General's Office (Army), entry 15, Court-martial Case File, file LL3125; Peck, p. 345.

33. *The Civil War Dictionary*, pp. 74–75, 172.

34. *Vermont Journal*, 2 Jan 1864

35. Valentine G. Barney letters.

36. Benedict, p. 225; Peck, pp. 344, 359, 362, 372, 375; Eugene Viele's compiled service record.

37. Edwin A. Kilbourne letters; Linus E. Sherman letters.

38. Benedict, pp. 225–226; OR, vol. 29, p. 990; Valentine G. Barney letters; Eisenschiml, pp. 175–176.

39. OR, vol. 29, p. 991.

40. OR, vol. 29, pp. 990–992; Valentine G. Barney letters.

41. Charles Noirel's compiled service record.

42. Charles Noirel's compiled service record; Ezra J. Warner, *Generals in Blue: Lives of the Union Commanders* (Baton Rouge: Louisiana State University Press, 1964), pp. 67–68, hereinafter cited as *Generals in Blue*.

43. Charles Noirel's compiled service record.

44. Benedict, p. 226; *Rutland Herald*, 6 Feb 64; *Report of the Adjutant & Inspector General of the State of Vermont, from October 1, 1863 to October 1, 1864* (Montpelier, Vt.: Walton's Steam Press, 1864), p. X, hereinafter cited as *Report of the Adjutant & Inspector General of the State of Vermont, from October 1, 1863 to October 1, 1864.*

45. Peck, p. 367; Charles A. Flanders' compiled service and military pension records. Established in 1855 as the Government Hospital for the Insane, St. Elizabeth's Hospital has had a distinguished history in the treatment of the mentally ill. The Hospital's early mission, as defined by its founder, the leading mental health reformer Dorothea Dix, was to provide the "most humane care and enlightened curative treatment of the insane of the Army, Navy, and District of Columbia." During the Civil War, wounded soldiers treated here were reluctant to admit that they were in an insane asylum, and said they were at St. Elizabeth's, the colonial name of the land where the Hospital is located. Congress officially changed the Hospital's name to St. Elizabeth's in 1916. By the 1940s, the Hospital complex covering an area of over 300 acres housed 7,000 patients. It was the first and only federal mental facility with a national scope In 1987, the federal government transferred the hospital operations to the District of Columbia, while retaining ownership of the western campus. The patient population has steadily declined, and the Hospital now houses 600 patients. The original 1850s building has been designated a National Historic Landmark, but it is not in use because of its state of disrepair. On the grounds of St. Elizabeth's, there is also a Civil War cemetery where 300 Union and Confederate soldiers who died here are buried. The Hospital complex is located on a hill in southeast Washington, overlooking the Potomac and Anacostia Rivers. However, it is closed to the public. St. Elizabeth's Hospital is located at 2700 Martin Luther King, Jr. Ave, Washington, D.C. http://nlm.nih.gov.hmd.mde tour/elizabeths/html.

46. Charles A. Flanders' compiled service and military pension records.

47. Charles A. Flanders' compiled service and military pension records; http://umaine.edu/history/site7.html.

48. Charles A. Flanders' compiled service and military pension records.

49. Benedict, p. 226; OR, vol. 29, pp. 992–994; J. Webster Stebbins letters.

50. Benedict, p. 226; OR, vol. 29, p. 992.

51. Benedict, p. 226; OR, vol. 29, pp. 992–994, vol. 33, p. 23; Valentine G. Barney letters, Eisenschiml, p. 183.

52. Peck, p. 348; Charles Morgan's compiled service record and military pension record.

53. Warren E. Stearns, Civil War letters. Special Collections, Bailey/Howe Library, University of Vermont, Burlington, Vermont.

54. Benedict, p. 226; OR, vol. 29, pp. 992–994; OR, vol. 33, p. 23; Valentine G. Barney letters, Eisenschiml, p. 183; Nelson L. Wandell diary.

55. Benedict, p. 226; *Rutland Herald*, 6 Feb 1864; Nelson L. Wandell Diary; Valentine G. Barney letters: Peck,

p. 361; Edward H. Lane's military pension record, After the war Lane moved to Castle Grove, Iowa where he married Jane Eliza Lane July 4, 1867. They had a son on June 18, 1868. Jane, with their son, left him in 1870 and moved in with a Mr. Joseph R. Valentine in Golden, Colorado. Edward divorced Jane in 1879, charging her with adultery. He then married Margaret M. Dalton of Northampton, Massachusetts, April 29, 1889. He was 38 and she 37. He died January 13, 1895 of typhoid fever. Lane was working as a gardener at the time of his death.

56. Eisenschiml, pp. 183–184; Valentine G. Barney letters.

57. Longacre, pp. 133–136, OR, vol. 29, part 2, pp. 881–882; *The Civil War Dictionary*, p. 601.

58. Longacre, p. 138, OR, vol. 33, part 2, p. 1061; John G. Barrett, *The Civil War in North Carolina* (Chapel Hill, N.C.: The University of North Carolina Press, 1963), pp. 202–203, hereinafter cited as Barrett; Richard B. McCaslin, *Portraits of Conflict; A photographic history of North Carolina in the Civil War* (Fayetteville, N.C.: The University of Arkansas Press, 1997), p. 273, hereinafter cited as McCaslin; Clifford Dowdey and Louis H. Mamarin, eds., *The Wartime Papers of R. E. Lee* (Boston: Little, Brown and Company, 1961), pp. 655–656, hereinafter cited as *The War Time Papers of R. E. Lee.*

59. Longacre, pp. 138–139; OR, vol. 33, part 2, pp. 1102–1103; James Lee Conrad, "a most realistic war college," *Civil War Times Illustrated*, Feb 2005, p. 55, hereinafter cited as Conrad; McCaslin, p. 273; Barrett, p. 203; *The Wartime Papers of R. E. Lee*, pp. 656–658. John Taylor Wood had been a lieutenant in the U.S. Navy before the war. When war broke out in 1861 he cast his lot with the Confederate government. At the end of 1861, since there were more navy officers in the Confederacy than there were ships, President Davis had been authorized by the Confederate Congress to assign army rank to navy men. On January 26, 1863, Davis appointed Wood, then his aide, with the rank of colonel of cavalry. On February 10, 1863, the appointment was confirmed by the Senate. Wood served as a liaison officer between the navy and army, and inspected costal defense sites and ironclad construction. During the remainder of the war Wood signed his reports with either his naval or army rank, according to the nature of the assignment. Royce Gordon Shingleton, *John Taylor Wood: Sea Ghost of the Confederacy* (Athens, Ga.: The University of Georgia Press, 1979), pp. 17, 69, 91, hereinafter cited as Shingleton.

60. OR, vol. 33, pp. 92–93; McCaslin, p. 273; Barrett, p. 203.

61. OR, vol. 33, p. 93; McCaslin, p. 273; Barrett, p. 203.

62. OR, vol. 33, p. 93; McCaslin, p. 273; Barrett, p. 203; Shingleton, pp. 92–94.

63. OR, vol. 33, pp. 82, 84; *The Civil War Dictionary*, p. 601.

64. Ezra J. Warner, *Generals in Gray: Lives of the Confederate Commanders* (Baton Rouge: Louisiana State University Press, 1959), pp. 213–214, hereinafter cited as *Generals in Gray*.

65. OR, vol. 33, p. 93; Barrett, pp. 204–205.

66. OR, vol. 33, p. 93; Barrett, pp. 205–207.

67. OR, vol. 33, pp. 50, 94, 102; Barrett, p. 209; Conrad, p. 56; Shingleton, pp. 94–108.

68. OR, vol. 33, pp. 84–85.

69. Benedict, p. 227; OR, vol. 33, pp. 84–85.

70. Benedict, pp. 227–228; OR, vol. 33, pp. 77, 81, 85; *Lamoille Newsdealer*, 24 Feb 1864.

71. Benedict, pp. 227–228; OR, vol. 33, pp. 77, 81, 85; *Lamoille Newsdealer*, 24 Feb 1864.

72. Peck, p. 369; *Lamoille Newsdealer*, 24 Feb 1864; Stephen Burrows' compiled service record.

73. Benedict, pp. 227–228; OR, vol. 33, pp. 77, 81, 85; Peck, pp. 340, 369–371.

74. Benedict, p. 228; OR, vol. 33, pp. 77, 81, 85; *Rutland Herald*, 17 Feb 1864; Peck, p. 340.

75. Benedict, p. 228; OR, vol. 33, pp. 77, 85.

76. J. H. Goulding, compiler, *Official Military and Naval Records of Rutland, Vermont, in the War of the rebellion, 1861–1866* (Rutland, Vt.: The Tuttle Company, Book and Job Printers. 1891) , p. 84, hereinafter cited as Goulding; Peck, p. 352; William P. Smith's compiled service record.

77. Peck, p. 350; Nathan DeForges' compiled service and pension record; Nathan DeForge's application for admission to the Soldier's Home in Vermont, Vermont Veteran's Home, Bennington, Vermont.

78. Peck, pp. 350–352; *Rutland Herald*, 17 Feb 1864; Franklin Caswell's compiled service record; William. B. Jenks's compiled service record; Thomas B. Ripley's compiled service record.

79. Peck, p. 351; Francis O. Sawyer, military files, Special Collections, Bailey/Howe Library, University of Vermont, Burlington, Vermont; Thomas Rudd's compiled service record.

80. Pohoresky, pp. 76–101; William Pohoresky, "The Ledged of Jonnie Ring." *Civil War Times Illustrated*, vol. 41, no. 7 (February 2003), p. 44.

81. OR, vol. 33, pp. 77–78.

82. Benedict, p. 228; Pohoresky, p. 54; *History of the Ninth Vermont Inf. Vols.*

83. Peck, p. 377; OR, vol. 33, p. 85.

84. Peck, pp. 354, 377; OR, vol. 33, p. 85; James H. Grace's compiled service and military pension records.

85. Peck, p. 352, 353; *Rutland Herald*, 17 Feb 1864; James F. Bolton's military pension record.

86. Peck, p. 255; Joseph Osier's compiled service record; Peter Osier's compiled service record; *St. Johnsbury Caledonian*, 26 Feb 1864.

87. Peck, p. 377; OR, vol. 33, p. 85; Charles W. Stoddard's compiled service and military pension records.

88. Peck, p. 367; Matthew Riley's compiled service record.

89. Peck, p. 357; Thomas P. Garry's compiled service record and military pension record.

90. Peck, p. 350; George F. Durkee's compiled service and military pension records; *Rutland Herald*, 6 Mar 1864

91. Peck, p. 348; Nelson C. Roberts' compiled service and military pension records.

92. Peck, p. 358; Nathan C. Smith's compiled service record.

93. Benedict, pp. 228–229; OR, vol. 33, p. 85; *Vermont Watchman & State Journal*, 19 Feb 1864; *St. Johnsbury Caledonian*, 26 Feb 1864.

94. Peck, p. 364; William Melcher's compiled service and military pension record.

95. Peck, p. 365; William C. Holman's compiled service and military pension records; John V. Handly's compiled service record; Orlando W. Dimick's compiled service record.

96. Benedict, p. 229; Pohoresky, p. 75; *Lamoille Newsdealer*, Feb 24 1865.

97. Benedict, p. 230; *Rutland Herald*, 17 Feb 1864.

98. Peck, p. 365; Alfred Tatro's compiled service and military pension record.

99. Benedict, p. 229 MOH

100. W. F. Beyer and O. F. Keydel, *Deeds of Valor* (Stamford, Conn.: Republished, Longmeadow Press, 1993), pp. 301–302, hereinafter cited as *Deeds of Valor*; MOH.

101. *Deeds of Valor*, p. 302.

102. *Deeds of Valor*, p. 302.

103. *Deeds of Valor*, p. 304; MOH.

104. Benedict, p. 230; *Deeds of Valor*, p. 304; MOH.

105. Benedict, p. 230.

106. OR, vol. 33, pp. 77–78; Linus E. Sherman letters; *Lamoille Newsdealer*, 24 Feb 1864.

107. Benedict, p. 230; *Rutland Herald*, 17 Feb 1864.

108. Linus E. Sherman letters; Nelson L. Wandell diary; Valentine G. Barney letters; OR, vol. 33, p. 85.

109. Peck, p. 355; Benjamin E. Stokes' compiled service and military pension records.

110. OR, vol. 33, p. 86.

11. Benedict, p. 231.

112. Benedict, pp. 231–232; Nelson L. Wandell Diary; Valentine G. Barney letters.

113. Valentine G. Barney letters.

114. *Lamoille Newsdealer*, 16 Mar 1864.

115. Benedict, p. 323, Eisenschiml, p. 186; Valentine G. Barney letters; OR, v01.33, p. 79; Nelson L. Wandell diary.

116. Benedict, p. 232; Nelson L. Wandell diary; *Rutland Herald*, 17 Feb 1864; Eisenschiml, p. 216.

117. Benedict, p. 232; Nelson L. Wandell diary.

118. Benedict, p. 232, Nelson L. Wandell diary; *Rutland Herald*, 6 Mar 1864.

119. Benedict, p. 233, Nelson L. Wandell diary.

120. Eisenschiml, p. 189.

121. Eisenschiml, pp. 191, 206; Steele, p. 150.

122. Steele, pp. 150–151.

123. Peck, p. 354; James H. Grace's compiled service and military pension records; Joseph Carl's compiled service and military pension records; Benjamin E. Stokes' compiled service and military pension records; Robert W. Waitt, *Confederate Military Hospitals in Richmond*, Official Publication #22, Richmond Civil War Centennial Committee, Richmond, Virginia, 1964, www.mdgorman.com/Hospitals/general_hospital_15.htm.

124. James H. Grace's compiled service and military pension records; Joseph Carl's compiled service and military pension records; Benjamin E. Stokes' compiled service and military pension records.

125. Nelson L. Wandell diary; Eisenschiml, p. 193.

126. Benedict, p. 233; *Vermont Journal*, 26 Mar 1864

127. Benedict, p. 233; Nelson L. Wandell diary; *Rutland Herald*, 26 Mar 1864.

128. *Vermont Journal*, 26 Mar 1864.

129. *Lamoille Newsdealer*, 16 Mar 1864.

130. Eisenschiml, p. 195.

131. Benedict, p. 233; *Burlington Daily Free Press*, 17 Mar 1864; Peck, p. 360.

132. *Vermont Journal*, 26 Mar 1864.

133. Gerard A. Patterson, "Hangman Pickett," *America's Civil War*, November 2002, pp. 39–44; Longacre, pp. 172–175.

134. Benedict, p. 233; Valentine G. Barney letters; Nelson L. Wandell diary; Edwin A. Kilbourne letters.

135. Benedict, p. 233; Peck, pp. 344, 362.

136. Linus E. Sherman letters.

137. Linus E. Sherman diaries.

138. Benedict, p. 234, Valentine G. Barney letters.

139. Peck, p. 351; National Archives Record Group 153, Records of the Judge Adjutant General's Office (Army), entry 15, Court-martial Case File, file NN1666; Rufus Nicholson's compiled service record.

140. Benedict, pp. 233–234; Peck, p. 345; Peck, p. 345; Erastus P. Fairman's compiled service record; Erastus P.

Fairman, Civil War Recollections, in the possession of Lewis Shattuck, hereinafter cited as Erastus P. Fairman Recollections.

141. J. Webster Stebbins letters.

142. J. Webster Stebbins letters; James Martin letters.

143. Longacre, p. 143; *The Wartime Papers of R. E. Lee*, p. 688; Sifakis, p. 531.

144. Benedict, p. 234, *The Civil War Dictionary*, p. 656; OR, vol. 33, p. 289; Barrett, pp. 213–220, 224.

145. Linus E. Sherman letters.

146. Ibid.

147. Benedict, p. 234; Valentine G. Barney letters.

148. *The Civil War Dictionary*, pp. 616–617; *Generals in Blue*, pp. 357–358.

149. Benedict, p. 234; Linus E. Sherman letters; Edwin A. Kilbourne letters; Valentine G. Barney letters; Eisenschiml, p. 212.

150. Edwin A. Kilbourne letters.

151. Benedict, p. 234; Linus E. Sherman letters; Edwin A. Kilbourne letters; Valentine G. Barney letters; Eisenschiml, p. 211.

152. Benedict, p. 234; Barrett, pp. 221, 224–225.

153. J. Webster Stebbins letters; Edwin A. Kilbourne letters.

154. Edwin A. Kilbourne letters.

155. Peck, p. 348; Seymour Trowbridge's compiled service record and military pension record.

156. Peck, p. 353; Franklin L. Forbes' complied service record; 9th Vermont regimental order book.

157. *The Civil War Dictionary*, p. 925; Edwin A. Kilbourne letters.

158. Valentine G. Barney letters.

159. Ibid.

160. National Archives Record Group 153, Records of the Judge Adjutant General's Office (Army), entry 15, Court-martial Case File, file no. NN2773; compiled service record; Vermont Gazetteer, p. 766.

161. National Archives Record Group 153, Records of the Judge Adjutant General's Office (Army), entry 15, Court-martial Case File, file no. NN2773; compiled service record; Vermont Gazetteer, p. 766.

162. National Archives Record Group 153, Records of the Judge Adjutant General's Office (Army), entry 15, Court-martial Case File, file no. NN2773; compiled service record; Vermont Gazetteer, p. 766.

163. Valentine G. Barney letters.

164. Edwin A. Kilbourne letters.

165. Nelson L. Wandell diary; Edwin A. Kilbourne letters; Valentine G. Barney letters; *Rutland Herald*, 16 Jul 1864.

166. Nelson L. Wandell diary; Edwin A. Kilbourne letters; Valentine G. Barney letters.

167. Edwin A. Kilbourne letters.

168. Nelson L. Wandell diary; Edwin A. Kilbourne letters; Valentine G. Barney letters; *Rutland Herald*, 16 Jul 1864

169. Valentine G. Barney letters; *Rutland Herald*, 16 Jul 1864.

170. Nelson L. Wandell diary; Edwin A. Kilbourne letters; Valentine G. Barney letters.

171. Peck, p. 359; George Strong's compiled service record.

172. Nelson L. Wandell diary; Edwin A. Kilbourne letters; Valentine G. Barney letters.

173. Nelson L. Wandell diary; Valentine G. Barney letters.

174. Benedict, p. 235; Linus E. Sherman letters; Nelson L. Wandell diaries; History of the Ninth Vermont Inf. Vols.

175. Valentine G. Barney letters; *Vermont General*, p. 221.

176. Eisenschiml, p. 222.

177. Eisenschiml, p. 224, 240.

178. Benedict, p. 235; Valentine G. Barney letters; Peck, p. 345; Erastus P. Fairman's compiled service record; Erastus P. Fairman recollections; The History of the Ninth Inf. Vols.

179. Valentine G. Barney letters.

180. Peck, p. 374; Benjamin C. Stones' compiled service record.

181. Michael Willisford's compiled service record.

182. Michael Willisford's compiled service record.

183. Nelson L. Wandell diary; *Vermont Journal* 23 Sep 1864; Edwin A. Kilbourne letters; Valentine G. Barney letters.

184. Nelson L. Wandell diary; *Vermont Journal* 23 Sep 1864; Edwin A. Kilbourne letters; Valentine G. Barney letters.

185. Ibid.

186. *Vermont Journal*, 23 Sep 1864.

187. *Vermont Journal*, 23 Sep 1864; Valentine G. Barney letters; Nelson L. Wandell diary.

188. Edwin A. Kilbourne letters.

189. Peck, p. 366; Clark J. Beede's compiled service record; National Archives Record Group 153, Records of the Judge Adjutant General's Office (Army), entry 15, Court-martial Case File, file NN2434.

190. Peck, p. 351; Spencer Green's compiled service record.

191. Edwin A. Kilbourne letters; Lucius C. Dickinson's compiled service record; Valentine G. Barney letters.

192. Edwin A. Kilbourne letters; Nelson L. Wandell diaries.

193. Benedict, p. 236; Edwin A. Kilbourne letters; Linus E. Sherman letters; Valentine G. Barney letters.

194. *Lamoille Newsdealer*, 14 Sep 1864.

195. Peck, p. 347; Dennis Cornin's compiled service record.

196. Benedict, p. 236; Edwin A. Kilbourne letters; Linus E. Sherman letters; OR, vol. 42, part 2, pp. 793–794.

197. Peck, p. 355; John Kinsley's compiled service record.

198. Benedict, p. 236; Edwin A. Kilbourne; Linus E. Sherman letters; James Arthur Emmerton, *A Record of the Twenty-third Regiment, Massachusetts Volunteer Infantry in the War of the Rebellion, 1861–1865; With Alphabetical Roster*; Company Rolls. Boston: W. Ware & Co., 1886, pp. 230–233; The History of the Ninth Vermont Inf. Vols; Eisenschiml, p. 235.

Chapter 6

1. Frank J. Welcher, *The Union Army, 1861–1865, Organization and Operations. vol. 1, The Eastern Theater* (Bloomington and Indianapolis: Indiana University Press, 1989, p. 218, hereinafter cited as Welcher; Edward G. Longacre, *Army of Amateurs: General Benjamin F. Butler and the Army of the James, 1863–1865* (Mechanicsburg, Penn.: Stackpole Books, 1997), pp. 33–34, hereinafter cited as *Army of Amateurs*.

2. *Generals in Blue*, pp. 60–61; *The Civil War Dictionary*, p. 109; Sifakis, p. 96.

3. *Generals in Blue*, pp. 60–61; *The Civil War Dictionary*, pp. 63, 109, 385, Sifakis, p. 96.

4. *Generals in Blue*, pp. 60–61; *The Civil War Dictionary*, pp. 109, 591–592; Sifakis, p. 96.

5. Welcher, p. 219.

6. *The Heritage of Virginia*, pp. 122, 123, 187.

7. Welcher, p. 219.

8. Welcher, pp. 220–221; *The Civil War Dictionary,* pp. 247–249.

9. Welcher, pp. 223–224; *The Civil War Dictionary,* pp. 644–646.

10. *The Civil War Dictionary,* p. 253; *Army of Amateurs,* pp. 192–195; *Battles and Leaders,* vol. 4, p. 575; Donald C. Pfanz, *Richard S. Ewell: A Soldier's Life* (Chapel Hill and London: The University of North Carolina Press, 1998), hereinafter cited as Pfanz.

11. Benedict, p. 570; Richard J. Sommers, *Richmond Redeemed: The Siege at Petersburg* (Garden City, N.Y.: Doubleday & Company, Inc., 1981), p. 14, hereinafter cited as Sommers.

12. Benedict, p. 570; Sommers, p. 14.

13. Welcher, pp. 229, 453, 483.

14. *The Civil War Dictionary,* pp. 371–372; Eisenschiml, p. 231.

15. *Lamoille Newsdealer,* 28 Sep 1864.

16. Benedict, p. 236; Eisenschiml, P. 237.

17. Eisenschiml, p. 237.

18. Benedict, p. 236; Eisenschiml, p. 237.

19. Edwin A. Kilbourne letters.

20. Ibid.

21. Eisenschmil, p. 237.

22. Benedict, p. 237; Peck, p. 341; History of the Ninth Vermont; Peck, 341.

23. Benedict, pp. 236–237.

24. Benedict, p. 237; *Lamoille Newsdealer,* 5 Oct 1864; Eisenschiml, pp. 231, 239–240, 247; *Richmond News Dealer,* 27 Apr 1939.

25. Edwin A. Kilbourne letters; *Lamoille Newsdealer,* 5 Oct 1864; Peck, p. 341.

26. Benedict, pp. 237–238; Eisenschiml, pp. 231–232; *Richmond News Dealer,* 27 Apr 1939.

27. Benedict, p. 238; Sommers, pp. 5, 18, 21, 23, 27–28; Welcher, pp. 229, 875.

28. *The Civil War Dictionary,* p. 609; *Generals in Blue,* pp. 349–350.

29. *The Civil War Dictionary,* pp. 391–392; *Generals in Blue,* pp. 226–227.

30. Benedict, pp. 238–239; Welcher, pp. 229, 875; OR, vol. 42, part 2, pp. 1058–1059, 1082–1088; *Army of Amateurs,* pp. 211–212; Eisenschiml, pp. 247–248; Sommers, p. 21; OR, vol. 42, part 1, p. 793.

31. Benedict, pp. 238–239; Sommers, pp. 14, 509.

32. Benedict, p. 239: Sommers, p. 21; OR, vol. 42, part 1, pp. 793–794.

33. Benedict, p. 239; *Richmond News Dealer,* 27 Apr 1939.

34. Sommers, p. 15, 17; Pfanz, pp. 412–413.

35. Benedict, p. 240; Sommers, pp. 23, 25–26; OR, vol. 47, part 1, p. 798; *Richmond News Leader,* 27 Apr 1939.

36. Benedict, p. 240.

37. Benedict, pp. 240–241; Pfanz, p. 414; Sommers, pp. 43–47.

38. Benedict, p. 243; Sommers, p. 63.

39. Benedict, p. 241; Eisenschiml, p. 249; Erastus P. Fairman Recollections; Sommers, p. 54; OR, vol. 42, part 1, pp. 793, 811; *Richmond News Leader,* 27 Apr 1939.

40. Benedict, p. 241; Eisenschiml, p. 250; Sommers, p. 54; *Richmond News Leader,* 27 Apr 1939.

41. Benedict, p. 241; Eisenschiml, p. 250; Erastus P. Fairman Recollections; *Richmond News Leader,* 27 Apr 1939.

42. Benedict, pp. 241–242; Eisenschiml, p. 250; *Richmond News Leader,* 27 Apr 1939.

43. Benedict, pp. 241–242; Peck, p. 347; Henry P. French's compiled service record; OR, vol. 42, part 1, p. 812; *Richmond News Leader,* 27 Apr 1939.

44. Benedict, p. 242; Sommers, p. 55; *Richmond News Leader,* 27 Apr 1939.

45. Benedict, p. 242; Eisenschiml, p. 250; *Richmond News Leader,* 27 Apr 1939.

46. Benedict, p. 242; Peck, pp. 22, 344, 345, 363; Henry D. Belden's compiled service record; *Richmond News Leader,* 27 Apr 1939.

47. Peck, p. 366; Allen J. Dearborn's military pension record.

48. Peck, p. 366; William Hatch Chamberlain's compiled service record; Chamberlain family history supplied by Pete Chamberlain.

49. Goulding, p. 77; Peck, p. 351; John Riley's compiled service record; *Richmond News Leader,* 27 Apr 1939.

50. Peck, p. 374; Benjamin F. Stones' compiled service and military pension records.

51. Peck, p. 365; John L. Newton's compiled service and military pension records.

52. Peck, p. 374; Horace H. Preston's compiled service and military pension records.

53. Peck, p. 351; Joseph Lafayette's compiled service record.

54. Peck, pp. 127, 375; 9th Vt. Regimental order book; Sylvester C. Burlingame's compiled service and military pension records; Nelson L. Wandell diary.

55. Peck, p. 369; Octave Bushey's compiled service and military pension records; Octave Bushey's discharge papers and note sent home to his parents, James T. Ticehurst.

56. Peck, p. 348; Nelson C. Roberts' compiled service and military pension records.

57. Peck. pp. 344, 365, 372; Josiah O. Livingston's compiled service and military pension record.

58. Eisenschiml, p. 258.

59. Benedict, pp. 242–243; Sommers, pp. 55–57; OR, vol. 42, part 1, p. 812.

60. Sommers, p. 74.

61. Sommers, pp. 77–78.

62. Eisenschiml, p. 253; *Richmond News Leader,* 27 Apr 1939.

63. Benedict, p. 243; Somers, p. 65; Eisenschiml, pp. 252–253; *Richmond News Leader,* 27 Apr 1939.

64. Benedict, p. 243; Eisenschiml, p. 253; *Richmond News Leader,* 27 Apr 1939.

65. Peck, p. 361; Daniel Dwyer's compiled service and military pension records.

66. Peck, p. 361; James Lung's compiled service and military pension records.

67. Peck, p. 360; George W. Davis' military pension record.

68. Peck, p. 362; Henry Sias' compiled service and military pension records.

69. Peck, p. 360; Edward R. Cook's compiled service and pension records.

70. John Mickman's compiled service record; Nickerson's compiled service records.

71. Peck, p. 364; George W. Patrick's compiled service and military pension records.

72. Peck, p. 363; Leroy L. Bryant's military pension record.

73. Peck, 369; Morristown Grand Army of the Republic book, p. 255; Freeman Baker's compiled service and military pension records.

74. Benedict, p. 243; Sommers, p. 65; Eisenschiml, p. 253.

75. Peck, pp. 376, 377; William Waters' compiled service record; Denny E. Mason's compiled service; Albert E. Newton's compiled service record.

76. Peck, p. 371; Oberon Payne's compiled service and military pension records.

77. Peck, p. 361; William Moranville's compiled service and military pension records; *Richmond News Leader*, 27 Apr 1939.

78. Benedict, p. 245; Eisenschiml, p. 253; *Richmond News Dealer*, 27 Apr 1939

79. Benedict, p. 245.

80. Peck, pp. 345, 353, 368; Theodore S. Peck's compiled service and military pension records.

81. Sommers, pp. 66–68.

82. Sommers, p. 68.

83. Gordon Berg, "Embattled Courage at New Market Heights," *America's Civil War*, vol. 19, number 1, March 2006, pp. 28–30, hereinafter cited as Berg.

84. Sommers, pp. 27–28, 34–38; Berg, p. 32; Pfanz, p. 416.

85. Benedict, pp. 243–244; Sommers, pp. 83–92; *R. E. Lee*, vol. 3, p. 501.

86. Benedict, p, 244; Peck, pp. 359, 361, 760; Linus E. Sherman diaries; Erastus P. Fairman Recollections; Calvin M. Jenkins' compiled service and military pension records; *Richmond News Dealer*, 27 Apr 1939.

87. Erastus P. Fairman Recollections; Calvin M. Jenkins' compiled service and military pension records.

88. Benedict, p. 244; Sommers, pp. 121–122.

89. *Richmond News Dealer*, 27 Apr 1939.

90. Benedict, p. 246; Erastus P. Fairman Recollections.

91. Erastus P. Fairman Recollections.

92. Sommers, p. 210; Pfanz, p. 417; *R. E. Lee*, vol. 3, p. 501.

93. Sommers, pp. 121–122; *Army of Armatures*, p. 217.

94. Sommers, pp. 123, 526, 581; *Generals in Blue*, pp. 548–549.

95. Benedict, p. 244.

96. Sommers, pp. 130–131, 135, 527; Linus E. Sherman diaries.

97. Sommers, pp. 140, 146, ; *R. E. Lee*, vol. 3, pp. 502–503.

98. Sommers, pp. 143, 146; *R. E. Lee*, vol. 3, p. 504; Eisenschiml, p. 251; *http://www.nps.gov/rich/ri_harr.htm*.

99. George J. Stannard's compiled service and military pension records; Maharay, pp. 165, 202–203, 223, 252

100. Sommers, pp. 146–147; *R. E. Lee*, vol. 3, p. 504.

101. Benedict, p. ??; Sommers, pp. 150–151, 168; Nelson L. Wandell diary; George W. Durkee's military pension record; Linus E. Sherman diaries.

102. Sommers, p. 150; *Lamoille Newsdealer*, 12 Oct 1864.

103. Benedict, p. 250; Sommers, pp. 156–158; Eisenschiml, p. 244.

104. Linus E. Sherman diaries; Sommers, pp. 172–173.

105. OR vol. 42, part 1, p. 812; *Lamoille Newsdealer*, 26 Oct 1864.

106. Linus E. Sherman diaries.

107. Peck, p. 371; George F. Sprague, *Soldier's Record, Town of Craftsbury, Vermont, 1861–1865* (Craftsbury, Vt.: s.n., 1914), p. 64; George W. Smith' compiled service record.

108. Linus E. Sherman diaries; Eisenschiml, p. 257.

109. Eisenschiml, p. 257.

110. *Army of Amateurs*, pp. 222–225.

111. Peck, p. 348; Horatio N. Stoliker's compiled service and military pension records; Linus E. Sherman letters.

112. Peck, p. 354; Samuel Hartley's compiled service record.

113. Valentine G. Barney letters.

114. Valentine G. Barney letters.

115. Zeller, pp. 222–229.

116. Valentine G. Barney letters; Linus E. Sherman diaries; Linus E. Sherman letters.

117. Linus E. Sherman diaries; Linus E. Sherman letters.

118. Linus E. Sherman diaries.

119. Valentine G. Barney letters.

120. Benedict, pp. 252–253; Welcher, p. 892; *Army of Amateurs*, p. 228; Valentine G. Barney letters.; Linus E. Sherman Letters; Eisenschiml, p. 266.

121. Benedict, p. 253; Welcher, p. 892; Valentine G. Barney Letters; Linus E. Sherman Letters; OR, vol. 42, part 1, pp. 795–796.

122. Benedict, p. 254; Peck, pp. 360, 362; Stephen B. Wing's compiled service record; *http://vermontcivilwar. org/units/9/burgess-s.php*; OR, vol. 42, part 1, p. 797.

123. Benedict, pp. 252–253; Welcher, p. 892; Valentine G. Barney letters; Linus E. Sherman letters; OR, vol. 42, part1, p. 814.

124. Benedict, p. 253; Welcher, pp. 892–893; *Army of Amateurs*, p. 230; Valentine G. Barney letters; Linus E. Sherman letters; Erastus P. Fairman Recollections; OR, vol. 42, part 1, p. 796.

125. Benedict, p. 253; *Army of Amateurs*, p. 230; Erastus P. Fairman Recollections; Valentine G. Barney letters; Linus E. Sherman letters; Eisenschiml, p. 265.

126. Valentine G. Barney letters; Linus E. Sherman letters; Peck, p. 376; Alonzo R. Grover's compiled service and military pension records; Nelson L. Wandell Diary.

127. Peck, 375; Edward B. Bissell's compiled service and military pension records; Nelson L. Wandell Diary.

128. Peck, p. 370; Grand Army of the Republic, Department of Vermont, Personal Sketches of the Members of J. W. Warner Post No. 4 of Morrisville; Peter Ladu's compiled service record.

129. Peck, p. 376; Young, D. K. *Echoes in the Forest, The Family History Supplement to the History Of Stratton, Vermont.* Published by the Town of Stratton, Vt., 2000, p. 195; Joel Grout's compiled service and military pension records.

130. Peck, p. 356; Alson N. Wheatly's pension record.

131. Peck, p. 377; Charles W. Stoddard's compiled service record and military pension records; Nelson L. Wandell Diary.

132. Peck, p. 350; David M. Buffum's military pension record.

133. Benedict, p. 254; Peck, p. 349; William A. Ellis, ed., *Norwich University, 1819–1911, Her History, Her Graduates, Her Roll of Honor*; Smith, H. P. and W. S. Rowe. *History of Rutland.* Syracuse, N. Y.: D. Mason & Co., 1886, p. 130; William A. Dodge's compiled service record.

134. Valentine G. Barney letters.

135. Erastus P. Fairman Recollections.

136. Benedict, p. 253; *Army of Amateurs*, p. 230; Valentine G. Barney letters; Linus E. Sherman letters; OR, vol. 42, part 1, pp. 796, 810, 812, 813, 814; Eisenschmil, pp. 266–267.

137. Benedict, p. 253; *Army of Amateurs*, p. 230; Valentine G. Barney letters; Linus E. Sherman letters; OR, vol. 42, part 1, pp. 796, 810, 812, 813, 814.

138. Benedict, p. 352; Valentine G. Barney letters; Erastus P. Fairman Recollections; Linus E. Sherman letters.

139. Valentine G. Barney letters.

140. Peck, p. 361; Edward Hawkins' compiled service and military pension records.

141. Peck, p. 354; Peter Brady's compiled service record.

142. Peck, p. 348; Alvora M. Sargent's military pension record.

143. *Army of Amateurs*, p. 231; Valentine G. Barney letters; Erastus P. Fairman Recollections.

144. *Army of Amateurs*, p. 231; Linus E. Sherman letters; Erastus P. Fairman Recollections.

145. Benedict, p. 253; Nelson L. Wandell diary; Linus E. Sherman letters; OR, vol. 42, part 3, p. 504.

146. Peck, p. 350; James Duggan's compiled service record.

147. Benedict, pp. 253–254; Nelson L. Wandell Diary; Linus E. Sherman diaries; Valentine G. Barney letters; OR, 53, part 1, pp. 559, 570.

148. Benedict, vol. 1, pp. 396–397; *The Civil War Dictionary*, pp. 245–246.

149. Benedict, p. 255; Nelson L. Wandell Diary.

150. Benedict, p. 255; Valentine G. Barney letters.

151. National Archives Record Group 153, Records of the Judge Adjutant General's Office (Army), entry 15, Court-martial Case File, file LL3125.

152. Emery S. Wilder's compiled service and military pension records.

153. Linus E. Sherman diaries; Linus E. Sherman letters ; Nelson L. Wandell Diary.

154. Benedict, p. 255; Nelson L. Wandell Diary; J. Webster Stebbins; Linus E. Sherman diaries.

155. Benedict, pp. 254–255; Valentine G. Barney letters.

156. Benedict, 256; Benjamin W. Carpenter's Compiled service record and military pension records.

157. Erastus P. Fairman Recollections.

158. Linus E. Sherman diaries; Valentine G. Barney letters; Nelson L. Wandell diary.

159. Benedict, pp. 255–256.

160. Linus E. Sherman letters; Nelson L. Wandell diary.

161. *Lamoille Newsdealer*, 8 Mar 1865.

162. Peck, p. 355; Nelson Stinehowe's compiled service record.

163. Benedict, pp. 256–257; Valentine G. Barney letters; Welcher, pp. 498–499.

164. Eisenschiml, p. 279.

165. Benedict, p. 256.

166. Benedict, pp. 256–257; Valentine G. Barney letters; Linus E. Sherman diaries.

167. Benedict, p. 257; Peck, pp. 344, 345, 346, 349, 352, 353, 359, 368, 372, 375.

168. Michael Willisford's compiled service record.

169. National Archives Record Group 153, Records of the Judge Adjutant General's Office (Army), entry 15, Court-martial Case File, file LL3125.

170. Valentine G. Barney letters.

171. Valentine G. Barney letters.

172. *The Civil War Dictionary*, pp. 509–512, 579.

173. *The Civil War Dictionary*, pp. 292–293.

174. James Martin letters.

Chapter 7

1. Benedict, p. 258.

2. George W. Durkee diary.

3. Welcher, p. 501; Valentine G. Barney letters.

4. Peck, p. 350; John Baker's compiled service record; Peck, Louis B. Benway's compiled service record; http://members.aol.com/_ht_a/BellwareD/page1.html.

5. Peck, pp. 350, 369; Louis B. Benway's compiled service record; http://members.aol.com/_ht_a/Bellware D/page1.html.

6. Benedict, p. 258; Nelson L. Wandell diaries; George W. Durkee diary.

7. Valentine G. Barney letters.

8. Peck, p. 361; Thomas Flynn's compiled service record.

9. Valentine G. Barney letters.

10. James Martin letters.

11. Valentine G. Barney letters.

12. James Martin letters.

13. Benedict, p. 258.

14. Valentine G. Barney letters.

15. *Lamoille Newsdealer*, 8 Mar 1865.

16. J. Webster Stebbins letters.

17. Valentine G. Barney letters.

18. Ibid.

19. Benedict, pp. 258–259; George W. Durkee diary, Linus E. Sherman letters; Linus Sherman diaries; Nelson L. Wandell diary.

20. Erastis P. Fairman Recollections.

21. Benedict, p. 260; Nelson L. Wandell Diary; Valentine G. Barney letters.

22. Benedict, p. 260; Peck, pp. 344, 736; Esienschiml, pp. 292–293.

23. Nelson L. Wandell diary; George W. Durkee diary.

24. Benedict, vol. 1, p. 574;*The Civil War Dictionary*, pp. 298–299.

25. Benedict, p. 261; Eisenschiml, p. 296; Nelson Lankford, *Richmond Burning: The Last Days of the Confederate Capital* (New York,: Viking, 2002), p. 113, hereinafter cited as Lankford.

26. Benedict, vol. 1, pp. 580–581; *The Civil War Dictionary*, pp. 282–284.

27. Benedict 262.

28. Benedict, p. 263; Abel E. Leavenworth to Theodore S. Peck, February 16, 1893, Vermont Public Records Division of the Department of Buildings and General Services, Middlesex, Vermont, hereinafter cited as Leavenworth; Joel C. Baker to Theodore S. Peck, February 11, 1893, roll 26151, Vermont Public Records Division of the Department of Buildings and General Services, Middlesex, Vermont, hereinafter cited as Baker.

29. Leavenworth; Lankford, p. 65.

30. Chris M. Calkins, *The Appomattox Campaign: March 29–April 9, 1865* (Conshohocken, Pa.: Combined Books, Inc., 1997), pp. 47–48, hereinafter cited as *The Appomattox Campaign*.

31. Ibid, p. 58.

32. *The Appomattox Campaign*, pp. 58–59; Lankford, p. 91.

33. Benedict, p. 263; Leavenworth; Lankford, p. 86.

34. Benedict, p. 263; Leavenworth; Baker; OR, vol. 46, part 1, pp. 1211, 1212.

35. Lankford, pp. 103–104.

36. Benedict, pp. 263–264; Leavenworth; Baker.

37. Benedict, p. 264; Leavenworth; Baker; OR, vol. 46, part 1, p. 1212.

38. Benedict, p. 264; Leavenworth; Baker; OR, vol. 46, part 1, p. 1211.

39. Leavenworth.

40. Benedict, pp. 265–266.

41. Benedict, p. 266; OR, vol. 46, part 1, p. 1227.

42. Benedict, p, 265.

43. Ibid., p. 268.

44. Ibid., p. 268.

45. Ibid., pp. 268–269.

46. Ibid., p. 268.

47. Ibid., p. 269.

48. Ibid., p. 271.

49. Benedict, p. 271; Nelson L. Wandell diary.

50. Benedict, p. 271; Lankford, p. 144.

51. Valentine G. Barney letters.

52. George W. Durkee diary.

53. Valentine G. Barney letters.

54. Lankford, p. 156.

55. George W. Durkee diary.

56. Nelson L. Wandell diary.

57. Nelson L. Wandell diary; Valentine G. Barney letters.

58. Nelson L. Wandell diary; Valentine G. Barney letters.

59. Peck, p. 371; Morristown GAR book, p. 213; Charles H. Sweeney's compiled service and military pension records.

60. Charles H. Sweeney's military record; Michael Sherman, Gene Sessions, and P. Jeffrey Potash, *Freedom and Unity: A History of Vermont* (Barre, Vt.: Vermont Historical Society, 2004), p. 629

61. Benedict, p. 272; Nelson L. Wandell diary; Valentine G. Barney letters.

62. Benedict, p. 272; Jeffrey M. O'Dell, *Chesterfield County: Early Architecture and Historic Sites* (Chesterfield County, Va., 1983), pp. 221–222, 393–394; Suzanne Smiley Wist, "A Union Officers Midlothian Romance." *The Messenger* (The Chesterfield Historical Society of Virginia), No. 21, April 1992.

63. Valentine G. Barney letters.

64. Ibid. .

65. Nelson L. Wandell diary.

66. James Martin letters.

67. National Archives Record Group 153, Records of the Judge Adjutant General's Office (Army), entry 15, Court-martial Case File, file 00792.

68. Peck, p. 355; Joseph H. Larock's compiled service and military pension records.

69. Linus E. Sherman letters.

70. Benedict, p. 273; Nelson L. Wandell diary; *Burlington Daily Free Press*, 19 Jun, 1865.

71. Ibid.

72. Benedict, p. 273; Nelson L. Wandell diary; *Burlington Daily Free Press*, 21 Jun, 1865.

73. Benedict, p. 273; Nelson L. Wandell diary.

74. Benedict, p. 274.

75. Peck, p. 351; National Archives Record Group 153, Records of the Judge Adjutant General's Office (Army), entry 15, Court-martial Case File, file 001150.

76. Peck, p. 366; National Archives Record Group 153, Records of the Judge Adjutant General's Office (Army), entry 15, Court-martial Case File, file 001147.

77. National Archives Record Group 153, Records of the Judge Adjutant General's Office (Army), entry 15, Court-martial Case File, file 001150 and 001147.

78. National Archives Record Group 153, Records of the Judge Adjutant General's Office (Army), entry 15, Court-martial Case File, file 001293.

79. Ibid.

80. Ibid.

81. Ibid.

82. National Archives Record Group 153, Records of the Judge Adjutant General's Office (Army), entry 15, Court-martial Case File, file 00679.

83. Ibid.

84. Ibid.

85. Peck, p. 377; George Pierson's compiled service record.

86. Benedict, p. 274; Herman A. Seligson's military pension record; Burnham Cowdrey, *The Capture of Richard B. Winder*, n.p., n. d. roll 26151, Vermont Public Records Division of the Department of Buildings and General Services, Middlesex, Vermont, hereinafter cited as Cowdrey.

87. Cowdrey.

88. Ibid.

89. Ibid.

90. Ibid.

91. Ibid.

92. Benedict, p. 274.

93. Ibid.

94. Benedict, p. 274; *The Free Press*, 8 Dec 1865.

95. Peck, p. 378.

96. Ibid.

97. Maharay, pp. 266–274.

98. Steel, p. 268; Eisenschiml, p., 323, Edward H. Ripley's military pension record.

99. Valentine G. Barney's compiled service and military pension records.

100. Ullery, part 3, p. 142; Galer Britton Barnes, "Jennie's Whitework, Jennie's Way," *PieceWork* (November/December, 1997).

101. Ullery, p. 40.

102. Ullery, p. 40; Wist.

103. Euclid D. Farnham, conservation with author, Jun 26, 2006.

104. Ibid.

105. Ibid.

106. Peck, p. 363; (Enosburg, Vt.) *County Courier*, 20 Nov 1987.

Bibliography

Published Primary Sources

Baylor, George. *Bull Run to Bull Run; or Four Years in the Army of Northern Virginia: Containing a detailed account of the career and adventures of the Baylor Light Horse, Company B, Twelfth Virginia Cavalry, C.S.A., with leaves from my scrapbook.* Richmond, Va.: D.F. Johnson, 1900.

Blakeman, Noel A., ed. *Personal Recollections of the War of the Rebellion: Addresses Delivered before the Commandery of the State of New York, Military Order of the Loyal Legion of the United States.* Fourth series. New York: G.P. Putnam's Sons, Knickerbocker Press, 1912.

Drake, J. Madison. *The History of the Ninth New Jersey Veteran Vols., A Record of Its Service from Sept. 13th, 1861, to July 12th, 1865, with a Complete Official Roster, and Sketches of Prominent Members.* Elizabeth, NJ: Journal Printing House, 1889.

Emmerton, James Arthur. *A Record of the Twenty-third Regiment, Massachusetts Volunteer Infantry in the War of the Rebellion, 1861–1865; With Alphabetical roster; Company Rolls.* Boston: W. Ware, 1886.

Morristown Grand Army of the Republic Book, Morristown Historical Society, Morristown, Vermont.

Peck, Theodore S. *Revised Roster of Vermont Volunteers and Lists of Vermonters Who Served in the Army and Navy of the United States during the War of the Rebellion, 1861–66.* Montpelier, VT: Watchman, 1892.

Pond, George E. *The Shenandoah Valley in 1864.* 1885. Reprint. Wilmington, NC: Broadfoot, 1989.

Report of the Adjutant & Inspector General of the State of Vermont, from October 1, 1863, to October 1, 1864. Montpelier, VT: Walton's Steam Press, 1864.

Sorrel, G. Moxley. Paul A. Hutton, ed. *Recollections of a Confederate Staff Officer.* New York: Bantam Books, 1992. First published 1905.

United States War Department. *Revised Regulations for the Army of the United States, 1861.* Harrisburg: National Historical Society, 1980. First published 1861.

United States War Department. *War of the Rebellion: A Compilation of the Official Records of the Union and Confederate Armies.* Various volumes. Washington: Government Printing Office, 1902.

Manuscripts

Barney, Valentine G. Civil War Letters. Vermont Historical Society, Barre, Vermont.

Bennett, John W. Civil War Letters. In the possession of Doris King.

Bisbee, George. Civil War Diary, 1863. Special Collections, Draughon Library, Auburn University, Alabama.

Bliss, Zenas H. Civil War Letters. Vermont Historical Society, Barre, Vermont.

_____. Civil War Letters. In the possession of Daniel T. Hebert.

Branch, Charles F. History of the Ninth Vermont Inf. Vols. Vermont Historical Society, Barre, Vermont.

Dickinson, Lucius C. Civil War Letters. In the possession of Steve Wakefield.

Fairman, Erastus P. Civil War Recollections. In the possession of Lewis Shattuck.

Grout, James. Civil War Letters. Russell Collection of Vermontiana at the Martha Canfield Library, Arlington, Vermont.

Grout, Joel. Civil War Letter. Special Collections, Bailey/Howe Library, University of Vermont, Burlington, Vermont.

Hazen, A. Wayne. Civil War Letter. In the possession of Doug Green.

Hodge, Charles H. Civil War Letter. Special Collections, Bailey/Howe Library, University of Vermont, Burlington, Vermont.

Kilbourne, Edwin A. Civil War Letters. In the possession of Robert E. Kilbourne.

Martin, James. Civil War Letters. In the possession of Daniel T. Hebert.

Phelps, Edward N. Civil War Letters. Special Collections, Bailey/Howe Library, University of Vermont, Burlington, Vermont.

Rumrill, Luman C. Civil War Letter. U.S. Army Military History Institute, Carlisle, Pennsylvania.

Sawyer, Francis O. Military Files. Special Collections, Bailey/Howe Library, University of Vermont, Burlington, Vermont.

Sherman, Elijah B. Civil War Letters. Vermont Historical Society, Barre, Vermont.

Sherman, Linus E. Civil War Letters. Vermont Historical Society, Barre, Vermont.

_____. Civil War Diaries: January 1, 1862; November 31, 1864; March 18, 1864; December 28, 1864. Vermont Historical Society, Barre, Vermont.

Stearns, Warren E. Civil War Letters. Special Collections, Bailey/Howe Library, University of Vermont, Burlington, Vermont.

Stebbins, J. Webster. Civil War Letters. In the possession of David Prentiss.

_____. Civil War Letter. Special Collections, Bailey/Howe Library, University of Vermont, Burlington, Vermont.

Tucker, Rufus B. Civil War Letters. In the possession of Pat and Jim Geary.

Wandell, Nelson L. Civil War Diaries: 1862–1865. Brooks Memorial Library, Brattleboro, Vermont.

General Works

Aldrich, Lewis Cass. *History of Windsor County, Vermont: with illustrations and biographical sketches of some of its prominent men and pioneers.* Syracuse, NY: D. Mason, 1888.

Barrett John G. *The Civil War in North Carolina.* Chapel Hill: University of North Carolina Press, 1963.

Benedict, George G. *Vermont in the Civil War: A History of the Part Taken by the Vermont Soldiers and Sailors in the War for the Union, 1861–5.* 2 vols. Burlington, VT: The Free Press Association, 1886 and 1888.

Beyer, W.F., and O.F. Keydel. *Deeds of Valor: How America's Civil War Heroes Won the Congressional Medal of Honor.* Stamford, CN: Republished, Longmeadow Press, 1994.

Boatner, Mark M., III. *The Civil War Dictionary.* New York: Vintage Civil War Library, 1991.

_____. *Military Customs and Traditions.* Westport, CN: Greenwood Press, 1956; repr., New York: D. McKay, 1976.

Carlton, Hiram. *Genealogical and Family History of the State of Vermont.* 2 vols. New York: Lewis, 1903.

Catton, Bruce. *The Army of the Potomac: Mr. Lincoln's Army.* Garden City, NY: Doubleday, 1952.

_____. *The Army of the Potomac: A Stillness at Appomattox.* Garden City, NY: Doubleday, 1953.

Coffin, Howard. *Full Duty: Vermonters in the Civil War.* Woodstock, VT: The Countryman Press, 1993.

Connelley, William E. *A Standard History of Kansas and Kansans.* Chicago: Lewis, 1919.

Cooke, John Esten. *Wearing of the Gray: Being personal portraits, scenes, and adventures of the war.* Baton Rouge: Louisiana State University Press, 1977. First published 1867.

Cormier, Steven A. *The Siege of Suffolk: The Forgotten Campaign, April 11–May 4, 1863.* Lynchburg, VA: H.E. Howard, 1989.

Dale, Raymond E, comp. *History of the State of Nebraska; containing a full account of its growth from uninhabited territory to a wealthy and important state; of its early settlements; its rapid increase in population, and the marvelous development of its great natural resources. Also an extended description of its counties, cities, towns and villages, their advantages, industries, manufactures and commerce; biographical sketches, portraits of prominent men and early settlers; views of residences and business blocks, cities and towns.* 2 vols. Chicago: The Western Historical Company, 1882.

Dowdey, Clifford, and Louis H. Mamarin, eds. *The Wartime Papers of R. E. Lee*. Boston: Little, Brown, 1961.

DuClos Katharine F. *The History of Braintree, Vermont*. Vol. 2. Published by the History Book Committee of Braintree, 1976.

Duffy, John J., Samuel B. Hand, and Ralph H. Orth. *The Vermont Encyclopedia*. Hanover, NH: University Press of New England, 2003.

Edwards, William B. *Civil War Guns: The Complete Story of Federal and Confederate Small Arms: Design, Manufacture, Identification, Procurement, Issue, Employment, Effectiveness, and Postwar Disposal*. Harrisburg, PA: Stackpole, 1962.

Eisenschiml, Otto. *Vermont General: The Unusual War Experiences of Edward Hastings Ripley (1862–1865)*. New York: Devin-Adair, 1960.

Ellis, William A., ed. *Norwich University, 1819–1911; her history, her graduates, her roll of honor, published by Major-General Grenville M. Dodge, compiled and edited by William Arba Ellis in three volumes*. Montpelier: The Capitol City Press, 1911.

Emmerton James Arthur. *A Record of the Twenty-third Regiment, Massachusetts Volunteer Infantry in the War of the Rebellion, 1861–1865; With Alphabetical Roster; Company Rolls*. Boston: W. Ware, 1886.

Fisher, Harriet F. *Hometown Album*. Lyndon, VT: Lyndon Historical Society, 1995.

Freeman, Douglas S. *R.E. Lee: A Biography*. 4 vols. New York: Charles Scribner's, 1936.

Goulding, J.H., comp. *Official Military and Naval Records of Rutland, Vermont, in the War of the Rebellion, 1861–1866*. Rutland, VT: The Tuttle Company, Book and Job Printers, 1891.

Guernsey, Alfred H., and Henry M. Alden, eds. *Harper's Pictorial History of the Civil War*. 2 vols. New York: The Fairfax Press, 1866.

Hagemann, James. *The Heritage of Virginia: The Story of Place Names in the Old Dominion*. West Chester, PA: Whitford Press, 1988.

Hearn, Chester G. *Six Years of Hell: Harpers Ferry during the Civil War*. Baton Rouge: Louisiana State University Press, 1996.

Heller, Charles E., and William A. Stoft. *America's First Battles, 1776–1965*. Lawrence: University Press of Kansas, 1986.

Hemenway, Abby Maria. *The Vermont Historical Gazetteer: A magazine, embracing a history of each town, civil, ecclesiastical, biographical and military*. 5 vols. Burlington, VT: Tuttle, 1923.

Hoar, Jay S. *New England's Last Surviving Civil War Veterans*. Arlington, TX: Seacliff Press, 1976.

Hobbs, O. Kermit. *Suffolk: A Pictorial History*. Norfolk, VA: Donning, 1987.

Hurd, John L. *Weathersfield: Century Two*. 2 vols. Canaan, NH: Phoenix Publishing, 1978.

Jeffrey, William H., comp. *Successful Vermonters: A Modern Gazetteer of Caledonia, Essex, and Orleans Counties Containing an Historical Review of the Several Towns and a Series of Biographical Sketches of the Men of Mark Who Won Distinction in Their Several Callings, and Who Have Become Conspicuous in the Professional, Business and Political World*. East Burke, VT: The Historical Publishing Company, 1907.

_____, comp. *Successful Vermonters, A Modern Gazetteer of Lamoille, Franklin, and Grand Isle Counties Containing an Historical Review of the Several Towns and a Series of Biographical Sketches of the Men of Mark Who Won Distinction in Their Several Callings, and Who Have Become Conspicuous in the Professional, Business and Political World*. East Burke, VT: The Historical Publishing Company, 1907.

Johnson, Robert U., and Clarence C. Buel, eds. *Battles and Leaders of the Civil War, Being for the most part contributions by Union and Confederate officers*. 4 vols. New York: Century, 1887–1888.

Kittel, Joe, and Marie Kittel. "A Randolph Civil War Mystery." Paper presented to the Randolph University Club, Randolph, Vt., March 15, 1999.

Lankford, Nelson. *Richmond Burning: The Last Days of the Confederate Capital*. New York: Viking, 2002.

Leech, Margaret. *Reveille in Washington, 1860–1865*. New York: Harper & Brothers, 1941.

Levy, George. *To Die in Chicago: Confederate Prisoners at Camp Douglas, 1862–1865*. Evanston, IL: Evanston, 1994.

Lewis, Thomas A. *The Guns of Cedar Creek*. Strasburg, VA: Heritage Associates, 1988.

Linderman, Gerald F. *Embattled Courage: The Experience of Combat in the American Civil War*. New York: Free Press, 1987.

Longacre, Edward G. *Army of Amateurs: General Benjamin F. Butler and the Army of the James, 1863–1865*. Mechanicsburg, PA: Stackpole Books, 1997.

_____. *Leader of the Charge: A Biography of General George E. Pickett, C.S.A.* Shippenburg, PA: White Mane, 1998.

Lord, Francis A. *Civil War Collector's Encyclopedia*. New York: Castle Books, 1965.

McCaslin Richard B. *Portraits of Conflict: A Photographic History of North Carolina in the Civil War*. Fayetteville: University of Arkansas Press, 1997.

McWhitney, Grady, and Perry D. Jamieson. *Attack and Die: Civil War Military Tactics and the Southern Heritage*. Tuscaloosa: The University of Alabama Press, 1982.

O'Dell, Jeffrey M. *Chesterfield County: Early Architecture and Historic Sites*. Chesterfield, VA: Chesterfield County Planning Dept., 1983.

Olson, Sherry H. *Baltimore: The Building of an American City*. Baltimore: The Johns Hopkins University Press, 1980.

Peterson, Harold L., ed. *Encyclopedia of Firearms*. New York: E.P. Dutton, 1964.

Pfanz, Donald C. *Richard S. Ewell: A Soldier's Life*. Chapel Hill and London: University of North Carolina Press, 1998.

Pohoresky, W.L. *Newport, North Carolina, during the Civil War: The True Story*. Newport, NC: Pohoresky, 1978.

Pond, George E. *The Shenandoah Valley in 1864*. Wilmington, NC: Broadfoot, 1989. First published 1885.

Reese, Timothy J. *Sealed with Their Lives: The Battle for Crampton's Gap, Burkittsville, Maryland, September 14, 1862*. Baltimore: Butternut and Blue, 1998.

Scarborough, Ruth. *Belle Boyd, Siren of the South*. Macon, GA: Mercer University Press, 1983.

Sears, Stephen W. *Landscape Turned Red: The Battle of Antietam*. Boston: Houghton Mifflin, 1983.

Sherman, Michael, Gene Sessions, and P. Jeffrey Potash. *Freedom and Unity: A History of Vermont*. Barre, VT: Vermont Historical Society, 2004.

Shingleton, Royce Gordon. *John Taylor Wood, Sea Ghost of the Confederacy*. Athens: University of Georgia Press, 1979.

Sifakis, Stewart. *Who Was Who in the Civil War*. New York: Facts on File Publications, 1988.

Sigaud, Louis A. *Belle Boyd, Confederate Spy*. Richmond, VA: The Dietz Press, 1944.

Smith, H.P., and W.S. Rowe. *History of Rutland*. Syracuse, NY: D. Mason, 1886.

Sommers, Richard J. *Richmond Redeemed: The Siege at Petersburg*. Garden City, NY: Doubleday, 1981.

Steele, Robert G. *With Pen or Sword: Lives and Times of the Remarkable Rutland Ripleys*. New York: Vantage Press, 1979.

Taylor, L.B. *The Ghosts of Richmond and Nearby Environs*. Williamsburg, VA: Progress Printing, 1985.

Teetor, Paul R. *A Matter of Hours: Treason at Harper's Ferry*. Rutherford, NJ: Fairleigh Dickenson University Press, 1982.

Ullery, Jacob G., comp. *Men of Vermont: An Illustrated Biographical History of Vermonters and Sons of Vermont*. 2 parts. Brattleboro, VT: Transcript, 1894.

Waitt, Robert W. *Confederate Military Hospitals in Richmond*, Official Publication #22, Richmond Civil War Centennial Committee, Richmond, Virginia, 1964. http://www.mdgorman.com/Hospitals/general_hospital_15.htm.

Wallace, William M. *Soul of the Lion: A Biography of General Joshua L. Chamberlain*. Gettysburg: Stan Clark Military Books, 1995. First published 1965.

Warner, Ezra J. *Generals in Gray: Lives of the Confederate Commanders*. Baton Rouge: Louisiana State University Press, 1959.

_____. *Generals in Blue: Lives of the Union Commanders*. Baton Rouge: Louisiana State University Press, 1964.

Welcher, Frank J. *The Union Army, 1861–1865: Organization and Operations, Eastern Theater*. Vol. 1. Bloomington and Indianapolis: Indiana University Press, 1989.

Wickman, Donald H., ed. *Letters to Vermont from Her Civil War Soldier Correspondents to the Home Press*. 2 vols. Bennington, VT: Images from the Past, 1998.

Wiley, Bell Irvin. *The Life of Billy Yank: The Common Soldier of the Union*. Baton Rouge: Louisiana State University Press, 1986.

Wiley, Bell Irvin, and Hirst D. Milhollen. *They Who Fought Here*. New York: Bonanza Books, 1959.

Wilkinson, Warren, and Steven E. Woodworth. *Scythe of Fire: A Civil War Story of the Eighth Georgia Infantry Regiment.* New York: William Morrow, 2002.

Witherell, John R. *The Civil War Service of Edwin S. Stowell, 1861–1863.* N.p., n.d. Antietam National Battlefield, Sharpsburg, Maryland.

Young, D. Kent. *Echoes in the Forest: The Family History of Stratton, Vermont.* Stratton, VT: Published by the Town of Stratton, 2000.

Young, D. Kent. *Echoes in the Forest: The Family History Supplement to the History of Stratton, Vermont.* Stratton, VT: Published by the Town of Stratton, Vt., 2000.

Zeller, Paul G. *The Second Vermont Volunteer Infantry Regiment, 1861–1865.* Jefferson, NC: McFarland, 2002.

Newspapers and Periodicals

Barnes, Galer Britton. "Jennie's Whitework, Jennie's Way." *PieceWork* (November/December, 1997).

Brattleboro Vermont Phoenix.

Burlington Daily Free Press

Conrad, James Lee. "A Most Realistic War College." *Civil War Times Illustrated* 43, no. 6 (February 2005).

Fordney, Chris. "A Town Embattled." *Civil War Times Illustrated* 34, no. 6 (February 1996).

Frye, Dennis E. "Through God's Blessing." *North & South* 7, no. 5 (October 2002).

Hyde Park (Vt.) *Lamoille Newsdealer.*

Marszalek, John F. "Second Union Misfire on the Peninsula." *America's Civil War* (July 2001).

Montpelier Vermont Watchman & State Journal.

Patterson, Gerard A. "Hangman Pickett." *America's Civil War* (November 2002).

Pohoresky, William. "The Legend of Jonnie Ring." *Civil War Times Illustrated* 41, no. 7 (February 2003).

Prokopowicz, Gerald J. "Word of Honor: The Parole System in the Civil War." *North & South* 6, no. 4 (May 2003).

Richmond News Leader, April 27, 1939.

St. Johnsbury (Vt.) *Caledonian.*

Windsor Vermont Journal.

Wist, Suzanne Smiley. "A Union Officers' Midlothian Romance." *The Messenger* (The Chesterfield Historical Society of Virginia) 21 (April 1992).

Yorktown (Va.) *Cavalier.*

INDEX

Numbers in **bold italics** indicate pages with photographs or illustrations.

Aiken's Landing, Va. 164, 165
Alabama units 83
alcohol, use 20, 61, 65, 68, 69, 73, 96, 106, 108, 124, 157, 171, 197, 213, 218
Alexandria, Va. 22, 23, 60, 83, 112, 219
Allen, Charles L. 8
Allen, Edward 214
Alligators 117, 145
Altoona, Penn. 55
American Legion 124
Ames, Brig. Gen. Adelbert 160, 162, 195
Ammen, Brig. Gen. Jacob 65, 66
ammunition: artillery 47, 189; infantry 21
Andersonville, Ga. 133, 137, 140, 195, 219
Andross, Col. Dudley K. 7, 63, 89; after the war 90; background 7; and Capt. Ripley 61; horse stolen at Harpers Ferry 52; in hospital 89; moves 9th Vt. to Suffolk 77; promoted to colonel 75; promoted to lieutenant colonel 7; resigns 90
Annapolis, Md. 34, 47, 52, 53, 54, 55, 62, 135, 141, 144, 195
Appomattox River 159, 160, 162, 163, 207
Aquia Creek, Va. 95
Army of Northern Virginia 81; in the Antietam Campaign 41; after battle of Fredericksburg 78; breakthrough at Petersburg 206; and Chancellorsville Campaign 88; in defense of Richmond 165; and Gettysburg Campaign 95; Lee reorganizes 33; surrender of 212
Army of the James 181, 198; in the Battle of Drewry's Bluff 159; in the Battle of Fort Harrison 163, 164, 180, 181; creation of 158; 9th Vermont ordered to join 157; reorganized 160; and Ripley's

brigade 204, 205; in the Second Battle of Fair Oaks 184, 191
Army of the Potomac 1, 23, 80; in the Antietam Campaign 44; in the Gettysburg Campaign 95; at Harrison's Landing, 33; loses battle of Fredericksburg 78; Maj. Gen Joseph Hooker assumes command 80; before Petersburg 163, 164, 206; before Richmond 158, 159
Army of Virginia 21
Atkins, Pvt. George 134
Atlanta, Ga. 198
Atlantic & North Carolina Railroad 118
Ausable Forks, N.Y. 63
Austine, Maj. William 19, 216
Averill, Corp. Charles **138**
Averill, Pvt. Franklin **138**
Avery, Pvt. Alfred **191**

Bacon, First Lt. Harrison K. **217**
Baker, Arad 176
Baker, Elisa 176
Baker, Pvt. Freeman 176, 181
Baker, First Lt. Joel C. **126**, 192, 196, 206
Baker, Pvt. John 199, 200
Baker, Pvt. Thomas G. 154
Balaw, Pvt. Edward 62
Ballard, First Lt. Alfred C. **10**; Asst. Surg. Goss and Vincent 86; background 19; in battle of Newport Barracks 131, 132, 140; in camp at Cloud's Mill 23; in camp of instruction 19; at Camp Tyler 56; and Corp Scott 79; death of Capt. Beebe 30; deaths at Yorktown 112, 113; and Edward Ripley 31, 89; on Gen. Ammen 66; guarding Confederate POWs 55, 70; hoe cakes 91; leaving Camp Douglas 76; leaving Yorktown 112; muskets 19; promotion of Col. Stannard 75; and Pvt. Greenslit 32; size of 9th Vt. 183; Suffolk 83; trip to Chi-

cago 55; voyage with Confederate POWs 77; wounding of Pvt. Newton 76; promotion to first lieutenant 94
Baltic (steamer) 195
Baltimore & Ohio Railroad 21, 25, 34, 37, 41
Baltimore, Md. 20, 21, 22, 24, 34, 37, 38, 40, 50, 53, 55, 57, 76, 77, 106, 158, 216, 220
Bamberger, Col. William W. 208
Barber, QM. Sgt. Edward D. 124, 197, 198
Barber's Crossroads, Va. 91, 92
Barden, Pvt. Herbert 109, 110
Barnes, Sgt. David P. 6
Barney, Col. Elisha L. 148
Barney, Francis (McKallor) 221
Barney, John (also known as John B. Sabre) 72
Barney, Maria 221
Barney, Lt. Col. Valentine G. **10**, 152, 153, 165, 184, 190, 203, 212; after the war 221; Battle of Harpers Ferry 50, 52; Battle of Newport Barracks 133–140; Bear Creek expedition 120; brigade command 199; Camp Douglas 75; camp in Washington, D.C. 22; camp in Winchester 28, 29, 31; camp in Yorktown 108; camp of instruction 19; Camp Tyler 57, 58; capture of Savannah, Ga. 198; Col. Stowell's resignation 89; command of Newport Barracks 129, 144; command of 9th Vt. 162, 185; conditions at Cloud's Mill 22; Confederate POWs 34, 52, 70; Corp. Noirel 127; death of brother 148, 149; death of Maj. Bartlett 143; death of Pres. Lincoln 214; death of Pvt. Bushnell 28; death of Pvt. Spafford 38; description 18; discipline 73, 87, 213; drilling his Co. 92; drowning of Pvt. Smith 116; execution of a soldier 155, 200–201, 202–203; expedition to

Barber's Crossroads 91; expedition to Gloucester Court House 104; first reconnaissance in N.C. 120; G.O. 154, 63, 64; health of 9th Vt. at Yorktown 105–106, 108, 112; hospital 95; inspections 202; Lt. Elisha B. Sherman 68; Lt. Linus Sherman 68, 94, 106; Maj. Jarvis' death 122; march to Annapolis 56; movement to Harpers Ferry 36, 37; movement to N.C. 116, 117; movement to New York City 192, 193; N.C. quarters 125; Negro village 103; promoted to lieutenant colonel 94; punishing members of 99th New York 95; Pvt. Gerard 53; Pvt. Green 203; Pvt. O'Brien 59; QM. Sgt. Barber 124, 197; reconnaissance on Nine Mile Road 212; reduces Sgt. Halbert 92; Second Battle of Fair Oaks 189, 190; sees Pres. Lincoln 205; Sgt. Cormin 157; Suffolk 84, 85, 93; Swansboro expedition 127; trip to Washington, D.C. 20; Winchester 26

Barrington's Ferry, N. C. 130

Bartlett, Maj. Amasa 11; death of 143; promotion to major 125; and Pvt. Davis 111; recruiting in Vt. 129; takes Maj. Jarvis' body back to Vt. 122; travels to Fort Monroe 129

Barton, Brig. Gen. Seth M. 129, 130, 146

Bascom, Capt. John T. 15, 73, 144, 193

Batchelder, Pvt. Charles M. 24

Batchelder's Creek 130

Batterys: Dantzler 159; Drawbridge 81; Mansfield 81; No. 11 1, 166, 169, 172, 173, 178; Onondaga 81; South Quay 81

Baxter, Henry H. 62, 175

Bay State (steamer) 20

Bear Creek 126

Bear Creek Inlet 126

Beaufort, N.C. 112, 117, 126, 134, 135, 138, 139, 141, 144, 146, 156

Beauregard, Gen. Pierre G.T. 146

Beebe, Capt. George A. 11, 30

Beechwood, N.C. 153

Beede, Pvt. Clark J. 73, 115, 156

Belden, Adjt. Henry D. 9, 169, 196

Belding, Pvt. Herman 143

Bell, Durant 120

Bell, Millie 144

Bellware, Cynthia Ann (Trimble) 200

Bellware, John Shirley 200

Bellware, Mary Margaret 200

Belouin, Francois 200

Belouin, John Henry 201

Belouin [Bellware], Louis Sebastian 200, 201

Belouin, Marguerite (Duquette) 200

Benedict, Major George G. 52

Bennett, Sgt. John W. 83, 124

Bennington, Vt. 3, 133, 172

Benway [Bellware], John Henry see John Henry Belouin

Benway [Bellware], Pvt. Louis see Louis Sebastian Belouin

Berger, Rebecca Ann 128

Bermuda Hundred, Va. 132, 159, 160, 162, 163, 164, 165, 191

Big Bethel, battle of 7, 158

Bird, First Lt. Elijah W. 217

Birney, Maj. Gen. David B. 160, 164, 178, 179

Birney, Brig. Gen. William 160

Bisbee, Corp. George W. 90

Bisbee, Capt. Lewis H. 66, 67, 72, 73, 94, 215

Bissell, Pvt. Edward B. 188

Blackwater River 79, 81, 90

Bliss, Sgt. Zenas H. 26, 69

Bogue Banks, N.C. 146

Bogue Sound 117, 131, 134

Bogue Sound Blockhouse 127, 131, 132, 134, 140, 141

Bolton, First Lt. James F. 66, 68, 134, 196

Bolton, Pvt. John 62, 111

Booth, John Wilkes 214

Bottoms Bridge, Va. 95

Boyd, Isabelle "Belle" 26, 28

Bradford, Vt. 3, 7, 11, 24, 36, 52, 90, 124, 197

Brady, Pvt. Peter 61, 190

Branch, Capt. Charles F. 197, 217; after war 222; Battle of Newport 139; and Bettie Jewett 214; brings 9th Vt. Battalion home 220; command of 9th Vt. Battalion 220; guarding Midlothian coal mines 213–214; on move to Cloud's Mill 22; promoted to second lieutenant 196; and Pvt. Steele 34; and Railey Hill house 214; at Redoubt Dutton 162, 194; theft of Lieut. Col. Andross' horse 52; at Winchester 26

Branch, Emma (Cook) 222

Branch, Ida H. (Burbank) 222

Branch, Brig. Gen. Lawrence O'B. 46, 47, 58

Branch, Martha J. (Stewart) 222

Brandon, Vt. 56

Brattleboro, Vt. 3, 6, 9, 11, 18, 19, 20, 47, 86, 112, 136, 142, 147, 153, 169, 175, 188

Bratton, Brig. Gen. John 188

Breckinridge, John C. 158

Brice's Creek 129, 130, 146, 153

Bridgewater, Vt. 29, 143

Briggs, Second Lt. Gordon N. 217

Brookfield, Vt. 136, 189

Brooklyn, Conn. 57

Brooklyn, N.Y. 171

Brooks, Maj. Joseph C. 12, 18; AWOL in New York City 193; battle of Fort Harrison 176, 177, 178; and Capt. Ripley 93; chosen as provost marshal 102; command of the 9th Vermont 199;

movement to Richmond 207, 208; ordered to New Bern 152; promoted to major 144; and Pvt. Town 148; returns to Vermont 216

Brownell, First Lt. Elias L. 103, 125, 213, 217, 218, 220

Brownington, Vt. 74

Bruce, Capt. George A. 207, 208

Bryant, Pvt. Leroy L. 176

Buehler, Col. Charles H. 86

Buffam, Corp. David 65

Bull Run: first battle of 3, 5, 37, 57, 146; second battle of 32, 33, 96

Burke, Vt. 137, 173

Burlingame, Second Lt. Sylvester C. 73, 97, 171, 196, 197

Burlington Daily Free Press 58

Burnham, Brig. Gen. Hiram 166

Burnside, Maj. Gen. Ambrose E. 33, 78, 79, 119, 164

Burrows, Pvt. Stephen 131

Bushnell, Pvt. Augustus 28

Bushy, Pvt. Octave 172

Butler, Maj. Gen. Benjamin F. 148, 193; Army of the James 157, 158; assigned to capture Richmond 164; attacks Richmond's Intermediate Line 184; background 158; Battle of Fort Harrison and New Market Heights 165, 180, 181, 182; commander of the Dept. of Virginia and North Carolina 119, 158; Dutch Gap Canal 162; makes two attempts to take Petersburg 159; Michael Willisford 197; on Negroes 120; relieved of command 198; saves Lt. Sawyer 129; Second Battle of Fair Oaks 185, 190; term contraband 119; to act in concert with Army of the Potomac 159; Wilmington expedition 198

Cahoon's Point, Va. 81

Calais, Vt. 26, 90

Cameron, Col. Daniel 62

Campbell, Second Lt. Oliver C. 11, 17, 66

Camps: Davis 19; Douglas 55, 56, 58, 60–64, 70, 72–75, 103, 105, 108, 109, 149, 155, 157; Hamilton 77, 83; Parole 34, 141, 142, 144, 190, 195; Sigel 25, 26; Sorghum 137; Sumter 133; Tyler 57, 58, 60–62, 144; Wood Tick 83

Canaday's Mills, N.C. 120, 124, 127, 133, 141, 147

Canby, Brig. Gen. Edward R.S. 12

Cape Fear River 150

Cappahosic, Va. 104

Carl, Pvt. Joseph 134, 141, 142

Carlisle, Pvt. Ara M. 60

Carpenter, Surg. Walter B. 8; after war 194; arrives in N.C. 117; Battle of Newport Barracks 137; as chief of Nelson General Hospital 102; Col. Andross 90; at execution 155; in charge of hospital in New Bern, N.C. 153; joins the 9th Vt. 30; post surg. at Newport Barracks 119; Pvt. Flanders 127; Pvt. Smith 62; rejoins 9th Vt. in Chicago 59; resigns 194; selected by Col. Stannard 8; stays with sick men in Winchester 35

Carrsville, Va. 81

Castle Grove, Iowa 58

Castle Thunder 141, 190

Caswell, Pvt. Franklin 133

Cedar Creek, Va. battle of 184, 185

Cedar Point, N.C. 121, 122

Cemeteries: Ash Grove 135; Bow 122; East Brookfield 189; Edson 171; Evergreen, Colorado Springs, Colo. 222; Evergreen, Rutland, Vt. 221; Green Mount 194; Highland 170; Hill Grove 200; Lake View 221; Marcellon 186; North Hyde Park 213; Oak Lawn 177; Pike Hollow 74; Rosehill 68, 70; St. Francis 172; South View 115, 124; Vermont Soldier's Home 133; Willis 174

Chaffin's Bluff, Va. 160, 164, 165, 192, 193

Chamberlain, Bill **170**

Chamberlain, Curtis **170**

Chamberlain, Edward **170**

Chamberlain, Emogene **170**

Chamberlain, Pvt. George C. 124, 197

Chamberlain, Harold **170**

Chamberlain, Herbert **170**

Chamberlain, Myra **170**

Chamberlain, Romero 170

Chamberlain, Pvt. William Hatch 169, **170**

Chamberlin, First Lt. George C. 217

Champion (steamer) 83

Chancellorsville, Va. 88, 95

Charles City, Iowa 221

Charles City Road 184, 185, 190

Charleston, S.C. 133, 135, 137, 158, 203

Charlotte, Vt. 137, 171

Chase, Pvt. George T. 215

Chase, Wagoner George A. 59

Chazy, N.Y. 72

Chelsea, Vt. 7, 112

Chicago Tribune 58

Chittenden, Vt. 135, 172

Church Hill 208, 209, 212, 213

Cincinnati, Ohio 149, 181

City Point, Va. 76, 77, 158, 159, 163, 191, 193, 200, 206

Claremont, N.H. 62

Clark, Capt. Asaph 10, **13**, 29, 30, 62, 94

Cleveland, Sgt. Edmund F. 92, **94**, 196

Clingman, Brig. Gen. Thomas L. 129

Cloud's Mill, Va. 22, 23, 60

coal fields 214, 215, 216

Coburn, Pvt. George A. 225

Coggin's Point, Va. 160, 163

Colby College 158

Cold Harbor, battle of 159, 165, 182, 212

Colorado Springs, Colo. 221, 222

Columbia (mail boat) 23, 77

Columbia, S.C. 137, 160, 203, 243

Commodore Jones (gunboat) 104

Concord, N.H. 169

Connecticut units: 57, 83, 85, 140, 155, 163, 209

Constitution (steamer) 191, 192

Conwell, Capt. Russell H. 133, 137

Cook, Pvt. Edward R. 174

Cooley, Pvt. Charles W. 113

Copeland, Pvt. Edgar F. 135

Corinth, Miss. 57

Corinth, Vt. 22, 127, 128

Cornin, Sgt. Dennis 157

Cottage Grove, Ill. 56

County Road 118

Coventry, Vt. 66, 222

Cowell, Mass. 72

Cox Farm 185

Craney Island, Va. 191

Croatan, N.C. 120, 133, 140, 147, 157

Cullen, Col. Edgar M. 185, 186, 188, 189

Cumberland, Md. 164

Cutting, Corp. Asa 69

Danby, Vt. 156, 203

Danville, Vt. 207

Danville, Vt. 63, 66

Darbytown Road 164, 182, 185, 190

Dartt, Second Lt. Justus 10, 35, 66

Davis, Pvt. Albert A. 217, 218

Davis, Lt. Col. Benjamin F. "Grimes" 39, 40

Davis, Qm. Gen. George F. 19

Davis, Corp. George W. **111**, 112, 174, 207

Davis, Jefferson 129, 143, 147, 158

Day, Pvt. Simon 134

Daylight (gunboat) 126

Dearborn, Pvt. Allen J. 169

Dearing, Col. James 130, 146

Deep Bottom, Va. 164, 165, 173, 191

Deerfield, N.H. 158

DeForge, Pvt. Nathan 132, 133

Department: Middle 38; of North Carolina and South Virginia 129; of Richmond 165; of Virginia 78, 80; of Virginia and North Carolina 119, 158, 159

Derby, Vt. 66, 111, 177, 222

Devens, Brig. Gen. Charles 195, 202, 206, 207, 209, 212

Dickinson, Chaplain Lucius C.: background 9; and Maj. Jarvis 122; men's disappointment in 69, 101, 110, 145, 156; on Pvt. Gerard 53; on sinful behavior 60

Dismal Swamp 79, 81, 88

Dix, Maj. Gen John A. 58, 80, 95, 99

Dodge, First Lt. William A. **94**, 189, 196

Douglas, C.F. 5

Douglas, Stephen A. 55, 56

Douglass, Pvt. Joseph 29

Douglass, Pvt. Joseph, Jr. 77

Dover, Vt. 135

Dracus, Mass. 171

Draft 29, 64, 124, 125, 191, 192

Draper, Col. Alonzo G. 185, 186, 188, 208

Drewry (ram) 200

Drewry's Bluff, Va. 159, 164

Drummondtown, Va. 219, 220

Dubose, Col. Dudley M. 178

Duggan, Pvt. James 191

Dummer, N.H. 174

Dummerston, Vt. 135, 171

Durkee, Pvt. Charles 222

Durkee, Pvt. George F. **135**, 136

Durkee, Pvt. George W. **182**, 199, 200, 212, 222

Durkee, Rosewel 222

Dunham, Norman 200

Dunham, Canada 221

Dutch Gap, Va. 159, 160, 199

Dutton, Col. Arthur H. 83, 162, 163

Dutton, Charles 3, 5

Dwyer, Pvt. Daniel 173, **175**

East Braintree, Vt. 123

East Brookfield, Vt. 189

Easton, Penn. 164

Edgerton, Principal Musician Edward M. 95

Eighteenth Corps: assigned to 157, 162; Battle of Fort Harrison 164–166, 173, 178, 181; disbanded 195; part of Army of the James 158; part of Army of the Potomac 159; relocates to Bermuda Hundred 159; Second Battle of Fair Oaks 1, 185, 186; Stannard's brigade 99; under temporary command of Maj. Gen. John Gibbon 162

election, presidential 191, 192

Eleventh Corps 88

Elizabeth City, N.C. 129, 130

Elliott, Pvt. Henry O. 190

Elmer, Pvt. Alva W. 109

Ely Plantation 91

Enos, Rufus 137

Escort (steamer) 157

Evan's Mills, N.C. 150, 153, 154, 157

Ewell, Lt. Gen. Richard S. 165

Execution 154–155, 200–203

Fair Oaks, Battle of 1, 186–194, 196

Fair Oaks, Va. 185, 186

Fairchild, Col. Harrison S. 165, 185, 186, 188, 189

Fairfax, Va. 75, 92

Fairman, Asst. Surg. Erastus P.: arrives in camp **144**; on Asst. Surg. Vincent 194, 204; background 144–145; on Battle of

Fair Oaks 188, 189, 190, 191;
describes wreckage of artillery
unit 166; enlists in 17th Vt. 144;
and Lt. Jenkins 179; and Lt. Liv-
ingston 172; and Pvt. Bissell 188;
sets up aid station at Fort Harri-
son 180–181; under fire 188, 189
Falling Creek, Va. 79
Farnum, Eulcid D. 222
Field, Maj. Gen. Charles W. 179
Fifth Corps 159
Finchon, Pvt. John 62, 105
firing squad 155
Fisk, Pvt. Orin J. 114–115
Five Forks, Va. 206
Flanders, Pvt. Charles A. 22, 127–
128
Fletcher, Pvt. Henry W. 133
Flint, Pvt. Royal 96
Floatilla, Nansemond 84
Flynn, Pvt. Thomas 202
Foley, Michael 219
Foot, Solomon 112
Forbes, Pvt. Franklin L. 147
Fort Anderson 130
Fort Clark 158
Fort Connecticut 83
Fort Corcoran 81
Fort Dix 81
Fort Fisher 198
Fort Gaston 153
Fort Gilmer 160, 165, 173, 176, 178,
179, 206
Fort Gregg 173
Fort Halleck 81
Fort Harrison 1, 164, 165, 166, 167,
169, 173, 178, 179, 180, 182, 183,
185, 189, 190, 191, 199, 203
Fort Hatteras 117
Fort Huger 83, 84, 85, 86
Fort Johnson 174, 178, 206
Fort Macon 144
Fort Malaria 109
Fort McClellan 81
Fort Monroe 76, 77, 78, 80, 95, 99,
106, 112, 113, 114, 116, 117, 129,
140, 144, 153, 158, 159, 170, 171,
173, 191, 193, 216, 220
Fort Nansemond 81
Fort Richmond 192
Fort Rosecarns 81
Fort Schuyler 171
Fort Sigel 26, 27, 31, 34
Fort Spinola 153
Fort Totten 155
Fort Union 81, 86
Foster, Brig. Gen. Robert S. 86,
104, 160
Franklin, Benjamin 123
Franklin, John 125
Franklin, Va. 79
Fredericksburg, Va. 78, 95, 148
Freeman, Pvt. James C. 65, 113
French, Pvt. Henry P. 167
French, Maj. Gen. Samuel G. 78,
79, 81, 85
Frenchburg, Ken. 200
Frisbie, Pvt. John 110
Fuller, Willard 5

Fulton Hill 211
Funk, Lt. Col. John H.S. 35

Gale's Creek 117, 131, 142
Garry, Pvt. Thomas P. 135
Gary, Brig. Gen. Martin W. 186
Gauthier, Sgt. Frederick 215
General Wool (steamer) 191
George, Pvt. Clement 190
Georgetown, D.C. 34, 219
Georgia, Vt. 6, 9, 28, 60, 86, 112
Getty, Brig Gen. George W. 81, 83,
84, 85, 99
Gettysburg, Penn. 98, 99, 182
Gibbon, Maj. Gen. John 162, 202,
205
Gleed, Charles L. 213
Gloucester Court House, Va. 104,
105
Glover, Vt. 173
Golden, Colo. 60, 244
Goldsboro, N.C. 141
Gorman, Capt. James T. 131
Goss, Pvt. Jason E. 32, 192
Goss, Asst. Surg. Story N. 86, 87,
112
Gould, Adjt. George W. 171
Gould, Louise B. 221
Grace, Pvt. James H. 134, 141, 142
Grand Army of the Republic
(GAR) 124, 222
Grant, Pvt. John 133
Grant, Lt. Gen. Ulysses S. 51, 163,
206, 212, 214; calls temporary
halt to operations 183; captures
Forts Henry and Donelson 3;
decides to attack South Side R.R.
185; gets permission to relieve
Maj. Gen. Butler 198; lengthens
lines 160; orders Maj. Gen. But-
ler to capture Richmond 164;
orders Maj. Gen. Butler to coop-
erate with Maj. Gen. Meade 15;
orders Maj. Gen. Butler to halt
rebel construction 184; and Maj.
Gen. Ord 164, 173; and Maj.
Gen. Pickett 143; and Maj. Gen.
Stannard 165, 221; reviews XXIV
Corps 205; and Sgt. Sweeney
193, 213; and the Wilderness
146–147, 149, 159
Granville, Vt. 113
Gray, First Lt. John 217, 218
Green, Corp. Spencer 156
Greenslit, Pvt. William H.H. 32
Gregg, Brig. Gen. John 165, 178
Gregg, Brig. Gen. Maxcy 46, 47
Grout, Caroline A. (Pike) 74
Grout, Ella 73
Grout, Corp. James: 29; arriving
in Chicago 55; death 73; de-
scribes his actions in the Battle
of Harpers Ferry 46–47, 49; for-
aging for food 32; march from
Harpers Ferry 54; picket duty at
Winchester 29; requests items
from home to sell 31; wanting
combat 32; weather conditions
at Winchester 29

Grout, Pvt. Joel 74, 188, 189
Grout, Leon 73
Grout, Martha Jane (Pike) 189
Grout, Pamelia 74
Grover, Pvt. Alonzo R. 188
Guyer, Capt. Guy H. 6, 11, 16, 28,
66, 72

Halbert, Sgt. John S. 92, 196
Hall, Asst. Surg. Horace P. 8, 9,
28, 30, 59, 60
Halleck, Maj. Gen. Henry W. 34,
42, 44, 95
Halstead, Isadora 128
Hampton, Maj. Gen. Wade 160
Hampton, Va. 93, 113, 116, 158,
169, 171, 179, 188, 194
Hampton Roads, Va. 26, 77, 79,
83, 95
Hanging 203
Hanover Court House, Va. 99
Hardie, Drum Maj. Robert G. 9
Hardwick, Vt. 218
Harpers Ferry, W.V. 24, 25, 32, 33,
34, 36, 37, 38, 39, 40, 41, 56, 58,
60, 62, 70, 73, 109, 121, 140, 149,
160
Harpers Ferry, Battle of 1, 41–54,
45
Harrison, Lt. William Elzy 165
Harrison's Landing, Va. 33
Hartley, Pvt. Samuel 108–109, 184
Haskell, First Lt. Charles W. 66,
94, 213
Hatcher's Run 160
Hathaway, Second Lt. Arthur W.
196
Havelock, N.C. 120
Hawkins, Pvt. Edward 190
Heckman, Brig. Gen. Charles H.
160, 164, 173, 176, 177, 190;
ascends to command of the
XVIII Corps 166; background
165; changes Ripley's orders 166;
ordered back to division com-
mand 185; orders Fairchild to
attack Fort Johnson 178; orders
Ripley to attack Fort Gilmer 173;
Second Battle of Fair Oaks 186
Henderson, Capt. William J. 7, 11,
15: and Pvt. Beede 156; resigns
66–67; sick on march to
Annapolis 36, 53
Hero (steamer) 99
Hibbard, Second Lt. Curtis A. 11,
14
Hickory Fork, Va. 104
Hickory Hill 99
Hill, Maj. Gen. Ambrose P. 45, 46,
47, 48, 49, 50, 51, 52, 58
Hill, Maj. Gen. Daniel H. 41, 78,
79
Hill, Pvt. David N. 113
Hills Point, Va. 81, 84, 85
Hinesburg, Vt. 30, 103, 125, 176
Hobon, Capt. Patrick 94, 217, 219,
220
Hodge, Sgt. Charles H.: on burn-
ing Fort Sigel 35; on camp at

West Point 98; on Capt. Bisbee 73; and cheering the 10th Vt. 22; on citizens of Chicago 59; complains of rations 57; describes alarm at Winchester 32; describes Belle Boyd 28; describes condition of railroad tracks 24–25; describes condition of the Mason House 28; describes rail cars 22–23; describes scenery 23; describes Suffolk 86–87; on destruction of houses in Suffolk 88; on Gen. White 26; on noise in Camp Douglas 60; and Pvt. Batchelder 24; on Pvt. Greenslit 32; on retreating to Harpers Ferry 37

Hoke, Brig. Gen. Robert F. 129, 130, 145, 146, 147, 181, 182, 186

Holbrook, Frederick 3, 6, 19, 93

Holman, Col. John H. 185, 190

Holman, First Lt. William C. 11, **16**, 67, 125, 134, 137

Hood, Maj. Gen. John B. 78, 79, 81, 83

Hooker, Maj. Gen. Joseph 78, 79, 88

Hospitals: Annapolis Junction 189; Baxter 112, 114, 132, 133, 136, 175, 202; Bermuda Hundred 132; Central Park 188; Chesapeake 95, 113, 116, 169, 171, 188, 194; Chimborazo 212; Crew and Pemberton Hospital 141; First Division 219; Government Hospital for the Insane 127; Hamilton 170, 171, 216; Hammond 135; Maine Insane 127; Mansfield 132; Marine 76; McDougal 171; Nelson 102, **108**; New Bern **154**; Point of Rocks 171, 174, 189, 203; Sloan 131, 136, 171, 172, 176, 216, 220; Smith 112, 136, 147, 153, 169, 188

Houghtalin, Pvt. James 217–218

Howe, Corp. Charles W. 68, 69

Howlett Line 160

Howquash (gunboat) 126

Hoyt, Pvt. Homer 222, **223**

Hoyt Memorial Park **223**, 224

huts 87, 194

Illinois units: artillery 42, 58, 61; infantry 42, 58, 62, 65, 73, 74

Indiana units 58

Isham, Pvt. Charles H. 113

Ives, Pvt. Franklin 133

Jackson, Lt. Gen. Thomas J. "Stonewall" 24, 25; and the Antietam Campaign 41, 42; and the Battle of Harpers Ferry 1, 43–50; and Battle of Second Bull Run 33, 96; captures Harpers Ferry 57; and Chancellorsville Campaign 88; notifies Lee of the capture of Harpers Ferry 52; and Shenandoah Valley Campaign 38; training troops at Harpers Ferry 37

Jackson's Corps 1

Jacksonville, N.C. 128, 131, 150

Jamaica, Vt. 36, 192

James River 33, 34, 76, 96, 158, 160, 164, 165, 179, 181, 182, 184, 185, 191, 193, 200, 206, 207, 212, 213

Jarvis, Maj. Charles 10, 124, 125, 145, 146, 152; in action at Suffolk 85; background 94; and Camp Douglas 58; death 121–122; promotion to major 94; and Pvt. Carlisle 60

Jenkins, Second Lt. Calvin M. **179**

Jenkins, Brig. Gen. Micah 79, 81

Jenks, Pvt. William B. 133

Jericho Canal 81

Jewell, Kan. 136

Jewett, Bettie 214

Jewett, First Lt. Erastus W. 10, **11**; and accidental shooting 28; awarded Medal of Honor 139; in battle of Newport Barracks 137, 138, 139; captured at Winchester 35; detailed to Redoubt Dutton 162, 193, 194; enlists a Negro 123; and G.O. 154, 163; helps build Slabtown 103; promoted to first lieutenant 94; resigns 194; returns to 9th Vt. 193; selected as garrison engineer 102

John Barley Corn *see* alcohol

John Rice (steamer) 115, 116, 117, 193

John Romer (steamer) 191

John Tucker (steamer) 55

Johnson, Andrew 143, 221

Johnston, Gen. Joseph E. 206, 207

Jones, Pvt. Jesse C. 192, 193

Jones, Pvt. Oliver 65

Jourdan, Col. James: and Battle of Newport Barracks 133, 134; and Battle of Fort Harrison 165, 166, 173, 178; and Col. Barney 140; and Col. Ripley 142 144; commander of the Sub-district of Beaufort 126; and expedition to Cape Fear River 150, 151, 152; and expedition to Young's Crossroads 128

Kautz, Brig. Gen. August V. 160, 164, 185

Kelley, First Lt. Edward L. **125**, 129, 134, 137

Kelley, Capt. Samuel H. 10, **11**, 156; and Col. Ripley 167; and expedition to Bogue Banks 146; and expedition to Neuse River 151; promoted to captain 75, 94; and Pvt. Duggan 191; retrieving wounded 177; stolen saber 52

Kelly, James W. 74

Kemper, Brig. Gen. James L. 79, 129, 145

Kennebec (steamer) 97

Kennedy, Pvt. Austin 116

Keyes, Maj. Gen. Erasmus D. 96, 99, 101

Kilbourne, Capt. Edwin A.: 11, **15**, 112, 148; artillery drill 108; in Battle of Harpers Ferry 40, 49, 51; in Battle of Newport Barracks 146, 147; camp in Suffolk 92; Chaplain Dickinson 69, 101, 110, 156; Confederate POWs 70; Confederate raid 156; death of Sgt. Morse 111; execution of soldier 154–155; Gen. Sheridan, victory 163; gets new recruits 156; Harpers Ferry camp 40; on health of 9th Vt. 107; heat at Yorktown 107; move to Harpers Ferry 24; N.C. residents 117; picket at Petersburg 162; promotion to captain 67; as provost marshal of New Bern 120, 126; and Pvt. Beede 155–156; questions serving in the army 149–150; retreat from Winchester 36; St. Patrick's Day 76; Swansboro expedition 150, 152; visits contraband camp 103; Washington farm 41; at West Point 97; at Yorktown 96, 112

King and Queen County, Va. 104

Kingsland Road 185

Kinsley, Pvt. John 157

Kinston, N.C. 129, 146

Kittel, Joe 114, 115

Kittel, Marie 114, 115

Ladeau (also spelled Ladu) Pvt. Peter 188

Lafayette, Pvt. Joseph 171

Lamoille Newsdealer 3, 25, 117, 157, 163, 195, 203

Lamson, Lt. (U.S.N.) Roswell H. 84, 85

Lane, Pvt. Edward H. 59, 129

Lane, Jane Eliza 59

Lane, Margaret M. (Dalton) 60

Larock, Pvt. Joseph H. 215–216

Laurel Hill, Va. 65

Lawrence, Angeline 24

Lawrence, Jonathan 24

Lawrence, Pvt. Joseph 24

Leavenworth, First Lt. Abel E. **102**; as acting assistant inspector general 102; and Corp. Cutting 69; and Corp. Grout 49, 74; in lines before Richmond 206, 207; promoted to captain 196; races into Richmond 208, 209

Lee, Gen. Robert E. 159, 165, 179; and the Antietam Campaign 33, 34, 35, 38, 41, 44, 48, 50; and the attack on Fort Stedman 206; and Battle of Fort Harrison 181, 182, 183; and Battle of Fredericksburg 78; and Battle of New Bern 99, 129; and Battle of Second Bull Run 33; and Battle of Second Fair Oaks 185; and Battle of the Wilderness 146, 147, 149; and Chancellorsville Campaign 79; and Gettysburg Campaign 95, 98; lengthening lines at Peters-

burg 160; and Peninsula Campaign 33; and Suffolk Campaign, 78, 79, 88; surrenders 212; and Union breakthrough at Petersburg 207
Lee, Maj. Gen. William H. F. "Rooney" 99
Lewis, Capt. Daniel W. 12, **17**, 35, 97, 106, 145
Lincoln, Abraham 192; assassinated 214; and Brig. Gen. White 25; calls for more troops 3, 6, 75; and early days of the war 3; and his wife 20, 205; investigates the loss of Harpers Ferry 54; and Maj. Gen. Butler 158; and Maj. Gen. Sherman 198; and Pvt. Barden 109–110; in Richmond 212; and Stephen Douglas 56
Livernoise, Jennie 133
Livingston, Capt. Josiah O. 11, **17**: and Battle of Newport Barracks 138, 139; heart attack 172; promoted to adjutant 94; promoted to captain 196; wounded at Battle of Harpers Ferry 49
Long Island (steamer) 76
Longstreet, Lt. Gen. James: and Antietam Campaign 33, 41, 48; and Battle of Gettysburg 99; probes XXIV Corps 195; and Second Battle of Bull Run 96; and Second Battle of Fair Oaks 186; and Suffolk Campaign 78, 79, 81, 83, 84, 85, 86, 88
Longstreet's Corps 33, 96, 78, 81
Louisville, Ohio 55
Loveland, Second Lt. Calvin R. 6, 11, **16**, 28, 66
Lowell, Mass. 171
Luce, Pvt. Charles A. 55
Lunge, Pvt. James 173

Macon, Ga. 137, 144
Maine units 162, 167, 173, 186, 188
Malaria 95, 109, 113, 114, 185, 189, 193
Malvern Hill, Battle of 70
Manchester, Va. 213, 214
Mann, Pvt. Benjamin, Jr. 60
Manny, Pvt. John 123
Maple Leaf (steamer) 117
Marston, Brig. Gen. Gilman 185, 186, 190
Martin, Brig. Gen. James G. 130, 131, 132, 134, 138, 139
Martin, Pvt. James 145, 198, 199, 202, 203, 214
Maryland units 195, 209
Mason, Pvt. Denny E. 176
Mason Town Road *see* County Road
Massachusetts units: artillery 117, 133, 135; cavalry 32, 74, 104; infantry 21, 157, 158
Matamora (steamer) 77
Mayo, Joseph 209
McClellan, Maj. Gen. George B.: 53, 78, 79, 97; and Antietam

Campaign 34, 44, 50; jettisons Maj. Gen. Keyes 96, 97; and Peninsula Campaign 3, 21, 33, 37
McGinnis, First Lt. John E. 217, 220
McGrath, Capt. Eugene 38
McGrath, Pvt. George H. 60
McKneel, Charles 74
Meade, Maj. Gen. George G. 98, 99, 147, 158, 164
Melcher, Rhoda 137
Melcher, Pvt. William 137
Mendon, Vt. 221
Meriden, Conn. 171
Metcalf, Musician William H. 99
Mexican War 37, 80, 130, 146, 164
Miami (gunboat) 145
Miamisburg, Ohio 200
Mickman, Pvt. John 61, 62, 111, 176
Middlebury, Vt. 3, 8, 10, 61, 124, 147, 184, 197, 221
Middletown, Md. 41
Middletown, Ohio 200
Middletown, Va. 184
Midlothian, Va. 214, 215, 216
Mill Road 178
Minday, Emma 186
Minie, Capt. Claude-Etienne 21
minie ball, description 21
Monkton, Vt. 135, 157, 184
Montgomery, Vt. 147, 200
Montpelier, Vt. 62, 87, 88, 131, 136, 171, 172, 176, 216
Montreal, Can. 143, 200
Moore, First Lt. Herbert H. **196**
Moore, John 108
Moranville, Pvt. William 177
Morehead City, N.C. 126, 128, 132, 133, 134, 135, 138, 139, 140, 144, 146, 147, 151, 152, 156
Morgan, Pvt. Charles 128
Morristown, Vt. 5, 6, 88
Morrisville, Vt. 5, 213
Morse, Pvt. Henry E. 110, 111
Morse, Marion 111
Mosby, Capt. John S. 75
Mount Holly, Vt. 76, 113
Mount Washington (gunboat) 84
Mower, Capt. Albion J. 11, **17**, 125
Mulberry Island, Va. 96

Nansemond County, Va. 79
Nansemond River 79, 81, 83, 84, 86
Nashville, Tenn. 149, 198
National cemeteries: Annapolis 135; City Point 191; Cypress Hill 171; Hampton 113, 116, 171, 179, 188; New Bern 135; Yorktown 99, **100**, **101**, 103
Nealy, First Lt. O.H. 218
Negroes: 97, 156, 202, 209, 219; building fortifications 119, 120, 142; in Fort Yorktown 102 103; Franklin, Benjamin 123; and New York City draft riots 191–192; Pvt. Gerard mistaken for

53, 111; refugees 95, 151; Robinson, Ben **123**, 124; as servants 97; and Slabtown 109; troops 129; units 158, 178, 179, 195; Virginia planters 53; Willisford, Michael 154, 196
Nelson House 102, **108**
Neuse River 129, 130 147, 150, 151, 152
New Bern, N.C. 79, 116, 117, 126, 129, 130, 131, 133, 137, 143, 145, 146, 147, 149, 150, 152, 153, 154, 156, 157, 185, 196
New Brighton Road 222
New Hampshire units 83, 85, 165, 195, 206, 207, 209
New Haven, Conn. 20
New Haven, Vt. 90
New Jersey units '83, 117, 119, 164
New Market Heights, Va. 164, 165, 173, 178
New Market Road 160, 164, 165, 181, 185, 206
New Orleans, La. 3, 26, 158, 181, 198
New York City, N.Y. 20, 22, 99, 145, 171, 188, 191, 192, 193, 213, 216, 219, 221
New York Tribune 20, 192
New York units: artillery 38, 39, 58, 98, 99, 104; cavalry 39, 117, 128, 150, 151; infantry 32, 38, 39, 42, 43, 46, 47, 48, 50, 58, 60, 72, 85, 86, 89, 104, 115, 126, 128, 150, 152, 154, 162, 165, 189, 190, 192, 195, 196, 209, 216
Newark, N.J. 131, 136
Newbury, Vt. 60
Newport, N.C. 126, 134, 137, 139, 141, 142, 144
Newport, Vt. 59, 174, 222
Newport Barracks, N.C. 115, 117, 118, 121, 122, 124, 127, 128, 129, 141, 142, 143, 144, 145, 152, 154, 156, 189, 195, 196
Newport Barracks, Battle of 130–140, **136**
Newport News, Va. 33, 78, 79
Newport River 134, 137, 138
Newton, Pvt. Albert E. 176
Newton, Pvt. Charles W. 76
Newton, Pvt. John L. 171
Nicholson, Pvt. Rufus 144
Nickerson, Pvt. John 176
Niles, Pvt. Albert A. 88, 113, 176
Niles, Pvt. Porter S. 113
Nine Mile Road 190, 212
Ninth Corps 44, 78, 83, 78, 79
Noirel, Corp. Charles 126–127
Norfolk & Petersburg Railroad 79
Norfolk, Va. 76, 77, 78, 79, 81, 83, 85, 95, 112, 214, 218, 219, 220
North Anna River 95
North Carolina units: cavalry 146; infantry 83, 110, 118, 130, 132, 141
North Hero, Vt. 176
North Hyde Park, Vt. 213
Northampton, Mass. 60
Nottoway River 159

Oakes, Pvt. Joseph 96
O'Brien, Pvt. Thomas 59
Ohio units: artillery 39; infantry 32, 38, 39, 43, 46, 47, 58, 60, 65
Onslow Co., N.C. 123
Orange, Vt. 73
Orange & Alexandria Railroad 22
Ord, Maj. Gen. Edward O.C. 162, 164, 165, 166, 173, 198, 202, 205, 206
Ordway, John 222
Osborne Road (also known as Osborne Turnpike) 160, 164, 165, 208
Osier, Pvt. Joseph 135
Osier, Pvt. Peter 135
Otis, Pvt. William A. 62, 63

Paconi (steamer) 95
Paine, Brig. Gen. Charles J. 160, 164, 178, 198
Paine, Corp. David 136
Palmer, Second Lt. Edson B. 217
Palmer, Brig. Gen. Innis N.: assigned as commander of District of N.C., 146; assigns Col. Jourdan a mission 150; background 146; replaces Brig. Gen. Peck 146; wife and Col. Ripley 152–153
Pamunkey River 95, 97, 99
Panton, Vt. 215
Pardeeville, Wisc. 186
Parker, Second Lt. Richard F. 196, **197**
Parker, Pvt. Stephen 30
Patrick, Ellen S. 176
Patrick, Elmer E. 176
Patrick, Pvt. George W. 176
Pattee, Commissary Sgt. Davis J. 9
Patterson, Col. Joab N. 185
Pawlet, Vt. 151, 189
Payne, Anna E. (Zuckschwerst) 176–177
Payne, Julia A. (Tula) 176
Payne, Pvt. Oberon 176, **177**
Pea Ridge, Ark. 25
Peck, Maj. Gen. John J. **81**, 84; assigns Col. Ripley as garrison commander 117; background 80; as commander of 1st division, VII Corps 80; fortifies Suffolk, Va. 81; and Hill's Point 85, 86; and Longstreet's forces 86; and not hiring Negroes 119; protects gunboats 83; and Pvt. Flanders 127; replaced by Gen. Palmer 146; requests reinforcements 81, 83; sends Gen. Corcoran in pursuit of rebels 88; stops Pickett's attack 81
Peck, First Lt. Theodore S. **10**; attends services 156; awarded the Medal of Honor 139; in battle of Newport Barracks 134, 138, 139; chosen as an aide 196; chosen as quartermaster sergeant 9; at Fort Gilmer 177; and Pvt. Joseph

Osier 135; and Pvt. Franklin 123; on saving 9th Vt. colors 51; wounded 178
Pelletier's Mills, N.C. 152
Pennsylvania Railroad 34
Pennsylvania units: artillery 162; cavalry 91, 160; infantry 89
Peru, Vt. 2, 176
Petersburg & Weldon Railroad 159
Petersburg, Va. 33, 76, 78, 79, 81, 141, 147, 157, 159, 160, 164, 165, 179, 185, 206, 207
Pettee, Pvt. Aurelius 135
Phelps, Corp. Edward N. 54, 55, 90, 91
Piatt, Brig. Gen. Abraham S. 23, 25
Pickett, Maj. Gen. George E.: 181, 206; charged with war crimes 143; as commander of the Department of North Carolina and South Virginia 129; at Gettysburg 81, 86, 99; hangs POWs 143; and New Bern Campaign 130, 131; pardoned by President Johnson 143; plans second New Bern Campaign 145; and Suffolk Campaign 78, 79
Pierson, Pvt. George 218–219
Piper, Pvt. William 69
pitch orchards 117
Pitkin, QM. Gen. Perely P. 216
Pittsford, Vt. 53, 113
Plainfield, Vt. 3, 11, 86
Plymouth, N.C. 145, 146
Plymouth, Vt. 47
Pomfret, Vt. 214
Pope, Maj. Gen. John 21, 24, 33
Portsmouth Road 81
Portsmouth, Va. 79, 109, 110, 159, 220
Potomac River 22, 37, 48, 50, 53, 219
Potter, Col. Joseph H. 195, 199
Poultney, Vt. 132
Powers, George B. 219
Preston, Pvt. Horace H. 171

Quimby, Capt. Elisha M. 11, **14**, 52, 59, 61, 62, 111, 125

Railey Hill 214
Railroads *see* specific name of railroad
Randolph, Vt. 114, 115, 123, 124, 135, 192
Ransom, Brig. Gen. Matthew W. 129, 145
Rappahannock River 33, 78, 79, 88
Raulston, Col. John R. 185, 186
Red House, N.C. 153
Redoubt Dutton 162, 193, 194
Rhode Island units: artillery 117; cavalry 38; infantry 83, 86, 110
Rice, Sgt. Franklin E. 195
Rice, Second Lt. Henry H. 12, **18**, 125
Richford, Vt. 92

Richmond & Danville Railroad 213
Richmond & Fredericksburg Railroad 79
Richmond, Va. 21, 29, 33, 34, 51, 70, 76, 77, 78, 79, 95, 96, 99, 100, 101, 104, 141, 149, 158, 160, 162, 164, 165, 166, 171, 178, 179, 183, 184, 185, 190, 192, 199, 200, 204, 207, 208, 209, 210, 212, 213, 214, 216, 218, 219
rifle, musket: Enfield 69; Springfield 21, 69
Riley, Sgt. John 170
Riley, Pvt. Matthew 135
Ripley, Brig. Gen. Edward H. 10, **11**, 23, 62, **93**, 140, 148, 204, **211**; aborts attack on Fort Gilmer 173–178; after the war 221; as signed to a board of examination 104, 112; assigned to XVIII Corps 162; on Asst. Surg. Hall 30; attack on Battery No. 11 169–173; background of 93; Battle of Fort Harrison 165–168; Battle of Harpers Ferry 43, 45, 46, 47, 49; Bear Creek expedition 126; on Belle Boyd 28; brigade command 162; on camp at Clouds Mill 22; at Camp Tyler 57, 58, 59, 61; on Capt. Beebe's death 30; on citizens of Winchester 26; Col. Stannard 180, 182; command of Newport Barracks 117, 118, 119; commanding sub-district of Beaufort 144; on Confederate deserters 183; Corp. Green 156; court-martial duty in Morehead City 152; death of Maj. Jarvis 122; describing camp at Winchester 26, 30; describing trip to Harpers Ferry 23, 24; on digging fortifications 180; employs Negroes 119; on Enfield rifles 69; enlisting Negroes 12; envies his brother 70; on expedition to Barber's Crossroads 90, 91; expedition to Coggin's Point 163; on expedition to Gloucester Couth House 104; expedition toward New Bern 150; on fatigue duty at Winchester 26; on fellow officers 31; fraternizing with Confederate pickets 162; on Gen. Ammen 66; Gen. Butler 180; Gen. Palmer's wife 152, 153; on Gen. White 25; G.O. 154, 163; at Harpers Ferry 40, 41; horse trading business 124; leads troops into Richmond 209; on lice 183; Lt. Col. Andross 61; on Lt. Col. Stowell 88, 89; Lt. Jenkins 179; on march to Annapolis 53, 54, 55; Michael Willisford 154, 196, 197; on mortar fire 183; on move from Winchester 34, 35, 36; moves 9th Vt. to Newport Barracks 114, 116, 117; moves the 9th Vt. to New Bern 153; moves the

9th Vt. to Petersburg 157, 160; N.C. scouting expedition 120, 146; 9th Vt. colors 51, 52; prepares for second attack at Newport Barracks 142, 145; promoted to brevetted brigadier general and permanent brigade command 202, 205; promoted to colonel 93; promoted to lieutenant colonel 89; promoted to major 75; as provost marshal of Richmond 209, 210, 212; Pvt. Elmer 109; Pvt. Kinsley 157; Pvt. Mann 60; Pvt. Ripley 65; Pvt. Williams 65; Pvt. Wood 109; receives gift from Co. B 75; returns from brigade command 195; returns to Fort Monroe 129; on scare at Winchester 26; Second Battle of Fair Oaks 185–194; Sgt. Stebbins 203; on Springfield rifles 21, 69; at Suffolk 84, 85, 86, 88, 89; Swansboro expedition 128; turpentine venture 141; at West Point 98, 100; at Yorktown 95, 100, 101

Ripley, Pvt. Thomas B. 133
Ripley, Lt. Col. William Y.: in Berdan's Sharp Shooters 70; joins 1st Vt. Inf. 93; joins his brother, Edward H., in the turpentine business 141
Roanoke River 145
Robbins, Grace A. 74
Robbins, Pvt. John E. 74
Robbins, Mary H. (Hubbell) 74
Robbins, Ralph R. 74
Robbins, Rebecca (Pirl) 74
Roberts, First Sgt. John W. 214, **215**
Roberts, Pvt. Nelson C. 136, 172
Robinson, Ben **123**, 124
Rouss, First Lt. Milton 32, 39, 40, 42, 45
Rowanty Creek 159
Roxbury, Vt. 51, 96, 171
Royalton, Vt. 55
Rudd, Pvt. Thomas 139
Rupert, Vt. 188
Rutland, Vt. 3, 10, 21, 50, 86, 93, 142, 170, 216, 221
Rutland Herald 19, 59, 66, 77, 91, 95, 112

Sabbeville (Sabberville), Pvt. John 29, 72
Sabin, Capt. Albert R. 10, **12**, 41, 66, 68
Salem, Mass. 221
Salem, Vt. 173, 177
Salisbury, N.C. 133, 190
Sander's House 122, 146, 152
Sargent, Pvt. Alvora M. 190
Savage, Col. James W. **151**
Savannah, Ga. 137, 198
Sawyer, Capt. Francis O. **8**, 91, 1021, 29, 196
Scott, Corp. Bradford T. 74–75
Seaboard & Roanoke Railroad 79

Second Corps 159
Seligson, Lt. Col. Herman 10, **12**, 66, 68, 108, 217, 219, 220
Seventh Corps 80, 89
Sharon, Vt. 68, 136, 172, 190
Shenandoah Valley, Va. 21, 25, 33, 34, 37, 95, 163184
Sherman, Clarence 221
Sherman, Second Lt. Elijah B. 10, **13**; after the war 68; charged with neglect of duty 41; complains about Camp Tyler 59; complains about not being exchanged 61; on foraging expedition 41; resigns 68; threatens to resign if not promoted 68
Sherman, Hattie G. (Lovering) 68
Sherman, Jennie C (Galer) 221
Sherman, Capt. Linus E. 10, 216; after the war 221; on Asst. Surg Hall 30; in Battle of Newport Barracks 139; on building winter quarters 194; on capture of Plymouth 145; captured at Winchester 35; on Confederate deserters 199; on Confederates trying to regain Fort Harrison 183, 184; on court-martial board 106; on death of Maj. Jarvis 122; describes conditions at City Point 76; describes effect of the war at Cloud's Mill 22; describes Hampton Roads 76–77; describes provost marshal duties 126; on drills at Suffolk 90; on field rations 22; on first frost near Fort Harrison 183; fraternizing with Confederates 185; on health of 9th Vt. at Yorktown 106; on living conditions under fire 183, 194; on Maj. Bartlett's death 143; on Maj. Brooks and Capt. Bascom going AWOL 193; and Michael Willisford 154; and Millie Bell 144; on moving camp in Suffolk 92; on N.C. women using snuff 117, 144; on New Bern 152; promoted Capt. 94; on Pvt. Stoliker 184; on rain at camp near Fort Harrison 182; on rations at Winchester 31; at Sanders' house 146; on Second Battle of Fair Oaks 191; on snakes 145; as viewed by Capt. Barney 68, 93; on Washington D.C. 22; witnesses wounding of Corp. White 28; wonders about Gen. Butler's views of contrabands 119; on Yorktown surrender monument 96
Sherman, Louise B. (Gould) 221
Sherman, Maj. Gen. William T. 198, 203, 204
Shono, Corp. John 152
Shrewsbury, Vt. 65, 132, 133, 189
Sias, Hattie L. (Yates) 174, **175**
Sias, Pvt. Henry 174, **175**
Sigel, Maj. Gen. Franz 25
Simmons, Pvt. Nathaniel 111

Sisco, Corp. William J. 132
Sixth Corps 44, 206
Slason, Sgt. James L. 65
Slayton, Capt. Abial H. 6, **16**, 11, 28, 66, 73
Sleepy Hole Ferry, Va. 83
Smith, Corp. Edwin R. 32
Smith, Pvt. George W. 183
Smith, Gov. John G. 112, 216
Smith, Pvt. Nathan C. 136
Smith, Pvt. Otis B. 62
Smith, Pvt. Vilas 116
Smith, Maj. Gen. William F. 159
Smith, Pvt. William P. 132, 133
Smithfield (gunboat) 145
Smoot, Mrs. William 218
Smoots, Capt. David L. 83
Snakes 23, 117, 145
Sneden, Second Lt. George W. **196**
Snow, Second Lt. Asa H. 94
snuff 117, 144
Somerton Road 79, 81, 86
South Anna River 95, 99
South Quay, Va. 79, 81
South Side Railroad 185, 206
Spafford, Pvt. John W. 38
Spaulding, Pvt. Nathan 56
Spicer, Musician George W. 157
Spotsylvania, battle of 149, 159
Squires, Pvt. David 68, 69
S.R. Spaulding (steamer) 140
Stannard, Maj. Gen. George J. **6**, 7, 38, 162, 164, 216; after the war 182, 221; amputation of right arm 182; background 6; at Battle of Gettysburg 99; at Battle of Fort Harrison 165, 166, 167, 173, 179, 180, 181; at Battle of Harpers Ferry 46, 48, 49, 50, 51, 52; at Camp Tyler 58, 61; on citizens of Winchester 26; as division commander 164; loss of regimental colors 51; and Lt. Rouss 42; move to Winchester 23; movement of 9th Vt. to Washington, D.C. 20, 21; moves 9th Vt. to Cloud's Mill 22; mustering of 9th Vt. 20; prepares for battle at Harpers Ferry 39, 40; promoted to brigadier general 75; and Pvt. O'Brien 59; and Pvt. Town 73, 149; and retreat to Harpers Ferry 36; and Second Vt. Brigade 75; selected to command 9th Vt. 6; Surg. Carpenter 8; wounded 99, 182; in XVIII Corps 99, 160
Stanton, Edwin McM. 38, 62, 126, 127, 205, 221
Starksboro, Vt. 134, 139, 141
Staten Island, N.Y. 192
Steady, Pvt. Timothy 103
Stearns, Adjt. John C. 7, **8**, 94, 156
Stearns, Pvt. Warren E. 128, 150
Stebbins, Sgt. J. Webster: on Chaplain Dickinson 69, 145; on Col. Ripley 203; on death of Confederate POWs 70, 74; describes picket duty 87; at Ely house 91; on guarding Confeder-

ate POWs 69; on health of 9th Vt. 113; on lice 74; and Pvt. Wilder 192; sending money home 86; on snakes 145; at Windsor 90
Stepping Stones (gunboat) 85
Stevens, Col. Aaron F. 166
Stevens, Capt. Hazard 84, 85
Stevens, Pvt. Leonard M. 62, 69
Stinehowe, Pvt. Nelson 195
Stoddard, Pvt. Charles W. 135, 189
Stokes, Pvt. Benjamin 134, 139, 141, 142
Stoliker, Pvt. Horatio N. 184
Stone, Pvt. Benjamin C. 153
Stone, Pvt. Benjamin F. **171**
Stone, First Lt. Stillman 6, 66, **67**, 94, 107
Stony Creek 159
Stoughton, Brig. Gen. Edwin H. 75
Stowe, Vt. 5, 6, 7, 29, 73, 77
Stowell, Lt. Col. Edwin S.: background **7**; at Battle of Harpers Ferry 45, 46, 49; and Capt. Ripley 31; on Confederate soldiers 52; leaves Camp Douglas 76; and Pvt. Town 73; promoted to lieutenant colonel 75; resigns 89; in riot at Camp Douglas 61; selected as major 7
Strait, Zerah W. 5
Stratton, Vt. 29, 32, 46, 74, 188, 192
Stribling, Capt. Robert M. 183
Strong, Pvt. George 152
Stuart, Lt. Gen. James E.B. "Jeb" 33, 41
Sturgis, Maj. Gen. Samuel D. 22
Suffolk Campaign 77–90, **82**, 117
Suffolk, Va. 91, 95, 99, 121, 163, 189, 220
Sunderland, Vt. 174
Sutler 73, 85, 102, 106, 108, 142152, 185
Swansboro, N.C. 120, 121, 126, 128, 130, 146, 150
Sweeney, Augusta Grout 213
Sweeney, Carroll Francis 213
Sweeney, Sgt. Charles H. 35, 193, 194, 213
Sweeney, Pvt. Eli 181
Sweeney, Mary J. (Hill) 213
Sweeney, Oliva 213
Sycamore Church, Va. 160
Sylvester, Pvt. Frank 62

Tatro, Pvt. Alfred 137
Tatro, Angeline 137
Tenth Corps: attempts to capture Petersburg 159; in Battle of New Market Heights 164, 165, 178; command structure 160; at Fort Gilmer 173, 179; in Second Battle of Fair Oaks 184, 185
Terry, Maj. Gen. Alfred H. 160, 185, 186, 195
Thayer, Dr. Samuel W. 144, 145216
Third Corps 99

Thomas, Maj. Gen. George H. 198
Thomas, Pvt. Harry B. 214, 215
Thomas, Sgt. John W. 196, 217, 218
Thomas P. Way (steamer) 216
Tinmouth, Vt. 19, 56, 144
Tobin, Corp. Albert S. 215
torpedoes (mines) 207
Town, Wagoner James C. 72, 73, 148
Towne, Larry 114
Trent River 146, 153
Trent's Reach, Va. 159
Trois Rivieres, Quebec, Can. 200
Trowbridge, Pvt. Seymoure 147
Troy, N.Y. 185, 216
Tucker, Betsy (Bates) 29, 30
Tucker, Pvt. Rufus 29, 30
Tula, Kan. 176
Tunbridge, Vt. 29, 62, 99, 105, 167, 182, 199, 222, 224
Twenty-Fifth Corps 195, 196, 206, 209
Twenty-Fourth Corps 199, 216, 219; formation 195; ordered to assault Confederate lines 206, 207; reviewed by Lt. Gen. Grant 205
Tyler, Brig. Gen. Daniel 57, 58, 59, 61, 62, 65, 149

Underwriter (gunboat) 130, 131, 152
United States (steamer) 116
United Sates Military Academy 146
United States units: artillery 85; cavalry 146; infantry 62, 63, 197
University of Vermont 94, 222

Valentine, Joseph R. 60
Vanderbilt (steamer) 192
Varina Road 164, 165, 166, 167, 176, 178, 180, 206
Vaughn, Second Lt. Alvan P. 66, **67**
Vermont Soldier's Home 133, 172
Vermont units: brigades 1, 3, 23, 48, 75; cavalry 77; infantry 1, 3, 5, 6, 7, 8, 9, 21, 22, 30, 75, 89, 97, 144, 186, 220, 222
Veteran Reserve Corps (V.R.C.) 60, 77, 123, 128, 132, 133, 136, 176, 196, 202, 220
Vicksburg, Miss. 99
Viele, First Lt. Eugene 11, **15**, 125, 135, 196
Vincent, Surg. Walter S. 86, **87**, 122, 194, 204
Virginia Central Railroad 99
Virginia units: artillery 83, 166, 169, 178; cavalry 32, 35

Wakeeney, Kan. 176
Wandell, Pvt. Nelson L.: on assignation of Pres. Lincoln 214; at Battle of Harpers Ferry 47, 52; on camp in Richmond 212; fortifying Newport Barracks 142; on Jacksonville 150; on march to

Annapolis 53; on New Bern 152; at Suffolk 89; on Swansboro expedition 128; on trip to Chicago 55; on Union POWs 77; on winter camp at Fort Harrison 200
Warboys, Pvt. Charles N. **186**
Warboys, Pvt. George 190
Wardsboro, Vt. 74, 131, 188
Washburn, Adj. Gen. Peter T. 51, 216
Washing, John A. 41
Washington, D.C. 19, 20, 21, 22, 23, 24, 25, 26, 28, 33, 34, 40, 42, 48, 52, 62, 75, 80, 83127, 134, 149, 158, 179, 184, 191, 213, 219, 220, 221
Washington, N.C. 79, 145, 146
Washington Irving (steamer) 191
Waters, Pvt. William 176
Watertown, Wisc. 186
Waterveliet Arsenal, N.Y. 192
Weathersfield, Vt. 66, 94, 122, 124
Webster, Pvt. Birchard E. 72
Weitzel, Maj. Gen. Godfrey: assumes command of XVIII Corps 181; background 181; enters Richmond 206, 208, 209, 212; in Second Battle of Fair Oaks 185, 186, 188, 190
Wells, Pvt. Joseph 62
Wells, Vt. 109, 110
Wells River, Vt. 111
Wessells, Brig. Gen. Henry W. 145
West, Col. Robert M. 185
West Boylston, Mass. 184
West Charleston, Vt. 173
West Point *see* U.S. Military Academy
West Point, Va. 97, **98**, 99, 100, 222
West Troy, N.Y. 192
Westford, Vt. 219
Wetherell, Pvt. Ephraim 25
Wetherell, Pvt. William V. 29
Wetherell, Pvt. Wyman 23
Wheatley, Pvt. Alson N. 189
Wheeler, Corp. Richard 215
Whitcher, Second Lt. John **67**, 111, 133, 150
White, Corp. Abner B. 28
White, Maj. Gen. Julius 25
White House, Va. 95, 97, 99
White Marsh Road 81, 86
White Oak River 128, 131, 146, 150, 152
White Oak Road 121
Whiting, Maj. Gen. William H.C. 130
Whitingham, Vt. 59, 176
Whitney, Able 222
Whitney, Albert 222
Whitney, James H. 222
Whitney, John S. 222
Whitney, Lewis 222
Whitney, Pvt. Milo S. 199, 222
Whitney, Pvt. Orlando 99, **100**, **101**, 222
Whitney, Orson 222
Whitney, Ransome 222

Whitney Hill 99, 222
Wilder, Pvt. Emery S. 36
Wilderness, Battle of the 112, 147, 149, 159
Williams, Pvt. William, Jr. 65
Williamsburg Road 185, 186, 188, 190
Willisford, Michael 154, 196, 197
Wilmington, N.C. 130, 140, 150, 151, 198
Winchester, Va. 23, 24, 59, 66, 163
Winder, Capt. Richard B. 219, 220
Windham, Vt. 171
Windsor, Va. 90, 91
Wing, George K. 186
Wing, Luthera Litchfield 186
Wing, Seth Burgess 186

Wing, Pvt. Stephen B. 185, **186**
Winnimsinet (ferryboat) 105
Winnona (steamer) 157
Winooski, Vt. 172
Wirz, Capt. Henry 219
Wisconsin units 86, **89**, 98, 102, 106, 107, 189, 190
Wistar, Brig. Gen. Isaac J. 108, 112; assigns Col. Ripley to board of examination 104; assigns 9th Vt. to punish 99th N.Y. 95; background 89; as commander of Eastern District of Va. 102; and condition of Fort Yorktown 95, 100, 103; and injuries 101; tries to get Lt. Sawyer on his staff 129; at West Point, Va. 97, 98
Wolcott, Vt. 35, 114, 193

Wood, Pvt. Hiram 109
Woodbury, Urban A. 5
Woodward, Pvt. Edmund A. 113
Wool, Maj. Gen. John E. 38, 39, 40, 43, 79
Wright, Pvt. William T. 60

York River 96, 97, 99, 102, 103, 104, 105, 112, 115
York River Railroad 188
Yorktown, Va. 78, 95, 96, 97, 100, 101, 102, 104, 106, 108, 109, 110, 111, 112, 113, 116, 125, 127, 129, 143, 144, 184
Yorkville, Ill. 74
Young's Cross Roads 128, 150

Zuckschwerst, Anna E. 177